## Also by David Andress

*French Society in Revolution, 1789–1799*

*Massacre at the Champ de Mars*

*The French Revolution and the People*

# The Terror

# THE TERROR

## The Merciless War for Freedom in Revolutionary France

DAVID ANDRESS

Farrar, Straus and Giroux
New York

*Farrar, Straus and Giroux*
*19 Union Square West, New York 10003*


*Printed in the United States of America*
*Originally published in 2005 by Little, Brown, Great Britain,*
*as* The Terror: Civil War in the French Revolution
*Published in the United States by Farrar, Straus and Giroux*
*First American edition, 2006*

*Library of Congress Cataloging-in-Publication Data*
*Andress, David, 1969–*
*The Terror / David Andress.— 1st American ed.*
*p. cm.*
*Includes bibliographical references and index.*
*ISBN-13: 978-0-374-27341-5 (alk. paper)*
*ISBN-10: 0-374-27341-3 (alk. paper)*
*1. France—History—Reign of Terror, 1793–1794. 2. Political violence—France. I. Title.*

*DC183.5.A53 2006*
*944.04′4—dc22*

*2005047217*

*www.fsgbooks.com*

*1 3 5 7 9 10 8 6 4 2*

# CONTENTS


*Acknowledgements* vii
*Maps* viii

Introduction 1
1 Night Flight 9
2 Hankering After Destruction 38
3 The Fall 71
4 The September Massacres 93
5 Dawn of a New Age 116
6 Things Fall Apart 149
7 Holding the Centre 178
8 Saturnalia 210
9 Faction and Conspiracy 244
10 Glaciation 277
11 Triumph and Collapse 312
12 Terror Against Terror 345
Conclusion 371

*Timeline of the French Revolution to 1795* 379
*Glossary* 385
*Cast of Characters* 391
*Notes* 403
*Index* 429

# ACKNOWLEDGEMENTS

Thanks first to my editor, Tim Whiting, for starting the ball rolling on this project, and for smoothing the path of its development with his enthusiasm and support. Thanks also to Bill Doyle for bringing me to Tim's attention. My agent, Charlie Viney, has been a great help in focusing my thoughts as I developed the project for a new kind of reader, and I look forward to future collaborations.

The Faculty of Humanities and Social Sciences at the University of Portsmouth granted me a sabbatical in the spring of 2004 to finish this work, and I am particularly grateful to my colleagues who shared the burden of teaching and administration around – notably Brad Beaven, Gavin Schaffer, Heather Shore and Matt Taylor. My colleagues in the international H-France network were also understanding of the necessary focus of my attentions to this work. Alan Forrest provided thoughtful words of encouragement, as he always does, and a number of other historians also helped me with this project and others, and deserve a note of thanks here: Colin Jones, Laura Mason, Sarah Maza, David Kammerling Smith.

My wife Jessica and my daughters Emily and Natalie help to give all my work meaning. Without the latter in particular I might have been able to get up a little later sometimes, and not needed to disappear to work quite so often in order to get things done, but it wouldn't have been worth it in quite the same way.

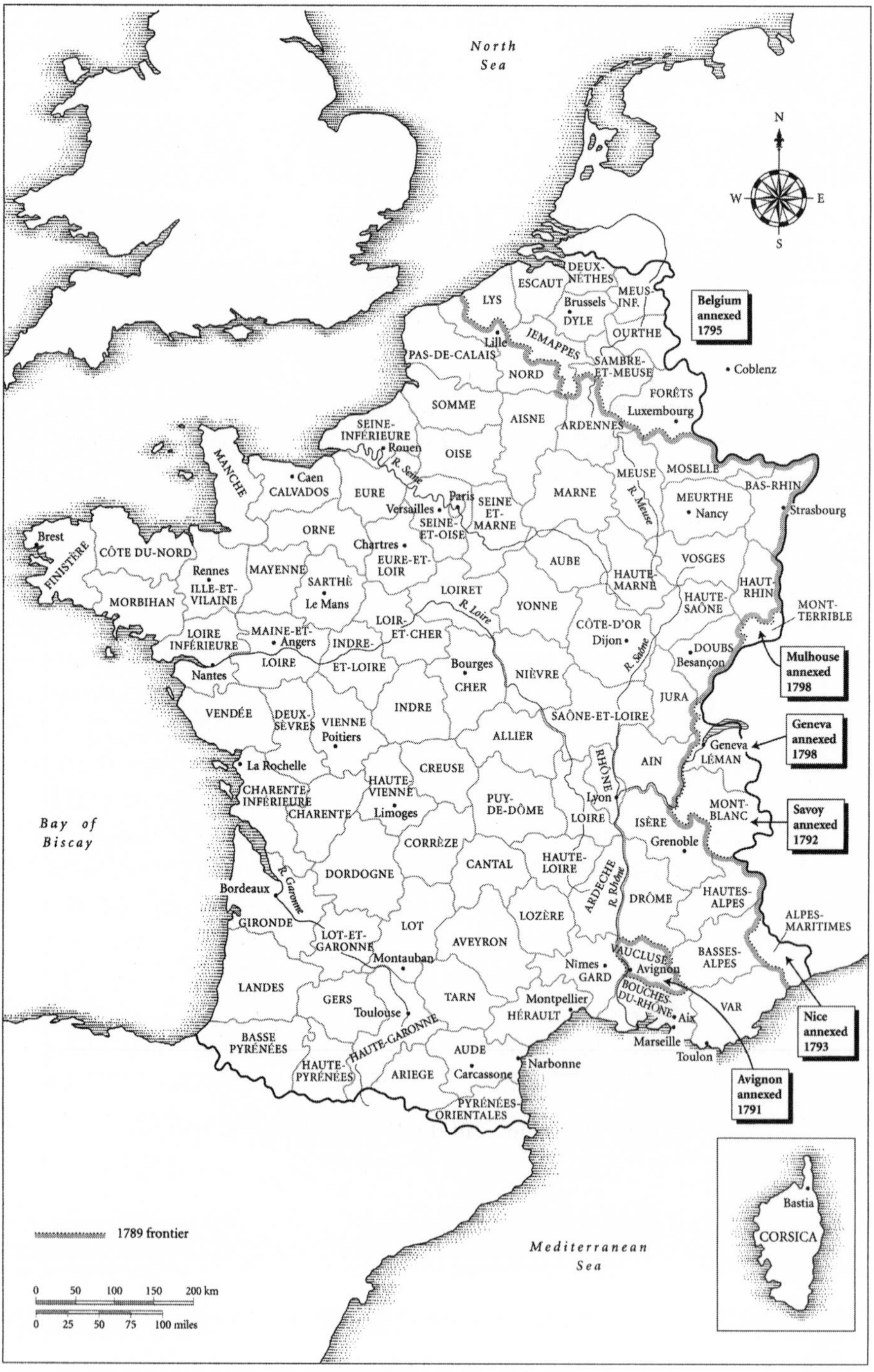


France in the 1790s

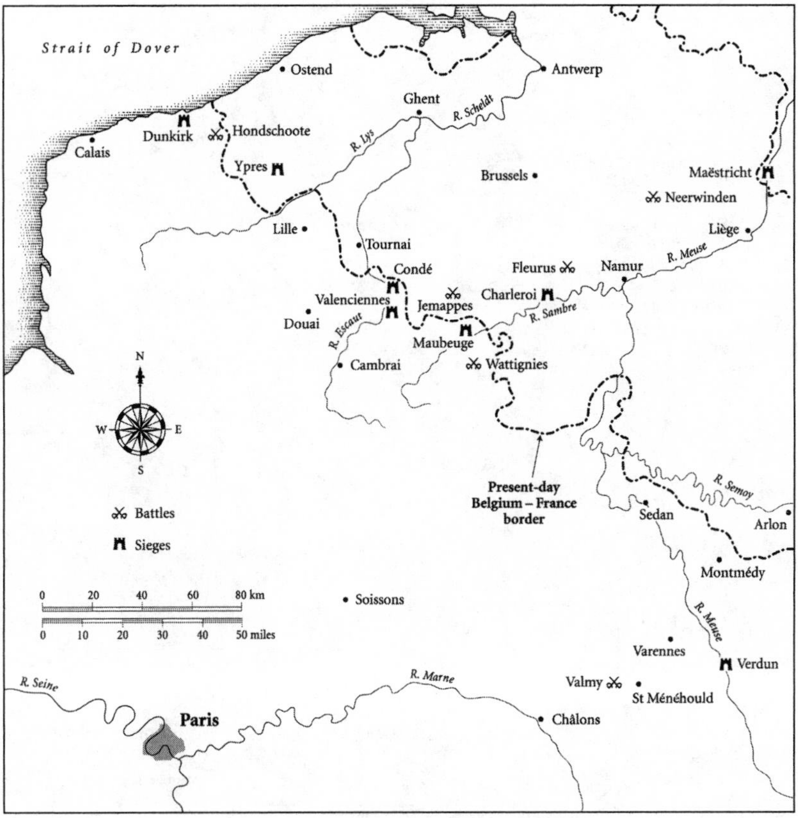


The Flight to Varennes and the War in the North, 1791–94

North Sea
N
W
E
S
Antwerp
Brussels
Jersey
Rouen
Caen
CHOUANS
Paris
Granville
Brest
R. Seine
R. Meuse
Rennes
CHOUANS
Le Mans
CHOUANS
Châtillon sur Seine
Quiberon
Savenay
Angers
R. Loire
Dijon
Besançon
Nantes
Saumur
R. Saône
Cholet
Bourges
Yeu
VENDÉE
Ré
Oléron
Lyon
Bay of Biscay
Bordeaux
Mende
R. Rhône
R. Garonne
Jalés
Nîmes
Avignon
Montauban
Toulouse
Marseille
Toulon
Vendéans' March to Granville, Autumn 1793
Vendéans' March from Granville
Minor Centre of Federalism, Summer 1793
Major Centre of Federalism, Summer 1793
Other Towns
Areas of Resistance to Central Authority
Mediterranean Sea
0 50 100 150 200 km
0 25 50 75 100 miles

Civil War in the Terror, 1793

# The Terror

# INTRODUCTION

How far can a state legitimately dehumanise its enemies? When is it right arbitrarily to detain those suspected of subversion? Can terror ever be justified as an instrument of policy? These are questions which ought not to need contemporary answers, and yet they do. We have supposed repeatedly over the last two hundred years that we live in a world attuned to the benefits of liberal civilisation – a world that ended slavery, regulated the humane conduct of warfare, created genuine democracy and held out the prospect of universal peace. A world, in short, where the almost sixty-year-old opening words of the Universal Declaration of Human Rights, that 'all human beings are born free and equal in dignity and rights', had meaning.

Yet that same world is also the world of the tyrannies of colonial rule, of eugenic experimentation in the name of modernity, of the horrors of two world wars, and the vile perversions of Darwinist science that spawned them, of racial annihilation and a half-century-long contemplation of deliberate nuclear armageddon. The new world order that was supposed to be born from the end of Soviet Communism (itself of course originally a project to better the lot of the oppressed) now seems no more than a morass of moral ambiguity and expediency.

The dawning of this troubled modernity saw two great upheavals in the political life of nations: the French and American Revolutions. The principles that underlay both have continued to resonate down the ages – whether the pithy 'no taxation without representation' or the varied assertions of 'natural and imprescriptible rights of man' to liberty, security, the pursuit of happiness and other goods. The leaders of both revolutions had a common grounding in the humanitarianism of the Age of Reason, members of a generation that across the European world was abolishing state torture, refining the process of justice away from punishment to rehabilitation, and gearing up to contest the legitimacy of slavery (though only the French tried at this point to abolish it, and that only temporarily, until Napoleon's more pragmatic reign).

From these common roots, the two revolutions are usually seen as diverging sharply. The Americans founded an enduring constitutional settlement on the separation of powers and the checks and balances of a federal system. The French plunged into an abyss of blood and fire, to emerge under the thumb of a military dictator crowned as emperor. The story, of course, is not actually that simple. France's decade of revolutionary strife was easily matched by the years of warfare in North America between the mid-1770s and mid-1780s. Of the colonies' 2.5 million inhabitants, one in every twenty-five fled abroad, far exceeding the proportion that left France during her Revolution. A third of the adult male population of the colonies were in arms, and many of those were in semi-official militias, or simple armed bands, that preyed on civilian populations for years at a time. Military fatalities reached perhaps one in thirty-five of the entire population, with uncounted tens of thousands of other deaths from violence and unchecked disease. The crude numbers of dead in the wars and repressions of the French Revolution – a half-million or more – are more horrific in their scale, but, in proportion to a population more than ten times greater, little worse than the American example.[1]

The sheer bloodiness of the American conflict is noteworthy because the rebels were trying to throw off a government that resided several thousand miles distant, and for much of the period were doing so with the active assistance of several other European powers. The French revolutionaries, by contrast, fought to overturn not merely a distant colonial power, but an entire social order, and to do so with virtually all of Europe in arms against them. What is astonishing is not so much that they tried but that, in a very real sense, they succeeded. When the French Revolution was over, the world was a very different place. The map of Europe was no longer drawn to suit the competing dynastic ambitions of ancient monarchical houses, and political debates across the continent no longer hinged on the selfish assertion of ancient privileges and prerogatives. Structures that were created by the powers of Europe explicitly to resist the threat of further revolution nonetheless were also by definition innovations, radical breaks with the past. Out of the destabilising threat of subversion from below came the 'Concert of Europe' agreed after the fall of Napoleon, an international system that for a generation governed the politics of the continent. New creations like the kingdom of the United Netherlands came into existence as buffer-states against French revolutionary contamination, and the map of central Europe took a decisive step towards the emergence of a modern Germany.

The French Revolution's impact was so deep seated that simply turning the clock back had become impossible, and the more profound recognition of this was in the birth of an entire new ideology – conservatism – designed to prevent further upheaval without being mere futile backward-looking reaction. Just as conservatism was born in revolution, so too more directly was liberalism, the crystallisation of the concern for the rights-bearing individual citizen that had animated the initial revolutionary pronouncements of 1789. Together, these two political currents would dominate the modern world, until with the growth of the marginalised industrial working classes of the later nineteenth century socialism intruded violently to join them.[2]

But socialism, too, was a child of the French Revolution. Intellectually, Karl Marx derived his entire picture of historical progress from liberal writers who saw in the Revolution the inevitable rise of the bourgeoisie.[3] Socially and politically, the example of the Revolution's radical phases produced a message of ineradicable commitment to human equality that demanded action against the injustices of an industrialising world. Meanwhile nationalism, without which the history of the last 150 years is simply inconceivable, was also born in its modern forms out of the aspirations and conflicts of the revolutionary era. The modern sense of national identity, of active belonging to a national citizen-body with its associated freight of rights and duties, is as much a product of this upheaval as is the tricolour or the *Marseillaise*. On a whole host of political, intellectual and structural planes, the French Revolution is the fount and origin of our modern world.

Here, of course, lies the heart of the historical dilemma we began with, for the French Revolution about which William Wordsworth rhapsodised 'Bliss was it in that dawn to be alive' is also the Revolution that brought the Terror to European consciousness, passing its thousands of victims beneath the modern, humane, death-dealing blade of the guillotine, turning an entire realm upside-down with paranoid pursuit of dissent and pitiless subjugation of individuals to a faceless national cause.

Many have argued that the Terror was inherent in the Revolution's project of innovation – a point made by countless reactionary and Catholic polemics – or that it was inherent in the political culture from which the Revolution itself sprang. That view is particularly prominent today, and has been since the late 1980s. In the declining years of the Cold War, and even more after the fall of the Soviet bloc, there seemed little value in earlier interpretations that put revolution at the heart of modernising change. Historical opinion instead focused on the supposedly unique and iniquitous qualities of revolutionary discourse – on how the power of the revolutionaries to reshape language, to give new names to old things, slid into a wild and erratic intoxication of power, to the commitment to change everything, and to remould humanity in an image so purified as to become perversely meaningless, merely a justification for further purges and executions of those who did not measure up.[4]

Along the way, it has sometimes become hard to see what the Terror actually was. In particular, it is seldom acknowledged now how far it was (much like the American Revolution) a civil war, deriving much of its grim impetus from the inevitable bitterness of conflict between former friends. Seldom, too, is it recognised just how important and active a role the enemies of the Revolution played in the aggravation of its politics – how eagerly, for example, the king and queen of France steered the country into foreign war, with the avowed intention of using the conflict to destroy the Revolution. In all the writings on the paranoid tendencies of the revolutionaries (tendencies which are, again, well attested in the parallel American experience too),[5] little attention is given to the issue of how such beliefs were given ample food by the betrayals, some real and deliberate, some clumsy and unintentional, that dogged the very heart of revolutionary politics.

On 14 July 1789, hundreds of ordinary citizens of Paris, called to arms by a universal alarm, invested, cannonaded and seized the fortress of the Bastille on the eastern fringe of the city. They sought not the handful of prisoners still confined in the dungeons of

France's most notorious prison, but the stocks of gunpowder they needed to load tens of thousands of muskets liberated from another arsenal the previous day. They did so in the sure and certain belief, which was far from entirely false, that the king of France had ordered his army to conquer the city, crushing the birth of a democratic agitation, and assisting a coup against the National Assembly that promised to give the nation a free and fair constitution. A hundred Parisians perished in the assault, many blown apart by cannon fire as a truce for negotiations broke down in chaos. In their subsequent moment of triumph, the crowd stabbed to death Bertrand-René Jourdan de Launay, the governor of the fort, helpless in the arms of his captors, hacking his head from his body and parading it on a pole for all to see and rejoice at. They likewise displayed as a trophy the head of the mayor of the city, whose loyalties were suspect, and who had failed to produce arms for the insurgents the previous day.

From the blood spilt in revenge on that hot July day to the moment five years and two weeks later when the head of the architect of the Terror, Maximilien Robespierre, was cut off amid scenes of popular jubilation in the heart of Paris, it is easy to portray events as a mere welter of carnage and mob violence. A long tradition has done just that, from Edmund Burke's 1790 *Reflections on the Revolution in France* to the late-nineteenth-century French writer Hippolyte Taine, who invented a whole new vocabulary of abuse for the 'refuse of the street' he blamed for revolutionary violence, to Simon Schama, who wrote in 1989 that 'In some depressingly unavoidable sense, violence *was* the Revolution itself.'[6] But this is simply not good enough. The crowd's actions on 14 July 1789 were reactions – they had no doubt about the reality of the threat they faced, and that reality did not diminish in later years. It is impossible in all conscience to absolve the revolutionaries of blame for their actions, especially in 1794 when the Terror proper was in train, and the judicial process itself was akin to a massacre of people who by any reasonable measure were innocent. But that historical moment was the outcome of a process, not its preordained goal.

The Terror was not some mysterious substance immanent in social upheaval, breaking to the surface unbidden to wreak havoc. It was above all the consequence in real civil war of a failure of consensus that had edged steadily closer to complete collapse for over three years. The monarch held to be plotting against his people in

July 1789 was allowed to cling on to his throne until August 1792, and for much of that time continued to be seen, with blind optimism, as the potential saviour of his people from aristocratic reaction. He was officially decreed to be the 'Restorer of French Liberty' only months after the Bastille fell. He was even allowed to resume the throne in 1791 after attempting to flee the country and incite a wider counter-revolution. So optimistic were the revolutionaries that crowds in the capital and elsewhere rejoiced in September of that year when the king announced (and perjured himself by swearing) that he would accept the new Constitution and rule through an elected assembly. A persistent belief in the abiding and abounding nature of their enemies also animated the revolutionaries, and for example provoked a massacre in the prisons of Paris in September 1792 often seen as a clear landmark on the road to Terror. But a further spiralling series of disasters and betrayals would be necessary to bring about the carnage of 1794, as a country at war with Europe shattered along a whole series of political, religious and cultural fault-lines. And in resorting to Terror, the revolutionaries preserved their country from the consequences of that disintegration, and went on to forge a military power that was to dominate Europe for twenty years.

Paradoxes like this abound throughout the period. Those revolutionaries who seem most imbued with human warmth – one thinks of Danton as memorably portrayed on-screen by Gérard Depardieu – are those who scarred politics with their corruption; those who lived blameless lives of moral purity – and none was more monastic than Maximilien Robespierre – were most willing to consign the innocent to a traitor's death. Those who ended the Terror, and ultimately handed France over to military dictatorship, were those who had most profited from it. The death-dealing of the Terror itself, so often seen as its defining quality, is not without ambiguity. The formal apparatus of the Terror that judged political enemies and traitors executed some seventeen thousand people across France. Military tribunals and *ad hoc* executions of captured rebels-in-arms disposed of some thirty or forty thousand more, and the general horrors of civil war (including unchecked epidemic disease) perhaps accounted for as many as two hundred thousand deaths. Yet almost as many perished fighting on the side of the 'terrorist' Republic in the same conflicts, and believed they gave their lives for a noble cause. The wars of the Emperor Napoleon exceeded these casualties by several times over, and most of those who died were young conscripts with no more choice in the matter than the most hapless victim of the guillotine. The victims of Austerlitz, Borodino or Waterloo are seldom lamented, and their killers never reviled. As with any historical account, when dealing with the Terror it is necessary to maintain a sense of proportion.

The notion of proportion brings us round again to our starting point, for the modernity bequeathed us by the French Revolution was irrecoverably scarred – if not by the Terror as some great and unparalleled event, then by the very fact that, in the cold light of history, the Terror is not, has not been, a unique aberration. To invoke another great phrase of the American revolutionary heritage – widely though inconclusively attributed to Thomas Jefferson – the price of liberty is eternal vigilance. Such a phrase is merely trite, however, unless we consider its deeper implications. For the French revolutionaries, as for so many regimes that have succeeded them across the world up to the present day, the call for vigilance against enemies, both external and internal, was the first step on the road to the loss of liberty, and lives. Of far more significance, and the true and tragic lesson of the epic descent to the Terror, is the summons to vigilance against ourselves – that we should not assume that we are righteous, and our enemies evil; that we can see clearly, and others are blinded by malice or folly; that we can abrogate the fragile rights of others in the name of our own certainty and all will be well regardless. If we do not honour the message of human rights born in the revolutions of 1776 and 1789, as the French in their case most clearly failed to do, we too are on the road to Terror.

Chapter I

# Night Flight

In the brief midsummer darkness of 20–21 June 1791, Louis XVI, King of the French, fled his capital and his people.[1] Using secret passageways in the Tuileries palace, the royal family were spirited away by a small band of loyal followers, leaving central Paris in a hired hackney carriage driven by Axel von Fersen, a dashing young Swedish knight, and rumoured lover of Queen Marie-Antoinette.[2] Outside the city walls Fersen left them to make his own escape, and the party embarked in a second-hand *berline*, a bulky coach pulled by a team of six horses. Louis had spurned the chance to flee in anything lighter and faster, because it would have meant travelling apart from his wife and their two children. Together, he reasoned, they were safer, but as the coach creaked and groaned eastwards towards the frontier fortress of Montmédy, laden down with the family, their attendants, bodyguards and luggage, it would prove a fatefully unwise choice.

The fugitives' schedule had been carefully plotted, and relays of cavalry were to see them to safety, once they had passed into the jurisdiction of the marquis de Bouillé, loyal governor of the frontier region. The departure had been delayed by several hours, however, by last-minute hesitations and confusions, and the *berline* was too slow to make up the time. The duc de Choiseul, commander of the first relay of horsemen, presumed the escape postponed (as it had been once already, after repeated earlier reschedulings), and ordered his men to withdraw to barracks, concerned that their presence was alarming the locals.[3] He passed the same instruction to all the later relays. Ignorant of this critical decision, the royal party proceeded towards the first rendezvous. Escorted by only two horsemen, and followed by another carriage bearing their maidservants, the *berline* meandered on across the rolling landscape of Champagne as morning turned to afternoon – twice the king ordered a rest-stop, and, casting aside all effort at concealment, chatted with passers-by as if nothing unusual was occurring.

Yet what was happening was amazing and traumatic. Not since the religious and political strife of the early seventeenth century had a king of France had to flee his people, and never had one made so brazenly – or so desperately – for the frontiers. This episode had been brought about by upheavals which were unprecedented in European history, with a long and tortured trail of antecedents reaching across Louis' reign into that of his predecessor. If the king and his companions regarded their move with insouciance, this was a symptom of the wider delusions that the entire court laboured under, long after events had first decisively challenged their right to rule France as they saw fit.

The flight had begun, ironically enough, on the second anniversary of another momentous day, 20 June 1789. On that day elected representatives of the 'Third Estate' – in other words, the mass of the population – took action to proclaim themselves the new constitution-makers of France. They were already locked in conflict with the royal administration, refusing to sit as merely one of the three chambers of the Estates-General, France's historic national consultative body. Tradition said their twenty-seven millions should have but one vote here, a permanent minority standing alongside the votes of the First Estate (some 130,000 Catholic clergy) and the Second Estate (the nobility – no more than 350,000 by even the widest count, and perhaps only half that).[4] On 17 June, however, the Third Estate gathering had declared itself to be a 'National Assembly', and summoned deputies from the other two to join its sessions. Royal actions to nullify this move, locking the deputies out of their meeting-chamber until a projected Royal Session could take place, sent them hurrying to a nearby indoor tennis-court, there to pledge their new oath, never to separate until France had a new constitution.[5]

For the Third Estate deputies, who had struggled for six weeks to persuade the other two Estates to follow their lead in creating one single representative body, meeting recalcitrant opposition from the nobility especially, this was all part of a grand struggle. The very existence of the Estates-General, holding its first meeting since 1614, reflected the depth of crisis into which France had been plunged. From some perspectives, the whole of the preceding two decades had been an era of catastrophe, leading up to this revolutionary moment. Louis XVI inherited the throne from his grandfather, Louis XV, in 1774. The old king had died covered in public odium. This was partly at least because for the previous three years the most powerful and vociferous vested interests in the land, the noble judges of the *parlements*, France's highest law-courts, had been banished from their place in public administration, replaced with bodies more compliant to the royal will. This act, the culmination of decades-long struggles over whether or not the *parlementaires* had any right to critique new laws and taxes, brought the judges into a paradoxical alliance with the self-proclaimed forces of Enlightenment and progress.[6]

While some, like Voltaire, condemned the judges as a feudal relic standing in the way of rational governance, most authors who spoke to the growing ranks of the reading public took them at their own valuation – defenders of the rights of the nation against royal despotism. Pamphlets, news-reports and secret scandal-sheets all portrayed the fight with the old king as one where virtue, and the public interest, lay with the recalcitrant judges, currently exiled to rural obscurity. Louis XV, an old man of sixty-four, made older by a life of excesses – of which the sexual ones were legendary, and almost all true – died of smallpox in the midst of this conflict. Louis XVI, ascending the throne when not yet twenty, a grandson thrust into the succession by the deaths a decade before of his father and elder brother, felt that he would earn the gratitude of the nation by restoring the *parlements*, which he did almost immediately.

It was with hindsight a great misjudgment – the first, unfortunately, of many. Nothing in his education had really prepared Louis for kingship, although he had been dauphin, heir-apparent, since 1765. There is no doubt that he was a good man and a loving husband and father, nor that he had the intellectual capacity to cope with affairs of state. He was, however, a vacillator, often unable to decide between conflicting courses of action, anxious to avoid confrontation, and inclined to give his backing to whoever had had the last word, whatever their merits.[7] He allied this with a conviction, at least in the early years of his reign, that 'I must always consult public opinion; it is never wrong,' and reportedly noted this as a paramount reason for restoring the *parlements*, adding that 'I wish to be loved.'[8] It was a humble desire, but harboured an ironic (and certainly unintended) reference to the nickname of his predecessor, 'The Well-Beloved', a tag Louis XV had thoroughly outlived by his last years. It was a pattern the new king seemed doomed to repeat.[9]

His troubles had begun even before he ascended the throne. He was married in 1770 to Marie-Antoinette, daughter of the Habsburg empress Maria-Theresa of Austria. The couple were both only fifteen. Since the 1750s the two powers had been allies, but it had been a disastrous partnership for France, dragging her into the Seven Years War of 1756–1763. This saw Britain smash French pretensions to empire in North America and India, while the Prussians under Frederick the Great survived the triple weight of France, Austria and Russia to become the arbiters of central Europe. By the 1770s, hostility to the Austrian alliance was a fixture of public opinion, and the new marriage was intensely disliked. Indeed, it seemed cursed from the outset – a crowd stampede at a firework show in Paris, meant to celebrate the wedding, left over 130 dead, one of the worst public accidents of the century, long and bitterly remembered.[10]

Worse still was to come. The gauche youth and his young wife proved unable to produce an heir. Before long all Paris, and all the world, knew that something was not right in the royal bedroom. Neither plain nor pious enough to sink into the background as Louis XV's queen had done, Marie-Antoinette had already begun to develop a reputation for frivolity, extravagance and sexual adventures: the latter essentially fictional, it must be said. Her portraits show a woman whose stout chin and distinctive nose do not conform to modern standards of beauty (though at least she did not suffer from the positive disfigurement of the lower jaw noted in the Habsburgs of earlier centuries), but she was certainly regarded as striking.[11] It seemed clear to the many interested observers that, under the circumstances, the fault must lie with the dauphin. He was shy, chubby and generally unprepossessing, and diverted himself with long hours of hunting and the unusual and solitary hobby of locksmithing. He had been encouraged to take this up as a child through fashionably enlightened ideas about 'useful' pursuits. All this made him a forlorn and slightly ridiculous figure, and one soon depicted, in public rumour, published slanders and pornographic engravings, as entirely impotent.[12]

The bitter irony was that nothing could be further from the truth. Although hectoring letters from Maria-Theresa insisted there could be no physical fault with her daughter, other high-level diplomatic and medical correspondence made it clear that the well-endowed Louis was just too much of a gentleman (albeit a sexually naive one) to force himself on a young and slightly built wife, whose hymen painfully resisted penetration.[13] For seven years the sad farce continued, into the new reign, when the provision of an heir became even more urgent, until at last Marie-Antoinette was persuaded to have a minor surgical intervention, and the couple could conceive. Their first-born was a girl, Marie-Thérèse-Charlotte, barred by ancient custom from the succession, but in 1781 they brought forth a new dauphin, Louis-Joseph-Xavier-François. Fireworks again lit up the Paris skyline, this time without fatal incident.

The boy was treasured by his adoring parents, but by the later 1780s he was succumbing slowly to the ravages of tuberculosis, reduced in the spring of 1789 to a tiny gaunt figure, mere skin and awkward jutting bones. His suffering ended, by terrible coincidence, on 4 June 1789, casting the king and queen into a paroxysm of grief at the height of the new political turmoil. They had suffered two stillbirths in the early 1780s, and lost a daughter, Sophie-Hélène-Béatrix, in infancy only two years before. They now clung fiercely to Marie-Thérèse and their younger son, Louis-Charles, the new heir, only four in 1789. By the time Louis XVI chose the fateful *berline* to carry the children to hoped-for safety, their lives would already have been imperilled once by the storms of revolution.

The Tennis-Court Oath of 20 June 1789, part of the crisis which forced Louis to drag himself out of mourning, spurred the royal court into already long-meditated action. For years, the queen and the king's brothers and cousins – the powerful 'Princes of the Blood' – had watched the country creep closer to what was, in their view, the overturning of the natural order. The roots of this turmoil were closely interwoven with the vacillating politics of Louis XVI's indecisive wish to do good. On coming to the throne, even as he restored the *parlements*, he had put in place a ministerial team bent on radical reform. Louis' own reading had led him to share some of the economic ideas of the *physiocrates*, a group of thinkers who had developed a version of free-market economics. The 'mercantilists' of previous generations had believed that wealth was a relatively fixed quantity, best increased by taking it from others: the outcome of this was a range of long-term state policies for colonial expansion, domination of overseas trade, and state sponsorship of strategically significant industries. Physiocratic thought, like modern economics, stressed the possibility of wealth creation. Rather ironically, on the verge of what we now see as the Industrial Revolution, such growth was thought to come primarily from the land, and physiocrats stressed the need to free agriculture from restrictions and liberate productivity. The need to free all sorts of economic activity from outdated regulations was nonetheless also part of their thinking.

The man Louis chose as his Finance Minister was ideally placed to carry forward reforms. Anne-Robert-Jacques Turgot was already a noted physiocratic author, whose essay *Reflections on the Production and Distribution of Wealth* had appeared several years earlier, arguing for economic deregulation. He was the son of a former mayor of Paris and of an aristocratic and intellectual mother, and had been destined for a brilliant career in the church until he switched tracks to become a state administrator. His portraits show a man at ease with his intellectual power, with a sardonic air that suggests well the intolerance he was to show to opposition. Turgot had served since 1761 as chief administrator, or *intendant*, for the Limoges region, and had successfully followed through some of his ideas at that level, boosting the local economy. Arriving in office determined to be a new broom, he immediately put into effect a series of edicts aimed at revitalising the national economy along identical lines. Two of the central pillars were the removal of the restrictive authority of local guilds over skilled labour, and the lifting of regulations that confined the trade in food grains to controlled markets, with prices that were monitored and manipulated to maintain public order.[14]

In May 1776, barely twenty months after the first of Turgot's measures had been promulgated, and little more than a year after they had been systematised in his famed 'Six Edicts', he crashed from office. There were many reasons, not least of which was that the previous year had seen food rioting across the Paris region so severe it was nicknamed the 'Flour War'.[15] The population saw the deregulation of the market as a government licence for exploitation, with artificial shortages created by greedy wholesalers to boost prices. The guilds and corporations had also mounted a tenacious defence of their rights and privileges, appealing to the natural hierarchy of society, and aided by police reports of the insubordination and riotous tendencies of 'liberated' urban workers.[16] Turgot's enemies higher up, the conservative-minded in the court, the *parlements* and even the clergy, represented his work as a threat to the structure of society itself, blackening his name with the stain of Enlightenment – already a byword for vice in such circles. The minister never hesitated to express his thoughts trenchantly, and many of his edicts carried detailed preambles making the case for reform in stern and urgent terms. The king, bombarded with such misinformation, and finding the reforming zeal expressed in some of Turgot's edicts too close to his enemies' characterisation, let the minister go, and he fell into provincial exile. Turgot himself, in a conclusion redolent of the suspicions that would dog the later revolutionaries, believed that the popular agitation of the Flour War had been purposefully created by his enemies to discredit him. He died in 1781, gout-ridden and embittered.

The end of the aspiration for thoroughgoing reform was also the beginning of the end for all those who had opposed such reform. At first, their victory did not seem so Pyrrhic, and it was even repeated five years later, when the Swiss-born Finance Minister Jacques Necker, who had guided France through a successful military intervention in the American War of Independence, made the mistake of publishing details of the royal accounts.[17] Necker had risen to political prominence after a successful banking career partly by taking an anti-physiocratic line in his own writings. Placed in power in 1777, but denied the Finance Minister's formal title (and thus a seat in the king's council) due to his Protestantism, he had run the finances on the basis of floating ever more loans to the state on the European financial markets, to avoid the crippling political difficulties of getting the *parlements* to authorise new taxes. His aim in publishing accounts had been to reassure the markets of France's creditworthiness. However, this move was just what the conservatives had been looking for to get rid of a man who was foreign, Protestant and too clever for his own good – his spiky assurance of his own financial genius, along with a sanctimonious air of moral virtue, made him few friends, and he never courted popularity within the elite. Loud voices proclaimed Necker's treachery in betraying the 'king's secret' to the outside world. This affair merged with a more internecine dispute over just how much power Necker could wield within government, as it became clear that he was being marginalised by his enemies. Louis again listened to those closest to him, and Necker was obliged to resign in 1781.

He left behind a public reputation for financial wizardry that would be much mourned in the coming years, although one could equally claim that his main skill lay in not attempting the impossible task of immediate structural reform. Although in his own writings Necker would claim to have left the royal finances on a sound footing, it did not take long for them to show a catastrophic deficit. France was locked into a desperate and increasingly forlorn attempt to reassert herself as both a continental and a maritime power – a status she had effectively lost in the disasters of the Seven Years War.[18] France should have been, according to her political elite, the arbiter of the world. Although there was great glee at the successful humbling of the English foe on behalf of the Americans, this long and costly war brought not one inch of territorial gain, and the new nation proved uninterested in a more enduring alliance. The debts that had been contracted, and the continued burden of maintaining a presence on the world stage, broke the back of the fiscal system. By August 1786, Necker's replacement, Calonne, a loyal and relatively colourless career administrator (though later colourfully defamed – he was always prominent on the list of Marie-Antoinette's alleged lovers), was forced to go to the king with the news that France would very soon be bankrupt, when a temporary tax increase sanctioned in 1782 expired at the end of the year.[19]

Structural reform was now the only route out. France's troubles were legion, and made all the more complex by being interwoven with the very nature of its society. Although it was no longer true to say, as it had been a hundred years earlier, that the nobility paid no taxes, they remained exempt from the *taille*, the main tax on land and personal wealth, and had bought themselves out of many other onerous financial obligations. Throughout every previous crisis the social elite – which included the *parlementaires*, who registered new taxes, and a wide range of other state officials – had insisted on maintaining this essentially privileged position. Their insistence was made more pointed by the fact that they actually owned their positions, and could frequently treat them as hereditary property: the crown had for hundreds of years boosted its finances by selling such 'venal offices' in the ranks of justice and administration.[20]

All this meant that every change to the finances of the state that had been effected in the previous century had been a complication or agglomeration to the existing system, rather than real reform. The elite, in fact, paid a number of the same taxes as the rest of the population, including a poll tax, the *capitation*, that was graduated by levels of wealth, and another form of property tax, the *vingtièmes*, or twentieths (so called because they were levied in chunks of 5 per cent on assessed value). It was a 'second *vingtième*' that was currently keeping state finances afloat. Nevertheless, the more powerful an individual was, the more say he had in the level at which he was assessed for these taxes – and consequently the less, proportionately, he paid.[21] Other dues that the state periodically extracted, including a whole range of fees for the continuation of rights to more general exemptions, were irritating to the elite, but could neither relieve the general inequity of the system nor provide enough income to the state.

With the knowledge of looming bankruptcy, Calonne obtained royal sanction to seek a drastic new way out: introducing more uniformity into taxation, cutting back on exemptions, and liberalising the economy to stimulate growth. All this was to be supported by a new network of local consultative bodies drawn from the propertied population without reference to pre-existing privileges. Unfortunately, to enact such changes, those with pre-existing privileges, at both the national and the provincial levels, would have to be induced to agree. Confronting the *parlements* was impossible. They collectively despised Calonne for his role in a royal dispute with the *parlement* of Brittany in 1765, and would take pleasure in sabotaging his programme for the sake of it, notwithstanding any principled disagreement they might also have.

In response to this impasse, Calonne reached back to the early seventeenth century for a precedent, and summoned an Assembly of Notables. This purely temporary gathering of 144 of the great and good, from the Princes of the Blood down, should have provided the rubber stamp he needed. It convened in February 1787, but by the time it dissolved in May not only had Calonne been ousted from office under a similar rain of opprobrium to Turgot, but his successor's modified package of reforms had also been spurned. This man, Loménie de Brienne, archbishop of Toulouse, was a favourite of the queen, and had led opposition to Calonne's agenda in the Assembly. A noted careerist, public friend of many Enlightenment writers, and widely alleged to be a secret atheist, Brienne was now sixty, but pursued reform in office with all the vigour he had opposed it with when opposition seemed profitable. For the next year he waged war on the privileged, especially the *parlements*, who continued to try to block change. This fight would earn him the richer archbishopric of Sens, and a cardinal's hat, but little else.

Unfortunately for all concerned, not only were their disputes worsening the state's fiscal plight, they also began to raise the spectre of significantly wider social and political discontent. To the conservatives of the royal court, Enlightenment may have been a dirty word, but to increasing numbers of their educated, propertied, but unprivileged subjects, it was a way of life. The term itself lacked the precision it would later acquire, and both opponents and advocates were more likely to speak loosely of *philosophie*, although the general idea of *lumières*, 'lights', signifying modern rational wisdom, was in wide use. More significant in this developing crisis were the channels of sociability through which such ideas circulated, and that had come to be associated with the idea of 'public opinion'. All sectors of propertied and leisured society, including ironically enough a broad cross-section of the highest elites, were participants in a network of both real and virtual affinities that was widely proclaimed as making up a 'tribunal' fit to judge the affairs of state – a belief that even the young Louis XVI shared, as the restoration of the *parlements* had shown.[22]

Such affinities began, most informally, but also with the highest social cachet, in the *salons* of the grand society hostesses of Paris. A subset of these had since the early eighteenth century devoted themselves to promoting high-level intellectual exchange. Although in many cases the conversation in such locations had become merely polite by the 1770s and 1780s, lacking the cutting-edge sophistication of a Voltaire, a Diderot or a Rousseau, they still fostered the idea that matters of great weight could be discussed openly. Perhaps even more significantly, and not merely in Paris but nationwide, circles of interested literati, meeting both in fee-paying reading rooms and as private clubs, dispersed knowledge of intellectual and political affairs across a broad educated 'public'. That public was a complex mix of individuals and groups. One arm extended from the judges of the provincial *parlements* and other local courts through a panoply of practising lawyers and legally qualified officials. Perhaps the majority of all those in France at this time who could be counted in the broad middle classes were men of the law in some sense or other. Some were barristers, who by the 1780s took for granted the use of 'enlightened' arguments and impassioned appeals to humanitarian sentiment in their work. More, however, were those petty local officials who ran a society still based around villages and small towns, down to the judges who sat on village tribunals, who might also be the land agents and overseers for absentee landlords. Even as men such as these judged criminals and debtors by the harsh and sometimes unjust letter of the law, they might be dreaming of new social and political utopias in their clubs and societies – safely set of course on fictional islands or in the realms of ancient history.

Men of the church were equally likely to join in such groups, especially in major centres, and indeed many of the leading thinkers of the Enlightenment were in holy orders. Placed there by their families as a respectable avenue of social progression, they had little connection with the church as a pastoral institution, and their free-thinking was less hypocritical than the atheism of archbishop Brienne, or the lovers kept by many another aristocratic prelate. Some among the local gentry might also join the realms of the 'public', but, along with the active parish clergy, the minor nobility was a bastion of traditional values, upholding a hierarchy that their 'betters' mocked even as they took it for granted. Those at the centre of economic innovation – from prosperous tenant farmers in the grain belt outside Paris to well-heeled merchants in the Atlantic ports and cotton-mill owners in Normandy and the north – usually had little time for leisured contemplation, but they were as likely as any to put their sons on the route to social respectability through office-holding and privilege, and thus to give them the leisure to think subversive thoughts from inside the system. Others who sought advancement into the ranks of the well-to-do frequently saw such subversion as a way ahead in itself, so long as it was confined to the sphere of literary and theatrical production. Countless clever young men (and a few women) sought to get ahead in the 1770s and 1780s by writing risqué novels and daring plays, though most languished in near-poverty as a result.

As such aspirations show, despite the existence of a complex network of state and religious censorship, potentially destabilising ideas circulated widely among this literate social stratum. One of the consequences of the all-pervasive tone of moral and political censorship, however ineptly applied, was that politics and morality (and especially the sexuality assailed by Catholic values) were often conflated – as Marie-Antoinette had already found to her cost, and as would continue to be the case in the coming years. The state itself acquiesced in these developments, oblivious to their underlying dangers. Louis XV's attempt to disband the *parlements* had been supported by a blizzard of government propaganda, covering both the weighty real issues and slanderous critiques of the king's enemies. At the same time, any work that was not seen as profoundly immoral was likely to get 'tacit permission' from royal officials to circulate, on the assumption that it would never fall into the hands of the common people, where thinking was truly dangerous. Both individual books and regular periodicals printed beyond the borders circulated clandestinely, their illegality merely a technicality to their readers, even while the visible edifice of censorship was maintained by occasional ritual book-burnings.[23]

In the crisis which had emerged from Calonne's failed reforms, the 'public opinion' formed in all the salons, book clubs, reading rooms and discussion circles of the educated classes fell in behind the opposition. The *parlements*, which sought essentially to reinforce their own powers, had so successfully represented royal authority as despotic that they led the public into a state of profound resistance to change – or, at least, to these particular changes. In late 1787 the government had agreed to its opponents' demands for a future meeting of the Estates-General, as the only historically sanctioned way forward. By May 1788, however, faced with continued *parlementaire* intransigence, it launched an all-out institutional assault on the *parlements*, abolishing them more thoroughly than in 1771. Mayhem ensued, with real revolt in several outlying regions, made worse by the beginnings of a food shortage caused by a disastrous harvest. The disorder could be contained by troops, but the loss of public faith was insurmountable. The state had to suspend debt payments in August, shortly after which Brienne was forced out of office (by yet more conservative intriguers), to be replaced by Necker, recalled to favour out of desperation. Necker resorted to his old policy of borrowing to cover immediate expenditure, and temporarily reinstated the *parlements*, while awaiting the Estates-General and its deliberations, hastily brought forward to the spring of 1789.

Up to this point, from the perspective of the king and his ministers, what was happening was only a more severe version of the kind of privileged resistance to change that had gone on throughout the century. What they could not yet see was that public opinion was about to take a dramatic turn. On 25 September 1788, the *parlement* of Paris, as France's highest law-court, decreed that the coming Estates-General should take its historic form – and that, therefore, there should be one chamber each for clergy, nobility and commons, voting separately and equally. At this point, the anti-despotic alliance of privileged and unprivileged shattered. For the unprivileged (and for a thin crust of liberal aristocrats who shared their views), it was out of the question for there not to be some recognition of their numerical weight – 96 per cent of the nation, by many contemporary reckonings (and probably more, in reality). Hundreds of pamphlets made the point repeatedly and vociferously. Elite opinion splintered over the issue – Necker called a second Assembly of Notables to discuss this very point, but it was unable to reach any conclusion. While some eminent figures, such as the king's cousin, the duc d'Orléans, were emerging publicly as liberals, from this gathering also came the first open voices defying the call for change, and championing a recalcitrant conservatism. On 12 December 1788 the majority of the Princes of the Blood issued a collective memorandum demanding that the king preserve privilege at all costs, and defend his nobility against the 'threat' to their existence. Social war now loomed.

The electoral process for the Estates-General began in January 1789, after the king's council had decreed that Third Estate numbers would be doubled (although it had been silent on whether or not these extra votes would be counted by head). An unprecedented mobilisation saw overtly political clubs develop in many centres, with lawyers, merchants and landowners coming together to press the demands of propertied opinion. Vociferous pamphlets stated their case. Some, like the abbé Sieyès' *What Is the Third Estate?*, condemned the privileged at great length and with profound effect as parasites on the real productive social order. The formal statement of collective grievances in documents called *cahiers de doléances* was integral to the electoral process, and here again some of the more 'enlightened' and politically astute groups began distributing model drafts for such texts, demanding a more rational administration and a fixed role for representation in the order of the state.[24]

Out beyond the charmed circle of the educated, propertied and leisured, the wider nation was also embroiled in the electoral process, with grievances being formulated even in the individual rural parishes. Here the weight of privilege was more immediate and onerous, in the form of seigneurialism, an intricate and widely variable burden of fees, dues and quit-rents paid on land and crops to those who had inherited or bought such rights. This was a relic of medieval feudalism, but also a key source of income for the nobility, who defended it ardently. Whether scions of ancient lineage or newly ennobled merchants and officials, the *seigneurs* of France showed little concern for their vassals' well-being, and treated their rights over them as both valuable property and a crucial marker of social status. In 1777, when a humble farm servant might earn only 60 livres in a year, Charles-Eugène-Gabriel La Croix Castries, a well-connected future Marshal of France, paid 770,000 livres for a package of feudal rights over a swathe of the Cévennes hills near Nîmes. For that sum he obtained the right to dues on crops across fifty parishes, to tolls on local bridges, a milling monopoly, and even the right to charge for the use of his seigneurial courts in litigation. He had no difficulty in subletting the rights to collect these dues to eager middlemen, confident that there were fat profits to be made.[25] For the poor cottager or sharecropper, the weight of rents, dues, tithes and taxes was so heavy that even fertile and well-stocked farms only yielded enough for a bare subsistence to those who worked them.[26]

In the grievances of the rural parishes, the voices of the scorned peasantry cried out for liberation from this burden and its abuses, as they suffered the effects of a dire harvest, on the heels of which came the worst winter in decades. In the short term, this had little political effect, as their representatives went forward only to local assemblies, where the leaders of propertied opinion imposed their more politically refined agenda on the final *cahiers* of grievances that went with their deputies to Versailles. The great palace-complex built a century earlier by Louis XIV, precisely to avoid contact with the turbulent masses (of Paris especially), was now to be confronted with their demands. The consequences would be shattering, especially as the general population became more and more convinced that the shortages they were enduring were caused by an 'aristocratic plot' to hinder reform and re-subjugate the masses through famine.[27]

All this agitation from below produced its inevitable reaction, and the representatives of the nobility elected to the Estates-General were generally of the most conservative coloration. The *parlementaire* administrative class was scorned in favour of the rural and military nobility, who made up over 90 per cent of those chosen, and who would prove for the most part more conservative even than the crown. Although some were modest country gentlemen, more were the wealthy products of the royal court and provincial elites, controlling resources beyond even the dreams of the Third Estate's lawyers, doctors, writers and merchants – and determined to hold on to most, if not all, the sources of that wealth and distinction. All the previous decades of shared 'enlightened' sociability were forgotten in a body which met with its membership set on radically different goals.[28] The country at large awaited an outcome in a state of unprecedented tension. Food prices were soaring, aristocratic estates on the fringes of Paris had been looted of their game, overtly anti-seigneurial rioting had racked the south-east, and, only weeks before, Paris had been convulsed by a major riot of workers protesting alleged attempts to put them on starvation wages. Popular disorder seemed to threaten a general breakdown, and the propertied elements bent on confrontation with the crown and nobility also began to set up local militias to defend their property, reinstating historic urban rights in some places, and in others simply asserting the right to take actions appropriate to the circumstances. The authority of the state to act seemed almost to have collapsed already – there was virtually no money in its coffers, and since the previous winter its only policy had been to wait for the Estates-General.[29]

From 5 May 1789, the Estates-General met at Versailles, its Third Estate members ritually humiliated, placed last in all processions, compelled into dowdy black while their aristocratic foes paraded in gold and silks, standing when they sat. To the controllers of royal protocol, this was just how things were – the natural order of hierarchy – but the Third Estate fought back. Their refusal to be just one of three chambers, their persistent calling on the clergy and liberal elements in the nobility to join them, their gradual adoption of a new language in speaking of themselves – first as 'the commons', then as the 'National Assembly' – led them down the path to their Tennis-Court Oath, and a confrontation not just with the nobility, but with the monarch.

On 23 June, in the aftermath of that dramatic pronouncement, the deputies of the three estates were again herded together, in their ritually determined order, to hear the will of the king. In hindsight, it would be the last time Louis XVI felt he had spoken to his people without constraint and from his own mind. What he presented was a plan which showed that, yet again, he had allowed himself to be influenced by those nearest him who shouted loudest. The royal council had met on 21 June, and the king's brothers had vociferously condemned the plans of Necker, supported by several other ministers, to offer the Third Estate something of what they wanted. Despite the warnings of the moderates that a plan which offered the Third almost nothing would never be accepted, and that the state lacked all means of enforcement, the conservative voices won out.[30]

After making a few hesitant opening remarks himself, the king had a speech read for him which made provision for regular meetings of the Estates, and all manner of other administrative reforms, but which treated the privileges of the nobility as immutable and central to the 'ancient constitution' of France.[31] A year earlier, the measures he proposed would have been revolutionary change, but to the ears of the National Assembly they now seemed to scorn what had already been demanded as of right. Defying royal orders to disperse, the deputies reaffirmed their earlier 'illegal' decisions. The comte de Mirabeau – a larger-than-life debauched aristocrat elected by the Third Estate of Provence for his advanced views – told the royal master of ceremonies that it would take bayonets to shift them against their will.

For Louis the programme of 23 June remained his final view on the appropriate reordering of France. When he fled Paris in 1791 he left behind a detailed memorandum explaining his actions and condemning the events of the intervening two years.[32] This text dwelt for almost as long on the personal indignities to which Louis and his family had been subjected as it did on the alleged defects of the new constitution. It said nothing of the attempt to throw out the popular minister Necker on 11 July 1789 in favour of a more solidly royalist administration, which together with alarming troop movements around Paris was taken by the capital's citizens to be the first move in an aristocratic coup. The subsequent massive three-day uprising which had seized the Bastille for the forces of revolution became merely 'sparks of revolt' which the king had braved to appear 'alone among the citizens of his capital' on 17 July. The dramatic shift in the balance of national power that forced the royal court to order troops away from the city became a royal concession 'to remove all cause of mistrust' between king and people.[33]

Louis blamed the 'men of faction' for all the ills of the country, and such never-named figures flitted through his account of the humiliations he had suffered. They were behind the events of 5 and 6 October 1789, when the ongoing crisis over food prices and simmering anger in Paris at political stalemate led to a massive march of Parisians on Versailles. The king lauded his own courage in remaining in the palace, claiming to have been forewarned of this nefarious plot, but not wishing to stir a civil war by withdrawing to a safer distance from the capital. His reward was to see an enraged crowd storm the palace after shots had been fired by Royal Bodyguards, and Marie-Antoinette placed but one locked door from a raging mob.[34]

It was a raging mob which calmed down with remarkable speed – suspicious speed, no doubt, to royal eyes – when informed that the royal family would be moving to Paris. That deal seemed to Louis to have been the goal of the whole movement, brokered as it was by the marquis de Lafayette, commander of the armed forces of revolutionary Paris, whom the king suspected of being a chief agitator. Louis and Marie-Antoinette came to loathe this haughty liberal, still only thirty-two in 1789, who prided himself on his good looks and heroic record in the American War. Their coerced agreement with him left the royal family prisoners in the Tuileries palace, which as Louis pointed out in 1791 had not had a royal occupant for nearly a hundred years. Its Renaissance splendours, dividing the Tuileries gardens from the older palace of the Louvre in a long row of pavilions, had been allowed to decay, and the rooms were 'far from providing the comforts to which His Majesty was accustomed in other royal residences'. Being guarded not by his own Bodyguard, but by detachments of Lafayette's forces, the boldly named Parisian National Guard, was yet another imposition. Louis was later careful to praise the individual citizen-soldiers for their 'attachment to his person', but this was displayed only when they were not 'led astray by the clamours and lies of the men of faction'.[35]

Points such as these reveal the overall pattern of Louis' manifesto – quite simply, he had tried to work for the good of the country, and to find 'wise men' among the new political class to collaborate with, but evil 'men of faction' had raised the people up against such sensible endeavours, mindlessly trampling on ancient prerogatives, doing vicious harm to the social and religious structure of the country, and raining personal insults on the king and his family. Such was the accumulation of defects in the body politic as a result that the king could no longer view the proposed constitution as in any meaningful way monarchic – all real power would lie with elected representatives, and his sacred royal duty to oversee the affairs of the state was being laid aside in a fashion that he could no longer pretend to accept. He admitted in the first passages of the manifesto that his apparent acceptance of changes made since October 1789 had been such a pretence, forced upon him by his 'absolute lack of liberty'.

Louis ended his text with a stirring appeal to the people of France: 'Scorn the suggestions and the lies of your false friends; return to your king; he will always be your father, your best friend. What pleasure he will have in forgetting all his personal insults, and in seeing himself again amongst you.' The price of this return was to be a constitution that Louis would feel able to accept freely, one that would respect 'our holy religion' and ensure that 'the goods and condition of each shall no longer be troubled, the laws no longer infringed with impunity, and finally that liberty shall be placed on a stable and unbreakable foundation'.[36] As the tone of the whole document made clear, for Louis the events of the past two years had been about him. For the people of France, however, the Revolution was about them.[37]

What had evidently escaped Louis' attention as his carriage rumbled across northern France on 21 June 1791 was that the country he was travelling through was not the one he had inherited almost two decades earlier. The summoning and subsequent deadlock of the Estates-General in 1789, in combination with the dire economic crisis, had stoked alarm in every corner of the country, and built up an enormous popular demand for change. Unleashed by the explosive events of mid-July, this had produced an epoch-making transformation. Louis' visit to Paris on 17 July had marked the effective collapse of the 'aristocratic' party before the force of mass revolt. His youngest brother, the comte d'Artois, had already fled the kingdom, leading the first of the *émigrés*, the 'emigrated' who would by 1790 be campaigning openly for a war on the triumphant Revolution. Within France, the National Assembly had become the dominant force in politics. The nobles and clergy, united with the Third Estate by disingenuous royal order as preparations for the 11 July coup began, found themselves bound into a body carrying out a total political and social transformation. Censorship of news had been lifted as the Estates met, and dozens of new journals spread the message of the events at Versailles far and wide. With many deputies at the Estates also conducting diligent and impassioned correspondence with the anxious constituents who had sent them, the whole country was primed for radical change. Within weeks of the Bastille's fall, forces from among the legal and propertied classes that had made up the Enlightenment 'public', seconded by a popular rank and file, had co-opted or replaced pre-existing administrations in almost every major centre, demonstrating the truly national dimensions of the upheaval.[38]

The political ambitions of the unprivileged and the epidemic of popular alarm at aristocratic plotting that redoubled after 11 July came together within weeks to create even more revolutionary change. Widespread fear of attacks on the slowly ripening harvest was largely created by anti-aristocratic propaganda, a staple of the liberated revolutionary press, but also drew on deep-seated beliefs about the ever-present danger of brigandage, the fear of strangers in isolated rural communities, and a genuine sense that starvation would follow if this crop was lost. It also followed naturally from a fear of reprisal after the widespread popular disorder of the past year. Rumour and propaganda came together to create an atmosphere in which almost anything – an unknown horseman on a local road, the noise of cattle moving through undergrowth, a particularly surly beggar – became the harbinger of the feared brigands, paid by the aristocrats to burn the harvest. For several weeks after the fall of the Bastille, normal life across much of France was suspended by this

'Great Fear', a current of emotionally charged popular mobilisation that rippled in waves across the landscape, neighbouring communities triggering each other into alarm and defensive agitation.[39]

The idea that the failed coup at the centre would be seconded by a wider assault on the population drove some regions of France into overt attacks on seigneurial chateaux, especially where antagonisms had been festering since the drafting of the parishes' *cahiers* of grievances. News of such determined actions by peasant communities merged with the flood of less definite information from fear-struck regions, giving the impression at the centre that the whole country was in arms against the old order. Thus began one of the first examples of the profound ironies that dogged revolutionary social relations into the Terror and beyond. The National Assembly was horrified by the news from the countryside. Such spontaneous popular mobilisation, lacking any 'respectable' leadership (unlike in so many towns), posed a threat to private property and public safety, and to the security of the revolutionaries themselves. Throughout the years to come, popular unrest was always more likely to be seen as aristocratically inspired anarchy than as legitimate desire for change.

At the same time, the members of the National Assembly could see that aristocratic and seigneurial privileges were at the heart of both peasant anger and noble power. A move to abolish such privilege, at least in principle, might calm popular anger, and weaken the Revolution's enemies. A motion proposing a move against seigneurial rights was quietly introduced into the Assembly on the evening of 4 August 1789. It was seconded by another, slightly different, proposal, which triggered an accelerating wave of suggestions from all sides of the Assembly for privileges which could be done away with. Overnight, carried away by enthusiasm, the Assembly agreed not just to eradicate the 'feudal' burdens on society and the distinctions they supported, but to remove the privileges of the different towns and provinces of the kingdom, to universalise taxation, to end the sale of state offices as a route to power and nobility, to make justice free, to abolish the burdensome tithe of the church, to prohibit the clergy from charging for their services, to wipe out the massive range of state pensions and sinecures enjoyed by the nobility, and thus, ultimately, to assert that France would become a society of equal citizens.[40] A year later, completing the logic of the event, the very concept of nobility and its associated titles and distinctions was abolished.

The 'Night of 4 August 1789' was a breathtaking moment, an enterprise begun almost certainly with no idea of the scope of change it would necessitate, or of the opposition it would create.[41] Many of the higher clergy and nobility, after all, had been there to propose reforms themselves, although in some cases what they suggested was the abolition of each other's privileges, as they saw their own slip away. A week later, the Assembly codified its measures on the initial question, the 'feudal' regime of the seigneurs, in a formal decree. The system was declared 'entirely abolished', but the most substantial financial burdens on lands and harvests were made into redeemable assets, not swept away as so many peasants had already demanded. The seigneurs, stripped of privilege, were yet to be allowed to demand twenty years' dues in redemption payments, with unredeemed dues to be paid *ad infinitum*.[42] This made perfect sense to the educated defenders of private property in the Assembly, but no sense at all to the peasantry – why should rights which derived fundamentally from abolished noble privilege still give such figures a claim on their harvests?

This problem was to rumble on through the following years, with perhaps a majority of all rural communities more or less ignoring their continuing 'feudal' obligations, and many taking part in waves of punitive action against seigneurs and chateaux, despite continued state attempts to restore social discipline.[43] Disorder and discontent of this sort cut across the restructuring efforts of the National Assembly, which nonetheless worked to build a fundamentally new society on the principles implicit in the abolition of privilege. At the end of August 1789, they agreed to a Declaration of the Rights of Man and the Citizen, which in seventeen brief articles codified that society's foundation: free, equal, individual citizens, subject to law, protected in their property and opinions, and entitled to political participation. The king's refusal to sanction this, or the earlier decree on feudalism, contributed significantly to the crisis which saw him transported to Paris in October. Even before that, moderates in the Assembly had lost the battle to create a noble upper house for the new legislature, or to give the king more than a temporary 'suspensive' veto on legislation. The power of a democratically elected chamber was to be almost absolute.

The National Assembly went on over the next year to construct a system of democratic representation of astonishing thoroughness. It began by wiping the map of France clean. Centuries of piecemeal acquisitions by conquest or treaty, hallowed local and regional traditions of autonomy or difference – all evidence of backward-looking historical particularity was erased. Eighty-three new 'departments' made up the new administrative jigsaw, roughly equal in size, and themselves divided into an orderly pyramid of districts, cantons and municipalities. Election was the mode of appointment for new officials of all stripes – not merely the councillors of the different bodies, but also their administrators and legal officers, and the judges of local courts.[44]

For municipalities – and this included even the tiniest village – the local autonomy offered was remarkable (and would prove an enduring headache for higher authorities). At a stroke were swept away the statist traditions of royal absolutism, which had seen top-down authority exercised through appointed officials as the only way to deal with the unprivileged general population. The radicalism of this electoral system was tempered, however, by the imposition of differing levels of taxpayer franchise – some two-thirds of adult males qualified to vote, but only directly chose officials at the municipal level. For higher posts, these 'active citizens' chose 'electors' from those who paid a higher level of tax, a cohort of less than a tenth of the four million voters, to go forward to the departmental electoral colleges that actually made appointments. Thus real electoral power was restricted to those who might reasonably be expected to respect private property.

By the summer of 1790, as they were settling into office, this cohort of electors acquired a new role, one that was to add a further dimension of dissent to the revolutionary landscape. They were made responsible for electing parish priests and bishops. In a Catholic system that had relied for almost two millennia on top-down, 'apostolic' authority, this was a stunning change. To the National Assembly, it seemed perfectly logical, because at the end of 1789 the vast lands and endowments of the Catholic church – including almost a tenth of all farmland – had been effectively nationalised, as part of the effort to resolve the fiscal meltdown that was the original cause of the revolutionary crisis. The clergy were to become salaried state servants, while the confiscated assets would back a new paper currency, the assignat, which would be used to pay back many of the state's creditors (including the holders of privileged 'venal offices', all of whom were slated for hefty compensation). They could then use the paper at advantageous terms to buy parcels of the former church land – *biens nationaux* or 'national property' as it was called. The paper could be burned, and thus the debt would be erased; meanwhile the market for agricultural land was stimulated, and more such land put to productive use by new profit-maximising landlords.

By early 1791 the monetary dimension of this system was already beginning to crumble. The paper money, rather than being dissolved into the land market, was reaching wider and wider circulation. Hard currency was in woefully short supply as the wealthy, seeing the disorder around them, and in some cases planning for emigration, hoarded their resources in tangible coin. Instead of burning already issued notes, the treasury was having to print more and more, and they were devaluing steadily – a few per cent so far, but with far worse to come.[45] The religious dimension, which should have been merely a rational restructuring of an old and unwieldy system, was meanwhile threatening to trap the revolutionaries in a nutcracker of popular and elite opposition. The clergy had voiced fundamental objections to becoming salaried officials, especially in an electoral context where Protestants, Jews or 'enlightened' atheists might be among the voters, and when the revolutionaries refused to allow the pope to be consulted. Although the new status of the church was enshrined in law through the 'Civil Constitution of the Clergy' in July 1790, agitation against it continued, attracting widespread support in some regions.

Stung by this criticism, and fundamentally unable to accommodate such objections within their outlook, the National Assembly had imposed a loyalty oath on all existing parish priests and bishops in January 1791. Half of the priests (and almost all the bishops) refused to take it, and these 'non-jurors' were supported by substantial parts of the population, especially in regions of the west, north-east and south where they formed the majority. Violence flared on all sides – loyal priests were stoned, and even shot at, in dissenting areas, dissenting priests likewise assaulted elsewhere, and civil authorities hauled into a wide range of antagonisms that ranged from the local and personal to the overtly ideological.[46]

The religious issue gave 'counter-revolution' something that the grievances of dispossessed seigneurs never could: a popular constituency. In the south, where sectarian rivalries with a Protestant minority were entrenched, the preservation of the Catholic religion had already proved its value as a rallying-cry in several bloody urban confrontations throughout 1790.[47] Overt counter-revolutionaries, in contact with the comte d'Artois' exile network, had been behind much of this agitation. From now on, intransigent Catholic believers across France were to dog the Revolution's footsteps, earning themselves the label of 'fanatics' and an unending torrent of scorn from the 'enlightened' elite.

Religion also carried Louis XVI a step closer to his final break with the National Assembly. Although he publicly sanctioned the Civil Constitution and its subsequent oath from his Parisian 'captivity', he was privately unreconciled, and took Palm Sunday communion on 17 April 1791 within the Tuileries from a non-juror. The following day, the royal family attempted to leave the city for the chateau of Saint-Cloud, their summer residence. Departure now would evade the king's planned and highly public Easter communion in the city. Word of the events of the 17th had spread, however, and what followed demonstrated that 'patriotic' alarms could still produce massive popular responses. A crowd blockaded the Tuileries, marooning the royal family in their carriages. Rumours that a royal flight beyond the frontiers was planned swept the city, and the Parisians stoutly resisted the entreaties of the municipal leadership to let the royal family pass.[48] Giving in rather than sanction violence, Louis and Marie-Antoinette became convinced that a more secret flight was now their only hope.

As they plotted escape, and Louis drafted his manifesto, the king and queen looked out on a world that seemed to have gone mad, where groups who simply had no right to a place in the political process had usurped proper authority, and used it to wreak havoc. The king was particularly critical of the Societies of Friends of the Constitution that had sprung up in growing numbers over the last year and a half. Spiritual heirs of the Enlightenment reading clubs, and of the more political groups hastily convened in the Third Estate agitation of 1788–1789, they formed according to Louis an 'immense corporation', a divisive interest opposing the will of the monarch, just as the *parlements* had done to disastrous effect through the century.[49]

Such clubs orbited most clearly around the agenda set by the Paris club, which had begun among members of the Estates-General itself, and which met in a monastic building not far from the Tuileries. The nickname of that monastic order, the Jacobins, gave this club and the whole movement its everyday title.[50]

The Jacobins were, for Louis, the public face of the shadowy 'men of faction' he devoted so much energy to condemning. He attributed to them enormous powers over public opinion, and claimed that they had successfully hounded out of existence any rival organisations. This was a gross exaggeration, although it was true that in Paris popular hostility to a group of nobles who called themselves the 'Friends of the Monarchical Constitution' had forced the group into effective dissolution, unable to meet without attendant crowd disorder.[51] Less exaggerated were Louis' other claims: that the clubs often met publicly, exposing state policy to criticism before a humble audience; that they corresponded among themselves across the nation on matters of public business; and that they passed decrees and motions that were often placarded and published, even – especially – when harshly critical of authority.

The Jacobin Club movement was in many ways the French Revolution's substitute for a political party system. The latter was widely regarded as unthinkable, because it would institutionalise something that even radicals called 'faction' – groups organising against each other to contest for power. The clubs, however, saw themselves not as such a faction, but simply as patriots gathered to discuss what was best for the nation. In the smaller localities where clubs formed, and to a certain extent even in larger cities, there was an element of truth in this, and the clubs accommodated a broad swathe of the patriotic elite emerging from all the new structures of political engagement. Nonetheless, the overt forces of counter-revolution remained far beyond the pale for the Jacobins, and the movement spent much of its energies on denunciation of aristocratic and clerical enemies.

For the king, of course, those 'enemies' were among the most cherished of his subjects, and from his perspective there is no question that Jacobinism represented the horrors of an institutionalised insurrection against all he held dear. In this context, Marie-Antoinette in particular was blithely and indiscreetly enthusiastic about the restoration of proper subordination once the monarch was again 'free'. She had been so for some time, writing as early as February 1791 to the comte de Mercy-Argenteau, an Austrian diplomat and long-time confidant, that 'we have decided to take as a basis for the constitution the declaration of 23 June', and that they were 'grappling together with the very difficult choice' of ministers in a new monarchical government.[52] Such correspondence indicates quite clearly that, if the precise contours of the 20 June flight were arranged after the Easter débâcle, the underlying intention had long been present. As that flight unfolded, the unreality of the royal understanding that lay behind it would become dramatically apparent.[53]

It was 6 p.m. on 21 June by the time the royal party reached the isolated posthouse at Pont-de-Somme-Vesle, near Châlons, where they had been supposed to meet their first escorts three hours earlier. The withdrawal of that escort had been brought about at least partly by the suspicious and threatening actions of the local peasantry, who having seen the troops arrive had left their fields. Seigneurs had in the past used troops to enforce the collection of feudal dues, and in this harvest season there was much alarm at a possible revival of that practice. The decision Choiseul then took, to withdraw his troops cross-country, rather than to precede the royal party on the road, merely widened the area of alarm through the long summer evening.

The royal family's carriage meanwhile rumbled on after its change of horses, towards the next rendezvous, the small town of Sainte-Ménéhould. By now, the first misgivings were beginning to dawn, and an outrider was sent into the town to look for the escort. He found them, eventually, in their billets, their commander horrified to find the royal party arriving even as he reported his orders to stand down. This officer perhaps grasped the urgency of the situation better than anyone, urging the carriage on as the horses were again changed: 'Leave, hurry, you are lost if you do not leave quickly!'[54] The *berline* and its outriders departed as fast as they could, its occupants unaware that a real race for their freedom was now on. They had been recognised as they departed by Drouet, the postmaster, returning from an engagement elsewhere. Unwilling to act alone, he gathered Sainte-Ménéhould's mayor and councillors and reported the news. This small group, the unremarkable local worthies of a peaceful rural town, now showed the true impact of the Revolution. As one, they authorised Drouet to pursue the carriage and to halt it.

Meanwhile, they arrested the commander of the cavalry detachment, who had already discovered to his chagrin that, once the truth of the situation became apparent, his men were unwilling to saddle up and ride out to protect the king's party.

One loyal sergeant did make for the next post, bidding to outrace Drouet – himself an ex-cavalryman who knew the country well – and alert the king to his peril. He arrived there, at Clermont-en-Argonne, too late. The drama was not yet over, however. The *berline* had gone on its way after its outrider had warned the detachment commander there not to stand to, for fear of a general alarm. Once the carriage was away, the officer's attempt to rouse his men brought not only a mutinous refusal from them, but the summoning of the local National Guards by the municipality.

It was at the next relay, Varennes, that all hope was to be lost. Darkness was falling as the royal voyagers arrived at half-past ten, to discover not only that the troops meant to guard them had been withdrawn, but that they had taken with them the fresh horses for the carriage, placed in their care here as an extra measure of security. It was only by a combination of pleas and threats that the party were able to persuade the postilion to drive his horses a little further, and it had required an equally humiliating personal plea from the king for a local officer to grudgingly direct them to the billets of the cavalrymen. These desperate efforts were in vain, for Drouet had arrived, and the municipality of Varennes proved as decisive as that of his home town. The bridge out of town was blockaded and the local National Guard stood on alert. As the *berline* rolled up, the town's procurator – the council's legal officer – demanded to see the party's passports, which had been completed in the name of a Russian baroness, a role played by the children's governess, Madame de Tourzel. The king was disguised as her steward, and the queen as governess to the children, both of whom were dressed as girls. As they waited for the documents to be scrutinised, the Royal Bodyguard who was their closest outrider turned and asked Marie-Antoinette – tellingly not the king – for permission to 'charge this rabble', but she demurred.[55] The passport was technically valid, but Drouet intervened, claiming it lacked a necessary signature.

The objection was enough for the procurator to insist that the party descend from the carriage and move to his house.[56] His name was Sauce, and he was a merchant grocer – the cause of much satirical comment in coming weeks, given the king's predilection for fine foods. Meanwhile, Drouet's insistence that the 'steward' was Louis caused the summoning of a local worthy who had lived at Versailles. His spontaneous recognition, falling to one knee before the king, ended all pretence. For the king and queen, military rescue now seemed their best hope. That hope was briefly raised when Choiseul's original detachment of forty horsemen, which had been meandering across country for over five hours, arrived at Varennes and made themselves known. But by now almost the entire population of the town had appeared, a crowd surrounding Sauce's house, agog with the news of the king's presence. With every passing minute, as the circle of alarm spread, the crowds got larger. Peasants dressed in smocks and clogs mingled with townsfolk dragged from their beds in hastily donned coats and jackets, and a growing contingent of revolutionary blue uniforms, as more and more National Guards, by the handful and by the dozen, were arriving from neighbouring communities. Many others who wore no uniforms were nonetheless armed, if not with muskets, then with shotguns, pitchforks or flails. Choiseul's gallant offer to force a passage was vetoed by the king, fearing for the lives of his family in the wild firing that would certainly break out.

In vain the king attempted to rally his subjects, appearing at the windows, trying to engage the crowd, playing the tender father. He claimed that it was among his loyal country folk that he sought shelter from the dangers of Paris, he invited them all to travel to Montmédy with him, to see that he had no intention of leaving France. His pleas fell on deaf ears. There was no riotous anger, few threats, just a stone wall of popular determination that his journey should not be allowed to continue. The officers of the municipality, initially overawed by the king's presence, had promised him that they would help him reach Montmédy in daylight. The gathering crowds, however, seemed to have no intention of letting that happen. The officials dispatched a rider to Paris for instructions, and the night passed as the royal family fell further into despair. At six the next morning, unexpectedly, orders came from Paris – the National Assembly had formulated instructions to all officials as soon as the flight had been discovered, and these had crossed with the courier from Varennes.

The orders were unambiguous: the king had been kidnapped by

counter-revolutionary forces, and was to be detained and returned to Paris forthwith. Much rapid thought had gone into this phrasing. On the one hand, to admit that the king might have left of his own free will would stir up radical hatred against him, and make an accommodation very difficult – he was still the keystone of the constitutional order, and most leaders of the Assembly wanted him back in that role. On the other hand, it was only by claiming that the king had been taken against his will that the Assembly could offer a legal justification for his capture: the royal person was constitutionally inviolable, and his choice of residence could not be officially gainsaid. One way or the other, he had to be reduced to a puppet in order to be restored.

The legal niceties meant little at Varennes – the king had been stopped, travelling incognito towards the frontiers, that was all most of the thousands now thronging the town, turning it into a virtual armed camp, had known until this moment, and all they had cared about. The counter-revolution that lurked across the Rhine was not to have him, whether he willed it or not. Even so, it was the sight of the orders from Paris that drew from Louis' lips the mournful comment that 'there is no longer a king in France'.[57] Despite this tone of resignation, he held on to a slim hope of rescue by Bouillé, the military governor and commander of Montmédy. For over an hour, he tried to delay departure, feigning exhaustion, but the *berline* turned down the road to Paris at 7.30 a.m. on the 22nd, two hours before Bouillé rode up to the blockaded bridge with his rescuing forces. The strength of the mobilised population at Varennes prevented him pursuing the king further, and he turned about, fleeing the country himself within hours. Louis was left to travel in the hands of ordinary Frenchmen, become revolutionaries, down the road that wound back to a capital in arms, and wound forward into an era of war, regicide and Terror.

CHAPTER 2

# Hankering After Destruction

The city that awaited the return of the king sprawled for miles along the banks of the Seine, and housed more than six hundred thousand people. At its heart it remained a medieval metropolis, a dense maze of tiny streets, paved with mud and overhung with timber-frame houses that reared unevenly to five or six storeys (and occasionally collapsed on themselves without warning). These streets bore names redolent of an earlier era of narrow economic specialities and tight-knit communities – the Street of the Weavers (rue de la Tixeranderie), the Quay of the Leather-dressers (quai de la Mégisserie) – and others that reminded the walker constantly of the profusion of religious houses and orders – the Street of the Girls of St Thomas, of the Unshod Carmelites, of the Little Fathers. Many of the convents such names marked were by 1791 in the hands of the revolutionary state, which had abolished monasticism a year before, but around them the same populations crowded into apartment houses and tenement blocks. Traditionally, the ground floors of such residences were given over to workshops, with people of means renting large apartments on the first couple of storeys above. As the buildings rose, so rooms became smaller and more numerous, cheaper to rent, and home to more and more impoverished workers. The centre of Paris still preserved much of this mixed character, but newer developments were producing a more sharply divided social landscape.[1]

To the west and south-west sprawled the new developments of the wealthier classes, in the Faubourgs (or suburbs) Saint-Honoré and Saint-Germain. Here the aristocracy had come to congregate over the eighteenth century in newly built townhouses that walled out the urban bustle, and the bourgeoisie increasingly to concentrate in less grand but equally exclusive new residential districts. Around them were the great open spaces of the city: the long formal rectangle of the gardens of the Tuileries palace, open to respectable strollers, at the west end of it the immense square of the Place Louis XV (now Place de la Révolution, eventually Place de la Concorde), and beyond that the Champs-Elysées, still as their name implied open fields landscaped as pleasure-grounds. South of the river stood the Champ de Mars, drill-ground of the national military school that stood nearby, transformed in July 1790 into an open-air arena for 250,000 participants and half a million spectators to salute national unity in a 'Festival of Federation' on the anniversary of the Bastille's fall.

Eastwards from the tangled centre, the city presented a different aspect. Equally sprawling, but lacking in architectural grandeur, the Faubourgs Saint-Antoine and Saint-Marcel extended north and south of the river. The former, once overawed by the looming fortress-prison of the Bastille, was home to the city's carpenters and furniture trades, and also legendary for its independence. For over a century, workers who wanted or needed to work outside the control of the guilds that dominated the city centre could find refuge under the 'privileges' of the Faubourg Saint-Antoine. By 1789, this made it the haunt of licence, or of the most fervent defenders of revolutionary liberty, depending on your reading. Its citizens in 1791 certainly lauded their leading role in revolutionary events, supporting a society named unequivocally the Conquerors of the Bastille, Defenders of Liberty. Saint-Antoine, for all its allure of marginality, was a relatively salubrious region. Less so Saint-Marcel. For decades before the Revolution, it had been universally regarded as the haunt of the lowest plebs, a *populace* in the contemporary jargon, ready to rise up and trouble public order on the lightest pretext. Home to the tanners of Paris, whose stinking effluent polluted the Bièvre stream that flowed into the Seine, everything about the area spoke of decay and turpitude. Whenever trouble loomed in the years before and after 1789, rumour would place the 'brigands' of Saint-Marcel at the heart of it.[2]

With areas such as this lurking within walking distance, and a floating population of tens of thousands clogging the rooming-houses of the centre, Paris had always been a nervous city. Fear of crime was everywhere. Crowds who strolled in the gardens of the Palais-Royal not far from the Louvre, or took themselves to the melodramas and burlesques of the popular theatres that stood on the boulevards where once medieval ramparts ran, were preyed upon incessantly by pickpockets and tricksters. Handkerchiefs, pocket watches and snuff boxes vanished, to reappear on the second-hand stalls that lined the riverbanks, and once a week took over the Place de Grève that sloped down to the gravelly shore in front of the central City Hall. There also once a week those thieves unfortunate enough to be caught were flogged and branded, and if recidivists hanged. Before the Revolution more dire crimes were punished by breaking on the wheel – death by the smashing of limbs and skull.[3]

On another day of the week, unemployed artisans used the Place de Grève as an outdoor labour-exchange, meeting to await masters in need of workers. The city's industries were dominated by the skilled tradesmen who made up this milieu, many of them organised over the centuries into guilds that had defended their privileged control of specific activities – from goldsmithing to glazing, tailoring to spit-roasting – through the courts. Raised up to their trades from adolescence as apprentices, and serving as journeymen to refine their art for years until they could buy into the ranks of the masters, such artisans traditionally safeguarded order and subordination as the backbone of urban society. The reforms of Turgot in the 1770s had dramatically challenged this role, and the guilds reinstated after his fall had lost the right to insist upon an apprenticeship for new masters – turning them much more into capitalist employers of labour rather than true 'master craftsmen'. Resentment stoked up over the coming years by the enforcement of new rules against the workers had helped encourage the concern with their liberty that animated such artisans by 1791. The guilds were formally abolished in March, allowing the workers to press for fairer treatment by employers, freed from 'oppressive' regulations. But the revolutionary state was no more welcoming of economic subversion than had been the Old Regime, and on 14 June 1791 passed a law banning all workers' associations. Workers who had been at the forefront of the fight for liberty were now seeing that quality redefined against them, criminalising them for restraint of trade.[4]

For over a century Paris had been rigorously policed, its mechanisms for controlling both simple crime and the wider subversive potential of the masses lauded as an example to all of absolutist Europe. Local neighbourhood magistrates dealt with complaints and accusations, troops of the royal guards and city watch lent their forces to the law, and a more sinister force of Inspecteurs de Police ran former thieves, among others, as secret agents to root out nefarious plots. All of this was the empire of the infamous Lieutenant-General of Police, a senior government official with the ear of the king himself, charged with preventing the forces of the vast urban morass from ever threatening the stability of the kingdom. This of course the police had signally failed to do in July 1789, and superficially at least they had been swept away.[5]

Paris was now policed instead by its Sections, elected neighbourhood bodies with their own police commissioners and magistrates, and with the power of the citizens' militia of the National Guard to enforce order. All this was widely recognised by the population as right and proper. But Paris in 1791 was increasingly agitated by the continued existence of a secret police, whose agents sometimes took on National Guard uniform, and who continued to spy on those they viewed as subversives: in some cases, continuing a career that had started as servants of the Old Regime. The nature of subversion – and how far it existed, and was 'counter-revolutionary' by definition – had occasioned violent confrontations between the forces of order and many ardent radicals numerous times already in 1791, even before the king presented his capital with a whole new set of problems to deal with.[6]

The Paris that the royal party returned to on 25 June 1791 was a solemn and divided city. Municipal orders had banned public expressions of anger as the *berline* rolled through the streets, but countless thousands who stood silent to watch it go by, hats firmly on heads, made their feelings plain enough. On the journey, one man had already paid with his life for an expression of loyalty. The comte du Val de Dampierre had tried to ride up to the carriage and salute the king, only to be gunned down by locals for whom he had once been a harsh and untouchable overlord, and to whom his conduct confirmed his nature as an *aristocrate* and counter-revolutionary.[7] The monarch's fall from grace had been reinforced when they reached

Epernay by the intrusive presence in the carriage of two members of the National Assembly. From then on they rode in literal physical contact with the royal family, and made it clear that they controlled the progress of the journey – it was they, not the king, who ordered the meals and rest-stops. The apparent ease with which the fugitives had been taken in hand, however, masked the real and perilous dilemmas that the revolutionaries now faced.

A rolling carnival of revolutionary enthusiasm had accompanied the journey, with tens of thousands marching in relays around the royal coach, men, women and children alike, the whole populations of many communities turning out to witness the spectacle. They were not there merely as spectators, however, and arrived armed, even if only with pitchforks, axes or scythes, to guard against any hint of counter-revolutionary rescue. Constant cries of 'Long live the king' resounded around the carriage, but this goodwill was accompanied by equally fervent hostility towards his alleged kidnappers. A boiling torrent of personal invective was hurled at the three Royal Bodyguards seated prominently atop the *berline*, as were countless stones and handfuls of dung. The queen was intermittently reviled as well – the dauphin's paternity was loudly called into question countless times, and when she tried to give a piece of chicken to a solicitous guardsman, a huge cry went up that it was poisoned. At all the frequent stops along the way, local mayors and other dignitaries used the opportunity to parade their own revolutionary credentials, forcing the king to endure public harangues on his thoughtless conduct as the local National Guards strutted in their tricolour regalia.[8]

One of the key themes of such speeches, and of the abuse directed at the Bodyguards and the queen, was the real fear that the flight had inflicted on the country, and the dread consequences of the king's departure. If the crowds had known that, when the royal party stopped for the night at Châlons-sur-Marne, yet another escape plan had been put to the king by local sympathisers, their fears would have known no bounds. Louis naturally refused to flee alone. As it was, the royal family was hustled away from Mass the following morning by National Guards newly alarmed at reports that Varennes had been put to the torch by invading Austrians, and only the meeting with the National Assembly deputies shortly afterwards calmed spirits that were close to a dangerous hysteria. The royal governess, Madame de Tourzel, had almost fallen into the hands of an angry mob at a rest-stop just hours before.[9] Rumours of the effect of this treatment on the queen were rife – the American minister in Paris, Gouverneur Morris, recorded reports that 'the queen's hair is turned grey by her late adventures', while a letter to a British diplomat from his daughter claimed that 'she has scarcely any hair left; in her despair she tore it off'.[10]

One of the two deputies who joined the king in the carriage, and was to have a key influence on the royal family's fate, was Antoine-Pierre Barnave, a twenty-nine-year-old former barrister who had been prominent in revolutionary events as far back as 1788, when he led pro-*parlementaire* opposition in and around Grenoble. His early participation in politics seemed to mark him out as a fiery radical, and in late July 1789 he had earned a scandalous reputation by questioning whether the blood of two royal officials, lynched in ghastly fashion in the middle of Paris, had been so 'pure' as to make their deaths regrettable. Active participation in the expanding political influence of the Paris Jacobin Club, and hostility to the relatively centrist political disposition of Lafayette through 1790, added to this impression.

In August 1790 a maverick right-wing deputy, Jacques-Antoine de Cazalès, had challenged Barnave to a duel after calling him 'the greatest rogue of all the rogues' on the left of the Assembly. Barnave defended his honour as a gentleman, as well as boosting his radical reputation, by exchanging pistol shots with Cazalès in the Bois de Boulogne. He fired first, and missed. Cazalès' pistol misfired three times before he, too, missed. On the reload (demanded by Cazalès), Barnave shot him in the head. Cazalès' hat cushioned the blow, but left him with a fractured skull, from which he would recover to become an *émigré* in later years.[11] By early 1791 Barnave was one of a 'triumvirate' of leaders widely perceived to be steering the Assembly's destiny from their base in the Jacobins. The other two were Adrien Duport, a former Paris *parlementaire*, and Alexandre de Lameth, a senior cavalry officer before his election to the Second Estate. Alexandre's brother Charles, an Assembly deputy as well, had also fought a duel for the radicals' honour, being wounded by the duc de Castries in November 1790.[12] The fact that such figures, 'respectable' enough to exchange blows with haughty aristocrats, could be seen as radical leaders says much for the limited effect that social change had yet had at the heart of the political system.

The crisis of the Flight to Varennes, however, crystallised many of the social and political tensions that underlay the influence of the 'triumvirs', and revealed stark ideological clashes within the ranks of the revolutionaries. The dread provoked by news of the king's flight, embodied in the harangues he endured on the return trip, marked the point where the residual enthusiasm of 1789, the belief that the country could indeed be remade anew for the betterment of all, yielded dominance in the public mind to the other side of the political coin: fear that such gains as had been made would be overturned by the active plots of the Revolution's enemies, and bloody revenge exercised upon the patriots who had dared to challenge the rights of the aristocrats. From this came two themes that would drive the Revolution relentlessly forward from now on: a belief in the need for more change to consolidate what had gone before, and a growing and increasingly violent willingness to engage in open conflict with the ever-swelling ranks of the perceived 'counter-revolution'. At the forefront of these trends, immediately after Varennes and in the years ahead, were the men and women of the radical clubs of Paris.

The Jacobin movement may have been the face of radicalism on the national political stage, but within Paris many had gone beyond it, both in the policies they advocated and in the personnel they recruited. First among these was the Cordeliers Club. Named like the Jacobins for the monastic cloister in which it met, this club descended directly from one of the most radical of the sixty districts into which Paris had been divided for the Estates-General elections. In mid-1790 the campaigners for direct democracy who had led this district had been decisively defeated, as the city was remodelled into forty-eight Sections with no deliberative powers. The formation of the club had been their immediate response, taking the formal name 'Society of the Friends of the Rights of Man', and with that making the clear suggestion that the national and municipal leadership had already begun to scorn those rights.[13]

The leadership of the Cordeliers was a mixed grouping. Louis Legendre, for example, was a local master butcher, but one who had earned a reputation for radicalism by active participation in the July and October risings of 1789. Antoine Momoro was one of the few licensed printers in Paris before 1789, a prosperous businessman whose transition to radical politics seems to have been a matter of principle. For Jacques-René Hébert, a provincial goldsmith's son who had joined the stream of ambitious young men into the capital in the 1780s, radical politics, and more specifically radical journalism, had been an escape route from a somewhat marginal existence as, among other things, a theatre box-office clerk. François Robert, by contrast, had been a lawyer before turning to revolutionary journalism and organisation, the former especially in partnership with his wife, Louise Kéralio, an accomplished author in her own right. All of these figures were under forty when the Revolution broke out – in Robert's case, under thirty. Similarly young, and still only thirty-two in 1791, was possibly the most eminent early Cordelier, Georges-Jacques Danton.

Danton was a barrister, son of a lawyer, prosperous but unsatisfied, who saw in the Revolution a chance for distinction. He was a natural adventurer, larger than life in many senses, whose forceful personality and sparkling charm overcame the handicap of his face, brutally scarred by a childhood encounter with an angry bull. His leadership had been one of the major factors in making the original Cordeliers district a thorn in the side of higher authority. A pithy and aphoristic speaker, by early 1791 he had graduated his talents to the Jacobin Club itself, and his restless quest for both distinction and material gain would ultimately bring his downfall. For now, however, he remained an inspirational figurehead to a growing movement.[14]

Just as the leadership of the Club drew indiscriminately on the professional and artisan circles of its locality, so it had a membership that made no distinction between citizens' economic status – there was an entry fee, but a mere fraction of the sum that deterred all but the prosperous from joining the Jacobins. From its origins, the Cordeliers movement set itself against the principle, adopted back in 1789 by the National Assembly, that political participation should be limited to taxpaying 'active citizens'. The rank and file of the Cordeliers itself did not stretch down very deeply into the realms of domestic servants, seamstresses, labourers, laundrywomen, apprentices and journeymen artisans that made up so much of the Parisian population (and indeed membership of the club was not formally open to women), but they certainly encouraged such people to attend freely as spectators to their debates. Early in 1791, moreover, Cordeliers activists launched a wave of new organisations specifically designed to attract just such people, of both sexes, to political consciousness.[15]

A 'Fraternal Society of Both Sexes' had already begun to meet in late 1790, sharing the premises of the Jacobin Club, and initially dedicated to relatively uncontroversial political education for its plebeian members. In the atmosphere of spring 1791, with growing rumours of the king's disloyalty, raging conflict over the priesthood and a rising tide of radical political comment in the press, this group was caught up and transformed into one of the leading 'popular societies'. Alongside others such as the Society of the Carmes (named for yet another monastic locale), the Halles (in the market district) and the Indigents (making an explicit political statement about the capacities of the poor), the Fraternal Society became a noisy presence on the Parisian political stage.

The popular societies drew together a membership that was probably in the low thousands, and that included precisely the sort of labouring people formerly cut out of political life – right down to porters, serving-maids and day-labourers.[16] The trajectory of this grouping over the coming months, and their fate after the Flight to Varennes, illustrated again the complex ironies of revolutionary social conflict. By the time of the Flight, popular societies were in a state of semi-proscription. A law passed by the Assembly on 10 May had prohibited them from petitioning public bodies collectively – that is, in the name of the society, rather than as a list of individual signatories. Although the societies continued to meet and agitate, they had clearly been marked out as dangerous and disruptive, and in the atmosphere of the time such danger was understood through the language of counter-revolution. The reasoning behind this had been made clear by the Paris Municipality when it petitioned the Assembly in advance of the 10 May measure:

> For a long time, the enemies of the constitution have placed their hopes in anarchy; they have counted on the exaggeration of patriotism and on the excess of that impatient ardour produced by the rapid conquest of liberty. They have calculated on the habit of mistrust in a people always abused; that so-long repressed hatred of an oppressive government; those movements of fear and of scorn inspired by all acts of authority, when it is usurped. They have employed these sentiments, which they must have found everywhere, with the most fatal cunning against all the legitimate powers conferred by a free people.[17]

In other words, being more radical than the established authorities was a counter-revolutionary act, especially when it stirred up the 'people', by whom is meant here the allegedly ignorant and easily duped common people, who had been excluded from the franchise for precisely that reason. At a time when refractory priests were clearly leading a groundswell of resistance to revolutionary policy in the provinces, and aristocratic plotters had been adept at exploiting sectarian tensions, any agitation which disrupted public loyalties was subsumed into the same pattern. What appeared to be radical idealism was in fact, the authorities claimed, a mask for an aristocratic campaign of provocation, seeking the collapse of the revolutionary settlement by fostering impossible popular expectations that would inevitably lead to violence.

Nowhere was this more clearly felt than in the authorities' antagonism towards the radical press. Hundreds of new journals had sprung into life since 1789 (and almost all collapsed swiftly for want of readers) as formerly draconian restrictions on freedom of expression could no longer be maintained. They covered a spectrum from the most farouche counter-revolution to violent and uncompromising radicalism. In the savage competition for readers that marked the trade, some flourished, to become instant institutions.[18] Jacques-René Hébert, for example, would from 1791 on become a leading radical journalist. At the time of Varennes, however, he was eclipsed in the eyes of the aggressively anti-aristocratic Parisians by the idiosyncratic figure of Jean-Paul Marat.

A trained doctor who had once hoped to forge a career among the scientific academies of the capital, only to be scorned (he claimed) for his humble origins and radical views, Marat was already forty-five in 1789, and had been producing republican and 'anti-despotic' writings since the late 1770s. He soon found his niche in the new political landscape, producing a newspaper, *L'Ami du Peuple*, 'The People's Friend', that claimed to enlighten the population about the dire threats to their new-found freedom. Constantly harassed by the authorities, forced into hiding on several occasions, Marat continued a stream of denunciations against the Paris municipality and the 'traitors' in the National Assembly, demanding new uprisings and thousands of heads to make the Revolution safe.[19] Yet while his extremism made him a bogeyman of the centre and right – and even led some to believe that 'Marat' was a character confected as part of the aristocrats' provocations – he became an icon for the radical population. He claimed with some justification that 'I am the anger, the just anger, of the people, and that is why they listen to me and believe in me.'[20] Men and women gathered in the streets and squares to read 'the latest Marat' to each other, and his columns often contained virulent denunciations of the authorities' wrongdoings, sent in by readers themselves. His pages were in part a forum for a developing sense of radical popular identity, something the authorities simply could not accommodate in their world-view. From Marat, and their own experiences, many on the streets of Paris learned to share the view he put pithily four days before the king fled, apostrophising the National Guard's General Lafayette and the municipality: 'The people should have the good sense to hang you high and dry. That's how all the villainy of the public functionaries, plotting with the king to re-establish despotism, must be ended.'[21]

Thus the ironic belief of the authorities in the counter-revolutionary nature of radicalism was made into an even deeper and more unresolvable problem by the corresponding view, on the radical side, that the politics of the National Assembly were themselves in danger of undermining the very revolution they had created. This confrontation became starkly visible in the aftermath of the king's flight. Paris was cast into turmoil by the escape, and all the fears of subversion that lurked behind the façade of citizen unity rapidly boiled to the surface. The prisons were patrolled with new vigour, as were the lodging houses that accommodated the suspiciously rootless elements of the population, widely feared to be 'brigands' in the pay of the *émigrés*. The National Guard, organised in no fewer than sixty battalions across Paris, stood to on all sides, primed for confrontation.

The first clashes, however, were with those who blamed the Guard itself for the situation. To many on the streets, it seemed that only collusion could have allowed the royal family to slip out of what was allegedly a watertight security cordon. Even as some sections of the city were enrolling all-comers in emergency militias, others were hearing cries for General Lafayette and the mayor, Jean-Sylvain Bailly, to be hanged. Like many others, Jean-Baptiste Duthy, a waggoner, said as much and was arrested for it near the Place Vendôme. While in custody he went on to rip the epaulettes from an officer's uniform, a gesture of contempt for the signs of alleged distinction that was echoed, verbally and physically, by several others across the city.[22] Near the Palais-Royal, a servant and a jeweller went round tearing down the posted National Assembly proclamation of the king's 'kidnapping'. Arrested by several outraged citizens, the former asserted bluntly that 'the king had gone away of his own free will', and the latter claimed that, seeing the word *enlèvement* in the notices, he thought it 'inflammatory' and 'had thought it right to suppress them'.[23]

The Cordeliers Club sprang into action, and by the afternoon of the following day, with news of the king's recapture filtering through, had declared that 'Louis had abdicated the throne; from now on Louis is nothing to us, unless he becomes our enemy.' The text went on to more categorical assertions, culminating in an explicit challenge to the constitutionalists: 'monarchy, hereditary monarchy above all, is incompatible with liberty'.[24] François Robert himself was arrested in the Palais-Royal as he tried to distribute posters with this announcement, and was soundly beaten by a National Guard patrol whom he enraged with his stiff-necked pose: 'I know my Rights as well as I do my Duties, I know only the law, I have not violated it . . .'[25] After his informal punishment, he was hauled up before the police magistrate of the local section, and allowed to go free – partly perhaps because his home Section, the Cordeliers and the Fraternal Society all sent delegations attesting his patriotism and demanding his release.

The continual effort of the authorities to exclude the lower orders from politics was reinforced in the days after the king's return by concerted moves to sweep away several tens of thousands of men from municipally funded relief work in Paris. The city, saddled with huge numbers of unemployed, had since 1789 intermittently provided work for them at such tasks as ditch-digging, quarrying and heavy construction, and the latest wave of 'public workshops' were eating into public funds that were already overstretched. Such fiscal concerns were accompanied in the press and public pronouncements by scaremongering about the potential for aristocratic subversion of these men, and occasional reports of nefarious and suspicious activities among them. Neither Bailly nor Lafayette hesitated to deploy the troops of the National Guard to disperse demonstrations that arose when the workshops were officially closed down at the end of June.[26]

Outside of Paris, the slowly disseminating news of the flight caused panic and a spontaneous xenophobic and anti-aristocratic reaction. There were invasion-scares along almost every frontier, and further waves of attacks on non-juror priests and suspect nobles – Dampierre was not the only one to die. Local authorities, often themselves staffed by men who shared popular suspicions, did little to restrain violence, and even used it in some cases as a pretext to place further restrictions on the clergy. Through the summer, around a third of all departments instituted the detention, relocation or administrative surveillance of 'suspect' non-jurors.

With the royal family back in the Tuileries, under even heavier guard than before, the National Assembly pondered what to do with them. In effect there were few real options. Only the Cordelier fringe of Parisian politics favoured a republic, supported by a few idealists such as the intellectual marquis de Condorcet and the English radical exile Thomas Paine. A few provincial clubs demanded a republic – in one case, a petition to this effect from the southern university town of Montpellier achieved some brief fame, circulating nationwide, but only five other localities officially endorsed it.[27] Some provincial addresses and petitions called for Louis to be tried, perhaps deposed in favour of a regency for his young son: that opened up its own can of worms, for who should be regent – Marie-Antoinette? The king's *émigré* brothers?

Most of the country was willing to let the National Assembly judge the matter, expressing confidence in the deputies in dozens of messages. In this general context, a claimed thirty thousand Parisian signatures on the Cordeliers' republican petition was not enough to shift the perception among the deputies, and elite opinion generally, that France required a monarchy, for both internal stability and external peace. On the right of the Assembly, around three hundred largely noble deputies opposed even the temporary suspension of the king that was effectively now in place. Acrimonious debates ensued when an investigating committee reported on 13 July, but the majority agreed to follow the line taken on 21 June, and to sanctify the myth of a royal kidnapping. On 16 July, the king's personal inviolability was upheld, and he was exonerated of blame for the episode (shifted onto the conveniently departed Bouillé, who chivalrously had already publicly declared his guilt). Louis, however, would only be reinstated to his constitutional prerogatives once he had ratified the completed constitution.

At this moment, the Jacobin Club of Paris, the king's bugbear of opposition, split decisively. Almost all the members who were deputies to the Assembly – including the triumvirs and their supporters – left the Club when radicals refused to accept this decision without some form of appeal to public opinion. Moving to another nearby monastic building, and like the Jacobins taking on its obscure name, the moderates formed a 'Feuillant Club' that for the next few months would assume a commanding position in national politics. That command was reinforced the next day when the popular societies tried to organise a mass signing of a petition for a referendum on the king's fate. In events which horrified onlookers, the city's National Guard turned out under the red flag of martial law, and the citizen-volunteers charged down a crowd of over ten thousand gathered on the Champ de Mars.

Although some among the crowd had thrown stones, and one or two shots may have been fired, this event was really a police riot. Senior Guard officers admitted to a later inquiry that they had been unable to maintain discipline among the volunteer troops. It was noteworthy that the companies of paid professional soldiers that were also present held back, and even on one occasion threatened violence to officers who tried to order them in against the crowd.[28] They were far less inclined than the taxpaying volunteers to be incensed against the 'rabble' confronting them, presumably because they gave less credit than them to claims that popular protest was necessarily counter-revolutionary. Despite surrounding the crowd on several sides, and rampaging across the site for some hours, the Guard almost certainly inflicted well under a hundred fatalities, and possibly no more than a dozen. The men were angry enough to charge, and to shoot in a disorganised fashion, but they lacked the stomach or the skills to finish off their targets. One unemployed cook, Nicolas David, was picked up from the field and questioned about his injuries: trapped before a charging unit, he had been knocked down and stabbed at by several men with fixed bayonets, but they had succeeded only in scratching him above one eyebrow and giving him a small cut on his side.[29]

The confrontation, however, was sufficient for the authorities to drive many of the leading radicals into hiding. The Cordeliers' leader Danton fled briefly to England, and the popular societies fell into abeyance for much of the rest of the summer. The press, even of a relatively left-leaning stamp, was filled with lurid tales of aristocratically funded brigandage behind the clash. This was exactly the kind of misinformation that had prompted the over-reaction of the Guard in the first place, even if, for some on the left such as the fire-breathing Marat, it was the municipal and national authorities who had paid such brigands to provoke violence and justify the suppression of the radicals.

Several weeks of martial law allowed the dominant Feuillants to work undisturbed at finalising the constitution. They were engaged in a process which, had it become public knowledge at the time, would probably have provoked violence to make the Champ de Mars look like a tea-party. Barnave had struck up a remarkable rapport with Marie-Antoinette during their slow coach-ride back to Paris, perhaps in part due to her deliberate effort to charm, and his considerable personal vanity. When the queen smuggled a letter to him at the beginning of July, suggesting they discuss political solutions, he and his fellow triumvirs leaped at the chance to consolidate constitutional monarchy. The correspondence would go on, initially through notes tucked in the pocket of the comte de Jarjayes, husband to one of the queen's maids, until the following January.[30] While this remained hidden from the eyes of the suspicious Parisians, the evident rapprochement between the triumvirate and the court that followed led the American *chargé d'affaires* to note unambiguously: 'There is no doubt that they have secret communications.'[31]

The Feuillants sought to achieve three things: a finished constitution, but one in which the role of the royal executive had been strengthened; open agreement from Austria, as the leading continental power, on the validity of this settlement; and the reconciliation and return to France of the king's brothers. Artois, who had fled in July 1789, had now been joined by Provence, the older of the two, who had co-ordinated his departure with Louis, but had made a faster and more successful trip to the Austrian Netherlands disguised as an English merchant. As leaders of the *émigré* movement, they were a thorn in the side of French policy, especially as they saw fit to disregard both open and covert appeals from Louis to abandon their sullen opposition to every aspect of the Revolution. Artois, as early as April 1790, had been fomenting counter-revolutionary unrest in southern France through networks of agents, and the princes now stood at the head of a veritable court-in-exile, unwilling to see the king as anything other than a prisoner in need of liberation.

This was especially galling for the royal couple, as they were in fact conducting their own secret foreign policy through the baron de Breteuil, a former government minister. Breteuil, sixty-one in 1791, had had a long diplomatic career, and had been minister of the king's household – effectively Interior Minister – from 1783 to 1788, before playing a key role in the abortive attempt to restore royal authority in July 1789 that led to the taking of the Bastille. As a minister, he had worked closely with the king, and implemented some significant reforms: restraining the use of secret royal warrants, or *lettres de cachet*, to detain individuals without charge, and legislating in 1787 to improve the status of Protestants, who lived under severe legal handicaps. Nonetheless, as the events of 1787–1788 unfolded, Breteuil became increasingly convinced of the need to restore royal authority. Although he had resigned in the summer of 1788 ostensibly in protest over increased use of *lettres de cachet* against opponents, his private opinions were far from liberal – he was recorded as saying that 'we are unleashing passions that will lead to far more permanent and incurable ills' than the supposed 'abuses' being reformed.[32] He was thus a natural candidate to be summoned back to power when Necker was forced out of office on 11 July 1789, and royal troops ringed Paris with every appearance of using force against the capital. Although there is some ambiguity about the true intentions of this move – and it seems likely that no immediate assault was planned, more a slow process of intimidation and consolidation of authority – the Parisians' explosive reaction sent Breteuil hastening into exile among the very first waves of *émigrés*.[33]

Breteuil had been given plenipotentiary powers to represent the king in late 1790, having been in correspondence with Louis and Marie-Antoinette since his arrival in the Austrian Netherlands. The 1790 document stated that 'I approve everything you may do to achieve the aim which I have set myself, which is the restoration of my legitimate authority and the happiness of my peoples.'[34] This echoed the sentiments of another even earlier text, smuggled out to Charles IV of Spain (Louis' closest ruling relative) in October 1789, a 'solemn protestation against my enforced sanction of all that has been done contrary to the royal authority since 15 July of this year'.[35]

It appears that the Breteuil document, although allegedly in the king's own hand, was actually written by the queen, perhaps acting out of necessity during one of the bouts of near-paralysing depression that the king had been increasingly prone to, ever since the collapse of the first Assembly of Notables in 1787. Although contemporary opinion would doubtless have seen this as evidence that the crown was being manipulated by the devious foreign woman, seen more objectively it attests that she and Louis were acting with one mind during what they indeed regarded as a captivity, albeit not the helpless one asserted by Artois and Provence.

The turn to the Feuillant leadership for assistance was thus one more manoeuvre in the royal couple's increasingly desperate efforts to restore royal authority. Although there can be little doubt that Barnave and his colleagues genuinely believed that France needed Louis at its head, it is also clear that the queen, who took the leading role in all these negotiations, was using them. A letter of October 1791 to Axel von Fersen, safely in exile, made her feelings plain: 'Have no fear, I am not joining the wild men; if I see or have dealings with some of them, it is only in order to make use of them, and they fill me with too much horror to think of ever going over to them.'[36] The queen's view of the triumvirs as 'wild men', when many in the radical movements of Parisian and national politics were coming to see them as little better than counter-revolutionaries, is a fitting depiction of the vast gulf of incomprehension, always present but ever-widening, between the royal family and the Revolution.

In any case, all the discussion and plots with the Feuillants came to almost nothing. The revision of the constitution – in reality the arduous process of deciding which of the hundreds of decrees passed by the Assembly in the previous two years was actually part of that document, and whether any should be amended – hardened some of the social exclusions of politics. Membership of the National Guard was now explicitly confined to active citizens, and the franchise to become an 'elector' was raised considerably. Little else substantive, however, was changed. The project of repeated waves of moderate leaders since 1789, to introduce an English-style second chamber to the legislature, was briefly revived again. However, it was hated as much by intransigent aristocrats as by impatient radicals, and could gain no significant support. Although the Feuillants succeeded in getting the king rebranded as the 'hereditary representative' of the nation, rather than the scornful 'first functionary' of an earlier pronouncement, they were unable to secure any active legislative powers for him. He kept the 'suspensive veto' agreed in 1789, but the right to introduce legislation was restricted to the Assembly itself – a terrible blow to Louis' own sense that law-making was at the heart of royal prerogative. When on 14 September he appeared before the Assembly formally to swear loyalty to the new arrangements, he was further humiliated. All but one of the assembled deputies refused to stand or bare their heads before him (the aristocrats were boycotting the whole affair). While Paris and the nation rejoiced at the completion of the Assembly's task, Louis wept openly before his family in the Tuileries, unable even to speak coherently, such was his distress.[37] The British ambassador, Lord Gower, noted with cruel brevity that 'the sincerity of his acceptation is doubted by many'.[38]

The process of electing the deputies to man the new Legislative Assembly was already in train. Indeed, it had begun days before the Flight to Varennes, only to be suspended by the emergency. Active citizens in their primary assemblies, and then electors in their departmental colleges, met and voted through the late summer. Declared candidacy or canvassing was officially prohibited; electors were supposed to be left free to judge in their own minds which worthy individuals to nominate. The Jacobins, however, had begun to drop heavy hints about the kinds of individuals to avoid, and even in some areas bent the law by suggesting names to favour through papers and pamphlets. Those who were interested in the electoral process were in any case those likely to take an activist view of the Revolution – as with every election from this point on, only a minority of those eligible troubled to take part, and thus inclined the result towards radicalism.[39]

The members of the outgoing Assembly had barred themselves from re-election by decree back in May – a measure which has often been called 'self-denying' by spurious parallel with a decree of the English Civil War Parliament.[40] It was in some respects more 'self-loathing', however, the fruit of bitter antagonism towards the aristocratic minority of the old Assembly, and radical efforts to deprive the triumvirs and their ilk of a prolongation of their power-base in national politics. In both respects, it was eminently successful. The 'new men' of the Legislative Assembly had no more than a scattering of nobles and constitutional clergy among them, all of whom had proved their attachment to the Revolution. Moreover, although almost half of the new deputies attached themselves initially to the Parisian Feuillant Club on arrival, compared to scarcely a sixth joining the Jacobins, it was the latter group that showed immediate political distinction, and was to triumph in short order.[41]

The leaders of the Feuillant grouping had been, without exception, men of the old Assembly. The summer had proved their command of politics to be ephemeral. While they strove to dictate the Assembly's agenda in its final weeks, the Jacobins had been summoning the national network of clubs to renewed loyalty to their original 'mother society', with almost unbroken success.[42] A vigorous campaign of correspondence had portrayed the Feuillants as schismatics, attempting to divide and destroy the Jacobin movement for their own self-interested ends. Key to the Jacobins' national resurgence was the figure and image of Maximilien Robespierre, best known among the small group of deputies who remained with the Club. A barrister from Arras, thirty-one in 1789, he had been a nonentity when the Estates-General had opened, elected to it almost by chance. A slight figure, whose features grew more sharply drawn as the pressures of revolutionary politics drained him of health, but remaining always neatly turned out under a powdered wig in a style that was old-fashioned even at the start of the Revolution, he had struggled to make an impression, cursed by a weak, high voice in a chamber dominated by stentorian orators.[43]

Nevertheless, in speech after speech to the Assembly and in the Jacobins, Robespierre had steadily built a reputation. The twin cornerstones were his unshakeable, and unquestioned, personal morality and probity, and his equally solid conviction that counter-revolution was everywhere. He was dubbed 'The Incorruptible', a telling epithet in a political climate where accusations of counter-revolutionary bribery and unscrupulous self-enrichment formed a fog of denunciation around almost all politicians. He lived a near-monkish existence, displaying a rather priggish sense of his own purity in an era when the material comforts of wealth were understood naturally to accompany the exercise of power. Initially a humanitarian and almost a pacifist – he opposed the retention of the death penalty when a new penal code was debated in June 1791, and would decry bellicose developments in the Legislative

Assembly – his conviction of the need to combat counter-revolution would gradually overcome his scruples against violence.

Robespierre had proposed the 'self-denying' measure of May, convinced that otherwise the leaders of the old Assembly would use their prestige – undeserved in his eyes – to dominate the new political scene and exclude true patriots. At almost the last meeting of the Assembly, he vigorously denounced a Feuillant proposal to ban political clubs, denying the claim that they were no longer needed, that the Revolution was finished. He insisted that enemies remained on all sides, and, in a classic trope of his style, sought to unmask the hypocrisy of those who claimed otherwise – the overt counter-revolution was always, in his mind, attended by hidden cohorts that lurked among the apparently patriotic. He instead lauded the clubs as sites where patriotic surveillance of the authorities could be maintained, and where the self-serving ambitions of politicians could be checked by the true patriots among the people.[44] The measure to ban the clubs passed, but would never be enforced, and on the following day Robespierre was carried shoulder-high through the streets by a huge adoring crowd to celebrate the end of the Assembly. His return to Arras was a triumphal procession, his carriage mobbed in every town he passed through. He soon returned to Paris and the Jacobins, establishing himself as a journalist and municipal politician.

The approach to politics pioneered by Robespierre was far more attractive to provincials who had founded their own clubs, and fought their own battles against local counter-revolutionaries, than the Feuillant line, so successfully portrayed as the power-hungry manoeuvres of an elite that remained afraid of the people. The men of true political distinction and drive that were sent from the provinces, as opposed to the freight of mediocrities that weighs down any large assembly, came from the resurgent Jacobin network. The clash of perspectives this engendered was apparent from the very opening days of the Legislative.

Following the king's humiliation on 14 September, Barnave and the Feuillant leadership, who now took up a covert but rather obvious role as royal advisers, strove to avoid a similar scene when he made his opening speech to the Legislative. In one of its last acts the National Assembly had specified a simple but dignified ceremonial to be followed for the king's presence in the new Legislative Assembly. However, on 4 October, after the new deputies had ratified their own credentials, they sent a deputation to inform the king that they were ready for business. Through nerves, its leader kept his remarks to the king extremely brief, and was so flustered when Louis said in answer that he could not attend for three days that he withdrew without making a reply. In the Assembly, this news, delivered in words which suggested a frosty royal reception (contrary to other reports), provoked uproar, alongside well-informed guesses that Louis was waiting for Barnave to write his speech. On the 5th, Jacobin influence made itself felt in a harsh decree which threatened to strip Louis' presence of all dignity, and only frantic Feuillant manoeuvring the next day restored the original protocol, at the cost of outcry on the streets. The American diplomat Gouverneur Morris mocked the Feuillants' outrage at Jacobin manoeuvres, given their earlier attitudes to the king before his flight: 'Are they indignant that any others should exceed them in marks of indignity?'[45] The queen drew an immediate and summary conclusion from the events: 'There is nothing to be gained from this Assembly: it is a pile of rogues, madmen and beasts.'[46]

The speech that Louis made on the 7th was direct and statesmanlike, taking as its starting point that idea that the Revolution was now, evidently, completed. He (or Barnave, who was indeed the author) called on the Assembly to take up the important issues left unresolved by its predecessor: to establish a system of national education; to reconstruct on firmer lines the network of public assistance devastated by the conflict with the church; and to promote economic regeneration through suitable public works, the improvement of communications and the stabilisation of the monetary climate. On more directly political challenges, the tone was calming – Louis foresaw no aggression from other powers, but committed himself to a restoration of order and subordination in the armed forces, while passing over in silence the divisions over the clergy and their property. From the Feuillant perspective, this was just what was required – order, tranquillity and a return to normal internal and external relations for France.[47]

Unfortunately, pacific statesmanship was thoroughly out of fashion, not least among the royal family itself. Louis' and Marie-Antoinette's own secret diplomacy was pressing even now for the powers of Europe to go beyond the 'Pillnitz Declaration' made by Austria and Prussia on 27 August, which made vague threats to intervene if royal authority were not restored. Their goal was an 'armed congress' of the powers, bringing to bear considerable numbers of troops as a direct threat to the revolutionaries unless Louis was given back his legitimate status. There can be little doubt that, despite the necessity of appearing resigned to the constitution, the king and queen intended their acquiescence to be no more than a stopgap measure to allow them to rally external support against those they never ceased to call 'rebels'.[48] Louis' silence in the historical record, and the apparent dominance of the queen, merely reflects the fact that the king no longer committed his thoughts to paper on anything if he could avoid it, whereas Marie-Antoinette was conducting several secret correspondences as outlets for her rage against their captors. The queen was by now very far from the flighty teenager of the 1770s, and her active involvement in the machinations of the coming months showed her as an individual of considerable mettle. Louis' intermittent depression must also be taken into account in obliging her to act for her family's safety – as he was restored now to his role in the council of ministers, he also resumed, and intensified, his habit of sleeping through many discussions. What was once perhaps a tactic to avoid entanglement in acrimony now also reflected an increasing disengagement from the distressing context of his existence.

That context, as the autumn wore on into winter, was increasingly dominated by a new grouping that had emerged from the Jacobin cohort in the Legislative Assembly. At the time they were frequently referred to as 'Brissotins'. Their leading light was Jacques-Pierre Brissot, thirty-eight years old, from an artisan family in Chartres, who after brilliant success in education had made his way in the world as an author and journalist. Here he was rather less successful, as he seems to have been embroiled by dubious associates throughout the 1780s in a variety of money-making schemes in Paris and London, one of which left him with little choice but to supply information to the French police – although he was probably never a 'police spy', as others charged.[49] Work for a prominent new anti-slavery society from 1788 gained him a more respectable public reputation, and throughout the life of the Constituent Assembly he had forged a significant career as a journalist, Parisian municipal politician and speaker at the Jacobins. He was seen by some on the centre-right as the most threatening figure of the left, and was regularly vilified in their publications, but ascended triumphantly to the Legislative from the city's electoral assembly. He was joined by a cohort of equally notable revolutionary activists, including a trio of lawyers from Bordeaux. Armand Gensonné, Marguerite-Elie Guadet and Pierre-Victurnien Vergniaud were all also in their thirties, with promising legal careers that had evolved into roles in revolutionary public life and engagement with a Jacobin perspective. Coming as they did from the department of the Gironde, they gave this grouping the name by which it is most often remembered: the Girondins.[50]

For the Girondins, unlike the fading Feuillants, the Revolution was anything but finished. Whether through paranoia or perceptiveness, they intuited the truth of the royal position, and set out to force the king to show his hand by launching attacks on the *émigrés* and non-juring clergy. Aristocratic emigration had been given a dramatic boost by the apparent example of the king himself, and by continued and growing disgust with the whole course of the Revolution. The American *chargé d'affaires* reported at this point that some areas of the country were now empty of nobles of fighting age, many of whom had left with their whole families. Opinion among them was now so polarised, as he reported, that they believed 'that they are dishonoured if they remain in France, and that only those who go to join the princes will be considered as noble after the counter-revolution which they consider as certain'.[51] As early as 20 October 1791, Brissot stood up in the Assembly to counteract this trend, arguing for military action, if necessary, to disperse the growing numbers of *émigrés* gathering around the court of the exile princes in the Rhineland. At the end of the month, the Assembly decreed that the comte de Provence would be removed from the succession if he did not return to France by the end of the year. On 9 November it passed a punitive law against all *émigrés* – they were branded conspirators, and threatened with confiscation of their lands if they remained in exile. Louis' response was not long in coming. Only two days later he vetoed the measure against Provence and the *émigré* decree. The Girondins had succeeded in forcing direct opposition between the policy of the crown and the Assembly within only six weeks of its first meeting.

The radical screw on the court was tightened further a week later when the crucial post of mayor of Paris was won by Jérôme Pétion. A lawyer and former royal administrator, and like so many activists still only in his mid-thirties, he had been the other deputy along with Barnave in the royal coach in June, and was one of those few members of the old Assembly to stay loyal to the Jacobins. Administrative control of all the forces of the capital was now firmly in the hands of the Jacobin movement. Pétion defeated General Lafayette for the mayorship after the resignation of Bailly, worn out with the constant political feuding and attacks from the left. It is a note of the factionalisation of politics that, among an electorate of well over a hundred thousand, Pétion and Lafayette polled fewer than ten thousand votes between them. Nine out of ten active citizens took no part in the process. Lafayette's campaign had suffered attacks from both sides: hated by radicals for the Champ de Mars massacre, he was equally loathed by the court and its supporters for his perceived role in the October Days of 1789. Upon his defeat, he departed politics for his estates in the Auvergne, there to launch a new bid for glory, lobbying to be given command of an army.

Towards the end of November the political climate chilled further along with the weather. A new Surveillance Committee was established in the Assembly, charged with investigating crimes of *lèse-nation*, an adaptation of the old charge of *lèse-majesté*: anything which threatened 'harm to the nation', and an extremely broad drawing of the remit of potential treasons. On the 29th, the Girondins shrank Louis' room for manoeuvre even further with a deputation urging diplomatic action to remove the *émigrés* from the Rhineland, and a decree on the same day requiring all priests, including the non-jurors who had refused to join the constitutional church, to take a new loyalty oath, or be accounted as officially suspect. Louis was to veto this measure too, in mid-December. By then further aggressive moves were being made in the Assembly to pin the crown down on its relations with other powers, but the issue of the priests was one which penetrated to the heart of how 'counter-revolution' was perceived in the country at large, and was key to the wider impact of this ongoing crisis.

One of the ironies of the conflict being fought out between the Girondins and the royal family was that Louis and Marie-Antoinette paid almost no attention to the areas where the Revolution was in conflict with its own citizens, and where support could indeed have been rallied. Trapped in a diplomatic and political bubble, they saw their opponents as rebels who had to be put down from above, neglecting the potential for unseating them from below. One dimension of this, a fear of provoking further threatening crowd violence from the Parisians, is perhaps understandable. In general, however, it reflects the limited royal perception of what was actually happening in France.

In fact, large areas of north-western France – Brittany, western Normandy and the lower Loire valley – were substantially alienated from the Revolution. A profound cultural gulf had opened up between the urban elites, who effectively monopolised district and departmental office-holding, and the rural population, who in the vast majority were loyal to a non-juror priestly cohort. The Girondin Gensonné, before taking his seat in the Assembly, had been part of an official investigation into religious issues in the Vendée and Deux-Sèvres departments. He had found that 'constitutional' priests in the countryside could often attract no more than a dozen communicants in parishes of five or six hundred souls.[52] In the Maine-et-Loire department, the administrators reported to the Assembly in early November that seditious priests were leading thousands of peasants in regular gatherings and marches, and that at least three district capitals were 'in danger of night attacks, of being pillaged and burnt by these brigands'.[53]

Such so-called brigands very often felt that they had received no material benefit from the Revolution, while seeing their communities torn apart by the threat to the church. In areas south of the Loire, in and adjacent to the Vendée department, agriculture was predominantly carried out on small tenant farms. Here the abolition of feudalism had had little positive impact, especially when the original burdens had often been relatively light, and in some cases were transferred by Assembly decree onto tenants' rents and leases. Abolition of hated Old Regime taxes and tithes had been accompanied by legislation also permitting landowners to add their weight to rents. When the landlords were frequently members of the bourgeois stratum that was running the Revolution, and thus was also responsible for disseminating a considerable burden of new revolutionary land tax down to the villages, outright hostility was entirely understandable. Further north in Normandy, and particularly in Brittany, regional privileges over taxation were being ground out of existence, placing huge new demands on a resentful and increasingly hostile peasantry.[54] The National Guard militias that elsewhere offered a proud display of the patriotism of every small community were in the west equally likely to be used as the tools of the urban elite, raiding recalcitrant peasant communities in search of taxes and aristocrats.

If the king and queen chose to remain unengaged by this level of discontent, others within the counter-revolutionary fraternity were less reticent. Artois had been funding networks and abortive uprisings for almost two years, and their initial focus on the volatile sectarian conflict of the south-east was now expanding to new areas outraged by the clerical oath. One small-scale gathering in the Vendée, co-ordinated by the marquis de La Lézardière, had been broken up by revolutionary authorities in the summer of 1791. Thirty-six people were sentenced by the courts for an attempted armed gathering, although a general amnesty promulgated to mark the acceptance of the constitution cut short the investigation.[55] The network controlled by the marquis de La Rouairie was considerably more impressive. La Rouairie had been a hero of the American War, but lacked the charm and the cachet of Lafayette, and had been cold-shouldered by high society on his return to France. He became an outspoken advocate of the rights of the provincial nobility, and was thrown in the Bastille in the spring of 1788 for bringing to Paris the grievances of the *parlement* of Brittany. Although freed in the summer, he set himself against all change, and seems to have plotted counter-revolutionary revolt from early 1790. Within eighteen months, he had secured official support from Artois' exile court, and had built up a 'Breton Association' claiming cells across the four western provinces (Brittany, Normandy, Anjou and Poitou) – at least a dozen departments. The plan was for a guerrilla uprising, adopting tactics La Rouairie had learned in irregular warfare in America. It was to be co-ordinated with foreign invasion, and with other risings in the south-east, planned by groups also in touch with Artois. By early 1792, the Breton Association possessed six thousand firearms, and even four cannon.[56]

Revolutionary authorities were actively pursuing such conspirators, and indeed would effectively shut down the original Breton Association in the summer of 1792, but they still left their disturbing mark on the body politic. Beyond the counter-revolution, the politicians of the Legislative Assembly had to deal with a country that was far from content, even when the revolutionary leadership was not the immediate target. Economically the Revolution had been a calamity piled upon a disaster. The money that flowed into the urban economy through the pockets of the seigneurs had dried up, and spending of all kinds by the social elite, a mainstay of the artisan trades, was in critical decline – clients were either emigrating, or just hoarding their cash, planning to leave or hedging against uncertainty. Money itself was no longer a stable medium of exchange, as the assignat notes depreciated to below 80 per cent of face-value in early 1792, falling ever faster.

The Feuillant policy of stabilisation foundered on these economic and social rocks as much as on the political ones of court and Jacobin intransigence. The people of France had been actively taking charge of their own destinies ever since the collapse of royal authority in 1788–1789, and they had been doing so in a context of political and journalistic expression that associated all problems and all hardship with the twin forces of revolution and counter-revolution. Some areas of the country were learning to associate all revolutionary initiative with an attack on religion and their way of life. By the same token, the fall of the assignat, for pro-revolutionary writers and their audiences, was the consequence of deliberate hoarding, deliberate speculation and deliberate political effort to overturn the country's finances. Since, to take just one example, La Rouairie had been given forged assignats by the *émigré* court in June 1791 to fund his work, we can observe that there was more than paranoia to this perception.[57] In patriot eyes, economic destabilisation was part of a plot, ever ramifying and ever returning to public consciousness, to starve the citizenry into submission. Every challenge to the material well-being of the population was also a challenge to their political liberty. Moreover, it was a challenge which, since 1788, groups had never hesitated to meet with physical force.

So it was that, when heavy autumn rains depleted the harvest across many regions of France and prices began to soar, people took action. By November 1791, the Pas-de-Calais and the Haute-Marne in Champagne had seen price-fixing riots in urban markets. Along two of the major rivers of northern France, the Orne and the Aisne, shipments of grain were seized by urban populations threatened by economic decline and unwilling to allow 'their' food supplies to be exported. Riots came to Paris in January and February, with popular discontent at the soaring price of sugar – a colonial commodity badly affected by revolt among the slaves of France's Caribbean possessions, seeking their share of revolutionary liberty.[58] Comfortable middle-class revolutionaries proclaimed the virtue of abstaining from such 'luxuries' in times of shortage, but to many ordinary Parisians there was nothing luxurious about sugar, or its companion coffee.[59] Artificial stimulants had as significant a role in late-eighteenth-century urban life as they do today, and people were just as unwilling to do without them.

By the time this outbreak had died down, new unrest was stirring to the south of the city, in the grain-belt that produced much of the bread that was the Parisians' staple diet. Here, the commercialisation of agriculture for urban markets had produced significant social cleavage and tension – this was the epicentre of the Flour War of 1775 that had brought down Turgot. Now the agitation for the 'just price' of goods spread beyond grain to other staples, such as butter and eggs, and the raw materials of work: timber, iron and other supplies. Communities emerged from the countryside *en masse*, sometimes led by local mayors and other officials, or by employers such as forge-masters and glass-makers. Pin-makers, weavers, charcoal-burners, spinners and labourers, all doubly dependent on markets for food and materials, took part in large numbers.[60] As they marched under the proud tricolour banners of their patriotic communities and village National Guard units, their actions flowed from a sense of justice that had been renewed and redoubled by revolutionary experience, but also from a sense of endangerment that was equally part of that context. It was in this setting that Louis Simonneau, mayor of Etampes in the Seine-et-Oise, not far south of Paris, was lynched on 3 March 1792 for refusing crowd demands to fix 'just prices' in the town's market. He was later to become a symbol of growing political and social divisions when the authorities organised a funeral procession for him in the capital in June.[61]

Troubles were not confined to the counter-revolutionary west, or to the Parisian region. The inland departments of south-western France – from the Cantal to the Haute-Garonne, by way of the Lot and the Tarn – saw revolutionary unrest again between January and March 1792, matching in magnitude any of the upheavals of 1789. Seigneurs were again targeted by rural communities, sometimes now with the added specific accusation that they were planning to join the *émigré* armies. Non-juror priests and a variety of other counter-revolutionary 'suspects' were harassed, disarmed and occasionally lynched. Political concerns once again seem here to have predominated over economic ones, although the distinction remained hard to make, and the seizure and consumption of concealed stocks of food and wine was often part of the ritual humiliation meted out to popular enemies.[62] To the south-east, in the Gard, heartland of sectarian tensions, food riots and counter-revolution formed a complex tangle. Overt counter-revolutionaries tried to gather in the nearby Ardèche in late February, but were forced to flee before mobilised National Guard detachments that proceeded to take out their anger on local villagers. Both the Gard and the Ardèche were thereafter sites of endemic disorder, culminating through April in waves of uprisings by both Catholic and Protestant communities. The property of known counter-revolutionaries was destroyed, along with feudal records. Food was seized, and in some areas land enclosed or claimed by seigneurs was opened up or divided among villagers. Lord Gower, the British ambassador, referred to the region as in 'a state the nearest possible to civil war'.[63] As elsewhere, both National Guards and local officials could be found on the side of 'disorder', suggesting quite clearly that the Feuillant belief in peace and order had no connection to the way many perceived the perils and challenges surrounding their communities.[64]

By this point, the Feuillant cause was long dead. Parisian public opinion, orchestrated by the revived popular societies, had dealt the *coup de grâce*. Desperate to regain a public profile, the Feuillant Club had opened its hitherto private sessions to audiences in early December 1791. The result was a cacophony of barracking so loud that radicals in the Legislative Assembly, meeting nearby, complained that their work was being interrupted. Thrown out, the Feuillants could not even meet for several weeks, by which time the debates in the Jacobin Club and in the Assembly had moved on to entirely new ground.[65] Barnave, marginalised by events, withdrew to Grenoble in January, his dreams of influence in tatters. In contrast, in the words of Gower, 'The Jacobins are acquiring a popularity in a degree and manner that are truly alarming.'[66]

Increasingly prevalent as winter turned to spring were views entirely opposite to the Feuillant position: in essence, that war would be the Revolution's salvation. Girondin rhetoric had raised the prospect of a cleansing of the frontiers by war, and even many in the original Feuillant camp itself were coming round to this view, especially those closer to Lafayette. He was shortly to receive his desired military command, and joined in the general clamour for decisive action. Both he and the newly appointed War Minister, Narbonne, thought that action would give the army new vigour, and allow it to be used as a stabilising force in domestic politics. Thus Louis himself came to the Assembly on 14 December, to announce that the German princes on whose territory the *émigrés* were gathered had been given an ultimatum to disperse them. Two days later, Brissot at the Jacobins hailed this initiative as a great revolutionary opportunity, believing the ultimatum would be rejected, and the ensuing crisis would show the king in his true colours.

From the last days of 1791, Girondin rhetoric adopted an increasingly universalistic, even messianic, approach to the prospect of conflict. On 25 December, Guadet had called for the new year to mark 'the first year of universal liberty', while two days later, in a piece of oratory that convulsed the Assembly and its public galleries into a patriotic fervour, Vergniaud hymned the valour of the French and the perfidy of their enemies, 'satellites of despotism, carrying fifteen centuries of pride and barbarism in their souls', seeking to reconquer the gains of the Revolution. His peroration was epic, and addressed to the people itself: 'Glory awaits you. Hitherto kings have aspired to the title of Roman citizens; it now depends on you to make them envy that of citizens of France!'[67]

All this fell rather ironically flat when news began to come through that the rulers of Trier and Mainz, targeted by Louis' ultimatum, had caved in immediately and set about dispersing the *émigré* groups. The king had genuinely wanted Artois' court and its hangers-on removed, since they consistently refused to acknowledge that he was still sovereign and capable of free action, and their inveterate plotting merely continued to stir up radical hatreds, placing him in more peril. Fortunately for the war party, help was at hand in the person of the Austrian leader and Holy Roman Emperor himself, Leopold II. Upon news of the ultimatum, he had threatened to mobilise troops against France if they attempted to enforce their threats. When word of this reached Paris on 31 December, it immediately revived the flagging Girondins. For two months, they hectored the ministry into more and more aggressive threats against Austria, seeking a public renunciation of all hostile intent – in the kind of language no absolutist sovereign would dream of consenting to – and finally setting a 1 March deadline for satisfaction or conflict. On that very day, however, Leopold died suddenly (sparking wild rumours in his own court of a French poison-plot). News reached Paris just in time to stimulate the Girondins to further demands, in the expectation of temporary confusion among their enemies. On 10 March, pressure from the Assembly, including the inevitable accusations of counter-revolutionary collusion, produced a change of ministry, with the installation of a group of close associates of the Girondin position, all convinced advocates of revolutionary war.[68]

Almost nothing now stood between France and war. Over the frontiers, the *émigrés* revelled in their exile status and future glory. While the elite clung to the courts of Artois and Provence, and the monies dispensed through them by the sympathetic princes of Germany, the young and impoverished gentlemen who had fled France to save her rejoiced in the comradeship they found. One wrote in January 1792 that he slept regularly 'on straw laid out on the floor of a small sitting-room . . . five or six of us side by side', having nursed a half-pint of beer through a long evening in an inn – 'I never realised it was possible for a man of my sort to live for ten or twelve sous per day' – even as he and his fellows scraped together to buy horses for the spring campaign that was sure to come. He sympathised with the older and more pampered members of the emigration, who now found themselves demoted from well-sprung carriages to footsore marches through endless mud:

> There is nothing we would not do for such men, whose profession was never that of war . . . They had to leave their motherland and all that they held most dear to embark on this new crusade and to fight the perjured, ungrateful felons, who have issued from hell to thwart the fulfilment of good king Louis's promises to France.[69]

Even the king and queen had come actively to favour conflict. A month earlier Axel von Fersen had secretly visited the Tuileries, and reported back to his master, Gustavus III of Sweden, on a detailed discussion with the royal couple on the objectives of the still-planned 'armed congress'.[70] He had offered Louis and Marie-Antoinette two alternatives. The first was that the congress could demand that Louis be freed from Paris, placed in safety and allowed to negotiate an internal and external settlement freely, including a revised constitution. This would imply that Louis recognised the need for a 'constitutional' settlement with his people. The second option ignored the internal situation, and leaned on two areas where France was currently seen as being in breach of international law: the Assembly had annexed the enclave of papal territory around Avignon in September, and refused to honour the feudal rights of German seigneurs in Alsace, guaranteed by treaty since 1648. By presenting France with ultimatums on these two issues, and a demand for the honouring of all other existing treaties, the congress could undoubtedly drive the revolutionaries into all-out war. The king's role would be to go along with French sentiments, and even to lead them, in order 'to inspire enough confidence to put himself at the head of his army', whereupon he could negotiate with the powers of Europe 'and with the assurance of their support dictate laws to his people'.[71]

The king was initially hesitant about the risks involved in this latter strategy, but the queen was far more immediately eager, and together with Fersen seems to have talked Louis round to agreeing, once again, that 'he had no intention of negotiating with the rebels', and that therefore leading the country into war was the best route out of their situation. The blinkered arrogance involved in thinking that the revolutionary political class would allow Louis to leave Paris and join 'his' armies would be merely pitiful if it did not demonstrate so clearly the royal couple's persistent treasonous conspiracy against the constitutional order Louis had taken a solemn oath to uphold. As early as 17 January, the Austrian Council of State in Vienna had effectively already agreed to put the various ultimatums this plan involved to France, and went on to agree an alliance with Prussia, the other Great Power of central Europe, on 7 February. Not all their motives concerned the protection of monarchy. Both powers were anxious about rising Russian influence to the east, and Austrian diplomats viewed friendship with Prussia as a route out of insecurity and potential isolation (given that France was supposed to be their main European ally). Prussian leaders foresaw potential territorial gains in north-western Germany as one price of their friendship, and even the Austrians thought that their lands around the Low Countries might be augmented by a swift victorious war and a gratefully restored French monarchy.[72]

War, then, was agreed, and the formal declaration on 20 April against the 'King of Bohemia and Hungary', as the new Austrian ruler Francis II was styled, was almost an afterthought to this huge, multifaceted bellicose movement. Even the British ambassador had agreed, believing 'a war of some sort necessary' to quell 'the rapid increase of anarchy'.[73] Few voices had spoken against it, but one of those that had was Robespierre's. Back in the late autumn, when war had seemed still a fairly distant prospect, his disagreement with Brissot and the Girondins had been conducted in polite terms. As he saw the drive for war grow not just among patriotic Jacobins, but also in the court and the ministry itself, especially after Narbonne's appointment, his suspicions grew deeper and darker. What had been an unnecessary risk increasingly looked to him like a nefarious plot. Girondins waxed lyrical about a fictitious 'Austrian committee' in the Tuileries preparing to sell France down the river, but Robespierre could not agree that a course of action desired by everyone from Brissot to Marie-Antoinette, by way of Lafayette, was any way to safeguard the Revolution. Military dictatorship or total disaster were more likely outcomes. Ironically, although his suspicions of collusion were overwrought, and he was at probably the absolute low point of his political influence, Robespierre had never been more right.[74]

## Chapter 3

# The Fall

By mid-morning on 10 August 1792, the long elegant façades of the Tuileries palace looked down on a scene of carnage. Corpses in the distinctive red coats of the king's Swiss Guards were scattered across the courtyard below, and on the once peaceful expanse of the Tuileries gardens. Mingled with them were the blue-coated bodies of National Guards from Paris and across France, and the corpses of *sans-culotte* volunteers from the Parisian Sections, their working clothes garnished with red liberty caps and tricolour cockades. Most of these patriot victims were clustered close to the palace itself, marking where disciplined volleys of musketry from the Swiss professionals had cut them down in swathes. The bodies of the Swiss were more dispersed, showing where they had followed orders and attempted a withdrawal, only to be harried to their deaths in ones and twos. Some even managed to break out into the neighbouring streets, running for their lives, ordinary Parisians perhaps feigning incomprehension of their Germanic accents as they cried for help, until their pursuers caught up and cut them down. Many of them bore the grim slashing wounds inflicted by sabres and pikes; some were headless, having given trophies to the victorious invaders. Some showed the marks of further furious mutilations.

Around the abandoned palace the noise of the crowds had dulled from its earlier continuous roar, though partly replaced now by the crackle of bonfires. Smoke drifted across the centre of the city as the signs and symbols of royalty, dragged out of the palace, hacked from street signs and ripped from corpses, were burned in expiatory pyres. Within the shattered building itself, servants caught defenceless by the attack had also been struck down, their bodies scattered through the royal apartments along with the splintered remains of fittings ornamented with the fatal fleur-de-lys. Across the city, the walled and gated townhouses of the aristocratic elite, their famed *hôtels particuliers*, were also being assailed by the crowds, though their owners and other occupants had for the most part long fled.

The major occupants of the Tuileries, the royal family themselves, had departed the palace before a shot had been fired. Giving themselves into the custody of the Legislative Assembly, they had watched from safe but helpless seclusion as the victorious Parisians burst in, confronting the three hundred deputies that remained – barely two-fifths of the original total – with their imperious demands for a formal end to the monarchy. The leaders of the Girondins, who had pushed the country into war, now consummated this new stage in the Revolution's course, and by a show of hands secured the suspension of the king. What seemed like the logical outcome of their earlier policy of confrontation was, however, the first stage in their own downfall, and the triumphant rise of the radicals of Paris.

Tensions between the Parisian radicals of the club movement and the authorities had already been manifested on 15 April, five days before the declaration of war, when the release of forty soldiers imprisoned for a mutiny eighteen months earlier was celebrated with a massive parade, replete with radical slogans and alarming signs of popular vigour. The radicals' icon, Robespierre, and the Jacobin mayor Pétion attended, as did a crowd estimated by contemporaries at over four hundred thousand.[1] Such vigour was shown yet again in a massive upsurge of popular enthusiasm upon the actual outbreak of war, with almost all echoing the Girondin line that the enemies of France were about to be routed.

Unfortunately for the authorities – the uneasy coalition of pro-war aristocrats, former Feuillants now regrouping under the banner of General Lafayette, and the Girondin ministry – the war took a very different course. Defeat may have been the secret hope of the aristocrats, but the events it would shortly provoke were to be their undoing. Nowhere, except for small pockets in the east, did French forces succeed in advancing into enemy territory in the spring of

1792. In the north, on the main front against the Austrian Netherlands, General Dillon was lynched by his own troops after they had been driven into panicky withdrawal at their first attempted incursion – his body was dismembered, paraded through the streets of Lille and burned on a bonfire.[2] Four weeks after the opening of the war, France's three leading army commanders, Lafayette, Luckner and Rochambeau, all begged the Assembly to seek peace negotiations, fearful of utter collapse if they committed their troops to battle.

These events should have come as no surprise to anyone – the British ambassador had reported as public knowledge, back in January, that 'the whole army . . . is in a state of insubordination not very promising at the eve of war'.[3] France's politicians could not accept the generals' evaluation, however, and the armies were ordered onto the offensive again in mid-June. Such attitudes prompted a new wave of defections among the officer corps, already devastated by emigrations that had reached the thousands after the Flight to Varennes. Those that did not emigrate sometimes simply resigned in despair – like Rochambeau, the most senior general on the northern front. What followed was not quite collapse, but near enough – throughout July the situation of the French forces steadily worsened, and they found themselves at bay well within the frontiers by the beginning of August. Prussia had committed troops to the war in early July, threatening the eastern frontiers and provoking a new round in the vicious political exchanges that had broken out in Paris.

By the time of the Prussian engagement, the situation in the capital was already one of desperate division. In late May events had seemed to be following the pattern established by the clashes of the winter, as the leaders of the Girondins, most notably Brissot and Vergniaud, condemned an alleged 'Austrian Committee' around the queen for counter-revolutionary plotting, non-juring priests were threatened again with deportation, and the royal Constitutional Guard was dissolved because of its aristocratic 'contamination'. The American diplomat Gouverneur Morris saw developments as 'the high road to despotism', as 'the most ardent advocates for the revolution' began to 'cry out' for authoritarian solutions.[4] When on 28 May the Legislative Assembly put itself into continuous session to watch over these critical times, it was followed immediately by the

Jacobin Club and the Fraternal Society, the original mixed-sex popular society of the capital, determined to exercise their own surveillance over the authorities, and various Sections petitioned the Assembly for the same right over the coming days.[5] On 3 June, the national authorities imposed a 'Festival of the Law' on Paris, honouring Simonneau, the mayor of Etampes lynched in the food-riots of the winter. In part a response to the popular-radical 15 April demonstration, it marked the beginning of intensifying hostility between Girondins and radicals. Meanwhile, the Girondins were also fighting on their other flank, against royal intransigence. The May measure against non-jurors remained unsanctioned by the king, who also decided to withhold his sanction from a proposal on 8 June to bring twenty thousand *fédéré* – 'federated', that is, united – provincial National Guards to protect the capital, as regular troops were sent off to the front.

The growing desperation of the Girondins in the face of this intransigence was reflected in the action taken by the Interior Minister, Jean-Marie Roland. With the support of his fellow Girondin ministers Servan and Clavière he sent an open letter to the king on 10 June, pleading with him to sanction these measures. What may have been an entreaty – 'much more delay, and a grieving people will see in its king the friend and accomplice of conspirators' – could equally well be read as a public rebuke, or indeed a threat.[6] The letter was actually drafted by Roland's wife, Manon. Aged thirty-eight in 1792, she was twenty years his junior, an aspiring intellectual who had seized on the possibilities for advancement that the Revolution provided. She had driven on the political career of her husband, a former royal inspector of manufactures, using political connections in France's second city, Lyon, to bring him to official notice in the capital. Madame Roland was an eager participant in the developing political intrigues of the summer, and the hostess of a salon where Girondin-inclined figures met several times a week.

As a consequence of this intolerable public outburst (regardless of its authorship), all three Girondin ministers were removed from office by the king on 13 June, replaced with Feuillant nonentities. The following week saw a yawning gulf opening up between the Feuillant–court axis on the right and the radicals of the Paris clubs on the left, with the Girondins straining to bridge the centre. The

American Gouverneur Morris wrote on 17 June that 'we stand on a vast volcano', recording that one reason that the generals were afraid to attack was that a victory would occasion 'outrages of the most flagitious' – that is, deeply criminal – kind among the population stirred up by the Jacobins. Morris also noted that the Feuillants intended to strike back against the Jacobins and 'in favour of the constitution, and M. de Lafayette will begin the attack'.[7]

On 18 June, a long letter from General Lafayette, at the head of his army 'entrenched in camp, at Maubeuge', was read into the record of the Legislative Assembly. He began by abusing the fallen ministry – 'unmasked by its divisions, it has fallen to its own intrigues'. His main target, however, was the Jacobin Club network, whom he denounced unequivocally: 'Organised as a separate Empire within the capital and through its affiliates; led blindly by a few ambitious chiefs, this sect forms a corporation set apart at the heart of the French people, whose powers it usurps in subjugating its representatives and mandatories.'[8] He concluded by demanding that such clubs be closed down by force, a proposal greeted by uproar from radical deputies and their supporters. On the following day, the king officially applied his veto to the measures on the non-jurors and *fédérés*.

In anticipation of this, the leaders of the popular Paris club movement had already been planning a demonstration, ostensibly to plant a liberty tree – a sort of revolutionary maypole – near the royal palace of the Tuileries. An armed crowd of several thousand thronged the area on the 20th (which was, of course, the anniversary of the king's flight), and by four in the afternoon managed to force or cajole their way past the National Guards posted around the palace, and invaded the Tuileries. The crowd flooding through the building eventually confronted the king himself, cornered alone in a window-bay. There he was obliged to put on a red woollen 'cap of liberty' – another rising symbol of revolutionary ardour – drink the health of the nation and listen to long diatribes on his inappropriate behaviour. Throughout he displayed a passive stoicism that would mark much of his behaviour from now on, although he also stoutly resisted calls to rescind his veto there and then. The Jacobin mayor, Pétion, arrived around six to restore order, claiming to have only just been alerted to the situation. The king rather tartly said that was 'very surprising', given the length of time he had been under siege.[9]

Gouverneur Morris noted that 'the constitution has this day, I think, given its last groan'.[10]

The Parisian radicals, who were beginning to refer to themselves and their constituents as *sans-culottes*, the 'breechless' who wore the long trousers of the working man, went away feeling satisfied that their message had been put across. Many of the *sans-culottes* were members of the National Guard, and activists in their local Sections – and thus by definition taxpaying 'active citizens' – but they and their spokesmen played on the notion of a common plebeian identity. This was not proletarian, not a modern 'working class' of wage-earners, but more the kind of identity embodied by the Cordeliers Club activist and master butcher Louis Legendre (a key figure in the invasion of the Tuileries) – skilled men, possessed of their own resources, but grounded in popular neighbourhood life, demotic common sense and the hard-pressed consumer's suspicion of political and economic machinations.[11] Legendre's Cordelier colleague Hébert embodied this identity in the mouthpiece he chose for his journalism, *le père Duchesne*, 'Father Duchesne'. This foul-mouthed furnace-maker was borrowed from burlesque theatre and turned into the expression of popular printed radicalism as both title and main character of his newspaper. Hébert himself was a small and in some ways unassuming man, recorded by contemporaries as being well mannered and neatly turned out, and living in quiet domestic comfort with his wife, a former nun he had met at one of the popular societies, and who in February of 1793 was to give birth to a daughter. Hébert's journalism and his increasing role in Parisian politics were to create for him a public persona sharply at odds with this private image.[12]

Duchesne, who was used as a character by many authors, but whom Hébert made legendary, delivered bluff lectures, laced with a flamboyant use of profanity, to his readers, and sometimes to members of the political elite cornered in his pages.[13] His watchwords were patriotism and suspicion – that the people were right in their hearts, but always in danger of being misled by unscrupulous political leaders. His proposed solutions were usually direct and bloody. It should be noted, however, that Hébert's writings were very far from being simplistic. Appearing several times a week, they assumed, through their use of casual references and nicknames (Madame Veto for Marie-Antoinette, General Blondinet for Lafayette), an intense familiarity with political events and personalities, one that could only have been gained by his *sans-culotte* readers through an active involvement in local discussion, and probably a reading of less theatrical press genres. The *Père Duchesne* was not so much an introduction to politics for the ill-informed as an ongoing vernacular treatise on reasons to maintain a radical attitude. Hébert's solutions to the capital's political troubles were straightforward, but the reader needed a strong grasp of what those troubles were in order to make sense of his prescriptions.

To see the *Père Duchesne* in this light is to contradict most contemporary observers' perceptions, which tended to assume, as we have already seen, that the kind of people Hébert wrote for were ignorant, rather stupid, and easily swayed in their views by corrupt agitators. Only the month before, writing in his newspaper, the *French Patriot*, the Girondins' figurehead Jacques-Pierre Brissot had denounced the radicals as Enragés, or 'Madmen'. He defined such a person as a 'false friend of the people, and enemy of the constitution'. He contrasted such a position with a Patriot, such as himself, who was a 'friend of the people, and friend of the constitution'.[14] The collection was completed with the 'Moderate', who was an enemy of the people and 'false friend' to the constitution. Although the latter distinction was clearly intended to maintain the distance between Brissot's associates and the Feuillants, he also clearly sought to mark out the realm of politics as necessarily the home of a patriot political class who could talk down to the 'people' as their friends, but not necessarily their equals.

Such attitudes and suspicions of popular activity and its leaders were soon displayed even more clearly. After the events at the Tuileries on 20 June, radicals in the capital initially maintained the initiative, and a mass meeting in the Faubourg Saint-Antoine two days later circulated a petition calling for the king's immediate dethronement.[15] A plan for another major rally the next day fell flat, however. By this time news of what had happened on the 20th had reached other parts of France, and soon it became clear that public opinion was not yet on the side of such republican agitation. Although the Paris Jacobin Club had in fact, and contrary to Lafayette's proscriptive remarks, stood scrupulously aside from direct popular agitation, it was abused in a wave of denunciatory addresses that flowed into the capital from the provinces through the rest of June. Local authorities, and *ad hoc* gatherings of active citizens, united to pour obloquy on those who dared violate the sanctity of the monarch's residence. Whether through sentiment or necessity, the political class of France remained determined, at least for now, to hold on to their king. From within Paris itself, a petition reported to contain twenty thousand signatures condemning the invasion of the Tuileries was presented to the Assembly on 1 July. By now, Lafayette had sensationally intervened again, this time in person, abandoning his command to appear in the capital.

Lafayette was playing an immensely dangerous game, trying in effect to save the monarchy despite itself. In early May he had made the bizarre proposal to Mercy-Argenteau, the Brussels-based Austrian diplomat and confidant of Marie-Antoinette, that Austria should suspend hostilities against France until he, Lafayette, could use military force to secure peace within Paris.[16] Although this letter remained secret, his public attitudes and past record were enough to subject the general to intense radical suspicion. His trip to Paris, speaking in the Assembly on 28 June, confirmed such suspicions. He again demanded the closure of the clubs, along with new restrictions on press freedom and the right of petition. He got an unsympathetic hearing, with many on the left alarmed that this was the manifesto of a *coup d'état*. They were quite correct, though it was a coup so blithely ill organised that it evaporated before ever really beginning.

Lafayette had not prepared any troops to support his political moves, but rather intended to summon the National Guard to his aid at a review the following day on the Champs-Elysées. The notion that they would rally to him without severe internal conflict was pathetically optimistic, and in any case, the review was swiftly cancelled by Pétion's municipal authorities. In a final irony, the authorities had been alerted to Lafayette's intentions by a message passed from Marie-Antoinette herself, who had no desire to be 'rescued' by a man she so heartily despised, in the name of a constitution she and Louis were determined to overthrow. Despite confronting once more the threat of violent death on 20 June, the royal family remained fixed in their opposition to any form of compromise with the 'rebels'. The general found himself bereft of supporters, and facing a serious legal challenge – he had abandoned his command without permission, as radicals in the Assembly had declared to his chagrin on the 28th, and now faced moves to impeach him.[17]

The political situation in the capital was by now both electrically tense and turbulently confused. On the left, the radicals of the club movement and some of the more *sans-culotte* Sections continued to meet, petition and protest in favour of their agenda. By the end of June, this included the defence of Pétion, under investigation for his tardy arrival on the 20th, and subsequently suspended from office by the department administrators. Many Sections had begun to meet daily or thrice-weekly, their evening sessions shared with audiences of those formally excluded from political rights – 'passive citizens', women and children.[18] By the middle of July, over half the Sections had called for the mayor's reinstatement, with some adding demands for punishment of the authorities that had dared to suspend him. Pétion was restored to office by a vote of the Legislative Assembly on 13 July, in time to take part in the annual Festival of Federation on the 14th – an event which passed off peacefully enough, in the absence of the king, and as little more than a sideshow to the developing political crisis.

It was partly in the light of the Festival that the original proposals of early June to encamp twenty thousand *fédéré* troops in the capital had been put forward. Although the king had vetoed this specific move, the Festival still garnered delegations of National Guards from across the country. Many of these were selected and dispatched by their home cities and departments as if their mission were indeed to defend the capital against counter-revolution. The radical patriotism with which many delegations arrived was reinforced by activists of the Parisian clubs and Sections, who took up the *fédérés* as soon as they reached the capital and inducted them into the complexities of the threats facing all good patriots. The Jacobin Club itself formed a special committee to liaise with the *fédérés*, whose representatives also met together in the same premises. On 13 July, this grouping published a bitter assault on the king, a 'perfidious monarch' who would do better to flee now, and not be caught again, so ill had he served France.[19]

From the popular left, then, the situation was clear, and many had already settled in their minds the need for a republican solution. Among the broader population, too, the wave of anti-Jacobin feeling that had flowed forth after the 20 June molestation of the king had clearly gone into reverse. Both at the centre and across France, public opinion began to turn away from the monarchy. Within the political class itself, opinions were far less easily categorised. The Feuillants continued to try to save the king for the constitution. Lafayette, after his humiliating exit from the politics of the capital, came up with yet another plan. By force of personality, he had obliged the military high command to acquiesce in a scheme to transfer his troops from the Rhine front to Flanders, swapping places with those of general Luckner. This *chassé-croisé*, as it was dubbed, was militarily absurd, and a mere pretext for the two armies to be united, and then to march to the town of Compiègne, to where Lafayette would escort the royal family on 15 July. There, the Feuillants' pet scheme to revive the 'balanced' two-chamber legislature rejected in 1789 would be presented as the heart of a new constitution negotiated in 'freedom' by the king. Yet again, however, Marie-Antoinette's refusal to yield in her resistance won over an initially tempted king, and the scheme was called off only a few days before the 15th.[20] Lafayette returned to his military command in near-despair.

More complex yet than the Feuillant position was that of the Girondins. They found themselves facing an insurmountable dilemma on 10 July, when the Feuillant ministers who had replaced Roland and his colleagues were themselves driven into resignation by incessant political attacks. The king made no immediate move to replace them, and Girondin bids to take up the reins of government became increasingly desperate over the subsequent weeks. What it would mean to do so, however, grew more and more unclear. On 11 July the Legislative Assembly enacted a measure it had devised less than a week before. Declaring *la patrie en danger*, 'the fatherland in danger', it summoned all administrative bodies into daily session, and militarised the National Guard for front-line service. The decree also gave the Assembly the ability to negate a royal veto. In this respect, since the measure itself had not been ratified by the king, it was *de facto* an abandonment of constitutionality.[21]

Rather than recognise this, as many radicals already had, the Girondins were drawn into increasingly rancorous dispute with those radicals as they attempted, like the Feuillants before them, to save the monarchy despite itself. Through the last ten days of July the original 'Girondins', the Bordelais trio of Vergniaud, Gensonné and

Guadet, conducted an urgent but fruitless correspondence with the king concerning the need for patriots at the heart of government.[22] Their motivations for doing so were impugned then and later, but were in reality quite straightforward – they could not see France surviving the overthrow of the constitution when her enemies were already inside the frontiers. Their aim, however, was to place their own men in ministerial office, and to see off an already growing tide of republican agitation, which necessarily drew to them charges of personal ambition and counter-revolutionary intent. Those who had already decided that the royal family had betrayed the Revolution could not stomach the notion that the national interest required them to remain. Indeed, from the radical perspective, the Girondin attitude simply made no sense, unless one began to think in terms of conscious, self-seeking betrayal.

There was bitter irony in the fact that it was Vergniaud, master orator of the Gironde, who had launched the move to create the powers used on 11 July, in a speech on the 3rd in which he summoned all patriots to unite in the face of danger.[23] At this very moment, a group of Assembly deputies centred around the Girondin leadership, but also, attempting to reach out to others linked to more radical Jacobinism, formed a group identified as the 'Reunion Club'.[24] What started out as a bid to coalesce 'patriot' forces against still-active Feuillant and royalist manoeuvres was already coming under radical attack by the end of July as a vicious cabal of the selfish, perhaps crypto-royalist Girondins. Like the salons of Madame Roland and others where Girondin-inclined figures had met, the Reunion Club was a private gathering, without the public gallery that had become a fixed feature of the Jacobins, the popular societies and the radical Sections. What was, for the Girondins, a matter of privacy was for their enemies a commitment to secrecy that pointed inevitably to conspiracy. What, after all, could a true patriot wish to conceal from the people of Paris?

For much of France, the Girondins' ever more desperate attempts to take up the reins of constitutional power could only have been an irrelevance. On both sides of the political divide, loins were being girded for combat without quarter. In the embittered climate of the south-east, a suspected counter-revolutionary conspirator, the comte de Saillans, was arrested with four companions at Les Vans in the Ardèche on 12 July. Despite the efforts of the authorities to keep the five men safely in prison, they were killed by a crowd and their heads paraded on pikes. A day later, at Joyeuse in the same department, a counter-revolutionary priest and nobleman were seized and killed by a mob largely made up of National Guards and newly rallied volunteers for the army.[25] Between then and the end of July, there were attacks on counter-revolutionaries in eight other localities across the country, including the ceremonious killing of two priests in Bordeaux on the 14th, the murder in three separate incidents of six suspects in Marseille between the 21st and 23rd, and the massacre of a dozen local officials in Toulon between the 28th and 31st. These assaults were sparked by the authorities' apparent hesitation in ordering action following frenetic rumours of a plot to massacre local patriots and seize the naval base, home to France's Mediterranean fleet.[26]

This fear of massacre was endemic, and not without foundation. The counter-revolutionaries of the emigration had their say at the end of July, drafting a 'Manifesto' in the name of the Prussian and Austrian rulers for the Allied commander, the duke of Brunswick, leading the advance from the Rhineland. Written on 25 July, and reaching Paris at the end of the month, the full text was officially published on 3 August, and was utterly unequivocal:

> The inhabitants of the towns, *bourgs* and villages who dare to defend themselves against the troops of Their Imperial and Royal Majesties, and to shoot at them . . . will be punished immediately, according to the severity of the law of war, or their homes demolished or burned down . . .
>
> The city of Paris and all its inhabitants, without distinction, will be obliged to submit themselves, immediately and without delay, to the king, to give this prince full and complete freedom, and to guarantee for him, as well as for all royal personages, the inviolability and the respect which the laws of nature and of men oblige from subjects towards sovereigns . . . Their said Majesties declare . . . that if the chateau of the Tuileries is taken by force or insulted, that if the least violence is done to it, the least outrage to Their Majesties the king, the queen and the royal family, if their safety, their preservation and their freedom are not immediately provided for, they will wreak an exemplary and ever-memorable vengeance, by delivering up the city of Paris to

military execution, and total destruction, and the rebels guilty of assassinations to the execution that they have earned.[27]

On the very day that this was published, all but one of the forty-eight Sections of Paris united, unprecedentedly, to petition the Legislative Assembly for the dethronement of the king. Two days earlier, Parisian radicals had been hardened to their task by the arrival in the capital of a battalion-strong delegation of *fédérés* from Marseille. They had marched the length of France, leaving behind them in the south-east the aftermath of savage conflict. Counter-revolutionary nobles had tried to convene an armed assembly at the chateau of Jalès, in the Ardèche, at the time of the Parisian Festival of Federation. An ardent Catholic rank and file had responded to the call, gathering in the thousands. It was the third such gathering since 1790, and, in the climate of war, the revolutionary local authorities mobilised against it with ferocity. Battalions of hastily raised volunteers descended on the area, killing several hundred of the potential rebels, and torching nearby villages they suspected of aristocratic sympathies. It was from this repression that the comte de Saillans was fleeing when captured and lynched.[28] In the neighbouring departments of the Gard and the Lozère, suspected counter-revolutionaries were lynched in a series of incidents at the same time. The Marseille delegation brought with them to Paris this atmosphere of feverish near-civil war. They also marched in singing a tune that had begun life in April as the 'War Song of the Rhine Army', but which would now forever be associated with the southerners who had learned it as they passed through Alsace: *La Marseillaise.*

It is a song of dread and defiance, of betrayal, sacrifice, victory and liberty. From its first lines – 'Come, children of the fatherland, the day of glory has arrived!' – it evokes an almost millennial sense of drama. The rest of the first verse is sinister, and horrific in its import: 'The bloody standard of tyranny is raised against us! Do you hear from the fields the howling of their ferocious soldiers? They are coming among us, to butcher your sons and your wives!' Then it explodes into the chorus:

To arms, citizens!
Form your battalions!

We march, we march
So impure blood
May water our soil!

The imagery of unrelenting combat echoes through all the verses. The fourth warns that 'all of us are soldiers against you; if our young heroes fall, France will make others to take their place, ready for battle with you'. The sixth verse evokes heroic ancestors whose 'dust' the French may contemplate: 'We will take supreme pride in avenging them or following them!'

The politics of the war itself are also made clear – it is not foreigners as such, but 'a horde of slaves, traitors and conspiring kings' against whom the French struggle. 'Ignoble shackles and long-prepared chains' are awaiting them if they fail, but they should still be 'magnanimous warriors', and 'spare the sad victims armed against us despite themselves' in the ranks of foreign armies. No such pity is to be expended on 'these sanguinary despots, these accomplices of Bouillé, all these tigers who, pitiless, tear at their mother's breast'. It is a 'sacred love of the fatherland' that will 'guide and uphold our avenging arms', but it is also 'liberty, dear liberty' that the citizens fight for – 'That your expiring enemies should see your triumph and our glory!'[29] Although the lyrics owe a surprising amount to patriotic odes in circulation at the time of France's last great war on behalf of the American colonies, they are combined here into an uncompromising message both of the threat posed to the Revolution and of the resolve of the citizenry to extinguish that threat by force of arms.[30] The newspaper the *Chronicle of Paris* reported that the massed singing of the chorus in the theatres soon became ubiquitous, and was 'truly thrilling'. A young officer in the royal guards thought otherwise, and wrote that the 'invasion of brigands' from the south 'completed the emancipation of the criminal scum of the city'. The Marseillais were 'five hundred fanatics, three-quarters of them drunk . . . followed by the dregs of the people'. Their arrival was greeted with 'satanic dances' as they 'howled' the tune named in their honour.[31]

By the first week of August, as the Marseille *fédérés* settled into the club and Section networks of Parisian radicalism, it was becoming increasingly evident that force of arms was about to be used in the capital itself. The Legislative Assembly had shunted the

3 August deposition petition into a committee, which was due to report on the 9th. Further mass petitions, and abortive moves towards uprisings, punctuated the intervening days. The Girondins were in disarray. Brissot had advocated delay in a series of critical public speeches in late July, and a later memoirist recorded that the then foreign minister, Chambonas, had been authorised by the court to dispense enormous sums to purchase such opinions – upwards of two million livres, allegedly. Certainly, Mayor Pétion would claim openly the following year that Chambonas had offered him thirty thousand livres to order police action against potential insurrectionaries.[32]

Madame Roland berated Brissot and the three deputies from the Gironde in her correspondence, lashing out against their time-wasting and self-regard. She sought action from her husband to propose an immediate, but provisional, suspension of the king. One activist and friend of Brissot, Louvet de Couvrai, begged him in private correspondence to abandon his delaying line: 'The Court is toying with you. Brissot, I beg you in the name of our glory and the fatherland, lose not a day . . . vote without delay for suspension and we are saved.' A few days later, however, in his newspaper the *Sentinel*, Louvet begged the people of Paris not to 'give in to the misled or perfidious advisors who invite you to descend armed upon the Tuileries'.[33] Another Girondin-inclined journalist, Carra, was less equivocal, and on 4 August in his paper, the *Patriotic Annals*, published an article headed 'Upon the just and indispensable necessity of dethroning Louis XVI'.[34] All of this underlines just how far the Girondins were from being anything like an organised 'party'. There was more consistency, if also no one formal centre, further to their left.

Among those who had been republicans since Varennes, and those who had come round to this conclusion more recently, there was no doubt that the king was a perjured traitor, working with Marie-Antoinette, the *émigré* princes and the powers of Europe to arrange not merely the defeat of the Revolution but the massacre of all patriots. The image of a 'Saint-Barthélemy', recalling the St Bartholomew's Day slaughter in 1572 of thousands of Protestants by a Catholic court, echoed through the radicals' press writings and speeches. If they could have read the correspondence of Marie-Antoinette, who in March had discussed French military dispositions with the Austrian diplomat Mercy-Argenteau, and who continued to supply strategic nuggets of military information in letters to Axel von Fersen throughout the summer, their worst fears would have found added fuel.[35]

As it was, the radicals' own suspicions were quite enough to propel the dethronement movement forwards. To all appearances, it was not a movement in which major national leaders played a great part – Robespierre, for example, although he had called for 'regeneration' of both the legislative and executive branches of government in a speech to the Jacobins on 29 July, does not seem to have been directly involved in insurrectionary preparations.[36] The firebrand journalist Marat, although he had called in his pages for insurrections almost continuously since 1790, allegedly took fright at the risks of a real one, and sought protection from the Marseille *fédérés*.[37] The Jacobin Club rehearsed all the issues of dethronement and insurrection in its debates, but did not come to the fore in actual planning. Here, it was the Cordeliers Club, the leaders of the *fédérés* and radical leaders within the Sections and the Paris Commune itself that finally assembled to bring down the monarchy. A wave of petitions from the Cordeliers, *fédérés* and Sections had preceded the near-unanimity of 3 August, and the press and public meetings stimulated a growing sense that insurrection was to take place – the only questions being when and how. Even the royal family, more or less imprisoned in the Tuileries, sensed the atmosphere. Gouverneur Morris paid his respects to them on 5 August, and found 'nothing remarkable, only that they were up all night, expecting to be murdered'.[38]

To plot insurrection, a committee of around a dozen leaders began to meet at the end of July, using the office of the Jacobin Club's correspondence committee. It included several Cordeliers leaders, others who would be clearly identified as Girondins within the next year, and men from the sectional movement, but none of the great figureheads of radicalism. Nevertheless, the recorded meetings of this group, on 26 July, 4 and 9 August, each preceded an insurrectionary event. The first two were abortive, centred in the more radical eastern suburbs of the Faubourgs Saint-Antoine and Saint-Marcel, from where crowds failed to move towards the Tuileries.[39] There was real hesitation about commitment to an armed insurrection. Radical leaders were unsure how many of the more prosperous

National Guards from Sections in the city's west end could be counted on not to defend the king, and the professional competence of the battalion of Swiss Guards based at the Tuileries was widely feared. Mayor Pétion felt this dilemma particularly severely – he had legal responsibility for preventing disorder in Paris, and also worried at several points that an insurrection was bound to fail.[40]

Finally, on 9 August, the radical leaders of Paris decided that they had to act. The previous day the Legislative Assembly had decisively rejected a move to indict General Lafayette, and on this day failed to support the motion for dethronement. The national authorities seemed to offer nothing but pointless deadlock. The alarm was sounded that night in the Sections, and armed forces were summoned. Delegates of nineteen Sections (many others falling away in fear at the last moment) agreed at 3.30 a.m. on the 10th to a military plan – *fédéré* and Left Bank detachments to come up across the river opposite the Tuileries; eastern units, under Antoine-Joseph Santerre, a wealthy *sans-culotte* brewer and leader of the Faubourg Saint-Antoine, to make a direct approach. As dawn broke, these columns were on the move, at the same time as the defenders of the Tuileries were taking up position after a frantic night of organisation. Some eight hundred Swiss Guards stood ready, joined by over twelve hundred loyal National Guards, and some two hundred volunteers from the old Royal Bodyguards and the dissolved Constitutional Guard.[41] These forces were enough to give the insurgents real pause, and possibly even drive them off – although tens of thousands of Parisians thronged the streets, many of them bearing arms, the disciplined core of the two attacking columns probably numbered under three thousand.

It was to be a series of personal decisions which determined the course of the fateful day of 10 August. One such choice was that of the military leader of the Tuileries garrison, the marquis de Mandat, who opted to obey a municipal request to come to the City Hall at 4.30 a.m. He arrived to find the radicals in command, having proclaimed an 'Insurrectionary Commune', and was placed under arrest around 7 a.m. (and lynched later in the day), leaving the defenders without a unified command. The choices of Louis XVI, in his last hours of independent action, would be even more decisive in their outcomes, if not their content. He emerged from a few hours' snatched sleep in the early hours of the morning, dressed in undistinguished civilian clothes and appearing ruffled and concerned. He then disappeared into conference with his confessor, emerging some time before 6 a.m., and deciding to review his troops. Marie-Antoinette had already rebuffed one suggestion that the royal family should place themselves under the protection of the Assembly. The man whose advice she had scorned, Pierre-Louis Roederer, a former judge now an official of the department of Paris, wrote that her combativeness made it clear to him that 'there was within the palace a strong determination to fight and a faction who had promised the queen a victory'.[42] At this moment, a real fight indeed seemed likely. However, Louis naively chose to expand his review from the loyal troops paraded before the palace, and began to walk towards other groups further away. National Guard artillerymen drawn up by the river shouted '*Vive la Nation!*' (and not '*le Roi!*') as he passed, and as he moved into the Tuileries gardens, he encountered even more hostile formations, and an armed crowd that made a rush towards him from the other side of the gardens. Loyal officers formed a human shield to get him to safety.[43]

Within the palace, the shaken king was subjected to a browbeating by Roederer, who warned him, as he had warned Marie-Antoinette, that flight to the Assembly was their only hope of safety. The queen urged resistance, but Roederer told her bluntly that in that case, 'you will be responsible for the lives of your husband and children'. This was the final straw, and the king gave in. With the National Guards of dubious loyalty now fleeing to the other side, he could see no hope of a successful defence. At 8.30 a.m., the insurrection achieved its central goal before a shot had been fired, as some 450 of the defenders escorted the royal family on foot into the custody of the Legislative Assembly. With no established protocol to follow in such a crisis, the deputies accommodated them in the reporters' box behind a grille near the president's chair, while a temporising debate began.

What followed back at the palace was entirely unnecessary, therefore, to the resolution of the political situation. Left without overall leadership, the volunteers, and especially the Swiss Guards, stood by their sense of military honour, refusing to lay down their arms to the insurgents. Confrontation turned to scuffles, scuffles almost at once to random firing, and then to pitched battle. The military discipline of the Swiss told to deadly effect, and they laid out some three hundred insurgents across the main courtyard and the Place du Carrousel before their ammunition began to run low. They withdrew to the palace itself for a last stand, at which point a courier battled through the firing to bring them orders from the king to cease fire and withdraw. Although one party of some 150 Swiss were able to flee to the protection of the Assembly, the majority, trying to escape via the gardens and the square beyond, were cut to pieces. The wounded were finished off with bayonets and pikes, and as the crowds who had seconded the attack broke into the palace, domestic servants and anyone else caught within were considered fair game after the 'treacherous' refusal to surrender. As was customary, severed heads were paraded in triumph, and rumours of worse mutilations ran rife. The thoughtlessness of the king in leaving his defenders without orders, and his later pointless instruction to abandon their posts, had been prime factors in the massacre, although of course the counter-revolutionary press would make hay with the popular savagery on display.

It is worth noting, however, the archives of the Palais-Royal Section that neighboured the Tuileries. For five days after the battle, its records were littered with the deposition of objects from the fighting. Four groups of men, twelve in total, from a surgeon and a National Guard lieutenant to several journeyman artisans, handed in goods found on the bodies of dead Swiss. On nine occasions, similar individuals and groups reported that they had taken goods from others who seemed to be looting them from the palace, and deposited them in official hands; and no fewer than fifteen further individuals made official deposits of items that they had picked up or otherwise come across in and around the Tuileries.[44] Whatever judgments we make about the attack on the palace, it cannot simply be attributed, as so many counter-revolutionary authors wished to do, to a thieving, murderous rabble.

Back in the Assembly, it was once again the great orator of the Gironde, Vergniaud, who broke the stalemate of hesitations. Faced with Parisian delegations demanding a decision, he proposed the immediate suspension of the king from his constitutional functions, and manhood-suffrage elections for a National Convention to reorder the nation's affairs. There were by now no members of the royalist right in attendance, and precious few even of the Feuillant centre. None of the three hundred who did remain were going to dispute the Parisians' victory in the face of their bayonets. Accepted by a show of hands, this measure left France under the control of the victorious insurrectionaries. That, at least, was the theory, and certainly the case in Paris, as the deputies of the Legislative Assembly found themselves forced into an uneasy power-sharing arrangement with the radicals of the Insurrectionary Commune. A Provisional Executive Council, made up of the former Girondin ministers and the Cordelier, Danton, at the Justice Ministry, was appointed at once. A week later, radical demands produced an 'extraordinary tribunal' to deal with the crimes of the court on 10 August. It would guillotine a few officials, but was rapidly sidelined by events. Meanwhile, all three centres of power, the Assembly, the Commune and the ministries, began sending out delegations and commissioners into the provinces, to explain the fall of the monarchy and to cleanse the body politic of remaining royalists.

The 'second revolution' that took place over the following weeks was an administrative purge in some ways greater than that of 1789. Then, changes in personnel had been haphazard, and extended over a period of months, with widespread compromise between old and new orders in evidence. Now, royalism was anathema, and any hint of Old Regime loyalties not entirely effaced by later patriotism was enough to see politicians and administrators thrust from office, replaced by 'purer' patriots and newly minted republicans. As in the run-up to 10 August, this process was punctuated by crowd killings of suspected counter-revolutionaries, and occasionally suspected hoarders and profiteers, across the country. The south-east recorded the most incidents, but there were others from the Ariège in the Pyrenees to the Oise near Paris. Between 15 and 19 August, the Orne in central Normandy saw killings in four separate locations, three of which involved groups of men gathered to put forward volunteers for military service.[45] This move, required by a law of 22 July, frequently led to bloodshed against local counter-revolutionaries as volunteers psyched themselves up to leave their locality and commit themselves to war.

The aggression was not all one way, however. In the west, where the pursuit of non-juror priests by town-based local authorities continued vigorously, the rural population took violent exception to the militarisation of the National Guard and the call for new volunteers. In the Deux-Sèvres, a large gathering sacked the estates of one member of the departmental administration on 19 August, and on the 22nd over ten thousand protesters invaded the town of Châtillon-sur-Sèvre, burning district administrative records, while asserting that the foreign enemies of the nation were acting in defence of religion. At La-Roche-sur-Yon in the Vendée, crowds gathered demanding the release of interned priests. Two Breton departments experienced pitched battles between anti-recruitment groups and hastily mobilised urban National Guards, as did the neighbouring Mayenne. Here protesters declared that they would 'never consent to send soldiers against the king and the priests'.[46] Alarming reports of these attitudes filtered back to Paris, as they had done for over a year.

On 17 August, General Lafayette had tried one last time to save the monarchy despite itself, demanding that his troops follow him in a march on Paris. When they would not, he fled to the Austrian lines, to spend most of the rest of the decade in various forms of imprisonment. Two days later, Prussian forces entered France from the east, bringing with them the *émigrés* who had been instrumental in drafting the vengeful Brunswick Manifesto. The duke himself, as he prepared to lead the invasion, remarked to the comte de Provence that 'we shall have no obstacles to get over', which was to be regretted – it would be to the 'general good' if there was some serious fighting, 'for the French need a lesson which they will never forget'. Even Provence blanched at this assault on his national honour, replying that Brunswick should look out for 'some unforeseen obstacle. I presume that the French will defend their country. They have not always been beaten.'[47] Nonetheless, so confident were the *émigrés* of victory that they had already begun to argue over positions in the new government, and made sure that in every district their forces occupied the civil and religious Old Regime was restored to full force.[48] The marquis de Falaiseau, near the besieged town of Thionville, wrote to his wife that 'the former parish priests have been reinstated. Just now some gendarmes brought along a "constitutional" priest, bound and gagged – a great rascal, they say. I spoke to the man . . . he refused to retract.'[49] Falaiseau did not bother to record what became of him.

The major French fortress of Longwy surrendered to this army on 23 August, the suspicious haste of its fall after only a brief bombardment adding to an already near-hysterical atmosphere in Paris. On the 26th, the Commune of Paris ordered house-to-house searches for 'aristocratic' weapons-caches, and on the same day the Legislative Assembly voted for the deportation of all non-juror priests. Such individuals within the capital were swept up in a wave of arrested 'suspects' that began to strain the resources of the prison system – a system reputed for years to give shelter to corruption and counter-revolution. It was in this atmosphere that events which have entered grim legend as the September Massacres took place.

# Chapter 4

# The September Massacres

She received a sabre blow behind her head which took off her cap. Her long hair fell onto her shoulders. Another sabre blow hit her eye; blood gushed out; her dress was stained with it. She tried to fall down, to let herself die, but they forced her to get up again, to walk over corpses, and the crowd, silent, watched the slaughter. She fell again. A certain Charlat knocked her senseless with a club, and as she seemed lifeless, they attacked her perhaps still-living body relentlessly. Pierced through by sabre and pike blows, she was no more than a shapeless thing, red with blood, unrecognisable . . .[1]

They tore off everything, her dress, her slip, and naked as God made her she was spread out on the corner of a boundary-stone, at the entrance to the rue Saint-Antoine. They left her exposed there from eight o'clock in the morning till noon, then they cut away her head and the sacred parts of the body . . .[2]

Two individuals dragged a naked body by its legs, headless, its back on the ground and its abdomen laid open to the chest. The cortege halted. On a shaky platform, the corpse was ceremoniously spread out, and the limbs arranged with a kind of art . . . To my right, at the end of a pike, was a head that often brushed against my face because of the movements the bearer made when he gesticulated. To my left, another individual, more horrible, held against his chest in one hand the intestines of the victim, and in the other a large knife . . .[3]

In these accounts, and many others, contemporaries and historians recorded the horrible death of the princesse de Lamballe, favourite of Marie-Antoinette, outside the Parisian prison of La Force on 3 September 1792. Born Marie-Thérèse-Louise de Savoie-Carignan, she had been married at sixteen, and was presented at Louis XV's court in 1768, aged nineteen and already a widow. The gruesome early death of her husband from syphilis, contracted in one of his numerous and unconcealed affairs, left her childless and isolated (and reportedly the disease left her sterile), and she was forbidden to remarry by her father-in-law, the duc de Penthièvre.[4] When two years later Marie-Antoinette came to Versailles, in desperate need of friends in this new foreign court, she and the princesse rapidly became inseparable. Even before Marie-Antoinette became queen, there was diplomatic and other gossip that hinted at an improper connection between the two, growing in vitriol as Lamballe was given power in 1775 over the new queen's household affairs and revealed herself to be both an icy stickler for protocol and an apparent glutton for property and sinecures. However, another favourite, the comtesse de Polignac, eclipsed Lamballe in royal favour in 1777, and for twelve years she faded from public view.[5]

In October 1789, as Polignac fled abroad and the queen was 'imprisoned' in the Tuileries, the princesse rallied to her side, once more taking charge of the ceremonies of the court, and becoming closer to Marie-Antoinette than ever before. She may even have been the go-between in some of the queen's increasingly desperate political manoeuvres. Revolutionary propaganda and pornographic libels reiterated all the old rumours of her sexuality, coupled with charges of duplicity, stupidity, greed and counter-revolutionary intent. Lamballe's public image, the famously milky-skinned blonde ice-maiden of unshakeable hauteur and hidden perversity, made her an iconic hate-figure second only to the queen herself. She perished at the height of an episode that marked the final end of all hope for the French monarchy, the culmination of a ruthless patriotic mobilisation at a moment of grave national peril, and the birth of a grim legend of radical bestiality and carnage: the September Massacres.

Lamballe's death is undisputed, but its manner is not. On 3

September 1792, a small group of Parisian men reported to the administrative office of the Quinze-vingts Section, one of the forty-eight neighbourhood political districts of the capital. One was a labourer, two were carpentry craftsmen, and two were artillerymen of the Parisian National Guard. They had struggled along the Grande rue du Faubourg Saint-Antoine, main thoroughfare of the eastern side of the city, with a troublesome burden, which they now wished to place in the hands of the authorities. The Section's clerk noted that they were the 'bearers of the headless body of the former princesse de Lamballe, who had just been killed at the Hôtel de La Force'.[6] The clerk itemised the contents of the corpse's pockets, and also noted that the head was currently elsewhere, being paraded on the end of a pike. Within hours, corpse and head were reunited, and soon after both were collected by servants of the princesse's family and taken for private burial. Thus, without fanfare or rigmarole, in the records of a minor part of the revolutionary political apparatus, the favourite of Marie-Antoinette was put to rest – her corpse fully clothed, decapitated but otherwise unmutilated, challenging in its cold physicality, all the quasi-pornographic specifics of her legendary demise recorded dispassionately by the Section clerk.[7]

It had taken less than four months for war to produce the collapse of the monarchy, and it required less than a month more for that fall to become massacre, as the people in arms exercised their right of self-defence against those they felt were betraying them to the counter-revolution. In return, the uprising from below that sealed this period would be the ammunition that the people's enemies, of every stripe, needed to condemn categorically such a brutal engagement with the politics of their betters. The legends that began to accrue around the September Massacres even as they were taking place marked out the epoch-making nature of the 'second revolution' that France underwent in the summer of 1792.

On the afternoon of Sunday 2 September 1792, a small convoy of hired carriages left the Ile de la Cité in central Paris, heading south through the city streets on a short journey to the Abbey of Saint-Germain-des-Près. The carriages contained prisoners, some twenty-four in all, who had been locked up in a converted attic in the Palais de Justice since the great insurrection of 10 August. Like several hundred others detained in the city since that date, these were a mixture of associates of the royal court, politically suspect functionaries and Catholic priests who had refused loyalty oaths. This particular batch were being moved to join a substantial cohort of their fellows in the prison known as the Abbaye. They were, as current understanding saw it, dangerous counter-revolutionaries, and were given an armed escort of the National Guard, the Parisian citizens' militia.[8]

The convoy rolled along the riverside quay and crossed the open space of the Pont Neuf before swinging into the narrower confines of the rue Dauphine. The streets were busy with the usual bustle of pedestrians, and also with groups gathering to exchange the day's news and alarms. There was nothing unusual in such gatherings: Parisians liked to keep up to date, and word of mouth was their favoured medium. Today, however, there was a more sombre tone than usual to such exchanges. As the carriages passed, shouted insults, and the occasional threat, followed them, their occupants' clerical robes and dishevelled condition marking them out as captured enemies of the people.

Conditions in the city were, in fact, almost unbearably tense. The successful insurrection of 10 August that brought down the monarchy had been an act of desperation for a nation facing military defeat. On this very day, 2 September, Paris was alive with the news that the fortress-town of Verdun was hopelessly besieged (it had, indeed, already fallen, as the Parisians would later learn). The loss of this stronghold would leave an open road to the capital for the advancing foe. Meanwhile, the rumour ran through the city that the population of the prisons could, at a moment's notice, be broken out and armed by the still-active cells of the hydra-headed counter-revolution.

The convoy's journey was almost over when, within a few hundred yards of the prison, it was intercepted by a crowd of armed men. Ordinary working people of the city, in their everyday clothes, with perhaps a smattering of National Guard blue coats, the crowd would have personified, in the prisoners' eyes, the faceless mob that had carried out so many ghastly deeds already in the past years. Their weapons – swords, knives, hatchets and bludgeons – were a chilling reminder that such groups had decapitated many of the Revolution's enemies since the fall of the Bastille in 1789. The crowd commandeered the coaches and led them to the headquarters of the local Section committee, which, like almost all such bodies, met in requisitioned religious buildings. The terrified prisoners were herded up a flight of steps into a large room, where they stood before six local committee-men who had been summoned by the ringing of the alarm bells. The leaders of the crowd that packed into the room confronted this group with their demands: these prisoners were enemies of the nation, villains who required instant justice, and the committee-men had been conscripted into the role of judges.[9]

As the local worthies considered this, two or three of the prisoners, who had perhaps tried to break loose or dispute with their captors, were struck down before them, and their bloodied corpses dragged into the courtyard. Numb with terror at the sudden violence, the remaining prisoners offered no resistance. Reluctantly or otherwise, the local committee took on its new judicial role – in later self-justification, one member would assert that there truly was no choice. The original armed escort for the prisoners held them in the room with the newly constituted 'tribunal', while the executioners formed up on the steps outside. There was no question of acquittal – each of the prisoners was sent out alone, and stabbed or bludgeoned to death. The executions lasted around a half-hour: no sudden frenzy, but a brutally matter-of-fact procedure. The only suggestion of a lack of organisation was that two of the original prisoners were concealed by the committee among its members, and survived.[10]

From this beginning, the crowds wished to move on to a more general dispatch of the prisoners at the Abbaye, but disagreement arose among them – should they all be put to death as quickly as possible, or should there be at least a scrutiny of the individual reasons for imprisonment, with clemency for any innocents that were found? This was a debate that raged for much of the afternoon in and around the locality of the prison, prolonged, and perhaps guided to its final conclusions, by the arrival of delegates from the Paris Commune, the municipal council, that had seized much of the executive power in the region on 10 August. While this debate went on, another group burst into the monastery of the Carmes, a mile or so to the east, and killed some 115 of the 160 prisoners who had been held there. Most of these were priests, and most died after being 'judged' in another impromptu tribunal.[11]

As evening drew in, this bloody process finally began in earnest at the Abbaye, as it also took shape elsewhere in three of the great prisons of Paris – the Châtelet, the Conciergerie and La Force. On the following morning, two temporary prisons would be visited – one holding priests in the seminary of Saint-Firmin, and a depot of condemned felons destined for the chain-gangs, held in a convent on the rue des Bernardins. On the afternoon of the 3rd, death came to the thieves' prison of Bicêtre, and on the following day to the final site of massacre, the women's hospital-prison of La Salpêtrière. Most of these events were rapid, lasting no more than a few hours, but the workings of the tribunals at the Abbaye went on for over twenty-four hours, those at Bicêtre almost as long, and those at La Force, though begun among the earliest, did not conclude until late on 6 September.

Everything about these extraordinary events seemed to demand prodigies. It was reported in the streets, and even in the Legislative Assembly, that at Bicêtre a pitched battle had broken out, and cannon had been turned on the prisoners. At La Force, prisoners who had barricaded themselves in dungeons were supposedly drowned by deliberately flooding the building. Ghastly violence was everywhere in the accounts of supposed witnesses – victims decapitated slowly with saws, impaled, tormented with fire, skinned alive, their hearts torn out; victims and bystanders forced to taste the blood of the dead; killers dipping their bread in blood, or even in the wounds of their victims; rapes by the score, and 'unspeakable acts' that could only be hinted at in the prisons that housed women and children.[12] However, while the true picture of the September Massacres is a grim one, it is nevertheless one in which bizarre sexual mutilations, sadistic tortures and the dark passions of the frenzied mob have no place.

The story of the Massacres is inseparable from the consequences of the earlier 10 August insurrection. This rising had cost the lives of some six hundred troops loyal to the king, including a number, perhaps as many as a hundred, who had been executed summarily. But in return, some three hundred Parisians, from forty-four of the forty-eight Sections of the city, had been killed or wounded, along with nearly ninety of their *fédéré* comrades from other regions. The rank and file of the attackers came from the core of the Parisian working population. Later authors would condemn them as brigands, bandits and the dregs of society, but the lists of the dead and wounded are dominated by a roll-call of respectable working men, master craftsmen, shopkeepers and other small traders. Between a third and a half of the casualties appear to have come from the two great artisan districts of the city, the suburban Faubourgs Saint-Antoine and Saint-Marcel. Some of them were in their fifties, and many left widows and orphans, as shown by the petitions that emerged when the revolutionary authorities later voted to provide these with pensions. Pierre Dumont, aged fifty, was maimed in the attack and lived on for two years before succumbing, but his wife was refused support. The master glazier Antoine Lobjois left a wife and five children when he was killed, but the authorities for some reason refused to support three of them. Even younger casualties left dependants: Louis Le Roy was twenty-one and a journeyman goldsmith, supporting his mother and father along with a wife and two small children, when he was killed.[13] The bloody impact of this rising struck home in every neighbourhood. As Parisians gathered to ponder these events, both in the course of their everyday business and in the Section assemblies that met in emergency daily sessions, the stakes facing them were also clear.

Overthrowing the king had been seen as the Revolution's last chance. So long as the royal court controlled the executive and the military high command, the catalogue of defeat that had ensued since the declaration of war in April would continue. Disposing of the baleful influence of the court, however, still left Paris balanced on a knife-edge. The unambiguous threat issued a month before in the Brunswick Manifesto, to put Paris to fire and sword if the royal family were assaulted, was now, presumably, fully to be carried out. The forces of the duke of Brunswick were still on the advance, subduing France's border fortresses with a thoroughly professional and merciless efficiency. Paris faced the need to send its own men out to meet them, while leaving behind a counter-revolutionary prison population that rumour elevated to many thousands. A new government was only formed in outline, new elections only just under way, and the hold on power of the revolutionaries seemed shaky indeed. The need to secure the rear was pressing. As early as 11 August the Paris police had warned the authorities that there were moves afoot by unspecified groups to enter the prisons and 'render prompt justice'. The revolutionary mayor of the city, Pétion, reported a rumour on the 17th that the Saint-Antoine and Saint-Marcel areas had been alerted overnight for a mass raid on the prisons 'to immolate the persons detained there'.[14] The continued flow of bad war news through the rest of the month did nothing to calm fears, and much to harden resolve.

The national and municipal authorities would always indignantly deny any direct incitement or organisation of the Massacres, but there can be no denying that they were as swept up in the spirit of last-ditch resistance and fear of internal subversion as any other Parisians. On 25 August the Provisional Government issued a proclamation which put the situation in stark terms:

> Our enemies prepare the last blows of their insane rage . . . they wish to open a route to Paris, they may succeed. Who is there amongst us whose soul does not rise up with indignant pride at this idea, with a just sense of our strength? Citizens, no nation on earth ever obtained its freedom without fighting. You have traitors in your bosom; well, without them the battle would be soon finished; but your active surveillance cannot fail to defeat them . . .[15]

Two days later, as the Interior Ministry sought to promote measures of defence – the fortification of every town and village, demolition of bridges, blocking of roads – it observed that:

> The French people . . . know that, apart from the loss of their liberty, they should expect the cruellest vengeance if they weaken before the atrocious men who have meditated this revenge for so long . . . Every measure of preservation is good in the extreme crisis of our danger . . . Is there any place for holding back when we must save the country?[16]

Heirs as they were of Enlightenment humanitarianism, it is perhaps true that ministers and legislators could not bring themselves openly to take the last step of advocating immediate massacre, but it is evident that the language of official pronouncements, let alone that of the press, which was far more alarmist, led its audiences almost every step of the way down that very path. One of the more violent newspapers, the *People's Orator*, gave a particularly clear message in the last days of August:

> The first battle we shall offer will take place within the walls of Paris, and not outside. All the royal brigands that this unhappy city shelters shall perish in one day. Citizens of the provinces, you hold the families of the emigrated aristocrats: at that moment they should fall beneath the weight of popular vengeance: burn the chateaux and the palaces, spread desolation and horror everywhere that the traitors have fomented civil war . . . The prisons are full of conspirators: see how we judge them . . . Will you not reflect that if these villains triumph, they will unleash every excess of barbarity . . . ?[17]

Georges-Jacques Danton, hero of the radical Cordeliers Club and of the Paris Commune, installed as Justice Minister on 10 August, took a less paranoid and more optimistic tone in a speech to the Legislative Assembly on 2 September itself – a speech that became legendary for its grandiose peroration, but which contained nonetheless seeds of the looming massacre. Speaking when news of the fall of Verdun had not yet arrived, he lauded the self-sacrificing virtue of that town's garrison, sworn to kill the first to propose surrender, and its patriotic inhabitants who committed themselves also to the fray:

> Paris shall second these great efforts. Commissioners of the Commune shall go to proclaim the solemn invitation to the citizens to arm themselves and march for the defence of the fatherland . . . We ask that you [the Assembly] work alongside us to direct this sublime movement of the people . . . We ask that whoever shall refuse to serve in person or to give up his arms [for another] shall be punished with death . . . We ask that an instruction be drawn up for the citizens to direct their movement . . . The tocsin that shall sound will not be an alarm, but the call to charge upon the enemies of the fatherland – to defeat them, Messieurs, we must be daring, more daring, ever daring, and France is saved![18]

Sixty thousand volunteers were to be raised at once, from a Parisian population summoned to rally on the Champ de Mars, home of the 'Altar of the Fatherland', patriotic centrepiece of the Festivals of Federation.

Danton's public lauding of popular courage and ferocity, in a moment when the radicals' association with militant popular action had never been plainer, can be contrasted with the private reflections of Madame Roland. Writing on the same day of the 'superhuman exertions' that 'we' (presumably herself, her husband the minister, and her fellow Girondins) were making, she nonetheless reported that 'we can only save ourselves by a kind of miracle . . . What makes me despair is the cowardice of the municipalities . . . Our mad Commune hampers everything . . . If this continues we are bound to expire soon and even more likely at the hands of the people of Paris than at those of the Prussians.' She bewailed popular suspicion and stupidity: 'Frenzied detachments of the people rush here demanding arms and think themselves betrayed because the minister is not at home at the moment they choose to visit him . . . All the horses have been seized and, because this is a "popular" operation, many have been lost through sloppy organisation.'[19] Throughout all that followed, the Girondins would retain a deep contempt for the radicals of Paris and their powers to stir popular action. In this, they situated themselves on the opposite side to their more radical fellows, across one of the most profound gulfs of the era. In her fears of the madness of 'popular' action, Madame Roland had more in common with the British ambassador, who wrote of the 'influence of the rabble' over the capital, than she did with Danton's summoning of the citizenry to action. Lord Gower went on in a dispatch of 3 September to record that 'as the multitude are perfect masters, everything is to be dreaded'.[20]

Within the city itself, stoked up with the alarming messages of politicians and journalists, which merely reflected their own fears, the general population indeed had no truck with the humanitarian concerns of their 'betters'. On 2 September itself, one Section passed a resolution which explained the prevailing spirit, even as the killings began elsewhere in the city: 'There are no means available, to avoid danger and to augment the zeal of citizens to depart for the armies at the frontiers, other than to carry out immediate prompt justice against the criminals and conspirators detained in the prisons.'[21] Prompt justice – this was to be the watchword of the unfolding events. Bloodshed held no terrors for the Parisians. Like most other eighteenth-century populations, they had treated the rituals of public execution as a form of spectacle, in which authority enacted itself on the suffering bodies of those who offended it – at best a hanging, without the benefit of the neck-breaking quick drop, not developed until the humanitarian nineteenth century, at worst a long-drawn-out ordeal of beating, burning and dismemberment, as memorably inflicted on Robert-François Damiens, a weak-minded servant who had wounded Louis XV with a penknife in 1757.[22]

Even lesser punishments often revolved around bodily suffering, from the temporary unpleasantness of the pillory to the flogging and branding that were inflicted on all but the most petty of thieves. All of this took place on the Place de Grève outside the City Hall, a weekly public ritual, just as on another day markets for second-hand clothes drew bargain-hunters, and on yet another crowds of labourers and journeymen gathered to seek work, news or companionship.[23] In the crowd actions and lynchings that had punctuated events in Paris and elsewhere since 1789, the ordinary people had already shown that they had learned the lessons of the public display of death well from their erstwhile masters. Ironically, however, when the veil of legend is pulled aside, the September Massacres would show a more instrumental, less spectacular approach to revolutionary killing.

No clear identification of the individuals who actually carried out the September Massacres has ever emerged. For the eighteen months after the events, to claim to have taken part was a badge of honour and a means of advancement, while for the years after that it was an invitation to persecution and potential murder. A few dozen men were tried for these acts, but all frantically denied participation, and there is no way of definitively ruling either on their cases or on those of any other self-proclaimed or alleged *septembriseurs*, as they were tagged. What we can say is that, of all those alleged or reported to have taken part, most would have been equally at home on the casualty lists of 10 August – no sinister agitators from the higher classes, and no assemblage of shadowy brigands, but a cross-section of the established working population of the city.[24]

It is most likely that, whatever nudges the Parisians received from higher authorities, the main nexus of organisation for the September Massacres was the network of Sections.[25] These neighbourhood councils had been meeting every evening since the start of the emergency in July. They were the self-proclaimed home of the patriotic Parisian, and while their composition reflected the varied social make-up of the various districts of the city, they had achieved a memorable moment of near-unity on the eve of 10 August, when all but one had called jointly for the overthrow of the monarchy. They were the nursery of popular militancy, and the only official organs of revolution that displayed an unambiguous call for massacre – when the call for prompt justice cited above was circulated, several other Sections pronounced in its favour, and several more had already made, or were in the process of voting for, resolutions of a similar stripe. Nevertheless, these declarations were not indications that the Sections were proceeding to carry out a plan – their language is one more of incitement than of organisation. Even at this neighbourhood level, it seems that no one was prepared to go down on paper as the direct advocate of what was, even at this critical moment, mass murder.[26]

And yet the Massacres had already begun. Perhaps those who were attending Section meetings on 2 September were those too timid, or too concerned with official forms, to have already taken the first steps, but others had not been so hesitant. As we have already noted, by that evening the process had spread to most of the prisons of Paris, and we must now consider more closely the grim details of its unfolding. The first and most striking observation to make is that, for all the horror of the events, over half of those detained in the prisons where killings occurred were spared. Between 1200 and 1500 died, but even at the Abbaye, where the crowds had gone first in search of the notorious counter-revolutionaries thought to be there, at least 250 of the 450 detainees were freed. The lowest proportion of the saved came from the chain-gang prisoners held on the rue des Bernardins – only three of seventy-five were freed. The highest was at La Salpêtrière, where of some 270 women detained, only some 35 were killed, and these were a minority of the 87 branded felons that had been singled out for scrutiny. A quarter of the priests detained at the Carmes convent were freed, and a similar proportion from Saint-Firmin, around half the inmates of Bicêtre, a fifth of the criminals in the Châtelet, and somewhere between a third and three-quarters of those in the Conciergerie (where accounts differ, but agree substantial numbers were saved). Two-thirds, finally, of the diverse inmates at La Force were released in the course of four days of activity.[27]

On every occasion that a prison was invested, at least some semblance of judicial procedure was invoked. At a bare minimum, as on the rue des Bernardins, the documentation of the prisoners was checked by someone among the crowds, and some reason for discerning guilt or innocence found. The same appears to have been the pattern at the Châtelet and Conciergerie. At La Salpêtrière, a slightly more formal consultation of registers took place, separating out the branded felons, who were then examined to determine who merited death. At the Abbaye, at La Force and at Bicêtre, at least, the crowds went further, and constituted tribunals.[28]

No trustworthy record survives of the personnel of these organs, although we know that as many as ten or a dozen individuals served as the panel of judges, and that, logically, to keep up these numbers over a period of time, there was probably some rotation among a larger group. The only named individual who undoubtedly served as a leader in this process was Stanislas Maillard, a clerk who had made himself a revolutionary hero by risking his life to treat with the Bastille garrison on 14 July 1789, and who had augmented his reputation by assuming leadership of the famous march by Parisian women to Versailles in October of that year, protesting at high bread prices and political deadlock. A leading figure in Parisian street politics thereafter, Maillard found himself presiding at the Abbaye tribunal, but since he would die before the end of the Terror, he left behind no reliable hint as to how willingly he had taken up this role.[29]

We know the name of the man, Jean-Denis Violette, who handled the documentation of the Carmes prisoners, and that he served on the committee of the nearby Luxembourg Section. A survivor from La Force noted that he had appeared before a court of ten, seven of whom were in National Guard uniform, one was a prison clerk, and the other two market porters. A court bailiff would later confess to having acted as secretary to this body, reading out prisoners' details from the registers. These, however, are virtually all the details that remain. An eyewitness recorded that at Bicêtre a crowd of three thousand invested the prison in almost complete silence, the prisoners were confined to their rooms and the prison records scrutinised before individuals were called up for judgment – but those who took these systematic actions remain unknown.[30]

If the tribunals' membership remains obscure, a general pattern of their operation is more clear. All seem to have had a chair or president, though this may have been a rotating function. Mayor Pétion, when he visited La Force on 6 September (trying, unsuccessfully, to reassert regular authority), reported seeing a full division of judicial labours: three men scrutinising the registers and summoning the prisoners, others questioning them, others still sitting as judges and jury.[31] Besides the members of the tribunal, there was an interchange of views with others present – a 'public gallery' seems to have constituted itself around each tribunal, so far as there was space. This audience applauded the passing of sentence, but sometimes went further, shouting out condemnations of some figures, or calling for clemency for others: at the Abbaye, at least two men seem to have been saved by appeals from the audience. On the other hand, Maillard would claim, perhaps disingenuously, to have been threatened with death by those present for his work to moderate this tribunal's condemnations. The pressure of the crowds seems to have slackened over time, as the novelty and urgency of the situation died down, and at La Force the prison buildings were under the control of the National Guard for much of this period, admitting only those known to the local commanders.[32]

This participation of the audience, however it may have shifted between places and times, was a resonantly typical revolutionary experience. From the first meetings of the National Assembly in 1789, when it met at Versailles under the old name of the Estates-General, audiences had engaged with the debates, applause or catcalls greeting radical or conservative remarks. Even when the Assembly moved to Paris, when a smaller public gallery reduced attendance, and when more rowdy elements were deliberately excluded, crowds of both sexes gathered outside the meeting-hall, listening attentively for word of the proceedings passed from inside, cheering their heroes and sometimes jostling unpopular figures as they entered or left. This behaviour was matched at every level of public meeting – right down to the individual Sections, whose sessions might have to contend with an audience of women and the poor, kept from the actual chamber but keen to participate. The Jacobin Club, at first a meeting-place of politicians, by 1792 the ideological powerhouse of republican revolution, had held its sessions with a public gallery open to all comers, and had thereby been accused of propagating its seditious doctrines to a gullible populace – yet it was the populace that chose to come and listen, cheer, heckle, comment, praise and condemn.

The Parisian population had learned to take a close and critical interest in public events through the course of the eighteenth century. Although they lived under an absolutist regime, in which their voices were never officially recognised except as the background cheers to royal ceremonial, those voices nonetheless had become louder. The policies of the absolutist state had steadily cranked up the tax burden on the general population, as France waded through a series of long and mostly unsuccessful wars. Alongside this, repeated seismic shifts in state policies over the regulation of the food supply had caused fears of deliberate famine, fears that broke out into rioting on a number of occasions. Parisians in particular lived in dread that the huge inflow of grain to the city would be cut off by nefarious means, and their hunger be used as a pawn in some devious political game. In response, they learned to be extremely attentive to the rules of the political game – who was in, who out, what it all might mean – and to keep a canny eye on the forces of law and order delegated to keep an official eye on them (and, as was well known, to feed them reassuring but false official news).[33]

The attitude that it was the Parisians' right to be informed, and increasingly to criticise, developed across the century, and was profoundly ingrained by the start of the 1780s. As the absolutist state fell apart into revolution, those rights of knowledge and criticism bloomed into rights of action – defensive action above all. The fall of the Bastille on 14 July 1789 happened because the Parisians were in search of guns and gunpowder to arm themselves against troops that the royal court had reportedly ordered into action against the city. The instinctive response of the city had been to take action, and though a respectable political class rapidly tried to take control of the new situation, the popular rights to know, to criticise and to act persisted, and merged with more overtly radical political agendas to become a forceful, forthright and above all active doctrine of direct popular sovereignty.[34]

The version of popular sovereignty acted out on the streets of Paris was very different to that which was articulated under the same label by the politicians. For them, popular sovereignty meant that the people's representatives, at the national level, had absolute power. For Parisians, less concerned with constitutional niceties, it often meant that a crowd or an audience could demand action, or take action themselves, on the grounds that they were 'the people', acting locally in a way that they claimed, implicitly, would be approved by the rest of the people. This is clearly capable of leading to nightmarish complications, from the point of view of a nationally based administration, and indeed over time it would do just that. In September 1792, it licensed individuals to talk themselves and their fellows into direct action against the imprisoned counter-revolutionaries.

Once again, however, we must remind ourselves that the direct action taken was not a simple mob attack. From its earliest moments at the Abbaye, it demanded the sanction of procedure, and there is every indication that the tribunals were genuinely concerned to determine an individual's guilt or innocence. If the audience also demanded a role, it was clearly not a hectoring agitation for universal condemnation. The tribunal chaired by Maillard at the Abbaye questioned one police agent for three-quarters of an hour, by his own account, before acquitting him. Many other freed prisoners recorded that they had been subject to 'many questions' or a 'most serious examination' before their discharge. It was claimed by Section officials that the princesse de Lamballe had been interrogated for four hours before her dispatch, though this may be an exaggeration, attempting to stress her guilt in the effort to mitigate the frightful reports of her demise.[35] Some prisoners said that they had been recalled more than once before the judges prior to release, and this seems to indicate that prisoners' stories were checked with their home Section authorities. Two Royal Bodyguards obtained a temporary reprieve by spinning some such story, but were condemned on a second hearing when it was revealed that they had given a false address. On the other hand, it is said that those prisoners too terror-struck to respond to questioning, or in some cases even to stand unsupported, were condemned – after all, what did the innocent have to fear?[36]

Clearly, not all prisoners received a long investigation. On the evening of the 2nd, one prisoner awaiting trial, Madame de Tarente, recalled later that she could judge the proceedings of the Abbaye tribunal by the death-cries that resounded through the building every five minutes.[37] The felons of the rue des Bernardins, and their female fellows at Salpêtrière, once identified, were executed without individual hearing. It is said that a party of Swiss Guards held at the Abbaye, believed to have been participants in a massacre of patriots on 10 August, were killed in similar summary fashion. On the other hand, women were, in general, spared. All eight held at the Abbaye were returned to their cells, perhaps for their own safety. Of seventy-five women at the Conciergerie, only one was killed, Madame Gredelier, notorious for having killed and mutilated her lover. At La Force, the women's side of the prison had 110 inmates, including nine prominent political prisoners. Of all of these, only the princesse de Lamballe died; the rest were released, probably for the most part after a simple reading of their records. Only at Salpêtrière did the hardened nature of the female criminals singled out, or some other movement of opinion, lead to a real female 'massacre'.[38]

Men imprisoned for debt had already been subject to a hasty defensive order from the Paris Commune as news of the Massacres broke – they were to be segregated from other prisoners and protected, a measure which seems to have been successful.[39] Likewise, those locked up for minor matters, assaults, disorderly behaviour and so forth were summarily dismissed. Three categories perished: those adjudged 'real' political counter-revolutionaries, professional criminals and forgers. The latter category, though relatively small, tells of the hatred felt by the Parisians for those who preyed on their reliance on paper money. Since the start of the Revolution, good solid coin had become ever harder to find, and the assignat paper money that began to be issued in 1790 was supplemented by the promissory notes and tokens of many local authorities and agencies. This heaven-sent opportunity was not neglected by the criminal fraternity, and forged notes of all kinds circulated freely. Moreover, it was publicly notorious that the actual production of such notes took place within the loosely guarded prisons themselves. Forgery injected a terrible uncertainty into everyday economic transactions, it encouraged a spiralling inflation that was steadily stripping paper money of its value, and it was widely reported to play a role in the destabilising plans of the counter-revolutionaries.[40] September 1792 was not a good time to be a captured forger.

The other two types of detainee, the political counter-revolutionary and the professional criminal, lived in a sinister symbiosis in the revolutionary culture. Professional criminals were 'brigands', believed to inhabit a coherent underworld structure that lived and worked hand-in-glove with the aristocrats who plotted the downfall of the people. In the summer of 1789, the countryside had been convulsed with rumoured reports of brigandage: armed gangs attacking ripening crops, promoting a famine to serve the interests of counter-revolution. Throughout the intervening years, Paris had rung to repeated alarms that the city was filling with shadowy figures, flitting over the frontiers or rising up from an unknown netherworld. There were always thirty thousand of them, for some reason – this seemed almost a talismanic figure, and no matter how many times in 1790 or 1791 the brigands of Paris failed to launch their dastardly blow, at the next alarm the same fears were trotted out, as much in the pages of the press and the mouths of politicians as in the language of the streets.[41] In September 1792, it was self-evident that, if there was a prison plot, its rank and file would be provided by the brigands. If an individual 'brigand' were actually imprisoned for pickpocketing a handkerchief, it did not matter: a thief was a thief, who was a brigand, who was a counter-revolutionary, and in the final tally of deaths, seven of every ten who perished were condemned for just this association.

The 'political' counter-revolutionaries probably condemned themselves out of their own mouths, if they deigned to answer the charges put to them. By this stage, many Catholic priests who refused to compromise with the Revolution had come to regard it as the work of the Devil, and its defiance an act of martyrdom. Figures from the administration or the royal court who would not forswear their loyalties to the crown, or who could not deny their public acts of favour towards the monarch, had no defence to offer when told that these things were crimes. Some perished defiant, others terrified – but all adjudged guilty died.

It is to death, finally, that we must return. In the eighteenth century, every system of justice dispensed death, but generally delegated the function of meting it out to the hangman, that figure of folkloric allure. Even if, as in Paris, it was part of the hangman's duties to flog, brand, and sometimes beat the condemned to death, he was always just doing his job, in his sinister, otherworldly but almost gentlemanly way.[42] Regular systems of justice segregated judgment from the actual practice of doing to death, when they did not also accompany that practice with the presence of a ministering priest, whose work to save the soul of the condemned seemed to ignore the awful fact of what was being done to their bodies. If execution was a public spectacle, it was thus also detached from reality – no august judge had to step over splashes of blood to leave his chambers.

The September Massacres were more brutally pragmatic. After being stripped of any valuables, the condemned were pushed outside the tribunal's place of judgment, and there, waiting, were a group of executioners, who struck them down without further ado. If they had time to scream, it was soon cut short. Grim silence from the killers and their audience greeted the condemnations, only broken by cheering when an acquittal was announced, and the newly freed citizen stumbled out, perhaps to be embraced by the very blood-splattered killers who would gladly have hacked him to death if guilty.[43] A British agent, Colonel George Munro, reported seeing the executioners at the Abbaye: 'A single file of men armed with swords, or pikes, formed a lane of some length . . . And when I saw them seemed much fatigued with their horrid work.'[44] A lawyer, Maton de la Varenne, jailed on an official's grudge, wrote of being called up from his cell before a 'terrible court', but when there was found to be no charge against him in the prison register 'frowns vanished from every face, and a cry was raised of *Vive la Nation!* which was the signal for my release'. Fainting with relief, 'I was carried out of the gate by men who held me up under the armpits and assured me that I had nothing to fear and that I was under the protection of the people.'[45]

In all the horror of massacre, it is perhaps here that we find the greatest apparent incomprehensibility. The reprieved were welcomed, and the victims were killed calmly, their still-bleeding bodies dragged away and stripped in nearby courtyards, from where municipal carts, hastily summoned, would deliver them to mass graves in various cemeteries. Their clothes were washed, and that which was salvageable would later be sold to the benefit of municipal and Section funds. Such sales would recoup expenditure, again hastily ordered, on straw to soak up the blood and cover the naked bodies on their journey to the burial pits. It was all rather orderly.[46] The mode of killing itself, with its physical contact and its dramatic bloodshed, was most likely dictated by pragmatic thoughts: arms and ammunition were in gravely short supply, and firing squads would have been an unpatriotic profligacy. They would also, of course, have made far more noise, and perhaps set further alarms and rumours afoot.

Prompt justice was done, with sound practical considerations in hand. That is the real horror. It is easy to come to terms with the idea of irrational carnage carried out by sadistic mobs: such acts fit neatly into the concept of a radically 'different', almost subhuman crowd, safely distanced from the self-image of the observer. Far less comfortable is the realisation that bloody murder could be committed by upright citizens in the name of their country's freedom. If we quite fairly object that the victims of September were not, in fact, the active partisans of a fatal plot against Paris, we must also agree that believing them so was a mistake shared almost unanimously everywhere from Legislative Assembly to street-corner tavern.

Before leaving the story of the September Massacres, a further dimension of the violence must be considered: its consequences within the new republican political class. The outcomes of 10 August had essentially fallen in favour of the Girondins. They had their suspended king (not simply deposed, as radicals had wanted), their majority of the key government ministries, and their domination of a Legislative Assembly from which all hint of royalism had fled. An insurrection orchestrated by the most radical elements of the capital had therefore given power over to a group who were, by comparison, decidedly centrist. Suspiciously centrist in the eyes of some, not least Maximilien Robespierre, who emerged from his political reticence on the evening of 11 August to have himself elected by his home Section as a substitute-member to the Commune. His arrival in office coincided with the rigorous banning of all royalist and other suspect publications within Paris by the Commune. Four times in the next ten days he personally led deputations from the Commune to admonish the laxity of the Assembly, even while the Girondin leadership strove first to get the department of Paris to reassert control over what was, in theory, only a municipal council, and when that failed tried in vain to get a replacement Commune elected over the 'insurrectionary' one that had become essentially self-appointed and self-perpetuating. The Assembly decree abolishing the Commune was promulgated on 30 August, but withdrawn on 2 September.[47]

Robespierre seems to have decided that the 'faction of the Gironde', a label he began to use explicitly at this time, were set on compromise with royalism, following on from their vain attempts to form a patriot ministry under the king at the end of July. In the near-paranoid political atmosphere, this was the seed for recurrent accusations that the Girondins were in fact royalist counter-revolutionaries in disguise. With the royal family now, since

13 August, under the Commune's guard in the keep of the Temple, Robespierre set his sights on the process of election to the new National Convention that had been summoned on the 10th, to ensure that only 'true' radical patriots were in a position to decide France's future. In Paris at least he would be eminently successful.

The electoral assembly met on 2 September in the Bishop's Palace near Notre-Dame, but was adjourned to the following day after radical complaints that there was no public gallery there – crucial for democratic scrutiny, or intimidation. On the 3rd, the electors processed to the Jacobin Club, passing of necessity the scenes of massacre at the central prisons of the Conciergerie and Châtelet. Once in their new home, the electors agreed under further radical promptings to purge themselves of those who had belonged to the Feuillants, or who had been part of the protests against the 20 June invasion of the Tuileries. This discarded some 200 of the original 990, and on 4 September Robespierre became secretary of an assembly which proceeded to elect to the Convention twenty-four deputies of impeccably radical connection. Robespierre himself headed the list, defeating Mayor Pétion, who quit the assembly in disgust and was elected from a neighbouring department. On at least two occasions, strong hints from Robespierre about the kind of person who should be chosen influenced individual results. The notion that voting should be a private reflection was out of the window.[48] Girondin-oriented candidates had to look elsewhere for support, and were returned from departments both far and near, creating a great rift between the politics of the capital and those of the country at large.

Yet more significant for future conflict is the suggestion that Robespierre and other key radical leaders, most notably the firebrand journalist Marat, had actively sought to sweep up the leaders of the Girondins into the process of the massacres. It is clear that, under the looming threat of murderous action, various individuals were rescued from the prisons of Paris in the first days of September by order of the Commune's surveillance committee – among them one member of the Legislative Assembly, and the head of Robespierre's old school – suggesting that the radicals had clear foreknowledge of the intended killings. It is also the case that, as the massacres began on 2 September, Robespierre himself spoke in the Commune of a Girondin plot to put the duke of Brunswick on the throne, and that night warrants were issued by the Commune's surveillance committee to arrest Brissot, Interior Minister Roland and over two dozen other Girondin members of the Legislative Assembly.[49]

Those warrants were not executed, of course. At the height of the Terror Robespierre was to accuse the then Justice Minister Danton of blocking them, but by then he was accusing all his enemies of being part of a vast royalist conspiracy. Moreover, as we have seen, it is also the case that not all those put in prison were to die, and that most of the killing was already over by 3 September, when the Girondins might have been detained. Nevertheless, the accusation that the abortive arrest of the Girondins was designed to see them dead was believed implicitly by the intended victims. Madame Roland wrote on 5 September to Jean-Henri Bancal des Issarts, a colleague of Brissot soon to be a Girondin deputy, that 'Robespierre and Marat have a knife to our throats . . . they have a small army paid from the proceeds of what they found or stole from the [Tuileries] palace.' She reported the existence of the arrest warrants, and even said that Brissot's home had been searched, but the searchers 'were ashamed to find only material refuting their claims', and dared not go on to the homes of actual ministers. Although this reticence rather challenges the assertion that the warrants were a ruthless attempt to kill off the Girondins, Madame Roland repeated that claim, and went on: 'We are not safe, and unless the departments send a guard for the Assembly and the Council [of Ministers], you will lose both.'[50] The sense of grim conflict and paranoid plot-mongering that permeates these exchanges was to play a significant part in shaping the French political landscape over the coming year.

The story of September 1792 does not end with the last blood-soaked corpse pitched into a pit of quicklime. Its final act opens with events at Valmy, in the wooded hills of the Argonne between Verdun and Chalons, little more than two weeks later. Ironically, this was the very territory that the Flight to Varennes had been decided over: the French army was headquartered at Sainte-Ménéhould, Valmy itself being the site of a windmill near by.[51] There, on the misty morning of 20 September 1792, the advancing forces of the duke of Brunswick, who had summoned the French to return to their natural allegiance, and threatened Paris with exemplary destruction, finally brought their foe to decisive battle. The French won. To be fair, it was not much of a battle, since the Allied armies, over-extended by their advance, opted to call a truce after the size and discipline of the French forces were revealed by an initial artillery exchange.[52] Those forces had been rallied in the knowledge that they defended Paris, and that Paris stood firm behind them. They held fast, and history was transformed. The British minister Lord Auckland observed that 'it will be resounded through France (and through other parts of Europe) that a mere horde of undisciplined freemen has been able to foil the efforts of a combined army of veterans, greatly superior in numbers and appointments, and directed by the best commanders in Europe'.[53]

A letter found a few weeks later on a dead Prussian officer reveals the extent of the shock felt by the Allied forces:

> The French *émigrés* have deceived our good king . . . in the most infamous fashion. They had assured us that the counter-revolution would take place as soon as we showed our faces. They had also told us that the French troops of the line were a collection of riff-raff and that the National Guard would take to their heels at the first shot fired. Not a word of this was true.[54]

The poet Goethe was in the Prussian army, and as they encamped that night his dispirited comrades prodded their pet intellectual for his thoughts on the day's events. He had no doubts: 'From this place and from this day forth commences a new era in the history of the world.'[55] The French would echo him: in Paris the very next day, the newly elected National Convention unanimously voted the abolition of the monarchy, and the day after declared it now to be Year One of the French Republic. A new era indeed, though it was to be a far more troubled, and briefer, one than they imagined.

# Chapter 5

# Dawn of a New Age

The French National Convention that met for the first time on 20 September 1792 was an extraordinary body. It was elected when France was technically still a monarchy, and in its first sessions declared royalty abolished. It was home to vicious political infighting: almost half of its members would remain resolutely uncommitted to any faction. As a body dominated by lawyers (they made up almost half its membership, with no other occupational group exceeding a tenth), its decrees would invoke special powers far beyond the bounds of law. Elected by a tiny minority of the potential voters (barely one in six participated), it declared itself repeatedly at one with 'the people'. Intended to write a constitution, it found itself the sole legislative authority of the country, issuing unchallengeable decrees in an unprecedented flood of transformative lawmaking. When it finally gave birth to a constitution after nine months' labour, it immediately suspended its implementation, and continued to rule by fiat for another two years. Although it was dedicated to principles of unanimity and national unity, declaring the French Republic 'One and Indivisible' on 25 September 1792, its actions and policies drove wounds into the body politic that endure to this day.

And yet the Convention also spawned legends. Its members criss-crossed France as 'representatives-on-mission', their proconsular powers bringing revolution to every locality. The measures the Convention took raised the nation up against an ever-growing list of surrounding enemies, and forged a new republican tradition of military prowess. Above all, the Convention created the foundations for two hundred years of republicanism in France, a much disputed and often unstable heritage, but one which would ultimately come to dominate the nation's modern history.

The Convention met in the Manège, the converted indoor riding arena that had housed its predecessors since the start of 1790. Adjacent to the Tuileries palace itself, the Manège was suitable only because of its size – it had very poor acoustics (something which had hampered the oratorical career of Robespierre, among others), and at eighty metres in length, but fewer than twenty in width, was not designed to facilitate face-to-face debate.[1] Its undistinguished interior held tiered benches in a long 'racetrack' oval. Speakers at the central rostrum, positioned below the president's chair and secretary's desk midway down the chamber, could barely be heard at the far ends, and the occupants of those two ends could sit all day without taking notice of the debate at all. This disconnection, paradoxical as it was for a body with such grave responsibilities, echoed the surprising detachment that the French citizenry at large showed towards the political process.

As noted above, barely one in six of the electorate took part in the initial voting for the Convention at village and town level, producing departmental electoral assemblies that, much like that of Paris, could easily fall into the hands of partisan organisation. The irony was that the complex arrangements which discouraged so many from taking part had been expressly designed to defend the process from the perils of 'faction'. Overt electoral canvassing, and candidacy as such, were banned. Electoral assemblies were designed to be spaces for individual contemplation, where electors nominated the men of their acquaintance that they thought would be best for the job, rather than choosing between declared candidates who might have nothing to commend them except their forwardness. Ever since this system was introduced in 1790, however, and applied endlessly to the election of mayors, councilmen, magistrates, municipal prosecutors, town clerks, regional councils, and even the clergy, it had led to uncertainty and rancour. Numerous cycles of votes and revotes (all laboriously transcribed by hand from the ballots into registers, in the groaning presence of the electors) might be necessary to gain a majority for the most minor vacancy – and a chosen nominee might have no wish actually to take up the post, leading to a new cycle in quest of a replacement. Every electoral assembly meant at least a day or more – and sometimes closer to a week – of attendance, with all the inconvenience and cost that implied. With elections called at close intervals for various posts – some regions experienced seven or eight separate ballots in 1790–1791 – the process swiftly degenerated. Either local worthies co-opted the system to insert themselves relatively painlessly into office by prior agreement, or political factions came to dominate proceedings.[2]

Such factions were of course incarnate in the Jacobin Clubs, which by 1792 had successfully put to flight most of their former enemies to the right, and were now proceeding to divide bitterly over the developing antagonism between the Girondin leadership and the more radical groups personified by Robespierre, Danton and the bloodthirsty followers of Marat and the Paris Commune. If they seldom openly defied the laws against candidacy, local Jacobins became expert at defaming their perceived enemies, and at calling attention to the virtues of their own men. Since all this was done in the name of proclaiming themselves the only true patriots, and in an atmosphere of war emergency, the numbers repelled by the process, or unwilling to expose themselves to possible charges of treason, grew ever larger.

The claims of unity with the sovereign people that were soon to be the stock-in-trade of the Convention were thus particularly ironic, but they enabled its members to deploy unblushingly an unchecked control of the whole political and legislative process. The old National Assembly of 1789–1791 had become accustomed to passing rafts of legislation without an external restraint, once the king's early reluctance to sanction such measures had been overcome by his 'imprisonment' in the Tuileries. The executive veto he regained under the 1791 Constitution had proven to be his downfall, of course, as he used it without hesitation to block (in patriot eyes) urgent measures of national security. Now, the Convention operated without even an executive as such. With the king suspended and a republic proclaimed, but one without a constitution, the Convention gathered to itself all the powers of the state. Motions passed on its floor became decrees with the immediate force of law, whether their substance emanated from long rumination in a committee of deputies or reflected the momentary effervescence of debate. The committees of the Convention oversaw all aspects of government, and the ministers of state answered to it alone – they did not even have the collective identity of a cabinet to shelter behind, and had to fight hard to avoid constant interference and challenge. The Convention would even, as Louis XVI was to find out, assume the powers of a supreme judiciary. For the first year of its existence, the question of how to deploy these vast powers would drag the Convention through turmoil, before they crystallised into a system the deputies did not shrink from labelling as Terror. As its outcome implies, that turmoil reflected not just administrative uncertainty, but also a real battle for the soul of the new Republic.

The divisions that had already marked politics after the toppling of the monarchy resurfaced almost immediately in the Convention. Mass enthusiasm for the war effort, including the melting down of iron pots for cannon balls, had shaded by early September into confiscatory attacks on the rich, and thus into actions indistinguishable among the propertied classes from overt criminality. The British agent George Munro, who lived discreetly in Paris observing radical exiles from across the Channel, reported on 14 September that 'the blackguards of Paris have begun this day to stop people publicly in the streets, and take their watches and buckles from them; they have even taken the ladies' rings from their fingers and from their ears'.[3] News of Valmy calmed the immediate crisis, but on 24 September a proposal to formulate new measures against 'brigands and assassins' was supported by Brissot and Vergniaud, joined by others becoming prominent in the Girondin camp. These included Charles Barbaroux, who had led the *fédérés* of Marseille to Paris in July, but had rapidly migrated away from his original fierce radicalism; Antoine-Joseph Gorsas, a Parisian journalist, also once a friend of the capital's radicals but becoming increasingly alienated from their violence; and François Buzot, a lawyer who had sat in the National Assembly, a republican since 1791, soon to be notorious as the lover of Madame Roland. Buzot proposed a further measure on this day that divided the Convention for weeks to come, seeking the installation of a corps of National Guards drawn from across France to guarantee the Convention's safety. The measure was eventually voted down, but not before exposing yet more festering antagonisms towards the Parisian activists and *septembriseurs*.[4]

Standing out on the other side of these debates were a small core of committed radicals, centred on the Parisian delegation whose election had been overseen by Maximilien Robespierre. Alongside him, and pre-eminent in Girondin accusations at this moment, was Jean-Paul Marat, the ex-doctor whose journalism was held by many to have been a prime instigator of the September Massacres – indeed, he was believed by some to have actively plotted the events from within the Paris Commune. Others who were notably active in opposing the Girondin moves included Jacques-Nicolas Billaud-Varenne, a teacher and lawyer with an active career in the Jacobin and Cordeliers Clubs behind him, and who had served as deputy-procurator on the 'Insurrectionary Commune' that toppled the throne; Jean-Marie Collot-d'Herbois, a dramatist from Lyon who had moved to Paris in 1789, become a journalist and club activist, and also served on the Insurrectionary Commune; and Philippe Fabre d'Eglantine, another playwright and Cordelier, with close links to both Marat and Danton.

Danton, who stood down from his role as Justice Minister to sit in the Convention, was repeatedly rolled up by Girondin attacks into an unholy trinity with Marat and Robespierre. Much of this assault continued to focus on the idea that Brissot, Interior Minister Roland and others had been marked for death by these men in the September Massacres, and only escaped by happenstance. The animus between Danton and the Rolands, husband and wife, had begun when Danton interfered with Roland's area of administration in the Provisional Government, and rapidly escalated into vociferous hatred. Danton thought Roland was a vacillating incompetent, and his wife a harridan. The Rolands thought Danton both personally corrupt and the leader of an avaricious faction, out to exploit the Revolution for personal gain. Danton had, for example, split the secretaryship of his ministry between Fabre d'Eglantine and another journalist and Cordeliers colleague, Camille Desmoulins. He gave the post of chief of staff to the activist François Robert, put Billaud-Varenne on the Council of Justice, and also found a place there for his old clerk of chambers, Jules-François Paré (who would go on to become Interior Minister as a result). Old Cordeliers colleagues were also used as emissaries to the departments during the summer crisis – over a dozen Club members were dispatched on various missions, which for some were the start of new political careers on the national stage. Madame Roland later denounced this entire apparatus as:

> a swarm of unknown men . . . patriots out of fanaticism, and even more out of self-interest, most of them with no livelihood except what they hoped to pick up from political agitation, but devoted to Danton their protector and imitators of his licentious habits and doctrines.[5]

It was on such grounds that the Rolands led the charge that Danton aspired to dictatorship, while he scorned the notion that he had anything in common with Marat, and on 26 September made a scathing attack on Roland. He ridiculed his wife's influence – 'everyone knows that Roland is not alone in his department' – and dismissed his calls to move the Convention out of Paris for its own protection. Before the assembled Convention, Danton slated Roland as 'an old driveller who sees ghosts everywhere, and who is frightened by the slightest popular demonstration'.[6] These attacks rallied others such as Brissot, Gorsas and Buzot to outraged and vigorous defence of the Rolands, and brought on a further round of hostilities. As Justice Minister, Danton had laid out funds for secret and unrecorded purposes during the pre-Valmy crisis. Roland charged him with embezzling at least some of these funds, a charge against which his only defence was to cite the extraordinary circumstances and to put up a front of outraged patriotism. Danton was forced to fall back on the partisan support of the Parisian delegation in a row which rumbled on through the following month.[7] The effect was to distance him decisively from the Girondins, and turn a pragmatic figure who could have been a valuable bridge across the personal and political divide into a bulwark of the left.

That political divide continued to grow, and at the end of September the focus switched to Brissot. The occasion was the regrouping of the Jacobin Club, which had been experiencing difficulties since the fall of the monarchy. Many of its members had been engaged with the business of government, or with the Insurrectionary Commune, or on missions to the provinces on behalf of one or other body. Meetings had become desultory, not helped by the continuing popularity of the rival Girondin-oriented 'Reunion Club' among legislative deputies, and to which some two hundred continued to go in late September, while in many cases remaining nominal members of the older club. The more extreme Jacobins regarded this body as no better than the old Feuillants – schismatics with a dangerous agenda – and some called for such individuals to be barred, but voices of moderation prevailed, and the Reunion seems to have voted peaceably to wind itself up and rejoin the 'Mother Society' at the end of the month.[8] The Jacobins' renewed vigour, however, merely provided the opportunity for further animosity.

An outright attack at the Club on Brissot's journalism was launched by the conspicuous radical François Chabot, a former Capucin monk and 'constitutional' priest who had sat on the far left of the Legislative Assembly and now the Convention. Reputedly as dissolute in his habits as anyone condemned by Madame Roland, Chabot was unrelenting in his pursuit of both personal advantage and what he saw as the plots of the counter-revolutionaries. Brissot continued to edit his successful newspaper, the *French Patriot*, and his editorials had denounced repeatedly the dangerous influence of the forces he saw behind the September Massacres. On 23 September, even as the Convention was still in its opening sessions, he had written against the 'anarchic, demagogic deputies' pulling it off course, calling them a 'disorganising party' – an ominous charge in time of war. In response to this, Chabot spoke of a 'conspiracy' against the popularity of Danton, Robespierre and others, and placed Brissot at the centre of it. Several times over the next fortnight Brissot was summoned to appear and defend himself at the Jacobins, and it seems there were many who were willing to give him a hearing, but he never arrived. On 12 October, with Danton now president of the Club, Collot-d'Herbois took up the assault, condemning Brissot's writings against the Commune, and reaching into the past to accuse him of supporting Lafayette and the Feuillants and preaching war unnecessarily. On a vote to expel him, agreement was almost unanimous.[9] Ironically, or perhaps ominously, it was only at this point that Marat joined the Jacobins, having previously been kept away by the majority's attitude to his unsavoury reputation.

Three days later, the Club sent a circular to its many provincial affiliates explaining and defending its decision against Brissot. To the charges mentioned above were added the claims that Brissot had tried to prevent the insurrection against the monarchy, and had published incessant attacks on the Commune using Roland's Interior Ministry funds. He was placed at the head of a 'faction' manipulating events to their own ends. No stone was left unturned in the condemnation – it was even claimed that the infamous 20 June invasion of the Tuileries, a move orchestrated by the far left, had been plotted by Brissot, a claim that implicitly acknowledged the unpopularity of this event in the country at large. This propaganda was not always successful, and at least ten significant clubs objected to its language. One, the Recollets in Bordeaux, went so far as to make Brissot an honorary member. The coming months were to demonstrate ever more plainly how different politics looked in Paris and the provinces.

Meanwhile, the autumn wore on with yet more vicious personal attacks. Opinion among many leading political figures seems to have been steadily hardening, and the tendency for even relatively minor proposals to be met with stinging critique and personal slanders created a clear divide, reinforced as the Jacobins purged their internal committees of Brissot's friends and allies (and would expel them *en masse* later in November). Brissot himself took up the cudgels in a pamphlet produced little more than a week after his expulsion. Here, he explicitly called the activities of the Insurrectionary Commune criminal, charging it again with being a 'disorganising' influence. Its emissaries had preached pillage and the division of property, and had sought to accustom the people to 'the effusion of blood and the spectacle of decapitated heads'.[10] He named all his leading accusers as his enemies, adding them to Robespierre and Marat, and saying that the Parisian election to the Convention had been 'prostituted . . . to the most vile of factions'. Brissot repeated the charge that Robespierre had sought his death in the September Massacres, events he called a 'day of shame for Paris', and which he claimed were only part of a wider plot to dominate the government and legislature – a plot controlled by a clique within the Jacobins that rendered the renewal (that is, the purging) of that Club imperative. His view was seconded in print by Gorsas on 29 October, abandoning his former position of friendship towards Parisian radicals, and now associating all such activism with the bloodthirsty diatribes of Marat.

The day of Gorsas' attack also saw the Girondins strike back in the Convention, in what may have been a co-ordinated strategy. Jean-Baptiste Louvet de Couvrai, yet another politician-journalist and friend of Roland and Brissot, issued a long condemnation. While assailing Danton for failures in office, and calling for Marat to be arrested, Louvet's venom was essentially directed at Robespierre.

After rehearsing what were by now standard accusations about the plot behind the September Massacres, Louvet perorated in epic style:

> Robespierre, I accuse you of having for a long time calumniated the purest and best patriots . . . I accuse you of having, as far as you could, scorned, persecuted and reviled the national representation, and of causing it to be scorned, persecuted and reviled! I accuse you of having put yourself forward as an object of idolatry, of allowing it to be said before you that you were the only virtuous man in France, the only one who could save the *patrie*, and twenty times of having given to understand this yourself! I accuse you of having tyrannised the electoral assembly of Paris by all the means of intrigue and horror! I accuse you of having evidently aimed at supreme power; which is demonstrated by the facts that I have noted, and by all your conduct, which speaks for itself to accuse you![11]

If the slightly bathetic follow-up to this was to 'request that examination of your conduct be sent before a committee', it nevertheless was a direct attempt to indict Robespierre, and by implication all those who chose to stand by him.

Naturally, Robespierre's allies did stand by him, and yet another round of by now familiar accusations flew. Robespierre himself spoke to rebut Louvet's charges on 5 November, a performance noteworthy only for its defensive tone, and for his efforts to distance himself from Marat, claiming to have done no more for him than for other patriot writers, and indeed to have told him as far back as 1791 that his bloodthirsty writings 'revolted the friends of liberty'.[12] The round of charge and counter-charge ended by bringing Jérôme Pétion, mayor of Paris throughout the summer, into the fray. He and Robespierre had been the two most notable radical figureheads in the capital since their membership of the National Assembly of 1789, and it was with visibly deep regret that he entered the fray now. On 7 November a letter from Pétion was read to the Jacobins, in which he defended his own conduct as mayor through the turbulent events of recent months, while at the same time denying that there was any 'faction' around Brissot active at the time. He had known Brissot since childhood, and could not credit the ludicrous attacks being made on his patriotism now. In a speech to the Convention on 10 November, he went further, publicly criticising the Insurrectionary Commune for its illegal and unnecessary assumption of political power, and squarely stating that Robespierre had been its guiding light. Ultimately, he reinforced the case already made by Brissot and Louvet against Robespierre, in another instance from this time of political bridges being decisively burned.

There were those who tried to be conciliatory, as indeed Pétion had been until the last moment. The Girondins' great speech-maker, Vergniaud, saw no point in these senseless quarrels, a position shared with his fellow Bordelais Armand Gensonné. The eminent philosopher-politician Condorcet, a close political ally of Brissot, objected like these two to the escalation marked by Louvet's speech. From across the growing divide, in the debate on Robespierre's reply to Louvet, Danton spoke out for reconciliation, while Bertrand Barère, a noted lawyer from the Pyrenees who had sat in the National Assembly, subsequently (like so many) entered journalism and was a rising figure of influence in the Convention, called from the centre ground for an end to 'single combats of vanity and hatred'.[13]

There was a whole range of reasons why political life in the Convention was so immediately poisonous. Some are clear products of circumstance – the aftermath of the September Massacres and the 'patriotic' manipulation of the Parisian electoral assembly could only foment bitterness born of fear and outrage. Other reasons emerged from the structures which revolutionary politics had already adopted before the fateful summer of 1792. The fact that so many of the leading figures in politics were also political journalists – as even Robespierre had been during the Legislative Assembly – often competing to sell newspapers on the strength of their individual perspectives, added venom to many interchanges. It also provided additional outlets for unrestrained assertions about the activities of groups and individuals, while enshrining such claims in print for later use, by friends or enemies.[14]

The existence of multiple forums for political speech-making was a further dimension of the problem. While the Convention was clearly the national representative body, and its legitimacy went unchallenged, the Paris Commune remained a key force for channelling the energies of radicals in the capital, and for many the

Jacobin Club had a parallel claim to a place on the national stage, as the home of true patriots, and centre of a national network of such figures. The agenda of the Jacobins, though imbued with concern for the fate of the *patrie*, tended inevitably more towards issues of what we would now call ideology. This for the revolutionaries meant questions of virtue, patriotism and *civisme* – the 'civic spirit' at the heart of arguments about what defined a good citizen – and was given decisive priority, at the expense of a focus on the practicalities of government and administration. With its pedigree of patriotism since 1789, and its institutional links across the country, the Jacobin Club was in a position to prioritise questions of the personal morality of public figures over issues of political pragmatism, and thus to force such questions onto the agenda of more official political bodies.[15]

In so doing, it echoed recurrent themes of French political culture throughout the late eighteenth century. As we have seen in earlier chapters, individuals from the king down, via ministers such as Turgot, to politicians of all stripes, journalists and popular activists all associated public activity and political events with the clash between virtue and vice. On both sides of the gulf between revolutionaries and counter-revolutionaries, the persistent assumption was that one's enemies, be they 'men of faction', *aristocrates*, or 'fanatics', were consciously and manipulatively seeking to do evil. Such beliefs had many sources. Some harked back to the common assumptions about the politics of royal courts: that public service was an avenue for private gain through patronage and favour; that opposition to royal policy was treacherous; that the wickedness of ministers was the appropriate element to emphasise when mounting opposition (in the hope of replacing them); and that, ultimately, nothing happened in politics without some factional, manipulative agenda at work.

Broader cultural beliefs also fostered such divisive attitudes, however. The commitment of Enlightenment thinkers to the power of human reason, and to the uniformity of human perception, had the ironic unintended consequence of blinding them to the very notion of 'unintended consequences', at least in matters of grave import. The role of fate or providence in human affairs was steadily downgraded through the later eighteenth century in the eyes of many 'progressive' thinkers, while their emphasis on human potential focused their attention on conscious action as the motor of great events. And when things were going wrong, as they had so manifestly done since the later 1780s, conscious action spelt 'conspiracy'.[16] The widespread acceptance of such views is seen in the otherwise incomprehensible remark of the British agent George Munro, who saw an unsuccessful move to expel all the Princes of the Blood from France in December 1792 as a Girondin attack on the radicals. His reasoning was that 'this blow is intended at the Duke of Orléans, who is the soul of Robespierre's party'.[17] The vast success and political influence of the otherwise obscure leaders of the radical 'faction' only made sense, to Munro as to many other observers, if the enormous wealth and significance (to their eyes) of the king's cousin could be put behind it. Many of Jacobinism's enemies would charge that it had never been more than an effort to put Orléans on the throne – even when, as we shall see, it would end by putting him on the scaffold.[18]

Two further significant dimensions of belief also had an impact on the actions of French public figures. The first was the obsession with unanimity that had run through revolutionary debates since their beginnings. Local and regional diversity, particularism, division, these were all hallmarks, even before 1789, of the 'aristocratic' mode of thought that was trying to defend individual and group privileges against the greater claims of the whole. That whole had been the monarchy in the 1760s and 1770s, and was now the Nation itself. Even before the proclamation of the 'one and indivisible' Republic in 1792, that assumption of unity had run through all the Revolution's acts. The Nation, the People, and their representatives were conflated in countless pronouncements, as sovereignty was vested in a national body politic that could only have one will, and which, according to some more extreme views, could not be wrong when matters of its own interests were at stake. Even more problematically, that conflation left elected politicians in the position to assert that, in some near-literal sense, they were the Nation, and their views therefore the infallible ones of the whole.[19] While this was in part simply a reproduction of the monarchy's own assumption that the king 'represented' the body politic in and through his own person and will, it drew additional strength from a second dimension of advanced and fashionable thinking of the time.

In the last decades of the eighteenth century, the 'sensationism' of many Enlightenment thinkers – the notion that uniform rational conclusions could and should be drawn from the evidence of the human senses – was joined in the minds of many with a new 'sentimentalism' that tied this idea into the realm of emotional relations and experiences.[20] Strange as it may seem to a modern reader, many educated people in late-eighteenth-century France believed that a frankly melodramatic acting-out of emotional experiences was 'authentic', and the mark of an honest and virtuous character. Men and women alike were expected to be moved to tears by sentimental passages in plays and books – and not merely to discreet moistening of the eyes, but full-blown sobbing.[21] A radically open-hearted approach to life was widely asserted to be both wholesomely natural and socially desirable. Whole-hearted emotional commitment was quickly translated into revolutionary political commitment. Here, for example, is the future Girondin Louvet describing the moment he learned of the fall of the Bastille in 1789:

> At that very moment, I put on the tricolour cockade which had been won at such a bloody price. How can I paint the emotional transports with which this cockade was given me and with which I adopted it? I was at the knees of my tender friend. With my tears I drenched her hands which I then placed upon my furiously beating heart![22]

In this classic example of a sentimentalist *tableau*, strong emotion is translated into vigorous gesture, emphatic pose and the inevitable tears. His 'tender friend', incidentally, was his mistress, whom he had renamed 'Lodoiska' after the sentimental heroine of one of his own novels, and whom he would marry after the Revolution legalised divorce – such was the intertwining of literary, personal and political life that revolutionaries could achieve. The key motif that sums all this up, and leads towards its deeper political repercussions, is 'transparency'. By Louvet's own account, his authorship of several sentimental novels stood him in good stead in 1791, when the Paris Jacobin Club held that to be sufficient credential to elect him to its important Correspondence Committee. Emotional honesty (or, to be cynical, the acting-out of such openness) was taken to represent political honesty – the strangeness of this concept to modern eyes again bearing repetition, that authorship of works of fiction could point to virtue in the factual world of politics. But thus it was.[23]

In the writings of Jean-Jacques Rousseau, the novelist, dramatist and political philosopher who had died in 1778, revolutionaries of all stripes found a grounding for these beliefs. Rousseau was a strange and outlandish figure, lionised by the elite society of the Enlightenment salons, but driven by his own inner demons to see hypocrisy and scorn all around him, and to attribute his own internal miseries to the machinations of others. By the time of his death, although he remained protected by some of the most powerful people in France, he thought of himself as a persecuted martyr for the cause of virtue. This bizarre, charming, but abominably self-regarding man became the centre of a veritable cult after his death: pilgrimages to his last resting-place were a popular activity among the refined population of the capital in the 1780s. In Rousseau's writings, beside political concepts such as the infallible 'General Will' of the nation, people found justification for their own worship of virtue and transparency. Shortly before his death, Rousseau produced his *Confessions*, a form of autobiography in which, while appearing to confess all sorts of weaknesses and vices, he also succeeded in projecting himself as an innocent abroad, a maligned hero who lived for the cause of personal authenticity in a hostile and malicious world. Such was the power of this perspective, and the charm of his writing for the readers of the 1780s, that it overcame shocking details like the abandonment of his children at birth to foundling hospitals – where they almost certainly died. Rousseau's protestations that fatherhood was not for him carried more weight with a broad mass of readers, inclined by appreciation of his novels to sentimental sympathy, than did actions which, to more sceptical reviewers, were simply monstrous.[24]

The cultural appreciation of transparency and sentimentality carried over directly into revolutionary political culture. For the Girondins, their 'transparent' appreciation of each other's virtue and honesty was cemented by the private gatherings that had gone on for years among Brissot's circles, and now continued to draw in new members. In late September 1792, for example, Madame Roland had hosted a dinner to celebrate the declaration of the Republic, inviting Brissot, Pétion and Condorcet, the Bordeaux trio of Vergniaud, Gensonné and Guadet, and others we have already encountered, including Louvet and Barbaroux.[25] The perspective of this group on politics, and their appalled reaction to the threats to their life and reputations proffered by the radicals of Paris, were both reinforced and made more intransigent by their implicit belief in their collective merit, cemented by close and continuous private discussions. As we have already seen on several occasions, the Girondins were far from agreement on all aspects of policy, either before or after the fall of the monarchy, but as they were steadily demonised by their political opponents to the left, they began to pull together ever more tightly to resist what they saw as baseless and murderous slander.

The Girondins' more radical opponents, although sharing many of the same views as them on issues of transparency, placed a contrasting emphasis on the public facets and performance of its virtues. For radical Jacobins, what mattered was the visibility of political action, and its connection to the interests of the watching population.[26] The continually recurring charge against the Girondins was that they were plotters against the public welfare – ever since their eagerness for war had proved so disastrous, and they had hamfistedly failed to install themselves as the king's ministers in early August. Radicals prided themselves on never concealing their moves from the virtuous 'people', even if that 'people' was actually the self-selecting group that chose to watch the sessions of the Jacobin Club, or to haunt the Convention's meeting-place. Of course, for the Girondins, that 'people' was actually a corrupt clique, the same private army they held responsible for the September Massacres. Louvet had loudly boasted in his speech against Robespierre that he knew the Parisians, because he had lived among them all his life: 'They know how to fight, the people of Paris; they don't know how to murder.'

Unfortunately for the Girondins, whatever the truth of that claim, it was also the case that the most active groups of Parisian democratic partisans, those most assiduous in attending both their own popular societies and the public galleries of the Jacobins and the Convention, were those who roundly supported the action taken in September, and who would not have been sorry to see the Girondins go the same way. Conditioned by the history of the past four years to expect betrayal from on high, they breathed a quality Robespierre was to dub *défiance* – a revolutionary mistrust of all public figures who did not repeatedly and openly acclaim and demonstrate their popular and radical credentials. Revolutionary transparency, for those who attended the Fraternal Society or the Cordeliers Club, and who sat in the Paris Commune, had come to mean a continual effort to root out the wicked, aristocratic, counter-revolutionary elements that still infested the body politic. Denunciation, of the blatant kind pioneered by Marat's hysterical journalism, and which others such as Chabot were developing a taste for within the Jacobins and the Convention, was the route towards purity. The Girondins repeatedly accused the radical leadership of stoking up these sentiments, but they themselves were masters of inflammatory rhetoric when the occasion demanded, and it would be fairer to say that all parties in the new republic were bathed in a flood of fear and suspicion.[27]

It is also true that idealistic beliefs about transparency and virtue were not the only motors of activism and conflict. The rumours that continued to swirl around Danton – accusing him through the winter of misappropriating funds and property on a mission to the armies in the north – demonstrate the striking attention to self-interest that revolutionary politicians could deploy. His feud with the Rolands continued to rumble on, and meanwhile new factional allegiances were being cemented within and outside the Convention. The Parisian elections to that body, morally dominated by the figure of Robespierre, had drawn heavily on Danton's Cordeliers associates – no fewer than ten club members, including Danton himself, Marat, Fabre, Billaud-Varenne, Collot-d'Herbois, Robert, Desmoulins and the butcher Legendre, had been included in the twenty-four-man delegation. Along with Robespierre, the other Parisians and a few provincial emulators, these men provided the heart of the left wing of the Convention. They soon came to be called 'the Mountain', and by extension the Montagnards. The name derived immediately from their habit of sitting on the highest of the tiered benches in the Convention, from where they could look down on those associated with the Gironde. In an extension of the geographical metaphor, the centre-ground of politics was occupied by several hundred unaligned deputies referred to as the Plain – or more disparagingly, as time went on, *le marais*, the marsh or swamp. The Montagnards' elevation could thus mark their scorn for the speakers of the Gironde and the Plain, but their name had strong connotations of moral virtue: in the language of romantic sensibility, just as the natural countryside was preferred to the corrupting city, so the mountains were seen as the purest location of natural communities and honest individuals.

Ironically, however, those whom the Montagnards left behind in their ascent to national politics soon came to look suspiciously on the whole machinery of the Convention. There were more than just ten Cordeliers who would have liked a seat on the national stage. Jacques-René Hébert, author of the fiery *Père Duchesne* newspaper, for example, was defeated several times in the electoral assembly, never receiving more than a handful of votes. Charles-Philippe Ronsin, an ex-soldier, playwright and more or less full-time Cordeliers activist, had explicitly sought Robespierre's endorsement for election, but without success. Pierre-Gaspard Chaumette, a former medical student who had become a journalist and activist; François-Nicolas Vincent, a clerk and Cordelier who had been a leader of the insurrectionary preparations; Antoine Momoro, the printer who had been one of the most eminent early Cordeliers – all of these watched their erstwhile colleagues ascend to grander things.[28] They would all remain vigorously active in politics, and would retain the Cordeliers tradition of *défiance*, eventually even of the activities of the Mountain. Chaumette became the chief procurator – prosecutor and legal officer – of the Commune of Paris, Hébert his official deputy (and unofficial political superior). Vincent rose to prominence within the offices of the War Ministry, from where he would send Ronsin out as a newly minted general officer on several critical missions of military and political repression.

Across France, politics shared the acrimony of national debates. In Lyon, France's second city, tensions between hard-pressed urban consumers and the authorities produced a breakdown of conventional law and order in late September, with the pillage of food stocks controlled by self-appointed popular 'police commissioners', often women. Among the tens of thousands of working people who thronged the dense heart of the city, pinned on a promontory between the Rhône and Saône rivers, and the sprawling suburbs to the north and west, where silk-weavers' houses dotted the slopes in search of light to work by, a precocious politicisation since 1789 had raised up neighbourhood political clubs with an intense radical agenda for justice. Bitter grievances over the management of the silk trade created vicious disputes between artisans and the monied men of the local elite, compounded by fears that counter-revolutionary aristocrats were using the city as a refuge from their own aggrieved vassals in the surrounding countryside.

The local municipality, Girondin in outlook due partly to close links with Roland, who had lived there until 1790, was powerless to intervene in the troubles of late 1792, and was repeatedly lambasted by self-appointed agents of the 'sovereign people'.[29] The Convention ordered new local elections for the city in October, which resulted in a municipality of hardline radicals paradoxically sharing power with a moderate mayor, elected on a much higher turnout at the same time. Lyonnais politics divided sharply between radical club activists and the propertied elites, who had shunned political engagement over the last year, but who from this point on would focus their efforts on taking control of the neighbourhood Sections. For them, the radical activists were little better than scum, 'presumptuous through ignorance, ambitious through [self-]interest . . . mostly illiterate, many receiving charity handouts', and their quest for power was no more than a plot to plunder the city's coffers, and its richer inhabitants, as one correspondent of Roland wrote in December.[30] This characterisation was far from accurate – many radicals were artisans or businessmen on their own account, and their leaders were the same lawyers and men of letters that led every revolutionary faction – but their aggressively plebeian posturing and open contempt for the wealthy fostered an atmosphere of social hatred that would erupt with fatal consequences in the year ahead.

In Marseille, the other great city of the south-east, home of the *fédérés* who had helped topple the monarchy, there were also rising tensions. Jacobin activists from the city seized the departmental administration from its official home in Aix and forcibly relocated its members to Marseille in August 1792, rectifying a slur on municipal pride that had existed since 1790, but also unhesitatingly defying national political authority. They would shortly also establish an unofficial 'revolutionary tribunal' to judge the local accessories of monarchy and counter-revolution. As the Marseillais had done since 1789, they continued to use both civic deputations and armed expeditions to spread their message of revolutionary purity into neighbouring towns. As the autumn and winter wore on, this process, often funded, like the military expeditions to Paris, by 'revolutionary' levies on wealth, became ever more divisive as its rhetoric grew ever more extreme.

The rising extremism of approaches to social division was also on display across a wide swathe of rural France. In late August, the Legislative Assembly had formally abolished all feudal dues on the land except those for which an original written title-deed existed. While this move encouraged the peasantry, it was a distinctly limited step – notwithstanding the efforts of peasants actively to destroy the signs and documents of feudal obligation since 1789, many such original titles existed, and many indeed were in the hands of revolutionary authorities. The feudal holdings of the Catholic church were still being turned to profit by the state, as for example were the extensive rights of the Municipality of Bordeaux. Feudal rights were far from the only concern of country-dwellers by late 1792, moreover. By November, the grain-growing lands around Paris were already seeing major collective protests against high prices, just as a year previously, and a further movement was developing, demanding *partage* – the division and distribution of lands from landlords to the peasants.

Some of this had been foreshadowed in those earlier protests, and partly in response to widespread sentiments in its favour, the division of common lands had been allowed by a decree of 14 August, passed in somewhat sketchy form in the confusion after the fall of the monarchy. The Convention suspended this decree in October, largely because of its lack of clarity, but a wave of written protests through the winter placed a harsher interpretation on the legislators' hesitations. One commune in the Gard expressed what was a common view: 'Royalty, clergy and nobility have been abolished for ever, but the great landed proprietors remain to be destroyed, for it is in this very moment that they bear down with their full weight upon the poor inhabitants of the countryside.'[31] A notary from a village in the Somme indicted the 'rich class who have seen with pleasure the former nobles become their equals, [but] who have not admitted those unfortunates below them as equals'. By mid-winter, there were reports from the Paris basin that radical activists were proposing the egalitarian redistribution of all land, while hundreds of individual incidents of the occupation and redistribution of seigneurial commons and enclosures took place. A language of 'despotism' and 'bloodsucking' associated the wealthy with the aristocrats and the counter-revolution, echoing the divisive fears of the urban consumers of Paris, Lyon and elsewhere.

Ironically, this internal dissent came at a time when French armies were scoring spectacular successes on almost all fronts. The initial victory at Valmy had held out the brief prospect of a negotiated peace, something to which the commanding general Dumouriez appeared at first receptive. He spun out talks over several days, while the Allies used up their last supplies, and he gave out strong but misleading signals of his intentions. The duke of Brunswick was recorded by one *émigré* aide-de-camp as believing that 'Dumouriez is our man. In two days he will come over to us with all his troops.' The *émigrés* seriously doubted this, witnesses as they were to the rapid deterioration of the Allied army.[32] News of the declaration of the Republic reached the opposing forces quickly, ending negotiations abruptly. Brunswick talked up the possibility of a renewed attack, but yielded to practicalities. His army fell back, effectively abandoning all the Allies' gains in northern France as his ill-supplied and unhealthy troops sought secure winter quarters. Dumouriez even lent them some troops to assist the withdrawal, manhandling Prussian artillery back down the roads it had advanced along.[33] The *émigrés*, male and female alike, who had 'filled the roads' with their carriages on the advance, presenting as one titled lady wrote a 'remnant of Parisian elegance', now found themselves in dire straits. As the writer went on:

> The chaos of the retreat was horrible. We were overrun by the troops who swarmed all over the roads . . . We fought for accommodation in barns and were content to sleep on the straw. The sight of a church tower gave us hope of asylum, but our hopes were dashed when we read the words 'No admittance to Jews and *émigrés*'.[34]

Like many *émigrés*, this writer would be hounded by French advances through the winter, finally finding refuge in England in the spring of 1793.

With this disaster for the Allies in the east, Dumouriez was able to capitalise on the wider war front. His main forces left the Prussians to their own misery, swung north and entered the Austrian Netherlands (modern Belgium) on 27 October, winning a major victory on 6 November at Jemappes. This hard-fought battle, which saw the French advancing through cannon fire and grapeshot to overrun entrenched Austrian positions, and fighting off repeated enemy cavalry charges, consolidated the reputation of the Republic's armies as a formidable foe. One of the generals present, Maréchal-de-camp Dampierre, who had himself commanded from the front line, wrote with pride of the heroism of the volunteers, 'the soldiers from Paris and other towns of the Republic, who for more than two months have been sustaining incredible hardships, sleeping in bivouacs, frozen with cold and drenched with rain'.[35] The victory secured Belgium for the Republic, and allowed the French to consolidate an occupation of the territory throughout the winter. Meanwhile to the east the Rhineland was invaded and overrun by a French army through October and November, and although Frankfurt fell to a Prussian counter-attack in early December, the advantage remained with the revolutionaries. Basle in Switzerland was also occupied, and in the south-east the state of Savoy, in the western Alps, was occupied and then annexed to France on 27 November.

With such a run of crushing victories under way, the initial Girondin enthusiasm for revolutionary war began to revive, and on 19 November a decree of 'Aid and Fraternity' from the Convention pledged to assist all peoples seeking liberation from monarchic tyranny. This contradicted earlier assertions that the Revolution would fight only defensive wars, and was reinforced on 15 December when 'revolutionary' administration was imposed on all occupied territories – including the abolition of feudalism, seizures of church and 'counter-revolutionary' assets, extraordinary taxes on wealth and revolutionary loyalty oaths. A less flamboyant but equally significant measure had reopened the River Scheldt, in northern Belgium, to international shipping. This had been closed by international treaty for almost 150 years, and was a direct challenge to the commercial interests of Holland and Britain. Along with the more propagandistic elements of French public policy, this seemed to place the new Republic at odds not merely with overt counter-revolution, but with all the other powers of Europe. The issue that the Convention had been debating since early November, the fate of the imprisoned king, could only open this chasm wider.

On 7 November, a report to the Convention from the deputy Jean-Baptiste Mailhe swept aside the monarchist argument that Louis was constitutionally inviolable unless and until he had been declared to have abdicated – which he had never been, having merely been suspended until the establishment of the Republic made the point moot. Mailhe's long and prolix argument dismissed such notions as quibbling technicalities that had no place in the discussion of great crimes such as Louis', and ended with a project for the trial of the king, introduced with a melodramatic flourish typical of the time:

> The tottering of thrones that once seemed most secure, the active and happy prosperity of the armies of the French Republic, the political current which is electrifying all humanity, everything announces the imminent fall of kings and the reestablishment of all societies on their original foundations.[36]

Debate on the trial project opened six days later and revealed wide divergences of view. A few deputies, some of whom in their hearts probably still believed in the natural inviolability of kings, held out against a trial, the main alternative they offered being banishment. Some Girondins questioned the wisdom of a public hearing, preferring to hold Louis discreetly to avoid the necessary hardening of positions this would occasion, although perhaps also as a hostage in the minds of the Great Powers. Most were agreed on the need for a trial, however, as the opportunity publicly to expose Louis' crimes with documentary proof. A 'Commission of Twenty-Four' had already been scouring the Tuileries and the inner workings of royal government for just such proof.

Others to the left found the whole idea of a trial ludicrous.[37] Louis-Antoine Léon Saint-Just, at twenty-five one of the youngest revolutionary politicians, who had lived his whole adult life in the turmoil of political innovation, made his maiden speech to the Convention on the opening day of debate. He was a scion of the officer class, and in his teenage years had seemed bound for a life of idle dissipation, producing semi-obscene writings and embarrassing his family with his debts. Revolutionary politics took hold of him, however, and transformed a languid youth, with a widely noted almost feminine beauty, into an icy republican ideologue. It was this new Saint-Just who revealed himself clearly in this speech, cutting to the heart of the issue. The king, he said, 'should be judged as an enemy', not as a citizen. He mocked the idea that a king, one of 'the lowest class of humanity . . . the class of oppressors', should be 'raised . . . to the rank of citizen' in order to be tried before the justice of the Republic.[38]

Saint-Just discussed the crimes of Louis himself, how he 'oppressed a free nation', and had 'intended that the people be crushed' in the assault on the Tuileries. He even managed to turn Louis' hesitant behaviour on that day against him: 'Did he not review the troops before combat? Did he not take flight rather than halt their fire?'[39] Going further, the speech revealed the depth of transformation that the end of the monarchy had brought about in at least some minds:

> With whatever illusions, whatever conventions, monarchy cloaks itself, it remains an eternal crime against which every man has the right to rise and to arm himself. Monarchy is an outrage which even the blindness of an entire people cannot justify . . . all men hold from nature the secret mission to destroy such domination wherever it may be found.[40]

As he pithily summarised, 'No man can reign innocently. The folly is all too evident. Every king is a rebel and a usurper.'[41] And so, Saint-Just went on, Louis must be judged promptly, but only by deciding whether or not he is 'the enemy of the French people', and if he is, then putting him swiftly to death with no more ado.[42]

To more moderate politicians, such a position was pure madness, inviting as it did war without end until the last crowned head of Europe (or the world) had been toppled. It was one thing to make enthusiastically vague pronouncements about coming to the aid of oppressed peoples, as the Convention was to do less than two weeks later, but quite another to put extrajudicial murder at the heart of the Republic. That, after all, was exactly what their enemies had accused them of doing only two months before. Those who advocated summary execution remained a small minority, and the majority in favour of a trial continued to harden, all the more so after 20 November when the stunning news of a secret repository of royal papers in the Tuileries was revealed. Hidden behind panelling in a corridor, the size of a modern kitchen cabinet, this secret *armoire de fer* or 'iron cupboard' had been constructed in the spring of 1792 on the king's personal orders by the locksmith who now denounced its existence, firstly to the Inspector-General of Royal Buildings, and then to Interior Minister Roland himself.[43]

Roland was so electrified by this claim that he went with the locksmith to the palace and had him force open the cupboard. Inside he found hundreds of documents, which he rifled through, making hasty notes of some of their main topics before taking the bundled papers direct to the nearby Convention. Roland announced that he had found papers 'of very great importance' – so important that he had bypassed, on his own authority, the Commission of Twenty-Four already at work on the royal records in the palace, and now requested the formation of a new special commission to examine this find.[44] Unfortunately for the minister, his hasty zeal had only brought him more trouble. On the following day, he had to appear at the Convention again, angrily to rebut charges that he should have taken deputies from that body with him to investigate what was then only one man's report, and the wilder claim that he had pocketed jewels found with the papers – an assertion made by Marat, and soon picked up by other radicals in the press and Parisian assemblies. Although that was probably the most far-fetched accusation, it was by no means the most damaging. Robespierre in the Jacobin Club, on the very evening of the discovery, voiced fears that 'not only could Roland have removed documents, he could also have added them', firstly to hide evidence of Girondin duplicity, and then to incriminate various Montagnards and their allies. Marat's paper soon had Roland receiving his orders direct from Louis XVI himself, and on 26 November the Commune of Paris established a committee specifically to investigate Roland – once again showing the influence that this mere municipal council continued to claim in national affairs.[45]

The contents of the cupboard eventually provided about half the documents used for the king's trial, but these were only about 5 per cent of the total found. It seems likely that they were simply sifted for the most incriminating individual statements that could be produced for dramatic effect. This neglected the more structurally sinister nature of the archive as a whole. It appears that Louis was envisaging a time when he would have triumphed over the Revolution, and his records could re-emerge as the definitive account of governmental activity, and as a record of those who had stood by and advised him in the times of trouble. As well as memoranda and drafts in his own hand, it contained extensive correspondence on religious affairs, and on the problems of the nobility and the armed forces. It also revealed the extent of negotiation between the king and the various Feuillant leaders, and shockingly exposed the comte de Mirabeau, hero of the Estates-General, who had died in 1791 hailed as the greatest man of the Revolution, as having been paid to give secret advice to the court throughout 1790.

Although the evidence it provided helped secure agreement at last to proceed with a trial of the king, the 'iron cupboard' episode thus also contributed to the continuing decline in political relations within the Convention and government. On 3 December, a speech by Robespierre echoed Saint-Just's argument before the Convention that the king should merely be disposed of. He repeated the call the next day, but by then the motion to proceed with a trial had already been carried, and on the 6th a committee was formed to draw up an indictment, which was presented on the 10th. On the following day Louis himself was summoned to the bar of the Convention and questioned about his alleged high crimes.

The indictment reached back to the fateful day of the Tennis-Court Oath, 20 June 1789, charging that it was then he had first 'attacked the sovereignty of the people' by driving the Estates-General from its meeting-place. The royal session of 23 June 1789 was denounced as 'subversive of every liberty', and the events of July interpreted as a plot for the military destruction of the capital. The Flight to Varennes also featured, as did the king's evident perjury in taking the oath to the new constitution in September 1791. He was also held responsible (as he and the queen had long feared they might be) for his *émigré* brothers' counter-revolutionary excesses, and charged with bribery and corruption on a massive scale, all with the intent of defeating the Revolution, and in general 'of having committed a multitude of crimes in order to establish your tyranny'.[46]

When Bertrand Barère, presiding over the Convention, questioned Louis about his deployment of troops against the people, the ex-king gave the only answer he could: 'I was the master . . . then, and I sought to do what was right.'[47] He responded with dignity to all thirty-five of the chief heads of indictment against him, and after his questioning the trial was adjourned for almost two weeks as a hastily assembled legal team worked on his defence. The team included the eminent barrister Tronchet, who had reluctantly agreed to take the case, a junior from Bordeaux, Raymond de Sèze, who was far more ardent in his loyalty, and the remarkable figure of Chrétien-Guillaume de Lamoignon de Malesherbes. Aged seventy-one, a former government minister who had used his control of censorship in the 1750s and 1760s to favour the publication of 'advanced' works, he was a relic of the days when humanitarian progress seemed to be the goal of enlightened monarchy. He volunteered his services, and unlike de Sèze would perish for his pains in a later stage of the Terror.[48]

For now, the defence team set to work with the former king, who had been living an almost surreally tranquil existence in the keep of the Temple with his family and sister, provided with books and servants by decree of the Legislative Assembly. The prisoners' only troubles came from the guards inflicted on them by the Paris Commune. Although forbidden any brutality, they commonly spoke in crude terms of Louis' fate – all were certain, of course, that he would be executed – and were a jarring intrusion in an otherwise domestic round of meals, lessons for the children, daily walks and reading. At the start of the trial, however, the Commune tightened the regime, segregating Louis from his family except for brief supervised visits – and these were only allowed after the intervention of the Convention. Not all of this was due to pure malice, and the Commune repeatedly represented to the Convention the urgency of the need to settle the king's fate, fearing escape or rescue, and the burden that continual watchfulness was placing on the jailers.[49]

Louis was widely observed to have entered a state of almost preternatural calm during his imprisonment. Seen by his later supporters as evidence of his acceptance of martyrdom, it may also reflect an intensification of the intermittent depression he had long been subject to, a further blocking-out of the harsh realities of the situation. This is perhaps reflected in his choice of defence strategy. Malesherbes advocated a tough realist position, challenging the presumptuous and illiberal claim of the Convention to act as prosecutor, judge and jury, and raising the wider issue of its authority to try him at all, thus forcing into the open the whole question of the legality of Louis' overthrow. Louis, however, favoured a reiteration of his first spontaneous reaction to the charges levelled against him. He would seek to deny all wrongdoing, insist on his constitutional prerogatives as the executive power, and continue to claim inviolability as king. Given the undeniable evidence of bad faith accumulating from the revelations of the iron cupboard (rendered more telling by the fact that Louis continued evasively to deny knowledge of the whole archive), and the fact that the indictment implicitly rejected the validity of such claims anyway, it was a hopeless case.[50] Nevertheless, it was one which de Sèze pleaded with magnificent eloquence on 26 December, despite the four sleepless nights of work that had preceded it. With Louis again standing at the bar of the Convention, he rehearsed the king's response to each of the charges, and to the claim of the Convention to be able to try him, emphasising at each point that the king had stood for legality and order against naked, illegal force. His final peroration opened with words that would later prove ominously prophetic: 'Citizens, if at this very moment you were told that an excited and armed crowd were marching against you with no respect for your character as sacred legislators . . . what would you do?'[51]

The members of the Convention at present had no interest in answering that question, being already exercised about the possible consequences of executing 'Citizen Capet'. This was the name that radicals insisted on, reviving that of a medieval dynasty of French kings, the last time they had not borne the aristocratic territorial titles abolished by the Revolution back in 1790. From the opening of the debate on 27 December, it soon became clear that the bitter partisanship of the autumn months was still in full force. Louis' guilt was not seriously disputed, but two issues really engaged debate – should he be executed or imprisoned; and should any sentence be referred to the electorate for approval? This option, the 'appeal to the people' (*appel au peuple*), came to dominate almost to the exclusion of the issue of sentence. Debates were in any case disjointed and often confused, and on 7 January a week's adjournment was decreed, to give time for the printing of deputies' speeches and reflection on their content before the final votes.

The appeal was a question which had appeared settled by Mailhe's original proposal for the trial – he had considered, and ruled out, trial by referendum. Such a procedure would be enormously divisive and impractical. In a situation of continued religious turmoil, with regional authorities still regularly banishing non-juror priests from their flocks, and rising tensions of all kinds in the major urban centres, it is hard to see how six thousand town and cantonal primary assemblies could reach a verdict that would not itself provoke further conflict. But to the Girondins, who seem implicitly to have assumed that the Convention would vote for death under

Parisian pressure, the appeal offered the hope of retrieving the Revolution from an irrevocable break with Europe, and of preventing the king's fate serving to consolidate that iniquitous Parisian grip on the Republic. Their speeches dismissed with bland and empty reassurance the notion that France would be divided, while dwelling on the outrages offered to the Convention by those 'calling themselves Sections of Paris, believing they have the right to dictate the law, voting decrees that threaten the Convention itself'.[52] Vergniaud spoke of the capital being in 'ignominious servitude to a handful of brigands', in a speech filled with veiled references to the perfidy of Robespierre and Marat, the 'men of ambition' who would make themselves new Cromwells over Louis' corpse. He denied that discord could break out in the primary assemblies, claiming that 'agitators' did not exercise there 'the same empire that a shameful weakness has allowed them to usurp in Paris'.[53]

Unfortunately for the Girondins, while the majority in the Convention might agree that the September Massacres had been unsavoury, and that there was a whiff of extremism about the Commune and its Montagnard allies, they were not prepared to go down the road of associating all this together with the king's sentence. There were those, like the obscure lawyer Chaillon, who could fit it all into a pattern that demanded the king live, as he put it, 'to disappoint the hopes of the foreign powers who disdain him, the émigrés who detest him, of Rome that would like to have beatified him already, of the factions that surround us and of the Cromwells who lead them'.[54] It was a convoluted argument, but found an echo in the cold evaluation of the American ambassador Gouverneur Morris: 'The monarchic and aristocratic parties wish his death', believing that the impact of the execution would 'turn into the channels of loyalty the impetuous tide of opinion'.[55]

Many speakers were troubled by the thought of regicide and its consequences, and pointed to English history as a parallel: Charles I executed in 1649, leading to military dictatorship and restoration; James II exiled forty years later, establishing an enduring political settlement. Many more, however, felt that the king was a criminal who must be punished, and that the powers and the *émigrés* were unlikely to be deterred by a royal hostage that the Republic had already once refused to execute. Nevertheless, the range of opinion was extremely wide, and it is a tribute to the strategic ineptitude of the Girondins that they managed to set themselves so squarely against the population of the capital that surrounded them yet again, and gained nothing but greater exposure to hostility for so doing.

The session of 14 January was taken up, until late into the night, with wrangling over whether to vote on the appeal to the people first, and thus implicitly to suggest that the Convention's subsequent decision about Louis' guilt was provisional. Girondin efforts to secure this result failed, after several hours of what one newspaper of record could only note as 'tumultuous indecision', and which seems to have been violent argument.[56] The vote that rejected the appeal on 15 January, by 424 to 283, was by far the most emphatic of those where the issue was actually in doubt – the king had been declared guilty earlier the same day by a unanimous roll-call vote. After these votes the Convention turned to other business until the evening of the 16th, when from eight o'clock the deputies processed one by one to the tribune to cast their votes for Louis' sentence. The roll-call took thirteen hours through the cold winter's night, though the hall, packed with some 721 deputies and numerous spectators, remained stuffy throughout. Louis' defence team had been refused seats, and stood through the entire process.[57]

Ironically, for such a momentous decision, both the nature of the vote itself and its outcome were complex. No restrictions were placed on the deputies' votes – the question was not 'Shall Louis be executed?', but rather 'What penalty shall be imposed on him?', and the answers provided were various. In the end 361 deputies voted unambiguously for death: some, like Marat, adding that it should be within twenty-four hours. Some 321 voted for sentences of imprisonment, usually adding that the king should be exiled once peace was made, though two wanted him locked up at hard labour. A small middle group voted for death, but with various suggestions as to a reprieve. This included twenty-six who followed Mailhe, presenter of the original report on the trial, who said that his vote was for death, but that the Convention itself should have a further vote on a reprieve. Depending on one's perspective it is possible to present the majority for execution as no more than one (the 361 unconditional votes for death versus 360 that were not), or as high as seventy-five, but it is clear that the will of the Convention, albeit not in any great majority, was that Louis should die. His lawyers then read a letter in which Louis rejected his conviction, and the elderly Malesherbes, exhausted and distraught, broke down in tears as he tried to plead for compassion. A subsequent vote called on a reprieve through 19 and 20 January gave a clear majority of seventy against it, and on the 20th the execution was decreed for the next day.[58]

The king had been told of his fate by Malesherbes, who again broke down, on the morning of the 17th. The old minister was thereafter barred from seeing him, and Louis remained in isolation until the evening of 20 January, when a deputation of the Convention gave him the news that he was to die in the morning. He asked for a confessor, and to see his family. Thus he was able to break the news to them himself. For an hour and three-quarters they remained together, racked with grief, Louis' eight-year-old son clinging to his father's knees. As the king was finally led away his teenage daughter flung herself towards him and fell in a dead faint. Louis had time to help revive her, then he was gone. A loving father and husband, he was to die a Christian martyr, his great tragedy being that, perhaps only through the impossible dilemmas placed before him, he perished also a perjured traitor to his own people.[59]

The next day dawned foggy and chill. Louis was roused before six and took communion from his Irish priest, Edgeworth de Firmont. His valet was refused permission to crop his hair – that was the executioner's job. At eight the brewer Antoine-Joseph Santerre, *sans-culotte* hero of the Faubourg Saint-Antoine now elevated into a National Guard general, came to collect Louis. After some hesitation, it was Louis himself who broke the deadlock with a brisk 'Let's go!' Under the escort of twelve hundred troops, his shuttered carriage began a long trip counter-clockwise from the Temple around the northern boulevards towards the Place de la Révolution (today Place de la Concorde). Paris had been turned into an armed camp for the occasion by order of the Commune. Its gates were closed, artillery was stationed at strategic points, and tens of thousands of National Guards were on duty, lining the route to the scaffold four deep. All windows and shutters along the way had been ordered closed, muffling all signs of normal life, and the usually vociferous Parisian crowds were still and silently watchful, as they had been when the captive king had ridden back from Varennes eighteen months before.[60] The security may seem somewhat overdone, but there were in fact plans to rescue the king, plans which reveal incidentally how fragile the distinction between republicans and royalists could still be.

The baron de Breteuil, the former minister that the king had charged with his secret exile diplomacy years earlier, had been working hard to retrieve the situation ever since the fall of the monarchy. He had even plotted with an *émigré* royalist journalist, Antoine Rivarol, to use the latter's sister, mistress of General Dumouriez, as a go-between to induce the general's surrender, before Valmy rendered such a suggestion absurd.[61] As the fate of the king looked more grim through the autumn, Breteuil turned to yet more desperate measures, and enlisted the services of the baron de Batz. A Gascon nobleman, descendant of the real d'Artagnan, and with much of the latter's legendary swagger and adventurism, Batz had been a financial speculator in the late 1780s, working in a 'bear' syndicate to manipulate and profit from falling prices during this period of crisis. Alongside him in the syndicate were Breteuil himself and Etienne Clavière, a Swiss-born banker and associate later of Mirabeau, then of Brissot, and who after 10 August 1792 was serving as Finance Minister of France. Clavière was far from Batz's only interesting association. He had been elected as a noble deputy to the Estates-General, and had already been involved in several shady schemes with counter-revolutionary intent. One, to set up a 'slush fund' for royalist purposes from the proceeds of compensation paid for abolished state offices, raised over half a million livres, the king himself making a note of this in July 1792. At this point, Batz had emigrated, but he left behind a wide circle of friends and acquaintances across the political spectrum, and offered his services to Breteuil in the autumn via Axel von Fersen, then based in Brussels before its fall to the French. Fersen was wary of Batz's flash reputation and disreputable contacts, but he agreed he could be of use.[62]

Into the winter of 1792, Breteuil continued to attempt to work on the members of the Convention, but he was crippled first by the success of the French military, removing the incentive for a negotiated surrender, and then by the revelations of the iron cupboard, which compromised at least one individual revealed to be a correspondent of the king. By the end of the year, Batz, who remained extravagantly willing to run risks, was his only hope of immediate action to save the king. Breteuil accordingly gave to Batz, who was intent on setting off for Paris anyway, a letter of authority to 'use all possible means to

The end of the Flight to Varennes. Louis XVI is arrested, 22 June 1791.
(Engraved by Reinier Vinkeles and Daniel Vrydag, after Jan Bulthuis, Bibliothèque Nationale, Paris, Archives Charmet/www.bridgeman.co.uk)

The taking of the Tuileries, 10 August 1792.
(Jean Duplessi-Bertaux, Chateau de Versailles/www.bridgeman.co.uk)

Georges-Jacques Danton, barrister, Cordeliers activist, Minister of Justice: the statesman with an eye for the main chance.
(French School [18th century], Musée Carnavalet, Lauros/Giraudon/ www.bridgeman.co.uk)

Antoine Barnave, leader in Grenoble's 'pre-Revolution', charmed by Marie-Antoinette, architect of the failed 'Feuillant' settlement.
(Leonard de Selva/Corbis)

Counter-revolutionaries of Fouesnant, Brittany, rounded up by the National Guard in 1792.
(c. 1886–87 by Jules Girardet, Musée des Beaux-Arts, Quimper, Giraudon/www.bridgeman.co.uk)

Jacques-Pierre Brissot. Journalist, Parisian municipal politician and acknowledged unofficial leader of the Girondins.
(Bettmann/Corbis)

'The Incorruptible', Maximilien Robespierre.
(1791 by Pierre Roch Vigneron, Chateau de Versailles, France, Lauros/Giraudon/www.bridgeman.co.uk)

The corpse of the Princesse de Lamballe, former favourite of Marie-Antoinette, September 1792, displayed according to legend.
(Leon-Maxime Faivre, © Photo RMN – © Gérard Blot)

Architect of the Flight to Varennes, Axel von Fersen, who returned from exile on several occasions for secret discussions with Louis XVI and Marie-Antoinette.
(Noel Halle/Private collection, Giraudon/www.bridgeman.co.uk)

The royal family imprisoned in the keep of the Temple. For a time a surreally tranquil existence.
(1851 by Edward Ward, Harris Museum and Art Gallery/www.bridgeman.co.uk)

Bertrand Barère, eternal compromiser, member of the Committee of Public Safety, during Louis XVI's trial, January 1793.
(Jean Louis Laneuville/Kunsthalle, Bremen, Lauros/Giraudon/ www.bridgeman.co.uk)

'Every king is a rebel and a usurper.' The words of Louis-Antoine-Léon Saint-Just, one of the youngest revolutionary politicians, November 1792.
(Musée Carnavalet, www.bridgeman.co.uk)

The triumph of Jean-Paul Marat, idiosyncratic icon of the radical press, after his acquittal by the Revolutionary Tribunal, April 1793.
(Louis Leopold Boilly, Musée des Beaux-Arts, Lille, Lauros/Giraudon/www.bridgeman.co.uk)

Madame Roland, wife of Interior Minister Roland, ardent organiser of Girondin resistance to radical 'madness'.
(French School [18th century], Bibliothèque Nationale, Paris, Giraudon/ www.bridgeman.co.uk)

liberate the king, the queen and their family', signed on 2 January 1793.[63] Thus it was that on the morning of the 21st, Batz and a handful of loyal companions stood at the top of an embankment where the boulevard Bonne-Nouvelle met the rue de Cléry, awaiting the appearance of some five hundred royalist contacts that he had summoned, intent on forming a phalanx to rush Louis' carriage as it passed and sweep him away. Unfortunately, none but the original handful showed up – whether the Commune's elaborate precautions had done their deterrent work, or whether some or all of the five hundred existed only in Batz's imagination, we cannot know. The remaining handful did their best, plunging down towards the road as the carriage appeared. Batz's cry of 'To me all those who want to save the king!' went conspicuously unanswered, and the serried ranks of National Guards blocked their route before they could even trouble the close escort. Batz slipped away in the confusion, to reappear as a shadowy conspirator in years to come. Louis went on his way to the scaffold, probably unaware of the incident, as he was when a former secretary to the queen also tried to fight his way to the carriage.[64]

At ten, Louis reached his final destination, his dignity only ruffled when the executioner made to bind his hands – the confessor had to intervene to prevent a struggle, reminding Louis that he would thus resemble even more Christ in martyrdom. On the scaffold itself, coatless and with his hair cropped, Louis attempted a speech. He declared himself once more innocent, but pardoned 'those who have brought about my death', and seemed about to say more about the shedding of his blood – probably to hope forlornly that it would not lead to more – when Santerre ordered the drums to start up, and his words were drowned out. The executioners moved Louis swiftly into the machinery of death: he was strapped to a tilting plank, which dropped his head into a brace, and the blade of the guillotine plunged from above. Death in this manner was undoubtedly quick, and more painless than other forms of execution, though debate continued in medical circles about whether the head retained consciousness for a few seconds as it dropped into the basket. One or two accounts of Louis' death suggest the blade did not sever his whole neck in one go, and had to be borne down on by the executioner to get a clean cut. With his spine severed already, it is nevertheless unlikely that Louis could have uttered the 'terrible cry' that one account claims.[65]

What this method of execution did produce, however, was fountains of blood, spurting around the lowered blade, and running out onto the scaffold as the body was retrieved. Many accounts agree that people ran forward to dip handkerchiefs in the blood – others, more extreme, assert that pikes and sabres were baptised in it, or that some tasted it, demonstrating cannibalistic lusts or republican virtue, depending on the author's viewpoint. People also eagerly bought up the locks of hair that it was the executioner's perquisite to sell, and possibly also scraps of the king's last garments. Again, commentators differed widely on how to treat this – relics of a sacred king, or mementoes of the end of tyranny? However the end of 'Louis the Last' was treated, it was clear that a bloody Rubicon had been crossed, and that France could never be the same again.[66]

## Chapter 6

# Things Fall Apart

Even as Citizen Capet journeyed to his final appointment, intent on emulating Christ's sacrifice, the new Republic was consecrating the first of its own pantheon of martyrs. Louis-Michel Lepeletier de Saint-Fargeau was a symbol of the universal appeal of the Jacobin and republican ideal. He had been elected to the Estates-General at the age of just twenty-nine, a member of the highest ranks of the so-called 'robe nobility' that staffed France's law-courts. Although his position as a *président* of the Paris *parlement* might have inclined him to conservatism, he rejected the lure of counter-revolution, and became an enthusiastic reformer. Lepeletier worked in the areas of education and justice, helping to map out an ambitiously humanitarian penal code of graduated punishments, and drafting a wide-ranging and visionary plan for compulsory national education. Re-elected to the Convention from the department of the Yonne, he had followed the Montagnard line, and was one of those to vote unreservedly for the king's death.[1]

It is unclear how far any of this, except perhaps his general background and his fatal vote, were of interest to the former royal bodyguard named Pâris who found Lepeletier in a restaurant in the Palais-Royal on 20 January 1793, and hacked a gaping hole in his chest with a large knife. While Pâris made his escape, the Republic went to work on Lepeletier's image, refining it to suit the moment. Details of his death were shifted – from eating with another regular customer to dining frugally alone, even from an ornate dining-room to a spartan one, in some images. Plaintive last words – 'I'm cold' – were transformed into a stern statement of patriotism: 'I am content to spill my blood for my country; I hope it will serve to consolidate liberty and equality, and to reveal their enemies.'[2] Lepeletier's own image underwent a remarkable transformation at the hands of Jacques-Louis David, Montagnard deputy and France's pre-eminent neoclassical artist. David orchestrated a Romanesque funeral rite, with the body exposed outdoors for four days in the Place Vendôme on a pedestal that had until recently held a statue of Louis XIV, with stairs added for patriots to process by and pay their respects. The blood-soaked shirt of the martyr was draped over a pike at the foot of the bier, and subsequently led a funeral procession that took in both Convention and Jacobin Club on the way to burial.[3]

To immortalise the event, David completed a painting that hung thereafter in the Convention itself. This image, later destroyed by Lepeletier's royalist daughter, turned the pop-eyed and hook-nosed young nobleman into the Christ of a *pietà* with the head of a Greek god. Over his improbably muscled torso hung a blood-dripping sword, emblem of his gory death, and also of the Damoclean threat of the counter-revolution. As the first months of 1793 were to prove, that threat was indeed everywhere, and capable of penetrating not merely to the heart of a Paris restaurant, but to the remotest corners of the country, and of stirring unrest that would drive the Revolution further into the fratricidal horrors of civil war.

Much of what the revolutionary leadership was to describe as counter-revolution was, however, the collision of dissent and paranoia. The political war between Montagnards and Girondins continued apace, with a notable scalp being secured on 22 January, when Roland quit the Interior Ministry, still under attack for his mishandling of the iron-cupboard affair. His old enemy Danton had used a eulogy of Lepeletier delivered in the Convention the previous day to assert that 'for the good of the Republic, Roland should no longer be a minister'. It was the last in a long line of almost gratuitous attacks, against which Roland's repeated protestations of innocence had counted for nothing.[4] Roland was replaced by Dominique-Joseph Garat, who had failed to investigate the September Massacres after replacing Danton at the Justice Ministry, and was thus a safe pair of hands (dubbed a 'political eunuch' by Madame Roland) to lead the ministry out of the Girondin–Montagnard crossfire. Roland's own political humiliation was completed three weeks later, when he stood for the mayorship of Paris, and received barely four hundred votes. The victorious candidate, Jean-Nicolas Pache, gained over eleven thousand (as with the election of Pétion a year earlier, this was under 10 per cent of the electorate, Parisian politics being ever more the preserve of the *sans-culotte* activists). Pache was a former civil servant who had been promoted by Roland himself, to compound the bitterness with irony, and had served as War Minister since the previous October. He had steadily abandoned his early Girondin sympathies, turning to the Mountain and the *sans-culottes* of Paris, whom he was to represent from now into the heart of the Terror.[5]

The difficulties of reconciling Parisian and national priorities were illustrated within days of this election, as food prices rose to new heights at the same time as the assignat currency fell ever further. Radical activists in the Paris Sections petitioned the Convention on 13 February for state action to control the price of bread in particular – something which the Old Regime had sought to do as a matter of course, but which most revolutionary leaders had long regarded as the business of economic laws, not political ones. Failure to act on this plea presented the Convention ten days later with a widespread outbreak of disorder in the capital, as the population resorted to its age-old right in times of crisis and carried out a *taxation populaire*: a food riot in which a 'just price' was set (though not always actually paid). Every quarter of the city was swept up in the agitation that lasted four days, with hundreds of shops stripped of their stock, surpassing by far the magnitude of similar troubles a year earlier. The local authorities fought back, although their own National Guards, especially in poorer parts of the city, sometimes resisted efforts to stem the crowds. Dozens were arrested, both men and women from every rank of the working population. To Maximilien Robespierre, however, there could be only one conclusion to draw from such a series of events – crowds which disrupted the capital over something as insignificant as bread, sugar or coffee were not 'the people of Paris', but 'a mob of women, led by valets of the aristocracy'. He was not alone in such disparagement. Bertrand Barère, who stood for the neutral ground, the Plain, between Mountain and Gironde, heaped scorn on the protesters, speaking in the Convention of 'the perfidious incitement of aristocrats in disguise', and noting that 'where I see no respect for property, there I can no longer recognise any social order'.[6]

The hand of the counter-revolution was apparently therefore at work even in the actions of the common people of Paris, and by late February 1793 the members of the Convention had already begun to strike out at the wider manifestations of that insidious network. One way was to make the generalising anti-monarchic rhetoric of the king's trial into a bitter reality of conflict. Although British diplomatic opinion had feared the expansion of the war – recognising astutely that it might be best to leave the Republic to stew in its own factional juices, rather than give them further material for patriotic mobilisation – the government of William Pitt the Younger had found it necessary to mobilise the militia on 1 December 1792. Partly concerned with the threat posed by Jacobin-inspired 'corresponding societies' in the British Isles, this was also a necessary measure preliminary to further hostilities, and British political opinion was cemented in its antagonism to the French by the sentiment of outraged horror that greeted the king's execution.

Conscious of this, but believing that Pitt's government was already working to topple the Republic, and buoyed up by anglophobic rhetoric about the instability of the British Empire, perched on the tottering pile of the National Debt, the leadership of the Convention moved steadily through January towards a declaration of war on England, as they persistently referred to the old enemy. War against what were more realistically evaluated as the world-spanning forces and deep pockets of Pitt's government was viewed with something like horror by many moderates in the Convention – one reported to the American Gouverneur Morris in December 1792 that 'a majority of the Convention would give Mr Pitt the French West Indies to keep him quiet'. The English agent Colonel Munro reported in early January 1793 that 'the king's friends of course wish' for war, 'in hopes of creating a counter-revolution', while republicans 'wish by every means to avoid it, though at the same time they talk exceeding big, and even seem to threaten England'.[7] Such big talk was soon to prevail, though the king's friends were to be sorely disappointed.

Meanwhile, tensions were also rising on the border between newly conquered Belgium and the Dutch Republic. The opening of the Scheldt was cause for diplomatic alarm, but internal Dutch politics were also raising the spectre of French intervention. The old

France had had to sit by impotently and watch in 1787 as Prussian troops, with English backing, reinstalled the Stadtholder, *de facto* monarch, over a 'Patriot' and French-oriented rebellion from the urban elite.[8] Now that restoration was itself trembling on the brink of a new wave of Patriot mobilisation, one which the new Republic could hardly resist engaging with. Thus, when the Republic declared war on England on 1 February, spreading the conflict to the high seas of the world, it also declared war on the Stadtholder's regime, and ordered General Charles-François du Périer Dumouriez, former Foreign (and briefly War) Minister in the Girondin ministry of early 1792, and now commander of French forces on the northern front, to launch a winter offensive.

Dumouriez's position was complex. He was widely regarded as a leading political actor – much diplomatic correspondence, for example, referred to the government that he had been part of as 'the Dumouriez ministry'.[9] When he was ousted from political office, military service appeared to offer new avenues for distinction, as the Valmy–Jemappes campaign seemed to demonstrate. Moreover, when he had liberated Belgium in November, Dumouriez had hoped to install an independent republic (as had the several thousand exile Belgians, survivors of a radical movement suppressed by Austrian troops in 1790, who went with him). Whether Dumouriez had seriously thought of setting himself up as ruler of this new republic is a moot point, but he had been inconclusively implicated, with Danton, in shady political and financial dealings after the decision instead to incorporate the territory into the French Republic under 'revolutionary administration'.[10] While these rumours of scandal and faction were unfolding through the winter, Dumouriez had also had to watch his victorious armies begin to dissolve: the one campaign that ended at Jemappes was the term of enlistment many volunteers raised during the summer had thought they had agreed to.

One Parisian volunteer recorded the casual terms on which such enlistments were treated by some. He joined up on 1 October 1792, but finding the march north rather fatiguing, took a stage-coach instead, rejoining his battalion on the border. He disdained to join them in bivouacs, taking lodgings in an inn, but as 'I continued to spit blood' he left the service on 30 November, leaving behind a letter of intentions only later endorsed by his officers. Service was, as he commented, 'in no sense obligatory. Two hundred young men had already left this battalion before it reached Belgium ... Moreover, there had never been any question of fighting except for the express purpose of driving the enemy out of France ... None of us was regarded as a professional soldier.'[11] While tens of thousands of men drained away from French forces, those of the enemy were steadily growing in strength. Straightforward numerical superiority had been a key factor in the French victories of the autumn, and the weight of revolutionary volunteering had been made more significant still by the siphoning of Prussian and Austrian troops into eastern Europe. Here, aggressive Russian intervention in Poland seemed to threaten war, and the Prussians virtually abandoned the western front for several months, leading to the swift French seizure of the Rhineland. Austrian forces were diverted to a lesser extent, but both were allowed to refocus on the French problem by the partition of Poland agreed on 23 January – Austria got little, except an end to uncertainty, while Prussia and Russia carved up the remains of the independent state between them.[12]

Dumouriez was thus a general politically disappointed and militarily overstretched. It was a dangerous position to leave him in, as events would prove. There had already been rumours in the diplomatic community in early January that he was plotting a *coup d'état*, or had intended to rescue the king, or had entered into a secret treaty with the king of Prussia after Valmy.[13] Obeying his orders, he launched the offensive against the Dutch, avoiding the complex waterways and marshes of the coastline and striking at the inland fortifications of Breda and Maastricht. Dumouriez succeeded in driving north to take Breda on 25 February, after a week's siege, but an advance to the east under his subordinate Francisco de Miranda, a Spanish-American military adventurer, stalled at Maastricht, where Prussian reinforcements had stiffened the garrison. On 1 March, Miranda was outflanked by an Allied army twice his twenty thousand effectives, forced to abandon the siege and make a hasty and disorganised retreat. He lost three thousand men to Austrian cavalry charges, for only a few dozen enemy casualties.[14]

What followed was both military and political collapse. While the Convention at home broadened the war by declaring against Spain, on 7 March, Dumouriez left his forces in Holland and tried to rally troops further south to stem the Austro-Prussian tide. At the same time, he nullified by decree some of the measures of revolutionary administration, and closed Jacobin clubs as a source of unrest, attempting to get more conservative elements of the Belgian civilian population on his side. Angry correspondence with the Convention reinforced the impression that both the situation and the general were out of control. An attempted counter-attack at Neerwinden on 18 March turned into a decisive French defeat, and five days later Dumouriez agreed to an armistice with the Austrian general Coburg on his own authority, conditional on a French evacuation of the Austrian Netherlands, which was complete by the end of March.

Triumph was turned to disaster, and now compounded by base treachery. Coburg had agreed to the truce because it was Dumouriez's avowed intention to do as Lafayette had sought to do: turn his troops on Paris and install a sensible, moderate regime, devoid of expansionist tendencies and wild rhetoric. As he plotted, Dumouriez took the desperate step of arresting the current War Minister, who had come to his camp with four Convention deputies to investigate the situation (and most likely detain him, Dumouriez having openly declared himself against the Convention on 27 March). He handed all five of them over to the Austrians on 1 April. Now Dumouriez outlined his plans to the forces still under his command. The troops, however, refused to march. Trapped, the general gave himself up to the Austrians on 5 April, his treason consummated by emigration, that cardinal sin of the revolutionary catechism.

So it was that a former Girondin minister had betrayed the Republic in blatant terms. The implications of the astonishing events on the northern frontier could not have found a more receptive audience than the politicians and radical activists of Paris. February and March 1793 had seen a continued escalation in the ferocious conflict between Mountain and Gironde, with the radical forces of the Paris Commune and Sections increasingly weighing in the balance against the latter. Gouverneur Morris reported on 7 March that 'already they begin to cry for a dictator', and that 'great exertions' were being made to 'bring about a new revolution' against the Girondins.[15] News of the looming disaster in Belgium had caused frantic alarm in Paris by 8 March, when Danton called for volunteers to march north – perhaps opening the way to new massacres, as in September.[16] On 9 March, the printing presses of Girondin newspapers were smashed by armed militants, inspired by a small radical club with close associations to the journalist and municipal prosecutor Hébert. The next day saw a wider but disorganised movement, ultimately a failed attempt to launch a purge of the Convention, encouraged by the well-established Cordeliers Club and joined by a new group of ultra-radicals, rapidly dubbed by their opponents the 'Madmen', or Enragés.

These were an amorphous group, their leaders lacking the solid institutional base that Hébert and his ilk had by now secured in the Commune. Two of the most notable figures were Jacques Roux, a provincial priest based in Paris since 1790, who preached a radical economic egalitarianism based on his experience of serving a vast and impoverished inner-city parish; and Jean-François Varlet, a full-time activist with independent means who nonetheless shared Roux's message, with its concomitant dimension of conviction that the Revolution and the *sans-culottes* were being betrayed by the wealthy class for their own selfish interests.[17] Although these individuals held only a fluctuating influence over a loose grouping of the more radical Sections and clubs, their views were coming ever more in line with the times. They had already gained support from the journalism of Marat, who had announced during the food riots of late February that 'the exorbitant rise in prices of goods of the first necessity' was a plot 'to desolate the people', led by a vast coalition of 'the capitalists, the speculators, the monopolists, the luxury merchants, the instruments of chicanery, the old judges, the ex-nobles, etc.'.[18]

For those such as Marat and the Enragés, the Girondins were incontestably part of this conspiratorial morass, and were primarily responsible for blocking moves to regulate the economy in favour of the poor, precisely to maintain the effectiveness of their 'famine plot'. The fact that almost all members of the Convention found it hard to break free from the straitjacket of political economy passed the Enragés by as they sought a clear target for popular wrath. As the views of the Enragés gained support in Paris, in mid-March the Convention established the death penalty for at least one measure of economic egalitarianism, threatening with the guillotine anyone who advocated the forcible redistribution of land.

Acts such as this were part of an astonishing programme of draconian legislation that the Convention embarked on from the late winter of 1793. Even as its internecine hatreds continued to gnaw at its innards, that body threw out measures of unprecedented rigour that would reshape the whole social and political landscape of

France. The tone had been set in mid-February, with the rapid rejection of a 'Girondin Constitution' that was largely the work of the philosopher Condorcet. The project was scorned by Montagnards as insufficiently centralised, a recipe for weakness and division in the One and Indivisible Republic.[19] It was strength and unity the Republic needed, and in the last week of February the Convention set out to give France's degraded military establishment just that. The armies were currently organised in *ad hoc* groupings, some understrength regular regiments, some National Guard units, and some totally new formations of the volunteers of 1791 and 1792. The latter, known as 'blues' from their new uniforms, had considerable tensions with the regular troops, who still wore the white of the old army, and were known derisively as 'white-arses'. Meanwhile, the emigration of noble officers had gutted the officer corps. Although a backbone of professional officers and senior NCOs remained, and some branches, notably the artillery, were still in good shape, the overall effect was one of disorganisation, with a steady shrinkage in effective numbers. The hard winter of 1792–1793 left the glories of the victorious campaigns of Valmy and Jemappes as little more than happy memories.

The extraordinary testimony of 'the woman Favre', who served as a soldier on the front line in the north, reveals the spirit, but also the dissatisfactions, of the troops who had stuck to their posts over the winter. Favre was captured by the enemy on 1 March 1793, and only revealed to be a woman when they stripped her of her outer garments – preparatory, she said in a deposition upon returning to Paris, to her execution, 'in the same way as the other prisoners, whom the enemy slaughtered by slicing with their swords'. A cavalry captain protected her when her sex was revealed, and she feigned ignorance of German when officers tried to interrogate her. Within a few weeks she was back inside French lines, able to report on overheard conversations at the enemy headquarters. Favre, incidentally, was far from the only woman who had put on a soldier's uniform and gone to the front. Serving not far from her over the winter of 1792–1793 had been Félicité Duquet, known as 'Vadeboncoeur', or Go With Good Heart, a cheery martial nickname. Her commander wrote that he had been 'apprised . . . that she is of the female sex' only when ill-health brought on by the winter weather induced her to ask for a discharge in February 1793, and he testified in her release papers that she had 'conducted herself with valour and courage in all the actions' of the unit.[20]

At least forty other women are known to have served in the ranks in 1792–1794, and there may well have been hundreds of others. Some were impetuous youngsters, like Anne Quatresols, a cavalry trooper at the age of thirteen who won honours in half a dozen battles. Rose Bouillon, by contrast, enlisted alongside her husband, 'wishing to also contribute to strengthening the Republic', leaving two children at home with her mother, and fought on when he died at her side. Others became old campaigners, and even, in the case of Ursule Aby, an officer. A decree of 30 April 1793 ordered all such women home from the ranks, but it was widely ignored – many of the women continued to be successfully disguised as men – and those who were recognised might be lionised for their courage even when it was seen askance as something not quite natural.[21]

Favre, who had joined the ranks after taking comforts to her husband, a captain of gunners in a Parisian battalion at Liège, was lauded in Paris and brought before the Convention for praise – but once there, she launched into a patriotic tirade against the incompetence, and possible treasons, of the generals:

> They leave our brave defenders without arms, without clothes and without boots . . . Many of the soldiers have no muskets and those which the others have are in very bad order, often lacking triggers or locks, although very good ones have been given to enemy soldiers who have infiltrated into our armies. There are whole battalions without breeches . . . the 7th battalion of the Paris army went on parade in this absolutely denuded state under the eyes of citizens Danton and Lacroix, who could not refrain from saying, 'Oh! This lot are really and truly *sans-culottes*.' When this battalion asked Dumouriez for arms, he merely replied, with an impatient gesture: 'Ah, very well, we shall look into that.'[22]

It was not just ordinary footsoldiers who complained. The citizen Beauge, elected to command the third battalion of Paris volunteers, wrote in the spring of 1793 directly to the War Minister, lamenting the destruction of his unit. Already at half-strength after the privations of the winter, it had been left in an exposed position guarding four miles of front near Aachen. The commanding general had scorned requests for the unit to be relieved or reinforced, and soon after they were surprised on the march and overwhelmed by strong enemy cavalry forces – 'None of my men would surrender. In a moment I saw the enemy seize our colours . . .' He rode at them, 'resolved to sell my life dearly', but his horse bolted through the enemy line to safety. He ended with a series of questions:

> Why was the general unaware that the enemy had crossed the river? Why had not the posts along the river been reinforced? . . . Why were we abandoned by the rest of the force at a distance of only six leagues from headquarters? Why were isolated battalions left exposed to attack? . . . Cannot the person or persons responsible for our advanced positions at least be blamed for criminal negligence?[23]

Under the circumstances, the continual drain of personnel from the front-line units was entirely understandable. Remedying the issue of supply would come to be the central concern of the Terror – although the spectre of treason in the high command also remained close to fearful patriots' hearts. To begin to solve the surface issues of organisation, the Amalgame law was passed on 21 February, creating new 'half-brigades' that would unite regular and volunteer forces side by side, allowing each to draw strength from the other. For the wider problem of numbers, the Convention resorted on 24 February to a new policy, reminiscent of Old Regime practices: the Levy of Three Hundred Thousand. This was effectively a measure of conscription. Each department was to meet a quota of new recruits, by volunteering if possible, but by ballot or drawing of lots if necessary, just as the peasants of the eighteenth century had been polled for the hated militia.[24] Given that the 'volunteers' of 1792 had often had to be bribed by local officials with enlistment bounties, or cajoled into enrolling to avoid trouble with the law, the proportion of genuinely new volunteers in 1793 was small (though some discharged former volunteers patriotically re-enlisted, to great political fanfare).

In Paris, and in the northern and eastern regions of the country, where fear of invasion was real and immediate, and where in any case there were often long traditions of military service, the levy was relatively unproblematic, met at worst with resignation and grumbling.

Further west and south, however, it was a different story. Many areas of southern and central France saw considerable discontent, expressed sometimes in conscious efforts to enrol the local patriot elite (or their sons) by force of ballot, obliging authorities to insist on a drawing of lots. At Beaune, near Dijon, the prescribed assembly of those eligible for enrolment attempted to insist that officials, purchasers of nationalised church lands and members of the local Jacobin Club should be the first to be selected. One town's young men even voted to send the local patriot priest off at the head of the list.[25] While such moves reflected a clear antagonism to the Republic, especially from peasants gathered in the towns for the enrolment, they seldom led to overt violence: an outbreak in the Aveyron on 17 March that wounded the mayor of Rodez was almost unique in the south. In the west, however, things were different.

The north-western corner of France was very far from the armies of the Austrians, and very far also from the superheated patriotic atmosphere of Paris. Here, the peasantry remained in large part loyal to the non-juror priests that revolutionary authorities had now been hounding for over two years. They were also steadfast in their antagonism to those town-based, property-owning and openly anti-rural authorities themselves, with their punitive tax assessments and National Guard sweeps of 'unpatriotic' districts. When previous calls for military volunteers had gone out, the peasantry of the west had been happy to ignore them (when they did not respond, as in August 1792, with violence), but this new conscription could not be ignored. Across an arc of territory encompassing some twelve departments, from western Normandy through Brittany and south of the lower Loire, the idea of coerced military recruitment was the spark to a powder-keg of bitterness.

In Normandy the resistance was diffuse, and not always openly violent, but as the news reached further west at the start of March, the Breton peasantry rose up, especially in the Morbihan and Ille-et-Vilaine departments, threatening over half a dozen district capitals, and even the major city of Rennes. Local authorities and National Guards struggled for several weeks to contain a brushfire of rebellion, and though they succeeded in suppressing open revolt, they left behind the seeds of greater troubles for the future. One speaker in the town of Champeaux in the Ille-et-Vilaine had bluntly explained the peasants' attitude: 'We shouldn't pay taxes any more; since there is no more king, there are no more laws . . . The nation is fucked, and all the laws it made are only good to be fucked.'[26] Conscription was indeed only the spark, and the peasant marchers had been calling for the restoration of the old church, and of the crown, and for the end of the urban authorities that now ruled them – and thus for the return of the generous tax exemptions that Brittany had enjoyed for centuries. Marching under the white flag of the Bourbon monarchy, they struck out at signs and emblems of the 'Nation', tearing down the liberty-tree maypoles that many communities had erected, and stamping on tricolour cockades torn from captured patriots' hats. Some of the patriots were even forced to take an oath 'no longer to be national'. For the Breton peasantry, both those who farmed the land and the labourers and craftsmen who lived among them, the 'Nation' was an alien revolutionary intrusion in their way of life, a word that meant nothing in itself, and had merely come to stand for all the impositions and unwelcome changes since 1789.

To the south of Brittany, in what had once been the provinces of Anjou and Poitou, now divided between the Deux-Sèvres, Loire-Inférieure, Maine-et-Loire and Vendée departments, hatreds were even more intense. Here, the poor sharecroppers who made up the backbone of the rural population had seen their tax assessments rise, while the urban landowning elite had piled the abolished tithes and feudal dues on to their leases, by explicit permission of the National Assembly. Their parish priests, to whom they looked as the spiritual centres of far-flung and isolated settlements, were three-quarters non-juring, and already long engaged in cat-and-mouse evasion of revolutionary and republican repression. News of the levy reached here around 3 March, and, from that day on, calls were heard for the 'blues' of the National Guard to be the ones to leave, taking the local administrators with them. Ill-feeling fermented for a further week, and then burst out into paramilitary action. The Republic had only a feeble military presence here: some 1300 soldiers, mostly guarding ports and coastal islands against British invasion.[27] Strategic centres were seized by peasant bands that rapidly gathered into an army, and by the 14th the town of Cholet had been overrun by a force of ten thousand. Only five days later, a column of National Guards attempting to penetrate to the heartland of the revolt was repulsed in full-scale battle at Pont-Charrault, and the War of the Vendée was born.

From its very origins, it was a war of atrocity and counter-atrocity. Years of festering hostility erupted into massacre. In their first weeks of victory the rebels killed dozens of republican captives in each of the towns they seized: hundreds in total. Vengeful National Guard columns slaughtered captured rebels in turn – as on 23 March at the small town of Pornic, for example, where after a republican counter-attack many rebels were found insensible from the town's looted supplies of wine. Even in major centres of republicanism like Nantes and La Rochelle, under no immediate threat of combat, enemies were killed and mutilated as rumours of approaching peasant armies ran wild: in the latter city, six priests were hacked to pieces and their grim remains paraded through the public spaces. At Machecoul in the Loire-Inférieure, the rebels who escaped from Pornic executed over 150 captured republicans with the same quasi-judicial thoroughness shown in the September Massacres.[28] Reasons were found to spare a few dozen others, but the reports of carnage flew back to Paris, and across the nation. Even before the news of Pont-Charrault and Machecoul reached the capital, a decree sentencing all captured rebels to death without appeal had been passed on 19 March.

Between the passage of the Levy of Three Hundred Thousand and the outbreak of the Vendéan War, the Convention had already been busy erecting further draconian measures of mobilisation and control. On 10 March – the day of the failed Enragé rising – it created the Revolutionary Tribunal, a single court to embrace the punishment (by death) of counter-revolutionary offences across France. Based in Paris, it took the form of a normal court, even with a jury, an innovation the Revolution had borrowed from England. But judges and jurors alike were hand-picked from the ranks of revolutionary activists, and it was the Tribunal's chief prosecutor, Antoine Fouquier-Tinville, who wielded the real power. The Tribunal would become a death-machine, its name enough to evoke fear in every corner of the country. It joined another new revolutionary institution, formalised only a day earlier: the representatives-on-mission.[29]

Members of the Convention had been dispatched as commissioners to investigate and communicate with the provinces since that body's inception, but usually only in small numbers, and with limited and specific mandates. On 9 March 1793, however, no fewer than eighty deputies were invested with revolutionary authority, sent out in pairs to designated groups of departments, there to take whatever measures were necessary to ensure the success of the Levy of Three Hundred Thousand, and in general to rally the country to the war effort. Others were sent out soon after, well over a hundred in total within the first month of the concept's operation. Out in the provinces, their arrival would yet again 'revolutionise' local politics. Even where there were no immediate counter-revolutionary disturbances, representatives-on-mission did not hesitate to purge local authorities of those deemed insufficiently patriotic, to raise new local armed forces to hunt down subversives, to levy forced loans and 'contributions' from the wealthy, to imprison suspect figures, and to appoint their own *ad hoc* delegates and commissioners from the ranks of local activists to follow up all these measures with intensified general surveillance.[30]

Surveillance was another key theme of the Convention's measures in this critical season. On 21 March Surveillance Committees were ordered to be formed in every single municipality – including individual villages – and in every neighbourhood Section of larger towns. Every community would thus now have a body specifically charged with monitoring the movements of strangers and suspicious figures. These committees were also given charge of an invention of the previous month, the *certificat de civisme*. These 'Civic Certificates' were mandatory for all public officials, attesting to their patriotism, and would in time become essential for anyone wishing to move around the country, lest they be accounted a suspect at their destination.

In the week following the formation of the Surveillance Committees, the Convention went on to decree that certain categories of person, notably ex-nobles and clergy, were officially 'suspect', and liable to detention and deprivation of civil rights. It declared that all *émigrés* were legally dead, and their properties therefore forfeit. It finally, on 29 March, imposed the death penalty for a variety of press offences: advocating the dissolution of the Convention or the re-establishment of the monarchy, and also for incitement to murder or criminal damage. As this suggests in the light of the Parisian events of 9 and 10 March, despite the heroic measures it was decreeing for the country at large, the Convention still remained caught between its conflict with overt counter-revolution and the ever more bitter faction-fight that pitted the Gironde against the Mountain and its Parisian allies.

This double-edged conflict was highlighted again on 5 April, as Dumouriez was fleeing to the Austrian lines. Marat, serving as president of the Jacobin Club, published a circular to the hundreds of affiliated provincial clubs calling on them to demand the dismissal of Girondin deputies who had voted for the appeal to the people on the king's fate in January. On the same day, the Convention established a new committee, formally empowered to oversee all government activity, and to pass its own decrees for the administration of the country and the war effort. Its name, the Committee of Public Safety, had already been in use for a body with lesser powers, originally set up in January as the Committee of General Defence. This had had over twenty members, including Brissot, Gensonné and Guadet, several other Girondin-inclined figures and a range of others from across the Convention's political spectrum. Its public sessions and large membership (with their political hatreds) had constrained its effectiveness as an instrument of government, and the 'new' Committee of Public Safety was very different. Established initially with just nine members, it would meet in secret, and was granted power to take 'all measures necessary for the internal and external defence of the Republic'.[31] Its very name suggested the power it would ultimately take on – *salut public* in French is the *salus populi* of the ancient Roman tag, that which is the 'supreme law', justifying all actions. In voting on 6 April for the Committee's membership, the Girondins were shut out in favour of a few centrists (including the prominent Bertrand Barère) and a majority that leaned to the left, embodied in Danton, who rapidly became its unofficial leader.

As the Committee of Public Safety bedded in to its new role, the Girondins embarked on another of their disastrous strategic errors. It had been they who had suggested to the Convention, in the panicked atmosphere of 1 April following the first intimations of Dumouriez's treason, that the immunity of Convention deputies from arrest be revoked. Despite that pretext, many at the time saw in this measure the foundation for an attack on the influence of the Mountain, and especially of Marat, whose journalism continued to call unabashedly for the lynching of the Girondins.[32] With immunity revoked, the Girondins found themselves under attack ten days later, when Robespierre indicted 'Brissot, Guadet, Vergniaud, Gensonné, and other hypocritical agents of the same coalition' as members of a 'profoundly corrupt' criminal conspiracy, and demanded that the

Revolutionary Tribunal deal with them alongside a range of fellow criminals, from Marie-Antoinette to Dumouriez's friends, and the duc d'Orléans.[33]

This extraordinary figure, first cousin to the king, had been a background influence and source of funds for radical politics all through the early Revolution, though his obvious eminence made him a target for right-wing conspiracy theorists as soon as unrest began in 1789.[34] Orléans had maintained his leftist connections, changing his name in September 1792 to Philippe Egalité ('equality'), sitting on the left of the Convention, and voting for his cousin's death. Although as we have seen many viewed him as the puppet master of the Jacobins – a reputation that would long outlive him – the Convention turned on him for his close association with Dumouriez (Orléans' son, the duc de Chartres, had gone into emigration with the general), his parliamentary immunity was revoked and he had been arrested on 6 April.[35]

The impact of Robespierre's speech on the 10th, linking the Gironde to the widest possible net of counter-revolution and treason, was electric. While as a formal indictment it fell flat, as a political manoeuvre it pushed the Girondins into hasty action. On both 10 and 11 April, physical fights broke out in the Convention, and on the latter day one deputy even drew his sword, claiming another had pointed a pistol at him. On 12 April Guadet made a counter-attacking speech, denouncing Marat's 5 April circular, and calling for his indictment before the Revolutionary Tribunal. Girondin supporters turned this into a formal proposal, drafting a nineteen-page document detailing Marat's scandalous accusations against the Gironde, and his unhesitating calls for the use of violence against them. Bidding to force the issue into the open before the eyes of all France, they called for a roll-call vote, as had been used to condemn the king, and got one on 14 April. The twin impacts of the national crisis and the bitter atmosphere in the Convention were evident in the voting figures. No fewer than 128 deputies had been sent on mission, including ninety-six identifiable as Montagnards or their sympathisers. Another 238 deputies simply absented themselves from the vote, but over a hundred Girondin supporters and a further hundred neutrals of the Plain pushed through Marat's impeachment against only ninety-three objectors. Fifty-five members registered a formal abstention.[36] Faction and emergency were eating away at the heart of the august body that had voted in such massed solemnity for or against the death of the king.

Marat's trial opened on 24 April. He had evaded arrest for three days (as he had more than once evaded the police of the old Bailly-Lafayette municipality in the Revolution's early years), and when he surrendered he had been put in the Conciergerie prison, in a spacious room where he received guests. These included deputations from the Paris Commune and many others pledging him their loyalty. At the trial, the public galleries applauded him to the rafters, so much so that he had to ask them to be quiet so that his defence could be heard. That defence mixed justification with rebuttal – his denunciations had been right and proper, aimed at enemies of the Revolution, and had neither targeted individuals for murder, nor preached pillage, as the indictment charged. Prosecutor Fouquier-Tinville did not press very hard on these matters, and the newly appointed judges and jury demonstrated that they understood the atmosphere of Paris better than the Girondins, acquitting Marat that same day.[37] Crowned with a triumphal laurel-wreath, Marat was carried back to the Convention by a cheering crowd, and two days later a celebration hosted by the Jacobin Club was so overwhelmed with people that a set of benches collapsed under the weight.

The Girondin attempt to reassert the majesty of the law through manipulation and personal attacks had therefore resoundingly failed, and the magnitude of the failure was already apparent by the date of the trial. Over a week earlier, on 15 April, Mayor Pache and Deputy Procurator Hébert had led a delegation that presented a petition from thirty-five of the forty-eight Sections of Paris to the Convention, asking that a list of twenty-two named Girondin leaders be thrown out of the Convention. The Montagnard leadership recoiled from this, partly because of its nature as an apparent proscription against the sovereign Convention, but also because the petition sought to poll the departments on the expulsion, and Robespierre and others feared the unrest such a consultation would encounter. This allowed the Girondin leadership to scorn the proposal, but the tide of Parisian hostility continued to rise.[38] On 18 April, the Commune itself published a petition with twelve thousand signatures against the 'Twenty-two', a figure rapidly becoming totemic in the politics of the capital. Gensonné in the Convention condemned this as 'a veritable conspiracy against the sovereignty of the people'. Two days later, the Paris Jacobin Club called on its provincial associates to identify and condemn local 'Federalists', a name gaining recognition as labelling those Girondin sympathisers who sought, in Montagnard eyes, to decentralise the Republic out of existence. In response, the former mayor of the city, Jérôme Pétion, once a radical and now firmly aligned with the Gironde, summoned good Parisians in an open letter to cast out the 'venomous insects' dominating the city's politics.[39] Marat's acquittal was therefore confirmation that a struggle to the death, a struggle now clearly between Paris and the Gironde, was under way.

The internal politics of Paris had been evolving rapidly through the spring of 1793. The influence of the Enragés continued to grow, although they remained outside the main lines of municipal power, and meanwhile the individual Sections were beginning to take a stronger lead in radical developments. Those most consciously *sans-culotte* in orientation were advancing two parallel developments. The first was a series of meetings of sectional delegates at the old archbishop's palace, the Evêché, on the Ile de la Cité, where co-ordination of radical action could be done without the burden of the Commune's official responsibilities. The second was the 'fraternisation' movement, in which delegations from the more radical central and eastern Sections effectively coerced the election of new, more *sans-culotte* committees in the less ardent neighbourhoods of the western and northern suburbs. This process could lead to fist-fights, denunciations and even arrests. Not only the Commune but the individual Sections now enjoyed powers of arrest, through their Surveillance Committees, invariably referred to as 'revolutionary committees' in the Parisian context, and a key site of activist *sans-culotte* zeal.[40]

The patriot enemies of the Gironde never secured a complete dominance in the Sections, due in part to the sheer complexity of the power-struggles under way. Sections' general assemblies, their normal 'civil' committees and the revolutionary committees could all be swayed one way or another, and induced to counteract the measures of the other bodies. The personal loyalties and actions of individual Section presidents and secretaries could likewise affect the records, and hence the outcomes, of turbulent events – events often taking place late at night, after the traditional long working day of the artisans. The National Guard headquarters and the officers and men of its sixty battalions – the senior figures often, but not always, the same men as the Sections' leadership – all had a political role to play. The Montagnard-oriented Commune could sometimes be enjoined to intervene, but so too could decrees of the Convention, where a Girondin majority for individual measures was still possible.

Nevertheless, it was clear that the Gironde had lost the capital. Bitter arguments early in May over the passage of price controls on food grains, a so-called 'Maximum', showed that the Girondins remained prepared to stick up for free trade and economic liberalism in the face of *sans-culotte* claims of real starvation and counter-revolutionary conspiracy – and indeed in the face of mass demonstrations, with a reported eight thousand from the Faubourg Saint-Antoine surrounding the Convention on 1 May.[41] On this occasion, unlike earlier in the year, the Girondins lost, driven to defeat by a growing Montagnard realisation that popular anger must be appeased, even if its demands went against the grain of educated thinking, to further both the war effort and the internal security of the Republic. The Gironde did not give in, however, and in response to further waves of *sans-culotte* agitation and threats, they went on the offensive. Louvet wrote in Brissot's paper, the *French Patriot*, on 10 May, condemning 'brigandage and anarchy' and pledging 'between virtue and crime, implacable war, eternal war!'[42]

The Gironde secured a Convention majority on 18 May for the creation of a special 'Commission of Twelve', charged to investigate and repress subversion within the government of Paris. Of the twelve appointed, nine had voted for the appeal to the people in January, and nine also for the impeachment of Marat, while only three had voted for the death of the king – it was, therefore, clearly packed with Girondins.[43] On the same day, Guadet had gone so far as to suggest that a 'substitute Convention', made up of men nominated as replacements at the time of the original elections, be called to Bourges in central France as a measure to preserve national sovereignty against the capital. Brissot called in a pamphlet for the dissolution of the Paris Commune and of the Jacobins, a move that so infuriated the radical journalist Camille Desmoulins that he published a *History of the Brissotins* in which he accused Brissot of having fomented the Revolution itself as part of nefarious plot to ruin France and exalt England. The debate had progressed so far into vitriol that few absurdities seemed unwarranted.[44]

The context of the quarrel, for the enemies of the Gironde, justified all accusations. The Austrians were advancing across the northern frontiers, and were shortly to put two major fortresses at Condé and Valenciennes under siege. In the east, the fortress-city of Mainz was already surrounded, and in the west the rebels of the Vendée had consolidated into a Royal and Catholic Army and were capturing new territory throughout May, defeating even the small numbers of regular troops able to be committed against them. Their fluctuating and ill-equipped forces would nonetheless sometimes reach numbers of up to a hundred thousand, and posed a terrifying threat to the Republic.[45] Meanwhile, the Girondin deputies had openly sided with 'moderate' Parisian Sections in an effort to sabotage the Commune's plans to recruit an additional twelve thousand conscript troops from within the city. A bid to have the choice of men made by local political authorities (and therefore to give the *sans-culottes* the chance to send off their opponents to the front) was condemned by Pétion, and called 'anarchy' by Brissot's *French Patriot*. Vergniaud, Guadet and Buzot were also among those openly supporting resistance to this move, including a demonstration on 6 May in which a crowd of young men chanted 'Down with the anarchists! Marat to the guillotine! To the Devil with Robespierre, Marat, Danton!'[46] With the Girondins' leaders openly abetting what seemed like treasonous resistance in Paris – little better, in effect, than the actions of the Vendéans themselves – things were made worse by reports that those leaders were also encouraging provincial resistance to the acts of representatives-on-mission. Several Girondins wrote advising local authorities to sit in permanent session to safeguard themselves against disbandment, and calling on the propertied classes of the major cities to resist depredations. Vergniaud even advised the good citizens of Bordeaux to arm in their own defence against the anarchists.[47]

The battle between the Girondins and their enemies had now entered its endgame. Ironically, those whom they had initially vilified as aspiring dictators, the Montagnards of the Convention, were stepping back out of the picture as confrontation approached – just as they had on the eve of the assault on the monarchy ten months earlier. It was the activists of Paris itself who would dare to assail the Convention, as they had assailed the Tuileries. Danton, continually swept up with Robespierre and Marat into the diabolical triumvirate of the Girondins' imagination, was in fact playing his usual game of pragmatic ambiguity. On the external front, in his role as unofficial leader of the Committee of Public Safety, he had even made secret overtures towards a truce with the Austrians, but to no avail. Earlier in the year, he had tried to reconcile the two factions, and he continued to make public appeals for fraternal unity within the Convention, and helped to block or divert some of the wilder demands emerging in petitions from the Sections. He supported the need to act for the material well-being of the hungry *sans-culottes*, and even advocated forming a special militia to police the food supply, but he held out against repeated Parisian calls for purges through April and May.[48]

Robespierre's public policy was little different, to the extent that some Parisian activists were criticising him by May as an *endormeur*, lulling them to sleep with false assurances.[49] The Montagnard leadership knew, however, that the risks of allowing an insurrection against the Convention were enormous. The Girondins who would be its target did, after all, command considerable provincial loyalties – and indeed had a significant following in Paris itself, as 6 May had shown. Handled badly, a rising of the *sans-culottes* would look like nothing so much as the anarchist coercion that the Gironde had been warning against all year, and risked destroying the sovereignty and legitimacy of the 'rump' Convention that would remain. The Republic could be shattered, and the counter-revolution flood in triumphant – which, of course, is what the Montagnards suspected the Girondins of wanting.

The Convention itself, stripped of nearly half its members by official missions and unofficial absenteeism, swung back and forth between the factions. On 20 May an eminently *sans-culotte* motion for a billion-livre 'forced loan' from the wealthy was carried, while on the 23rd a Girondin motion authorising the Commission of Twelve to secure an armed guard for the Convention was supported, as was a measure to adjourn all sectional assemblies by 10 p.m. each day. In response to this, the *sans-culotte* Sections merely interrupted their session at ten to reconvene in the same instant as 'popular societies', immune to such regulation. On 24 May, the Twelve struck at the heart of the Parisian movement, arresting Hébert, the Enragé Varlet and several other leading activists. The pretext for Hébert's arrest was an article in which he had accused the Girondins of being paid by Prime Minister Pitt, and of starting the Vendéan Revolt. Interior Minister Garat had pleaded for Hébert to be left alone, openly citing the inflammatory precedent of Marat's acquittal a month before.[50] The Twelve reported to the Convention that plans for an insurrection had been uncovered. When on the 25th a delegation from the Commune protested the arrests to the Convention, its president, the Girondin businessman Maximin Isnard, uttered a dire threat against those who challenged the national representatives: should they harm the Convention, he roared, 'Paris will be annihilated, and men will search the banks of the Seine for traces of the city!'[51]

Such a threat, with its desperate echoes of the Brunswick Manifesto of August 1792, played directly into the hands of the *sans-culottes*, who by now were virtually besieging the Convention with deputations, petitions and increasingly peremptory demands for patriotic action. On 10 May the Convention had moved from the long, narrow hall of the Manège, which had always retained traces of its origins as a riding arena, to a newly created chamber within the Tuileries palace itself, rebuilt from the former private theatre of the monarch. Although this afforded more commodious accommodation to the deputies, it also gave even freer rein to the Parisians to invade repeatedly the space of the national representation.[52] As this pressure was piled on the deputies, the assembly of delegates at the Evêché palace was growing both in size and influence, and, from the middle of the month on, was effectively acting to plan an insurrection. Much of its impetus came from another parallel with the summer of 1792, as a major force of *sans-culotte* volunteers was being prepared to leave for the Vendée under General Santerre of the Faubourg Saint-Antoine. Already stripped of many young men by the Levy of Three Hundred Thousand, the Parisian Sections responded to this new call with remarkable vigour – one Section alone, that of the Place Vendôme, enrolled 277 men in two weeks.[53] With such extraordinary demands being placed on its manpower, Paris needed to be secured for the Republic, and specifically for the *sans-culottes*' vision of that body.

Tumults continued to challenge the Convention from day to day – on 26 May the Twelve had to use National Guards from a nearby 'moderate' Section to clear the chamber after an invasion of *sans-culottes* demanding the Commission's dispatch before the Revolutionary Tribunal. As the Guards worked, Montagnard deputies chorused, 'We are oppressed! We will resist oppression!' That night the Mountain filibustered the session until they had a majority of those with the stamina to remain, and then hastily cashiered the Twelve and released its prisoners. On the 28th the Gironde struck back, asserting that the previous session had not been properly constituted, and the vote inadequately recorded. They forced a formal roll-call vote on the Commission's reinstatement, and won by 267 to 228, with 99 deputies on mission, and 133 elsewhere.[54] This vote, like others recorded in this period, demonstrates that the Girondins were without doubt a minority – a fluctuating group of between 140 and 200 individuals with relatively consistent voting patterns, with a hard core of fewer than a hundred.[55] By contrast, the Mountain could call on some three hundred who were either openly Jacobin and sympathetic to Paris, or who kept a lower profile, but never voted for Girondin or other 'moderate' proposals. With a third or more of these regularly on mission by the spring of 1793, the balance was held by the Plain, some 250 deputies with a low level of political engagement, available to be swayed by arguments and circumstances.[56] One hundred and twenty-seven of these had given the Gironde its majority to reinstate the Commission: their last, and Pyrrhic, victory.

The Sections were now on the march. In the Commune, the freed Hébert spoke in stark terms of purging moderate 'intriguers' from the city and seizing suspects, but his official superior, Pierre-Gaspard Chaumette, procurator of the city, publicly opposed violence: 'no arms, no blood', he had said on 27 May, to loud applause. The legal responsibilities of the Commune made it impossible for an insurrection to be openly planned there, whatever the views of individuals, and it was at the Evêché that more forceful action was plotted. There were two groups operating in the palace in the last days of May. An open assembly of popular-society members, with some five to six hundred attendees, was paralleled by a closed congress of delegates from thirty-three Sections now aligned with the *sans-culotte* movement. The larger body heard debates on what should be done, but its elected leaders, claiming the need to protect their plans, consciously suppressed discussion of real action – action that was being organised by the sectional congress at the same moment. A series of different committees and commissions were formed by these bodies, finally resolved into a nine-member committee on the night of 30–31 May.[57]

Yet another parallel gathering, called by the department of Paris (as opposed to the municipality of the Commune), included delegates of the Commune, the Evêché assembly, and the other districts of the department outside the city walls. Brought together on 31 May at the Jacobin Club, they voted to add eleven members to the nine from the sectional congress, and meanwhile the Commune itself appointed a further four delegates. The final total reached twenty-five, adding Claude-Emmanuel Dobsen, president of the Cité Section (site of the Evêché), and one of those in the custody of the Twelve, who had joined the original nine-member group in the early hours of 31 May, fresh from prison. The expanded body now named itself the Central Revolutionary Committee, and proceeded between 6 and 7 a.m. on 31 May to dissolve, on its own revolutionary authority, all the constituted bodies of the municipality and department. This included the regular General Council of the Commune, immediately reappointed as the 'Revolutionary General Council', thus shorn of legalistic obligations to public order.[58]

The insurrectionaries were nonetheless concerned to reject the image of anarchy thrust upon them by the Girondins. Section Cité, soon followed by the rest of the *sans-culotte* Sections, had explicitly placed all private property under its protection as the movement began. The Central Revolutionary Committee itself was very far from being made up of the sub-proletarian 'brigands' that featured so heavily in social fears of the time. It contained only three men who could be described even loosely as workers: a printer, a shoemaker and a painter-gilder. They were outnumbered both by six lawyers – including Dobsen, who had sat as a district-court judge – and by five other professionals, including two engineers and a doctor. Two men had noble connections, two others were merchants, and most of the rest had long careers in revolutionary activism and public office that had obscured their origins – including the Enragé Varlet with his independent wealth. One of the merchants, Jean-Baptiste Loys, had even denounced his own two brothers as royalists in his home town of Arles, before arriving in Paris in January 1792 with a delegation from Marseille that also included the future Girondin Barbaroux. Alternating between the politics of the south-east and the capital, he had been wounded in the assault on the Tuileries on 10 August 1792, and served as a zealous advocate of popular power on various public bodies.[59]

Although one could argue that the preponderance of professionals and the educated on the Committee had something to do with the delegations sent by the departmental assembly, even the central grouping derived from the Evêché shared the basic attributes of this group, which were far more about ideological commitment to a radical view of popular republicanism than they were about a particular version of social identity. The *sans-culotte* image remained, in political fact, just that: an image projected by advocates and enemies alike, each seeking to frighten the other with a vision, according to taste, of the unruly plebs or the righteous anger of 'the people'. Many thousands of the working people of Paris marched in the rank and file of the insurrection, and no doubt shared the ardent patriotism their leaders expressed on their behalf, but those leaders were still, in the majority, from the educated political classes.

What followed through the daylight hours of 31 May was, despite the determination of the Central Revolutionary Committee, a confused and ultimately inconclusive affair. Some in the Commune, including the influential Chaumette, continued to argue against the folly of armed action against the Convention. Mayor Pache, although acquiescing in the rising, also sought to prevent it degenerating into a new September Massacres. Armed clashes between some radical and moderate Sections were only averted at the last minute when the radicals' own eyes showed them that the moderates, contrary to reports, were not wearing the white cockades of royalist counter-revolution. Within the Convention itself, the rising was far from unexpected. Leading Girondins including Louvet, Buzot, Barbaroux and Guadet went to a secluded room they had prepared in advance during the night of the 30th–31st, and emerged armed in the morning.[60] In the Convention's chamber, some hundred deputies were present as alarm bells rang through the city around 6 a.m., and Montagnard leaders demanded the definitive suppression of the Commission of Twelve. They were countered by Girondin attacks on the Sections and on the new commander of the Paris National Guard, Hanriot, legally responsible for the city's security, and for the alarms currently sounding. Sectional forces, petitioners from the Commune and onlookers gradually pressed into the hall, until deputies sitting on the left moved across to join those on the right, freeing space for the interlopers to sit. In the midst of this process, Vergniaud proposed a motion that the Sections of Paris had 'merited well of the country' – whether he was speaking of the moderate Sections, under the impression they were coming to the Girondins' rescue, or was trying to appease *sans-culotte* anger, or was simply thankful that no overt acts of violence had occurred, remains unclear. He had also sought to leave the hall, only to return, and again whether his aim had been to flee or to appeal in person to the militant crowds is unknown.[61]

The goals of the insurrection were put to the Convention by a delegation that arrived some time after the crowds had invested the hall. They went far wider than the issue of the Commission of Twelve, although the arrest of its members and of the Girondin 'Twenty-two' were prominent demands. The Parisians also wanted a new fixed ceiling on bread prices, a paid 'revolutionary army' of *sans-culottes* to deal with hoarding and subversion, the establishment of state-run arms factories for the war effort, and the arrest of others, including the Girondin Finance and Foreign Ministers, Clavière and Lebrun. The first draft of this address, written by the activist Loys, had gone even further, calling for aid to the old and the sick, public works for the unemployed and the poor, subsidies for soldiers' families, and a thoroughgoing purge of all public administrations. Little of this found favour with the Montagnards, who were deeply conscious of the dangers of being seen to be coerced. Even a spokesman for the Commune sought to portray what was happening as an 'extraordinary movement' and a 'moral insurrection', as opposed to a physically threatening 'brutal' one.[62] After inconclusive debate, in which Vergniaud heckled Robespierre's lengthy and denunciatory speech with demands for a conclusion, a motion put forward by the centrist Bertrand Barère for the abolition of the Commission of Twelve was adopted, the only concrete measure to come from the day.

It was clear that even the most ardent Montagnards in the Convention would not accept the wider demands of the Sections, but the core issue of the fate of the Girondins could not long be postponed. The armed forces of Paris remained in a state of alert, effectively investing the Convention through the next day, in which the question of the Gironde was debated in the Committee of Public Safety. On 2 June, with a massive force of insurrectionary National Guards drawn up around the Tuileries, the Convention listened as Barère again put forward a compromise: a list of deputies would voluntarily suspend themselves from office for a time, removing their apparent threat to national unity. Four Girondins offered to resign on the spot. However, this was not enough for the Sections. The Commune (where Marat was participating in debates) and the Central Revolutionary Committee wanted proscriptions, and had already sought to arrest ex-minister Roland overnight – he was not at home, but the police took Madame Roland to the Abbaye prison. The troops who surrounded the Convention grew restive, and deputies began to report that they had been blocked from leaving the Convention, and in several cases manhandled by angry Parisians. Danton spoke of the 'Majesty of the Convention' being outraged, and it adopted a decree ordering the troops to withdraw. When this message was brought to Hanriot, the son of poor peasants from Nanterre, he responded with a passage worthy of Père Duchesne himself: 'Tell your fucking president that he and his Assembly are fucked, and that if within one hour he doesn't deliver to me the Twenty-two, I'm going to blast it!'[63]

With the reality of the situation beginning to sink in, even some Montagnards grew alarmed, and Barère proposed that the deputies should march out and assert their freedom. This they did under the leadership of Marie-Jean Hérault de Séchelles, an aristocratic Montagnard in the mould of Lepeletier, who had taken up the presidency of the session after Hanriot's outburst. Several hundred deputies, including all but thirty of the Montagnards present, trooped out into the Tuileries gardens, where Hanriot waited on horseback before his troops. He greeted Hérault as a 'good patriot' and one of the Mountain, and asked him to swear that the Twenty-two would be surrendered. Hérault refused, and the general's reply was to signal his troops to make ready. Cannons were primed, cavalrymen drew their swords and the infantry levelled their muskets.

This was the fatal moment. The Parisian troops had been stood to arms for three days. Pay they had been promised had not yet been voted for, despite repeated demands. Their rage at the Girondins was unequivocal. At the Champ de Mars on 17 July 1791, and at the Tuileries on 10 August 1792, it was at moments like this that undisciplined shooting from National Guards had instituted massacre. Paris, the Convention and all of France trembled on the very brink of an abyss. The discipline of the *sans-culottes* held, and before their ranks the deputies gave in and abandoned their initiative. Helpless, they filed back into the hall, where they were joined, as on 31 May, by Parisians who freely mingled among them. Georges Couthon, a wheelchair-bound Montagnard lawyer, now proposed that the Girondins' arrest should be voted. Vergniaud tartly replied that perhaps he would like a glass of blood to slake his thirst, but the list of the expelled was drawn up nonetheless. Marat took an active part in editing the final version.[64] Twenty-nine deputies were listed – twenty of the totemic Twenty-two, and nine from the Twelve – plus the ministers Clavière and Lebrun. The vote was carried by an uncertain majority: the record was later tampered with, and most opponents of the Mountain abstained. With the issue decided, the forces of Paris finally released the Convention, but only after receiving orders to do so from the Commune.

The expelled Girondins were held in surprisingly lax house arrest, from which many escaped over the following weeks. They fled to the provinces, to the departments whose wrath they had collectively threatened Paris with on so many occasions. As they fled, they helped to send France down a terrible slope towards a civil war between republicans, adding to the woes of a country already assailed from within and without. One of the demands of the insurrection of 31 May had been for action against a reported anti-Jacobin coup by the citizens of Marseille, and the movement of 2 June had been strengthened in its determination by the first reports of armed insurrection against the Jacobin authorities of France's second city, Lyon. Despite the bloodlessness of the coup against the Convention, and its much vaunted 'moral' nature, the actions of the Parisians had worsened the already precarious condition of the Republic. If France had stepped back from one abyss when the deputies retreated unscathed from Hanriot's troops, the triumph of the Montagnards would prove little less perilous. The fight between Paris and the Gironde, between the much mocked 'statesmen' and the despised 'anarchists', was about to become a war for France herself, and for the fate of the Revolution.

# Chapter 7

# Holding the Centre

Three months after the Convention had been purged, it was once again under siege. Thousands of *sans-culottes* surrounded the Tuileries on 5 September 1793, in a movement that had begun the day before as a popular demonstration against the scarcity of bread.[1] Protests outside the City Hall had been co-opted by the radical leadership of the Commune into a march on the Convention to petition for new measures against hoarders and other political enemies. The Commune even ordered workshops to close the next day, a Thursday, so that workers could attend the demonstration. A swelling tide of activity through the night resulted in a huge mobilisation, incorporating not just the municipal delegation, but a combined petition from the Jacobin Club and the forty-eight Sections of the capital. They came together quite literally in the shadow of an extraordinary phenomenon. A major eclipse, covering three-quarters of the sun's disc, cast Paris into an eerie twilight just before noon on the 5th, causing the worldly-wise Parisians some amusement as they prepared their insurrection. Not for them the superstitious fears of earlier generations at such natural events. The ancient Romans, whom so many revolutionaries revered for their republican virtues, would not have laughed so easily at such an omen, on such a day.[2]

As petitioners thronged the Convention, many issues were put forward, but the tone of the day was set by a delegation from the Jacobins:

> It is time that equality bore its scythe above all heads. It is time to horrify all the conspirators. So legislators, place Terror on the order of the day! Let us be in revolution, because everywhere counter-revolution is being woven by our enemies. The blade of the law should hover over all the guilty.[3]

In the aftermath of these words, a great revolutionary moment took on its definitive contours. From now on the Republic would be officially engaged in terror, and the landscape of social and political relations, already transformed more than once by Revolution, would be radically changed once again. Unlike the demands that brought down the Gironde, however, these moves did not split the Convention, nor did their bloodthirsty implications even occasion much immediate concern among its members. A long hot summer of civil war had hardened the hearts of good republicans, and reinforced all of their beliefs and goals. Despite significant continuing differences, the experience of a fight for survival would send republican France into the Terror with a population mobilised to an unheard-of extent, and ready to commit remarkable crimes in the name of liberty.

The *sans-culotte* Sections that had risen up against the Girondins on 31 May and 2 June did not limit their zeal to the twenty-nine culprits expelled from the Convention. In the days after, several hundred 'suspects' were seized by sectional activists and other officials, often resulting in complex exchanges between all the competing authorities of the city. The journalist Louis-Marie Prudhomme, for example, had begun (like many Girondins) as a radical in 1789, but was now suspiciously centrist to some. He was arrested, released, rearrested and re-released, all in the few days after 2 June. Such was the determination of his home Section, Unité, to have him in custody that the municipal leaders Chaumette and Hébert had to deliver his second release order personally to have it carried out. In a token of the confusion of the time, Prudhomme himself then took an active part in the lengthy discussion that this final release brought on in the Section's revolutionary committee.[4] Madame Roland, arrested before the insurrection began, was released at some point in its course, and was at home with her husband over the following days as he resisted arrest by the simple recourse of claiming to need to address the Convention. The sectional delegates sent to seize him were nonplussed, and considerable to-and-fro resulted. Both the Commune's General Council and the Central Revolutionary Committee had to be consulted before the couple were finally taken under the 'care' of the Sections.[5]

Those Girondin leaders who had surrendered themselves to Parisian custody were held in a slipshod form of house arrest for most of the following month: not until 24 June did the Convention decree that they should be moved to a central location, and even that move was not speedily executed. It seems that some in the Convention, a poorly attended body through much of June, intended that the expelled deputies should be treated well, and perhaps even ultimately reintegrated with it.[6] As a consequence of their loose guard, the majority of them slipped away from Paris. This included Roland (who left his wife behind in custody), Gorsas, Buzot, Barbaroux, Guadet, Louvet and Pétion, most of whom fled to join and encourage growing anti-Parisian sentiment in Normandy over the course of the month, as did several other less well-known deputies.

Jacques-Pierre Brissot, arch-enemy of the radicals, had been among the first to escape, but was also the first recaptured. He had passed through his home town of Chartres and was en route for Caen, centre of the Norman resistance, when he was arrested travelling on false papers on 10 June and shipped back to the capital.[7] Only two of the Gironde's leading figures, Vergniaud and Gensonné, elected to remain voluntarily in Paris. The latter, however, incited trouble in Bordeaux by writing an address to the city's inhabitants, received there on 8 June, claiming that the Parisian rising had been an attempt at legalised assassination of himself and others. Vergniaud remained more passive, although at the end of the month he would publish a pamphlet accusing Bertrand Barère and Robert Lindet, two relatively moderate politicians who had sided with the insurrection, of refusing to confront the Girondins with charges they could defend while smearing them with accusations of fomenting revolt.[8] Given the words of Gensonné, and the actions of those in Caen, including Barbaroux, who wrote home to Marseille on 18 June urging a new march on Paris and the 'punishment of the assassins', this was disingenuous in the extreme.[9]

On the other hand, the leadership of the Convention now found itself in a very sticky situation. On 5 June, Mayor Pache of Paris had reported to the Committee of Public Safety that no incriminating evidence against the expelled Girondins had been found during the searches of their papers, and the Committee had to admit this to the Convention the next day. Explaining the actions of the Parisians to the rest of the country thus grew much harder. Danton, as the Committee's unofficial leader, and the centrist Barère, another key member, together proposed a number of measures that effectively conceded the Convention's awkward position: the suppression of the Sections' revolutionary committees and the dismissal of Hanriot from command of the National Guard, and the dispatch of twenty-nine deputies to the expelled Girondins' home departments as hostages for their safety. This was an extraordinarily overt admission of the tensions the expulsion was creating, and intolerable to more earnest supporters of the insurrection. Robespierre and others condemned the proposals, and, with stalwart Montagnards the only consistent attenders in the Convention, this agenda was buried. For the rest of the month, however, the Convention would continue to hesitate over the Girondins' fate, and indeed over the best way forward for the country as a whole. It was events elsewhere that would settle the matter, and drive the Republic further into peril.[10]

Although the escaped Girondins concentrated in Normandy, and campaigned to raise an army there against Paris, the most severe threats to the power of the Convention and the unity of France arose in a very different region, and one long troubled already by social and political conflicts. The two great cities of the south-east, Lyon and Marseille, had begun a slide into confrontation long before the Parisian insurrection. Both held over a hundred thousand people, and both had faced great economic troubles: Lyon's staple silk industry was in dramatic decline, while Marseille's Mediterranean trade links were severed by war with Britain, Spain and the Italian states. Both cities had faced unrest through the winter, with popular hunger increasingly poorly addressed by a Jacobin political machine that continued to consolidate power through municipal elections and Club apparatus. Both cities were also riven by political dissent. Supporters of the Girondins had become convinced that the local Jacobins were intent on pillage in the name of 'anarchy', and in self-defence had begun to assert their political voice through neighbourhood Section meetings. In Marseille, in response, the Jacobin club and city leadership had by March 1793 begun to disarm and arrest those it designated as 'suspects', and was forming a new armed force of six thousand men, with the authority of two recently arrived and sympathetic representatives-on-mission. Although the levy was superficially prompted by reports of widespread Catholic and royalist unrest in nearby departments, the fears of the moderate Sections were that these troops would be turned on them in a Jacobin coup.[11]

April in Marseille saw crisis turn to confrontation, as news arrived in the second week of the month that the duc d'Orléans and his family were to be imprisoned in the city by order of the Convention. Arrested after Dumouriez's treason, Orléans represented to local Jacobins the spectre of counter-revolution in the guise of moderation, and there was radical disquiet at the tensions his presence might arouse. Moderates, however, were equally traumatised, as Orléans' murky connections with radical journalists and politicians made him just as likely in their eyes to turn Marseille into the epicentre of an 'anarchist' coup against the Girondins in the Convention, perhaps with the six thousand new troops from the city as its nucleus. Ten days after this news broke, the representatives-on-mission in Marseille ordered the closure of the Sections in nearby Aix, after reports that the latter intended to charge some local Jacobins with the murder of prisoners earlier in the year. This was enough for the Marseille Sections to take action in their own defence, first by protest, and then by trying to abort the formation of the six thousand. The representatives fled the city at the end of the month in fear of their lives, and on 2 May issued a decree condemning the Sections as counter-revolutionary, noting that they 'openly manifest a tendency towards federalism'.[12]

Throughout May the new authorities in Marseille purged the Jacobin presence in the city, including a wave of arrests on 18–19 May, and then attempted to justify themselves to the Convention. Their delegation was booed in the Convention on 25 May, as they presented a petition against the excesses of the Jacobins with a reported twenty-five thousand signatures. The representatives, they claimed, had 'surrounded themselves solely with the factious and the disorganisers . . . they have been nothing but apostles of discord and anarchy . . . In every Section they have tried to erect a wall of separation, which . . . could produce nothing but the fomentation of hatred and the ignition of civil war.'[13] All too prophetic, this news from Marseille had been one of the factors spurring on the original *sans-culotte* rising of 31 May. The more successful one of 2 June drew determination from events in Lyon which had gone even further.

For reasons very similar to those of Marseille, political tensions in France's second city had reached the boiling point on 29 May. A Jacobin municipality led by an extremist demagogue, Marie-Joseph Chalier, was using the support of a pair of representatives-on-mission to see off a challenge from the moderates grouped in the Sections. Orders had gone out to the Army of the Alps in Grenoble to send a column of troops to the city's aid. To pre-empt their arrival, the sectional movement struck out, seizing the city's fortified arsenal on the morning of the 29th and making it the headquarters for a military advance by the local National Guard on the City Hall in the late afternoon. Two hours of pitched battle followed, with Jacobin supporters turning artillery on the besieging infantry before their final rout. There were only a few dozen verifiable casualties, but the slaughter of eight hundred patriots featured in the report of the rising read to the Convention on 2 June. Even as this hardened Parisian hearts, the Lyonnais had consolidated their victory by replacing the council with moderate appointees, and forcing the two representatives, captive in the arsenal, to order the troops approaching the city to reverse their course.[14]

Although the events in Marseille, Lyon and Paris all fed off each other in the lead-up to the fall of the Gironde, after 2 June politics briefly sank into stunned inaction. Suddenly, through a whole combination of local and national factors, political confrontation had been resolved by brute force – as of course it had been so often since 1789, but never so close to the heart of a political class that only months before had seemed staunchly republican and revolutionary. And for much of the country, it was the Parisians who were in the wrong. The assault on the national representation was protested in writing by no fewer than forty-seven of France's departments, as against only thirty-four who expressed support for the Montagnard position, or kept silent.[15] Virtually the whole of southern and western France participated in protest, with only the north-eastern frontiers and the centre, south of Paris, being more or less solidly behind the capital. As things turned out, for the majority written protest from local authorities was as far as their dissent would go, but around

Lyon, Marseille, Bordeaux and Caen there was real revolt in over a dozen departments.

As we have seen, it was in Caen, closest of these four centres to Paris, that the escaped Girondins concentrated. Although by far the smallest of the four 'federalist' cities, Caen and its surrounding Calvados department provided a relatively secure base for anti-Parisian agitation. Throughout the winter and spring the department and its deputies had been conducting a regular correspondence laced with denunciation of the Parisian 'disorganising party', and the department administrators, only days before the Parisian insurrection, had promised to raise an armed force to protect the Convention, pledging 'war to the death against anarchists, proscribers and factionists'.[16] A delegation dispatched to the capital arrived in time to witness the end of the 2 June events, and to confer for several days with expelled deputies, returning to Caen on 8 June, where they painted a grim picture of the factional forces at work in the capital. By the end of that day, orders had gone out from the town to arrest two representatives-on-mission in nearby Bayeux, and an invitation was made to the local military commander, General Félix Wimpffen, to confer with the authorities. By the next day, the Girondin deputies had begun to arrive, further hardening attitudes – the special general assembly of the town's councillors voted to reject all measures emanating from the Convention, and to form an armed force in conjunction with neighbouring departments to march on the capital. No fewer than eight such departments quickly sent delegates to Caen, and plans were laid to gather the force at Evreux (home town of the deputy Buzot, guiding light of the movement). It was at this point – when individuals had to commit themselves to marching against Paris – that things began to stall. Despite enthusiastic claims that the troops would enter Paris welcomed as liberators, it was not until 10 July that a meagre force of two thousand assembled under Wimpffen's command, raked up from a few regular forces, various departments' small contingents of volunteers and a battalion originally raised in Calvados to go to the Vendée.[17]

While the Girondins and their supporters were struggling to mobilise manpower in the north-west, the region that had given their 'faction' its nickname, around the city of Bordeaux, was also facing a crisis in its resistance. The politics of Bordeaux before 1793 had been relatively tranquil compared to the other great cities of

France. The wealth of the city, lying on the banks of the Garonne river just to the south of its opening into the broad estuary of the Gironde, came from the slave trade. Over the eighteenth century the profits of shipping sugar from the Caribbean colonies of Martinique, Guadeloupe and Saint-Domingue – wealthiest of all the sugar islands – had built fine new boulevards, squares and public buildings along the Bordeaux waterfront. Since 1791 unrest in those colonies had curtailed the profits of the local elites, and war with Britain in 1793 effectively shut down normal transatlantic trade (although some would continue to prosper by fitting out privateers to assail British merchantmen). The attitudes of the Bordelais elite turned around the values of secure constitutional government and free trade. Their rising horror at the treatment of their leading spokesmen in the Convention was thus compounded by the evolving details of the draconian legislation of the spring.

Reaction in Bordeaux to news of 2 June had been furious, and sectional assemblies had reportedly been flooded with aggrieved citizens intent on acting against the usurpations of the capital. By 7 June, scarcely twenty-four hours after reports from Paris had reached the city, and with news also in hand of the events in Lyon and Marseille, a 'Popular Commission for Public Safety' had been formed to take over the running of the city and department, and to organise revolt. Two days later the Commission dispatched messages to the communities of the department calling on them to help form an armed force to resist 'tyranny', and on the 11th delegates were sent out in nine teams, destined for over three-quarters of France's departments, to spread word of the insurrection and summon support. However, by 14 June, when the Commission ordered the city of Bordeaux to raise six hundred men as a contribution to their forces, there were already recalcitrant protests from some urban Sections. Just as in Caen, it proved impossible to meet the original goals of this recruitment, and indeed it was not until early July that some four hundred men marched out of the city. Most of them were labourers signed on for a daily wage agreed in desperation by the Commission. By this time the potential for active resistance in Bordeaux was waning fast – there had not even been sufficient impetus to arrest two representatives-on-mission in the city at the start of June, although they were closely watched, and a further pair of deputies visited the city later in the month, to a hostile welcome, but no threats to their persons or liberty.[18] Bordeaux's earlier political tranquillity appears to have reflected a general unwillingness of individuals to commit themselves to violent political action – a reluctance noticeably absent in the capital, or France's other great cities. The feeble 'departmental army' never left the boundaries of the Gironde, and broke up at the end of July.

To focus on the efforts of Caen and Bordeaux to raise military forces against the Convention is to suggest that the 'Federalist revolt' was no real threat to Montagnard control of France. That is of course not true. Between them the two cities had taken nearly a dozen departments out of the control of the capital, in regions which both stood between the centre and a war front: the Vendéan Revolt was in full flood, and Spanish forces had joined hard fighting in the Pyrenees. With the counter-revolutionary enemy active on every frontier (thanks in part to the Convention's zealous extension of the scope of the war – something for which the Girondins could still be blamed), losing contact with major regions of the country could have fatal consequences.

What was true of the western cities was true in spades for those of the south-east. Lyon was a supply centre for armies in the Alps, Italy and the eastern Pyrenees, and a key hub of road communications. With its surrounding department, it was also a major centre for arms manufacture and stockpiling. Losing Lyon for the Republic could mean the collapse of all southern France.[19] This was especially the case as the cities of Provence, including Nîmes, Avignon and the naval port of Toulon, were showing every sign of following Marseille into Federalist revolt. The armies on the frontiers were in serious danger of being caught between converging fires. Edmond-Louis-Alexis Dubois-Crancé, the former professional soldier who was representative-on-mission with the Army of the Alps near Grenoble, had seen the danger clearly, and as early as 2 June had ordered the advance of several thousand troops towards Lyon. Although stymied by a meeting with the two deputies who had been in Lyon on 29 May, who persuaded him to await developments, Dubois-Crancé's aggressive attitude was well known in Lyon, and a decree on 7 June from the Convention placing him in charge of measures to 'restore calm and public tranquillity' in the city raised fears further.[20]

Nevertheless, for several weeks the situation stalled. The Convention sent a more moderate deputy, Robert Lindet, on mission to Lyon to see if relations could be maintained. He remained in the city for a week from the 8th to the 16th, shunted from one provisional authority to another, and unable to gain a solid purchase on the politics of the city. He did at least hold off the threat of a more decisive immediate break, but he left empty-handed.[21] In Lyon itself, the aftermath of insurrection had been remarkably similar to that in Paris – sectional militants, in this case of an anti-Jacobin persuasion, rounded up several hundred of their political enemies, often under confused circumstances, while politically suspect units of the National Guard were stripped of their weapons, and a general atmosphere of uneasy anticipation prevailed.[22] In the second half of June, the situation began to deteriorate further. With news arriving of the apparent success of Federalist movements elsewhere, the Lyonnais were emboldened to begin formalising new power-structures outside the Convention's authority, and the summoning of new electoral assemblies towards the end of the month allowed further grassroots anti-Jacobin hostility to find expression. The rhetoric emanating from Lyon's Federalist bodies grew ever stronger – one address to the Republic on 14 June swore that the city would 'march against the rebels opposing the national will' in Paris.[23] Unfortunately, this was exactly the same kind of rhetoric that the Lyonnais were hearing from centres such as Bordeaux and Caen, thus giving the impression of a swelling tide of national resistance when there was in reality almost no coherent military preparation.

Lyon's municipal government began to plan an armed force on 19 June, but the wider department administration did nothing, and by the end of the month plans for independent military action had been shelved in favour of waiting to join forces supposedly advancing from Marseille. Those forces would never succeed in moving up the Rhône, and Dubois-Crancé's troops were already taking position to isolate the two centres of revolt. Within a few weeks, on the symbolic date of 14 July, the Rhône bridgehead at Pont-Saint-Esprit would be retaken from Federalist forces based in Nîmes, cutting even the possibility of a link-up. Meanwhile, as they sought out military leadership for their troops, the Lyon Federalists were increasingly turning to men whose views were not those of the Gironde. On 8 July the comte de Précy was made commander of the departmental army (such as it was), and secretly exempted from taking a republican loyalty oath.[24] By the middle of July, Précy had pulled together a headquarters staff of ex-nobles, including one, his nephew, who was an outright *émigré*.[25]

With Lyon increasingly isolated, and drifting into association with overt counter-revolution, things already looked bleak for the Federalists' original ambitions. On 12 July, the city was declared to be in a state of rebellion by the Convention. On 13 July, one day before the southern cities were sundered at Pont-Saint-Esprit, two events occurred which further sealed their doom. At Pacy-sur-Eure in Normandy, Wimpffen's meagre Federalist force that had assembled three days before was routed as it attempted to advance towards the capital under a subordinate general, the comte de Puisaye. With Caen wide open to the Montagnard advance (and its citizens soon to make a swift and politic renunciation of their Federalist allegiance), Girondin leaders fled. Some, notably Buzot, Barbaroux and Pétion, headed for Bordeaux, others just went on the run. Meanwhile in Paris a strikingly attractive dark-haired young woman from Caen named Marie-Anne-Charlotte Corday d'Armont arrived at the lodgings of Jean-Paul Marat, the journalist and deputy demonised by Girondin propaganda. He was bathing at the time, seeking to ease the pain of psoriasis, a disfiguring skin condition. Wearing a vividly striped dress shortly to be immortalised in prints and paintings, she gained entry to his room with a note promising information on the Federalist rebels. Once there, they talked until Marat's fiancée left to fetch more water. Charlotte Corday, as she is known to history, pulled out a large knife and stabbed Marat to death with one blow to the chest.

Arrested at the scene, Corday was interrogated repeatedly over the following few days by a succession of officials convinced that, as a mere woman, she could only be the tool of some political conspiracy, but she stubbornly insisted (to no avail) that what she had done was an act of individual determination. At the first interrogation, the unsavoury ex-monk François Chabot, badgering her with questions, caught sight of a paper in the bosom of her dress. He snatched at it, and she resisted by twisting away, her bound hands preventing any other defence. In so doing, she ripped her dress apart, leaving herself huddled forward over her knees in a vain effort to preserve her modesty. Alone in a room full of men, she had to be untied in order to cover herself. Despite this, as a witness from the Convention recorded, she retained the composure to amend from memory the record of individual answers she had given, when the notes of hours of interrogation had been read back to her. The deputy recorded this, and her 'imperturbable presence of mind', as 'worthy of admiration'. When the session closed, she asked only that she might put on gloves to protect her wrists from the chafing of the ropes they bound her with.[26]

Charlotte Corday came from a family that moved in royalist circles – her own two brothers were *émigrés* who had left to fight with the armies of the exiled princes. However, she found the moderate republicanism of the Gironde more to her intellectual and moral taste. From her own accounts, and those of witnesses, it is clear that she had been inspired to admiration of the Girondins by their speeches, and by meeting some of them in Caen, and to hatred of the Montagnards by their excesses – and no doubt by the propaganda of both local and national moderates. Seeing the desperate weakness of the Federalist forces, she had attempted to aid them by striking at the heart of the anarchist monster. She viewed herself much as Madame Roland did, as a tragic heroine, and was eminently prepared for a martyrdom that the Revolutionary Tribunal inflicted upon her after a short hearing on 17 July: she even had her portrait painted in her prison cell. Her defence lawyer, who was later to act for Marie-Antoinette, could only observe to the court that Corday 'does not even seek to justify herself'. The 'sublimity' of her 'imperturbable calm', he added, could only be explained by 'the exaltation of political fanaticism'.[27] Corday's own words at the trial give this an ironic slant, as she revealed her eminently revolutionary motives for the slaying:

> I knew that he was perverting France. I have killed one man to save a hundred thousand. Besides, he was a hoarder; at Caen they have arrested a man who bought goods for him. I was a republican well before the Revolution, and I have never lacked energy.

Asked to define that latter quality, she went on, 'Those who put their own interests to one side and know how to sacrifice themselves for the *patrie*.'[28] There is nothing here that would not have been at home in the thoughts and deeds of Saint-Just or Robespierre (though both were unlikely to have mustered the force of will to match

Corday's self-sacrifice). This commonality of language and perception reflects the truly extraordinary nature of the internecine conflict that had opened up across France. Corday went unrepentant to her death, as so many other republicans were to do. She was executed on the afternoon of her trial, wearing the red shirt of a parricide and soaked by a sudden summer storm; counter-revolutionary legend had it that her virgin cheek reddened in outraged modesty as the executioner contemptuously slapped her severed head.[29] The slap itself was well attested by eyewitnesses and the guilty man, an assistant named Legros, was jailed and publicly rebuked by the authorities for this 'indecent behaviour'.[30]

Thus the hydra of Federalism and counter-revolution had struck at the heart of the capital, once again confirming, as Lepeletier's martyrdom had in January, that nowhere was safe from the enemies of the Republic. Marat's death spurred Parisian activists to new heights of grieving commitment. Like Lepeletier, Marat was laid out in public for several days of mourning: in this case in the church of the Cordeliers on the Left Bank, home to the eponymous Club, and Marat's most ardent supporters. Unlike Lepeletier, Marat was exposed in the sweltering heat of July, and although the painter David, again master of ceremonies, paid 7500 livres to the city's best embalmer, the corpse rapidly began to rot, and the stench in the packed church was insufferable. The funeral had to be brought forward a day to the 16th, which may be why members of the Convention were conspicuously absent, engaged on business. There again, it had only been since the previous autumn that Marat had been thought respectable enough to join the Jacobin Club, and many less ardent deputies had still looked askance at his lust for blood, and scorn for property.

When David immortalised him in oils 'at his last breath', he made Marat's preoccupations respectable, beautifying his scabbed and discoloured skin, posing him in the bath where he died with the hand that held his pen draped languorously downwards. Before him on a simple wooden box was a letter from a poor woman begging for aid, and an assignat note he clearly intended for her relief. He clutched a note in which his killer begged admission with the fictitious phrase 'It is enough that I am unfortunate to have the right to your benevolence'. David had to work hard to create the image of antique virtue out of a man who once lectured Robespierre:

> Learn that my reputation with the people rests, not on my ideas, but upon my boldness . . . my cries of rage, of despair and of fury against the rascals that impede the action of the Revolution. I am the anger, the just anger, of the people, and that is why they listen to me and believe in me.[31]

The avant-garde of the *sans-culottes* felt no need to pacify such rage, and Cordeliers and other club activists dominated the funerary rites, including the female radicals who bore his body, still in the bath which had been made into a tableau of death, to a hastily prepared grotto in the garden of the Cordeliers Club. Marat's heart was extracted and embalmed separately, to hang in an urn from the ceiling of the Club's meeting-room. The language of the speeches echoed such extreme gestures, often devoted to the immortality of the 'prophet' Marat, and the potency of his 'martyred' blood to revive the Republic. The funeral oration itself began 'O heart of Jesus, O heart of Marat', and went on to assert that 'Jesus was but a false prophet but Marat is a god. Long live the heart of Marat . . .'[32]

If such language was for now confined only to the most ardent disciples of Marat, it was soon to have its much wider echoes in the rising extremism of the verbal and physical confrontation between republicans and their ever-present enemies. One bitter irony of the situation in the early summer of 1793 was that the Montagnard Convention spent much of this time reining in the activism of the Parisians who had 'purified' it, and refusing to yield to the demands of impatient Enragés such as those who swarmed around Marat's grave. Just as the Paris Commune itself had restrained some of the Sections from overzealous persecution of suspect patriots in the first weeks of June, so on the wider stage of political and journalistic activity the urgent need had been not to pursue indiscriminate revenge but to stabilise a Republic that seemed to be crumbling.

The Convention rushed ahead with the new constitution that had been delayed by the disputes of the spring, producing a document on 24 June that was dramatically radical, by comparison with that of 1791, and yet could also be read as assuaging the fears of the Federalists. Sent out for ratification by nationwide primary assemblies, the Constitution enshrined adult male suffrage and annual elections, and allowed voting in the electoral assemblies to be by voice rather than ballot, if the voters so chose – a coded version of the 'vote by acclamation' that *sans-culottes* used to dominate the Sections. But the four 'natural and imprescriptible rights' at the head of the text were 'equality, liberty, security and property', with security further defined as 'the protection given by society to each member for the preservation of his person, rights and properties'.[33] Well aware that the Federalist leadership branded them as anarchists bent on pillage, the Montagnard leadership fought back by emphasising this element of the new order. Even Hébert's *Père Duchesne* was enrolled, the title-character meeting up in one number with an aged bourgeois, who upon learning of the new constitution remarks that 'I had thought you a man of faction, a disorganiser, I see to the contrary that you organise the Republic well, you *sans-culottes*, since you safeguard my property.'[34]

Such a conversion was unlikely to be convincing to many so long as the Cordeliers and other Enragé forces were still raising the spectre of spoliation. Only two days before the Constitution's promulgation, the Cordeliers Club had heard calls for a new revolution, like that which toppled Louis XVI, if stricter economic regulation was not put in place. On 25 June, as the Convention was supposed to be celebrating its master-work, the priest Jacques Roux appeared before it at the head of a Club delegation and harangued the offended deputies with a series of charges:

> Liberty is but a vain phantom when one class of men can starve another with impunity. Equality is but a vain phantom when the rich exercise the power of life and death over their fellows through monopolies. The Republic is but a vain phantom when the counter-revolution is accomplished daily through the price of provisions which three-quarters of the citizens cannot pay without shedding tears.

His lengthy and condemnatory speech also contained a stark warning, which could equally well be read as a threat: 'It is only by putting foodstuffs within the reach of the *sans-culottes* that you will attach them to the Revolution . . .'[35] As if to ram home his point, the last days of June saw extensive disturbances in the capital over the price of soap. Although the Commune had regulated the price of bread to its pre-revolutionary level, all other prices still floated free, and in the desperate air of the time they soared ever higher.

With the country collapsing around them, and threatened from within the capital by the Enragé agenda, the Convention was in dire straits. The Montagnard leadership struck back at the Enragés, and particularly at the temerity of Jacques Roux. He was compared to the rebel priests of the Vendée, and condemned as one of the 'three chief enemies of the state' alongside Austria and Britain by Robespierre at the Jacobins. Robespierre and Hébert united to expel him from the Cordeliers Club, the Commune censured him, and, with bitter irony, one of Marat's last acts was to have a public dispute with Roux – sufficient for him to be rounded up for questioning about any possible links with Marat's death.[36] Upon his release, with the icons of radicalism turned against him, Roux was a spent force, his attempt to enter journalism in the guise of the 'shade of Marat' merely summoning further Montagnard attacks through August. Nonetheless, the demands at the heart of the Enragé agenda did not go away, and would revive in new forms – and from new mouths – as the Federalist civil war ground on.

Hopes that the new Constitution would salve the Republic's wounds faded through July. The text did form part of a successful propaganda offensive that brought most of the more passively resistant regions of the country back to the fold, but, where conflict was already under way, it could not change entrenched attitudes. The Federalist authorities of Lyon turned decisively away from reconciliation on 17 July when they executed the demagogue Chalier, who was rapidly admitted into the Jacobin pantheon of 'martyrs of liberty'. A botched execution, with the guillotine falling four times before Chalier's head rolled free, added to the horror of the account. The city's formal acceptance of the new Constitution two weeks later, although perhaps seen from Lyon as a measure towards peaceful resolution, now meant nothing.[37] On all fronts, meanwhile, the war went badly for the Republic. The Vendéan rebels, although driven off from Nantes at the end of June, had an unbroken run of victories through July, ending by threatening the city of Angers. The southern fronts in the Alps and Pyrenees were forced onto the defensive by the diversion of anti-Federalist forces, and Savoy was reinvaded by its Piedmontese former masters. The key fortresses of Condé and Valenciennes, besieged in the north since May, now fell, and new targets further into France were threatened by Austrian and British troops. To the east, the city of Mainz surrendered to the duke of Brunswick on 23 July, its garrison forced to accept terms that barred them from further combat against the Allies.

Now, with the fortunes of the Republic at their lowest ebb, Robespierre took centre stage. Under pressure over the growing crisis, the membership of the Committee of Public Safety had been overhauled by a Convention vote on 10 July, removing Danton and most of those who had served with him. They were replaced by a group which included some of the Mountain's most ardent men – Couthon, who had moved the final vote against the Girondins; Saint-Just, who had called for the king's execution without trial – and others of rising eminence. On 27 July, exceptionally, Robespierre was added to their number. His membership would last precisely one year. Although previously a sceptic about the value of the Committee, he would be substantially responsible for turning it into the powerhouse of revolutionary government during that year. Indeed, it was a bare fortnight after his appointment that he personally intervened in a Convention debate to block the implementation of the 1793 Constitution.

This had been ratified by the primary assemblies with a creditable two million votes – among the higher turnouts of the 1790s – and promulgated on 10 August 1793 in a Festival of the Unity and Indivisibility of the Republic. In this festival, pikes carried from each department, the *sans-culottes*' favourite weapon, were bound into a gigantic republican *fasces*, ancient Roman symbol of unity, and the constitution itself suspended in a cedar box from the roof of the Convention.[38] Nonetheless, as Robespierre argued the next day, conditions made it impossible to summon the primary assemblies necessary for new elections without the fear of their infiltration by conspirators and counter-revolutionaries. Thus the Convention, the Committee and the representatives-on-mission with their ever-lengthening list of powers would remain in charge throughout the emergency. Those powers included, since 17 July, the right to issue decrees on any subject and have them treated as if they came from the Convention itself – which is to say, not subject to challenge whatsoever. On 16 August, their powers to purge and replace all regular authorities were explicitly confirmed. On the same day, the Convention voted in principle to accept a proposal from the united Sections of Paris for the foundation of universal conscription – or as the petition put it, 'a spontaneous movement of a great people who will throw themselves *en masse* on their enemies to exterminate them'.[39]

Perhaps ironically, the immediate crisis of the summer may already have passed by the time of these decisions. The areas of Federalist influence were steadily shrinking, and in the west in particular the Vendéan menace assisted the restoration of order in the towns and cities of Brittany and Normandy (the countryside would be another story). Bordeaux's Popular Commission for Public Safety, panicking under the threats of retribution emerging from Paris, dissolved both itself and what was left of its 'army' on 2 August. New local authorities in the city undertook extensive face-saving measures of Jacobin allegiance through the rest of the summer, even honouring Marat, though to little avail in the face of hard-hearted deputies from Paris.[40] Those hearts had been hardened noticeably when two representatives-on-mission entered the supposedly penitent city on 19 August, and were accosted by a large crowd of sword-waving youths on the boulevards. The elegantly dressed young men hurled violent threats at the jostled deputies, threats that were repeated by the crowds surrounding the municipal council chamber, where the deputies were taken forcefully by their captors. Into the small hours of the morning the abuse continued, and the following day the representatives were hounded out of the city – and learned later that their coachmen had been offered bribes to drive them off a bridge en route.[41] It would be two months before the deputies re-entered the city, this time with troops, and the aimless and pointless defiance of Bordeaux's well-heeled youth would earn them nothing but harsh treatment.

Meanwhile, the progress of the Republic's armies continued. Lyon was encircled by republican troops on 9 August, and a siege begun – in fact more of a distant blockade, since the republican lines were stretched too thin for heavy action. Further south the Republic retook Avignon on 27 July, and troops closed in on Marseille through August. In the north, hesitations and divisions in the Allied command saw British troops turn west on 12 August to besiege Dunkirk – a prime political objective of Pitt's government, seeking an independent and defensible base on the continent – while Austrian forces turned east towards the fortress-town of Maubeuge, splitting a mighty force of some 160,000 men that could have driven on Paris, and confining combat to the frontier zone.[42] Meanwhile in the west the surrendered garrison of Mainz was committed to action against the Vendéans, leavening what had mostly been a war of National Guards and volunteers with a strong body of regular troops. The Vendéans treated this move as a breach of the troops' surrender terms, seeing themselves as part of the Allied armies the garrison was forbidden to fight, and decided to offer them no quarter in combat.[43] As if in anticipation of this, but far surpassing it in impact, from 1 August republican forces in the west had been authorised to use a strategy of devastation and depopulation – to lay waste the rebels' bases of support, even down to the 'woods, the copses and the undergrowth', and to deport any and all 'loyal' citizens, leaving a free-fire zone for counter-insurgency operations.[44] A heavy defeat at the town of Luçon on the 13th put the rebels on the defensive, and marked the beginning of the end for the Royal and Catholic Army.

Although the cumulative effect of these developments was to turn the tide in the Republic's favour, at least in its internal conflicts, this was not necessarily apparent at the time. Events in Lyon and further to the south-east, where Catholic hatred of the Revolution was almost as strong in some areas as in the Vendée, prompting a brushfire of revolt in the Lozère department particularly, continued to demonstrate the fundamental unity of the counter-revolution in Jacobin eyes, and the summer campaigning season on all fronts was at its height. French armies were holding their own, but the threat of collapse was still real. Pressure from Parisian radicals for more decisive measures on both the military and political fronts continued to grow, and anger at the apparent ineffectiveness of the administration was simmering in the Commune and the Cordeliers Club. Meanwhile similar pressures for very different reasons were coming from the economic and military experts on the Committee of Public Safety and elsewhere.

Throughout the summer, agitation from the capital's sectional movement and the Commune, at least partly in response to the extremists on the left, had already begun to shift the Convention's social and economic policies. They had secured the closure of the Paris stock exchange on 27 June, and a month later would gain from the Convention a decree imposing the death penalty on all hoarders, a measure which also empowered local authorities to search private premises for food and other commodities at will. Between these two measures, the Convention also passed an act of great symbolic significance, finally striking down without reservation all the feudal dues which had borne so heavily on the peasantry, and cancelling the elaborate plans for redemption and indemnities that had been in place since 1790. Although this act reached out to the rural community, and marked the historic end of the feudal burden, it had little immediate impact – most peasants had long since stopped paying such dues in the turmoil of Revolution, and those alienated by the Republic's religious policies would need more than a material sop to bring them back to loyalty. It joined measures taken in June to sell off the lands of *émigrés* in small plots, and to share out village commons: gestures towards the peasantry that were dramatic in principle, but of little more than propaganda value in the middle of a civil war.[45]

Other fundamental divisions continued to trouble the Republic. Emblematic of them had been the dismissal of the former duc de Biron from his general's post in the Vendée on 12 July, only shortly after he had taken the town of Saumur against the tide of Vendéan victories.[46] Despite this conspicuous success at a time of dramatic failures, Biron had been hounded out as an ex-noble, associate of the duc d'Orléans and general 'moderate'. His replacement was Jean-Antoine Rossignol, a former private soldier and *sans-culotte* jeweller appointed as his deputy by Charles-Philippe Ronsin. This was symptomatic of the complex entanglements of politics at this moment. Ronsin was an ex-army sergeant who had become a playwright before the Revolution, and thereafter an activist in the radical elements of the Parisian National Guard and the Cordeliers Club. He was sent to the west as an agent of the War Ministry. Since April 1793, the ministry had been led by Jean-Baptiste Noël Bouchotte, another former professional soldier (in this case a captain in 1789) who had helped to stabilise the northern front in the chaotic days after Dumouriez's defection. After his elevation to the ministry, he rapidly built a new revolutionary career on forging close links between his offices and the Parisian Sections. He was explicit in his intention to 'sans-culottise' the military hierarchy, writing in August 1793 to one general that 'when all those with talent show themselves to be against the popular system, the minister is forced to take other men to move it forward, who appear at first to have few abilities, but who finish by developing them, and who have in the end the prime one: the will to go forward'.[47]

Bouchotte made it his business to maintain the *sans-culotte* character of the struggle against the Vendéans, and Ronsin was a prime agent of this effort. Thus Rossignol's Parisian origins and his political attitudes made him a more worthy leader of men, in Ronsin's eyes, than Biron, despite his drunkenness and complete unfamiliarity with military operations. Rossignol's own military career had been largely confined to a series of brawls and duels on garrison duty in western ports in the 1770s. Nonetheless, with the agreement of the often feuding pack of representatives-on-mission that dogged the republican headquarters, Rossignol was now a general officer.[48] Biron would be far from the last ex-noble general removed under such circumstances, and in the same period the comte de Dillon was removed from command in the north and imprisoned, accused of a far-fetched plot to liberate Marie-Antoinette and set up a regency for her young son.[49] He and Biron would be guillotined within the year. The comte de Custine met an even swifter fate: recalled from the north in July, he would be charged, convicted and executed for treachery on 28 August.[50]

The assault on the military leadership by those on the far left was a sign of the growing restlessness with all forms of moderation. Danton's removal from the Committee of Public Safety in early July, although it appeared to come as a personal relief to him, also closed a period of relatively conciliatory political responses to the crises of the Republic. Always attuned to the possibility of deals and compromises (the counterpart to his less than puritanical approach to personal enrichment), Danton had, for example, envisaged a possible negotiated settlement to the Vendéan Revolt, and saw Biron as a potential agent in this. He had also been a prime mover in defusing tensions with some of the outlying areas initially sympathetic to Federalism, and stood out against the Enragé demands for total regulation of the food-supply, alarming to property-owners everywhere. He equally resisted demands from Paris for Marie-Antoinette to be put on trial, seeing her as a bargaining chip with the Austrians.[51] His removal seemed to mark the potential for greater radicalisation and a wider pursuit of the *sans-culotte* agenda, for which the funeral rites of Marat might stand as symbol.

However, the Convention still had other things in mind, and was shortly to reassert control of the capital and the country. By the end of July the Committee of Public Safety was firming up its identity as a controlling agent of state power, and would soon embark on measures that acknowledged, but did not always yield to, the agenda of the political radicals of the capital. Robespierre now sat on the Committee alongside Montagnard ideologues like Couthon and Saint-Just, military engineers like Lazare Carnot and Claude-Antoine Prieur (always called 'Prieur de la Côte d'Or' to distinguish him from Pierre-Louis Prieur 'de la Marne', also on the Committee but a more politically radical figure), and two prominent centrists of the Plain, Robert Lindet and Bertrand Barère (a survivor of the original Committee). Numbering twelve in total, the members of the Committee would never all meet at once, such were the demands of the war for their presence 'on mission'. Those that were present at any time came together around a plain oval table installed in what had been Louis XVI's private office in the Tuileries. Their longest sessions were often through the night, after debates at the Convention and the Jacobins had closed, and following further long hours of individual bureaucratic labours. Although they produced acres of correspondence, their actual discussions were unrecorded, guarding the secrecy of republican government from prying ears, just as two primed cannon guarded the entrance from the courtyard below.[52]

From out of the division of labour among this diverse group, commitment to a successful prosecution of the war and to a hardening of ideological control over the Republic began to converge inexorably. Barère demonstrated that his centrism was only relative by proposing a decree on 1 August that sent Marie-Antoinette for trial before the Revolutionary Tribunal. This move headed off radical protests from the Commune, where rumours of Danton's (and others') efforts to swap her for prisoners or other concessions had surfaced. Barère denounced the queen as 'the cause of all the woes of France' in a noticeably heated text which also called for the destruction of the centuries of royal tombs at Saint-Denis to the north of Paris, and sent all the Bourbons except Louis XVI's children into exile. The Committee's hardline credentials were thus, at least for the moment, firmly established.[53]

The effect of Barère's speech was reinforced by a remarkable *coup de théâtre*. In the course of his denunciations, he pulled out a letter, accompanied by a medal, found, he said, on a captured English spy in Lille. The letter told in a feebly transparent code of a network of agents and plans, approved by Prime Minister Pitt himself, and tying together the Vendée, Normandy, Bordeaux, Lyon, the war fronts and the unrest in the capital. It was all part of a grand plot, intended to come to a head on the symbolic date of 10 August, a plot now foiled, of course, but which confirmed all the revolutionaries' worst fears about the unity of their enemies.[54] It was also nothing but a crude forgery, and the extent to which the alleged English plans matched up exactly with even the most paranoid of the revolutionaries' fears was evidence enough of that, without problems of chronology and language observed by later more sceptical readers. Whether it was forged by someone eager to gain influence, and passed off as genuine to the Committee of Public Safety, or whether, even, they had ordered the forgery to 'prove' what they already believed true, is unclear. The 'English letter' served, nonetheless, to tighten the bonds of republican unity, a unity that the Committee and the Convention remained determined to focus on themselves.

In their own way, the festivities of 'Unity and Indivisibility' on 10 August, anniversary of the king's fall, were emblematic of the process of consolidation. Beyond the symbolic bundling of pikes into *fasces* and the consecration of the Constitution, the day had been a manifestation of the power and potential of the Republic on a grand, indeed operatic, scale. Jacques-Louis David had once again drawn on the artistic talents of the capital, and the resources available to the state, to drive home a message of syncretic power. The festival in Paris was only the grandest of many ordered to take place across the country by a decree sent out, ironically, on 31 May 1793, day of the insurrection against the Girondins. The whole imagery of the festivities displaced the rivalries of Federalism in favour of an organic conception of a national community being reborn in this moment – in some towns, real newborns were laid on patriotic altars alongside the tablets of the Constitution.[55] In Paris, with a more rarefied symbolism, the ex-noble Hérault de Séchelles celebrated a 'republican Mass', serving the pike-bearers from the departments with a chalice of water that had cascaded from the bared breasts of a massive pseudo-Egyptian statue – variously the goddess Isis, or the Republic, Nature or Liberty, depending on one's reading – and named the Fountain of Regeneration.

On the Place de la Révolution to the west of the Tuileries gardens, largest public square of the city, a female Liberty had replaced Louis

XV on the central pedestal, and as the festivities processed here, via a triumphal arch on the northern boulevards, a massive pyre of the relics of monarchy was assembled and torched. Most were actually theatrical props, as many of those who appeared in tableaux of patriotic triumph were employees of the theatres. Three thousand white doves were released as the flames took hold – a spectacular visual effect, and another measure of the resources devoted to the scene.[56] As with all the Republic's great festivals, the crowds were immense, marshalled into order by all the agencies of local government and military power. Enthusiasm, regardless of the possible incomprehensibility of the rites being enacted, was compulsory.

Less than two weeks after this statement about the power of the Republic, with its sequel of commitment to continued rule by the Convention, the organising forces of the state were set at a new ferocious pitch. On 23 August the Convention, on the initiative of the Committee of Public Safety, proclaimed the *levée en masse* – a term prosaically translated as 'mass levy', but which also conveys the sense of a 'mass rising', answering the Sections' call of the 16th, and exemplified in the first paragraph of the decree:

> Henceforth, until the enemies have been driven from the territory of the Republic, the French people are in permanent requisition for military service. The young men shall go to battle; the married men shall forge arms and transport provisions; the women shall make tents and clothing, and shall serve in the hospitals; the children shall turn old linen into bandages; the old men shall go to the public places, to stimulate the courage of the warriors and preach the unity of the Republic and the hatred of kings.[57]

To carry out these grandiose plans, former church property held as 'national buildings' was designated for barracks, and a wide range of other public sites for conversion into arms workshops. Draught animals and firearms were requisitioned, and to begin the mobilisation all single men between eighteen and twenty-five were ordered to march at once to district capitals, there to drill until further orders for deployment arrived. To feed them, and the cities, all agricultural producers were ordered to turn over the year's taxation on their land in kind, at once, along with any outstanding arrears. Given that tax collection had fallen to somewhere below a quarter of expected receipts in the past twenty-four months, this was a dramatic and ultimately problematic requirement.

The whole agenda of the mass levy was problematic, in fact, since the country remained bitterly divided, and the concerns and actions of the revolutionary leadership, radical activists and the great bulk of the population continued to drift apart. The areas of Brittany and western Normandy that had seen protests against the Levy of Three Hundred Thousand in March were further alienated by the new demands. Many young men found the only way to evade the call of the Republic was to join guerrilla bands that had flourished in the densely hedgebound *bocage* landscape since those protests. These *chouans* took their name from one of their leaders, a former smuggler named Jean Cottereau. His nickname, 'Jean Chouan', referred to the call of the owl, the *chat-houant*, used as a recognition signal for nocturnal rendezvous. Like the Vendéans, religious loyalties and rejection of the Republic fanned an overt counter-revolutionary commitment among these bands, which fluctuated wildly in numbers but counted at least several thousand active guerrillas. In their heartlands, most *chouans* nevertheless remained integrated members of their communities until the time came to stage a raid or a retaliation. The 'failure' of the *chouans* to coalesce into a workable military structure was their salvation, as it was impossible for them to be pinned down by conventional military action. In the meantime, the *chouans* traded in fear and the humiliation of isolated patriots. In late 1793, one outraged individual reported that he had been made to climb the local church tower and cry *Vive Louis XVII!* – the royalists' title for Louis XVI's surviving son, languishing in a republican prison. On another occasion, a female victim was made to kneel before an image of the Sacred Heart of Jesus, the adopted emblem of the more devout among the rebels. Public renunciations of revolutionary faith under threat of death were common, often accompanied by ritualised public abuse and beatings.[58]

Much about this pattern of *chouan* activity indicates clearly that they were attempting to defend a pre-existing set of local community norms against the alien republican values of those they fervently denounced as *intrus* or intruders. When 'converted' local patriots betrayed them again by reporting such acts to the authorities and appealing for aid, a more embittered confrontation set in, and between early 1794 and mid-1796 the *chouans* assassinated hundreds of local republican officials, and persecuted those they saw as profiting from the spoliation of the church through the purchase of its nationalised assets. In the later stages of their existence, they went so far as to collect the rents due on such property from the peasant tenants, diverting funds from patriots' pockets to the Royal and Catholic Army in whose name they issued receipts. The towns of the region became effectively armed camps, with the thin lines of the main highways kept open between them by military force alone. If active *chouan* militants constituted a tiny minority of the population, like active political militants of all stripes, it is clear that in the villages of the west they enjoyed a solid, if largely passive, popular support.[59]

The kind of rejection of the Revolution displayed by the *chouans* and their Vendéan brethren, framed so clearly in terms of Catholic commitment, began in late 1793 to turn some republicans' thoughts to a drastic settlement of the ongoing conflict with the church. As the festivities for the new constitution suggested, orthodox Catholic rites no longer had any place in the public ceremonies of the Republic, despite the latter's continued funding of the 'constitutional' church. With reports that Federalist centres were also drawing strong support from the priesthood, some activists began to feel that religion itself had failed the Revolution. One such was Joseph Fouché, a former schoolmaster who scarcely more than a year earlier had been an advocate of the role of the clergy in education. As a representative-on-mission to Nantes in the early days of the Vendéan Revolt, he had seen 'fanaticism' at first hand, and had almost been killed by rebels while returning to Paris. After that, he spoke of popular attitudes to religion (or 'ignorance and fanaticism') as 'the blind instruments of the aristocracy', and called for 'the odious influence of religion' to be offset by new republican educational systems.[60] Sent on mission again in the summer to the relatively tranquil central department of the Nièvre, by August he was presiding over the 'republican baptism' of his own daughter, named in honour of the department. Within two months, he was to order cemeteries in the department to carry the slogan 'Death Is But an Eternal Sleep', desacralising funerary rites: in effect abandoning the role of religion in society altogether in favour of 'the revolutionary and clearly philosophical spirit' he had first wanted for education.

What was to become 'dechristianisation' (in an enduring term first coined by its enemies) remained in its early stages during the summer of 1793, at least outside the zone of the Vendéan conflict, where priests and church buildings had already become prime targets for atrocity. Nevertheless, it reflected the wholesale transformation that Jacobin and radical leaders were beginning to see as necessary for the survival of the Republic, and the creation of a republican citizenry. The work to be done continued to be demonstrated by events in the strife-torn south-east. The siege of Lyon ground on, while representatives-on-mission rooted out Federalism in the surrounding departments, and further south forces under General Carteaux spent much of August steadily working their way towards Marseille. As they approached, disorder grew as granaries emptied in a city blockaded by land by the Republic and from the sea by the British fleet. The city's Federalist mask slipped, and its leadership displayed their fundamentally counter-revolutionary attributes – or so the Republic would see it. Imprisoned Jacobins were hastened to their executions, while priests prayed openly for deliverance from the encroaching forces, and the ruling council opened negotiations with the British forces under Admiral Hood cruising off the coast, for military assistance, or at least for the passage of food supplies.[61]

Such overt treason went beyond what some in Marseille's insurgent sectional movement could tolerate, and street-fighting broke out between two parties, those for surrender to Carteaux and those for collaboration with the British, on 23 August. Two days later, the city fell to Carteaux more or less without a fight, and the more uncompromising of the leaders fled eastwards to Toulon, home of the French Mediterranean fleet, and until this point almost isolated from the main conflict. The arrival of the refugees from Marseille panicked the Toulonnais, and they responded favourably to new overtures from Admiral Hood. After three days of desperate discussion had also convinced the personnel of the fleet that resistance was futile, and that the emissaries of Paris would bring carnage, the city and the fleet were handed over to the British and their Italian allies on 27 August.[62]

Yet another episode of monstrous treachery was therefore added to the balance-sheet of Federalism, and yet further evidence secured to show that all opposition had but one source. The Parisian reaction was to press still further for stern measures. A month after

Marie-Antoinette had been confined to the Conciergerie to await trial, there was still no sign of it taking place, and radicals suspected, quite rightly, that the Convention was still thinking vaguely of her value in diplomatic negotiations. A closed meeting of leaders from the Convention and Commune on the night of 2–3 September ruled that option out at last – Hébert, putting himself forward self-consciously as the figurehead of the *sans-culottes*, threatened to have her killed himself (presumably in his day-job as municipal prosecutor), if no action was taken. To raise the stakes still further, that very night a purported escape plan, involving officials of the prison administration itself, was foiled, causing security around the former queen to be tightened to obsessive levels, as the fear of plot, always part of the revolutionary mentality, escalated to the brink of hysteria.[63]

All this, then, was the background to the events of 5 September, when Terror became 'the order of the day'. With the crowds that had rallied to the Commune's call pressing into the meeting-chamber, Chaumette, procurator of Paris, spoke first before the Convention. His words revealed clearly that the grassroots agenda of the Enragés, despite their political isolation, had now penetrated to the heart of *sans-culotte* concerns. The food supply, he said, was under attack, warning of 'new seigneurs, no less cruel, avid or insolent than the old, who have arisen on the ruins of feudalism'. Those who had bought or leased productive farms were intent on a ruinous exploitation, 'to speculate on public misery, to shut off the wellsprings of abundance, and to tyrannise the destroyers of tyranny'. Others equally villainous had seized control of the markets in foodstuffs and other 'goods of the first necessity'. The blows struck against them by laws earlier in the year had not felled them, and their 'brigandage' continued. Internal enemies were everywhere: 'Every day we learn of new treasons, new crimes. Every day we are unsettled by the discovery and the rebirth of new plots. Every day new troubles agitate the Republic,' threatening to 'cast it into the unplumbed abyss of the centuries to come'.[64]

Under such circumstances, the people, ready to fight back, must have the means to do so, and the first of those was their own subsistence, 'and to get it, force to the law!' Chaumette came thus to the key demand of the Commune's petition – the formation of a 'Revolutionary Army' to hunt down internal enemies, and especially hoarders and speculators, an army (in fact a paramilitary militia) that would take with it an 'incorruptible tribunal' to judge its enemies, and a mobile guillotine: the 'fatal instrument that cuts off with one single blow both the plots and the days of the plotters'.[65] His words met with immediate acclaim.

Yet even these events reflected continuing tensions among the revolutionaries. The breaking news of the surrender of Toulon had stoked the flames of Parisian outrage, and for some time it seemed that the Committee of Public Safety might be a victim of the *sans-culottes*' anger. Jacques-Nicolas Billaud-Varenne, who had established a position for himself among the Montagnards as a strong advocate of the Parisian agenda, had already called in the Jacobin Club for a new committee to supervise, and if necessary purge, the executive, and he repeated this call in a heated debate that followed the arrival of the municipal petition. In retaliation another deputy, Claude Basire, launched into a series of extraordinary charges. He was a member of the Committee of General Security, charged by the Convention with countering internal subversion, and began by saying that 'a sectional revolution like those of Lyon, Marseille and Toulon is being prepared in Paris'. Billaud-Varenne angrily interrupted with a demand for a vote on his motion, but Basire went on:

> In the last few days there have been extraordinary movements in Paris, not occurring naturally, and with the object of making a sectional revolution, or better counter-revolution. Everyone knows that the sectional revolution is well established, well organised, and under preparation for some time: the counter-revolutionaries await only their moment to show themselves. If we deliberate in enthusiasm, let us take guard not to precipitate the people into the hands of their adversaries by ill-planned initiatives, to have their throats cut by their enemies.[66]

Basire ended with the claim that the Committee of Public Safety had new and valuable intelligence on these enemies, and begged for time to hear its reports later in the day before the Convention was wrong-footed. With events leaning dangerously toward confrontation between the Parisians and the Convention, it was Danton who stepped up next to the speaker's tribune.

Danton had been a target of Parisian wrath since his service on the

Committee earlier in the year, and the summer had seen repeated smears on his probity from Hébert, who blamed him for losing out on the Interior Minister's post in a summer reshuffle (the post, replacing the 'eunuch' Garat, went to Jules-François Paré, Danton's former clerk). Also on the attack was François-Nicolas Vincent, another former clerk now one of the key orators of the Cordeliers Club, as well as a senior figure in Bouchotte's *sans-culotte* War Ministry. Vincent was one of a group of leading Cordeliers who had been treading a fine line between acknowledging the supremacy of the Mountain and backing a full-scale Enragé demand for new purges – as early as 5 August he had declaimed against the 'monstrous power' of the Committee of Public Safety, while also calling Danton a conspirator.[67] Renewed attacks on the Enragés shortly after by Robespierre and others had served as an indirect warning to back off, but by the last week of August Hébert himself, straddling the line between his Cordeliers radicalism and municipal powerbase, had joined the left-wing assault.

Bouchotte's successful 'sans-culottisation' of the War Ministry was pushing such Parisian radicals into believing that it might be possible, and wise, to bypass the Convention and its committees, take control of the executive directly, and prosecute the war with true *sans-culotte* vigour. The fact that it would elevate the group of radicals denied election to the Convention to new heights of power was probably not incidental. Danton, on behalf of the Convention, and to defend his past record, had been one of those to fight back. On 26 August he had used the podium of the Jacobin Club to rebut Hébert's repeated charges of corruption, going into details to defend his own dealings.[68] His defensiveness earned only Hébert's scorn, and as the bad news flowed in from the south, and Parisian tempers rose, the Convention remained under pressure.

It was therefore a decisive moment when Danton reached the tribune. Almost exactly a year before, he had summoned the French to 'be daring, more daring, ever daring, and France is saved!' Acclaimed then, he had been lambasted since, but as he strode forward a wave of applause began, from the deputies and from the crowds of petitioners cramming the hall. The wave rose, and lasted, and he stood for some time under the hail of noise until he was able to speak. The moment was his, and he grasped it. In a brilliant disarming manoeuvre, he took on Billaud-Varenne's championing of the Parisian demand for a 'Revolutionary Army' to act against hoarders, and made it his own:

> We must know how to profit from the sublime *élan* of the people who press in around us. I know that when the people present their needs, when they offer to march against their enemies, we must take only the measures they themselves present: for it is the genius of the nation which has dictated them.[69]

The applause resumed as he called for the immediate voting of this measure.

Then he went on, and in a master-stroke assailed the power of the sectional movement while proclaiming its glories. He spoke of the 'industrious men who live by their sweat', unable to get to the daily sectional assemblies that the *sans-culottes* lauded under the right of permanence. 'It is only in the absence of true patriots that intrigue may seize hold of the Sections,' he continued, and asked the Convention: 'Decree then two great assemblies in the Sections each week, and that the men of the people who attend these political assemblies should have a just recompense for the time they take away from their work.' Outflanking the *sans-culottes* thus over their very power-base, he went on to redouble the gamble, and called brazenly for the impossible task of giving every Frenchman a musket to defend the *patrie*: 'It is the want of arms that enchains us. The *patrie* shall never want for citizens!' A vote of a hundred million livres towards this implausible goal, a vote soon to be conveniently forgotten, was passed by acclamation, and Danton had rescued the Convention.[70]

Danton acknowledged the *sans-culotte* agenda of subsistence, but only to announce that 'the people is great', as attested by their supposed lack of response to the ongoing 'false famine, arranged to lead them into counter-revolution'. His peroration turned division into unity at a stroke: 'Homage to you, sublime people, to your greatness you join perseverance . . . You fast for liberty, you must get it. We shall march with you, your enemies shall be confounded; you will be free!'[71] The hall came to its feet, wild with enthusiasm, hats waving in the air to cries of '*Vive la République!*' The day was not over, and indeed it was only after this critical moment that the Jacobins came forward with their own petition for Terror. But by then the atmosphere had shifted, and all attention was once again focused on the fight against enemies outside the capital.

From the events of 5 September came key components of the Terror. Danton's proposal to limit the Sections to twice-weekly meetings was the first step towards the reining-in of independent *sans-culotte* initiative, and reinforcing the exclusive political authority of the Convention. The Revolutionary Army would help spread Terror to the corners of rural France (while also diverting the most militant *sans-culottes* beyond the capital). Other measures approved in principle would multiply the scope and effectiveness of repression: the Revolutionary Tribunal was enlarged to work as several concurrent chambers, revolutionary and surveillance committees were to be purged of 'suspects' by higher authorities, and a general measure to intern all suspect persons was adopted. New regulations on economic control were also proposed, though the Convention would still hesitate over taking this measure forward for a few more weeks at least.

The delicate balance between the Convention and the radicals of the capital had tipped for the moment back towards the former, and emblematic of this was the arrest on this very day of the Enragé Jacques Roux. The scourge of moderates and hoarders had been arrested already on 22 August by the Commune for denouncing its handling of the food supply. Released on the 27th, his home Section demonstrated its continuing confidence in him by electing him to the committee co-ordinating the 5 September petition. When it met, however, in a typically *sans-culotte* move the committee at once purged itself, and Roux was one of the 'dubious' men thrown out. As such, he was therefore sufficiently suspect for his own Section reluctantly to order his detention, where he would linger uselessly until committing suicide the following February to avoid a show trial before the Revolutionary Tribunal.[72] By then, all of France had learned just how far a commitment to Terror as a political maxim could take them.

## Chapter 8

# Saturnalia

On 26 October 1793, on the Place Bellecour, heart of an elegant neighbourhood built less than twenty years before to house the grandest of Lyon's elite, the representative-on-mission Georges Couthon raised a silver hammer and struck three blows on a wall of one of the graceful townhouses that lined the square. Carried there in his invalid chair by four stout *sans-culottes*, Couthon had issued a condemnation in a voice that rang round the square: the Place Bellecour, and all the houses of Lyon's rich, were doomed. 'May this terrible example strike fear into future generations,' he proclaimed. 'The French nation, always great and just, knows how to reward virtue, so it also knows how to abhor crime and punish rebellion.' As his words and the subsequent hammer-blows died away, a crowd of men, women and children, recruited from the poorest of Lyon's working classes, ran forward and began to smash down the dwellings of the elite.[1] Formerly they would have been hustled from the very street before such buildings; now they rampaged inside them with sledgehammers. They did so in a city which had officially ceased to exist. Surrendering to the intensifying bombardment of an ever-closer siege on 9 October, Lyon had been wiped from the map of France by decree of the Convention three days later. Couthon's act of the 26th inaugurated a demolition that was planned to leave only the dwellings of the poor and buildings of 'public utility' standing, in a city renamed 'Freed Town' (Ville Affranchie). A triumphal column raised over the ruins was to bear a stark inscription: 'Lyon Made War on Liberty. Lyon Is No More.'[2]

France in the autumn of 1793 was a world turned upside down. By the end of October when Couthon's followers went to work, eventually razing some sixteen hundred of Lyon's finer houses along with the city's ancient fortifications, the country had been subjected to a two-month whirlwind of shocks and innovations under the name of Terror, and more were to come. With all of them, the tensions that had preceded the declaration of Terror on 5 September continued to resonate through the republican body politic, drawing its sinews ever tighter, but at the same time ever closer to their breaking point. Danton's intervention on that day may have saved the Convention from Parisian pressure (whether threatening or merely embarrassing), but that pressure did not relent. On the very next day further *sans-culotte* intervention obliged the Convention to elect Billaud-Varenne and Collot-d'Herbois to the Committee of Public Safety. Both men had a long history (in revolutionary terms) of being at the forefront of radicalism. Collot had proposed the motion to abolish royalty on 22 September 1792, and Billaud had followed up with the formal proposal to substitute the Republic One and Indivisible the same day. They had also helped to drive through the anti-hoarding legislation of the summer.[3] Billaud had been faced down in his intemperate demands for more scrutiny of the executive on the 5th, but would now be in place to carry out just such a suspicious overview. Collot, the ex-playwright and theatre manager from Lyon, was equally ardent in his politics, but had been on mission elsewhere through many of the capital's more recent crises, and was soon to undertake more such work, part of a new wave of vengeance as the Republic dealt with the fading remnants of the Federalist menace.

Carrying out the agenda of 5 September, the Convention produced a sweeping 'Law of Suspects' on the 17th, ordering the incarceration of all ex-nobles, women and children included, unless they could prove their attachment to the Republic, and of anyone who had expressed opposition to the Revolution. Also to be detained were those unable to justify their conduct or means of support to one of the ubiquitous Surveillance Committees, or to whom such a committee had refused to issue a *certificat de civisme*, the Civic Certificates now essential for public business and travel. Public officials dismissed from their posts in any of the Revolution's upheavals joined this list, as did all who were ever placed on a list of *émigrés*, regardless of their date of return.[4] In its spirit, this law clearly continued to target those figures that remained the Revolution's classic enemies: the aristocrats, corrupt public officials (like the parade of monarchists, Feuillants and Girondins drummed out of office in the last two years), and alongside them, those without substance or morals, the indigent and shiftless 'brigands' who had been the major victims of the September Massacres a year earlier.

Such a measure alone would indeed have been draconian, but it was intensified in the capital particularly by the zeal with which Surveillance Committees could find reasons to refuse Civic Certificates. On 11 September the Paris Commune had laid down extensive grounds for such refusals, in anticipation of the new laws. Their list included, naturally, declared enemies of the Revolution by word or deed, but also an entire range of other actions harder to classify: for example, 'those who pity the farmers and greedy merchants against whom the law is obliged to take measures', or who 'in assemblies of the people, arrest their energy by crafty discourses, turbulent cries and threats'; 'who speak mysteriously of the misfortunes of the Republic, are full of pity for the lot of the people, and are always ready to spread bad news with an affected grief'; or who 'received the republican constitution with indifference and have given credence to false fears concerning its establishment and duration'. One can see that a broadly drawn definition of sedition might just cover such activities, but the Commune's list went on: 'those who, having done nothing against liberty, have also done nothing for it', and, even more tellingly, 'those who do not attend the meetings of their Sections and who give as excuses that they do not know how to speak or that their occupation prevents them'.[5] In the Paris of the *sans-culotte* Terror, there was to be literally no excuse for not being an ardent patriot.

Within a few months, over fifty separate places of detention had been requisitioned in the capital alone, and over seven thousand individuals were detained at their own expense: if they wanted a bed and not just a pile of straw, they had to pay almost a livre a day, monthly in advance, to the guards. Those that could not afford it rotted amid their own excrement in overcrowded, rat-infested cells.[6] By the following summer, the number of detained suspects across

France would rise to some three hundred thousand. It is nonetheless worth reflecting on the fact that the vast majority of these suspects survived the Terror, whereas many more might have perished if the *sans-culotte* and Enragé calls of the summer, envisaging implicitly a new and greater September Massacres, had gone unchecked. As with the formation of the Revolutionary Tribunal, concerning which Danton had said, 'Let us be terrible, so that the people does not have to be,' the always ambiguous issue of the control of violence was an abiding concern of the Convention.[7] Like every other measure of the time, the Law of Suspects reflected the tensions within the coalition of revolutionaries, as well as the hatred of counter-revolution that supposedly united them.

In a telling example of such tensions, the *sans-culotte* activists of the capital moved swiftly to circumvent Danton's move to neuter them by restricting their meetings. The ruse already used to evade Girondin controls in the spring, of reforming as a 'Popular Society', enabled the twice-weekly Section meetings to be spun out into something very like the 'permanence' they were now officially denied. With the wave of such new 'societies' formed from the largely male activists of the Sections, the mixed-sex groups that had flowered under the Cordeliers' influence since 1791 went into eclipse. *Sans-culotte* Paris was a community based on close neighbourhood connections and local powerbases, with little place for the free association of the earlier groups – or for their prominent role for women.

While the enemies of the Republic, both real and merely suspected, were rounded up in the weeks after 17 September, the Convention was also finally pressurised into granting the *sans-culottes* their 'General Maximum' on foodstuffs on the 29th. What they got, however, was a two-edged sword. Prices on a wide range of goods were restricted to 1790 levels, plus one-third, plus transport allowances and a 15 per cent sellers' premium – something over a 50 per cent increase on the 1790 figure, but a cut of a quarter on what shops had been charging that summer.[8] Consumers stripped stores of goods as soon as the regulated prices were announced, and the difficulties of ensuring that producers would restock at these new rates were immense.

The report that introduced the Maximum made clear the exceptional circumstances that had occasioned it, noting that 'in normal times' the price mechanisms of supply and demand functioned perfectly: 'This balance is infallible. It is useless for even the best governments to interfere.' Such a doctrinaire statement of *laissez-faire* economics was wilfully blind to the persistent economic regulation of the Old Regime, but it reflected the pieties of enlightened thinking exactly. Not for nothing had successive revolutionary regimes tried time and again to free the grain trade from its police, only to be driven back by popular anger. In this ideological context, the Maximum could only be justified to the Convention politically: 'When a general conspiracy of malignancy, perfidy and unparalleled fury joins together to break this natural equilibrium, to famish and despoil us, the welfare of the people becomes the highest rule.'[9]

Thus those who sold over the new prices would be denounced as suspects, and markets would be overseen again as they had been only a few years before, only now in much greater detail. Much of the apparatus of the Terror would have to be devoted to just this problem – the Subsistence Commission's bureaucrats would soon outnumber those of the Committee of Public Safety – but meanwhile the urban consumer was also threatened by a Maximum on wages that notionally accompanied the price regulation, at a rate of only 50 per cent over 1790 levels. Even official statistics showed that the going rate for labour in late 1793 was up to twice that level, and this measure was effectively unenforceable in the private sector. The pay of the many who passed into the employ of the state under the mass levy was tightly regulated, however. It was also paid in the assignat paper currency which, despite rallying from 22 per cent in August, was worth only 48 per cent of its face value by the end of 1793. Montagnard sympathy for the working population, despite echoing the rhetoric of the *sans-culottes*, did not go so far as to offer them prosperity, merely survival.[10]

The provisioning of the Republic, and especially of its cities and armies, was one of the key justifications for the formation of the Revolutionary Armies demanded on 5 September. Recruiting for the Parisian force went on throughout September, producing a body of some six thousand infantry and cavalry and a large associated corps of artillery – although this group, the *crème de la crème* of militancy, were used more in battle in the Vendée than in tracking down food-hoarders. The cavalry were a strange grouping, in which more than one aristocrat hid himself – although one, the prince de Rohan-Rochefort, was caught the day after enrolling (and later sent to the guillotine) when a faithful former servant called him 'monseigneur' in conversation. Their recruitment would become the source of recrimination and hints of corruption, in contrast to the infantry, who were nominated from the Sections as examples of the finest *sans-culotte* virtues. What that meant in practice was that the rank and file of the Parisian force were artisans and traders in their thirties – too old to have gone off to the front – with a long experience of neighbourhood politics, and usually with an intimate conviction that the peasantry were determined to starve the city. Generations of hostility between producers and consumers were embodied in men who fanned out across the Paris Basin, sometimes in groups of no more than a half-dozen, to terrify the inhabitants of villages and individual farms in their pursuit of hoarding and other suspect activity.[11]

Across the country, further armed groups on the pattern of the Revolutionary Armies were raised by local authorities, and in particular on the initiative of the representatives-on-mission. These men continued to be sent out from the Convention in waves – fifty-eight individual commissions in August, twenty-nine in September, forty-five in October. In some cases, the same men were sent to different areas at different times, but over these three months only forty-five deputies were recalled to Paris, so the number of them at large in the country grew steadily.[12] The independent authority granted to these men by the Convention was to become a bone of contention between them and the Committee of Public Safety, as well as a general problem for the population of France. An order signed by the representative Laplanche, at Bourges in the quiet central department of the Cher, illustrates this. On 28 September 1793, 'by virtue of the unlimited powers invested in us by the National Convention', he named various citizens as his commissioners to each of the surrounding districts, each with powers 'to depose any weak, negligent or prevaricatory civil or military administrators'. These men were also authorised 'to tax the rich revolutionarily, to strike against bad priests, and to gather patriots and republicans into action everywhere against the oppression of egoism, moderatism, fanaticism and aristocracy'.[13]

As the coming months were to show, the licence to disrupt local politics on a whim, and to raise private armies to enforce those whims, would prove very difficult to contain. Nevertheless, it is worth noting that the Committee of Public Safety, in drafting individual orders for such representatives, gave them every reason to act with zeal. Maximilien Robespierre's younger brother and fellow deputy Augustin, ordered to Marseille back in August, had been told to take 'vigorous measures against the rebels', and to exercise 'the greatest severity', in a letter written by the military technocrat Lazare Carnot. In September, a representative sent to Nantes was warned that 'we can be human only when we are assured of victory'. When Laplanche, noted above, was ordered a month later to Caen, he was told to carry out 'dazzling acts of severity that spare no guilty person', and in November a representative sent to the Pas-de-Calais was reminded that 'all revolutionary measures are allowed, or rather commanded, to you'. These orders were all signed by diverse members of the Committee, including Robespierre, Carnot, Billaud-Varenne, Barère and the former noble Hérault de Séchelles, and their injunctions, with their edge of savage desperation, were the routine language of its correspondence.[14] The control of violence, if it meant on the one hand preventing aimless popular vengeance, meant on the other channelling the energies and fears behind the threat of such vengeance into supposedly more purposive, but sometimes little less bloody initiatives.

The weeks after the declaration of Terror on 5 September had already proved a difficult time for the Convention and the Committee. At first it had seemed that the moment had been crowned with a great military victory, when news came in a few days later of the battle of Hondschoote. In this three-day engagement, French forces under the recently appointed General Houchard – the first non-noble to hold the rank, replacing the guillotined Custine – finally drove off Anglo-Hanoverian troops threatening the port of Dunkirk. Carnot, the chief military man on the Committee of Public Safety, had set great store by this goal, believing that a decisive defeat for English arms could be the signal for a general popular uprising across the Channel. This wider goal of course went unfulfilled, and revolutionary rejoicing was further dampened as Houchard's forces became ensnared in the days after their 'victory' in a series of costly and indecisive engagements. The enemy had clearly not been crippled, as first reports had indicated. No fewer than twelve representatives-on-mission accompanied the French army, and it was one of these, returning to Paris on 20 September, who broke the news that all was not well: so much so, indeed, that he accused Houchard of betraying his own army. On the 22nd, the general was relieved of command and arrested by order of the Committee of Public Safety.[15]

On 25 September a two-day crisis ensued, as the rank and file of the Convention accused the Committee of keeping them in the dark about news from the front. A motion of censure was passed, and on the 26th Robespierre, Barère and two other members (the only ones actually present in the capital) appeared before the Convention to answer charges of inaction. Robespierre responded acidly, firstly lambasting the Convention itself: 'Whoever seeks to debase, divide or paralyse the Convention is an enemy of our country, whether he sits in this hall or is a foreigner. Whether he acts from stupidity or from perversity, he is of the party of tyrants who make war upon us.' After the telling-off he answered their complaints like an aggrieved parent to an ungrateful child:

> We are accused of doing nothing, but has our position been realised? Eleven armies to direct, the weight of all Europe to carry, everywhere traitors to unmask, agents paid by the gold of foreign powers to confound, faithless officials to watch over, everywhere obstacles and difficulties in the execution of wise measures to smooth away, all tyrants to combat, all conspirators to intimidate, almost all of them of that caste once so powerful by its riches, and still strong in its intrigues – these are our functions![16]

The Committee, therefore, must have the Convention's support in order to do its work – if not, then all of the twelve would resign. Cowed, the Convention gave in, and formally voted its confidence in the full Committee. By insisting on their unity, the disparate men who were ruling France stamped their authority over a body which, until then, had been more concerned with unmaking rulers than supporting them. It would be some ten months before the Committee's rights of political initiative and administrative control were to be challenged again.

The case of Houchard, the pretext for this row, was asserted by the Committee to be a clear-cut matter of treason. Their credibility rested on it, and the alternative was to blame failure, undiplomatically, on either the common soldiers or the interfering representatives. Thus there could be no going back. Polite correspondence with enemy commanders over prisoner-exchanges was elevated into evidence of treasonous intent. The general, a battle-scarred fifty-five-year-old who had been happily ensconced as a cavalry captain until the Republic brought him unlooked-for burdens, pleaded his innocence to no avail. He joined twenty-four other generals in prison, and like most of them went to the guillotine before the year was out.[17]

Despite the Committee's triumph in this matter, problems and uncertainties remained. The economic liberalism that still ruled many politicians' minds had baulked at the General Maximum. The threat posed by the capital's radicals was not eased when the hot-headed Ronsin was recalled from the Vendée to take charge of the Parisian Revolutionary Army. This was an appointment the Committee of Public Safety would have liked to go to Hanriot, commander of the National Guard – who despite his formidable role in the overthrow of the Girondins was a safer pair of hands, distanced from ultra-radicals like Hébert and Vincent. The Committee's agenda thus faced continued pressures from both left and right. With the Maximum and the Revolutionary Army in place, the next item of business was the dispatch of the great traitors and enemies still held in custody, and on 3 October twenty-two leading Girondins were sent for trial by the Revolutionary Tribunal (and an equal number, at large in the country, outlawed). Also dispatched to the Tribunal was Marie-Antoinette, still lingering in the Conciergerie prison under the obsessive eyes of the Commune's guards. Even the Convention session that ordered the trials saw controversy, as Robespierre had to fight off a motion by the radical Billaud-Varenne to take a roll-call on the vote – exposing potential new traitors, or further imperilling republican unity, depending on one's viewpoint.[18] Shockingly, trial preparations had revealed that some seventy-six deputies still sitting in the Convention had signed a secret protest against the expulsion of the Girondin leadership back in June, and it was politically necessary now to detain all of these men (Robespierre again had to resist efforts to put them all on trial as well, a move that would have endangered the fragile peace achieved with much of the country after the original purge).[19] With these figures out of the way, it is arguable that the remaining deputies were more radical, on balance, than the Committee itself, but as we shall see, defining 'radicalism' was to grow more problematic over the coming months.

One great radical move – in the original sense of going to the root – was to seize revolutionary control of the very notion of time itself. On 20 September Gilbert Romme, a mild-mannered but committed Montagnard ex-teacher who had suffered two months' imprisonment at Federalist hands in Normandy, reported to the Convention on a truly epoch-making project: the Revolutionary Calendar. Noting that the Convention had agreed a wide-ranging project to reform weights and measures (something not to come to fruition for several years, but which would ultimately give birth to the metric system), he observed that 'the arts and history' also needed a new organisation of 'duration . . . similarly free from the errors that credulity and superstitious routine have transmitted from centuries of ignorance to us'.[20] The Gregorian calendar was condemned as the record of the crimes of kings and priests, 'the era of cruelty, lies, perfidy and slavery; it ended with royalty, the source of all our ills'. Following through the logic which had begun with declaring 1792 to be the First Year of the French Republic, Romme then proposed that all dates should be revised:

> The Revolution has renewed the souls of Frenchmen; it educates them each day in republican virtues. Time opens a new book in history; and in its new march, as majestic and simple as equality, it must engrave with a new and vigorous instrument the annals of regenerated France.

The old years and months were to be abolished by decree, replaced by a system of twelve equal thirty-day months, while the extra five or six days at the end of the year, running up to the autumnal equinox (when, fortuitously, the Republic had been created), would be given over to national festivities. The week was to be replaced with a ten-day period (the *décade*, with just one day of rest – storing up trouble for the future popularity of the measure), and, within each day, the twenty-four hours would be replaced by ten segments, each themselves divided into ten smaller periods (of just under fifteen 'old' minutes), and then further subdivided as necessary *ad infinitum* 'down to the smallest measurable units of duration'. The changes to the internal measure of the day were postponed for a year, to allow the production of sufficient decimal clocks – which never actually happened, and so that part of the measure effectively lapsed. Everything else, however, took effect on 5 October. For several weeks the new system lacked a handy nomenclature, until on 'Day 3 of the 2nd month of the 2nd year of the French Republic', or 24 October, a second report was presented by Philippe Fabre d'Eglantine, another former teacher (and in this case also ex-playwright), friend of both Danton and Marat, who had been charged with naming the new divisions of time.[21]

Fabre had given himself the surname d'Eglantine after winning a symbolic dog-rose (or eglantine) crown in a poetry competition at Toulouse, and he brought his creative talents to bear on his new task. He took as his starting point the notion that it was essential 'to bring the French people back to agriculture'. It was a remarkable assertion, given the scorn of the most active republicans for the priest-ridden peasantry, but Fabre insisted that 'agriculture is the political element of a people such as we – a people on whom the earth, the sky and nature look with so much love and affection'. To reciprocate this bounty, the popular affection that the old liturgical calendar had managed to conjure up for 'imaginary objects, alleged saints' should be turned on to the real material influences on the population, 'to consecrate the agricultural system, and to lead the nation back to it'. This came down essentially to a system of naming the months, so that each season bore a certain ending, and each individual month recorded the key agricultural conditions or events (see Figure 1).

Although sometimes thought of as a manifestation of the revolutionaries' universalism – of which the metric system is a better example – the Republican Calendar was always intended to be very French. It was only in France that it could possibly be true, as Fabre concluded his report, that 'by simply pronouncing the name of the month one will be perfectly aware of the nature and implications of the season, the temperature and the state of vegetation'.[22] Even then, the further one went from the centre, towards the baking *garrigues* of the south-east, the high slopes of the Pyrenees or the windswept moors of Brittany, the further the calendar would retreat from its supposedly realistic references.

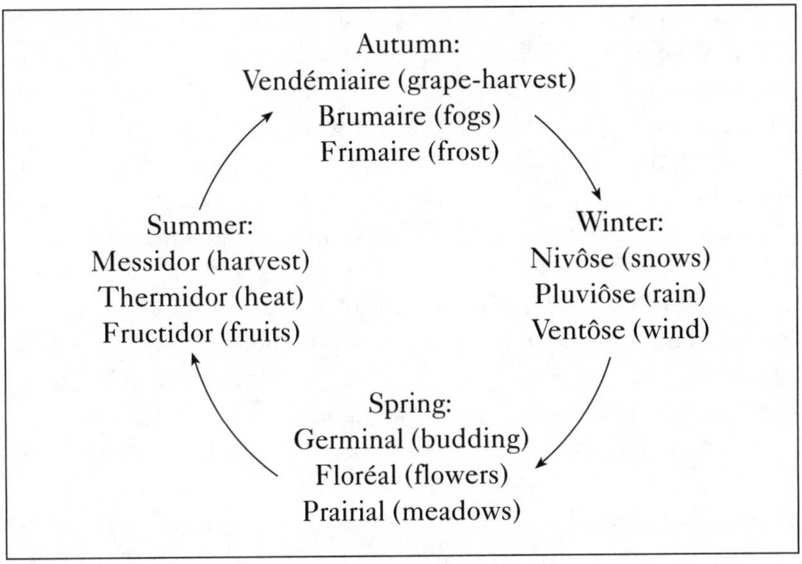


*Figure 1* The Revolutionary Calendar.

The Convention shrugged aside such quibbles, and adopted the new nomenclature immediately. It fitted well with a spirit of linguistic innovation that was making its mark in other ways. From 1 November (or 11 brumaire, Year II, as it was now), the Committee of Public Safety took up a practice that had begun with *sans-culotte* notions of equality, and abandoned use of the formal *vous* when addressing individuals in its voluminous correspondence. No one was now entitled to this mark of distinction, all were *tu*, the familiar form hitherto reserved for children, inferiors and intimates – after all, were the French not all brothers and sisters? The elaborate formal style of writing also passed away: no more 'I beg you, sir, to accept the assurances of my most distinguished sentiments', a simple *Salut et fraternité*, 'Fraternal greetings!', now closed good republicans' correspondence. *Monsieur* and *Madame* went the same way in common usage – at their roots were terms for 'squire' and 'lady' with no place in the new order. 'Citizen' was now the appropriate form of address, though this reserved the distinction of the sexes: women were *citoyennes*, an ambiguous term reflecting in part the fact that they were not simply *citoyens*, as was to be made even clearer in the coming months.

Such linguistic efforts to shape a uniform and united body politic were, in part at least, the ironic reflection of the chronic disunity that continued to afflict the Republic. Before the new calendar had been named, the authority of the Committee of Public Safety had been bolstered by the decision definitively to suspend the 1793 Constitution. Even this, however, had been the outcome of a tense and divisive process. Against *sans-culotte* calls for new elections, the Convention proclaimed that the government of the Republic would be 'Revolutionary until the Peace'. They did so on the initiative of the Committee, presented on 10 October by Saint-Just, the ice-cold ideologist of republican purity. This move itself was intended to head off a new rift with the Convention. On 4 October Billaud-Varenne had presented a report from the Committee to the Convention, perhaps against his radical political judgment, that complained of the persistent initiative of local authorities, their willingness to interfere in each other's jurisdictions and arrogate powers to themselves, and the extent to which the representatives-on-mission aided and abetted this process with their own unhesitating recourse to exceptional measures and personal discretion. The Convention had rejected the report, and its proposals to rein in all these figures and bodies, particularly bridling at the implied collective insult to the Convention in the persons of its roaming members.[23]

When Saint-Just spoke on 10 October, he avoided the touchy subject of the powers and prerogatives of the representatives. In doing so, however, he found it necessary to expose an even more shocking and dire state of affairs. Saint-Just pulled no punches in an extraordinary speech:

> You have had energy; the public administration has lacked it. You have wanted thrift; public finance has not seconded your efforts. Everyone has pillaged the state. Generals have waged war against their armies. Those possessing goods and provisions, together with everything that was vicious in the monarchy, have joined in league against you and the people.
>
> A people has only one dangerous enemy, and that is its government. Yours has constantly made war against you with impunity.[24]

The charges rolled on: 'It is possible that there is not a single military commander who is not secretly basing his fortune on betrayal in favour of kings.' 'Bad choice of government officials is the cause of our misfortunes. Positions have been bought ... The schemers perpetuate themselves ... Government is therefore a perpetual conspiracy against the present order of things.' 'It is possible for France's enemies to have your entire government occupied in three months by conspirators.' 'The rich have got richer ... They have doubled their wealth; they have doubled their means of seduction ... they are the ones who are everywhere in competition with the state for its purchases.' 'You prosecute hoarders, you cannot prosecute those who appear to be buying for the armies ... The majority of men declared suspect have an interest in provisioning. The government is the underwriter for every act of plunder and for all crimes.'[25]

Saint-Just's analysis, while rhetorically overblown, was not wholly inaccurate. General Houchard, the victor and scapegoat of Hondschoote, had written dejectedly to the Committee of Public Safety before the battle listing some of his problems: reinforcements turning up ten thousand fewer than promised, no new horses to move his artillery, no feed for a fortnight for those he already had. Food reserves for the men were rapidly depleting, there was no co-operation from local political authorities, his quartermaster-general was under arrest as a suspect, and the newly appointed replacement had no relevant experience. Ten million livres in paper money had just arrived from Paris, but there was nothing to spend it on. A second letter, penned as the first shots of the battle were fired, complained that his subordinate general officers were all either cowardly or shirkers, refusing assignments, quibbling over details and frankly incompetent.[26]

In the situation summarised by letters such as this, echoed by reports from every war front, France thus faced a clear dilemma. The people with the technical skills to organise a war economy, the experience to draw up multi-million-livre contracts and run them successfully, were not the frugal *sans-culotte* republicans that the new state was intended to appeal to. They were either venal by habit, because the business of government finance in previous decades had been run as a venal enterprise, or they had acquired venality through their weakness when confronted by great sums. Those that were not greedy, those most likely to have come new to their positions under the Republic, were often incompetent (and some of course were both), and inclined like any bureaucrat to fight furiously to conceal such failings – especially when they might owe their position essentially to political rectitude and factional allegiance.[27] Incompetence was not an explanation that Saint-Just and his colleagues favoured, however, as Houchard himself had found to his cost. Over all of this the shadow of counter-revolution loomed in its all-consuming enormity – to fail in one's duties was to betray the Republic, and such a crime did not happen by accident. Saint-Just's prescriptions were therefore emphatic:

> There is no prosperity to hope for as long as the last enemy of liberty breathes. You have to punish not only the traitors, but even those who are indifferent; you have to punish whoever is passive in the republic, and who does nothing for it. For, since the French people has manifested its will, everything opposed to it is outside the sovereign; all that is outside the sovereign is the enemy.[28]

The decree on Revolutionary Government passed after this speech gave the Committee of Public Safety the power directly to supervise the Revolutionary Armies, the regular armies, the ministers and all other local authorities, and to requisition anything necessary to the war effort, on a nationwide scale. It also clearly acknowledged that the Committee sat at the heart of a real 'government', requiring regular reports from all local authorities back to the centre, taking charge of the appointment of generals, and setting deadlines for the enforcement of new laws and 'measures of public safety' – violation of which would constitute 'a crime against liberty', and be appropriately punished.[29] The government was 'revolutionary' not merely in the sense that it was the consequence of revolution, but that it would act as it saw fit, outside the bounds of any written laws, to defend the Republic against all the many threats to its existence.

All these enactments, while diplomatically continuing to pass over the role of the representatives-on-mission, harked back to a phrase that Robespierre had written in a memorandum about the state of France back in June: 'There must be one single will' – *une volonté une*.[30] As he went on, for this will to be republican, 'there must be republican ministers, republican newspapers, republican representatives, a republican government'. This followed through the logic that the French had found so compelling ever since the 1760s in the writings of Jean-Jacques Rousseau on the *Social Contract* – that a political community had a 'general will' which represented the best interests of the community as a whole, and that individual wills had to be subordinated to that.[31] The twist that the Revolution, and especially the Republic, had added to Rousseau's formula was to vest the General Will in a body of elected representatives, while still asserting that individual representatives who dissented over the correct course of action to follow could be excluded thereby from the political community, as the Girondins had been. It was a formula for an ever-narrowing definition of political purity and legitimacy, in a political climate that already assumed the worst of all opposition.[32]

The great trials of the autumn before the Revolutionary Tribunal would make this abundantly clear. That of Marie-Antoinette in particular was a showpiece of revolutionary hatred. Orchestrated by both the Tribunal's prosecutor, Fouquier-Tinville, and the Commune in the person of Hébert, it left no stone unturned in its bid to defame the former queen. Fouquier-Tinville's opening charge on 14 October set the scene:

> In the manner of the Messalinas-Brunhildes, Fredegund and Médicis, who were called in previous times queens of France, and whose names, forever odious, will not be effaced from the annals of history, Marie-Antoinette, widow of Louis Capet, has been during her time in France the scourge and the bloodsucker of the French.[33]

The actual charges were a diverse and self-sustaining catalogue of vice and treachery. Since her teenage years, she had allegedly squandered the wealth of France on her own 'disorderly pleasures', while also diverting secret funds to Austria. Since 1789, she had animated every major counter-revolutionary threat, exercising her influence in the supposed manner of the classic female intriguer, through a series of sexual liaisons with everyone from the king's brother Artois to the marquis de Lafayette. Given her utter loathing of Lafayette, and distaste for Artois' political posturings, such charges were a tissue of absurdities, but they were also the common currency of public perceptions of the queen, retailed in countless pamphlets and pornographic illustrations, and the Tribunal was not about to let them pass unreinforced.[34] From all of this emerged her key treason, that of influencing the king against his people. She had caused him to appoint treacherous and 'perverse' ministers, and more generally she had taught him to dissimulate, to go against his own public word in plotting the downfall of the French.

The final charge was designed to show that, even in prison, the 'widow Capet' continued to conspire against the good of the country. She was 'so perverse and so familiar with all crimes' that she had even committed incest with her own son, alongside his aunt the king's sister, in a bid to debauch a child who they thought might yet be brought to the throne, 'and on whom they wished, by this manoeuvre, to assure themselves the right of ruling afterwards over his morals'.[35] It was Hébert himself who introduced this charge to the court, claiming to have it from the lips of the queen's eight-year-old son himself, who had been caught masturbating by a guard, and said the two women had taught him to do it. We can only speculate on whether he ever said such a thing, and what pressures might have been put on the terrified, isolated and guilty child to this end. Hébert went on to charge that the boy's health had been seriously compromised (and one of his testicles physically injured), but that he had recovered much of his natural vigour since separation from his mother during the summer.

Marie-Antoinette herself, who had been denied access to her children for several months, had been left aged and gaunt by her prison ordeal. Such was the paranoia of the Parisian authorities that an armed guard had stood over her even while she slept in the days before the trial. After the so-called 'Carnation Plot' of early September – when supposedly a note with escape plans was found inside a flower dropped in her cell – her first custodians were jailed, and those that replaced them were so fearful that they were driven to harshness even against their will. A serving-maid recalled later that one such jailer begged her forgiveness for not letting her attend to Marie-Antoinette's hair: 'The least thing makes me tremble . . . don't do anything imprudent or I'm a lost man.'[36] The former queen was deprived even of sewing-needles, though she kept busy by making a form of tapestry from rough yarns torn from the canvas panelling in her cell. She was given only a cardboard box to hold her possessions, and not allowed to keep so much as a drinking-glass unsupervised. Nonetheless, she remained calm and dignified, complaining only at the cold and damp as October drew in. Her health was suffering – her menstrual flow grew excessive, and the loyal serving-maid, Rosalie Lamorlière, had to discreetly prepare extra linen for her. On the day of the trial's opening, Rosalie was deprived of one of her last opportunities to serve the queen by a further indignity. As she went to take her a bowl of soup, a visiting *sans-culotte* official seized it and gave it to his companion to deliver, 'an overdressed young creature' who wanted an excuse to see the queen in her misery.[37]

Marie-Antoinette was only thirty-eight, but now looked ten or twenty years older. She nonetheless bore herself with dignity through the further and more public ordeal of the trial. A hostile gallery of male and female *sans-culottes* ringed the courtroom, and the attitudes of the personnel present left no doubt as to what her fate would be. Much of the damning evidence produced – including copies of personal correspondence in which she betrayed French military plans – was lost beneath the torrent of character assassination. She was supposed, for example, to have loaded the muskets of Swiss Guards in the Tuileries, biting open the cartridges with her teeth so they could pour fire on the patriots of Paris – all at the time when she was actually in the custody of the Legislative Assembly.[38] Only at the accusation of incest did she bristle, declaring that she would not lower herself to answer 'such a charge against a mother'.[39]

Not every revolutionary saw the value in these assaults: Robespierre himself spat that Hébert was an 'idiot' for pursuing his vendetta against the queen to such obscene lengths, his own puritanism rebelling against their lascivious details.[40] Others saw in the absurdities of the trial a more sinister design. The American ambassador Gouverneur Morris noted his belief that 'this execution will, I think, give future hostilities a deeper dye, and unite more intimately the Allied Powers'. It would also 'silence the opposition' of those who had failed to rally to the counter-revolution, 'and therefore it may be concluded that the blow by which she died was directed from a distance'.[41] Once again the revolutionary generation here shows itself adept at inferring the causes that most interest it from consequences that were manifestly overdetermined in numerous ways.

It made no difference: Marie-Antoinette was tried for two days, convicted, and on 16 October driven through the streets of Paris to the guillotine in an open cart, her hands tied behind her, wearing only a simple shift dress and cap. Once again, a gendarme had watched her closely, even as she changed her bloodstained linen for the last time. Without the chance to choose her own confessor, she had refused the services of the constitutional priest sent by the authorities.[42] Jacques-Louis David, the Montagnard artist-politician, sketched her cruelly, hatchet-faced and grim, as she took her last journey, exposed to the jeers of the crowd. On the scaffold she kept her composure until the last moment, cold and fear only then combining to make her visibly tremble. The press reported that she trod on the executioner's toe, leaving thus as her last words the ironically self-effacing 'I beg your pardon. I did not do it on purpose.' The radical journal *The Revolutions of Paris* commented uncharitably that she might have contrived this 'to add interest to her memory, for there are some people whose vanity persists as long as life itself'.[43] She had neither time nor inclination to make a speech – she would not repeat her husband's offer to pardon her killers – and Hébert was left to rejoice in the next edition of his *Père Duchesne* with 'the greatest of all joys . . . having with his own eyes seen the head of the female veto separated from her fucking tart's neck'.[44]

With Marie-Antoinette out of the way, attention could turn to the imprisoned Girondins, targets of radical wrath on 5 September for their allegedly cosy confinement in the Luxembourg palace. The decision to commit them for trial on 3 October followed a report to the Convention from the Committee of General Security that had accused them of a catalogue of crimes, rolled up into the charge that they were agents of the counter-revolution and of the foreign powers, especially Britain. When the trial of the twenty-two detained men opened, this theme was played out extensively in the prosecution speeches: William Pitt, British prime minister, 'wanted to vilify and dissolve the Convention, they have worked to dissolve the Convention; Pitt wanted to assassinate the faithful representatives of the people, they have assassinated Marat and Lepeletier'.[45] The Montagnard leadership, Robespierre included on this occasion, wanted to make of this a grand show trial, to draw a line under all of the treacheries of previous power-holding 'factions', and to drive home the message of the counter-revolutionary import of Federalism. Unfortunately, the accused were still allowed to speak in their own defence, and they included not just some of the best political journalists of the 1790s, but also men whose careers were founded on forensic and political oratory. Brissot was notably able in his own defence, rebutting point by point the absurdities of the charges, while Vergniaud also rose to the height of his powers, as usual extemporising his speeches from brief notes.

Vergniaud's surviving notes are almost plaintive in their brevity. He began with the central charge: 'I belonged to a faction. There was a conspiracy.' His reply is straightforward: 'I knew B[rissot] at the Jacobins. The others unknown to each other: how in coalition? Diversity of our opinions on various issues.' As we have seen, there is little evidence for according the Girondins anything close to a party line on most policies, until driven into unity by their opponents. Vergniaud noted cryptically some of the moments when the Gironde had stood out against the majority, principally over the king's trial, but then passed on to more morose reflections, as if acknowledging the hopelessness of the situation: 'If the blood of a Girondin is required, let mine suffice. They will be able to make amends by their talents and their services . . . Besides they are fathers, husbands. As for me, schooled in adversity . . . My death will make no-one unhappy.'[46] He was only just forty, and others were younger still: Brissot thirty-nine, Gensonné thirty-five.

Just as Vergniaud's thoughts fade into melancholia, so the trial was abruptly cut short. Alarmed at the inroads the defendants were making into the paper-thin case against them, the Committee of Public Safety (on Robespierre's proposal) obtained a change in the rules of the Revolutionary Tribunal from the Convention on 29 October. Prosecutor Fouquier-Tinville was now empowered to end a trial after three days by securing the jury's agreement that their 'consciences had been sufficiently enlightened' as to the facts.[47] On the very next day, this came to pass, and the inevitable death sentences were pronounced. One witness, on the jury itself, recalled the drama of the moment of Brissot's sentence: his head fell forwards onto his chest, and the Montagnard journalist Camille Desmoulins, whose *History of the Brissotins* had systematically defamed Brissot's career, cried out from the gallery, 'My God I am sorry for this!'[48] Desmoulins was a violently emotional character, soon to be as caustic in his condemnation of terrorist excess as he had been ardent in promoting the destruction of Brissot: this moment may have been an epiphany on the road to that transformation.

Most of the convicted men shared Vergniaud's stoic resignation – only one protested at the sentencing – but another, Charles Dufriche-Valazé, made up for his previous lack of political distinction with a melodramatic gesture. As sentence was pronounced, he pitched backwards from his bench, and blood poured onto the floor: he had stabbed himself with a knife concealed in his papers. Dead within minutes, he nonetheless would not cheat the executioner. The Girondins spent their last night together along with his corpse, and it travelled with them to lose its head on the Place de la Révolution. The stark contrast between the Girondins' self-image as martyred patriots and their condemnation as traitors was again on show as they met their deaths. They sang the *Marseillaise* together in the tumbril, and strode defiantly forward to the scaffold, crying '*Vive la République!*' as they entered the guillotine's bloody embrace. But the assembled crowds rejoiced at their demise: it took less than forty minutes to execute them all, and loud cheers greeted the last head to fall.[49]

Throughout the next month, the Revolutionary Tribunal saw a series of individual show trials. Philippe Egalité, the former duc d'Orléans, perished on 6 November, guilty essentially of being himself – member of the royal family, friend to disgraced figures such as Mirabeau, Dumouriez and Brissot – and by inevitable extension, therefore, a plotter against the Republic. Having voted for the death of his royal cousin (an act he reportedly repented of on the scaffold) could not save him.[50] Three days later Madame Roland was beheaded. At her trial little more had been done than to point out that she was the wife of the minister Roland, notorious hostess of the Girondin salons, and notorious lover of the deputy Buzot. A few hints as to her 'unnatural' female concern with political activity were sufficient for the jury to convict without further ado. She was thirty-nine. Her husband, twenty years her senior, had hidden successfully in Rouen throughout the turbulent summer and autumn. He emerged from his hiding place when he heard of her death and set out on the Paris road. At a peaceful spot, he sat down beneath a tree and, in true Roman fashion, fell on his sword. The note found with him ended with the words 'I left my refuge as soon as I heard my wife had been murdered. I no longer desire to remain in a world covered with crime.'[51]

The political executions continued on 12 November with that of Jean-Sylvain Bailly, the former mayor of Paris responsible for the Champ de Mars Massacre that had followed the Flight to Varennes. Condemned for this, and for having supposedly aided the king's attempted escape, he was more broadly reviled as a representative of the closed and arrogant academic caste of the Old Regime. Taken to a specially erected guillotine on the site of the massacre, he was assailed and spat upon by angry crowds along the route, and mocked as he stood coatless for an hour in freezing rain while the executioner struggled to burn the symbolic red flag of martial law – 'Bailly, you are trembling!' one onlooker cried out. 'Because I am cold,' he spat back. He went to his death stoically, resisting the role of terrified victim in a drama of revenge put on especially for the Parisian crowds.[52]

At the end of the month there was another flurry of political victims. Antoine Barnave, the Feuillant leader whom Marie-Antoinette had charmed into a secret correspondence on the carriage-ride back from Varennes, was dragged from the provincial prison-cell he had lingered in since the fall of the monarchy and done to death on 29 November, aged thirty-two. Jean-Paul Rabaut Saint-Etienne, an eminent Protestant pastor who had become a leading Girondin, was guillotined in Paris on 5 December. The drive to hunt down the Girondins would not end here, however. Half a dozen had fled Caen when it fell to the Convention, and most finished up in Bordeaux. Fleeing there too, they spent some eight months on the run in the Gironde department. Guadet, the last survivor of the original Girondin trio, hid in a well in his home town of Saint-Emilion with a colleague, fed by his family. Betrayed in June 1794, the two deputies were executed without ceremony once identified by the authorities, along with six members of Guadet's family. Three other notable Girondins were hiding in the same town, and went on the run cross-country when they heard of the capture. Madame Roland's lover, Buzot, leader of the drive to create the original Federalist army, shot himself as escape became impossible. So too did Jérôme Pétion, once mayor of Paris, and fêted by the crowds only two years earlier as the radical equal of Robespierre, before their dramatic parting over the September Massacres. By the time their bodies were found, they had been half eaten by wolves.[53] The third man, the Marseille patriot Barbaroux, failed to kill himself outright, and was dragged dying to the guillotine to pay properly for his crimes.[54]

If the wave of executions that began with Marie-Antoinette took one direction towards explicit political revenge, it also took another, less immediately explicable, towards the persecution of women. Even before Madame Roland, another prominent female activist had been beheaded on 4 November. Marie-Olympe de Gouges was an outspoken feminist author who had written a 'Declaration of the Rights of Women' during the early Revolution, but had compromised her revolutionary credentials with public sympathy for the king around the time of his execution, and later. Arrested in July 1793, she could have been left to rot in prison, but she was brought out and dispatched only days after the Convention had decreed a crackdown on all female political activity. This decree of 30 October had as its pretext the activities of the Society of Revolutionary Republican Women, the female wing of the loose 'movement' of the Enragés. Several hundred strong, it had survived the persecution of the individual male leaders of the movement, and had settled in the autumn of 1793 on the issue of symbolic items of clothing to express its ardour.

In a city where queuing for provisions had become a way of life, especially for women with families to feed, and where so many men had left for the front lines, or the Revolutionary Army, or spent their time tied up in the business of committees, the crowds in the public spaces of Paris were increasingly female. They were also increasingly vocal in their objections to the hardships they were placed under. Some would become party to radical *sans-culottisme*, but others were too prone to bewail the good old days when the king, supposedly, ensured the supply of food to his people. The Republican Revolutionary Women seem to have decided that women's loyalties could be brought back into line by changing outward appearances – a street-level manifestation of the psychological 'sensationism' so commonplace at the time. On 21 September, with *sans-culotte* support, the Society had extracted from the Convention a decree obliging all women to wear the tricolour cockade (a small rosette of ribbons pinned to the hat or lapel) that had symbolised patriotism since 1789. Such a move earned these activists the enmity of many ordinary Parisian women – unsurprisingly, since no such formal compulsion was placed on men – and the situation deteriorated as the Society went a step further, and tried to assert that patriotic women should adopt the red cap of liberty as their everyday headgear. Violent scuffles, notably with the formidable *poissardes*, the women who ran the stalls of the central markets, led to a political investigation.[55]

The outcome of this was a report to the Convention, read by André Amar on behalf of the Committee of General Security. It was laced with the sentimental effusions of the philosopher Jean-Jacques Rousseau, whose cult status under the Revolution extended beyond the pure politics of his *Social Contract*. His views about the sweet, tender and maternal nature of 'real', natural women, and the gross dangers of allowing them to meddle in masculine affairs of state, were emphatic, and accepted without question by the Convention:

> Should women exercise political rights and meddle in affairs of government? To govern . . . demands extensive knowledge, unlimited attention and devotion, a strict immovability, and self-abnegation . . . Are women capable of these cares . . . ? In general, we can answer no.

Amar went on, 'Do women have the moral and physical strength' to govern and defend society? 'Universal opinion rejects the idea.' The passions of public discussion were 'incompatible with the softness and moderation which are the charm of their sex'. Such assertions appeared in Amar's speech mere minutes after his revelation to the Convention that 'almost six thousand women' had gathered to demonstrate violently against the Republican Revolutionary Women.[56]

It was declared as a matter of established fact that no good could come of female political engagement, and indeed that it positively weakened the body politic, and thus all purely female political associations were closed down, and women were forbidden to be members of any political club. This finally and formally ended the honourable role of the 'Fraternal Societies', in Paris and elsewhere, whose admission of both sexes to political debates had been a turning point in the radicalisation of politics back in 1791. The active assistance of such women was no longer desired in the new Republican Jacobin order, and they were banished to the sidelines. *Citoyennes* were emphatically decreed not to be citizens. Procurator Chaumette of the Paris Commune made the point explicit when a women's deputation attempted to petition the municipality two weeks later:

> Remember the haughty wife of a stupid, perfidious husband, *La Roland*, who thought herself fit to govern the Republic, and who rushed to her downfall; remember the impudent Olympe de Gouges, who was the first to set up women's societies, who abandoned the cares of her household to meddle in the Republic, and whose head fell beneath the avenging blade of the laws.[57]

All this, however, could not banish hundreds of Parisian women from one key site of activism – their cherished presence in the public galleries of the Convention, the Jacobin Club, the Commune and other revolutionary gatherings. Seamstresses and washerwomen, servants and stallholders, craftswomen and midwives, they crossed the spectrum of female labour. Many had male relatives in the assemblies and clubs of Paris; almost all had them in the armies. Readily caricatured as the bloodthirsty *tricoteuses*, the 'knitters' who clustered around the guillotine in anticipation of fresh victims to provide entertainment, such women were eager followers of revolutionary politics. Many did indeed knit, or sew, or shredded linen for bandages in the galleries (as the decree summoning the mass levy had called for). Some even nursed their children there. They might claim, if challenged, that their presence served to avoid paying for candles and firewood at home as they worked, but they were also known to form their own groups of friends and neighbours, and to take an active role in the barracking and cheering that marked political speech-making throughout the period. Such women may have been acceptably passive in the eyes of politicians, but as one later asserted, by attending the Jacobins and maintaining the tradition of popular surveillance 'I served my country like my husband and my children serve it in the armies.'[58]

On 8 December, no doubt to the joy of her good *sans-culotte* sisters, another lesson in female depravity was given with the trial and execution of Marie-Jeanne du Barry. The last great 'official' mistress of Louis XV, she had retired to a convent after his death in 1774 – not by choice, but through the ruthless politics of the court – and had continued to live the frivolous, and indeed debauched, life that had brought her into the late king's affections. It was widely believed that she had been a professional prostitute, whose talent for sexually arousing the elderly and jaded monarch had been deployed by a political faction to gain influence, and to harm the true interests of

France. Under the Republic, her contacts with emigrated former associates, largely relating to incompetent attempts to smuggle her extensive collection of jewellery out of the country, were the pretext for accusations that she was actively seeking to finance *émigré* forces.[59] She died essentially as a symbol, like Marie-Antoinette, of all that the Revolution had come to hate.

While in Paris the machinery of execution was digging deeper into the past to find its victims, in the provinces the all too current crimes of the Federalists were being expediently judged. Central authority had finally returned to recalcitrant Bordeaux on 17 October, the representatives-on-mission entering the city at the head of 1600 troops, to be greeted by a nervous provisional council, elected a month earlier and desperate to stave off republican revenge. One of the representatives, Jean-Lambert Tallien, was scathing: 'They celebrate, it is true, festivals in honour of Marat; but these are pure hypocrisy. Hunger and fear are all that have rallied even for a moment the twenty-eight Sections.'[60] Tallien had begun the Revolution as a humble clerk, but rose to be a notable radical journalist and a leader of the fraternal society movement before playing a prominent part in the Parisian organisation of 10 August 1792. Tallien was an ardent Montagnard, and his experiences in Bordeaux were to take his politics in an entirely unpredictable direction, but not quite yet. The day after their arrival, he and his colleague, the former constitutional priest Claude-Alexandre Ysabeau, placed the city under martial law, having already decreed draconian measures of conscription for all those under thirty-five, and begun to deport some leading figures in the revolt to Paris for judgment. A 'Military Commission' of seven was appointed, its role bluntly to 'recognise the identity of the persons outlawed by various decrees of the Convention' – in other words, to send to their deaths without further trial any and all confirmed rebels.[61] Alongside it a new Surveillance Committee, drawn from the surviving ardent patriots of the city, acted to enforce *sans-culotte* orthodoxy in all aspects of administration, and to weed out suspects of every kind. To one lawyer who had never attended his Section, they declared that 'indifference is a crime'; when it was revealed that another suspect spoke three languages, that was enough to colour him as 'a dangerous aristocrat'.[62]

In practice, however, the repression of the Gironde was not

especially severe – from the arrival of the representatives through to the following spring, there were only 104 executions in Bordeaux, although there were many more cases of fines handed down to the rich, imprisonment of suspects and other penalties.[63] The population of Bordeaux was bullied, and some individuals paid a high price for their crimes, but overall, in this phase of the Terror at least, the city was not brutalised. The same cannot be said of Lyon. It had been decided, in the Jacobins, the Committee of Public Safety, and the Convention, that a terrible example had to be made of France's second city. So intense was the corruption of Lyon, according to this view, that it was not possible to find good local patriots, as at Bordeaux, to staff the instruments of repression. Outsiders would have to be brought in to purify the city. Furthermore, as the representative Couthon was warned by letter on 12 October, after news reached Paris of scenes of reconciliation between besiegers and the vanquished, 'you must unmask the traitors and strike them down without pity . . . have the salutary decrees we have sent to you executed with an inexorable severity'.[64] Couthon himself had replaced Dubois-Crancé, recalled on 1 October for not bringing a swift enough end to the siege. He shared the view that there was something wrong with the Lyonnais: 'One is stupid here by temperament', he wrote, blaming the fogs from the local rivers for 'thickening the ideas' of the inhabitants.[65] Nonetheless, he was of an essentially humanitarian temperament, and he could not steel himself to go further than the demolitions that were set in train on the 26th. Under pressure from Paris, he asked to be replaced.

At the beginning of November, representatives Collot-d'Herbois and Fouché arrived in Lyon. The former was fresh from two months' service as an ultra-radical on the Committee of Public Safety, the latter buoyed up in his aggressive righteousness by the success of his 'dechristianisation' measures in the Nièvre. They were accompanied by a steady flow of outside patriots, some appointed by the Parisian authorities, others brought in from more loyal neighbouring departments, but all animated by the conviction that the Lyonnais were inherently corrupt. The Temporary Commission for Republican Surveillance, the central organ formed by Collot and Fouché to run the city, informed the local bodies beneath it, staffed with the best patriots Lyon could offer, that 'you all have great wrongs to expiate, the crimes of the rebels of Lyon are your crimes'.

At the end of November, a contingent of almost two thousand of the Parisian Revolutionary Army marched into the city, under the personal leadership of the firebrand Ronsin. He reported back that 'in this city of 120,000 inhabitants, one can scarcely find . . . 1500 men not complicit in the rebellion'. Collot and Fouché were soon of the same view, indeed going further to note that 'there are no innocent men in this city, save those who were oppressed or held in irons by the assassins of the people'.[66]

The city and its surroundings were terrorised in short order, making up for the 'indulgence' that Couthon had displayed with a ferocious round of detentions, exactions, night raids on suspects' homes, requisitions and dechristianising vandalism. On 23 November, Collot and Fouché declared the city to be in a 'state of revolutionary war', and sought to accelerate what to them was an unsatisfactory rate of executions by the local courts: 'The justice of the entire people must strike down its enemies all at once, and we shall forge their thunderbolt.'[67] In direct response, the Temporary Commission ordered that arrangements be made to execute rebels *en masse*, by cannon fire. This 'thunderbolt', so impressive in theory, turned into a bloody shambles. On 4 December, 60 men, chained together, were blasted with grapeshot on the plaine de Brotteaux outside the city, and 211 more the following day. Grotesquely ineffective, these *mitraillades* resulted in heaps of mutilated, screaming, half-dead victims, who had to be finished off with sabres and musket fire by soldiers physically sickened at the task. The political abstractions of the people's justice did not translate well to reality; as the Commission wrote, 'this method has not had the execution that one would have desired', and 'other more sure means' should be adopted.[68] More normal firing squads supplemented the guillotine in future, in carrying out over 1800 executions in the coming months.

Meanwhile, further south still, republican cannon thundered about the walls of Toulon. The city's population had swelled to some fifty thousand – double the normal complement – with refugees from Marseille and other rebellious towns, and a sizeable influx of British and Italian troops.[69] Within the city, the surrender to the British had also heralded the return of the Old Regime in a variety of forms: the clergy were restored to their place as arbiters of civil existence, the white flag of the Bourbon monarchy was hoisted, and the nobility began to play a growing part in the politics of the town. The Sections that, as in other Federalist cities, had led revolt were pushed aside, becoming a rubber stamp for the decisions of the city's general council and the occupying authorities.[70] Defensive lines around the town and its natural harbour initially safeguarded the inhabitants from direct bombardment, but the siege was maintained ruthlessly: streams were dammed to cut off power to Toulon's watermills, and grain supplies in the city had to be shipped as far as the Balearic Islands to be ground. Sickness grew among the cramped population, and mortality rose to record levels. Maintaining contact with the sea was of course the city's lifeline, and fierce but indecisive fighting went on throughout the autumn in an effort to control the harbour.

On 17 December a young artillery major named Napoléon Bonaparte catapulted himself to glory with a brilliantly executed capture of the 'Little Gibraltar' fortress that commanded the anchorage. This feat was witnessed by Jean-Nicolas Paul Barras, a former *vicomte* and himself a military officer (with a rakish reputation) before 1789, but now one of the Montagnard representatives-on-mission overseeing the siege. Bonaparte's reward was immediate promotion to major-general, and to see the Allied fleet begin to pull out the very next day. Defensive lines broke down, and republican artillery was soon raining fire on the very centre of the town. Civilians and military alike fought to flee, struggling into overloaded rowing boats at the quaysides and begging to be pulled aboard the departing ships. As many as twelve thousand may have left this way, half the original population, made up of every social class (though of course the higher echelons, most implicated in the revolt, and also able to call in favours from the Allies, fled in greater proportion).[71]

Republican revenge was, naturally, terrible. A belated and only half-successful attempt by the British to burn what remained of the French fleet in harbour only enraged patriots further. The representative-on-mission Louis-Stanislas Fréron, rebellious son of a noted anti-Enlightenment literary critic, and author from early 1790 of the incendiary *People's Orator* newspaper, wrote unashamedly to Paris that 'we are killing everything that moves'.[72] He exaggerated, but the town's surviving population were forced to parade across an open space outside the walls, where local Jacobins picked out the guilty for immediate execution. They were shot in batches, perhaps eight hundred dying in this 'last judgment', as one observer called it. A further three hundred were executed by order of a Military Commission that sat until the following March, although, like other such tribunals in the south-east, this did acquit at least as many as it convicted. Of identifiable victims, the highest proportion were soldiers, officers and administrators, clearly guilty of armed rebellion, but the greatest numbers after that were the artisans and shopkeepers who were the mainstay of sectional politics – those who in Paris were the *sans-culottes*, and here as in Bordeaux, Lyon or Marseille had found themselves on the opposite side for the same motives of patriotic self-defence.

The eradication of Federalism should have marked a decisive stage in the consolidation of terrorist power. The centre and all the major war fronts were now joined together once more, their communications no longer threatened, and republican unity – albeit enforced with gun and guillotine – could be directed against external enemies more effectively in future. In the west, of course, the war against the counter-revolutionaries of the Vendée went on, and indeed expanded, as we shall see in the next chapter. To many revolutionaries these benighted and priest-ridden peasants might as well have been foreigners anyway. However, the ironies of revolutionary politics did not take long to reassert themselves, and the issue which had most fundamentally divided the Vendéans from the Republic – the vexed question of religion – was now coming to divide even the terrorists themselves.

Dechristianisation burst into French politics through a whole series of independent initiatives. Prior to his posting to Lyon, the representative Fouché in the quiet central department of the Nièvre had given the most famous example of its early phase, declaiming against the symbols of religious superstition and proclaiming that 'Death Is But an Eternal Sleep'. Even he, however, had been influenced by the similar moves of the lesser-known representative Laplanche in the neighbouring Cher. Local connections also spread the movement to the nearby Allier department. Meanwhile, Fouché's initiative had been witnessed with interest by Chaumette, procurator of the Paris Commune, on a visit to his native town of Nevers. To the north of Paris, in the Somme department, a representative named André Dumont, on mission with the ex-monk François Chabot, was harassing 'patriot' parish priests into abandoning their vocations. On 7 October in Reims, the representative

Philippe-Jacques Rühl, a former Lutheran minister from Alsace, wrote his name in history by smashing the *sainte ampoule* in the city's cathedral. This vessel contained the holy oils used to anoint French kings upon their coronation, and reputedly had replenished itself miraculously throughout a thousand years of use.[73]

Fabre d'Eglantine's report in late October on the naming of the republican calendar was saturated with anti-religious sentiments. In it the 'universal and definitive goal' of the clergy was said to be 'to subjugate the human species and enslave it under their dominion'. They were 'the enemies of human passions and of the sweetest sentiments', continually turning natural phenomena like the passing of the seasons into the backdrop for 'superstitious reverence', intended to place both power and wealth in their own corrupt hands.[74] Political initiative was clearly turning against the very institution of priesthood, and therefore against organised religion as such, but already the process was creating frictions within the Convention.

Only three days after Fabre's report, the Committee of Public Safety itself censured Dumont for his over-zealous and disruptive initiatives in the Somme, but a day later the Convention voted to bar all priests and former monks and nuns from school teaching. A week after this, on 5 November, the movement gathered pace when Marie-Joseph Chénier, Montagnard brother of the more famous, and counter-revolutionary, poet André, made a speech calling for the 'religion of patriotism' to replace Catholicism, and the Convention voted to order it printed for public distribution. On the following day, the Convention was treated to the sight of a parade of patriotic municipalities from the Seine-et-Oise, just north of the capital, denouncing 'fanaticism and superstition' before it in a pantomime display of religious artefacts and vestments. The good *sans-culottes* at the head of the delegation formally petitioned for the right of each community to renounce the Catholic religion, which the Convention thereupon voted. When the delegates from one of the townships, Mennecy, reached home, however, they were arrested by order of the Committee of General Security for their disruptive initiative.[75]

Dechristianisation posed all number of perils for the leaders of the Republic. Its first flowerings had been one of the motives for the Committee of Public Safety's intemperate criticism of representatives' initiative on 4 October. To set local commissioners and

Revolutionary Armies to work hunting down priests who had never been other than loyal, or dragooning locals into watching visiting *sans-culottes* mocking the ceremonies of religion, all diverted valuable resources away from actually enforcing the economic, political and military objectives of the Terror. Not only that, but it of course antagonised the rural population in particular. The more practical-minded men on the Committee of Public Safety, and in the Convention in general, knew that centuries of belief could not be eradicated overnight, and especially not by external coercion. When so much depended on putting the population to work, and when it was already necessary to coerce so much from them, an all-out assault on the very foundations of their lives could not be useful.

At a more philosophical level, the revolutionary leadership did not all share the emerging view of the key dechristianisers that religion was a sham. Robespierre in particular believed fervently that outright atheism was a trait spawned in the decadence of the aristocratic salons of the Old Regime. He was devoutly attached to the view that all truly moral individuals should recognise, if not the bullying Jehovah of the scriptures, then at least the hand of a somewhat more distant but undoubtedly benevolent creator in the works of nature. That had been Jean-Jacques Rousseau's view, and if others subscribed to the more cynical Voltairian belief that if religion was good for anything, it was undoubtedly the maintenance of order, the end result was the same.

More pointed still as an objection to the eruption of dechristianisation was the character of those who were its most zealous advocates. The maturing movement had by early November come to centre on the very forces within the terrorist coalition that the leadership found most problematic. It was the intemperate, violent and enduringly suspicious figures around the Paris Commune and the Cordeliers Club who led the way. The scorn of individuals such as Vincent and Ronsin for the Convention's leadership continued unabated, and the journalism of Hébert continued to warn of new changes that might become necessary, and to bemoan the lack of true conviction at the head of the Republic. Such men had very little by way of a positive agenda, other than to tear down all that remained of counter-revolution, and to keep on guillotining the 'suspect' until the most bloodthirsty *sans-culotte* caricature would be satisfied. In advocating all this, their commitment to seeking power for themselves had not abated, meanwhile, and they eyed the Convention darkly.

The dark gaze was returned. In the eyes of Robespierre and others, there were many things deeply suspicious about the foremost advocates of this 'ultra-radical' line. On 6 November, the day of the *sans-culotte* parade before the Convention, a delegation of such men visited the archbishop of Paris and 'persuaded' him to renounce his own ministry, which he did the next day. Among that delegation had been some very odd figures. One, 'Anacharsis' Clootz, was a German baron who had settled in France in 1789. A zealous advocate of the international expansion of the revolutionary message, and after August 1792 an honorary Frenchman, he nonetheless had any number of connections with dubious foreigners. Another member of the group was Pierre-Jean Proli, a Belgian adventurer widely rumoured to be the bastard son of the Austrian Chancellor Kaunitz. Resident in Paris for a decade or more, and also active in radical politics since early in the Revolution, he nonetheless was also far too 'foreign' for the taste of the more austere and increasingly xenophobic republicans.

Despite these deep, and ultimately fatal, suspicions, the agenda of the dechristianisers could not be easily baulked. The archbishop's renunciation of the faith before the Convention on 7 November was followed by the majority of clergy in that body itself, and spread in a wave across the capital – the politics of intimidation at the neighbourhood level were by now a fine art to the activists of the clubs and Sections, especially when an even slightly uncooperative priest had every chance of immediate arrest as a suspect. Displaying impressive organisational skills, the Commune drew up plans for a 'Festival of Liberty' that took place in the former cathedral of Notre-Dame only three days later. Renamed the Temple of Reason, the building witnessed elaborate theatricals centred on an actress who profaned the building (in Catholic eyes) in the guise of pike-wielding Liberty.[76] The movement to defrock, and in many cases to marry off, the clergy now began to spread in earnest across the country, adding to and building on the waves of confiscatory raids on church valuables that had begun as a purely military-economic initiative in the late summer. A temporising measure to declare the freedom of religion, sponsored by both Robespierre and Danton, was passed by the Convention on 6 December, but did little to stem the tide of local activism. Throughout the winter, France was to be 'dechristianised' in earnest, but by the end of that season, even as the list of the Republic's victories grew ever longer, the jagged claws of faction had raked new wounds in the tattered and shrunken body politic.

## Chapter 9

# Faction and Conspiracy

On 23 December 1793, near the small town of Savenay close to the marshy northern shores of the Loire estuary, the Royal and Catholic Army of the Vendée was brought to bay. Trapped on the wrong side of the river, cut off from their home territories to the south, the Vendéans were by now less an army than a crowd of armed refugees, resembling nothing so much as a wandering horde from some ancient migration. In the depths of a savage winter they had left their home ground and marched north, commanded by the twenty-one-year-old Henri, comte de La Rochejacquelin. Flamboyantly brave, and possessed of great charm and the elements of a military education – he had served under arms, albeit mostly ceremonially, since the age of thirteen – La Rochejacquelin had been elected by the Vendéans' council of war to replace Maurice-Joseph d'Elbée, himself only thirty-one, whose brief military career (which had ended ten years earlier) had commended him to the leadership in July. The Vendéans had begun to look to the nobility for leadership after the death in battle of Jacques Cathelineau, a pious weaver whose zeal and devotion had brought him to prominence early in the summer, but who had perished in an unsuccessful assault on Nantes.

That assault and its failure were to be emblematic of the decline of the Vendéans to their desperate state by December. On their home territory, among the woods and hedgerows of the *bocage*, the Vendéans were almost indestructible. Time and again Republican columns endeavoured to penetrate the countryside, strung out along the narrow sunken lanes and blind to the surrounding landscape, only to fall into devastating ambushes. Rebel troops who lived most of the time in their own homes could be summoned through a network of scouts and observers, and by signals such as the stopping of the sails of nearby windmills. Hurrying through familiar byways, they surrounded the intruding 'blues', and at a given signal, poured fire into their flanks. To the Republicans, it seemed as if the very hedges exploded with smoke and bullets, and many later claimed that the Vendéans had an almost supernatural facility of rapid musket fire. One general, Turreau, wrote in his memoirs that the Vendéans could unleash a 'rain of fire more massive than anything we can produce', and could pursue a beaten foe 'with inconceivable fury and speed', firing even as they ran.[1] When the column was sufficiently depleted and demoralised, the Vendéans themselves began to steal away, so that any rescuers or reinforcements would find only the dazed survivors.

This kind of warfare was essentially defensive – it sought not to enlarge the conflict further, but merely to hold the Vendée apart from the Republic, away from 'national' contamination. Many Vendéans built their understanding of what was taking place around this defensiveness, allied to their deep piety. Although the early months of the revolt had been marked by grisly massacres and mutual reprisals against local Republicans, many rebels had little personal animus against the soldiers they now faced. They were reluctant to keep prisoners, but rather than execute them were known sometimes to simply release them, albeit with their hair shorn so that, if they returned, they could be marked out for a harsher fate. The rebel 'general' Charles-Melchior de Bonchamps, dying after battle in October, ordered the release of five thousand republican prisoners as a gesture of pious mercy.[2]

This limited and unconventional approach to warfare, while on its own terms remarkably successful, did not satisfy the new noble leaders of the Royal and Catholic Army. Schooled in the conventions of eighteenth-century warfare, they understood that an army must capture strategic locations if it is to inflict defeat on its enemies. They also saw the Vendéan revolt as part of the larger conflict against the Revolution, in which it was vital to cause the most extensive disruption to the Republic, and if possible to combine their forces with others to make a general victory possible. Bonchamps had proposed before his death that a slow extension of the guerrilla campaign, linking up with the *chouans* among the sympathetic peasants of Brittany and Normandy to the north, would be a sound approach to this goal, but the rebels' chosen leaders disagreed. Under d'Elbée, the Vendéans repeatedly gathered their main forces into one place and hurled them against urban centres. Victories and defeats alternated through July, August and September, but the fundamental problem went unnoticed. The Vendéans, despite their early six-figure strength, were drawing on a limited pool of volunteers, shrunk by the casualties of every engagement, while the surrounding Republic's forces grew and grew as the mass levy and the Revolutionary Armies were gathered.

On 17 October the rebels suffered a critical defeat at Cholet, the home of the original rebellion, and one of the few urban centres actually within the rebel zone. Three days later the young and headstrong La Rochejacquelin was elected as the rebels' new general. He always put himself in the forefront of battle, wearing the locally produced vivid red handkerchiefs around his head, neck and waist. Others followed his lead, further adding to the distinctive appearance of the rebels, who marched in their peasant smocks and broad-brimmed hats under the banners of the five wounds of Christ and the Sacred Heart. Even La Rochejacquelin's widow later noted that their neckerchiefs and sashes 'made them look like brigands, and that is what the republicans called them'.[3]

The rebels' main force, now numbering some forty thousand combatants and at least as many dependants, had already been pushed north of the Loire in their retreat from Cholet. Their ranks had swelled as the Republic hounded the civilian population of the rebel zone from their homes – for over two months, 'devastation' had been an official policy, even if only patchily implemented in the rebel heartlands under fear of ambush. But the Royal and Catholic Army was now cut off from these heartlands, and La Rochejacquelin chose to make the situation worse by ordering an advance northwards. Rather than scattering among a Breton peasantry that was basically sympathetic, and who were from this point to intensify their own *chouan* campaign of guerrilla resistance, the Vendéans held together and trekked slowly for four weeks towards the western coast of Normandy. They were under the misguided belief, forwarded by over-optimistic *émigré* agents, that British troops and naval support would meet them at the port of Granville, but when they arrived on 13 November there was nothing to be found. A small force of *émigrés*, with the grudging support of England, had intended to link up with them, but missed the rendezvous.[4] After lingering for a day, desperately short of food, the rebels turned for home. Even on this bitter southward leg of their trek, the rebel leadership could not escape the delusion that they were fighting a 'proper' war, and launched their starving troops hopelessly against the well-garrisoned town of Angers on 3 December, and Le Mans ten days later. The latter was an especially heavy defeat, seeing the rebels driven out of town with severe casualties in savage street-fighting. The Vendéans were by now effectively surrounded and trapped north of the Loire. They drifted westwards for another ten days, until cornered, routed and crushed at Savenay.[5]

Hundreds of rebels who threw down their arms were shot or bayoneted out of hand, hundreds more were rounded up and shot in batches. Yet more were hounded to their deaths by cavalry as they attempted to flee through the freezing marshes of the estuary, and thousands of prisoners accumulated in the nearby city of Nantes, all under equal sentence of death. As the rebel army dissolved, the widow of the Vendéan general Bonchamps fled with her two young children at her side, finding shelter with a series of loyal peasant families. Her desperate attempts to bring them to safety through the cordons thrown out by the 'blues' were tragically thwarted by smallpox, which struck down all three of them as they sheltered at a farm. Forced to hide in a cow-shed as a patrol approached, they spent a freezing night, during which her son's condition worsened 'and the following day my darling child died in my arms'. For two days she bore his body, until she could arrange for a secret burial in the consecrated ground of a nearby churchyard.[6] Later captured, she would win pardon from a republican court as a humble camp-follower, her real identity concealed beneath the disfiguring scars of the smallpox, and further obscured by the ordeal which had added over a decade to her appearance. Her months on the run, terrible as they were, had nonetheless preserved her from a savage fate.

The Republic's approach to this war was made immediately clear by the victorious General Westermann, a close political ally of the 'moderate' Danton. After the battle of Savenay he wrote to the Committee of Public Safety in self-congratulation that 'I have crushed children beneath my horses' hooves, and massacred the women, who thus will give birth to no more brigands . . . We take no prisoners, they would need to be given the bread of liberty, and pity is not revolutionary.'[7] The prisoners of Nantes, at the instruction of the representative-on-mission Jean-Baptiste Carrier (an undistinguished lawyer, like so many other Montagnards, before he found fame in this episode), were executed out of hand. Several thousand were killed, including a number disposed of in the Loire in infamous events known to history as the *noyades*, or drownings. Barges were towed out into the river, laden with bound prisoners, and then scuttled. Other prisoners were said to have been bound in pairs naked, one man and one woman, and flung into the waters in 'republican marriages'.[8]

The Vendéan Revolt had terrified the Republic for nine months, and underpinned all the savage insecurities of the Federalist period. The Convention's leaders responded with unrestricted vilification. Two months before Savenay, speaking for the Committee of Public Safety, the supposedly centrist Bertrand Barère had asserted bluntly that 'the brigands are in service from the age of ten to sixty-six . . . The women are their scouts, the whole population of this revolted land is in armed rebellion.'[9] There was a grain of truth in this, of course, especially as the Republic's repressive tactics increasingly uprooted the rebel population from their homes. Some women, moreover, just as in the Republic's armies, managed to serve in the front lines. Madame de Lescure, wife of a Vendéan leader, herself followed the troops, and wrote that one day a soldier revealed 'himself' to her as a young woman, Jeanne Robin. She had gone off to join the fighting despite the advice of her parish priest, and against a strict order from the Vendéan leadership. Jeanne fought in the front line, until 'at last she was killed in the hand-to-hand fighting into which she had dashed like a fury'. Another thirteen-year-old girl served as a drummer, and 'had a name for courage' until killed along with another female relative, and in another group 'there was a girl, who had got into the cavalry to avenge her father's death. She performed prodigies of valour in all the campaigns of the Vendée.'[10]

Westermann's brutal triumphalism was no more than the logical outcome of the claim that every Vendéan was a rebel. Since August, the loyal population of rebel areas had been summoned to leave, and on 17 January 1794 the overall commander in the west, General

Turreau, issued orders that would bring the 'devastation' policy to terrible fruition. With most of the Vendée's fighting men wiped out, the area was to be cleansed of all rebels by a series of *colonnes infernales*, 'hell columns', marching in parallel across the landscape. Six such columns were ordered into existence, and Turreau's written instructions were explicit:

> All brigands taken under arms, or convicted of having taken them up, are to be run through with bayonets. One will act likewise with women, girls and children . . . Those merely suspected are not to be spared. All villages, settlements, heathlands and all that can burn are to be put to the flames.

When Turreau, himself of noble origins, and fearful of the personal price of failure, requested written approval of this action in February, the Committee of Public Safety pronounced his measures 'good and pure, but, far from the theatre of operations, we await results before judging . . . Exterminate the brigands down to the last one, that is your duty.'[11]

The hell columns lived up to their names, and not just in the fire that they brought to the villages and smallholdings of the Vendée.[12] The village of Montbert in the Loire-Inférieure had lost some eleven men in the rebel armies throughout 1793. On 11 February 1794, a hell column killed seventy-two individuals, including forty-nine women. Another column passed through on the 24th, and killed a further twenty, including fourteen women. Throughout the spring, those who had survived were picked off by roving patrols – the men in ones and twos, the women left clustered together in a nearby forest. Over 175 died at republican hands, and the village lost an equal number to epidemic disease that the war allowed to ravage unchecked.[13] A further savagely ironic twist to the horror of the hell columns was that they assailed patriot communities (of which there were some, even in rebel heartlands) with equal blind fury. The troops, most of whom were brought in as temporary reinforcements from elsewhere during the winter break in conventional campaigning, lacked the local knowledge to make any distinction. They had been deluged with propaganda about the savage nature of the rebels, their awful fate if captured and the wider counter-revolutionary goals of the rising. They became so consumed with the killing that some patriot mayors, decked out in their tricolour sashes, were cut down along with their helpless constituents as they came out to greet their 'liberators'.[14]

The representative-on-mission Joseph-Marie Lequinio wrote a year later, in his own account of the Vendéan war, that:

> We saw republican soldiers rape rebel women on the stones piled by the sides of the main roads, and then shoot or stab them as they left their arms. We saw others carry nursling infants on their bayonets, or on the pikes which had pierced mother and child with the same blow.[15]

Lequinio, however, was merely reporting such behaviour, not execrating it. He had personally blown out the brains of a rebel leader responsible for a failed prison breakout, and was far from squeamish about any form of killing – perhaps his upbringing, as the son of a surgeon, had steeled him to the sight of blood.[16] Time and again, he and his fellow representatives reiterated orders to kill captured rebels without distinction of age or sex, and echoed Barère's theme that all of them were incorrigibly dangerous. Two other representatives, Hentz and Francastel, reported to the Convention uncompromisingly: 'We are convinced that the Vendéan war will be finished only when there will no longer be a single inhabitant in this miserable land.'[17] That goal was never reached, but almost a quarter of a million did perish, a fifth of the region's population, including almost all the eighty thousand men, women and children who had set out on the march to Normandy in October. Disease, especially dysentery, killed many, but the bullets and bayonets of the Republic almost certainly accounted for at least half this vast figure.[18]

The devastation of the Vendée, like the planned demolition of Lyon, marked the utter divide that the republican leadership saw between itself and 'counter-revolution' in all its forms. Later, General Turreau could write of the Vendéans that 'their courage was indomitable, proof against danger, hardship and privation', and that overall they 'only needed an infusion of humanity and a better cause to possess all the characteristics of heroism'.[19] But to say such a thing out loud in 1794 was unthinkable. Revolutionary politics had put all sentiments of human compassion and mercy beyond consideration, and entrenched death as the only outcome of conflict. With bitter irony, just as the Vendéans and the Federalists had been finally crushed, and this attitude seemed to be bearing fruit in victory, the revolutionary leadership itself was gearing up to implode under the weight of factional division.

Throughout the previous year, politics and national survival had been bound up together. From the death of the king to the expulsion of the Girondins, on to all the measures of Terror, the great political battles of the Republic had been fought in support of a stronger war effort, a clearer revolutionary agenda, all intimately connected to the real violent struggles going on within and across the borders of France. What came to the surface at the end of 1793, however, was a baser kind of politics, where personal animosities and the quest for self-enrichment sat alongside arguments over the future course of the Republic, and where members of the Convention and the Commune of Paris could denounce their enemies as moderates one moment, and dine with suspected royalist agents the next.

Maximilien Robespierre, guiding light of the Montagnards and hero of the *sans-culottes*, lived in simple lodgings on the rue Saint-Honoré, not far from the Convention and Jacobin Club, with a respectable artisan family, the Duplays. The father of the family, Maurice, was a prosperous *sans-culotte* cabinet-maker in his late fifties with a wide circle of Parisian friends, and had met Robespierre at the Jacobins. His wife and daughters doted on the Incorruptible, who by now had lodged with them for two years. Images of him decorated the apartment, and he was taken care of in every respect: throughout the food shortages of the Terror, white bread and jam were secured for him, and a conspicuous pile of costly oranges on the family's table were kept to aid his digestion.[20]

Early on the morning of 14 November 1793, the Montagnard ex-monk François Chabot burst into this tranquil setting, dragging Robespierre from his bed with tales of counter-revolution and conspiracy, and waving a hundred thousand livres in assignat notes under his nose. These, Chabot said, had been given to him by a gang of royalist plotters to bribe Fabre d'Eglantine – architect of the Republican Calendar – into complicity in a major fraud a month earlier.[21] Those royalist plotters, according to Chabot, included figures no less eminent than Hébert – the Père Duchesne himself – the painter and pageant-master David (who was also a member of the important Committee of General Security), and a further leading member of that committee, Jean-Baptiste André Amar. Fearful that he was now being framed by these same plotters for a complicity he said had been forced on him, Chabot now tried to give the whole thing up to the authorities. Over the following weeks and months, at first in testimony to the Committee of General Security, later in letters written from prison, Chabot named literally dozens of figures in a hugely ramifying plot to corrupt half the republicans and defame the remainder, all in the cause of a royalist restoration.

Chabot himself was a poor witness to protest at such affairs: already well known as an unsavoury scandal-monger, he had been removed from the Committee of General Security in September on suspicion of corruption, the same month that he had married the sister of the brothers Frey, ennobled Austrian bankers of Jewish origin whose very presence in republican Paris was a paradox. There were whispers that the 'dowry' of the marriage came from Chabot's own corrupt machinations and was thus being laundered.[22] The fraud that he spoke of regarding Fabre had been carried out in early October, when the French Indies Company, an overseas trading concern, had been liquidated in accordance with the anti-capitalist legislation of the summer. The decree doing so, it would emerge later, had been falsified to improve the terms on which the liquidation was to be carried out. The directors of the company were then blackmailed into turning over the half-million-livre profits of this exercise to the cabal of Convention members responsible. Among these were indeed Amar and Fabre d'Eglantine.[23]

Fabre thus hardly needed bribing to participate in a deal he was already part of. Chabot was ill informed on this point, and his tendency to confabulate what he did know with what he guessed or feared would work against him in the coming months. What made Chabot's situation even worse was that on 12 October 1793, a bare week after perpetrating the Indies Company fraud, Fabre had stood before the Committee of General Security in secret session and denounced a sweeping plot, led by foreigners, to destroy the Revolution by leading it into internecine massacre. Fabre was covering his back, of course, and it worked in the short term, as the accusations against him later in the autumn simply bounced off. But between them Fabre and Chabot had salted what was already a thoroughly poisonous political atmosphere with the deadly taint of counter-revolutionary conspiracy. One Convention member who returned from the front in mid-November later recalled that he 'could scarcely recognise' his colleagues in the Mountain. Their unity had been replaced by 'a swarm of rival factions that dared not fight each other in the open but waged underground warfare'.[24]

Fabre's 'plot' had included the shadowy foreign radicals we have already seen – the Belgian Proli, protégé of the ex-noble Montagnard (and member of the Committee of Public Safety) Hérault de Séchelles; his close associate Pereira (a Portuguese Jew); the outspoken cosmopolitan baron Clootz; a Spanish nobleman named Guzman; and more than one English renegade. All of these were tied up in various ways with Parisian radical politics, whether through the Jacobins, Cordeliers or Commune. All were already viewed by some in the Convention with growing suspicion. The controversies that erupted in November over the excesses of dechristianisation only redoubled such fears.

Dechristianisation proved the catalyst for a wider eruption of factional discord. On 21 November 1793, Robespierre spoke out against the practice as aristocratic and immoral, and on the same day persuaded the Jacobin Club to expel a group of suspect individuals including Proli and Pereira. A day earlier, Danton had arrived back in the capital after spending a month in rural retreat with his new wife. It is possible, but unprovable, that he was brought back by a concern that Chabot's denunciations would embrace him – and indeed further possible that he was actually involved, if not in the Indies fraud, then in earlier financial machinations. It is certainly true that throughout his absence Hébert and his supporters had continued to lambast publicly his record and his friends, including figures like Fabre, accusing them of sympathy for the Republic's enemies.[25] Danton began to gather around himself, almost by default, all those whose opposition to the radicals and dechristianisers was even stronger than Robespierre's, and on 26 November he openly declared against dechristianising practices, calling them 'anti-religious masquerades'. He went on to tread the fine line between criticising excess and requesting unthinkable clemency for counter-revolutionaries:

> We must pursue traitors everywhere, whatever their disguise, but we must be careful to distinguish between error and crime.

> The will of the people is that Terror should be the order of the day, but that it should be directed against the real enemies of the Republic and against them alone. It is not the people's will that the man whose only fault is a lack of revolutionary vigour should be treated as though he were guilty.[26]

To Hébert and his radical colleagues, of course, such a statement was far over the line into the unthinkable – back in September the Commune had made it clear that any lack of revolutionary vigour was precisely grounds for considering someone suspect. The battle-lines between those Robespierre was to dub *ultras* – because they went too far in attacking the Revolution's enemies – and *citras*, who would not go far enough, were being drawn.

Naked political manipulation was at work in at least some aspects of this conflict. Fabre d'Eglantine, despite not being a member of the Committee of Public Safety, and despite being at the centre of Chabot's accusations, worked his way into interrogating the ex-monk, held in custody since 18 November. He did so alongside Amar, his fellow fraudster (who had unblushingly preached only weeks earlier on women's lack of the 'strict immovability and self-abnegation' necessary for political life). The report Fabre produced managed to shift the focus of Chabot's charges away from them and onto the dechristianisers – even repeatedly mentioning Commune procurator Chaumette, a key ally of Hébert, who did not appear in Chabot's own accounts of wrongdoing.[27] Among the radical *ultras*, however, there was developing an equally unscrupulous urge to gain victory over their opponents. Their difficulty was that they were far less practised in behind-the-scenes manipulation, and far more adept at forms of face-to-face intimidation which increasingly alienated the Convention.

Some of the conflicts had already become decidedly personal during the previous summer, when the hardline *sans-culotte* leader Ronsin was bullying the military leadership in the Vendéan war. Several representatives-on-mission became bitterly hostile to Ronsin and his fellow Parisians as both the representatives and the *sans-culotte* leaders tried to interfere in military strategy, dividing the command and leading to several defeats. It is worth noting how precariously the fate of the Republic had hung in the balance here, as it accounts in part for the savagery of the conflicts it engendered. The rebel army, for all its strategic disadvantages, considerably outnumbered the Republic's forces in the area through much of 1793. Such were the demands of guarding the cities and the coastlines that hardly more than fifteen thousand troops could be concentrated in the field for long periods. The backstabbing of the republican leadership both was prompted by the feelings of desperation these facts occasioned and served to intensify that very desperation as victory remained elusive.[28]

One otherwise undistinguished representative, Pierre Philippeaux, a lawyer from Le Mans, had witnessed Ronsin's activities at first hand. Soon after, he began a vendetta that started with accusations of incompetence – he tried to block Ronsin's appointment as leader of the Paris Revolutionary Army on these grounds in October – and moved on shortly afterwards to charges of extravagance with the Republic's resources, and outright corruption. Ronsin was being paid a salary of forty thousand livres to lead the Parisian force, twice that of a major-general at the front, and even some of his political allies criticised his expenditure on gold-braided uniforms. His violent pursuit of the defeated rebels of Lyon, where he was sent at the end of October, offered up further ammunition for criticism by the ranks of the *citras*, or 'Indulgents' as they were becoming known.[29]

Ronsin was targeted by the Indulgents alongside François Vincent, the general secretary of the War Ministry and Cordeliers orator who had been one of the most outspoken critics of moderation since the previous summer. The verbal violence that was such a feature of *sans-culotte* rhetoric seems to have dominated Vincent's conduct by the autumn of 1793, to the exclusion of any rational political calculation. He made little secret of the fact that he sought to overturn the rule of the Committee of Public Safety in favour of the kind of good *sans-culottes* he actively recruited into the War Ministry, where their aggressive incompetence alienated long-serving clerks. He was prone to rage, especially when drunk, and then to threats of death against any who stood in his way. War Minister Bouchotte had tried unsuccessfully to move him to a less prominent post, but was unwilling to challenge such a fiery figure – one who moreover had an active following in the Sections of Paris.[30] When the criticisms raised by Philippeaux and others persuaded the Convention to launch a commission of inquiry into the conduct of the Vendée fighting,

Vincent personally accosted Philippeaux at a dinner on 28 October, and told him bluntly: 'I have denounced you to the Cordeliers; we will make short work of your commission, and we will bring down the deputies who, like you, dare criticise the conduct of generals invested with our confidence.'[31]

Actions such as this formed the backdrop to rising pressure from the assorted Indulgents for their own restructuring of the Republic's politics – a movement in which individuals like Fabre were probably as concerned to save their own skins as anything else, but where others such as Philippeaux wanted primarily to do away with the extremists, and still others, notably Danton, may have had genuinely mixed (or indeed noble) motives. Danton's personal involvement in major financial wrongdoing remains enigmatic, but he certainly believed that the *ultras* were doing France no good. One friend later recorded that, in a characteristically pithy turn of phrase, he compared Hébert, Ronsin and others to 'so much internal wind that a misplaced sense of decorum prevents a man from blowing off'.[32] The former Interior Minister Garat claimed in his memoirs that Danton had a fully formed plan to win round the majority of the Convention and Committee of Public Safety to a course of salutary moderation and international peace, while condemning radical figures on the Committee of Public Safety like Collot d'Herbois and Billaud-Varenne to the outer darkness along with the Hébertist leadership. According to Garat, Danton bewailed the fate of the Girondins, who had doomed themselves by their own blind stubbornness: 'It was they who forced us to throw ourselves into *sans-culotterie* – which devoured them, which will devour everyone, which will devour itself.' Although he recorded the plan in detail, Garat also noted that its aims and method were 'carefully concealed', and he was surmising the details from his own partial view.[33]

Whether such a rounded plan existed or not, Danton's friends began to intensify the political pressure on the *ultras* in December 1793. On the 5th, a new newspaper appeared, entitled the *Old Cordelier* – a deliberate provocation to the 'new' Cordeliers such as Vincent from those who had been in at the Club's foundation, and who saw themselves as better men. The editor, and indeed the writer of the entire paper, was Camille Desmoulins. He was a strange, volatile figure, highly gifted in the inflammatory rhetoric of revolutionary pamphleteering, but otherwise seen by his contemporaries as almost a child (although, at thirty-three, only a year younger than Danton, and two years younger than Robespierre). The Incorruptible, an old schoolmate of his, was known to view him with an almost brotherly solicitude. Of all the well-known members of the Convention and Jacobins, however, Desmoulins was virtually alone in never being given any serious political or administrative role, and he was habitually referred to by his first name, further belittling him by implication.[34] Danton had charged him with this new task, knowing that it would suit his talents, but Camille's prime talent was for allowing his pen to run away with him, as the future would shortly show. The first two issues of the *Old Cordelier* had been seen by Robespierre in proof, and echoed some of his own views – that extremists were the tools, and probably knowingly so, of Prime Minister Pitt, and that atheism was a moral and political evil that must be stopped.[35]

The third issue of the paper appeared on 15 December, with a change in rhetorical tack. What was presented as a translation from the ancient Roman author Tacitus offered a terrifying vision of a society given up to suspicion and fear, living under a tyranny driven by denunciation, betrayal and violence, mocking the brutalising ignorance of *sans-culotte* functionaries with the careless arrogance of the classically educated. Everyone knew what Camille was saying, and he loaded the work with praise of Robespierre and Philippeaux, and abuse against Vincent and his superior Bouchotte. The work flew from the hands of its sellers, and had all Paris agog for further developments. They were not long in coming, as in a dramatic session of the Convention on 17 December Fabre d'Eglantine (still furiously working to protect himself) led a charge against Vincent and Ronsin, bypassing the Committee of General Security (whose business it was), to secure decrees of the Convention itself for their arrest.[36] Denunciations of their malicious conduct, and reports of their drunken boasts of power and of the coming doom of their enemies, rained down through the session, until even the virtuous Couthon, wheelchair-bound emissary of the Committee of Public Safety, could declare, 'Do not doubt it, all these ultra-revolutionary measures taken by the men denounced to you tend only to halt the revolutionary movement in order to organise counter-revolution or some private movement, thanks to which they could seize power.'[37]

He obtained a further vote from the Convention that the administrative apparatus itself, into which so many men had been inserted by *sans-culotte* bureaucrats, should be subject to a 'purifying scrutiny' under the watchful eyes of Jacobins everywhere: 'All those salaried by the republic must be known to you, and recognised as worthy of the public trust.'

The seesaw battle of the factions was very far from over, however. On 21 December, only four days after Ronsin and Vincent had been swept up into the Luxembourg prison, Collot-d'Herbois, the ultra-radical former playwright and Committee member who for two months had been occupied with the repression of Lyon, returned to Paris to defend himself. The purifying committee that the Jacobins had set up cleared him at once, and under the chairmanship of Hébert the Club invited him to justify his conduct, which he did with vigour, hurling accusations of counter-revolutionary sympathy at the *ultras*' opponents. By the end of the session, the Jacobin Club of Paris had passed a vote of confidence in two men, Vincent and Ronsin, arrested on the orders of the Convention, and summoned members of that body, including Desmoulins and Fabre, to justify themselves before the Club. Collot had made a sharp personal break with Robespierre, and for the moment at least had carried the Jacobins with him. Hébert rejoiced in print: 'The giant has returned, and all the dwarfs that have been annoying the best patriots have scurried a hundred feet underground.'[38]

Despite the ongoing strife of the factions, Robespierre still maintained relative neutrality. Danton, who had not committed himself publicly to the fight, joined him on 23 December at the Jacobins to call for Philippeaux to back down from his continuing assault against Ronsin, and both abstained from actively tangling with Collot's defensive agenda. Nonetheless, the pressure was immense, and Robespierre added to it on 25 December (the prosaic 5 nivôse for the republicans) with an address to the Convention in the name of the Committee of Public Safety, 'On the Principles of Revolutionary Government'. That revolutionary government had been implied in Saint-Just's speech on the suspension of the Constitution back in October, and had been regularised in its institutions on 4 December in a measure known simply as the 'Law of 14 frimaire'. Once again the central role of the Committee of Public Safety in all aspects of public life was confirmed, but, more significantly, the law strove to replace the relative anarchy of rule by representative-on-mission with a strict hierarchy of local bodies.

The representatives themselves, for the first time, had their powers reined in instead of constantly augmented, and in particular their right to remould local institutions with their own irregular creations of commissioners and committees was tightly limited in time and space. No more were such groups to prolong themselves in power after a representative's recall, or to allow their remit to wander into the terrorisation of neighbouring districts and other jurisdictions. They were explicitly banned from raising irregular armed forces, including their own Revolutionary Armies, and such forces in existence were to be disbanded. The Convention's laws and decrees were to be followed to the letter, not glossed by local discretion or bent to factional agendas. All elected local authorities – which by this stage often meant groups appointed by representatives or co-opted by local radicals – were subordinated to a strict network of 'National Agents', whose appointment was subject to ratification by the Convention itself (which meant in practice the Committee of Public Safety).[39]

The sharp contrast between this vision of a well-ordered revolutionary state – indeed a police state in all but name – and the play of factions at the centre was obvious to all. To the Indulgents, this measure was primarily an opportunity to rein in the *ultras*, who had flourished in the 'anarchy' of civil war. To radical *ultras* themselves, it was a sign that the Convention was full of dangerous dreamers, immune to the need for vigorous action across the nation, and lulled into a false sense of security by corrupting influences that required elimination. To Robespierre, however, as he set out on the 25th, this revolutionary government was something genuinely new, and a remarkable creation in its own right. The aim of constitutional government, he noted, 'is to preserve the Republic. The aim of revolutionary government is to found it.' The 'civil liberty' cherished under a constitution must yield to defence of the 'public liberty' now under attack: 'Under constitutional rule it is almost enough to protect individuals against the abuses of public power' – echoes of Saint-Just's claims in October that the government is the people's enemy – but 'under revolutionary rule the public power is obliged to defend itself against all the factions that attack it'.[40]

Those factions he then identified with two essential failings:

'moderatism which is to moderation what impotence is to chastity; excess, which is to vigour what inflammation is to health'. These great failings had all the vices of humanity on their side, and against them stood only virtue – he did not say as much, but he thought of himself (as his listeners well knew) very precisely as embodying that latter quality. But it was not only plain human weakness that assisted the looming triumph of vice, it was, above all else, the perfidious influence of France's foreign enemies. Foreign spies were everywhere, not merely observing the republicans from the sidelines, but woven into the fabric of their organisations. 'They gnaw all about us; they take our brothers by surprise; they caress our passions; they try to sway our opinions; they turn our own resolutions against us.'[41] This was the language of a man under tremendous pressure – indeed over the coming six months he would be prostrated by illness for several extended periods. His vision was highly personal, but it resonated with its listeners. Their world-view was shaped by the continuing revolutionary conviction that counter-revolutionary plots had accompanied the patriots like a grim shadow ever since the Bastille fell, and was egged on by the terrible realities of factionalism that had seen so many fail the test of republican resolve and pass under the hot hand of the guillotine as forsworn traitors.

There were, of course, foreign spies in France, and indeed in Paris. Espionage was an accepted facet of eighteenth-century war and diplomacy, and all the powers were running agents into and out of France, as the Republic was running agents abroad.[42] The British agent Colonel George Munro had lived as a Jacobin in a hostel for expatriate English, Irish and American radicals in Paris until January 1793, when a newly arrived English Jacobin bookseller recognised him as a government man, and he fled back to London. Most of his work, however, had been concerned with keeping tabs on just such expatriates, and reporting on political events, not plotting to undermine the Convention.[43] Some aspects of diplomacy were best carried on secretly, especially in the feverish atmosphere of the Republic. British diplomatic correspondence mentioned as a matter of routine the meetings of one agent, Baldwyn, with the French Foreign Minister and with Hérault de Séchelles (who took charge of foreign policy for the Committee of Public Safety) in October 1793. The letter also mentioned that Baldwyn had met, less immediately explicably, with Hébert. Correspondence the following February would indicate that the agent had subsequently been extracted from a republican prison by the Commune's authority, 'without the wish of the Committee of Public Safety, and despite Robespierre'.[44] Nonetheless, there is little evidence to suggest that any agents were concerned with actively promoting counter-revolution, as opposed to information-gathering, and almost none to suggest that England, at least, had more than a patchy and *ad hoc* network in France before 1794 at the earliest.[45]

It was not only foreign agents, however, who had mysterious influence within Paris. The daredevil Gascon baron de Batz, last seen fleeing from his unsuccessful rescue of Louis XVI, was in the city from at least the summer onwards. He was well enough known for Chabot to have included him as a prime mover in the plots he described, and was able to operate a network of personal agents, and probably also to penetrate the workings of the Commune. What Batz was doing in Paris remains essentially mysterious – he would later claim, for different audiences, that he was either concerned merely to survive or working actively for a royal restoration.[46] With his past record of financial speculations, he was almost certainly mixed up in the corrupt networks around the Indies Company scandal. How far he was still involved in a counter-revolutionary agenda, and actually working to undermine the Republic, is questionable. Chabot linked him firmly to Hébert, and certainly the Commune was capable of some odd decisions at this time. At least one prominent counter-revolutionary nobleman, the duc du Châtelet, obtained a false certificate of non-emigration from its officials. But it strains credulity to see Hébert and his associates, as some have done, as genuine royalist agents. Such a restoration would undoubtedly have treated the Père Duchesne to all the refinements of cruelty that judicial execution in the Old Regime had been capable of, and the man who had rejoiced obscenely at the fall of Marie-Antoinette's head seems unlikely really to have wanted her to escape. On the other hand, he did make an odd proposal at the end of September to have her moved back to the less central location of the Temple, after himself pressing for her trial earlier the same month. Chabot in his plot-mongering attributed this to the influence with him of the duchesse de Rouchechouart, a charge taken up later by Desmoulins in the *Old Cordelier*.[47]

A further mystery occurred immediately after Chabot's first

denunciations. Eleven men were ordered to be arrested, but only Chabot himself (who wanted to be arrested, to divert suspicion from his denunciation) and two other members of the Convention were actually caught. Batz, the Belgian adventurer Proli and a number of others including various wealthy bankers evaded the normally efficient agents of the governing Committees – one of whom was later executed for complicity in this escape.[48] None of this, however, is conclusive evidence for anything. What it should remind us is that the Republic of the 1790s was not a modern police state, despite the ambitions of the Law of 14 frimaire. The surveillance of individuals was almost impossible to maintain consistently. The networks of police agents that the government ran were most effective when simply listening in to public conversation in cafés and bread-queues, and reporting on *l'esprit public*, the 'public mood'. As the Terror ground on, and more and more people were detained on mere suspicion, it became easier for other agents to spy on them in their prisons. But even these *moutons de prison* often reported a blend of the completely banal and confabulated tales of gruesome plots that only meant something because of the increasing paranoia of those who read such reports – and sent hundreds to the guillotine as a result. Those citizens who remained at large, and could avoid the overt behaviours that made one a 'suspect', kept a remarkable level of freedom, if not without fear. Even those detained could sometimes retain influence – Vincent and Ronsin, who had been sitting in the Luxembourg prison since mid-December, were visited by over a hundred individuals from the Jacobin and Cordeliers Clubs, and others including senior officers of the National Guard, and had the effective freedom of the prison, to the extent of terrorising some other prisoners of more moderate views.[49]

With this, we come back to plots in earnest, because they were soon to destroy the *ultras*, and then the Indulgents, and lay the foundations of fear that would bring down Robespierre himself. The problem that confronted the revolutionaries was on one level a clash of personalities and political styles, on another a genuine difference of agendas. But both of these aspects were translated by the prevailing political language into issues of honesty versus criminality, patriotism versus counter-revolution. There was never a point at which all sides could be rallied to a common goal, because all were already convinced that such a move, made by those they distrusted, would be duplicitous. Throughout January and February 1794, a series of political incidents reinforced this perception.

On 5 January, Collot-d'Herbois used the platform of the Jacobin Club to assail Philippeaux for his critiques, and to accuse Desmoulins' journalism of anti-Jacobin principles. Desmoulins himself leaped up in response, but his answer was to accuse Hébert of fraud in receiving tens of thousands of livres in publishing subsidies. Two days later, Robespierre tried to calm the furious row in progress by distinguishing the essentially innocent Camille from his words, the 'political heresies, the erroneous and evil-sounding propositions' that an excess of acclaim for his journal had provoked him to produce. But Desmoulins remained defiant, and Robespierre lost his temper with this irresponsible boy-man: 'How can you dare to justify a writing that is the joy of the aristocracy? You must learn, Camille, that if you were not Camille you would not be treated so lightly.'[50] Meanwhile, on this same day, 7 January, Philippeaux also struck out, launching a formal indictment of twenty-six separate charges in the Convention against Vincent and Ronsin, and calling for the entire War Ministry to be reorganised.[51]

Robespierre, who had remained sympathetic to some of the Indulgents' views, especially when they pointed to possible counter-revolutionary plotting among Hébert's cohorts, faced an enormous shock at this point. Fabre d'Eglantine was finally exposed for his financial corruption, and arrested a few days later. With him was detained Hérault de Séchelles, a member of the Committee of Public Safety itself, and they were committed for trial by the Revolutionary Tribunal, along with the arch plot-monger Chabot himself and several others, on 17 January.[52] Robespierre, who had believed Fabre's protestations of innocence, and his claims about the true nature of the plots, turned on him furiously as soon as the news was made public. He also began to doubt the innocence of other Indulgents – there are hints of a private quarrel with Danton in this period, who was concerned to save his friends. Robespierre could only be suspicious of a man who would put personal ties above the elimination of proven traitors. His own decision to force the Jacobins to reinstate Desmoulins after a motion to expel him earlier in the month now left a bitter taste.[53]

The political pendulum seemed to be swinging towards the *ultras*, and this was marked on 2 February by the release of Vincent and

Ronsin. On 12 January the Convention had decided that they had no charges to answer, rebutting Philippeaux's detailed indictment, but hostility to them among the ruling Committees had kept them detained until a number of protests, both within the Convention and on the streets of Paris, had forced the issue.[54] On those Parisian streets, feelings were running high over an even more fundamental issue, as the General Maximum that was supposed to provide food for the *sans-culottes* was visibly collapsing. The harvest of 1793 had ripened in the chaos of civil war, and had been hunted out of its owners' barns by the Revolutionary Armies and the representatives-on-mission. While in the short term this had met the needs of the cities, by the end of the winter the incessant persecution of all food-producers had reached a point of diminishing returns. Bread could still be got in Paris at controlled prices, but almost every other commodity was only readily available if one paid a black-market rate. Meat, sugar, eggs, butter and other essentials were traded by a new army of clandestine street-sellers, slipping from door to door and charging two or three times the Maximum price. Popular anger bubbled in the queues and the marketplaces among those who could not meet such prices. It was all, in their eyes, a betrayal of the people, a return by stealth to the old famine-plot that had obsessed the revolutionaries since 1789. On the Place Maubert on 20 February, a woman went unrebuked for declaiming that 'If I wasn't holding myself back, I'd send the whole new regime to be fucked!'[55]

The very next day, here and in the central markets of Les Halles, angry crowds of women and men stripped stallholders of their supplies of butter, and forced carters to sell off their loads of eggs at prices not seen since 1790. Recognising the problem, the Committee of Public Safety acted immediately, but what Bertrand Barère announced to the Convention was not what the *sans-culottes* wanted. His speech began with an observation that demonstrated clearly how far the plot mentality had penetrated the internal disputes of the revolutionaries: 'The law of the Maximum was a trap set for the Convention by the Republic's enemies; it is a gift from London.' After this remarkable rewriting of history he went on, acknowledging the impossibility of backing away from the measure entirely: 'Its counter-revolutionary origin is forgotten'.[56] However, rather than tighten the persecution of sellers and suppliers with more raids and more executions, he proposed a revision of the Maximum itself.

'Commerce must be healed,' he announced, 'not killed.'[57] The middle-class free-marketeers of the Committee and the Convention felt that the Maximum could only work if it allowed reasonable profits to the supplier, and also more pragmatically knew that an excess of intimidation would simply lead to further hoarding. The *sans-culotte* obsession with rooting out such hoarding, which saw thousands of locally appointed commissioners rummaging in every barn and attic, had already been a significant factor in driving so much trade into the black market. Those in authority were also aware that the critical needs of the armies were often met by its agents offering well over the Maximum price to suppliers, compounding civilians' difficulties – a point ignored in the aggressive rhetoric of the *sans-culottes*.[58]

While the economic pragmatists of the Convention set a collision course with *sans-culotte* fears, others in the leadership offered solace to those fears. The icy young ideologue Saint-Just made a speech on 26 February (8 ventôse) in which he lashed out at the self-conscious 'moderates', while asserting that the Republic itself had been moderate in all but name – claiming, for example, that the three hundred executions so far ordered by the Revolutionary Tribunal were a fraction of those routinely carried out by other governments. Nonetheless, he announced new principles for the future:

> Wealth remains in the hands of numerous enemies of the Revolution. Want makes people who work dependent on their enemies . . . The Revolution leads us to recognise this principle, that those who have proven themselves to be enemies of their country cannot be property holders in it . . . The property of patriots is sacred, but the property of conspirators belongs to the needy.[59]

He went on to announce a measure to liberate all wrongfully imprisoned patriots, and to confiscate the property of counter-revolutionaries. Five days later, he confirmed in a second speech that this property would be shared out among poor patriots identified as such by every municipality in France.

These 'ventôse decrees' were greeted with immediate rejoicing, and seemed to be a definite step towards prioritising the humble patriots, whom all *sans-culottes* imagined themselves to be, whatever their actual sources of income. Nonetheless, tensions continued with the *ultra* leadership and the Convention. Vincent and Ronsin, after their release, had refused offers, put by Saint-Just himself, to leave the capital for other posts, and through the Cordeliers Club they and their allies were aggressively campaigning for tougher action on prices, and for the release of a number of individuals arrested, they said, for opposing the plots of 'moderation'.[60] By the time of Saint-Just's second decree, anger was rising to new heights on the streets and in the committee-rooms and clubs of Paris. There was talk that it would soon be necessary to kill cats and dogs for food, and one ardent *sans-culotte* proposed to his Section committee apparently in all seriousness that a new September Massacre in the prisons could offer a valuable source of meat. Beyond such extravagant threats, there was widespread murmuring of the possibility of a new purge of the Convention by armed insurrection, like that which toppled the Girondins.[61]

On 2 March, Ronsin called openly in the Cordeliers Club for an insurrection. Opposed at this point by Hébert, he protested to the Club that all he had meant was the removal of the leaders of the 'moderates' – though how this was to be achieved was unclear. On the 4th, the Cordeliers went further. They held something of a gala session, attended by a number of provincial patriots, officers of the Revolutionary Army, various leaders' wives, and the sister of the martyred Marat. The pretext for this was the launch of a new journal by the Club, reviving Marat's old title of the *Friend of the People*, intended to carry 'useful information and denunciations against the public functionaries and especially against the unfaithful mandatories of the people': thus targeting enemies at the heart of the Convention.[62] The atmosphere seems to have led the Club's leaders on to ever greater heights of excess. The Club decreed that the tablet of the Rights of Man that adorned its hall should be veiled in black 'until the people shall have recovered their sacred rights' with the destruction of the moderates. Vincent then made a speech denouncing a number of moderates by name, and claiming that their faction was more dangerous to patriots than the Girondins had been. He was followed to the podium by Jean-Baptiste Carrier, the representative-on-mission who in Nantes had presided over the summary execution of several thousand imprisoned Vendéans. Recalled in February after a dispute with local patriots and other central agents, he lashed out at the new men he had found in charge on his return: 'They don't want the guillotine because they sense that they deserve it!' He applauded the decision to publish the new paper, but called it a 'feeble resistance' against 'those who want to swamp the Republic . . . The insurrection, a holy insurrection, that's how you should resist the scoundrels!'[63]

In the thunderous applause that followed, Hébert came to the podium. He worked himself up by declaiming against Chabot and Fabre, and named Amar as shielding them from immediate prosecution. He then announced his willingness to name others even more guilty, and was egged on to fulfil this boast by Vincent, among others. He launched into a general attack on the Indulgents, and went on, in an excess of imprudence, to criticise Robespierre's efforts to protect Desmoulins from attacks in the Jacobins. Although he called Robespierre 'misled, no doubt', he still argued that his actions defied 'the will of the people, who had expressed themselves clearly on this traitor'.[64] This was the high point of the session's audacity, and it closed in a further orgy of self-congratulation. But the seeds of doom had been sown.

On 6 March 1794 Bertrand Barère, the Committee of Public Safety's perpetual spokesman, stood up in the Convention and denounced, yet again, 'foreign conspiracies' afflicting the Republic. Prime Minister Pitt was directly behind the 'seditious provocations' of recent weeks, which sought to save the wealthy counter-revolutionaries threatened by the ventôse decrees. He was followed by Jean-Lambert Tallien, the conqueror of Federalist Bordeaux, who warned that plans were afoot to install a dictatorship, and demanded that the people be enlightened: 'They will see that these men, despite their pantaloons and clogs, are nothing but aristocrats.' The fate of the agitators was put in the hands of the public prosecutors by Convention decree.[65] Tallien's remark was telling. For months now the political elite of the revolutionary government had grown increasingly suspicious of those who paraded the *sans-culotte* costume as a mark of patriotism. Too easily adopted by anyone, the long trousers, short *carmagnole* jacket and red woollen 'cap of liberty' bore more resemblance to theatrical, indeed pantomime, representations of the common people than to the everyday clothes of a working man. Parisian workers in particular had for several decades taken pride in decking themselves out in gaudy finery acquired through the second-hand clothes trade. The attempt by many who were not workers to pretend that they were by 'dressing down' was often ridiculous – the scapegoated general Houchard had once attracted sniggers by appearing before his troops in a particularly oversized red bonnet – and increasingly seen as sinister, a mask for counter-revolutionary intentions.[66]

On the night of 10 March, the prosecutor Fouquier-Tinville of the Revolutionary Tribunal was summoned to the Committee of Public Safety and told to prepare an indictment against Hébert, Vincent, Ronsin and the printer Momoro, a long-time leader of the Cordeliers. His response that there was no evidence against them met a one-word answer from Saint-Just: 'Amalgamate.' The fate of the 'Hébertists', who were rounded up on the night of 13–14 March, was to be rolled up into the tangled threads of vague conspiracy allegations that already enmeshed the body politic.[67]

The trial of Hébert and his alleged co-conspirators would have been absurd had it not demonstrated the utterly ruthless commitment of the Convention and its leaders to the maintenance of their control over the Republic. In addition to the four Cordeliers leaders, the trial drew in three 'dangerous' foreign radicals already under arrest: the baron Clootz, the Belgian adventurer Proli (on the run since November, but captured finally in February) and the Portuguese Jew Pereira. Two ultra-radicals already long under suspicion, Desfieux and Dubuisson, were thrown in, along with an outspoken requisitioning agent, Antoine Descombes, who had made too many enemies in his efforts to bring food to the capital. A dandyish and insubordinate cavalry officer in the Revolutionary Army, Albert Mazuel, joined them, charged with lending his forces to the planned insurrection. Four other minor *sans-culotte* activists rounded out the *ultra* component of the conspiracy. To show a clear royalist connection, the prosecution dragged in Antoine Armand, a medical student who had launched an insane one-man campaign to assassinate revolutionary leaders including Chabot and Barère, alongside Michel Laumur, an elderly general known to have been friendly with the great traitor Dumouriez. A neighbour of Armand, Marie Anne Latreille, was roped in through her frantic efforts to secure the release of her husband, one of the many arrested generals. Her conversations with Armand on this subject and others were turned into evidence of hopes for an insurrection. The final victim was Jan de

Kock, a Dutch banker and social acquaintance of Hébert and Ronsin. His wealth and origins, alongside reports of meetings with the various Cordeliers leaders at his suburban house, made him a perfect candidate to tie the whole conspiracy together.[68]

The trial itself opened on 21 March. No written evidence was put forward to support the key charges: a plot to starve Paris and overthrow the Convention by opening the prisons, accompanied by the distribution of demoralising information in print and posters, all co-ordinated through meetings at de Kock's residence. Instead, a parade of witnesses, some of whom were paid agents of the Committees, others political enemies, or those under suspicion themselves, offered up incidents, charges and alleged activities almost at random. After three days of this, on the morning of 24 March, the jury confirmed that they were sufficiently enlightened to proceed to the necessary guilty verdict. Pleas from some of the prisoners, notably Vincent and Momoro, to call defence witnesses were rejected out of hand, and the executions were scheduled for that very afternoon.[69] At 4 p.m., three carts transferred the condemned to the scaffold, accompanied by the hostile cries of a large crowd. Most of the condemned went to their deaths still bewildered by the whole process. The old soldier Ronsin was applauded for his calm demeanour, even bantering with onlookers. Hébert, on the other hand, was widely reported as being terrified at the fate he had so joyously called down on so many others. Spectators mocked him – 'this is no man; he's a little runt' – and the executioner waved the red cap of liberty, the now-tainted radical emblem *par excellence*, under his nose as he lay helplessly screaming beneath the waiting blade.[70]

By the time the Père Duchesne finally shook the hot hand himself, it seems likely that the Committee of Public Safety had already decided to follow up by removing the threat posed by the Indulgents. It would be a blatant attack on the sovereignty of the Convention, but the prestige of that body had survived such attacks before, and there were many points of good political logic in favour of such a move. In relation to the fall of the *ultras*, it would reassure the remaining *sans-culotte* leadership that their rulers had not lapsed into counter-revolutionary moderatism. That moderatism itself was seen, moreover, as a real danger, especially by figures such as Saint-Just, who saw his 'ventôse' programme of property redistribution threatened. Danton's efforts to shield his corrupt friends had made him enemies on the ruling Committees, while Desmoulins' incautious journalism, which continued to produce ever more dangerous editions of the *Old Cordelier*, was overtly treasonous in the eyes of many. Left intact, moreover, the immense political and personal prestige of Danton, by its mere existence, could leave the Committees compromised in the Convention. Willingly or not, Danton's presence provided a cover for those, like Philippeaux, who remained intent on attacking radicals, and whose attacks edged ever closer to a direct (and necessarily 'counter-revolutionary') challenge to the Committees' dominance.[71]

Rumours of Danton's looming demise were in the air from the time of the Hébertists' trial. Several individuals later claimed to have warned him of what was coming. He reportedly met Robespierre more than once in this period, and on one of these occasions was reduced to tears as he argued for a general reconciliation among republicans. Robespierre himself, though he never warmed to Danton, seems to have been deeply reluctant to take the last step towards proscription. It was, after all, an assault on the Convention itself, and not merely to purge it of long-standing enemies like the Girondins, but to drag from its heart men who had been staunch Montagnards. Robespierre may have hoped weeks earlier to have used his personal prestige to manage the play of factions without recourse to trials and executions, but he fell ill early in February, during which time the campaign of the *ultras* went beyond the point of no return. By the time Robespierre returned to health, around 9 March, it was too late to halt that particular doomed course.[72] Shortly before his illness, moreover, he had read to the Convention on 5 February a long report 'On the Principles of Political Morality', which made an eventual clash with Danton's style of politics inevitable.

The report was a manifesto for the Republic, intended to explain why it was that events were following the course they were, and to lay down their intended destination: not least, as Robespierre remarked, so that if government 'lapses into the hands of corrupt individuals . . . the light of recognised principles will illuminate their treachery, and so that every new faction will discover death in the mere thought of crime'.[73] The goal he laid down was nothing less than human happiness itself, to be established by the very nature of the state:

> We seek an order of things in which all the base and cruel passions are enchained, all the beneficent and generous passions are awakened by the laws ... We want, in a word, to fulfill nature's desires, accomplish the destiny of humanity, keep the promises of philosophy, absolve providence from the long reign of crime and tyranny.[74]

This was to be achieved by the cultivation, or the liberation, of virtue – a sublime, self-sacrificing love of country that had been commonplace in the ancient republics of Greece and Rome, but which needed nurturing and defending in the modern world. The means to do this led Robespierre to one of his most famous pronouncements:

> If the mainspring of popular government in peacetime is virtue, amid revolution it is at the same time both virtue and *terror*: virtue, without which terror is fatal; terror, without which virtue is impotent. Terror is nothing but prompt, severe, inflexible justice; it is therefore an emanation of virtue.[75]

Much of the rest of the lengthy speech was a diatribe against the factions – those who cry, supposedly, 'Indulgence for the royalists ... Mercy for the scoundrels', and those, equally wicked, who are 'false revolutionaries', *ultras* who 'would prefer to wear out a hundred red caps than to do one good deed', and who were brought back to the endemic theme of foreign conspiracy: for such an *ultra*, 'what he will think tomorrow is set for him today by the committees of Prussia, England, Austria ...'.[76]

Having failed to browbeat the *ultras* into silence, and seen them go to the guillotine, Robespierre was now to be forced by his colleagues to confront the implications of his own rhetoric for the Indulgents. Ideologues like Saint-Just and Couthon and the radicals Billaud-Varenne and Collot d'Herbois joined forces with those for whom the challenge to Danton was more personal. André Amar of the Committee of General Security was still successfully concealing his own complicity in the Indies Company Affair, while his committee colleague Marc Vadier, a bluff ex-army officer and former magistrate, nursed a powerful hatred of Danton over his shielding of Desmoulins and others. Vadier had called him a 'fat stuffed turbot' and threatened to 'gut him' – Danton's retort when he heard of this had been to propose to rip off Vadier's head, eat his brains and shit in his skull, but unfortunately Danton was not serious, whereas Vadier was.[77] On the night of 30–31 March, a joint session of the two committees finally faced the issue. Robespierre was argued round to supporting the necessary arrests, on the grounds of a long report from Saint-Just on the Indulgents' perfidy. Saint-Just wanted to read this in the Convention the next day to Danton's face, before having him seized. In his unbending righteousness (beneath which we can detect a streak of the melodrama which coloured so many revolutionaries' speeches), he seems to have been determined on a great scene of triumphal confrontation. When others objected that this was simply too dangerous – Danton might easily turn the Convention on his accusers – Saint-Just threw his hat in the fire in fury, and almost sent the report after it, Vadier and Amar lunging to save the text.[78]

Eventually the two committees agreed to order a night raid on the homes of Danton, Desmoulins, Philippeaux and another close ally, Delacroix. The centrist Robert Lindet, who had attempted to reconcile Federalist Lyon to the fall of the Gironde, and later helped ease Caen back into the republican fold, showed the delicacy of his sentiments by refusing to sign the warrants. Indeed, he went further and sent word to warn Danton of what was coming. Danton, however, had become weary, either of the repeated rumours of his demise, or of life itself – 'I am tired of humanity,' he said a few days earlier, according to one report, and another indicated his refusal to flee: 'You can't take your country with you on the soles of your shoes.'[79] Thus he and his colleagues were taken up with little difficulty in the small hours of the morning of 31 March. Desmoulins wrote from his cell of finding a crack in the wall through which he could call out to Fabre d'Eglantine in the next cell. Fabre's reaction spoke volumes about the tragic myopia of the revolutionary mentality: 'Oh God! . . . But what are you doing here? Has the counter-revolution come?'[80]

While Desmoulins discovered the anguish of imprisonment, Robespierre worked through the night to correct and elaborate on Saint-Just's draft report. The charges against Danton were extremely general – that he had not been implacably opposed to all the other factions and later 'proven' counter-revolutionaries, from Mirabeau and Orléans to the Gironde; that he had in some unspecified way aided in the treachery of Dumouriez in the spring of 1793 – along with a few more absurd accusations, such as the notion that his move to abolish colonial slavery was intended deliberately to injure France's position in the world. Much of Robespierre's text consisted of character assassination against a man who had a 'black and ungrateful soul' – though this turn of phrase might easily be the projection by Robespierre of his own guilt onto his victim, since he had maintained cordial relations with him until mere hours before this fateful night. Perhaps most damningly, Robespierre recorded that 'Danton laughed at the word virtue and said there was no virtue more substantial than what he showed to his wife every night.' Though it came from Robespierre's pen, such a bawdy jest was very much Danton's style, and probably therefore accurate. Given the principles Robespierre had proclaimed at such length in February, there really was no place for this kind of thinking in his Republic.[81]

Even with Danton and his friends in custody, the risks were not over. The Convention was being chaired by Tallien, active in condemning the *ultras*, but himself only recently returned from Bordeaux under a cloud of possible 'indulgence' towards prisoners and suspects. News of the arrests was brought to the session by Louis Legendre, former *sans-culotte* artisan butcher, founder member of the Cordeliers Club and possessor of impeccable patriotic credentials. He denied Danton's guilt, and demanded that both the prisoners and their accusers – the full membership of the Committees of Public Safety and General Security – be summoned before the Convention at once. The Committees came, though the prisoners did not, and Robespierre laid into Legendre's motives, accusing him of seeing Danton as a 'privileged being', not subject to the same laws that had condemned Fabre, Chabot and others to arrest. Although Legendre's speech had received some cheers from the safe anonymity of the Convention's benches, no one was willing to step up and continue the debate after this slating. Barère followed Robespierre to bring the assembly to heel: 'There is talk of dictatorship . . . it is essential to destroy such an idea. I notice that the friends of the accused are the only ones trembling for liberty.'[82]

The Convention was now sufficiently cowed for Saint-Just to read his redrafted report in silence. He seems to have still been in a sulk, and droned it out impassively, his only movement the raising and lowering of one hand: like a guillotine-blade, according to one witness. All the accused were comprehensively defamed, and held responsible for misfortunes as diverse as the state of the assignat, unrest in the colonies and the outbreak of Federalism. In short, as he concluded, 'Those I denounce have never been patriots, but aristocrats more adroit and more guileful than those at Coblentz' – home of the *émigré* princes.[83] The Convention voted unanimously to send them for trial: what choice did they have? The American Gouverneur Morris wrote scathingly at this point of the lack of true leadership that had emerged from the Revolution's travails – 'It is a wonderful thing, sir, that four years of convulsion amongst four and twenty millions of people has brought forth no one, either in civil or military life, whose head would fit the cap that fortune has woven.' He pointedly noted what all agreed, for good or ill: 'Robespierre has been the most consistent, if not the only consistent.'[84]

Two days later the trial of the 'Dantonists' began. To hurry things along, the prosecutor Fouquier-Tinville had been ordered to bundle the four new detainees into the group already held on corruption charges over the Indies Company Affair. He was given no evidence beyond Saint-Just's report, and was unable to gather any in the time available. An enormous crowd surrounded the Tribunal, overflowing into neighbouring streets, and the atmosphere was electrically tense. Vadier and Amar of the Committee of General Security attended to monitor the proceedings on behalf of their anxious colleagues. The first day went reasonably well, as it concentrated on the real financial wrongdoing of half the accused, but at the end of the day the defendants proposed a list of defence witnesses, including the mayor of Paris and a dozen Convention members, among them Robespierre. On the second day, Danton spoke in his own defence, and even the scanty and scattered recollections that survive reveal a performance of epic proportions, ranging from self-justification to caustic irony, but also veering into desperation: even offering his own precious information on plots against Robespierre, if he were given an 'undisturbed hearing'.[85] His performance dominated the whole day, his stentorian voice carrying easily beyond the confines of the chamber. The crowds were with him, and the looming disaster of an acquittal suddenly seemed very real. That evening Fouquier conferred with the Committee of Public Safety, and was ordered to allow no defence witnesses. The next day the defendants raged for their right to be

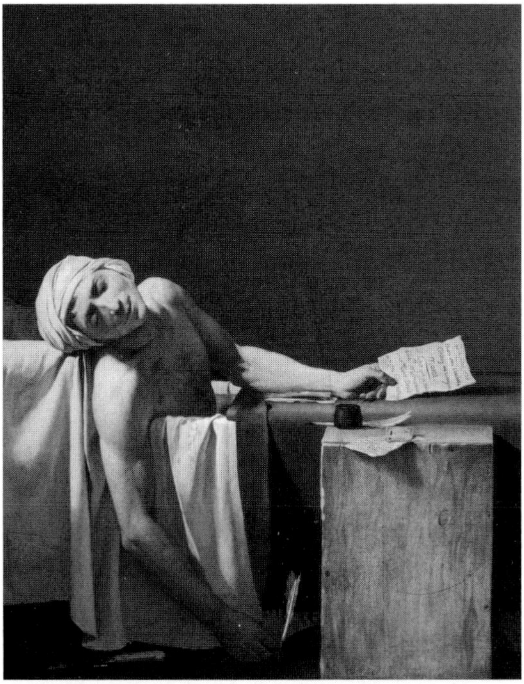

The death of Marat, idealised into a timeless icon.
(Jacques-Louis David, Musée des Beaux-Arts, Reims, Roger-Viollet, Paris/ www.bridgeman.co.uk)

'I have killed one man to save a hundred thousand.' Charlotte Corday on trial at the Revolutionary Tribunal, 17 July 1793.
(James Gillray, courtesy of the Warden and Scholars of New College, Oxford/ www.bridgeman.co.uk)

Pierre Vergniaud, most eloquent of the Girondins, indicted by Robespierre as an agent of counter-revolution.
(Louis Jean Jacques Durameau, Musée Lambinet, Lauros/Giraudon/ www.bridgeman.co.uk)

Robespierre at the tribune. Election to the Committee of Public Safety in July 1793 placed him at centre stage.
(Engraved by Stephane Pannemaker, Viollat, Eugene Joseph [after], Private collection, Ken Welsh/ www.bridgeman.co.uk)

Marie-Antoinette and her four children, painted in 1787.
(Marie Vigee-Lebrun, Chateau de Versailles, Giraudon/www.bridgeman.co.uk)

Antoine Fouquier-Tinville, the Revolutionary Tribunal's chief prosecutor and orchestrator of the trial of Marie-Antoinette, October 1793.
(Engraved by Blanpain, Private collection, Ken Welsh/ www.bridgeman.co.uk)

Marie-Antoinette in the tumbril, on her way to execution, 16 October 1793.
(Jacques-Louis David, Private collection/ www.bridgeman.co.uk)

Henri, comte de La Rochejacquelin, twenty-one-year-old leader of the Army of the Vendée. The Vendéan Revolt had struck fear into the Republic for many months.

(Pierre Narcisse Guerin, akg-images/Erich Lessing)

The rout of Cholet, 17 October 1793, after which La Rochejacquelin had been elected leader of the rebels.

(Jules Girardet, Musée d'Histoire et des Guerres de Vendée Cholet, Giraudon/www.bridgeman.co.uk)

'Don't forget to show my head to the people: it's worth seeing.' Danton led to his execution, April 1794.

(Pierre Alexandre Wille, Musée Carnavalet, Lauros/Giraudon/www.bridgeman.co.uk)

A sans-culotte standard-bearer – in fact, an actor dressed to lead a parade, such was the ease with which this 'costume' could be adopted.
(Louis Leopold Boilly, Musée Carnavalet, akg-images)

Sans-culottes sketched from life: an image almost beyond caricature.
(J.-G. Wille, 'Les moustaches républicaines ou les bons patriotes,' Photothèque de Musées de Paris)

The night of the 9th thermidor (27–28 July 1794), when Robespierre passed from moral centre of the republican universe to hunted outlaw.

(Jean Joseph Weerts, Musée d'Art et d'Industrie, Roubaix, Giraudon/www.bridgeman.co.uk)

heard, prompting a frantic note from prosecutor and judge to the Committee: 'The accused are denouncing to the people what they say is the rejection of their demand . . . Judicial procedure gives us no motive for rejecting it.'[86]

Public safety, the old 'supreme law', was now called on once again to work its magic – Saint-Just told the Convention that the prisoners were in revolt against the court, seasoning the announcement with a spurious report of a prison plot linking Desmoulins' wife Lucile and the imprisoned general Dillon. Lucile and her associates were seized, and the Revolutionary Tribunal was authorised to proceed in the absence of prisoners who 'insulted' it. When this was made known, in a note conveyed by the enormously relieved Amar, the game was obviously up, though before being led out Danton tried to appeal to the audience to see that they had offered no such insults. Fouquier declared that no more witnesses would be called on either side. The next morning, the Tribunal convened ninety minutes before its usual time, to wrongfoot the crowds. The jury conferred for two hours, sparking a brief rumour of a miraculous acquittal, but soon returned the inevitable verdicts.

The executions were carried out the same day, before an audience of Parisians whose sympathy for the condemned had evaporated as their guilt became official. Most of the victims went despondently to the scaffold, but the emotional Desmoulins, who had been devastated the previous day at news of his beloved wife's arrest, fought the executioners until the shirt had been half ripped from him before yielding to their bonds. His melodramatic soul cried out in the last words he wrote to his wife from prison – words that never arrived, thanks to her own incarceration: 'I see the shores of life retreating before me. I still see Lucile. My arms embrace you still and I hold you with my fettered hands, while my severed head rests in your lap. I am going to die.'[87] He seems to have been genuinely surprised to hear jeers from the crowds along the route to the scaffold.[88]

Nothing surprised Danton anymore. He had cursed the whole apparatus of the Terror as he passed his final night in prison: 'There's not one of them who knows anything about government . . . If I left my balls to Robespierre and my legs to Couthon the Committee of Public Safety could last a bit longer.' Below the scaffold, he watched impassively as his dozen co-defendants were decapitated, and mounted the steps at last drenched in their blood. It was sunset, and the whole scene was bathed in crimson light. As he passed into the machine, he could not resist one last pithy epigram: 'Don't forget to show my head to the people: it's worth seeing.'[89]

As the blade fell, the Terror had less than four months to run. Gouverneur Morris, as American ambassador one of a handful of neutrals left in the capital of Terror, wrote starkly, 'God only knows who is next to drink' from the poisoned cup of fate, 'but as far as I can judge, there is no want of liquor.'[90] Prophetically, Danton had named two of the three men on the Committee of Public Safety whose fall would mark the end of the Terror, but that end would not come before an acceleration of death that would make the travesty of Danton's trial seem positively mundane by comparison.

## Chapter 10

# Glaciation

On 25 January 1794 (6 pluviose II), the representative-on-mission Pierre-Louis Bentabole reported back to the Committee of Public Safety on his actions in the town of Châteaudun, a quiet district capital in south-eastern Normandy. On his arrival, he had gathered together what he called 'the surveillance committee of the local popular society' ('affiliated to the Jacobins', as he pointed out assiduously), 'and with their advice and that of all the patriots they indicated to me, I have purified the constituted authorities'. An earlier passing representative had already changed the municipal officers of Châteaudun, so Bentabole, a Montagnard lawyer and former public prosecutor from Alsace, had to content himself with purging the town council, along with 'a part of the district administration, the local bench of magistrates and the higher officers of the National Guard' and with forming a new District Surveillance Committee, 'in place of the old one, which was too weak'. He went on to observe that he had not followed the procedure laid down for carrying out such purges, which was to gather the citizens together in an assembly and question them about their officials. 'Many people would not dare to make important denunciations in public, or give information on the morals of individuals,' either through timidity, or lack of proof, and it would be difficult to arrive at a clear majority. He felt, however, that 'through the mode I have adopted, I have put in place only the best and warmest patriots . . . and I have removed only those who deserved it'.[1]

Bentabole's letter reveals a key aspect of life for the majority of the French during the Terror. They were prey to the arbitrary intervention of outside agents in their lives, prepared to purge and restructure local politics and community relations almost on a whim. This particular purge came as part of the national process of scrutiny decreed after the arrest of Ronsin and Vincent in December – what was essentially an issue of factional politics at the centre becoming a wave of abrupt and sometimes almost random change across the country. And all those removed from office in such a purge automatically became suspects, of course: under surveillance at best, in house arrest, or prison, if they were less lucky.

In the early months of the Terror, until the Law of 14 frimaire had bedded down, the local impact of such interventions was highly variable. Some representatives were more interested in dechristianisation than local government, others carried their zeal to hunt down counter-revolution to grotesque lengths. The former schoolteacher and cleric Joseph Le Bon, on mission to his home region in the Nord, summoned the inhabitants of Lille to make denunciations 'on pain of being treated as accomplices', and wrote that 'the guillotine is waiting imperiously to receive its prey' – which in this case was to be twenty 'counter-revolutionary' workers and artisans.[2] Many missions were carried out by deputies like Le Bon, native to the regions involved, which could result in sensitivity to the local conditions, or translate old feuds into new reasons for hostility. Arriving representatives, whether locals or strangers, were often dependent, like Bentabole, on local clubs for their political information. Such clubs could themselves significantly affect the tone of events. Some sought to avoid extremism, counterparts to municipal authorities like those of Roanne in the Loire or Elbeuf in Normandy, always ready to congratulate authority on its latest moves, after a prudent delay to ensure that such moves were not immediately overturned. Other local clubs were themselves motors of radicalisation, denouncing the rich and the aristocrats in the same breath – and even in some cases attacking the representatives as their accomplices. The club of the small town of Agde in the Hérault turned on the representative Joseph Boisset after he had seemed reluctant to pursue those they perceived as enemies at the end of 1793: 'We denounce you to the Mountain which had chosen you to be the exterminating angel of those bastards whom you are openly favouring and whom you are stirring up, even against us.' Boisset was replaced in March 1794.[3]

Such revolutionary zeal was often genuine, but in other cases the powers unleashed by the Terror fell into the hands of local factions. In the case of Tonnerre, a small town in the Yonne in western Burgundy, two such factions, both led by former land agents and bailiffs, had fought for political power all through the Revolution in a vendetta that went back to the 1760s, and enrolled over a hundred active partisans on each side. No nuance of intimidation or electoral fraud was beyond either of these. In mid-1793, when open violence between them had broken out, the two factions were labelling themselves as 'Montagnards' and '*sans-culottes*', formed opposing popular societies and sought to outbid each other in radical rhetoric. The recruitment of the mass levy at the end of the summer provoked street fighting between the two sides' supporters. When a representative arrived to investigate, he gave full powers to one faction leader who had succeeded in outbidding the other in radical rhetoric, and who then seized many of his opponents as suspects. Those who escaped fled to Paris, appealed to the Jacobins and the Convention, and had these arrangements overturned by another commissioner in November. Only the detention of many faction leaders throughout the rest of the Terror kept a fragile peace in this community of some 3500 souls, in a region of France untroubled by civil war or foreign troops.[4]

If in some cases the revolutionary agenda was taken up for very obviously selfish and local motives, in many others it was ignored as far as possible. The newly appointed National Agent of the rural district of Cany, not far from Rouen, noted at the end of 1793 that 'rich egoists' were everywhere in his jurisdiction, outnumbered, admittedly, by the 'true *sans-culottes*', but these latter were themselves heavily outweighed by 'the indifferent, of whom the countryside counts a great number, incapable of having an opinion of their own'.[5] Such a National Agent therefore had charge of a constant effort of propaganda, just to get the locals to understand what was going on around them, and to show the appropriate level of republican enthusiasm at news of victories (especially those victories that were over increasingly hard-to-distinguish Parisian factions).

There were areas of the country where the disconnection between people and politics ran even deeper. The representative Jean-Baptiste Bo, a qualified doctor and an energetic and efficient organiser, almost met his match in the district of Murat, high in the snowbound Massif Central, early in February 1794. Having struggled through snowdrifts to the local capital of Saint-Flour, he was able to report back to the Committee of Public Safety that his work in Murat was complete: 'As everywhere, I found the administrators more weak than unfaithful, and the people disposed to hear the truth. I told it to them everywhere with patience and kindness, and everywhere they felt this and thanked me.' He had gathered, he said, the National Agents together (and 'renewed' several), but he found that 'none were aware of the law of 14 frimaire' – the law which founded the office of National Agent over two months earlier! Doubtless the local communities had sent whichever municipal officer seemed most appropriate to answer what must have been Bo's incomprehensible request. Bo had explained matters to them, and 'engaged them in their own interests to be penetrated by the law, to keep up a detailed correspondence with the district agents, and I think that they will do all that one might expect from a near-illiterate cultivator' – the polite revolutionary word for peasant.[6]

The tendency constantly to remake local administration had begun with the fall of the monarchy and its accompanying 'second revolution' against royalists in office everywhere. When representatives-on-mission began to be sent out in early 1793, purging was already a routine part of the revolutionary mentality. The Federalist episode, of course, dramatically enlarged the scope of possible treasons, and hardened the attitudes of those sent from Paris against recalcitrant locals. By the time that the Revolutionary Armies were unleashed in the autumn of 1793, the combined impact of further harvest problems and the ongoing Vendéan Revolt had placed relations between centre and localities on what amounted to a permanent crisis footing. The actions of the Paris force, deployed in a large number of small detachments across much of north-central France, from where the capital's huge demands for food were met, formed a significant part of that ongoing crisis. The ardent *sans-culottes* of the Army were predisposed to identify peasants as their enemies – not merely did they hoard food 'meant' for the city, but they also rejected the dechristianising agenda so dear to the Parisian followers of Hébert and the Commune. In return, the *sans-culottes* inflicted the most brutal and scurrilous tendencies of dechristianisation on them: blasphemous parodies of the Mass and other ceremonies with confiscated robes and ornaments; scabrous denunciations of the frauds of religion delivered as lectures to captive audiences; and physical harassment of even the purest 'constitutional' priests.[7]

The men of the Revolutionary Army, experienced in the intimidatory politics of the Paris Sections, played up to the ferocious image of the *sans-culottes*. They wore the Republic's blue-coated uniform, but often augmented it with sashes, plumes, wide sword-belts and other piratical adornments. Many cultivated flamboyant moustaches, sometimes, it seemed, purely for purposes of intimidation – *les hommes à moustache* became a byword for violence across the country. In response to complaints from local authorities who saw themselves as good patriots, and the Army as a dangerous rabble, they issued their own accusations: denouncing such authorities as 'hoarders, men of the law, priests and agents of former nobles', as one wrote about the district of Pontoise, close to Paris.[8] The Army, like the representatives, relied on local popular societies to provide information and support for its missions. Such groups, especially near Paris, were often composed of those who had been excluded from local office by the wealthier landowners who dominated these 'breadbasket' regions. Social tensions of exactly the kind the Parisian *sans-culottes* expected to find were thus acted out for them and transformed, inevitably, into accusations of counter-revolution. On the other hand, in districts where the social cleavage was less distinct, the Revolutionary Army might end up victimising anyone that local activists did not like, or become embroiled in disputes akin to those that racked Tonnerre.

What made the presence of this force even more problematic was that it encouraged the outbreak of real crime. Existing criminal gangs and new ones sprung up from those who resisted conscription could take on the protective coloration of revolutionary authority to pillage isolated communities. A series of farms on the northern outskirts of Paris were attacked towards the end of 1793, in one case by 'a detachment . . . composed of twenty-five armed men as a kind of vanguard, wearing the national uniform, armed with sabres and pistols'.[9] Although the attackers were no more than bandits in disguise, their actions tainted the Revolutionary Army in the eyes of locals, and also provided ammunition for Indulgent condemnation of its very existence – denunciations that refused to distinguish between the real Army and its criminal imitators, and thus further inflamed public views of 'legitimate' requisitioning operations.

In addition to the Paris Revolutionary Army, there were numerous other local and regional formations operating by the winter of 1793–1794. It often required little prompting for revolutionary bodies, and men to lead them, to spring up. In the Nièvre, for example, a local magistrate, 'Marat' Chaix, established an ill-defined position for himself as a 'civil commissioner' during and after Fouché's notorious dechristianising mission in the department. Chaix led his own personal reign of terror for several months in late 1793 in his home district of Lormes. He ably exploited pre-existing tensions between village and town, and between local centres, and might be seen as no more than the equivalent of one of Tonnerre's factional leaders. But Chaix also embodied something found in many such men, who rose to spontaneous or manipulated positions of leadership at this moment – he was an ultra-revolutionary. Chaix preached war on moderates of every stripe in local administration, he spoke out for rapid, categorical, revolutionary justice against suspects, and called for the forcible redistribution of land (the *loi agraire* forbidden by law since unrest the previous winter). He supposedly once said that 'he would prefer to be a dog . . . than to be a bourgeois', due to their selfish and counter-revolutionary ways.[10]

Chaix gathered a small armed force around himself, drawing on the local popular societies, and went some way to redistributing wealth by terror, although largely only in terms of forcing requisitions that were state policy anyway. Where he acquired his political and social position is not clear, and it may have been a rationalisation of more personal vendettas. That he was himself a comfortable landowner, and some of his terrorist followers were his employees, clouds the picture further. He was far from alone, however, and similar speculation could be made about many other such figures in this and other departments. They and their fragments of Revolutionary Army and other irregular forces conjured up an image of total social war and the spoliation of the rich, even while actually doing little more than carrying out the state's intentions – requisitioning food, clothing, blankets, cutlery and valuables for the war effort. They made their share of arrests of 'suspects', but their efforts at repression were brutal and uncoordinated. Such lack of co-ordination, which had allowed many of them to seize power, was of course the target of the Law of 14 frimaire which abolished the local Revolutionary Armies and rescinded all the irregular and local mandates given out by representatives-on-mission. The new network of National Agents, and a revised pattern of representatives working only within the confines of centrally dictated decrees, was supposed to save the Republic from the perils of excess.

Consideration of ultra-revolutionary excess would be incomplete without a discussion of Claude Javogues. Scion of a family thoroughly ensconced in the legal office-holding classes of the Old Regime, and a lawyer himself, Javogues was, like so many of the radical revolutionaries, only in his early thirties by 1793. From Montbrison in what became the Loire department, he was undistinguished in his career, and genuine mystery surrounds his choice as a deputy to the National Convention.[11] Once there, however, and subsequently posted back to his native region as a representative-on-mission, he proved himself a truly remarkable character. He was part of the large team of representatives rallying surrounding areas during the siege of Lyon, and spent much of the autumn and winter of 1793–1794 in the Loire. One republican official likened him there to 'a mastiff that had broken its chain: he seemed always ready to throw himself on the first man he saw and tear him apart with his bare teeth; insults and threats were always on his tongue; he breathed blood and murder and burned to plunge himself into it'.[12] All witnesses (and there are many) agree that he was often drunk, but was just as prone when sober to lash out with feet and fists, slapping and shaking patriotic local officials as readily as he cursed and abused detained prisoners. An account from the delegates of three villages sent to treat with him depicts him holding court:

> His room was vast and full of people: mostly the poor of the town complaining of the rich. He paced between the fireplace and the window, taking from time to time handfuls of sweets from a large packet on the mantelpiece. He joked sometimes with his slut named Merlasse, or with a child that she held on her knee near the fire. At the same time, he distributed as he paced various punches and kicks to those present, cursing and swearing the whole time.
>
> Fontvieille made his petition, presenting papers for his signature. He took them and slapped him around the face with

them. Then, as his comrade Jean du Moulin Perrot had an air of good health, Javogues grabbed him by the chin with both hands, driving all ten of his nails into his face, and said to him, 'Ah, you buggering beggar, you eat all your bacon, your cheese and your chickens. I've the heart of a tiger, I will devour you!' Having regaled them both with several punches and kicks, he pushed them away.[13]

Equally famous was Javogues' obscene misogyny. A local Jacobin denounced his conduct in one town he visited to assess a revolutionary tax on the wealthy – a keystone of his policies. One 'old girl' who was charged more than her whole fortune ran to Javogues to complain. He told her loudly, 'You're a slut, a damned whore, you've fucked more priests than I've hairs on my head, your cunt must be so big I could get all of me in there.' The mayor's daughter on the same occasion was told that she was *une sacrée bougresse* and a damned whore, 'but a good patriot all the same'. Javogues meanwhile was groping a woman who sat beside him. He 'kissed her more than a hundred times', then put his hand on her breast. She slapped him and asked how a representative of the people could thus forget himself. 'Fuck it,' he said. 'Look here, I do less wrong in grabbing these tits than in stealing a halfpenny bit.'[14]

In these remarks, Javogues puts himself at least partially in the mainstream of the ultra-revolutionaries. However he progressed from undistinguished provincial lawyer to tyrannical revolutionary overlord, he was following a path charted by such epitomes of *sans-culottisme* as the Père Duchesne and Charles Ronsin, who made crude language and brutal machismo an effective requirement of radicalism, regardless of the speaker's social origins. Refinement in language and manners was, to *sans-culotte* eyes, a mark of aristocratic pretension, and thus of a counter-revolutionary spirit. True patriots should act and sound like the salt of the earth – even if that meant conjuring up crude fantasies from a drink-fuelled imagination. The old soldier Ronsin reportedly said in prison in December 1793 that perfect liberty would be reached when 'if I should meet a whore who pleases me' on the Pont-Neuf in Paris, 'I can tuck up her skirt and fuck her publicly'.[15] Ultimately, as Hébert, Ronsin and others discovered, such crudity would contribute to the downfall of the *sans-culotte* leadership, as other revolutionaries came to condemn it, ironically, as a mask for counter-revolution. The gross personal misogyny of figures such as Javogues and Ronsin was abetted, nonetheless, by the general repudiation by the Revolution of any solicitude for women except when they presented themselves as dutiful and obedient wives and mothers. Javogues' personal fondness for the bottle, subsequently elevated to legendary proportions, did not smooth his way with the locals, and nor did his harsh mockery of prisoners and suspects – but again, evidence for lethal personal cruelty, as opposed to casual brutality, fades away under inspection.

In sending subjects before a local revolutionary court which condemned them with little ado, Javogues was doing what all such representatives had been charged to carry out, even if he gloated about it publicly more than most. While he confiscated the fine carriages of suspects in order to arrive in new locations with an inspiring pomp, surrounded by the loyal *sans-culottes* of his own Revolutionary Army, and sometimes leading a train of chained prisoners behind, there is no evidence that he lined his own pockets – rather, indeed, as he put it so pithily above, his personal honesty in financial matters was both very real and central to his image of himself as a good Republican (unlike, it must be said, numerous other officials). He was operating in an area of civil war, where local elites had openly backed the armed resistance of Lyon in the summer of 1793, and had to be driven out with armed force in the autumn. His mission was to regenerate the area, weed out the enemies of the Republic and support the armies in the field. It was a hard task, and one he felt he did well.

He was impervious to the mounting tide of criticism that flowed back to Paris from local patriots, and even more dangerously felt entitled to criticise the decisions of the Convention, especially over the Law of 14 frimaire on Revolutionary Government. He wrote to Collot-d'Herbois on 4 February 1794 that the new National Agents were no better than 'dictators whose influence and authority could compromise the liberty and safety of the Republic', especially if their choice fell into the hands of the aristocrats (who of course, for a good terrorist, still lurked everywhere). He wrote of the 'absurdity' of the regular reports to the capital demanded of such agents, that it would need four or five thousand clerks just to process them. The result, he feared, 'if this monstrosity is not destroyed', would be the end of liberty for twenty-five million, and the rule instead of five hundred agents 'who will dispose arbitrarily of the life and fortunes of the citizens'. All the new 'mania for decrees' he likened to the behaviour of the Girondins:

> The miserable reptiles, who always want to lull us to sleep, should know, once and for all, that the good sense of the people is worth more than all their sophisms and their phrases. When their woes rise to a peak, they will rise up and crush the perjured men who have profited from their goodness and confidence only to betray them.

He feared a real 'plan for a counter-revolution' from within the Committee of Public Safety itself.[16]

Notwithstanding the irony, to his detractors, of Javogues' fears of arbitrary rule – he saw himself as immune to such suggestions, being a representative of the people and necessarily therefore acting for them – this kind of talk was intolerable. Added to the flood of complaints about his behaviour, which had been piling up slowly since the previous year, it forced the Committee of Public Safety to take action. Javogues was recalled on 8 February, the order reaching him four days later. He was fortunate not to be immediately swept up into the denunciations of the *ultras* that Robespierre was already working towards.

What Javogues had achieved was a thoroughgoing mobilisation, within a relatively small area, of the kind of people he was willing to recognise as patriots – urban artisans and minor office-holders, and the less overtly prosperous of the peasantry. He consistently favoured men of the Auvergne, the impoverished highlands which fringed the department (from where he came), over those of the Forez, its prosperous lowland heart – local prejudice neatly aligning with *sans-culotte* virtues.[17] Dozens of local 'patriotic societies', sometimes no more than a gathering of the householders of a village, were summoned into existence by his passage, as were a whole series of other revolutionary agencies and authorities. But this was an artificial activism, sustained largely by the threat of Javogues' infamous rages. Significantly, his extremism did not take root in wider local attitudes. He thought he was carrying out a social revolution, genuinely reforming relations between rich and poor with his 'revolutionary tax'. Many even of the poor by early 1794 were coming to see the constant requisitions and arrests as futile, and actually harmful to their livelihoods. By January and early February, more and more local agencies were becoming reluctant to follow his orders to the letter, and indeed some of them were complaining directly about him. His departure seems to have occasioned a collective sigh of relief, and revolutionary committees that had regularly been rounding up batches of suspects relapsed into relative torpor – some arrested only a few individuals in the next six months, and some scarcely met again.[18]

The excess that Javogues so violently embodied was also visible more widely in the mania for renaming that swept France in late 1793 and early 1794. The Convention had given the lead with its infamous pronouncement that 'Lyon Is No More', and the Sections of Paris were renamed by their own activists, some of them two or three times, as the political fashions changed. Out in the wider countryside, countless villages carried the marks of religious 'fanaticism' in the names of local saints, or the Virgin Mary. Dechristianisation demanded a transformation. Sainte-Marie translated easily to Sainte-Montagne, almost anything could be changed to 'Marat', and any mention of chateau or king could go in favour of 'Bonnet Rouge' (Red Cap) or 'Liberté'. Some imagination could also be shown. In the Loire, Javogues and his cohorts undertook a wholesale revolutionisation of the local geography. The town of Saint-Etienne became Commune d'Armes, marking its concentration of gunsmiths, while the Federalist centre of Montbrison, which had stubbornly resisted liberation, was renamed Montbrisé (Mount Broken). Saint-Just-en-Chevalet became Montmarat, and Saint-Germain-Laval, Montchalier-Laval, after the Lyonnais martyr. Charlieu was easily renamed simply Chalier. Saint-Chamond became Vallée-Rousseau after the philosopher, Sainte-Polgues simply Roche-Libre (Free Rock), and Saint-Haon-le-Châtel even more laconically Bel-Air.[19]

It was not only places that were renamed – Chaix in the Nièvre was far from the only activist to rename himself 'Marat'. French naming practices in the eighteenth century were remarkably narrow: many male children were called either Louis or Jean-Baptiste, and a substantial proportion of girls were Marie, Anne or Catherine. The names of the few favoured and familiar saints were by far the commonest choices, and this was problematic for the ardent dechristianiser. Roman names offered one route out – the favourite was probably Brutus, after both the assassin of the tyrant Caesar and an austere hero of the earlier republic celebrated in one of Jacques-Louis David's paintings. Those who renamed themselves in this period would usually choose such a heroic association, but for those who had children to name the choice was wider. Many unfortunates went out into the world bearing the name of a military victory, one of the homely virtues of the Revolutionary Calendar, or, worse, a favoured animal or plant – for, to revolutionary eyes, all that was natural was good.[20]

Not every revolutionary approved of the thoroughgoing nature of this process. From Cany, near Rouen, the National Agent of the district wrote to his superiors that a 'disorderly mania' for municipal renaming had taken hold locally by the spring of 1794. He lamented that 'most of [the communes] make these changes without reflection, and abandon insignificant names only to take on others even more insignificant'.[21] There were already signs by this stage that such renaming was falling from favour. Following the pattern of Lyon, the representatives in reconquered Marseille had announced in early January 1794 that it would henceforth be called Sans Nom, 'No Name', in a mark of the shame that should be felt by a city which had been the first to turn against the Convention and its representatives. Furious lobbying by Marseillais Jacobins who had remained loyal, aided by the support of other more sympathetic representatives, had the change overturned by the Committee of Public Safety on 12 February. The two men who had proposed it were the conquerors of Toulon, Barras and Fréron, and were to remember their thwarting bitterly, especially as an ongoing vendetta by the most radical of the Marseille Jacobins would soon see them recalled to Paris under a cloud of suspicion.[22]

The wider problem for the Republic, however, was that the 'excess' marked by such innovation, though labelled very clearly by Robespierre as the product of *ultras* driven by personal greed for Pitt's English gold, was often the only form of initiative present in the provinces that operated in favour of the Revolution. Rendering enthusiasm suspect, as was effectively the case by the spring of 1794, ran the risk of political paralysis. Saint-Just summed this up in a laconic private note – 'the Revolution is frozen' – but ironically he had in mind his conviction that the true patriots were being submerged, and 'all that remains are red caps worn by intriguers'. There was further bitter irony in his observation that 'the operation of the Terror has blunted the sense of crime', for this was to be nowhere truer than in the minds of Saint-Just and his fellows.[23] The bureaucratisation of republican life required increasing numbers of appointees to surveillance committees and commissions, while ever greater numbers of potentially suitable individuals were being branded as suspects in further rounds of compulsive purging. France after the fall of the factions was in danger of becoming one huge open prison, where the guards outnumbered the inmates, but could join their ranks at any moment.

The role of the Incorruptible Robespierre in the politics of the 'late Terror' is absolutely central. His major task in the division of labour within the Committee of Public Safety had always been the policing of orthodoxy, and the struggles against *ultras* and Indulgents had necessarily consumed much of his attention, in between his set-piece ideological lectures. In the practical matters of government he had neither experience nor aptitude – his idea of diplomacy was to denounce the machinations of foreign plotters, and of strategy to guillotine failing generals. Of economics he knew nothing and cared less. One former Montagnard colleague later wrote that Robespierre 'never had the faintest idea about government, administration and diplomacy'. Danton had been blunter: Robespierre 'couldn't even boil an egg'.[24]

What Robespierre could do was to spot a good patriot. In his private notebook he called the identification of such men a 'principal measure of public safety', and dispatched several trusted individuals to different regions early in 1794 to draw up lists of 'men who are worthy to serve the cause of liberty'.[25] By this stage, and increasingly after the fall of the factions, Robespierre had charge of a significant number of public appointments. How he was to fill them is exemplified by his handling of an earlier area of such patronage: the Revolutionary Tribunal. After its expansion decreed on 5 September 1793, Robespierre was able to move men of his choosing into significant senior positions. The presidency of the whole Tribunal was given to Armand Herman, a public prosecutor from the Pas-de-Calais. He was a childhood acquaintance of Robespierre, born not far from his home town of Arras, and the two had also known each other as adults, when Robespierre had pleaded before the courts Herman served. Herman corresponded with Robespierre on terms of familiarity, and was able to recommend several other men from their home region as 'good *sans-culotte* republicans' for service as judges or jurors.[26] The Incorruptible's own Parisian landlord, Maurice Duplay, was appointed as a juror to the Tribunal, and so too were the Duplays' doctor and their grocer. The man who printed Robespierre's newspaper during his earlier brief journalistic career also earned a place, as did a dozen or more other close personal acquaintances. The overlap of personal and patriotic ties is illustrated even more directly by the case of Marie Joseph Lanne, who had served as a prosecutor under Herman, and was later to become his deputy. Lanne stood as best man when Philippe Lebas, a Robespierrist who sat on the Committee of General Security, married the daughter of Maurice Duplay. With another daughter, Eléonore, Robespierre himself (still a youngish man of only thirty-six) was closely, albeit platonically, involved.[27]

Another set of individuals overlapped with the Duplay circle, but were based in the politics of Lyon. Two Lyonnais, resident in Paris and friends of Duplay, joined the jury of the Revolutionary Tribunal, and went on to introduce more of their friends and colleagues from the city to Robespierre. They formed part of a group that called itself the 'Friends of Chalier' – native sons of Lyon who had remained radical Jacobins throughout the Federalist era, revering the memory of Chalier, the demagogue executed in Lyon in July 1793, and seeking a positive role for their kind in the 'new' city of Ville Affranchie. While this network provided Robespierre with valuable individual recruits to his network of worthy patriots, it also entangled him in a more factional conflict that was to be part of his undoing. Lyon, it will be recalled, was heartily scorned by Parisian opinion after its fall, with figures such as Couthon and Collot-d'Herbois dismissing the Lyonnais as incapable of true patriotism. A hefty contingent of the Paris Revolutionary Army was joined in the city in late 1793 by a cohort of Parisian Jacobins dispatched to help populate the administration of the Terror. While Collot-d'Herbois seems to have avoided excessive friction between this group and the Friends of Chalier, his return to Paris in December 1793 left the city in the hands of Fouché, the ardent dechristianiser and (as it turned out) violent partisan of the Parisians in Lyon. Local patriots were turfed out of their posts in the Section surveillance committees in January 1794, depriving several hundred of them of paid employment in a city with virtually no functioning economy. These and many others could only find employment as lowly guards, little better than caretakers for property confiscated from the Federalist elite. Many felt that such property ought to be handed over to them in compensation for the 'oppression' they had suffered – and there were rumours, played on by the Parisians, that some helped themselves.

Scorned by the intruding Parisians, the Friends of Chalier lobbied hard in Paris for a return of their autonomy, which they were able to present by early 1794 as a call for the implementation of orthodox centralisation, given that Lyon was ruled by exceptional and temporary structures of the kind now firmly out of favour. This, allied to their personal contacts, put Robespierre on their side, and he acted to block Fouché when, in late March 1794, the latter tried to close down the Lyon Jacobins for 'slandering' the Parisians. Robespierre wrote out in his own hand the Committee decrees recalling Fouché and extending protection to the Lyon Club, thus making Fouché into a bitter personal enemy.[28]

The Incorruptible seems to have been blind to the self-interested element of the Lyonnais' struggle. The whole scenario was introduced to him through the circles of acquaintance where he felt most comfortable, by people whose stout patriotism was vouched for repeatedly – and in many cases proved by their robust willingness to sanction the execution of factionalists and traitors from the benches of the Revolutionary Tribunal. To be fair, the patriots of Lyon did not betray him by turning against his principles, as Camille Desmoulins and so many others had done, but the self-interested face of their actions, hidden from a man who, like so many other revolutionaries, could not believe that his friends were anything other than sincere, turned others against him.

There is a certain irony in noting the extent to which Robespierre depended on personal acquaintance for his work, given the apparently impersonal nature of the state he and his fellows were trying to construct. But they had in effect nothing else to work with. Only the experience of the last few years could reveal to them what people were like, and only personal association could provide some hope of discerning what they were *really* like. The Republic, in Robespierre's oft-repeated view, was not to be built on technical competence or military skill (qualities he really did not seem to understand), but on a sense of virtue. That virtue was a complex idea, embracing at the same time the solid family values of a respectable householder, and the willingness to order the death of anyone who deviated from the required orthodoxy. Robespierre's kind of patriot had to be as thirsty for the blood of enemies as any Père Duchesne, but resolutely unenthusiastic about his unflinching willingness to kill.

That willingness to kill, in its impersonal, bureaucratic manifestation, became ever more prominent as the spring of 1794 passed into summer. With the removal of the *ultras* and the Indulgents, serious political obstacles to the growing centralisation of power in the Committee of Public Safety were removed. At the beginning of April, the many thousands of locally appointed 'hoarding commissioners', agents of *sans-culotte* wrath who since the previous year had harassed those they suspected of stockpiling food, were stripped of their offices. Simultaneously, the organs of government itself were reshaped, doing away with the six large ministries of state, and replacing them with twelve smaller, less autonomous 'executive commissions', all of which reported to the Committee. Thus the *ultra* citadel of the War Ministry was wiped away, although few of its personnel were actively purged – there was far too much necessary work for them to do.[29]

Two weeks later, on 16 April, Saint-Just drove through the cowed Convention, still reeling from the deaths of Danton and his followers, a new Law of General Police, which among other things banned foreigners and ex-nobles from naval ports, fortress-towns and the capital itself, sanctioned deportation for those without gainful employment, and put together commissions to apply the ventôse decrees on property redistribution. A new 'bureau of general police' was formed in the offices of the Committee of Public Safety itself, giving it equal police powers with the Committee of General Security, and exclusive rights of scrutiny over the personnel of government.[30] Saint-Just seems to have been the architect of this structure, and briefly took charge of its operations. Five days after it began work, however, he went on an extended mission to the armies in the north, and Robespierre was to run the police bureau throughout May and June. His talent for drawing together cool-headed fanatics, and putting them ruthlessly to work, was thus given a new and extensive channel to run through.

He had already seen a personal friend, Claude Payan, appointed as National Agent for the City of Paris. Payan was an ex-artillery officer who had made his mark as a vigorous patriot in the vicious politics of the Federalist south-east, joining the bureaucracy of the Committee of Public Safety after being sent to Paris to report on the local situation in August 1793. Payan was a cool strategist, who as procurator of the Drôme department had deflected moves towards local Federalism in the summer of 1793 with careful warnings about the 'impolitic' nature of denunciations against Paris that used 'sarcastic language . . . to conjure up divisions'.[31] Only twenty-seven at the time, he was to prove himself as ardent a terrorist as the similarly youthful Saint-Just – who like him was in fact a member of the minor nobility, though such origins had long conveniently been forgotten by now.[32] With valuable allies like this already in place, Robespierre was able to shape the formation of the executive commissions extensively, placing men he approved of at the head of most of them.[33] The former judge Herman, most notably, moved from the Revolutionary Tribunal to the new commission for 'civil administration, police and courts', and hence bound the national bureaucracy closely into the Incorruptible's political police office.

Administrative centralisation went hand in hand with political centralisation. The Cordeliers Club, proud bastion of radical politics since 1790, could not survive the political pressures brought on by the fall of the Hébertists, and closed shortly after their trial. The Jacobin Club, where Robespierre and many of his Committee colleagues still spoke regularly, heightened the drive to ensure that orthodoxy had only one voice, allying with the agents of government to pressurise all the popular societies of the Parisian Sections out of existence through April and May. In the latter month, the mayor of Paris, Jean-Nicolas Pache, who had progressed from royal bureaucrat to Girondin minister, Montagnard supporter and finally *sans-culotte* figurehead, finally fell from office for his Hébertist connections. His knack for political survival stood him in good stead, however, and the imprisonment he now suffered was to save him from harsher vengeance later in the summer. His replacement as mayor, the thirty-four-year-old Jean-Baptiste Fleuriot-Lescot, was an undistinguished ex-architect and Parisian activist who came straight from the prosecutors' table of the Revolutionary Tribunal, and was imposed on the city by *fiat* of the Committee of Public Safety. He was, naturally, a dyed-in-the-wool

Robespierrist. The Commune of Paris and all the other organs of *sans-culotte* activism, for so long an independent powerhouse of the Terror, were now reduced to rubber stamps for government initiatives. The activist leaders not under arrest were by now largely swept up into the ever-widening networks of committees and administration, if they were not fully engaged in the massive programmes of war work that were transforming the Parisian economy. The Sections' official attentions for the rest of the summer were largely confined to three activities: preparing for the regular giant festivals the Republic continued to inflict on its population; gathering saltpetre, essential for gunpowder production, from the dungheaps and cellar walls where it crystallised; and collecting for the purchase of arms and equipment for so-called 'Jacobin cavaliers', a new force of cavalry to be raised by public subscription.

The power of the central authorities was also tightened in the judicial realm at the end of the first week of May, when all temporary and irregular tribunals and commissions judging cases of Federalism and counter-revolution in the provinces were dissolved, and their prisoners transferred to Paris for trial. Only one existing court, staffed by trusted patriots in Robespierre's home-town of Arras, was allowed to go on working for another two months. However, another tribunal was shortly to be summoned into being, simultaneously an exception and a prefiguration of the Terror's future direction. Etienne Maignet was a representative-on-mission in the region of Marseille and Avignon, replacing the recalled Fréron and Barras. An undistinguished lawyer from the Auvergne, Maignet was nonetheless well acquainted with members of Robespierre's circle, including the brother of Claude Payan. Through them, he was able to convince Robespierre, and thus the Committee, of the serious practical objections to the movement of prisoners to Paris from his region. His base of operations was a hotbed of Federalism, which of course by the time of its suppression had shaded into open royalism, and the country areas in particular were thoroughly disaffected from the Republic. Not only was the road to Paris a march of several hundred miles passing close to a number of zones of conflict, but it would require a small army to shepherd what he said were twelve to fifteen thousand detainees whose cases merited judgment, along with perhaps thirty thousand witnesses.[34] Maignet was therefore given the go-ahead on 10 May to form his own 'Commission' in the town of Orange.

The kind of justice Maignet envisaged the court handing out can be gathered from his treatment at this point of the village of Bédoin, near Avignon. A liberty tree planted by local patriots had been uprooted, and a red cap of liberty taken from it and flung down a well. Maignet's response was to assault the village with the forces of order, arresting all the local office-holders, burning the village to the ground (a conflagration that took three days to die down), then guillotining thirty-five people on the spot, and having a further twenty-eight shot. These totals included men, women and boys. A further thirteen women were sentenced to indefinite detention, and the remainder of the village's population forcibly resettled elsewhere. Maignet, in common with urban patriots from nearby cities, viewed the peasantry of villages like Bédoin as scarcely better than the Vendéans, 'dangerously gangrened' with fanaticism and aristocracy, and in need of harsh examples to suppress their wicked tendencies.[35]

The 'Popular Commission' set up at Orange operated under guidelines personally drafted by Robespierre. There were to be five judges and no jury, no written presentation of cases was necessary, and all that was required to convict was 'such information of any kind as is capable of convincing a reasonable man and a friend of liberty'. The court judged only one crime, whether individuals were 'enemies of the revolution', and the penalty for that crime was death. The majority of the judges came from lists of patriots drawn up by Robespierre himself on the advice of his inner circle: one had served already on the Paris Tribunal, and two were outspoken and bloodthirsty *sans-culottes* from Lyon. The court was not finally able to start operating until 19 June, and was closed down on 4 August. It convicted 432 individuals, but a hundred of these were spared the guillotine, mostly by the humanitarian sentiments of another judge, Roman-Fonrosa, aged sixty and with a previous judicial career to colour his assumptions. Such were his consistent objections to the streamlined process of the court that Claude Payan wrote personally from Paris to admonish him:

> Commissions charged with punishing conspirators bear absolutely no comparison with the tribunals of the Old Regime or even with those of the new. There must not be any forms; the judge's conscience is there to replace them. It does not matter

> whether an accused has been interrogated in such or such a manner . . . In a word these commissions are *revolutionary* commissions . . . They should also be *political* tribunals; they should remember that everyone who has not been for the Revolution has been by that very fact against it because he has not done anything for the *patrie*.[36]

This view from Paris crystallised the approach of the 'late Terror' to opposition – it was all to be eliminated, without mercy or compunction. It showed no regard here for the fact that, as even the chief prosecutor at Orange noted, many of those called before it were the victims of mutual denunciations for selfish or factional motives, and a choice had to be made between guillotining all, including the witnesses for the prosecution, or none. Robespierre's men would have preferred it to be all – for, after all, those embroiled in personal disputes were not giving their full attention to the struggles of the Republic, were they?

Nevertheless, as this example shows, the attitudes of the Robespierrists did not prevail unreservedly, even under the special circumstances of Orange. We must again remember that France in 1794 was not a modern police state, still less a totalitarian dictatorship. One of the reasons that the Robespierrists tried so ardently to shut down avenues of compromise and initiative was that so many agents of the Republic remained inclined to exercise both these faculties, to the detriment of central authority's view of their situation. As we have already seen, the discretion of representatives-on-mission, vested with all the dignity that membership of the National Convention still carried, was of critical importance in the local meaning of the Terror – and for some that meant the pursuit of an agenda quite distinct from the bloodlust on show in the Vendée and the south-east.

In areas of the country separated from the direct pressures of counter-revolution, invasion and Federalist strife – principally the centre and inland south-west – it was possible for a different kind of Terror to take root, one that in effect was not 'terrible' at all. Representatives-on-mission here could work more closely with the grain of local life, even when imposing momentous changes and emergency measures. In some cases, this ability must be attributed to the character of the individuals involved. Pierre Roux-Fazillac, for example, was a thoughtful former country squire and brigadier-general of cavalry, whose background gave him not just expertise in military matters, but also a real concern for education and for the economic conditions of the peasantry. Jean-Baptiste Bo, whom we met above in the snows of the Massif Central, had studied medicine as a philanthropic outlet from his wealthy origins, and was an active spokesman on welfare issues in the Convention before embarking on his missions. Gilbert Romme, who had designed the Revolutionary Calendar that Fabre d'Eglantine ornamented, had worked with the philosophical and philanthropic elites of Paris before the Revolution, earning an entry to their circles through his mathematical expertise. These men were ardent Jacobins and Montagnards, and there is no doubting their commitment to the Republic and the measures they were required to enact, but they and numbers of others like them were far from the despotic republican proconsuls of legend.[37]

In the spring of 1794, Gilbert Romme met with stubborn resistance from local communities in the Charente and the Dordogne, unwilling to provide information on their stocks of grain in the firm belief that it would be stolen from them by unscrupulous neighbouring areas. This was a common problem, and could have been resolved by force, raising the National Guard or some other army to raid villages' stocks. Instead, Romme ordered into existence a force of civil commissioners from each district, and got them to take a census of food stocks – but each team worked in a neighbouring district, to ensure fairness. In the Charente in March, and later in April in the Dordogne (where no fewer than 592 men had been used for the survey), hundreds of cartloads of grain were subsequently moved from one area to another without resistance, balancing supply and demand delicately. Bo followed a similar policy in the Tarn.[38]

Such careful management covered not just the basic subsistence of the population, but also the war effort – always the prime focus of the Terror, it must be recalled. Romme himself managed manufacturing arsenals in the towns of Ruelle and Abzac, introducing, along with many of his fellows elsewhere, special measures in the late winter of 1794 to supplement cash wages with controlled rations – the 'salary of subsistence', he called it, avoiding the workers having recourse to the black market. Their families were entitled to draw on the same stores for a ration every two days. Roux-Fazillac for some months was effectively the general manager of a major arms plant at

Tulle, where he worked within the confines of the General Maximum, but nonetheless managed to set generous piece-rates, significant salaries for senior staff and a monthly bonus system for proficient workers, and those who trained others. There were even provisions for retirement funds.[39]

The extent to which the Republic faced a real crisis in its stocks of food can be seen in a further measure that Romme had to introduce throughout the Dordogne in the spring of 1794: general rationing. Though the redistribution described above relieved absolute shortage, there were still only dwindling stocks to go round. In April 1794, flour was being dispensed to individuals at the daily rate of twenty ounces for manual workers, and only eight ounces for the unemployed, women and children – these rates had already been cut severely from twenty-four and sixteen only six weeks earlier. By the start of June the ration for workers was down to sixteen ounces, and that for children to only four – a single cupful.[40] While cynically one might suggest that a semi-starved population was one less likely to summon the energy for revolt, it is also true that rural populations in particular would not have tolerated the descent into such a situation without some unrest, unless they perceived the essential fairness of the measures put in place to alleviate it.

While acknowledging the serious agenda of equity and justice pursued by Romme, Roux-Fazillac and others, its limitations must be recognised as well. If, in contradiction to the trend in national politics, representatives in many areas liberated 'suspects' who were clearly innocent, and even insisted (as Romme did) on work and rations being given to the 'innocent members of *émigré* families', they never yielded in the political sphere. They might grant, as another representative did even while celebrating a dechristianising Festival of Reason at the end of 1793, that it was 'permissible to err', in matters of personal belief especially, but that did not license opposition.[41] Local communities were welcomed into the extended family that formed a frequent metaphor of republicanism, but there was no doubting that authority in that family lay with the *patrie* – the fatherland – and its agents. The enormous powers vested in a representative of the people made head-on opposition virtually unthinkable, especially after news of what had happened in the Vendée and the south-east was circulated. This of course is the context in which even the most humanitarian representative was operating – their fairness and consideration for the population were granted from the top down, in a system which continued to hold the shadow of the guillotine over every head, even if only from a distance.

The humane Terror of the peaceful zones thus continued to owe a great deal to its more brutal manifestations, even if Terror *à la* Javogues was clearly on the wane by the spring of 1794. Replacing it, as we have seen, was something no less deadly, and in some ways more sinister. Typical of this was the itinerary of Marc-Antoine Jullien, the son of a Convention deputy, and only nineteen in 1794, who became a trusted part of Robespierre's patriot network, and an influential roving agent.[42] Not only did he visit half a dozen significant centres early in 1794, helping to identify and list 'good patriots', he was also responsible directly for enforcing orthodoxy against the work of existing representatives in two significant areas. He travelled to the west shortly after the defeat of the Vendéan army, and witnessed the immediate aftermath of the drownings at Nantes. He found that the representative Jean-Baptiste Carrier had, like so many representatives, not fulfilled his duties punctiliously – he criticised him for 'oppressing patriots' in the local Jacobin Club, and found that the mass drownings in the Loire were insufficiently pure in intent to be truly revolutionary acts. As in many cases of such massacres around the country, reports of the looting of corpses and immoral treatment of prisoners before and after death were current, even if unverifiable. Although Jullien was effectively driven out of Nantes by Carrier's anger at these attitudes (Carrier later claimed that he could not credit the authority of a mere boy to criticise him), his reports contributed alongside the Jacobins' complaints to Carrier's recall in February – in time to help provoke the Cordeliers Club into its disastrous brush with insurrection the following month.[43]

Jullien's other major intervention came in early June, when he was sent to Bordeaux. Here, the two representatives Jean-Lambert Tallien and Claude Ysabeau were widely accused of being too lenient – notoriously, in this centre of Federalism, only 104 death sentences had been carried out on local rebels. Criticism of Tallien had run so high that he had returned to Paris on his own initiative in March 1794 to defend himself.[44] He took with him Thérèse Cabarrus, the captivating twenty-one-year-old daughter of a Spanish government minister and wife of an *émigré* noble judge, whom he reputedly found languishing in a Bordelais prison cell. As his mistress, and shortly his wife, she exercised considerable political influence, including over the release of prisoners known to have royalist leanings.[45] She was to be arrested again when she followed him to Paris, and her fate would hang over Tallien's head in the months to come. Meanwhile, when Jullien arrived in Bordeaux, he found Tallien's colleague Ysabeau, who had been removed from his mission by decree on 14 May, but was still in the city, wallowing in the 'asiatic luxury' it afforded him, and accepting the virtual worship of the city's wealthy inhabitants. Jullien put the matter scathingly in a letter to Saint-Just: 'He allowed the merchants to get near him, they told him he was a great man, and he believed it. He let his portrait be passed from hand to hand ... They called him the saviour of Bordeaux... applauding, even at the sight of his shadow, and crying out "long live Ysabeau, our friend, our father".'[46]

Jullien put a swift stop to all of this – Ysabeau was deposed and forced to return to Paris (though he dragged out the return for a further month), and the revolutionary administration of the city and its surrounding department was ruthlessly tightened up. He turned the apparatus of justice brutally against the wealthy of the city, whom he labelled 'an aristocracy of riches', and against the continued presence of religious refractories, and in less than two months oversaw the execution of 198 individuals – almost double the previous total.[47] What there was not, in the savagery of Jullien's own mini-Terror, was any suggestion of irregularity. He was a terrorist by the book, as was everyone that Robespierre had put in place – even if that book, as in the regulations of the Popular Commission of Orange, was sometimes very short indeed.

Throughout April and May 1794, while Jullien was between missions, a new vision of the Republic that was intended to endure from the Revolution had taken shape. On one side of this was an increasingly ruthless determination to cut the French off from their past, and to settle with all their former 'oppressors'. Batches of prominent individuals were processed through the Revolutionary Tribunal, accused of current counter-revolutionary plots, but largely guilty only of being the wrong sort of person. Chrétien-Guillaume de Lamoignon de Malesherbes, aged defender of Louis XVI at his trial, had perished as one such counter-revolutionary on 22 April. He had been rounded up with his daughter and her family in December, the initial pretext being his son-in-law's written protest three years earlier against the abolition of the old court system of the *parlements* – he was thus marked down for his membership of those 'corrupt' institutions, and for opposing the will of the Revolution. One of this man's daughters, Malesherbes' granddaughter, was married to a returned *émigré*: further proof, if any were needed, of the counter-revolutionary intentions of a family that had gathered all its remaining members together at Malesherbes' estate in the Loiret. Daughter, granddaughter and both their husbands accompanied the old man to the guillotine, and he had to watch them all die before mounting the scaffold himself. With them perished a princess and two duchesses, two moderate members of the old National Assembly, and Jean-Jacques Duval d'Eprémesnil, who had led the *parlements*' resistance to royal authority in the late 1780s that had paved the way for revolution, but who thereafter had come to epitomise reactionary insistence on such bodies' historical rights – Robespierre called him 'the most ardent defender of *parlementaire* stupidity'.[48]

Malesherbes and his family had shared their prison in the old Port-Royal convent – renamed, necessarily, and with no trace of irony, 'Free-Port' (Port-Libre) – with numerous other luminaries of the Old Regime. Among them were twenty-seven of the *fermiers-généraux*, the wealthy set of investors who had dominated the contracted-out collection of indirect taxes before 1789. One of their 'crimes', besides massive self-enrichment from the miseries of the poor, was to have built a wall around Paris in the mid-1780s to make the collection of tolls more efficient. This 'imprisonment' of the capital's population was bitterly resented in itself, but in the context of the food crisis that marked the Revolution it became seen as little more than a famine plot cast in stone. One of the imprisoned *fermiers* was Antoine-Laurent Lavoisier, perhaps the leading experimental and theoretical chemist of the eighteenth century, and discoverer of oxygen. This eminence did him no good once he had fallen into the jaws of the revolutionary machine, and nor did the consultations on technical matters that previous revolutionary assemblies had entrusted him with – including a critical role in industrialising saltpetre production for gunpowder. All connection with previous incarnations of authority was incriminating, and the *fermiers* were convicted on the moral certainty that they were plotting a counter-revolution in order to restore their previous ill-gotten fortunes. Lavoisier perished on 8 May.[49]

Alongside this extended and vicious settling of scores went a new programme for the future of the 'regenerated' French people. The ventôse decrees, with their avowed intention of permanently shifting the ownership of land towards the poor, had seemed to mark out a genuine agenda for social justice. If such justice (for patriots only, of course) was a fine thing in the abstract, difficulties nevertheless continued to arise in putting such principles into operation. The commitment to supporting 'poor patriots' through confiscations foundered on a number of rocks: inability to define such individuals (especially when the recent police law had threatened indigents with deportation); lack of understanding of the economic problems of urban workers, who could not just 'go back to the land'; and a real reluctance at the highest levels to actually go through with such an assault on property.[50] State confiscation was one thing – in 1789 the state had confiscated the lands of the church with hardly a murmur, except from counter-revolutionaries – but redistribution through any means other than the free market was troubling. This was not because revolutionaries feared the as yet uninvented ideas of socialism, but rather because, with such ideas not yet invented, the concept of giving property to those who had not earned it, and thus shown their ability to manage it, seemed simply mad, the product of 'anarchic' impulses that would result in the destruction, or at the very least criminal misuse, of that property.

The ventôse decrees just went away, all practical efforts at implementation ceasing within a couple of months. They were replaced, effectively, by a far more centralised, top-down and entirely conventional project of charity, unveiled by the perennial spokesman of the Committee, Bertrand Barère, on 11 May. The 'Great Register of National Welfare' was an attempt to replace the role of Catholicism in conventional charity – the support of widows, orphans, the aged, sick and crippled. A state fund replaced the wealth of the Church and its almsgivers, the local authorities replaced the parish priest, and patriotism replaced piety as a qualifying criterion, but beyond that the system of handouts was much as it had been before 1789, and threatened no social upheaval. Nevertheless, in its favour it should be said that the scheme worked, until the money ran out two years later.[51]

In the treatment of the demands of workers and peasants more generally, the Convention and the Committee in this period showed no signs of particular sympathy. Petitions from peasants to be allowed to subscribe collectively to the purchase of lands, or for the extension of the Maximum to the price of their long-term leases, were disregarded. The former went against the individualism of the Republic, and the latter implied that the Maximum might be more than a short-term emergency measure. On 30 May, with fears rising of troubles around the harvest, agricultural workers were declared by the Convention to be under requisition, subject to a uniform wage, and forbidden to leave their work. When farmers continued to offer higher wages, leading to fears that urban workers would be temporarily seduced into the fields from their workshops, the Committee again peremptorily banned any such movement without official permission.[52] Already on 1 May the *sans-culotte* Section Finistère in Paris had warned that armaments workers who 'fail to cooperate through negligence or a conspiracy to postpone the annihilation of all tyrants' would be arrested as suspects. On 10 June, the Revolutionary Tribunal was specially authorised by the Committee to prosecute as counter-revolutionaries any trouble-makers in critical industries.[53]

It should not be thought that the Republic was in thrall to big business – although repeated efforts to stamp out racketeering, especially in military supplies, were never very successful. Rather, the individualist approach of the employer was simply more congenial to the Committee's mindset, so long as that individualism did not extend as far as contradicting the wishes and needs of the Republic. Employers were nonetheless subject to severe and binding regulations, and sometimes compelled to operate at a loss on government contracts. The accommodations of private economic practice, which led so many on both sides of the shop floor to dodge around the Maximum as best they could, did not make sense in Robespierre's Republic of Virtue. Ever since the mass levy of August 1793, all the French had become soldiers in a national military effort, where self-interest should have become irrelevant.

The quest of the spring of 1794 was to institutionalise that attitude, to make it concrete and real, but just as the ideas at the heart of this goal were sterile and didactic, so too were the means chosen. On 7 May 1794, following a speech by Robespierre himself, the National Convention passed a decree that began 'The French people recognise the existence of the Supreme Being and the immortality of the soul.' As it went on, the only 'cult' worthy of this being was 'the practice of the duties of man':

> [The people] places in the first rank of these the duty to detest bad faith and tyranny, to punish tyrants and traitors, to aid the unfortunate, respect the weak, defend the oppressed, do unto others all the good one can, and to be unjust to no-one.[54]

Thus, quite simply, religion was reinvented to serve the needs of the Republic. As every good classicist knew, the very origin of the word 'religion' lay in the 'binding together' of the community. The incessant conflict between Catholics and dechristianisers that still lacerated the countryside was to be set aside, and a long series of festivals on each *décadi* – the once-in-ten-days 'Sunday' of the Revolutionary Calendar – would insinuate a proper civic morality into the hearts of the French. Ceremonies would honour such revolutionary concepts as the Martyrs of Liberty, and also a range of other, vaguer idols: the Human Race, Love of Country, Truth, Justice, Modesty, Friendship, Frugality, Disinterestedness, Conjugal Faith, Fatherly Love and Maternal Tenderness; and two dozen more, including Childhood, Old Age, Misfortune and Happiness.[55] The vague faceless deity once proclaimed by Rousseau, whose presence made itself felt in the glories of the landscape and the effusions of the sentimental human heart, would be dragooned into service to float over all of this, thankful no doubt for the 'recognition' of the glorious Republic.

The artistic talents of France were called forth in the same decree to produce hymns and 'civic songs' in a public competition for a state prize. On 16 May, another decree called upon poets 'to celebrate the principal events of the French Revolution' in hymns, poems and 'republican dramas' lauding 'the heroic actions of the soldiers of liberty, the courage and devotion of republicans and the victories won by French arms'. Historians were summoned to 'compose classic books', in which 'that firm and severe character appropriate to the annals of a great people conquering the liberty attacked by all the tyrants of Europe' could be displayed. This would 'infuse a republican morality into the works destined for public instruction', and once again a prize was offered. Within days, similar calls to painters, architects and sculptors went out, for a whole programme of cultural regeneration: from new public buildings, to statues for the public spaces of Paris, to a contest to design 'more convenient and healthy farms', reusing the materials from the demolition of 'castles, feudal structures and national buildings' – that is, churches and monasteries. Jacques-Louis David, the neoclassical painter who sat on the Committee of General Security, became the Renaissance man of this regeneration, taking charge of many of these competitions, and being given responsibility for drawing up new uniforms for the nation's representatives, and reporting on the dress of the nation in general, and means of 'adapting it to republican manners and to the character of the Revolution'.[56] The vision that was inherent in the grander aspects of the programme – that the population, in line with 'sensationist' psychology, could be remoulded to fit into the Republican ideal through external pressures – was spectacular in its scope and ambition, but it was to prove as hollow and fragile as any of the papier-mâché monuments so swiftly erected to the Republic's glory.

That vision, in the few brief months of its flowering, nonetheless ranged on ever wider, into the fields of language and education. For several years, revolutionaries had grown increasingly suspicious of non-French speakers, even though, if one included the various dialects of the south of the country along with the 'foreign' tongues spoken by Bretons, Basques, Alsatians, Flamands and others, those without French as their first language were probably in the majority. Anywhere from a tenth to a quarter, by some estimates, could not understand French at all.[57] Dialects were viewed askance, but real hatred had developed for some of the other tongues. Barère at the end of 1793 lambasted Breton as the tongue of 'federalism and suspicion', German as that of 'emigration and hatred of the Republic', and Basque as the language of 'fanaticism'. In March 1794, several thousand Basque villagers were forcibly deported from their homes on the mountain border with Spain, after reports of mass desertion of new recruits abetted by local non-juror priests. The local villagers' culture, according to Jacobins in nearby towns, made them immune to the benefits of the Revolution, and thus a danger to the frontiers of the Republic. Representatives-on-mission ordered their villages razed to the ground and their possessions confiscated. Thousands fled over the frontier to escape this persecution, and those that were deported to the interior were often incarcerated, herded into empty churches and left without the basics of life. Hundreds died of disease and neglect before being allowed to return to their ruined homes in the autumn.[58]

To 'save' such communities, the Convention decreed a new drive to make French universal on 4 June, calling forth a new generation of missionary teachers who would take the language into the benighted heartlands of ignorance and fanaticism. Unsurprisingly, few appeared, but the policy marked a final abandonment of compromise with minority languages. In the early years of the Revolution, the translation of decrees into the local idiom, especially in the south, had been a key item of radical proselytisation. Even at the end of 1793, a representative in Brittany could call for translations into 'low Breton' by local authorities of new laws to help lead the peasantry away from the *chouan* rebels, and ask popular societies in the towns to 'detach a member who possesses the country idiom' for propagandising activities.[59] Such adaptation to local circumstances was no longer acceptable, even as a short-term palliative. The measure of 4 June, incidentally, also denounced all forms of vulgarity and obscenity in printed works and public speech – a telling sideswipe from cultural puritans against the lingering vestiges of Hébertism.

Educational thought among the republicans of the Terror tended to focus heavily on its value in the crafting of citizenship, often in an overtly propagandistic, not to say brainwashing, style. This was sharply at odds with the educational ideas of their philosophical idol Rousseau, who had believed in education as the flowering of individual potential under intense but carefully crafted and unpressurised individual tuition. Revolutionary plans focused instead on public virtues and basic skills. Laws in December 1793 and February 1794 called for compulsory primary schooling, with the hatred of tyrants and love of the Rights of Man to occupy places of prominence alongside basic literacy and numeracy. Unfulfilled plans for developing secondary education would have placed an even more detailed emphasis on the glories of the Republic versus the evils of the past, while also striving to develop a practical, scientific and above all publicly useful curriculum. All the cultural products of the various artistic competitions under way would have had their uses here, no doubt. Though these plans fell into abeyance, what was founded, on 1 June 1794, was the 'School of Mars', bringing together three thousand teenage boys in a military academy in Paris.

All were chosen from the most ardently patriotic families, and drilled in a heightened atmosphere of republican patriotism, while learning about military manoeuvres and fortifications. They lived under canvas north of the bois de Boulogne, rose for their first drills at 5 a.m., and seem to have worshipped Philippe Lebas, the young Robespierrist representative (friend of Saint-Just, and son-in-law of Maurice Duplay) given charge of the school.[60]

Such a body of ardent youth might seem ripe for conversion into a republican (or Robespierrist) Praetorian Guard, but they were overtly intended simply to return to their localities at the end of the course, there to pass on what they had learned with due humility. There is no evidence, either, that this plan concealed more nefarious ends, and the School of Mars played no part in the politics of the period. Like so many of the republicans' plans, the school seems to have existed in a realm beyond irony and cynicism, where hidden motives could not be imagined by the progenitors of such projects, and ill-will or resistance formed no part of their make-up – such sentiments, of course, being the exclusive preserve of counter-revolutionaries.

The pre-eminent example of this republican dreamland is the Festival of the Supreme Being, envisaged in the decree of 7 May, and brought to fruition after a month's furious preparations on 8 June – the high holy day of Pentecost, in the old calendar. Robespierre had declared on 7 May that 'the true priest of the Supreme Being is Nature itself', and 'its festivals are the joy of a great people assembled under its eyes to tie the sweet knot of universal fraternity'. Thus the whole of Paris had been rigorously marshalled by David and his artistic team to present such a natural spectacle. Two thousand four hundred Parisians, divided into cohorts of old men, mothers, girls, boys and small children, were assembled into a chorus in an amphitheatre specially constructed in the gardens of the Tuileries. The choirs had been rehearsed frantically, and instructors from the National Institute of Music had drilled the population – expected and required to attend and participate *en masse* – in their home Sections for weeks. Paris and its region had been scoured for flowers to decorate the stage and the surrounding streets, and no expense, in an economy that ran on printing paper-money and coercion, had needed to be spared. To further beautify the scene, the guillotine was removed from the Place de la Révolution, continuing its work on the equally symbolic ground where the Bastille had once stood, until three days later protest from the loyal *sans-culotte* residents of the neighbourhood about the stench of blood and corpses sent it packing to the far eastern outskirts of the city.[61]

As in previous celebrations, the nationwide dimension was as crucial as the Parisian one for the authorities, and detailed instructions for the events had been dispatched to all corners of the country. Regimentation no less stringent than that of the capital was the order of the day. In Brest in the far north-west, the municipality drew up its own careful list of the individual children appointed 'to represent innocence and wisdom' in the parade. In Cambrai in the north, pregnant women were specifically summoned to a place of honour, and the husband of each 'must perform his duty of accompanying you and holding your arm'. The regulations of the festival dictated everything, even down to the arrangement of the women's hair most suitable to symbolise bountiful nature. In the obsessive concern with depicting harmonious family groups, and an equally determined insistence that any social distinctions should be effaced (hence the classical garb in which people were draped), the French were once again supposed to be reborn as children of nature.[62] Such was the determination to make a success of the event that the townsfolk of Troyes in Champagne were treated to a free feast outside the city walls, even when there were only eleven days' stocks of food in the town.[63]

Not everywhere greeted the new cult with the passive conformity that the Terror had drilled into the towns. In the village of Saint-Vincent in the Haute-Loire a local official had gathered the entire population into the former church, now Temple of Reason, to receive an oration on their duties to the Supreme Being. As he spoke, the female half of the congregation rose as one, turned, and presented him with their bared buttocks. For once, the wordsmiths of the Jacobins had no answer to such a manoeuvre, and had to endure a rash of such protests over the following days as news spread to neighbouring communities.[64] Wordless protest was by far the safest kind. Even as the ladies of Saint-Vincent were baring their souls, Léonard and Paule Meynard, a peasant brother and sister from the village of Romain-sur-Colle in the Dordogne, were languishing in prison in Paris, awaiting trial before the Revolutionary Tribunal as counter-revolutionaries. At the end of April, they had listened to one too many incomprehensible decrees read out in front of their own 'Temple of Reason', and had snatched a decree from the official's hands, calling on their neighbours to resist alongside them. The brief scuffle that resulted sealed their doom, and they would not survive the summer.[65]

At the Parisian Festival of the Supreme Being, meanwhile, Robespierre presided – officially only because he had been elected for a two-week stint as President of the Convention four days before, but it is hard to imagine any other figure filling the role. It was the first and only time that he appeared in the public guise of a political 'leader', and the impression he left among his colleagues was not favourable. The deputies of the National Convention marched in array, dressed in their new uniforms of cornflower-blue coats, tricolour sashes and plumed hats. They carried bouquets of flowers and ears of wheat. Some of them, professed atheists and dechristianisers, or just cynics, scoffed almost openly at the proceedings. Emblematically, the Jacobin Club had elected the dechristianiser Fouché, by now a clear personal enemy of Robespierre, for a term as its chair on the same day Robespierre was installed as President of the Convention – the artificial unity of Terrorist festivity remained fragile.[66]

Robespierre headed the march of the Convention, and others behind him hung back, so that he appeared sometimes to be walking alone ahead of them. He was reportedly radiant with happiness at the proceedings, which marked the apotheosis of his personal philosophy. After the massive choral performance at the Tuileries, he made another set-piece speech on virtue, then applied a flaming torch to a large effigy of Atheism – from it, gleaming or sooty according to the disposition of the observer, emerged a smaller figure of Wisdom. A deputy from the Pyrenees, Cassanyès, recalled that as he stepped forward to light the pyre with 'seven or eight members who were doubtless devoted to him', there were mutters from the ranks of the deputies that 'here come the lictors' – escorts of the Roman emperors.[67] The second half of the ceremonies took place across the river on the Champ de Mars, renamed the Field of Reunion for the day. As they paraded there, Cassanyès and his colleagues chatted about other things, pointedly ignoring the efforts of Robespierrist stewards to keep them in martial order. A vast mountain, symbolic of the Convention's Montagnards, had been built from plaster and board, and alongside it a fifty-foot column topped with the figure of the French people as Hercules. Crowned with a massive tree of liberty, and supplied with a convenient staircase, the mountain was ascended by the deputies in procession, as choirs, and some half-million spectators, boomed out more newly composed hymns. As this noise crashed to a halt, Robespierre descended like Moses himself, apparently blissfully oblivious to the disrespect of his fellows.[68] One, Thuriot, an old friend of Danton, put it bluntly: 'Look at the bugger; it's not enough for him to be master, he has to be God.'[69]

Such dissent was in fact a rising tide, although it would not make itself much felt for some time yet. But the Convention was growing restive with the plans of the Robespierrists. On 10 June, two days after the great festival, the Committee of Public Safety laid before it a measure that drew on the experience of designing the 'Popular Commission' in Orange. The prisons of the capital were becoming choked with the products of the centralisation of revolutionary justice, and more speed was needed in their judgment. Couthon, speaking for the Committee, made the matter plain: 'The delay in punishing the enemies of the *patrie* must be no longer than it takes to recognise them: it is less a question of punishing them than of annihilating them.'[70] His humanitarian sentiments that had excused him from the repression of Lyon had faded under the pressures of the past eight months. Thus the 'Law of 22 prairial' shrank the Revolutionary Tribunal by a quarter (surreptitiously purging the more punctilious members), and abolished the institution of defence counsel. As at Orange, the accused would now be judged on whether or not they were 'enemies of the people' (a slight amendment from 'revolution'), and sentenced to a swift end.

Various sweeping definitions of what qualified for such a status were given. The standard of evidence required was set as 'every kind . . . either material or moral or verbal or written, which can naturally secure the approval of every just and reasonable spirit; the rule of judgment is the conscience of the jurors enlightened by love of their fatherland'. Defendants had in essence no rights. Testimony would only be taken in the absence of other kinds of pre-existing 'proofs', and if there were 'important considerations of public interest' – such as, presumably, to ensnare further suspects. Only the prosecution could call witnesses, and might substitute written depositions if they could not attend. There was no one present to challenge such items except the accused themselves. Article sixteen was blunt: 'The law gives patriotic jurors to calumniated patriots as counsel; it does not grant them to conspirators.'[71]

Several Convention deputies quailed at this, and other phrases they perceived as dangerously imprecise: when the decree was reread on the 24th, there was briefly the semblance of a real debate in a body that had for several months done little more than pass the Committee's directives by acclamation. Couthon was driven to protest particularly at what he called 'the most atrocious calumny against the Committee', namely that it had sought through the law secretly to lift the immunity of Convention deputies, currently subject to arrest only after a decree of that body itself.[72] There is evidence, however, that that had indeed been one of the goals of the law, though it had now to be swiftly denied, and deputies' immunity affirmed by a further vote. Amid the wrangling, Robespierre launched an attack on the recalled representative Tallien, calling him 'one of those who spoke continually, fearfully and publicly of the guillotine, regarding it as something which had its eye on them for debasing and troubling the National Convention'.[73] This scarcely veiled threat lacked immediate consequences, however, and at the time, this episode seemed only a minor wobble on the road to a regenerated Republic. The new Tribunal got swiftly to work, its reduced bench of fifty jurors including no fewer than twenty-one newly risen through the ranks of Robespierre's patriot networks.[74]

The 'old' Revolutionary Tribunal had functioned for a year before its monthly total of executions reached a hundred, in March 1794. In April it had passed 244 death sentences, in May 339. June 1794 would see 659, rising to exceed 900 in July.[75] While revolutionary justice was being set on a new and even more ruthless course, the wider efforts of the Republic to save itself, in large part through the work of the representatives-on-mission, now came to fruition. The midsummer of 1794 would see the triumph of French arms, and the vindication of the overall economic and military drive of the Terror. But, at the same time, the country's politics edged ever closer to total collapse.

## Chapter 11

# Triumph and Collapse

Whatever else one may say about it, the machinery of the Terror had one undeniably formidable achievement: the army of the Year II. From the Levy of Three Hundred Thousand and the later mass levy came over three-quarters of a million effectives, plucked from every walk of life, including large numbers of illiterate or non-Francophone peasant boys. They were turned into a fighting machine that left Europe awestruck. The obstacles to this achievement had been immense. In the campaigns of 1793 – both internal and external – troops had sometimes been so ill prepared that they had to be herded into battle, and so ill equipped that the *sans-culottes*' favourite weapon, the pike, was more than just a symbol. It served in the ranks alongside swords, scythes, axes and even picks and shovels. The massive efforts of the representatives-on-mission to establish armouries and arsenals across the country yielded real results. By the spring of 1794, four huge plants in Paris, with three thousand workers, were turning out seven hundred muskets a day. At Commune d'Armes in the Loire, the former Saint-Etienne, the town's ironworks were placed under central control, and produced three hundred muskets and sixty pistols a day. There were over half a dozen similar large plants (including Roux-Fazillac's factory at Tulle) and numerous smaller concerns. Meanwhile, the *sans-culottes*' devoted search for saltpetre, critical constituent of gunpowder, was concentrated into no fewer than six thousand workshops for purifying the chemical, producing eight million pounds by the end of July.[1]

To satisfy the soldiers' need for uniforms, every tailor and shoemaker in the land was drafted into action – the latter had to produce a pair of shoes for the army at least every two days by order of the Convention in October 1793, and from 21 December to 8 February 1794 were forbidden to do any other work whatsoever. Uniforms remained a terrible problem, confected from every kind of cloth – in one department, mayoral robes surviving from the Old Regime were confiscated to give the required complement of red for lapels and facings – and often assembled poorly. One soldier wrote that:

> The weave was so poor and the lining so inadequate that geese could have grazed through the holes, the pockets so tight that a soldier couldn't get his handkerchief and tobacco-tin into them. The coats were so small that when they got wet they shrank so much you couldn't get them on.[2]

Some of the boots were likewise so ill made that it was more comfortable for the soldiers to march barefoot than to suffer debilitating corns, bruises and blisters. When soldiers drilled in close order, their wide-brimmed hats were often knocked off by their neighbours, and helmets issued to some units were so uncomfortable that they were thrown away: 'one saw the roads and fields paved with them'. The persistent difficulties of supply, already a marked feature of revolutionary campaigning in 1792 and 1793, did not abate despite the Republic's furious efforts. This sometimes left regiments and battalions short of literally hundreds of uniform items for months at a time – especially critical as many of the shortages occurred through the winter of 1793–1794, when coats, shoes, socks and breeches were vital defences against frostbite and exposure.[3]

Even as the campaigns of 1794 got under way, one soldier in ten, over seventy thousand, did not have a musket, and for those that did there was a constant danger of dilapidation. Oil, grease and cleaning materials were in critical short supply along with everything else, and masses of raw recruits had not yet internalised the discipline that kept seasoned soldiers' weapons clean and serviceable at all costs. Delicate flintlock mechanisms jammed, barrels rusted, unoiled wooden stocks split and fell off, and there was a fair chance that any such recruit's weapon, loaded and fired in the heat of battle, would blow up in his face.[4]

Nonetheless, things were better than they had been. The discipline of the armies in particular, which in this age especially had a critical impact on their ability to be marshalled for battle, had improved dramatically over the winter. Training camps had been set up behind the lines on the major fronts, where first the junior officers, then NCOs and drummers (crucial for marking the pace) were rotated through from serving units. The units themselves drilled furiously, especially as winter came to an end – almost non-stop through February. One sergeant noted, with typical military wit, 'Three hours of drill in the morning and three in the afternoon stopped them getting bored.'[5] As a result, the French armies no longer moved on the battlefields in unwieldy masses. Their operations still lacked the large-scale flair that would mark Napoleon's impact on warfare, but the soldiers of the Year II could manoeuvre in line or column and advance to the attack as well as any regular troops of the opposing armies. In some areas, indeed, the Republic possessed a certain superiority. French artillery benefited from cannon of an advanced 'Gribeauval' design, the most sophisticated in Europe, and a well-trained corps of engineers and artillerists – of whom the newly promoted general Napoléon Bonaparte was just one. The French development of light infantry, fighting in mobile and dispersed units to cover the advance and retreat of heavier columns, was to inspire the formation of the green-jacketed elite riflemen of Wellington's armies.

Unlike the forces of their opponents, the French were also spurred on by a continual diet of revolutionary exhortation. The representatives-on-mission were everywhere at the front and in the camps, and by 1794 their supremacy, with its message of the centrality of politics to victory, was evident to all. No longer, as Danton had complained after his missions with Dumouriez in 1792, could the troops mistake the representative for the general's secretary.[6] Doses of salutary Terror were not absent from this: in the Army of the Eastern Pyrenees, a general denounced for treason was executed in front of twenty thousand soldiers at Perpignan, which according to the representatives responsible gave them great 'energy and confidence'. At Landau in the east, another representative quelled defeatist talk among the garrison in the face of the enemy by shooting some of the ringleaders in front of their comrades.[7] The army in the north lost three successive commanders to the guillotine, including the unfortunate Houchard, scapegoat of Hondschoote, which must have been a great education to the troops in the virtues of success.

More restrained means of revolutionary education were more widely used, however. Until his fall from grace, the *ultra* War Minister Bouchotte used his official funds to distribute radical newspapers to the troops – over seven million copies, including no fewer than 1,800,000 of Hébert's *Père Duchesne* (at a cost for that paper alone of 118,000 livres). Official or semi-official army newspapers also appeared on several fronts, though they found it difficult to toe a safe political line, especially by 1794, without becoming anodyne. Soldiers themselves were encouraged, especially during the Hébertists' ascendancy, to attend political clubs in garrison-towns, or even to form their own among the ranks, despite the problems this could cause for conventional expectations of discipline.[8] Most difficulties with clubs, however, arose when local civilians, or occasionally politically active senior officers, clashed with administrators over policy, seeking to help the troops, but sometimes merely provoking wrangling. The Jacobin Club of Lille was a thoroughgoing thorn in the side of military and civilian administration in the north, despite, or indeed because of, its infiltration by radical officers based in the politics of the capital. In late 1793 the Club exercised wide-ranging powers, using control of the local Revolutionary Army to terrorise neighbouring communities, but it fell from favour along with the *ultras*, and was comprehensively purged in 1794.[9]

Despite such blips, there is every indication that the revolutionisation of ordinary soldiers' outlook succeeded. Indeed, as we saw in the Vendée, that propaganda success could overwhelm sentiments of common humanity. In that context, it is almost sinister to read the words of one soldier, Etienne Meunier, son of a cooper from the outskirts of Paris, who wrote to instruct his family after the slaughter at Savenay to 'go see my little boy [*mon fillot*], give him a gun and send him out to join me, for he must be big enough now to come and observe the Republic in action'. More understandably, the young trooper Barthélemy Lemain from Auxerre, serving on the snow-bound frontier in the depths of winter, reported that the daily arrival of enemy deserters lifted the soldiers' hearts: 'They come over the frozen river, because they no longer accept to be slaves, they want liberty. We are hoping that our troubles will end this year and that we shall emerge covered in the laurels of victory . . .'[10]

The road to that victory in 1794 opened hesitantly in the north, with an early Austrian advance, but this was quickly repulsed, and a pattern of French successes began, leading by late May to the beginnings of an advance into enemy-held territory. As in 1792, some help came from the disorganisation of the enemy, and from the fate of Poland. After that country had been carved up in January 1793, a patriot movement made a desperate bid to start a national revolt there in March 1794, temporarily drawing off the strength of both Austria and Prussia. Austria meanwhile vetoed a British proposal to subsidise the raising of a larger Prussian army to help in the west, fearing that any more significant military gains for the north-German state would come at the expense of Habsburg influence. The Prussian government therefore remained reluctant to commit major forces against France, needing them to keep order in Poland, and in its own territories in western Germany, where enthusiasm for French republican ideals was far from unknown.[11]

France suffered from no such overt military dissension. With food and other essentials in short supply, a ruthless procedure of official pillage in occupied territory was decreed in May, to be controlled by four special 'evacuation agencies'. The aim was not merely to supply the short-term needs of the armies, but also to leave a devastated zone around the frontiers, unable to support future enemy invaders. With her armies on the offensive from the Pyrenees to Belgium, this measure proved eminently successful, though in the south-east the pickings from the alpine territories of Piedmont were slim, and there was some discussion of an invasion of the richer territories of the Italian peninsula proper. This was turned down as an over-extension, but further west both Catalonia and the Basque country were opened to invading French troops.[12]

In late May attention switched briefly to the war at sea, where things had been going badly for the French. Their main fleet was bottled up in the Breton port of Brest, and the British Royal Navy had the run of both the Mediterranean (after the disaster at Toulon) and the Atlantic, allowing redcoats to seize the French sugar islands of Martinique and Guadeloupe. Now, however, a massive gamble was afoot. For the past year, French agents in the United States of America had been buying up grain with the Republic's precious few reserves of gold. Over a hundred merchantmen lay at anchor in the Chesapeake in the spring of 1794, awaiting the order to sail. Four French warships had managed to slip the British blockade in mid-winter, intending to shepherd the great convoy – what Barère called 'the food-bearing argosy' – across the Atlantic. But only a sortie by the main fleet could get them home past the blockade, and at sunset on 16 May twenty-five ships of the line sailed from Brest, watched by the whole town that had laboured unceasingly for months to have them ready. André Jeanbon Saint-André, a former Protestant pastor and member of the Committee of Public Safety, had taken personal charge of the naval preparations, and now sailed with the fleet on its death-or-glory mission.[13] While they were at sea, on 26 May, the Convention passed a decree ordering that no British prisoners were to be taken by land or sea: a measure of the utter hatred felt for the 'English', who subsidised all of France's continental enemies, blockaded her ports, sheltered the *émigrés* and were widely believed to be forging her currency; and who, worst of all, had failed to rise up against their rulers despite the fervent hopes of republicans.[14]

So new were the captains of the French fleet – all former junior naval officers or merchant skippers (as Saint-André had briefly been) – that they had to practise basic battle manoeuvres as they sailed. Rather ironically, given the 'blockade' they had been under, for twelve days they hunted the British fleet inconclusively, riven by poorly understood signals and incompetent zeal, and with some of the ships showing grim signs of the haste with which they had been finished off. On 28 May, the British fleet under Lord Howe came into view, and for the next three days the French desperately attempted to both keep in contact and avoid decisive engagement. Their orders were explicit on this, the safety of the convoy was paramount, and the French tried to lure the British northwards, assuming the convoy would take a southerly track. Late on the 31st, the British finally forced a general engagement, in a battle they were to dub the Glorious First of June (because the ships were too far out at sea to pick a convenient landmark). The French fought furiously but badly – their line was pierced in six places, many of their ships effectively surrounded – but their grim resistance left the outcome, by late on the 1st, something of a draw, with a dozen ships dismasted on each side. The British claimed the victory, as the French abandoned six of their crippled ships in their haste to regain port. They arrived on 11 June, to learn to their horror that the grain convoy was still at sea. Saint-André and his fellow representative Prieur de la Marne, who came on board with the news, immediately ordered what remained of the battered fleet back out, but before they could sail the convoy came in sight, and 116 ships carrying twenty-four million pounds of food entered harbour safely on the 13th.[15]

Although both Saint-André and the national authorities projected this as a great victory, Brest itself became a viper's nest of bitterness and suspicion. Saint-André's critical assessments of some officers were resented by them and their political allies, and the casualties to the fleet did not go down well with the population. With the British still ruling the waves, the Jacobin tendency to expect complete victory even against the odds, and to blame defeat on conspiracy, put Saint-André under a shadow, and he retreated to Paris ten days after the convoy's arrival. This ability to turn military triumph into political failure was about to be echoed on the wider national stage, as the armies of the Republic advanced northwards.

Operations on the Belgian frontier were initially a rather clumsy affair, with three separate armies manoeuvring in parallel, all reporting back to Lazare Carnot, who was by now effectively the 'war minister' on the Committee of Public Safety. Memories of the treason of Dumouriez, and the alleged treasons of so many other generals on this front, made the Committee reluctant by this stage to give one officer overall frontline control so close to Paris. For the same reasons, representatives-on-mission continued their close surveillance, and from 29 April 1794 the young ideologue Saint-Just had a roving commission to monitor all the generals' strategies in the north. For much of May he based himself with the army on the River Sambre, in the centre of the front, ordering a series of fruitless counter-attacks across the river every time the better-positioned Austrians drove off a French probe. If his initiative here was not particularly helpful, on a short visit to Paris at the beginning of June he may have been instrumental in securing a more fruitful change in strategy. Saint-Just rejoined the central army on 6 June, and two days later orders came from Carnot in Paris to unite this force with the eastern Army of the Moselle, producing a force of some ninety thousand effectives. After another repulse, this more co-ordinated force finally secured a beachhead over the Sambre on 18 June (for some it was their seventh crossing), and pressed on to besiege the

Belgian town of Charleroi, the same day that the Army of the North took Ypres further west.[16]

Saint-Just continued to exercise a ruthless authority. Only the day before the successful crossing, he and his fellow representatives had ordered the arrest of the whole senior officer corps, from captains upwards, of the second battalion of the Vienne, charged with responsibility for the unit's flight from the enemy. The order noted that 'seeing that valour and the hatred of tyrants are implanted in the hearts of all Frenchmen', only the officers could be to blame, either through their own cowardice or their failure to 'maintain discipline and to inculcate in their soldiers the love of glory, which consists in braving the dangers of war and conquering or dying at their posts'.[17]

Faced with grim ruthlessness, and overwhelming force, the commander of Charleroi yielded the town almost at once, after his offer to discuss honourable terms was rejected out of hand by Saint-Just: 'We can neither honour nor dishonour you, just as you have not the power to honour or dishonour the French Nation. There is nothing in common between you and us.' Nonetheless, the courtesies of war were observed in the surrender, something for which the victors of Ypres had already been rebuked by Carnot: a 'certain esteem' for enemies who deserved 'hatred and contempt' risked softening the French soldiers' attitude to 'hypocritical and bloodthirsty' foes.[18] Charleroi's eagerness to surrender provided the crowning opportunity of the campaign. The Austrian general Coburg, he who had conspired in Dumouriez's treachery, and who was lumped in by some republicans with the English Prime Minister as the two-headed monster 'Pitécobourg', was marching to the town's relief. He brought only fifty-two thousand troops, having to safeguard against further advances of the French from Ypres. His English allies showed the exaggeration of the French fears about their universal influence by refusing to join forces, remaining in positions near the coast.

A superior French force was thus able to engage the Austrians near the village of Fleurus on the morning of 26 June. The French were commanded by Jean-Baptiste Jourdan, a surgeon's son who had served as a common soldier for six years from 1778, fighting five campaigns in America, before returning, still only twenty-two, to run a draper's shop in his home town of Limoges. Made a lieutenant in the local National Guard in 1790, he rejoined the regular army and was rapidly promoted in the chaos of the 1792 and 1793 campaigns, fighting as a major-general under Houchard at Hondschoote. On 24 September 1793, with Houchard's fall, he had been given command of all French forces in the north. Modest but confident, and both tactically and strategically competent, he had fought a heroic campaign at the worst moments of the Republic's material shortages, saving the critical fortress of Maubeuge from looming assault at the battle of Wattignies on 16 October. As winter drew in, however, Jourdan was compelled to lament the state of his troops to the Committee of Public Safety, and threatened to resign in November if forced to go on the offensive. Relations deteriorated as the condition of the army did not improve, and on 10 January he was relieved of his command and sent home. The fact that he had not actually been defeated, along with his impeccably plebeian background, saved him from a worse fate. His merits remained well understood, and only two months later he was summoned back from his shop by Carnot (who had signed his dismissal in January) to take command on the Moselle, becoming overall commander in the centre in June.[19]

At Fleurus, Jourdan secured the Republic's future. The battle raged from before dawn until near sunset, a sixteen-hour combat that ended with Coburg's forces broken and straggling northwards to finally encamp twenty miles away, not far from Waterloo. The French were too exhausted and disordered to begin a pursuit at once, but the significance of the victory was clear, and Saint-Just commandeered a coach to ride for Paris with the news at once. The forces he left behind would soon rally, and by early July 180,000 French troops from the two advancing armies united in Brussels. The French victories confirmed the views of the Austrian high command expressed in May, that Belgium was indefensible against the might of France, and another season's campaigning in the low countries was futile. How far they had thus preordained their own defeat is unclear, but Austria was to withdraw decisively from the politics of north-western Europe after Fleurus.[20]

The capital that greeted Saint-Just when he arrived on 28 June was a city in sombre, indeed morbid mood. Eleven days earlier, a huge batch of fifty-four victims had gone to the guillotine dressed in the red robes that traditionally marked out parricides: literally father-killers, and by extension those who strike at sacred figures. They were the latest manifestation of the revolutionaries' insistence on the

Foreign Plot. On 20 May, a man noted variously as Ladmiral, Admiral or Admirat had shot at Collot-d'Herbois in the heart of the city. He missed, but announced that he would have shot Robespierre if he had found him. Only three days later, Cécile Renault, aged twenty, was found wandering the halls of the Tuileries, also asking for Robespierre. She said she wanted 'to see what a tyrant looked like', and was carrying two small knives.[21] The two would-be assassins were then rolled up into a grand trial which included half a dozen captive nobles, several bankers and financiers, and a whole series of discredited police agents and public officials. All were condemned, in the absence of anything that could meaningfully be described as evidence, 'as accomplices in a foreign conspiracy'.[22]

The day before this trial, 16 June, thirty-seven inhabitants of Bicêtre prison had been executed as enemies of the people, for an alleged plot to break out of the jail, stab the members of the Committees of Public Safety and General Security, 'tear out their hearts, cook and eat them, and to put the most patriotic representatives to death in a barrel lined with nails'.[23] These absurd charges resulted from the vague denunciation of one inmate about a planned breakout, passed from the prison administration to the Committee of Public Safety, and then by Robespierre to his acolyte Herman in his new role as chief of the public security administration. Herman appears to have added the details, and in the process began to think that such charges would be a useful way to clear the prisons. Thirty-six new accused were added to the list of those executed on the 16th, and a further 159 names resulted from a scrutiny of likely suspects in the Luxembourg prison, where senior political figures were held. These latter were all described as 'agents of general Dillon', who had himself been guillotined long ago on 13 April, in a batch with the widows of both Hébert and Desmoulins, and the former procurator Chaumette. The old and new Cordeliers had thus at last been brought together, confirming their mutual annihilation as the Committee cleared up the fictitious plot it had invented to end the trial of the Dantonists.[24]

The ever-increasing numbers of executions by the summer no longer carried away, as they had in April and May, figures of eminence – whether revolutionaries like Hébert and Danton or Old Regime stalwarts like Malesherbes and Lavoisier. Rather, the obscure victims of petty denunciations and the barely coherent suspicions of local Surveillance Committees were turned into the authors of absurd plots, as the machinery of Terror came almost to take on a life of its own. How far individuals like Herman and the prosecutor Fouquier-Tinville, or indeed Robespierre or Saint-Just, genuinely believed in the crimes of the people they were dispatching remains an imponderable question, but as time passed they clearly grew less and less interested in doubting a guilt which was presumed for the flimsiest of reasons. Intriguingly, few of those prisoners whose last letters survive seem to have bewailed the apparent madness of this system – most, indeed, did not see in it any system at all, blaming their fate on the vagaries of factional politics, or cursing the errors of the courts. Many such letters were taken up with settling of accounts in a far more mundane style, representing as they did last wills, and requesting the repayment of debts and disposal of assets. All in all, a truly remarkable stoicism seems to have pervaded the prisons of the Terror, where inmates sometimes rehearsed the whole ritual of execution, anxious to accustom themselves to its manoeuvres and not lapse into humiliating confusion at their last public appearance.[25]

The behaviour of the executioners itself aided this process. Back in July 1793, the assistant Legros had been jailed for slapping Charlotte Corday's severed head, a gesture held to be totally at odds with the solemnity of the ritual. By early 1794, with *sans-culotterie* the dominant mood in Paris, the executioner's assistant reportedly capered around the scaffold prior to the victims' arrival, and according to one witness his 'antics and grimaces entertained the crowd before providing them with the more substantial pleasure of seeing heads fall'.[26] Nonetheless, when the actual victims arrived, the mood was calmed – Hébert himself, in a deeply and perhaps consciously ironic performance, was among the few victims actually to be mocked on the scaffold by his executioner. By the summer, the ritual had become once more profoundly orderly. A priest hiding in Paris, the abbé Carrichon, risked his life to accompany a party of noble ladies to the scaffold, and secretly to give them their last rites by gestures from within the crowd. He noted that 'the businesslike promptitude of the executioners' mitigated the suffering of the victims, placing them out of sight of the fatal blade until their turn came, avoiding any 'mockery or insult for the victims' and generally preserving 'decorum'. He still recorded, however, that of the 'large circle of spectators', most were 'laughing and ready to be amused'.[27]

Although the notion of a 'good death' entered into calmly and lucidly by the victim may seem bizarre, it was well understood by the people of the eighteenth century, and there was nothing the crowd liked better than a brave and well-spoken final speech – even if at the height of Terror that might be reduced to a few bantering words from the tumbril. The revolutionary state itself had no interest in representing those to be executed other than as individuals of free will and rational demeanour: they were being executed for their counter-revolutionary intentions and acts, after all, not merely persecuted (so the Republic asserted) for their social or other identity.[28] Thus the changing aspects of the machinery of death maintained the sense of interaction and spectacle that public executions had possessed all through the previous centuries.

The grinding of this machinery could no longer conceal by the end of June that serious rifts had opened up within the revolutionary leadership. The Committee of General Security, and especially its leading spokesmen Amar and Vadier, resented the shift of authority away from themselves to Robespierre's police bureau, and genuinely feared a growing dictatorship by Robespierre and his creations: dictatorship that would end with all such dissidents on the scaffold. These tensions had been ratcheted up several notches on 15 June when Vadier used his policing role to launch a barely concealed assault on some of Robespierre's most cherished beliefs, and on him personally. The occasion was a report to the Convention on a 'conspiracy' that revolved around Catherine Théot, a seventy-eight-year-old self-styled 'prophetess' who lived on the rue Contrescarpe in Paris. Long known for her odd mystic beliefs (she had once been confined in the Bastille as a public nuisance before 1789), she had been arrested on 12 May 1794, having announced to her followers that there would be a great divine manifestation on the day of Pentecost, which was also of course the day of Robespierre's apotheosis in the Festival of the Supreme Being, a week before Vadier spoke. Théot had also reportedly claimed to be pregnant with a new Messiah, and simultaneously had asserted that Robespierre was the 'herald of the Last Days, prophet of the New Dawn'.[29]

There is some evidence that the wilder assertions about the connection of Robespierre to her divine schemes may have been encouraged by the eager receptiveness of several agents of the Committee of General Security, who had infiltrated her séances and were seeking political dirt on the Incorruptible. They did not need to invent the fact that Théot's activities were assisted, and to some extent managed, by Dom Gerle, a monk who had sat in the National Assembly and had become an outspoken advocate of Catholic supremacy. Somehow evading official attention until this point, he was now in custody, and could serve to taint all of Théot's circle with overt counter-revolution, should the need arise. Vadier's report to the Convention drew on all the scornful language of Voltairian Enlightenment cynicism about the 'mysteries' of religion to ridicule the 'Mother of God' Théot and her followers (and by implication, lost on no one, Robespierre's championing of the deity), while also painting them as a threat to the Republic that merited trial before the Revolutionary Tribunal. The Convention duly decreed that such a trial should be held.[30]

What made it worse was that Robespierre was still serving out his two weeks as president of the Convention, and had to sit very publicly, high on his official chair behind the speaker's rostrum, and take all this ridicule impassively. Had a trial gone ahead, it would also have revealed that among Théot's gullible disciples were the father of Fleuriot-Lescot, the Robespierrist mayor of Paris, and several friends of the Duplays. That same evening, Robespierre showed how determined he was to prevent further personal embarrassment, and how willing he was to bypass even the rudiments of formal procedure that endured. He summoned the president of the Revolutionary Tribunal (one of his own men), and the more independent prosecutor Fouquier-Tinville to see him alone, and browbeat them into dropping the case. Fouquier was furious at this blatant interference with a decree of the Convention, but had little choice but to hand over the file. Within days, Robespierre had got his acolyte Herman to sound out possible replacements for Fouquier, but he was able to survive, probably due to the support of other members of the Committee of Public Safety. Still not satisfied, the Incorruptible ordered Claude Payan, National Agent of Paris, to investigate the way the Committee of General Security had handled the Théot case, with a view to finding counter-revolutionary intent in the procedure itself. Several of the Committee's agents were rounded up for questioning, leading to further administrative rows, including threats to Payan himself from the Committee.[31]

On 27 June, the day before Saint-Just's return, Payan wrote to Robespierre, arguing that the time had come to prepare a report that would instigate a purge of the Committee of General Security, reducing its status firmly below that of the Committee of Public Safety, and recentralising authority. A strike at those who were 'jealous' of Robespierre's authority could be broadened into an opportunity to put down the lurking dissension that had marked the debate on the Law of 22 prairial:

> You cannot choose better circumstances for striking at all the conspirators; the leading public functionaries should then be directed by you, they should serve to centralise and render uniform public opinion, that is, the moral government, while as yet you have only centralised the physical, material government.[32]

We should be wary, however, of reading this as a call for personal dictatorship. Payan used *vous* for 'you' throughout, and at this time that could mean only a collective 'you' – the Committee of Public Safety was to govern this newly sterilised field of opinion, not Robespierre alone. Nonetheless, whether that Committee would include many of its present members besides the Incorruptible, in this vision, is an open question.

The news of Fleurus brought by Saint-Just enabled Bertrand Barère to brief the Convention on the battle in the approved style on 29 June: it was necessary to assert, for example, that 'not one Englishman reached by republicans continues to breathe', even though there were no British forces present, and that 'never was a combat more terrible, more stubborn, more bloody' – claiming implausibly that only one prisoner had been taken.[33] Under the cover of such boilerplate prose, however, things continued to be far from well with the Republic. Saint-Just on his arrival had been aghast to discover the hostilities permeating the two committees, and wrote in an undelivered speech that the government was 'not so much divided as scattered'. Yet he was as guilty as any of fomenting tensions: one of the first things he had done on rejoining the Committee of Public Safety was to remonstrate with Carnot about the kind of orders he was sending to Jourdan, condemning a bid to detach troops from his army in the strongest terms.[34] The scattering of the Committee came in part from practical considerations – Jeanbon Saint-André and Prieur de la Marne were busy on missions, Robert Lindet was 'buried' in the offices of the subsistence administration, Couthon had been ill – but it was also becoming an increasingly political dispersal. Lazare Carnot had less and less in common with the inward-looking fanaticism of Robespierre and Saint-Just; Collot-d'Herbois and Billaud-Varenne, once the spokesmen of the *sans-culotte* viewpoint, were keeping a low profile, but increasingly resentful of the marginalisation of their powerbase; Bertrand Barère, the former centrist now the Committee's mouthpiece to the Convention, knew that a storm was brewing, but could not decide which way to jump.

Robespierre himself had virtually nothing to do with the Committee's meetings from late June onwards, and similarly withdrew from active participation in the Convention as soon as his presidency expired on 18 June. Partly through ill-health, but also due to quarrels with his colleagues, he was backing away from public engagement just as a whole swathe of political forces were swinging into alignment against him, and by his refusal to debate them openly he hardened both their fears of a new purge and their determination to act. Robespierre had his own conceptions of who his enemies were, placing Carnot high on the list. The two had quarrelled over political interference in military orders, and over Robespierre's efforts to arrest 'suspect' individuals Carnot thought were essential in their administrative positions – and he called the Incorruptible a dictator openly in an argument on 30 June. In his notes for dealing with other enemies, Robespierre associated several of them with Carnot, and seemed in his mind to be placing the military organiser at the heart of an active web of conspiracy.[35]

One of those he linked to Carnot in his notes, François-Louis Bourdon de l'Oise, was in fact almost overtly plotting against him. Bourdon was a disreputable figure, legendary for his heavy drinking, who had performed poorly as a representative-on-mission in the west in 1793, and was suspected of personal corruption. Attacked by the Hébertists as an Indulgent, he had nonetheless survived the purge of the Dantonists, and now sought revenge for the fall of those he viewed as his closest political friends. He had extravagantly, but privately, boasted after the passage of the Law of 22 prairial that he was going to assassinate Robespierre himself, with a bloodstained sword that had seen action at the Bastille.[36] He was linked to a half-dozen other Convention deputies who felt similar ties to the memory of Danton, and also to three of the leading representatives-on-mission with whom Robespierre had clashed politically: Fréron and Barras, hounded out of Marseille by Robespierre's Jacobin allies there, and Tallien, who had fled Bordeaux, and whom Robespierre had openly accused of fearing the guillotine.[37]

These three in particular had great cause to fear for their survival, and were actively exploring means of turning the revolutionary government away from its terrorist course, but they were initially hampered by an overly cautious assessment of how much of a united challenge they would face from the Committee. The apparatus of the Terror had such men under surveillance: a report written on 7 July, for example, covered the activities of the 5th, when Tallien had, among other things, talked in the open air with 'a citizen who accosted him . . . always looking around from one side to the other, and even stopping short to turn around'; Bourdon de l'Oise had walked in the Tuileries gardens with 'five citizens whom we do not know', and a certain 'Th.', perhaps Thuriot who had lampooned Robespierre at the Festival of the Supreme Being, left the Convention after its session 'with three citizens, whom we presumed to be country folk, to judge by their dress', and spoke with them in his home for several hours.[38] All of this proved nothing, of course, but these men doubtless knew they were being watched, which can only have heightened their fears.

Also in action against Robespierre was Joseph Fouché, the fourth major recalled representative, against whom the Lyonnais 'Friends of Chalier' were still pursuing an active vendetta. While these men, who included some of Robespierre's closest associates through the Duplays, sought an indictment of Fouché before the Revolutionary Tribunal, he spent weeks virtually on the run in Paris, not daring to appear in the Convention or sleep regularly at home, and going about armed. Fouché had managed nonetheless to serve a term as president of the Jacobin Club in early June. Perhaps partially as a result of this, it was to the Club that Robespierre turned his attentions strongly after his effective withdrawal from the Convention and the Committee, making a dozen speeches there in the following weeks.[39]

The Jacobin Club of Paris was by now far removed from its origins. It had begun as an opposition group among deputies to the Estates-General in 1789, had swelled by late 1790 to represent a broad coalition on the left in the National Assembly, and survived the Feuillant schism of the summer of 1791 to become the ideological powerhouse of republicanism. As late as the end of 1793, important issues of national policy were still thrashed out in its sessions, and major speeches there were as much interventions on the national stage as those made in the Convention itself. But the fall of the factions and the rise of the bureaucratic Terror had numbed the Jacobins. Where once the delegates of provincial clubs might have been admitted as temporary guests alongside the elite of Convention members, now such men increasingly predominated. The 'Robespierrist' Jacobins that had been imported to fill the offices of the functionaries of Terror made up a significant proportion of the Club, although not enough to be always dominant – as Fouché's election to the presidency showed. The vendetta of some against Fouché was matched by an even more longstanding hatred acted out against Edmond Dubois-Crancé for failing to 'rescue' the oppressed Jacobins of Lyon in the summer of 1793. Robespierre, caught up in the Lyonnais' viewpoint, repeatedly denounced the representative he pointedly called 'Dubois de Crancé', emphasising the aristocratic *particule* within the name. He succeeded on 11 July 1794 in getting him thrown out of the Club in his absence. The Committee of Public Safety recalled him from Rennes in disgrace three days later, in a decree drafted by Barère, unwilling to break with Robespierre in case it brought down the whole government.[40]

One of the charges against Dubois-Crancé, outside his general perfidy and implied 'aristocratic' outlook, was that he had intrigued to bar public functionaries from membership of the Jacobins, a measure which would have crippled Robespierre's political power-base. Yet the rise of those functionaries, and even more the delegations that provincial clubs continued to send to Paris, meeting with such men and seeking to impose their own local interests over the will of representatives, National Agents and the government itself, was becoming intolerable. On 20 July the Convention itself was driven to act, after a speech by Barère denouncing these activities, and voted to declare the capital a closed city. All provincial officials (and of course these Jacobin delegates were virtually all holders of public office in their home towns) were supposed to return home – though there is little sign they did so in the turbulent days ahead.[41]

Meanwhile, Fouché was counter-intriguing furiously against the Friends of Chalier, and therefore against Robespierre. He declined to answer charges made at the Jacobins on the 11th in the wake of Dubois-Crancé's expulsion, insisting that a forthcoming report to the Convention from the Committee would clear him, and appeared at the Convention after a long absence on 13 July, perhaps to show his confidence in the national body. Renewed Jacobin fury was the result, that he should dare to dispute their revolutionary legitimacy, and he was expelled from the Club the next day. Robespierre spoke on this occasion in unhesitating terms: Fouché was 'a vile and miserable impostor whose action attests to his crime. His conduct is the same as Brissot and scoundrels like him.' He openly declared that Fouché was 'the chief of a conspiracy that had to be stopped'.[42] The fact that language like this failed to result in an immediate indictment before the Revolutionary Tribunal shows, however, that Robespierre no longer had a firm grip on power.

The memoirs of Barras, a former *vicomte* always conscious of his own grandeur, rather disdainfully record that Fouché was by now engaged 'actively and with a will with intrigues and machinations of the lowest kind'. Barras himself directed some of Fouché's energies into calls on various individuals, but Fouché went further: 'Rising at early morn he would run round till night calling on deputies of all shades of opinion, saying to each and every one, "You perish tomorrow if he [Robespierre] does not".'[43] Fouché himself in his memoirs painted his activities a little more flatteringly:

> Being recalled to Paris, I dared to call upon [Robespierre] from the tribune, to make good his accusation. He caused me to be expelled from the Jacobins, of whom he was the high-priest; this was for me equivalent to a decree of proscription. I did not trifle in contending for my head, nor in long and secret deliberations with such of my colleagues as were threatened with my own fate. I merely said to them . . . 'You are on the list, you are on the list as well as myself; I am certain of it!'[44]

He also claimed to have dissuaded Tallien, desperate about his imprisoned Thérèse, from assassinating Robespierre, as such an isolated act would not have broken the 'terrorist' faction, and might indeed have strengthened it. He did speak, he claimed, with men on the great Committee, including Collot, Billaud and Carnot, and persuaded them of the dangers of their situation. Thus, by Fouché's account, Robespierre was driven backwards onto the support of Saint-Just and Couthon. The latter seems to have decided to throw his lot in with Robespierre despite his earlier humanitarian reservations about the Terror – as we have seen he had by now been instrumental in forging several of its bloodiest decrees, while persistently denying that dictatorship loomed. On 11 July at the Jacobins, he had declared that he 'wished to share the blows of any daggers directed against Robespierre', and may have genuinely accepted the latter's view of the situation as a real threat of counter-revolution.[45]

That threat, however characterised, was growing ever more immediate as July dragged on. Barère himself recorded the level of dissension between the Committees of Public Safety and General Security, and within the former group itself. Throughout the month of messidor (late June–early July), by his later account, the two committees had met in conferences, and finally decided to revoke the Law of 22 prairial. Bringing in Robespierre and Saint-Just to a 'stormy' session, members of the Committee of General Security attacked the law with 'force and indignation', while those of the senior Committee 'disavowed it entirely'. The response of the two ideologues was to threaten to go public, claiming 'that there was a party formed to give impunity to the enemies of the people, and thus to destroy the most ardent friends of liberty, but that they knew how to warn the good citizens against the manoeuvres of the two committees'. They withdrew, 'proffering threats against the members of the Committee . . . It was as to a declaration of war between the two committees and the triumvirate' – by whom he meant Robespierre, Saint-Just and Couthon.[46]

Barère gives no date for this event, and it may be a later confabulation from two conferences which did take place on 22 and 23 July. At the first of these, where Saint-Just was present but not Robespierre, agreement was reached to go ahead with the redistribution of property envisaged in the ventôse decrees, in return for moves to set up 'popular commissions', also mentioned in those decrees, to locate and release unjustly imprisoned suspects. At the latter session, Robespierre joined the conference, souring the atmosphere with rants against the presumptions of the Committee of General Security, and vague assaults on the merits of Collot-d'Herbois and Billaud-Varenne. He forced through agreement to four 'revolutionary commissions' to judge and execute the suspects not cleared by the popular commissions – a new move, and a substantial acceleration of Terror, since the ventôse decrees called only for their deportation. After the session, however, he repudiated even this move, seeing conspiracy in any agreement with his enemies, leaving the committees with no clear policy on the suspects.[47]

Confrontation thus loomed ever closer. On 21 July Couthon had spoken overtly in the Convention about 'four or five' scoundrels in its midst, and on the 24th was even more open, denouncing 'five or six human pygmies whose hands are full of the riches of the Republic and dripping with the blood of their innocent victims' – in the lexicon of the times there could be no clearer indication that he meant the recalled representatives: Fouché, Tallien, Barras, Fréron, Dubois-Crancé. The latter reached Paris after his recall on this very day. Spurning the Jacobins, where Collot-d'Herbois had triumphed after his own recall seven months earlier, Dubois-Crancé had instead, even before going home, gone to the Committee of Public Safety and asked for an official investigation. He repeated the call in the Convention the next day for a report 'tomorrow if possible', and the Convention voted for it to be made ready within three days.[48]

On the same day, in a move which suggests considerable tactical awareness, André Amar of the Committee of General Security visited the Madelonnettes prison, where languished no fewer than seventy-three Girondin sympathisers expelled from the Convention the previous autumn. Amar had then been among those who demanded a trial for them, and Robespierre resistant, but now Amar was solicitous of their welfare. Tears reportedly sprang from his eyes as they complained of the conditions. These men were still influential – they had visitors and regular correspondence – and could help ensure unity when the time came to challenge Robespierre. Without some support from what remained of the centre and 'right', there was always the danger that an attack on Robespierre by fellow Montagnards would be allowed to turn into mutual carnage to the benefit of the onlookers.[49] But with sympathetic links established, Robespierre and his Jacobin power-base were in severe danger of being held to account for their actions by an increasingly hostile political assembly, and on 26 July the Incorruptible took action.

For a month he had dithered over Payan's call on 27 June for a 'great report' to crush opposition by exposing its true nature, but he was now ready, and arrived in the Convention, which had not seen him for six weeks, with a great speech. Its greatness lay only in its length and its impact, however. It took some two hours to deliver, and covers over thirty pages of close printing.[50] It was a wandering, sometimes allusive, sometimes repetitious diatribe, long on self-pitying and melodramatic declamations of his own impending martyrdom and willingness for self-sacrifice, short on concrete detail, but overwhelmingly directed towards a new purge. The report in the *Moniteur*, the Revolution's newspaper of record, gave a brisk summary that was clearly prepared a day or two later:

> He read a long speech in which he began by vaunting his virtue. He complained of being calumnied, and indicated that all those who appeared to him to oppose his projects were enemies of the people. He then, in a long diatribe, decried all the operations of the government; he declaimed successively against the committees of Public Safety, of General Security and of Finances. Without formally complaining of the civic opposition placed by this latter committee against his projects to invade the finances, he tried to include it in the proscription, in accusing it of having *counter-revolutionised* the finances of the Republic. He claimed next that the patriots were oppressed . . . He added that some have been trying to deceive us about the situation of the Republic; finally he announced that he would propose the only measures suitable to save the *patrie*.[51]

In tune with his unexpected focus on the finances of the Republic, Robespierre named three leading members of the Finance Committee as dangerous enemies, but he preferred merely to allude to others by their positions and alleged misdeeds. Nonetheless, such allusions were clear enough to those present, and included reference to Billaud-Varenne, Carnot and the trimmer Barère; to Marc Vadier (who in an earlier draft he had named explicitly, blaming his report on the Théot affair for turning a 'profound political conspiracy' into a 'mystical farce and misplaced merriment');[52] and to several

Dantonists, including Thuriot. He explicitly blamed many of the ills of the Republic on the attitudes revealed by the mockery he had suffered at the Festival of the Supreme Being – clearly he had not been as oblivious of it as he seemed. The Tallien–Barras–Fouché collection of recalled representatives were also given clear, if implicit, notice of their doom.

The Committee of General Security was assailed for its bitter turf-war over political policing, as was the reluctance of the Committee of Public Safety to take his salutary advice – thus he explained his long absence from its counsels over the past weeks. And yet, he went on, playing again on the chords of self-pity, that absence itself, along with his former stewardship of the police bureau, had served to produce further slanders from his enemies on both committees:

> There has hardly, perhaps, been one individual arrested, hardly a citizen vexed or harassed in any way, to whom they have not said of me, '*Behold the author of your calamities*' . . . How could I recount or divine all the species of impostures which have been clandestinely insinuated both in the National Convention and elsewhere, in order to render me an object of odium or terror?[53]

By the time he reached the final lines of the speech, Robespierre seemed to have assumed that he would be destroyed for making it: 'What can be objected against him who wishes to speak the truth, and who consents to die for it? . . . I am made to combat crime, not to govern it. The time is not yet arrived for honest men to serve the country unpunished.'[54]

As his listeners knew, however, all this was just Robespierre's standard fare – he had offered his breast to the assassin's dagger countless times by now, and warned again and again that traitors stood at the heart of the Republic, ready to immolate him along with all the patriots: thus had the Girondins, the Hébertists and the Dantonists all been demonised by his vocation of martyrdom. He probably really believed it, but whether he did or not scarcely matters. The real point of this speech had been made between his vow to die for truth and his pledge to combat crime: 'There exists a conspiracy against public liberty . . . in the very bosom of the Convention.' This conspiracy had 'accomplices on the Committee of

General Security, and in [its] offices . . . members of the Committee of Public Safety have entered into this plot'. The goal was 'to destroy the patriots and the country':

> What is the remedy for this evil? To punish the traitors, to renew [that is, purge] the offices of the Committee of General Security, to purify this committee itself, and subordinate it to the Committee of Public Safety; to purify the Committee of Public Safety itself; to constitute the unity of the government under the supreme authority of the National Convention . . . and thus crush all factions under the weight of the national authority, in order to raise upon their ruins the power of justice and liberty.[55]

This was almost word for word what Payan had proposed in his letter of 27 June. Beneath the rhetoric of liberty it represented the death sentence for all those who had even vaguely criticised the Robespierrists, and a vision of a future in which such dissent would become impossible. But Robespierre's enemies, all in their varying degrees fearing for their lives and for the Republic if he succeeded, had already begun to rally. The Convention which had heard the condemnation of the Dantonists in virtual silence, and raised only a few quibbles with the Law of 22 prairial, now found the courage of desperation.

The first flicker came when Bourdon de l'Oise jumped to his feet to oppose the printing of the speech – something which would normally have been decreed as a matter of routine. He said it contained 'matters serious enough to warrant examination', including perhaps 'errors', and the Convention should send it for investigation before the two Committees. Barère countered that its charges should be printed and debated as a matter of free speech (a curious standpoint in a country where 'anti-patriotic' writings had been banned for two years, but emblematic of the revolutionaries' lack of irony), while Couthon followed up with a demand for its immediate distribution to every municipality, as all 'should know that there are men here who dare to tell the entire truth'. He went on in a vein similar to Robespierre's, lamenting the slanders against the Committee of Public Safety by other bodies, noting that he had spoken out already against the 'immoral and unworthy' men sitting in the Convention, but that 'if I believed I had contributed to the loss of a single innocent man, I should destroy myself out of grief'.[56] A motion on his proposal was carried, as the opposition's forces still wavered.

This was almost the last sympathetic intervention, however. Vadier spoke coolly in self-justification: not only did he have more details that he would later use to explain his treatment of the Théot affair, he said, but he also rebutted the general charge of stirring conflict between the Committees. Pierre-Joseph Cambon, chair of the Finance Committee Robespierre had assailed, defended himself with more fire, ending with an explicit charge that met with applause: 'A single man has paralysed the will of the National Convention ... It is Robespierre, judge for yourselves.'[57] Robespierre replied inconclusively, and perhaps suddenly seemed vulnerable. The debate began to degenerate. Billaud-Varenne returned to the theme of examining the charges in committee, before Etienne Panis, a former member of the Committee of General Security, turned the matter aside: 'I reproach Robespierre with having the Jacobins expel whomever he chose. I wish for him to have no more influence than anyone else; I wish for him to tell us if he has proscribed our heads.' Panis went on, ever more melodramatically: 'It is time that I poured out my broken heart. I have been overwhelmed with slanders.' He was accused of being a profiteer, of despoiling the Republic, when he had not even the funds to buy new clothes for his children – 'I am described as a scoundrel, as a plunderer, as a man dripping with the blood of the prisons, I who have such a sensitive and tender soul.' He claimed to have heard from a man at the Jacobins that he was in the 'first batch' for the guillotine, and that others had confirmed this, and that 'it was Robespierre who made the list'.[58]

The debate returned to sensible ground with Bentabole, back from his Norman missions, who commented on the danger of printing unsubstantiated allegations. Over the objections of Robespierre and Couthon, but with the support of Amar, alongside Vadier the effective leader of the Committee of General Security (and still concealing his role in Chabot's Indies Company plot), this opinion prevailed. Barère, in true trimming style, changed his tune, calling for an end to the debate and commenting that 'if for forty days Robespierre had followed the activities of the Committee, he would have suppressed his speech.'[59] The original vote to print the speech for distribution was annulled, and it was referred to the two

Committees, to be printed only in sufficient copies for the members of the Convention itself.

The debate had shown Robespierre at his worst. He had probably hoped that his moral authority, returning to the fray after long absence, would have cowed the Convention and brought forth the necessary specific denunciations from others that would have doomed his targets. Placed on the back foot by the unexpected opposition, and challenged by several individuals to substantiate particular charges or make his vague allusions more concrete there and then, he spluttered out what amounted to near-retractions of some points, notably against Cambon and his committee. Had things gone on without cooler interventions such as Bentabole's and Barère's, he might even have faced charges himself for his 'slanders'. When the final vote for a limited printing was carried, he refused to hand over the speech, indicating allusively that the Jacobins would distribute it nationwide for him. This was a challenge to the Convention's authority, even if for the moment it slipped by almost unnoticed.[60]

What this session had also shown was that there was little evidence in practice of the grand plot that Robespierre alleged – no consistent line of opposition emerged from the debate, and each of the 'accused' who spoke had treated only of what concerned them directly. Whatever work Fouché had been doing, it had clearly not yet come to fruition. Time was now pressing, however. Robespierre took his affronted dignity off to the Jacobin Club, where to compound his outrage he secured the podium at the start of the session only after a tumultuous dispute between his supporters and a minority that wanted to give Collot-d'Herbois the floor. He opened by saying that this 'turmoil' made it clear 'that factious persons among us fear to be unveiled in the presence of the people'. Claude Javogues, the 'raging mastiff' representative recalled from the Loire for his ultra-terrorism, shouted out, 'We are neither factious nor conspirators, but we don't want the Jacobins dominated by one man!' Robespierre's reply was chilling: 'For that I thank you – for revealing yourself in such a pronounced manner and for permitting me to better know my enemies and those of the *patrie*.'[61]

He went on to repeat his speech from the Convention, to waves of applause and acclamations from his own supporters who packed the meeting. When he finished, the president of the Revolutionary

Tribunal, a loyal acolyte, spoke, asserting that there was now no doubt that 'the government was counter-revolutionary', and that those who challenged Robespierre's right to speak out were clearly 'the heirs of Hébert and Danton; they will also, I prophesy, inherit the fate of these conspirators'. Under the circumstances, Collot-d'Herbois showed remarkable courage in coming next to the rostrum, where he delivered a speech under a continuous barrage of heckling and jeers. His calls for a closer and more critical examination of Robespierre's charges were scorned, and he left the podium with an air of 'the most pervasive despair'. Billaud-Varenne, who sought to second him, was virtually drowned out, and cries of 'To the guillotine!' had begun. Silence fell as Couthon took the stage to demand examination, not of the speech, but of the conspirators: 'We will examine them, we will watch their embarrassment, we will listen to their vacillating replies, they will turn pale in the presence of the people, they will be convicted and they will perish.'[62] The Robespierrists went into ecstasies at this, and this motion was carried by acclaim, with hats flung into the air and wild cheering. A minority remained unmoved, however, and the session closed with deep hostilities unresolved.

It is at this point that, conditioned by the ruthless politics of the past century, a reader might expect either the Robespierrists or their enemies to have led a putsch, and murdered or rounded up their foes under cover of darkness. The fact that neither side seems to have made any moves in this direction illustrates the basic idealism, grotesquely misplaced as it had become, of the Jacobin revolutionaries. Everything continued to wait on decisions of the Convention, the properly constituted national authority. The next day at the Convention, Saint-Just was due to give a speech on the wider political situation, one he had worked at redrafting overnight into something like a repeat of Robespierre's. It was the ninth day of the revolutionary month of thermidor, a date shortly to pass into legend.

The meeting-hall of the Convention, still bearing the distinctive signs of its origins as the king's private theatre in the Tuileries, was as electrically tense as on any opening night as it convened. Saint-Just was recognised by the chair, but had scarcely begun with an affirmation of his own membership of no faction, and willingness to be flung from the Tarpeian rock – a laboured image of the ancient Roman mode of executing criminals – when Tallien leaped up on a point of order. The frantic networking of Robespierre's targets was finally about to bear fruit, as the impossibility of safe delay became clear. Tallien's hastily plotted intervention called Saint-Just to order on the grounds that his speech was simply going to open up more divisions within the government: 'They are coming to attack one another, to aggravate the ills of the *patrie*, to hurl it into the abyss.' He demanded, borrowing one of Robespierre's favourite images, that 'the veil be entirely torn away' from these intrigues.[63] He was applauded vigorously, and Billaud-Varenne followed with another point of order, charging that the previous evening's session of the Jacobins had been 'packed with planted agents' who were not legitimate members, who had 'deployed a plan for strangling the National Convention', and that one of these sat illegitimately on the Convention's benches – the unnamed individual was seized and dragged out. Billaud went on to develop his own criticisms, and Philippe Lebas, loyal follower of Robespierre, was threatened with arrest when he tried to insist on taking the floor from him.

Billaud charged Robespierre with oppressing patriots, protecting criminals and being alone on the Committee of Public Safety in wanting to preserve measures such as the Law of 22 prairial – 'that decree which in the impure hands he had chosen could be so fatal for patriots'. As he perorated, Robespierre himself could no longer sit by, and made a rush for the podium, only to hear the shocking sound of the National Convention echoing to cries of 'Down with the tyrant!' Collot-d'Herbois was in the chair, and there was no way this session would fall into Robespierre's hands like the previous night's Jacobin meeting. Tallien spoke again, seeking the arrest of the leaders of the Parisian National Guard and others of Robespierre's 'creatures', and calling for a permanent session of the Convention until its freedom was secured. This was voted to cries of *Vive la République!* Billaud and another member followed with calls for more such named arrests. Twice Robespierre sought the floor, and twice had to hear himself decried as a tyrant and denied it.[64]

Barère followed with a temporising speech in which he managed to call for unity against counter-revolution, and avoided almost all mention of Robespierre, while conceding that the military organisation of the Parisian National Guard had become problematic, and suggesting a decree to decentralise it. He also put forward a proclamation for national circulation, further calling for national unity.

Although these were voted, the direct attacks on Robespierre could not long be deflected. Vadier took the floor, and declaimed against 'the cunning individual who has been able to assume every mask' – turning to Robespierre's disadvantage his initial support and subsequent abandonment of men such as Chabot and Desmoulins. There was lively applause when Vadier blatantly called Robespierre a tyrant, and he then raged against his interference in the Théot affair, which he asserted was a real threat. Vadier struck perhaps one of the most telling blows when he began openly to mock Robespierre's rhetorical style: 'He is the only defender of liberty, he is giving it up for lost, he is going to quit everything; he is a man of rare modesty' – at which point laughter erupted, and continued as Vadier lampooned his self-pitying style and criticised his underhand denunciations.[65] The Incorruptible, already denounced as a tyrant, had now been laughed at in the National Convention. The end was indeed nigh.

Tallien resumed with an appeal to get back to the matter in hand, and in short order reminded the Convention of Robespierre's speech of the previous day, responding to its thrust by observing that Robespierre was a 'patriot' who had been nowhere to be seen when the monarchy was toppled on 10 August 1792, who had abandoned his post on the Committee of Public Safety at a time of pressing national danger, and who had had charge of the police bureau at a time when great crimes were committed in its name. At this Robespierre could only cry out in incoherent fury. According to some reports someone shouted out, 'Danton's blood is choking him!' He is said to have yelled back, in his last public pronouncement: 'So you want to avenge Danton? Why then you wretched cowards did you not defend him?'[66] It was a just charge, but irrelevant now, and two obscure deputies, Louchet and Loseau, seized the moment to propose and second his arrest. His younger brother Augustin, also a deputy and his devoted follower, demanded to be included in the indictment, while Maximilien (according to hostile reports) launched a tirade of abuse. The vote was carried unanimously (or so all would later agree). A few minutes later, after a speech from Fréron, another of those for whom proscription had loomed large, Saint-Just, Couthon and Lebas were also detained – the latter at his own request, a typically revolutionary gesture of martyrdom.[67]

These dramatic scenes were only half the story that was being played out. On the side of the Robespierrist administration of Paris, preparations had been under way for several days for a festival in honour of Bara and Viala, two thirteen-year-old boys killed fighting royalist forces in 1793, whose deaths had become staples of republican propaganda. The festival was to include a parade of all the wounded veterans in Paris, and thus provided an opportunity to fill the centre of the city with men from the Sections under arms. Permission had been gained from the Committee of Public Safety to convoke the Sections on the evening of 26 July to arrange a 'dress rehearsal' for the following morning. It seems likely that what was planned would be at least an intimidating spectacle, if not a direct threat to the conspirators Robespierre denounced in his speech that day. Unfortunately, these plans fell apart as soon as it became clear that Robespierre's speech had not been a triumph. The 'dress rehearsal' had no pretext to proceed without the plans for the festival itself, which were to come from the revolutionary pageant-master Jacques-Louis David.

David had been busy preparing a centrepiece for the commemoration, a third image to complete the trilogy of 'martyr pictures' begun with Lepeletier and Marat. The unfinished painting of Bara, however, lacked the political resonances so evident in the earlier images. It was of a nude and oddly androgynous youth, complete with flowing curls and crimson-tinted lips, writhing on the ground in what could have been death-agonies, or something else entirely. A tricolour cockade clutched to his chest was the only indicator of his identity. It suggests that David may have been finding his own imaginative outlets for the reality of living under the rule of the Incorruptible. In any case, he failed to deliver the plans for the festival (perhaps because he was no longer sure of the outcome of events), leaving the punctilious mayor Fleuriot-Lescot floundering, and the sectional meetings moot.[68] The mayor did, however, order troops to be ready for the 28th, the day of the planned festival itself, in case of trouble from the workers of the city. On 23 July the Commune had published a new Maximum on Wages, threatening a reduction of around a fifth in prevalent levels. Widespread rumblings of discontent were the immediate result, and this was a measure which showed the extreme lack of tactical foresight on the part of the terrorist bureaucrats.

Such disorganisation was repeated on the afternoon of the 27th. The arrests of Robespierre and his fellows had been decreed at around 2 p.m., but it was not until around 4 that they agreed to be escorted into custody, and were held in the offices of the Committee of General Security near by. Within an hour, orders for the arrest of Hanriot, Robespierrist commander of the National Guard, were being posted across the city. Hanriot, meanwhile, was in conference with Fleuriot-Lescot and the National Agent Payan. A regular meeting of the Commune had been taking place when news of Robespierre's peril arrived. Determining that what was under way was obviously a counter-revolutionary plot, they had sent out the council members to stir up their Sections and sound the general alarm with church bells and drums. Hanriot ordered four hundred troops from each of the six legions of the Parisian National Guard to assemble for immediate action. Payan was briefly seized by order of the Committee of General Security, but broke free, and Hanriot was similarly taken when he tried to rescue Robespierre with a handful of troops. The Parisian forces were slowly assembling, however. Four of the six legions refused Hanriot's order, but the remaining two mobilised in greater strength than he had asked, sending over three thousand troops to the Place de Grève in front of the City Hall by 7 p.m.[69] At Payan's orders, over two thousand of these occupied the offices of the Committee of General Security around 8.30, rescuing Hanriot, but failing to seize the committee members, or Robespierre. Hanriot, shaken by his detention, and reportedly the worse for drink, ordered a withdrawal back to the Place de Grève.

Militarily, the Commune was still in a position to crush the Convention, but the political situation was degenerating. Only a quarter of Sections sent delegates to the City Hall, and barely more than a fifth of Section general assemblies convened to give them unequivocal support. Without the support of the civilian 'people', the Robespierrist authorities were fearful of launching what would appear to be a military *coup d'état*, and became irresolute. Ironically, Robespierre and his colleagues were delivered into their hands at this point by their guards, who had been refused entrance to the Luxembourg prison by loyal Robespierrists in charge there. The prisoners were taken instead to the central police post, attached to the City Hall itself. They joined the deliberations of the Commune at around 11 p.m., Robespierre having declined a first invitation, viewing himself as still under arrest. He may have been hoping for a glorious acquittal, *à la* Marat, by the Revolutionary Tribunal, blind to the obvious fact that it would have been purged of his supporters long before he reached the bar.

Throughout the evening, the Convention's session had been chaotic, and sometimes panic-stricken, as word of the successive advances of Robespierrist forces filtered through. Deputies went out to some of the Sections, returning with the good news that most were rallying to legality. Bentabole travelled to the School of Mars with a colleague, fearful that the young zealots there would turn on them, but returned to report that the students 'all wanted to come to the Convention to make a rampart for it of their bodies'. They had left them in charge of a nearby artillery park, to safeguard it from use against the deputies.[70] At news of Robespierre's escape, he and his colleagues, along with Hanriot and the Commune's leadership, were placed outside the law, subject to execution upon arrest and identification. News of this, hastily distributed through the chaotic night-time streets, sent the last remnants of the forces that had been lingering in the Place de Grève drifting away – legality once more scoring an implausible triumph. The Convention dispatched Barras, the former army officer, to command the troops rallying to its cause. Throughout the chaotic evening, the Jacobin Club had also been in session, but proved itself even more paralysed by indecision than the Commune. Its members finally voted to make a demonstration of loyalty at the Commune in the middle of the night, but they arrived there in time to see the Convention's forces take charge, and melted into the darkness. The Club's meeting-hall was secured by order of the Convention – found empty, it was simply locked up. The motor of the radical revolutionaries had run dry.

Robespierre, his brother, Saint-Just, Couthon and Lebas had not given up. Around 1 a.m., as they sat virtually deserted in one of the Commune's offices, Couthon proposed a decree summoning the armies to their assistance. Legalism again reared its head. In whose name, Robespierre pondered, should they write? Couthon was firm: 'Why, in the name of the Convention, is it not always where we are? The rest are just a handful of factious persons who will be scattered . . .' Robespierre demurred, and after consulting his brother opined 'that we should write in the name of the French people'.[71] This blind infatuation with their own political virtue (or was it the bravado of pure desperation?) was snuffed out minutes later, as the Convention's forces burst in. Lebas shot himself dead there and then. Augustin Robespierre smashed his thighbone in a fall as he hurled himself from a window, and was left in agony. Couthon suffered multiple injuries as his wheelchair plunged down a stone staircase in the mêlée. Only Saint-Just was untouched, awaiting his captors nonchalantly, his eyes on a poster of the Rights of Man. Maximilien Robespierre himself had taken a pistol bullet in the jaw, smashing the bone and leaving him in agony – probably in a suicide attempt, though some said he was shot by the invading troops. In any case, he was carried on a makeshift stretcher into custody with his colleagues in the offices of the Committee of Public Safety, and there laid out on a table, bleeding profusely until a doctor was finally summoned to bind his wound. Bystanders mocked him, but he thanked one who passed him a handkerchief to wipe away the blood – thus his last recorded words were *Merci, monsieur*, the manners of an older age returning despite all his efforts at regeneration.[72]

Remarkably, legalistic quibbles still held up the final resolution of the drama. Fouquier-Tinville of the Revolutionary Tribunal complained to the Convention on the 28th that his court could not confirm the identities of the outlaw deputies, and thus permit their executions. Two municipal officers had to attest to the identification, and all the municipal officers of Paris had been outlawed the previous evening. This trifling matter required some debate in the Convention, before a simple decree resolved it. Around 6 p.m., the four surviving deputies, along with eighteen others including Payan and Hanriot (semi-conscious after being pushed out of a window in the struggles, and lying undiscovered for twelve hours on a dung-heap below), were taken to the guillotine, specially returned to the Place de la Révolution for the occasion.

It was a short trip from the Conciergerie prison, where they had been briefly lodged, but long enough for crowds to gather and insult them, and for some to dance a jig round the tumbrils. The previous evening, workers had gathered to protest the Maximum on Wages, coincidentally reaching the Place de Grève just as more political events overtook them. Fleuriot-Lescot had tried to curry popular favour with a proclamation that blamed Barère, 'who belonged to all the factions by turn', for the cuts, which he said aimed 'to make the workers starve', but the ploy did not work. Some saluted the executions of the Robespierrist Commune with jeers against the 'fucking Maximum'; others immediately began to plan strike action for pay rises.[73] The deputy Cassanyès, who had mocked Robespierre's apotheosis at the Festival of the Supreme Being, was present to chart his fall. As the Incorruptible sat groggily in the tumbril, pallid and visibly disfigured even beneath his bandages, a woman burst from the crowd and harangued him as a 'monster spewed up from hell . . . Go now, evildoer, go down into your grave loaded with the curses of the wives and mothers of France!' Even this brought no response, except to make him briefly open his eyes.[74]

There was no grandeur in these executions, no *Marseillaise* from these martyred patriots, no gallows humour or epigrammatic reflection – half of them were barely still alive anyway.[75] Augustin and Hanriot had to be dragged to the machine, as did Couthon, screaming as his crippled limbs were forced onto the plank. Saint-Just seemed elsewhere, perhaps already mentally inhabiting the perfect Spartan Republic of his dreams. Robespierre would not fit into the guillotine with the bandages applied to his wounds, so the executioner ripped them off. Thus the end of the Incorruptible, the great tribune of the people, the architect and prophet of the Terror, was signalled from his ruined throat by a ghastly, inhuman scream, only cut short as the blade fell upon his neck. The severed head presented, according to Cassanyès, 'an indescribably horrible spectacle'.[76]

# CHAPTER 12

# Terror Against Terror

The blade that cut short Robespierre's screams on 10 thermidor could not snuff out the Terror like a candle. The Incorruptible had been processed to his death by the same machinery that had accounted for his victims, and on the next day, 29 July, the guillotine was the busiest it had ever been in Paris, dispatching no fewer than seventy-one members of the Robespierrist hierarchy of the capital.[1] Fouquier-Tinville organised the prosecution material (in this case, merely to confirm the outlaws' identities), and Armand Herman, Robespierre's old friend from Artois, oiled the administrative wheels as usual. Herman had refused to join the Commune's rising on the 27th, falling back on a position of strict legalism – he even personally sent decrees of the Convention that evening to Claude Payan (who crumpled them up, cursing him as a 'base slave'), though this would not save him from eventual revenge, and execution in May 1795.[2]

Revenge and executions, albeit no longer on the scale of Robespierre's days, would mark much of the next year in French politics. How far the mentality of the Terror still governed the 'thermidorians', as Robespierre's foes would soon be known, is shown in perhaps the most remarkable of all the many rumours and plot-fantasies of the era. On the day of Robespierre's fall, and for some short time afterwards, it was common knowledge in Paris that he had plotted to make himself king. As one private diarist recorded, Robespierre was said to have sought acknowledgement as king 'in Lyon and in other departments' – emblematic of Parisian fears of provincial counter-revolution – and would then 'marry Capet's daughter', the teenage princess still suffering a miserable and orphaned imprisonment in the Temple.[3] All this would leave him, somehow, undisputed master of France, and accepted into the councils of Europe, bringing peace through the subjugation of all good republicans. The ex-*vicomte* and leading thermidorian Jean-Nicolas-Paul Barras wrote in his memoirs that such tales were 'hardly credible', but nonetheless 'not useless' in rallying the population to support the Convention. The whole thing becomes more than just the excesses of overinflated rumour when it is noted that a newly carved seal bearing a fleur-de-lys, emblem of French royalty, was discovered in the offices of the Commune by the invading Convention forces, and brought to the hall of the Convention itself to be displayed as evidence of Robespierrist perfidy.[4] Robespierre himself, as he lay in agony, was mocked repeatedly with his pretensions of monarchy: 'Isn't he a handsome king'; 'Sire your majesty suffers'; when his wounds were dressed with a bandage passed around his head, someone announced that 'his majesty receives a diadem'.[5]

Such language did not long endure – there was a palpable absurdity to it that soon caused attention to refocus on accusations of Cromwellian dictatorship – but there is evidence that it had been deliberately inflamed. The leader of the Committee of General Security, Marc Vadier, was said to have admitted decades later that the fleur-de-lys seal, and thus all its accompanying structure of belief, was planted in the Commune by his own police agents. The reason: 'The danger of losing one's head made one imaginative.'[6] In this cynical manipulation of public emotions and fears, done for the goal of self-preservation, we can see both the worst of the Terror and the emblematic logic of the thermidorian 'reaction' that was now to follow.

The survivors of the Committee of Public Safety initially hoped to retain their powers after what Barère called on 28 July 'a slight commotion which left the government intact'.[7] He pledged a revolutionary government 'a hundred times more effective' now that it had been 'invigorated and purified', and the following day brought forward three of the Committee's own candidates to fill the vacancies created by the dead 'triumvirate'.[8] But the Convention was not having it. The concentration of powers in the Committee had been the catalyst for the descent into the Robespierrist Terror, or so Tallien argued on the next day, when his motion substantially to renew the Committee, and to subject its members to periodic automatic removal, was passed. Tallien himself joined the Committee, alongside Thuriot representing the 'Dantonist' tendency, and others who brought it back to its original complement of twelve. Only days later, on 1 August, the Committee of General Security was purged of Robespierrists, including Jacques-Louis David, and on the same day the death-dealing Law of 22 prairial was repealed.

On 5 August it was ruled that generalised suspicion was no longer grounds for internment, and that only those who faced specific charges could be held in custody, and on the 10th a new law defined the remit of the Revolutionary Tribunal far more narrowly, and insisted that prisoners could be found guilty only if there was evidence of clear counter-revolutionary intent.[9] Chief prosecutor Fouquier-Tinville was incarcerated, and the machinery of official slaughter ground almost to a halt. As crowds celebrated the second anniversary of the fall of the monarchy with genuine joy, others waited for joyous reunions at the gates of Paris's many prisons. Over 3500 prisoners were released in the capital in August.[10] In the course of the same month, strong limits were put on the powers of representatives-on-mission, the Parisian and other Sections were limited further in their meetings, and finally on the 24th a new law on Revolutionary Government reversed the institutional centralisation within the Convention – the Committee of Public Safety was no longer to oversee the work of other bodies, individual committees would work with the twelve 'executive commissions' of government, and the nationwide network of 'revolutionary committees' was scaled back.

By the end of the summer, therefore, there had been an institutional reaction against most of the measures of the late Terror. While this in itself might have restored some humanity to administrative and judicial processes, it was accompanied, if at first only hesitantly, by a savage political and social reaction. The Convention, suddenly freed from the Robespierrist death-grip, was deeply uncertain about its future course: at the start of August, for example, a vote had been carried to bar all former nobles and priests from public office, only to be struck down the next day. Some, including the 'moderate' terrorist Robert Lindet, called unsuccessfully for a general amnesty to be proclaimed, and there were sufficient other moderates still on the benches to resist the more violent calls for vengeance, at least for the moment. In the name of the Committee of Public Safety, Lindet presented a report to the Convention on 19 September, in which he tried to promote a positive vision of the achievements of the Year II: 'You have won over the opinion of nations. They no longer ask if you have a government; they understand that to maintain the most numerous armies on earth . . . that is to know how to govern oneself.'[11] Traitors and conspirators had disfigured the 'measures of general security' adopted for national defence, but all was now well – 'Who would want to call us to account for those actions which are impossible to foresee and control? The revolution has taken place; it is the work of everyone . . . What happened to us that does not happen to all men thrown an infinite distance out of the ordinary course of life?'[12]

Lindet's position was, in the end, deeply disingenuous, though he doubtless earnestly hoped that a swift collective amnesia would come to France's aid. Others, however, were determined not to rest until the 'terrorists' had been made to pay for their crimes. Tallien on 28 August had already exposed a view of the wickedness of Terror as a 'system' that 'consists in threatening individuals . . . all the time and for everything . . . with whatever the imagination can conceive as most cruel', a self-perpetuating cyclone of fear that placed 'in each house a spy, in each family a traitor, in the service of a tribunal of assassins'.[13] On the next day, there was an attempt to impeach six remaining terrorists: Barère, Billaud-Varenne and Collot-d'Herbois from the old 'Great Committee', and Vadier, Amar and David from the Committee of General Security.[14]

How turbulent the political scene was can be judged from the fact that, only days after this unsuccessful move, the remains of the martyred ultra-radical Marat were exhumed and placed in the Pantheon, the national temple to 'great men', by order of the Convention. A few days later, several 'thermidorians', including Fréron and Tallien, were expelled from the Jacobin Club as that organ rallied from its near-extinction at thermidor to fight the growing reaction. On 5 September the Club proposed a return to the basics of Revolutionary Government, including reimposing the Law of Suspects and reinvigorating the Revolutionary Tribunal. It was to prove a forlorn effort, however: like Lindet's speech of the 19th, only a bump in the road to the repudiation of Terror, and to revenge on its actors. In this context, the spurt of hope among unrepentant Hébertists of a return to *sans-culotte* conceptions of Terror after Robespierre's fall, with several Sections petitioning in August for the imposition of the Constitution of 1793, showed only the pathetic isolation of their viewpoint. The clear trend of politics was now towards the right, even if the former Montagnards like Barras, Tallien and Fréron continued to ride the tiger of reaction.[15]

Much change came inevitably from the relaxation of the Terror itself. Former suspects now readmitted to society included many nobles and the wealthy who, if not previously actively counter-revolutionary, now had every motive to turn their thoughts to vengeance, and hence to royalism. The turncoat Tallien himself, with his beloved Thérèse freed from Robespierre's grasp, built a salon around her that soon gathered in much reactionary opinion, as well as ostentatious luxury offensive to *sans-culotte* eyes. Many other suspects were the victims of the kind of petty neighbourhood politics that had bred the absurd condemnations of the great Terror, and had no more thought now than to be personally revenged on those who had put them in prison. The individual terrorists of the neighbourhood Surveillance Committees were to suffer greatly at their hands over the coming years.

At first, the men who had run the Terror did not know how to react to such a turn of events. Those who still held office by July 1794, whether in local municipalities or in the 'popular societies' which had effectively replaced them as political institutions, had learned the virtues of extreme conformism over the previous year. Just as they had produced the required denunciations of Federalists, Hébertists and Dantonists, so they rushed to congratulate the Convention on the fall of the Robespierrists – and it is here, in the flood of addresses from every corner of the Republic, that the image of Robespierre's aspiration to dictatorship was solidified. He was 'the new Catiline' (another inevitable classical reference to a conspirator in ancient Rome) or a 'modern Cromwell', a 'monster', a 'hypocrite', a 'tiger corrupted by the taste of blood'; even, according to the loyal *sans-culottes* of the commune of Ernée in Mayenne, a 'reckless pygmy'.[16] But all this conformity came inevitably at the expense of broad-based political initiative, and in its absence, it was those who opposed the Terror most strongly who came to the fore.

On 31 August, a gunpowder factory at Grenelle in south-western Paris blew up, killing and injuring around four hundred people. Jacobins leaped to denounce it as the work of counter-revolutionaries, but for the first time in many months they were met by equally vociferous voices from another direction – the explosion, along with the renewed vigour of the Jacobin Club displayed a few days later, was part of a plot to reinstall the Terror. So claimed the leading thermidorians, who by now were gathering physical force to resist any new rise of the terrorists. Their main arm was a group known as the *jeunesse dorée*, the 'Gilded Youth', encouraged if not exactly led by Louis-Stanislas Fréron. This former extreme terrorist, who had boasted of 'killing everything that moves' in the ruins of Federalist Toulon, now showed the unscrupulous depths of his rabble-rousing talents. Where Tallien rallied monied opinion in his wife's salon, so Fréron courted the streets. His newspaper the *People's Orator* had competed with Marat in its incendiary vehemence before the Terror, but he now revived it as an equally hysterical anti-terrorist organ. The Gilded Youth found legitimation in its pages, and in an upsurge of other anti-terrorist (and sometimes openly royalist) papers that burst onto the streets of Paris at the end of the summer.

The Gilded Youth themselves were a difficult group to pin down. They were young men, many thereby of necessity deserters or evaders of the drafts of 1793, but others clerks in private or even governmental offices. They affected a dandyish costume, with wide collars, pinched waists and bizarre hairstyles, and an air of aristocratic disdain. Few were actually from the higher echelons of society, but they repudiated the whole culture of Spartan modesty that had permeated politics over the previous year.[17] That repudiation was openly violent. For all their raffish airs, in practice they were political thugs, who haunted the public spaces of Paris, attacking reputed terrorists and shouting down opposition in places such as the theatres, still a central venue for political displays.[18] Their existence, in numbers of perhaps two or three thousand, transformed the appearance of the capital, as did the steady reappearance of the released suspects.

By mid-September 1794, the political landscape began to be further transformed by a story being played out at the Revolutionary Tribunal. On 8 September, ninety-four alleged Federalists from the city of Nantes, survivors of a convoy of 132 prisoners dispatched to

Paris in mid-winter by the ultra-terrorist representative Carrier, came to trial. Rather than submit them swiftly to a bloody fate, the revised forms of the Tribunal gave them a hearing, at which they charged that the city's revolutionary committee were the authors of their misfortune. These committee-men were by fortunate coincidence also languishing in Parisian prisons, sent there during the great Terror as dangerous Hébertists.[19] Summoned as prosecution witnesses, they were transformed by the charges of the accused into defendants themselves, forced to relate the horrors of the thousands of executions committed in the city, and driven into mutual accusation and recrimination.[20] One of the defending counsel summed up the nature of the committee, 'composed of vile men, without morals . . . they have spilt torrents of blood; they continually invented new conspiracies in order to accuse the citizens and have them killed'. The whole episode of Nantes was a demonstration that 'foul assassins have profaned liberty'.[21] After five days of this, the accused Federalists were all acquitted. The new anti-terrorist press had wallowed in the tales of blood, and especially in the recitals of the infamous mass drownings in the Loire (exaggerating the toll by several orders of magnitude in the process), and pressure mounted insistently for the revolutionary committee and their accomplices to be tried.

The uneasy balance of forces in the Convention still endured, however, and it took a month for such pressure to bear fruit. On 13 October Merlin de Thionville, a formerly active Montagnard representative-on-mission, now sliding into sympathy with the Gilded Youth, reported on the ghastly nature of the crimes committed in Nantes: 'The Convention should, if possible, invent new punishments for these cannibals.' He went further, calling effectively for their trial to be a trial of the Terror itself: 'Let us not suffer the system of these men to continue any longer, for this would be to ensure for these monsters, these blood-drinkers, impunity for their crimes.'[22] The indictment itself was prepared in the first days of October and given enormous publicity in the days after Merlin's report, as the trial itself opened. Across France newspapers and placards spelled out the new official view:

> In the most remote annals of the world, in all the pages of history, even in the centuries of barbarism, one can hardly find deeds

> with which to compare the horrors committed by the accused . . . These immoral beings sacrificed honour and probity to their passions; they spoke of patriotism, and they crushed its most precious bud; terror preceded their steps, and tyranny sat amongst them.[23]

They were called, in the inevitable classical reference, 'new Caligulas', and damned for institutionalising in their mass drownings 'a crime Nero blushed at having committed once on a single person'.

The accused, much like those in the previous trial, tried to throw the blame elsewhere: initially onto two of Carrier's associates already guillotined through the ironies of Terror, and then on 22 October onto 'the man who electrified our minds, guided our movements, tyrannised over our opinions' – the representative Jean-Baptiste Carrier himself. On 30 October, responding to insistent public and political pressure, the Convention began the process of indicting Carrier, which required (since thermidor) a special internal commission to be appointed from its members. This reported on 11 November that there were grounds for a prosecution: it was the conscientious Montagnard Gilbert Romme who delivered the verdict. Once again the long-drawn-out process, so unlike the swift and almost silent machinations of the Terror, gave full play to the inflammatory potential of unofficial viewpoints. The revived right-wing press continually hammered at the Jacobins, a name rapidly becoming a catch-all term for the evil men that had supposedly taken over France under Robespierre. On 16 October this pressure had already resulted in a ban on collective petitioning and affiliation between clubs – something the Feuillants tried and failed to institute way back in 1791, but which could now be enforced more rigorously. On 3 November Billaud-Varenne had the temerity to speak out for the Jacobins after a long silence: 'The lion is not dead when it dozes, and when it awakens it exterminates all its enemies!'[24] Such signs of life in the Jacobin corpse were sufficient to provoke a storm of anger, and on 9 November a direct attack on the Club by the Gilded Youth. They assaulted the premises in force, smashing windows, beating the men present, and whipping women from the spectators' gallery. Another formerly ardent representative-on-mission, Jean-François Reubell, spelt out the contemporary mood in the Convention the next day: 'Where was tyranny organised? At the Jacobin Club. Who made the republican system so odious that a slave . . . would have refused to live under it? The Jacobins.'[25]

The rout of the Club was completed on the evening of the 11th, with the news of Carrier's indictment still fresh. Tallien and Fréron were personally present as another wave of Gilded Youth swamped the Club, and on the 12th it was closed down by order of the Convention as a threat to public order. Thus the thermidorians succeeded by brute force where all the other opponents of Jacobinism had failed. Then, as if to prove that they were still republicans, on 15 November the Convention voted to maintain all the existing sanctions against the aristocratic *émigrés*. Carrier, meanwhile, was allowed to answer the charges against him before the Convention on 21 November, and remained defiant: severe measures had saved the Republic in its hour of crisis, and if he was a guilty man, then 'all here are guilty, right down to the president's handbell'.[26] The Convention was not yet willing to raise that issue, and Carrier was sent before the Tribunal to join the members of the Nantes revolutionary committee. This necessitated an effective restart of the whole trial, producing yet more acres of publicity before the final verdicts on 16 December. Extraordinarily, only three men (including Carrier), were condemned to death. While the traditions of the Terror were upheld in guillotining them without delay, a vast breach was opened with the acquittal of twenty-eight other committee-men and two further accomplices, all guilty of complicity in the various oppressions and extortions that condemned the three leaders, but not guilty of acting 'with criminal and counter-revolutionary intent', and therefore free to go.[27]

Despite its remarkably lenient set of verdicts, the trial of Carrier and his associates opened up the political landscape to the prospect of legitimate vengeance against the terrorists. On 27 December the Convention appointed a commission to investigate four figures now singled out as the greatest of these still surviving: Barère, Billaud-Varenne, Collot-d'Herbois and Vadier. A week before Carrier stepped impassively to the guillotine, the Convention had bowed to the logic of its own ongoing repudiation of Terror, and readmitted the famous 'Seventy-five' deputies incarcerated for protesting against the fall of the Gironde. As we have seen these were already a factor in political calculations at thermidor, and they were now permitted to resume active political careers, of necessity swinging the

Convention sharply rightwards. Seventy-eight deputies in fact rejoined the legislature, sixty-seven of the original protesters, and eleven excluded for other reasons (including the English radical Thomas Paine).[28] Their readmission involved the Convention implicitly in questioning the legitimacy of the fall of the Gironde, and this was a difficult step to take, so much so that another three months would elapse before the Convention could continue on this path, and rehabilitate the outlawed survivors of the Girondin leadership. By the time this took place, France had already moved considerably further from the Terror, but was no closer to peace.

In purely military terms, the thermidorian period was a time of remarkable successes. In the north the Austrians were driven back steadily, and pushed to the far bank of the lower Rhine by late autumn. The French armies shunned the traditional pause in mid-winter, and carried the fight into Holland – thus on 23 January 1795 they were able to complete a truly memorable feat of arms, capturing the Dutch fleet with a cavalry-charge across the frozen anchorage of the Helder. With the country occupied, an assembly of pro-French representatives declared the 'Batavian Republic' in Amsterdam on 3 February. By the time a formal settlement with the Dutch was reached in May, binding them into an alliance, Spain was also well on the way to defeat, and the Prussian government had already concluded peace with France, leaving Austria (and her minor allies within the Holy Roman Empire) alone in continental Europe.

Within France, the situation in the rebellious west was also more under control by the end of the winter. Intermittent guerrilla outbreaks had grown stronger after thermidor and the apparent collapse of Republican initiative, and by September 1794 there appeared a real threat from *chouan* bands in Brittany and Normandy.[29] The former leader of the Norman Federalist force routed in July 1793, the comte de Puisaye, now sought to re-form a Royal and Catholic Army north of the Loire with British subsidies. A widespread re-eruption of the troubles of 1793 seemed likely, but a relatively intelligent strategy of pacification was implemented.[30] The republican general Lazare Hoche, himself fresh from incarceration as a suspect, won several engagements against Vendéan forces in the autumn of 1794, providing the impetus for a widespread acceptance by the rebels of an amnesty offered by the Convention on 2 December. On 17 February, a remarkable treaty was concluded with the Vendéans under François Charette, a former naval officer who had returned from emigration and fought in all their major campaigns. As their general, he now secured not merely amnesty, but the freedom of the Vendéans to worship under their own priests, and a general exemption of their communities from military service. Similar terms were accepted by the *chouan* leaders in April.[31] This astonishing reversal of previous attitudes, which had seen rebellion as a disease to be eradicated, might have brought a more lasting peace, but even as the negotiations took place the country was descending into new crises.

The harvest of 1793, which had barely fed the country through the Terror, had been a reasonable one, and the winter of 1793–1794 quite mild. These conditions were not to be replicated the following year. The winter of 1794–1795, and the whole terrible year that followed it, passed into legend as *nonante-cinq*, 'ninety-five' in the dialect of the northern regions where its effects were felt most harshly. Farmers, reluctant to grow crops that would be stolen from them by the state, had cut back on their planting, and what was grown was assailed by heavy autumnal rains. As winter drew in, what food had been saved in rural areas from the ruthless requisitions of the previous year rapidly ran out. Temperatures plummeted, adding to the near impossibility of transporting supplies on ice-bound rivers and snow-clogged roads. In the cities, artisans found themselves bereft of candles or firewood to light their workshops or fire their furnaces – they were thus unable to work and scarcely able to live. The economy was still catastrophically disrupted by the decline of the assignat, and hundreds of thousands found themselves effectively indigent, with no communal resources to fall back on. Old people stumbled out into the cold to die. Infants found no milk at their starving mothers' breasts. Suicides among the working people of Paris became so common that the authorities ordered the suppression of published figures, to avoid panic. Recorded death-rates in Rouen, normally under two hundred per month, soared to over four hundred in mid-winter 1794–1795, remained elevated all year, and peaked again at nine hundred in the late autumn.[32] The birth-rate, especially in the north, plummeted in the next year, as many women's menstrual cycles broke down due to chronic malnutrition, a condition which continued through another very poor harvest in late 1795.

What made all this much worse was that the Convention, despite assurances in early September 1794 that the General Maximum would be enforced for at least another year, had begun to abandon price controls as early as October, and on 24 December abolished the Maximum, and all restrictions on trade, outright. They also closed down the armaments workshops in Paris in January, after militant campaigns for higher wages had posed a threat to order.[33] The natural inclination of educated men of means to believe in the virtues of the free market reasserted itself, especially after police reports indicated that the population at large no longer believed in controls. But their abolition brought disaster. With the government now competing for supplies for the army on the open market, and forced to print assignats to meet all its bills (no one paid taxes in anything but paper, and most did not pay at all), prices soared.[34] The general cost of living was almost six times higher in Paris at the start of 1795 than it had been in 1790, but by April of that year it had risen by half as much again.[35] In Paris one could at least still get an official ration of bread at three sous a pound in the spring of 1795, but that ration was less than a pound a day, and on the open market one needed to pay almost ten times as much. Ever since the end of the Maximum, there had been waves of uncoordinated discontent, and arrests for individual outspoken attacks on the authorities. Police reports revealed a litany of complaint and desperation from men and women alike. Between 16 and 31 March there were at least five marches to the Convention to protest shortages, one of which, on the 28th, was violent, being dispersed by the National Guard. The previous day had seen food riots break out in two Sections, and illegal assemblies formed in several others. Further rioting occurred on the 30th, and a strike for bread broke out on the 31st.[36]

As the *sans-culottes* of Paris had felt the bite of famine, so they had also watched their political enemies rise in prominence. The Gilded Youth had grown ever more confident through the winter, and had begun a campaign to smash symbols of radicalism, notably the busts of Marat that were to be found in all public places, relics of his *sans-culotte* 'cult'. Their pressure led to Marat's remains being removed from the Pantheon on 8 February: the Gilded Youth seized them and hurled them into an open sewer.[37] From January they had a new anthem to sing: *Le Réveil du peuple*, 'the awakening of the people against the terrorists'. Soon to become as ubiquitous as the *Marseillaise* had been in 1793, its lyrics were unambiguous:

> Why this barbarous slowness? Hasten yourselves, sovereign people, to send all these blood-drinkers to the gates of Hell! War on all the agents of crime! Let us pursue them to their deaths! Share the horror that animates me, they shall not escape us. See already how they tremble, they dare not flee, the rogues! The traces of blood they vomit up will show us their steps. Yes we swear on your tomb, by our unfortunate land, to make a blood sacrifice of these frightful cannibals![38]

Men chorusing these words had marked the second anniversary of Louis XVI's death (to whom the 'tomb' above refers) by burning the effigy of a blood-soaked 'Jacobin' in the Palais-Royal. The implicit (and occasionally explicit) royalism of such events was tolerated by the authorities so long as it did not pose an active threat to the Convention's power. By contrast, attempts by *sans-culottes* to agitate against this trend were met with arrests, and new prohibitions on political meetings.[39]

Meanwhile, within the Convention, the wheels of revenge against the Montagnard terrorists continued to grind slowly. On 2 March 1795 the 'big four', Billaud, Collot, Barère and Vadier, were ordered under house arrest (though the latter was already in hiding). By the time they were sent for trial on the 29th after a week's debate, the formerly outlawed Girondins and Federalists were back in the Convention. On 8 March the Montagnard Bentabole, perhaps regretting his active role on 9 thermidor, had warned that such a move, implicitly attacking 'the insurrection of 31 May' that toppled them and its alleged eighty thousand patriotic participants, would 'rouse every passion', but the mood of the Convention was swinging away from even vague sympathy with such positions. The abbé Sieyès, who had posed the famous and ground-breaking question of 'What is the Third Estate?' in 1789, now emerged from two years of virtual silence on the Convention's benches – he replied once when asked what he had done in the Terror, 'I lived.' He riposted now that 'the fatal 31 May was not a work of patriotism, but an outrage of tyranny'.[40] Thus on 29 March men like Isnard, who once threatened the capital with annihilation, were able to have their say on the fate of Barère and his colleagues. Three days later, the desperation of the *sans-culottes* could no longer be contained.

On 1 and 2 April the protest movement already under way

through March escalated into a general, albeit uncoordinated, rising. The Convention itself was invaded by a crowd of both sexes demanding 'Bread and the Constitution of 1793' – the latter having acquired totemic power as a democratic document.[41] However, there was little difficulty in dispersing these protesters without further violence, once some loyal National Guards and Gilded Youth had been collected. Parisians who had almost worshipped the 'national representation', and cheered the fall of the various alleged factions that threatened it, could not yet muster sufficient contempt for the Convention as an institution to challenge its existence. The troubles had been widely foreseen: Fréron had been busy arranging for his followers to be on hand as an informal 'legislative guard', and ten days earlier harsh punishments had been decreed for any 'seditious' threats to the Convention.[42] Politically, this abortive 'Rising of 12 and 13 germinal' succeeded in the short term only in provoking the thermidorian leadership to arrest more Montagnards suspected of Terrorist sympathies (including Amar, who had evaded attention until now, and Thuriot, falling from grace after his earlier election to the Committee of Public Safety). Collot, Billaud and Barère were sentenced at once to deportation to Guiana – though Barère evaded the journey and went into hiding for the rest of the decade. Collot died in exile in 1796, but Billaud survived to become a comfortable farmer on the island of Saint-Domingue, living on until 1819.[43]

April and May 1795 produced yet more evidence that the thermidorians were moving away from the basic goals of the Terror. On 10 April, 'terrorists' everywhere were ordered to be 'disarmed' by local authorities, which licensed those now in power to strip such individuals of their civil rights, and expose them to further persecution. The Revolutionary Government itself, as defined in the Law of 14 frimaire and reorganised in August 1794, was suspended on 17 April, and on the 26th the institution of the representatives-on-mission, the mainstay of political and administrative initiative under the Terror, was abolished. On 6 May, the prosecutor Fouquier-Tinville of the Revolutionary Tribunal, and fourteen of the loyal jurymen who had returned so many guilty verdicts, were themselves sentenced to death, charged as partners in the necessarily 'counter-revolutionary' Robespierrist conspiracy. Fouquier in his last letter home continued to present himself forlornly as a wronged patriot, unable to come to terms with the grim ironies of the past year: 'Tell the children their father died unhappy but innocent.'[44]

As the *sans-culottes* of Paris watched their political idols being persecuted (though few probably regretted the passing of the coldly fanatical Fouquier-Tinville), they continued to suffer materially. The assignat was hovering somewhere between 10 and 15 per cent of its face value, and heading downwards. Meanwhile the price of open-market bread was going through the roof: from 25 sous a pound in late March, to 65 in early April, 120 sous two weeks later, and an astonishing 320 sous (16 livres) in mid-May. On the 20th, in response, a repeat of the germinal insurrection burst into the Convention several times, each time being driven out with whips and musket-butts until a third surge was joined by National Guards from the radical Sections of the eastern Faubourg Saint-Antoine. This movement seized control of the chamber, as the head of one deputy, Féraud, shot to death in scuffles at the doorway, was waved on a pike under the nose of the chairman.[45] After several hours of tumult, the enthusiasm of the crowds finally communicated itself to the remaining Montagnard deputies who had sat beleaguered in the hall for months, watching their political enemies gain the initiative. The deputies secured enough order to propose (and pass, under the gaze of the 'arisen people') a series of motions to secure the food supply, release imprisoned 'patriots' and begin to reorder government in their favour. This initiative proved fatally unwise, as yet more pro-thermidorian forces rallied from the more prosperous western Sections, retook control of the Convention and permitted its relieved members to order the burning of the Montagnard decrees and the arrest of the ringleaders. There were dark but plausible suggestions later that the thermidorian forces had held back just long enough for the Montagnards to incriminate themselves thoroughly.

An effort to rally *sans-culotte* forces the next day petered out – despite the presence of several tens of thousands of insurrectionaries, there was no active leadership available to coordinate action against the equally matched, but better-disciplined, thermidorians. Within two days the radical neighbourhoods of eastern Paris were overrun with loyal troops. Many militants were detained, along with eleven of the Montagnards.[46] Accused of plotting the insurrection they had merely sympathised with, six were sentenced to death by special commission on 17 June (the Revolutionary Tribunal having been finally abolished on 31 May). One of the eleven, Rühl, smasher of the *sainte ampoule*, had committed suicide before the trial, and others fled, including Prieur de la Marne of the Committee of Public Safety. The six convicted men attempted suicide with concealed knives on the steps of the courtroom, in what was undoubtedly a prepared gesture of collective defiance. Three, including Gilbert Romme, died there and then, the others were guillotined despite their wounds, all becoming the 'Martyrs of prairial' in republican legend.[47]

Several thousand arrests, although only a small number of trials and executions, followed as the thermidorian authorities finally quashed the influence of the *sans-culottes* in the capital. Workers and craftsmen without means were driven out of the National Guard, disarming the rank and file of militancy in addition to the continuing victimisation of its leaders. In one respect, the thermidorians' repression echoed their Jacobin forebears, paying special attention to the role of women in the disturbances as a sign of particular depravity. New laws banned all women from attending political assemblies, even as spectators, and they were prohibited from gathering outdoors in groups of more than five, under pain of arrest.[48] As the tide of popular *sans-culotte* republicanism went into full ebb, so a new flood of royalism began to gain force, in the capital with the Gilded Youth and the freed suspects who continued to monopolise the public spaces, but also, far more violently, out in the provinces, and especially in the strife-torn south-east.

As early as February 1795, anti-terrorist vengeance here had taken on bloody and brutal forms. One judge in the infamous 'Orange Commission' was attacked in Avignon, beaten, flung into the Rhône and finally finished off with a harpoon.[49] At Nîmes around the same time, local National Guards butchered the terrorist officials they were supposed to be escorting into custody, establishing a pattern of judicial and administrative collusion in killings that would endure for years. The word of a 'prisoner transfer' leaked to local activists was often to be a death-sentence, one frequently carried out with cold premeditation and no effort at concealment. The law of 10 April 1795 on the disarmament of terrorists placed many in the hands of their former victims, especially as in the south-east a number of rabidly anti-terrorist representatives-on-mission used it as an excuse for mass arrests. It added to a law of 23 February that stated, apparently innocuously, that officials purged from office since 9 thermidor had to return to their home towns and register for surveillance by local authorities. In practice, this was just another open invitation to death-squads, who aped the affected dress and manners of the Gilded Youth, and also shared much of their social character, but acted with even more deadly intent.

The most blatant of these took up the violent and vindictive sectarian Catholicism that had marked politics here since the early Revolution, calling themselves names like the 'Companies of Jesus', but they were rarely linked to the clergy, or to the wider counter-revolution.[50] At Marseille on 5 June 1795 a group of some forty carried out a massacre of almost a hundred terrorists, marching unchallenged into the prison, blowing the door off one cell with a cannon, and mutilating corpses to conceal (or erase?) their identities. All this was prefigured, and provoked, by Convention deputies, including the Girondin Isnard, who had rallied the city to self-defence against a march of several thousand patriots from Toulon ten days earlier. This itself had set off to 'save' Marseille after news of a previous massacre of imprisoned Jacobins at Aix on 11 May, but the column was defeated easily by the Marseille National Guard. The ensuing massacre was thus pure retaliation – some of those killed were among the three hundred captured Toulonnais, but many other were petty officials of the nearby towns. One deputy, Cadroy, is said actively to have encouraged the attack, and to have congratulated the killers when he visited them at work.[51]

The anti-terrorist companies of the south-east were to continue their work for years to come, with the politics of this region becoming an apparently never-ending series of assassinations, but they were only the most persistent manifestation of a wider vengeful mood. Lyon, with its blood-soaked revolutionary past, gave evidence of this on 4 May 1795, when over a hundred Jacobin prisoners were invested by crowds numbering up to thirty thousand. Anger at reports that individual Jacobins on trial might not be executed was escalated by rumours of a prison breakout, and of the Jacobin deployment of bizarre multi-bladed guillotines, that echoed the most absurd indictments of the Terror. This absurdity did not stop the crowds torching the prisons and hacking the prisoners to death as they fled to the rooftops.[52]

Violent anti-terrorism in the south-east would remain a problem of law and order for the rest of the decade, but it is fair to say that it no longer threatened counter-revolutionary upheaval in the way that local Catholic royalism had before the Terror. The repression of 1793–1794 had smashed local networks in a way that would take years to rebuild, and Jacobins would themselves take to violent vendetta as the 'White Terror' of early 1795 ran its course. One could even see the focus on vengeance against terrorists as something cynically manipulated by the thermidorians to inhibit more structured political moves towards royalist activity. The threat of a restoration remained real, nevertheless, and also served to maintain the republican allegiance of the propertied classes who had done well from the sale of church and *émigré* lands and property.

The spectre of a royalist triumph loomed most ominously in the west, where, despite Hoche's astonishing pacification, all was far from well. As early as May 1795 there were signs of unrest as smouldering hatreds on both sides flickered to life, and fate dealt peace a further blow on 8 June with the death of Louis XVI's son, Louis-Charles. Separated from his family since early July 1793, confined under conditions of the tightest security, the eight-year-old orphan had suffered a pitiful existence in the Temple throughout the worst months of the Terror, with continual rumours of plots to free him prompting harsh and intrusive surveillance. Poor food and little exercise took their toll. His fifteen-year-old sister, also locked up in the Temple, recorded that 'his bed was not made for six months . . . he was covered with bugs and fleas . . . His stools remained in his room. He never threw them out, nor did anyone else. The window was never opened.'

Although things improved after the end of the Terror, the damage had been done, though his sister wrote with the cruel candour of a child that 'my brother was inclined to be dirty and idle and might have taken more care of his person.'[53] The princess, named Madame Royale by her followers, would survive imprisonment until given in exchange to the Austrians for a batch of high-ranking republican prisoners in December 1795. Among them, ironically, was Drouet, the postmaster of Sainte-Ménéhould who had doomed the Flight to Varennes, and subsequently won election to the Convention. Madame Royale would marry the son of the comte d'Artois, and do her best to forget her suffering, though always remaining ardently counter-revolutionary. Her brother had no such future. Like his elder brother, who died so tragically almost exactly six years earlier, he had never been in robust health, and slowly faded away. He may have died from the same variety of tuberculosis as his brother, ironically known at the time as scrofula, the disease that legend said was cured by the 'royal touch'.[54] New romantic legends would insist for many years after the Revolution that he had in fact been rescued, and an unfortunate double perished in his place, but recent DNA evidence has proved these stories to be fanciful.[55] At the time few doubted the news of the death of Louis XVII, as royalists acknowledged him, and certainly his heir did not.

That heir was now Louis XVIII, formerly the comte de Provence, the elder of Louis XVI's two brothers, and himself childless – meaning that his heir was now the comte d'Artois, who had fled France as one of the first *émigrés* in July 1789. The hope that lingered in the back of some revolutionaries' (and indeed some moderate *émigrés*') minds, of raising Louis XVII as a constitutional monarch to respect his subjects' freedoms, was abolished at a stroke.[56] The line of royal inheritance now lay along a path of the most farouche counter-revolution. This was demonstrated unequivocally a few weeks later on 24 June, when Louis XVIII from exile in Verona published a 'Declaration' to his kingdom. In it he announced his objective as 'the restoration of the royal authority to the plenitude of its rights', and a desire to rule through the 'ancient and venerable constitution' – in other words, to restore the existence of the nobility, to raise the church up to its rightful place, and to rule by divine right. Assurances that 'abuses' of the old order would be put right, that public office would be open to all, and that new taxes would require the assent of an Estates-General added nothing more than his elder brother had been prepared to concede in June 1789, and the promise of a general amnesty specifically excluded those responsible for the latter's death.[57]

Almost simultaneous with the news of this message came a landing of an *émigré* force of some twelve thousand on the Quiberon peninsula in southern Brittany, delivered by the Royal Navy, and linking up with local *chouan* rebels. After the enthusiasm of their initial welcome, further advances were paralysed by a republican cordon orchestrated by general Hoche, against which they battled in vain until a final surrender on 21 July. Almost 750 rebels were executed, and the combat decisively ended the truce in the west, where conflict would rage on for another two years, eventually requiring an army of over a hundred thousand to strangle the last guerrilla bands.[58] The Quiberon expedition was only part of a much more grandiose plot by royalist networks for nationwide risings, including the subversion of Lyon by *émigrés* advancing from Savoy, and the undermining of the French position on the Rhine, designed to cut the country in two from east and west and bring down the Republic.[59] Much of this was the enthusiastic fantasy of agents hungry for the British gold that by now subsidised many such plots, but real acts of subversion were being carried out all the time. General Jean Pichegru, French commander on the Rhine, was visited by agents of the *émigré* prince de Condé, and seems to have allowed disgruntlement with his own position – ill supplied and out of the political limelight – to have undermined his republican loyalties. Nothing came of this in the short term, though Pichegru, once the favourite of the Committee of Public Safety in late 1793, would become a royalist agent by 1797.[60]

The *émigrés* were in fact far less of a threat in 1795 than they had been in 1793, when many tens of thousands of Frenchmen were in arms against the Republic, and a solid cordon of foes surrounded her territory. Nonetheless, their continued activities proved that it would be almost impossible for the Republic to come to terms with Europe except through the military victories that had already won peace with Holland and Prussia, and secured a favourable treaty with Spain on 22 July. Continued military aggression held out the hope of external peace, but internal peace was a far more intractable topic.

As the anniversary of 9 thermidor approached and passed, the mood on the streets of Paris was grim. Food remained abominably expensive, and in short supply – even the daily bread ration had been reduced to a few ounces, and prices of other goods rose through 1795 by anywhere up to 500 per cent.[61] Economic distress spread from the wage-earning classes up into the traders, small investors and property-owners who made up the backbone of the more conservative west end of the city. According to police reports, these were selling their 'last sticks of furniture' and having to 'eat up their capital' to stay alive, and even civil servants, paid in worthless paper money, were 'suffering the torments of privation'.[62] Crowds were reported as cheering when workers attacked sellers of costly bread near the Palais-Royal, and it was said that the view of the *sans-culottes* in the Faubourg Saint-Antoine was that the enemy might as well come for them, as 'unable to stand the cost of living, they didn't care if they were English or French'. 'A King or Bread' was a common cry, though others observed that 'we were happier under the reign of Robespierre' – a telling phrase – or that Terror should again be made 'the order of the day', and the 'time of the guillotine' become 'permanent'.[63] Official policy continued to swing around the poles of liberation from the Terror and ongoing repression of dissent. A new unified Paris 'Police Legion' was created in late June, but on 5 August the Civic Certificates that had governed individuals' political rectitude were abolished. On 8 August the arrest of the ultra-terrorist Fouché was decreed, along with several other Montagnards, and on the 23rd all political clubs and societies were closed down.

All of this was taking place as the new constitution of France was being completed – the Convention having finally decided to accomplish the task for which it had been summoned. The document it drew up, and published on 22 August, was in theory a model of liberal pluralism. There were to be annual elections, replacing one-third of legislators each year, and only a requirement to pay tax (however small a sum) or to have served in the Republic's armies as a first-stage franchise (though on the other hand the franchise to be chosen as an 'elector', and actually vote for representatives, was set high enough to exclude almost all those who did not own landed property). Voting was specifically to be by secret ballot, a necessity after the rampant intimidation of the past three years. Two chambers made up the legislature, with a delicate balance of powers between them, and also in relation to the executive, which was to be headed by a five-man 'Directory' in place of a single president, playing to fears of monarchical ambition. This executive was chosen through a ballot of the legislature, and strict separation of powers was envisaged.[64] However, well aware of the rising tide of royalist sentiment, which Paris shared with the country at large, the Convention simultaneously decreed that two-thirds of the new legislators should be chosen by the Convention itself. Popular anger at this measure, which was submitted for referendum along with the constitution, is reflected in the voting figures, announced on 23 September. Around 950,000 people cast votes on the constitution, 914,000 of them approving it. Although only 95,373 voted against the 'two-thirds' law, a mere 167,758 approved it – it passed therefore, but only through mass abstention.[65]

The Sections of Paris, like local primary assemblies everywhere, had been convened to vote on these issues, a long-drawn-out process that took up all of September, after which they were instructed to reconvene as electoral assemblies on 12 October. To assist in keeping a balance in Parisian opinion, the Convention had cynically rescinded the 'disarmament' (and thus civil disqualification) of many neighbourhood terrorists. They had also drafted in units of the army to keep the peace, no longer content to rely on the National Guard. Nonetheless, all but one of the Sections had rejected the two-thirds decree, the exception being the loyal *sans-culottes* of the Quinze-Vingts Section of the Faubourg Saint-Antoine (and even here there had been 139 dissenters from fewer than 600 voters). Rumours that the Convention was importing terrorists from outside to complete a coup were rife, and the formal gathering of the Sections as the sovereign people gave paradoxical strength and confidence to a genuinely royalist hard core to push others into action against the Convention, so clearly bent on violating that sovereignty. The Gilded Youth had by now escaped its thermidorian handlers (Fréron had been sent south to control, or foment, the White Terror), and its thuggish behaviour now turned against all republican personnel and symbols. They even clashed with troops, to cries of 'down with the bayonets' not heard in Paris since the early years of the Revolution.[66]

A classic uprising of the Sections followed, echoing many of the movements of 1792 and 1793 – from the repeated calls for unity and exchange of delegations and decrees to the slowly shrinking number prepared actually to take armed action. In the first days of October the Convention aggravated the situation by arming a special force of 1500 volunteers, many of whom were formerly disarmed terrorists. By the morning of 5 October, some 25,000 armed men of the Sections were on alert, though the majority rallied only to their own neighbourhoods, alarmed by new rumours of terrorist pillage and brigandage. The heartland of the movement was the west centre of the city, in four or five Sections around the financial district of the Palais-Royal, and it was from there that a march of some eight thousand insurgents moved on the Tuileries. In a striking vignette of the Convention's isolation, the military commander of the government forces had parleyed with the rebels the previous evening, and revealed his own sympathies for them. Arrested, he was replaced by Barras, the conqueror of the Commune on 9 thermidor. Five thousand regular troops, assisted by a few *sans-culotte* volunteers, drove the insurgents off with several hundred casualties on both sides. Barras' protégé from the siege of Toulon, the artillery general Bonaparte, commanded the fortified Tuileries, and became famed for the 'whiff of grapeshot' that had safeguarded the palace. Barras later had Bonaparte acknowledged as his second-in-command, though on the day he had been only one of several generals present.[67] The next day, 6 October, the fight was carried to the insurgents, and troops smashed easily through the barricaded heartlands of the rebels, a zone described in a typical revolutionary conflation as 'the home of royalism, speculation and anarchy'.[68]

The roles of Barras and Bonaparte in permitting the installation of the 'Directorial' regime, which took office formally on 3 November after a protracted electoral procedure, are emblematic of the future of France after 1795. The former *vicomte* became the only man to serve as a Director continuously throughout the four years that the regime endured. He never ceased to enrich himself at the Republic's expense, becoming in the words of one distinguished historian 'a byword for corruption and immorality'.[69] In government he presided over the persecution of unrepentant Jacobins and terrorists in 1796–1797; then in September 1797 orchestrated a *coup d'état* that cancelled widespread royalist electoral victories, and in the following weeks encouraged the formation of new left-wing political clubs as the persecution of priests and *émigrés* was resumed. Less than a year later, in May 1798, left-wing electoral victories were annulled in another coup and policy swung briefly to the right, only to swing savagely back against priests and royalists shortly after – Catholics and *émigrés* were attacked more harshly at the end of the 1790s than they had been at any time except the Great Terror, all the more cruelly since it came after several years of relative, and in some cases absolute, toleration.[70]

Meanwhile, the economy nosedived as inflation reached astronomic heights – the assignat was worth barely one three-hundredth of its face value by early 1796, and a new currency introduced to replace it collapsed within months. State bankruptcy followed in 1797, with creditors paid off in worthless bonds.[71] Only the reintroduction of hated pre-revolutionary indirect taxes – a stamp tax on paper, a tax on tobacco, tolls on the entry of goods to towns – along with innovations such as a tax on doors and windows stabilised the finances by the end of the decade. Resorting to such grossly unpopular economic policies, alongside its seesaw political repression, the Directory soon came to have no other power-base than the apparatus of the state itself, propped up on the self-interested loyalties of the prosperous class who had purchased the lands of the church and the *émigrés*, and who were still threatened with expropriation and death by royalists.

General Napoléon Bonaparte, the scion of Corsican gentry, meanwhile consolidated his position in the pantheon of republican heroes with his astonishing Italian Campaign of 1796, smashing the minor Italian states and the Papacy out of the war in a few months, and continuing into 1797 to gain the favourable Peace of Campo Formio with Austria in October 1797 (cynically handing over the age-old Republic of Venice to Habsburg rule in return for French domination of Italy). Although earmarked to lead an invasion of England, he persuaded the Directors instead to launch him on a nakedly imperialistic adventure into Egypt, where he landed in mid-1798, after capturing Malta en route. Nelson's naval victory at the Nile on 1 August cut him off from seaborne support, but he nonetheless ran rampant through Egypt and the Holy Land into 1799. Although driven back from Syria, he still managed a crushing victory over Turkish forces at Aboukir in July 1799, after which he callously abandoned his army and returned to France on his own initiative. War had already broken out again with Austria, who joined an alliance with Britain, Naples and Russia (committed to fighting revolution by Tsar Paul I in December 1798). Bonaparte did not reach French soil until October 1799, by which time the Directory was furiously fighting off royalist insurrections in the south and west, as well as continuing to purge the political class ruthlessly to sustain its own power – another emblematically unscrupulous figure, Joseph Fouché, had just been recalled on the initiative of his protector Barras to become Minister of Police. Political infighting was pushing the Republic towards ungovernability, even as its external enemies' assaults were broken by new victories in Switzerland, from where French troops would push back into both Germany and Italy before the year was out.

General Bonaparte reached Paris on 14 October, and four weeks later, assisted by that other great survivor Sieyès, he was raised to the newly created position of First Consul by the military coup of 18 brumaire. In 1802, he was nominated as First Consul for Life, and on

2 December 1804, in the cathedral of Notre-Dame in Paris, the coronation of Emperor Napoléon I of the French took place. Taking the imperial crown from the hands of the Pope himself, Bonaparte showed that he yielded to no other power than himself by placing it on his own head. Moments later, in a scene immortalised on a vast ten-metre canvas by the ex-Jacobin painter David, he compounded this hubris by crowning his own empress, Josephine. Although in his coronation oath he swore to rule 'with the sole aim of the interests, happiness and glory of the French people', it would be for the new emperor to interpret what that meant, as absolutely as Louis XVI had felt himself free to judge what was for the good of his kingdom.[72]

Had the Revolution come full circle, and left the Jacobinism of the Terror marooned in a bubble of exceptionalism? In the short term, perhaps it had. Napoléon made peace with the Catholic church even before becoming Life Consul, and went on to make peace with many, though not all, of the nobility (and adding to it his own imperial creations out of the military and civil leadership of his fluctuating domains). Though he continued to safeguard the property of those who had bought church and *émigré* lands, he scorned democracy and popular sovereignty, reducing elections to a charade, imposing nomination from above for most significant civic roles, and introducing the formidable figure of the Prefect at the core of local administration – directed by, and reporting directly to, central government. One could see here the shadow of Robespierre's National Agents, but the more usual parallel is with the Intendants who had done the same thing for the monarchy since the time of Cardinal Richelieu in the 1620s. In the short term, the 'security state' that the Empire perfected, and that had been under construction throughout the later Directory, left ordinary citizens with fewer political rights than they had enjoyed ever since the summoning of the Estates-General.[73] The wider human costs of the emperor's determination that his writ should run from Lisbon to Moscow were of course immense.

But a hundred years after the taking of the Bastille, as the citizens of Paris contemplated the mystifying metal obelisk of Monsieur Eiffel, the centenary of Revolution seemed less meaningless. France was again, as it had been in 1792, a Republic of manhood suffrage – alone among the Great Powers in shunning monarchy and in granting such unrestricted power to its electorate. Its citizens, after three-quarters of a century of upheavals, including two monarchies, a Second Republic and a Second Empire, were coming to terms with a republican heritage that seemed now the most enduring of all these alternatives. Even so, their Third Republic had had to be born out of the carnage of the efforts of a new Commune of Paris, self-consciously glorying in the memory of the *sans-culottes*, to establish a proto-socialist regime in 1871. The memories and interplays of revolutionary politics had continued to echo destructively through the French body politic, with royalist and militarist coups threatened, but by the later 1880s things seemed at last to be settling down (though how far they did is a question for another time).[74] Out of the morass of slogans coined in the 1790s, the leaders of the Third Republic condensed in three words the essential principles that had been fought for by the vast armies of the Republic, raised up by the instruments of Terror, that cast fear into the hearts of absolutist Europe. The French Revolution was again, as the great statesman Georges Clémenceau was to remark in 1891, 'a bloc', the Terror was part of it, and it stood for Liberty, Equality, Fraternity.[75]

# CONCLUSION

If it seems paradoxical to invest the architects of the Terror with the mantle of liberty, equality and fraternity – and there was certainly partisanship in the assertion, with republicanism only one of France's possible routes forward out of the nineteenth century – it is nonetheless an association worthy of examination. As one major study has recently phrased it, the Terror was *politique* – both politics and policy – and grew out of a language of politics that largely concerned itself with the means of fighting counter-revolution, leaving the question of ends sometimes unspoken, and sometimes, as we have seen, reduced to platitudes of harmony.[1] For the French republicans of later generations, the most significant ends came to be those of national glory. Thus the easiest and most common way to remember the Terror was to promote the military bureaucrat Lazare Carnot as the 'Organiser of Victory', and to immortalise Danton with a statue for his rallying of the volunteers of 1792 – already themselves immortalised in stone in the 1830s, sheltered by the wings of victory as they rush forward on the Arc de Triomphe. Clad in antique armour, one of the central figures is of a youth whose nudity recalls Danton's reported jest about *sans-culottes*. Like those they purport to represent, the figures on the Arc embody the timeless nation, that most unproblematic point of unity for modern states.

A school textbook published in 1877, *La Patrie* (The Fatherland), illustrates this thinking. After excursions into the ancient origins of the nation, and a monarch-by-monarch treatment from the tenth century on, the Revolution was woven into the fabric of continued national existence. On the same page that Robespierre and Marat, 'terrible and ferocious men', were accused of organising a 'plot to overturn the monarchy' in 1792, the author noted that 'all of Europe, excited by England, was arming against us', and that 'a sublime élan took hold of all of France . . . Young men ran to take up arms,' producing the 'glorious' victory of Valmy and the 'immortal battle' of Jemappes.[2] Although the September Massacres were described in a single line as 'frightful', the author depicted the whole period of the Terror as 'an unheard-of effervescence, a sort of burning fever' in which 'those who sought liberty and equality before the law' saw their 'zeal' become 'exaltation' 'and exaltation too often give way to delirium'.[3] Thus delirious, presumably, the French need not be held accountable for their actions. All the deeds of the Terror – the war in the Vendée, the execution of king and queen, the conflict with the Girondins, the fall of the factions, and of Robespierre – were passed over in two pages, before we read that 'while mourning reigned in the interior, our armies were covering themselves with an immortal glory'.[4] In passing on to the period of the Directory, military triumphs and the rise of Napoléon become the key constituents of the account.

For many later republicans, the consecration of national glory was thus key to resolving the dilemma of how to treat the Terror – as well as a means of defending the republican heritage against still-significant challenges from royalist and Bonapartist traditions. This focus on the 'Frenchness' of the terrorists can, ironically for us, obscure their wider significance, just as the later insistence by twentieth-century Marxist scholars that the Revolution was all about class struggle can make it seem irrelevant in a post-Soviet world.[5] But underpinning the resort to Terror were also ideas that resonate more strongly today: a vivid commitment to a notion of civil society, of personal equality and dignity, and of meaningful individual rights. This, after all, was the point of not letting the counter-revolution win, and it reveals itself even in the unlikeliest settings.

When at the height of the Terror Claude Payan rebuked the judges of the Orange Commission for their misplaced humanitarianism, calling for them to remember such courts' nature as '*revolutionary* commissions' and '*political* tribunals', he was making an explicit contrast with 'the tribunals of the Old Regime', but also 'with those of the new'.[6] In matters of ordinary civil and criminal justice, the terrorists were never less than punctilious about the rights of citizens. The debates of the Convention itself were occupied with fine points of judicial procedure even in the murderous summer of

1794. Only the day before passing the Law of 22 prairial that rendered the Revolutionary Tribunal a killing-machine, the Convention had held a careful debate on the question of whether someone against whom a criminal grand jury had refused an indictment could be brought before a police magistrate on a lesser charge for the same act. Almost a month later, it explored potential conflicts in legislation concerning the delivery of indictments by such *jurys d'accusation*. Even as late as 22 July, when the Terror was in its final paroxysms, the Convention could find time to debate rules for trials held *in absentia*.[7]

The problem of the Terror was that its unrelenting quest to preserve and protect the fragile flower of personal liberty was also the engine of the destruction of that very thing. What use is liberty, after all, unless one can dissent? There is some sign that those at the heart of Terror were aware of this tragic paradox, even if only semiconsciously. The speeches and writings of Saint-Just over the last months of his life offer a turbulent mixture of reflections on liberty, tyranny, justice and Terror. In his speech introducing the redistributive 'ventôse decrees' in February 1794, he explicitly contrasted the latter two terms: 'Justice is more formidable to the enemies of the Republic than terror alone . . . terror is a double-edged sword, used by some to avenge the people, and by others to serve tyranny; terror filled the prisons but left the guilty unpunished.'[8] When he indicted Danton at the end of March he seemed less uncertain, proclaiming against those who warned, in a phrase coined by Vergniaud, that the Revolution would 'devour its children': no, he said, instead 'the Revolution will devour every single friend of tyranny; not a single patriot will perish through justice . . . Leniency is ferocious because it threatens the fatherland.'[9]

Saint-Just's personal solution to the problem of the Terror was to look forward, as he did in the same speech, to the day when all the *patrie*'s enemies would be destroyed, and the Convention 'will give itself over to legislation and government . . . sound their depths . . . and bring down the fire of heaven to animate the Republic'.[10] In his private notebooks, discovered after his death, he worked on a series of propositions, known as his *Republican Institutions*. It was in these notes that he wrote the famous phrase, already cited, that 'the Revolution is frozen', and went on to more sinister observations:

> No doubt it is not yet time to do good. The individual good that we have done has been no more than a palliative. We must await a general evil great enough for opinion to sense the need for appropriate measures to do good. *That which produces the general good is always terrible . . .*[11]

The doing of good was Saint-Just's prime concern; his very next note read, 'The Revolution must end at the perfection of happiness and public liberty by laws.' In this cause, he produced in his notes a model constitution for a society run by 'institutions', by which he meant not just the conventional organs of government, but also new arrangements for civil laws, family relations, education and all the dimensions of social life. In his utopia, male children would be raised by the state from the age of five (on a vegetarian diet), and trained in 'military and agricultural' arts. Anyone who struck a child was to be banished, but by the same token offspring were never to be 'caressed'.[12] Uniforms appropriate to different stages of life would be worn, and men would have to declare their friendships annually at the public temples – those who had no friends, or broke a friendship without explanation, were to be banished. Friends were to dig each other's graves, and 'scatter flowers with the children on the tomb'.[13] The whole thing was an imaginative re-creation of the kind of ancient utopia which writers such as Rousseau had made popular throughout the eighteenth century, with even more of a Spartan devotion to unflinching public virtue than he had advocated. As a model for regenerating an actually existing society, it was patently absurd. Nonetheless, the raft of decrees that accompanied the Festival of the Supreme Being came close to echoing its inspiration, and Saint-Just's final speech to the Convention at thermidor, cut off after his opening remarks, would have ended with a call for that body to issue decrees concerning 'institutions that shall be drawn up at once' – and he had the model prepared.[14]

Reading much of Saint-Just's last writings, one can come away with the impression that he was totally absorbed by his own perceived virtue and rectitude, but there are also hints that he realised the precarious nature of the terrorist project. At one point he wrote of death: 'One loses little in leaving an unhappy life, in which one is condemned to vegetate as the accomplice or helpless witness to crime.'[15] Shortly afterwards he observed that 'there are some men labelled as dictators and ambitious, who devour these outrages in silence. Who is more powerful, the one who calls another a dictator with impunity, or the one so called?'[16] His misgivings crept out in another note, superficially defiant: 'The day that I am convinced that it is impossible to give the French people morals that are gentle, energetic, sensitive and inexorably opposed to tyranny and injustice, I will stab myself.'[17] Why write this, we might ask, if the thought had not occurred?

A final series of notes were taken from Saint-Just upon his arrest. They are disconnected, concerning everything from the relationship between the Convention and the Jacobins, laws on education and the employment of former priests, to the conduct of the people in insurrection and the division of agricultural property, all within a few pages. But the last note of all is telling: 'The misfortunes of the fatherland have spread across the whole country a sombre and religious hue. Silent reflection is necessary in these distressing times; it must form the disposition of every friend of the Republic.'[18] The young man of twenty-six, who went to his death beneath the guillotine in just such a silent and reflective mood, had perhaps finally realised the enormity of what had befallen his dreams of liberty and happiness.

So we return, inevitably, to the present day, where all histories begin and end – because they are written, and read, in the here and now. Here, where the rights of citizens to be protected by the law, to be compensated for the slightest wrong (if they can find a good lawyer) and to pursue their personal freedoms – whether guaranteed by hallowed constitutional amendments or new-fangled Human Rights Acts – are taken for granted. Where governments are constantly chased in the name of Freedom of Information, and where the slightest personal failing of a legislator is dissected obsessively. And now, when non-citizen suspects are detained indefinitely without trial, when new powers of surveillance and public control are hurried into being unchecked, when police ministries endlessly proclaim that only the wicked have anything to fear from subjection to their regimes of scrutiny – as if we are to believe, like Saint-Just, in the unquestionable virtue of these legislators. To draw a comparison from Terror to the War on Terror may be no more than a facile slippage of words, until we recall the devout dedication of Robespierre and his cohorts to the well-being of their fellow citizens, their earnest conviction of their own capacity to see clearly to the truth, and their stark certainty that devotion to the cause of liberty and justice licensed them to eliminate opposition by means beyond the rule of law.

It is the close parallels between our own age's concern with individual rights and the French Revolution's invocation of that concept that make the comparison yet more pointed. The French revolutionaries knew that they had been unfree, they understood the bloody price they were paying for their new freedom, and they saw in stark terms the oppressive fate that awaited them if they relented. All this gave them a dread determination that the clock would not be turned back, and imposed a momentous burden on their leaders – as Danton had put it at the establishment of the Revolutionary Tribunal that would later condemn him, 'Let us be terrible so that the people will not have to be.'[19] However awful the consequences, the revolutionaries clearly believed that they had something worth fighting for. Under the rule of Robespierre and Saint-Just this principle was driven further, as Terror and liberty became inseparable within the political process. As their pronouncements increasingly showed, 'liberty' for them meant in fact the unflinching embrace of a form of fraternal equality where the freedom to act as an individual became meaningless: it was enough to be *free from* the tyranny of the aristocracy; being *free to* act other than strictly patriotically was a nonsense to them.

We live in societies where the positive freedom to act as we wish is perhaps our central concern. Whatever the professed fears of global warming, or the expressed sympathies with the poor and downtrodden, the willingness actively to change our way of living is the province of only a small minority. For most, the everyday rhetoric of politics, with its perennial twin foci of security and prosperity, matches closely our lifestyles and desires. Positive freedom to choose between an ever-widening spectrum of goods and services is maintained as an unqualified good, as consumer-citizens claim as their rights what the revolutionaries would have dismissed as selfish luxury bordering on debauchery. And at the same time, of course, choice in politics is confined to a narrowing spectrum of appropriately 'patriotic' viewpoints, for all but those prepared to expose themselves to vilification by stepping outside the mainstream. Protecting the unparalleled prosperity of the West is the unashamed goal of those who foster the continuing unchecked spread of the security state, with its increasingly autonomous ability to decide who is and who is not entitled to rights that we think we can take for granted. Saint-Just's final thoughts return unbidden.

# TIMELINE OF THE FRENCH REVOLUTION TO 1795

Events are indicated by the month(s) in which they occurred; particularly notable individual dates are given as numbers in the text. For simplicity, this chronology does not record 'revolutionary' dates as used after October 1793, except to note the names by which certain events were known.

| | | |
|---|---|---|
| 1770 | | The future Louis XVI marries Marie-Antoinette. |
| 1771 | | *Parlements* are abolished; massive political protest. |
| 1774 | | Louis XVI comes to throne. *Parlements* restored, Turgot's experiment in deregulation begins. |
| 1776 | | Turgot falls from office. Replaced by Jacques Necker. |
| 1778–83 | | Massively expensive involvement in American War of Independence. |
| 1781 | | Necker falls from office. |
| 1786 | | State finances become clearly close to collapse. |
| 1787 | Feb.–Apr. | First Assembly of Notables rejects plans for reform. |
| | Jun.–Oct. | Reforms introduced after dismissal of Assembly; *parlements* begin to protest. |
| | Nov. | Convocation of Estates-General agreed for 1792. |
| 1788 | Jan.–Apr. | Opposition from *parlements* and public opinion grows. |
| | May | 8: *Parlements* are abolished by edict. |
| | Jun.–Jul. | Widespread protest by privileged groups, supported by local populations in many areas. |
| | Aug. | Summoning of Estates-General for 1789 conceded as state approaches bankruptcy. |
| | Sep.–Oct. | *Parlement* of Paris loses public favour after taking traditionalist stance on format of Estates-General. Pro-Third-Estate pamphleteering reaches epidemic proportions. |
| | Dec. | After second Assembly of Notables fails to agree on a format for Estates-General, Princes of the Blood declare against any concession of the rights of the privileged. |
| 1789 | Jan.–Feb. | Elections to Estates-General produce political ferment |

| | | |
|---|---|---|
| | | in general population, while food prices and supplies reach critical levels following several years' difficulties. |
| | May | Estates-General meet at Versailles; stalemate between nobles and Third Estate deputies over forms for meeting. Riots and disturbances continue in many areas; some peasants claim that the Estates-General has already abolished feudal abuses. |
| | Jun. | 17: Third Estate renames itself National Assembly, swears to form a constitution (20); the three Estates are ordered to unite (27), but court begins to plan military action. |
| | Jul. | 12–14: Parisian mass rising, including capture of the Bastille, prevents use of troops against Assembly. 15–17: king concedes existence of new situation. |
| | Jul.–Aug. | Across France, self-government seized by 'revolutionary' groups in towns, while countryside experiences 'Great Fear' of aristocratic brigands, and continued substantive unrest. |
| | Aug. | 4–11: National Assembly pronounces abolition of feudalism to calm the countryside; produces Declaration of the Rights of Man (26) enshrining revolutionary liberal principles. |
| | Sep.–Oct. | Assembly stalemated after king refuses to sign decrees, resolved by march of Parisians, led by women, to Versailles. Royal family and Assembly move to Paris. Jacobin Club established soon after. |
| | Oct. | Tax-payment requirements for voting rights ('active citizenship') are laid down. |
| | Nov. | Church property is nationalised to solve financial crisis. |
| 1790 | Jan.–Feb. | Elections to c.44,000 new municipal councils, and division of France into eighty-three uniform departments. |
| | Mar. | Laws ending feudalism reveal that compensation will have to be paid by peasants: widespread rejection of this in countryside. |
| | Apr.–Jun. | Counter-revolutionaries lead risings, especially in south, but are easily defeated. |
| | May | Radical political clubs begin to form, especially in Paris – the Cordeliers Club. |
| | Jul. | Catholic church reorganised under state control, including controversial provisions for election of clergy. |
| | | 14: 'Festival of Federation' celebrates anniversary of Parisian rising with mass military–religious ceremony. |
| 1791 | Jan. | Half of all priests refuse to swear allegiance to new Civil Constitution of the Clergy. |
| | Mar. | Guilds abolished. |
| | Mar.–Apr. | Pope condemns Civil Constitution; clerical opposition becomes increasingly divisive, provoking violence in Paris and elsewhere. |

| | | |
|---|---|---|
| | Apr. | 18: Paris crowds prevent royal family leaving the city. |
| | Jun. | Workers' organisations or unions are banned.<br>21: Royal family attempt to flee to eastern frontiers, 'Flight to Varennes'. |
| | Jul. | Radical protests at decision to reinstate the king are put down violently, 'Champ de Mars Massacre' (17). Various laws passed against social unrest. Feuillant grouping splits from Jacobins. |
| | Sep. | 13: King accepts Constitution. Elections carried out for new Legislative Assembly. Feuillants seem initially dominant. |
| | Oct.–Dec. | Calls from Girondins in Assembly for military action against *émigré* nobles; laws passed against *émigrés*, vetoed by king. Measures against non-juror priests, also vetoed by king. |
| 1792 | Jan.–Mar. | Growing demands for war, coinciding with widespread protests against food shortages; moderate revolutionaries caught between political radicalism and social conservatism. |
| | Apr. | 20: War declared on Austria, initially disastrous, leads to increase in political tensions. |
| | Apr.–Jun. | Republican sentiments grow among Parisian and other radicals; demonstrations against the king. *Sans-culotte* movement begins to develop. |
| | Jul. | 11: Assembly takes emergency powers as war crisis grows. Prussia enters war. |
| | Aug. | 10: After weeks of hesitation, Parisian radicals and *fédéré* troops storm the Tuileries palace; royal family are detained. |
| | Sep. | 2–6: Massacres in Paris prisons due to fear of treachery. New 'National Convention' elected, declares France a Republic (22). Victory at Valmy (20) sends French armies on to offensive. |
| | Oct.–Nov. | Conflict between Girondins and radicals over blame for September Massacres, and over action to be taken with the king. |
| | Dec. | 10: Trial of king begins. |
| 1793 | Jan. | 14: King is unanimously convicted, subsequently sentenced to death.<br>21: Publicly executed. |
| | Feb.–Mar. | War is declared on Britain, Spain and Holland. Austrians and Prussians counter-attack successfully. |
| | Feb. | 24: 300,000 men to be recruited to army. Revolt against conscription, aggravated by Catholic-royalist sentiments, in Vendée. |
| | Mar.–Apr. | Series of measures establishing censorship, draconian penalties for rebellion, etc.<br>Rising political conflict between Girondins and radicals in Paris, along with tensions provoked in provinces by commissioners dispatched from centre. |

| | | |
|---|---|---|
| | Apr. | 5: Defection of Girondin general Dumouriez to enemy compounds internal hostilities. |
| | May | Jacobins and others plan overthrow of Girondins, assisted by mass demonstrations. 29: anti-Jacobin rising in Lyon; 31: anti-Girondin rising in Paris. |
| | Jun. | 2: Convention purged of Girondins – triumph of *sans-culotte* militants. |
| | Jun.–Jul. | Girondin sympathisers in major cities reject outcome of Parisian purge, branded 'Federalist' rebels; situation moves towards civil war. New 'democratic' Constitution agreed by Convention. |
| | Jul. | 17: All feudal dues abolished definitively, without compensation. 21: Plans to divide *émigré* lands among the poor (not widely pursued). |
| | Jul.–Aug. | Open conflict with Federalists, especially in south-east, compounds critical war situation. |
| | Sep. | 5: Convention responds to radical demands and votes to declare 'Terror'. Suspects will be interned; food prices are controlled ('General Maximum'); new armed forces to monitor supplies. |
| | Oct.–Dec. | Violent repression of Lyon and Toulon, where Federalism has merged with royalist revolt; Vendée rebels put to flight, take up guerrilla campaign. |
| | Oct. | Republican calendar is adopted, government declared 'revolutionary until peace' (10). Implementation of 1793 Constitution suspended. |
| | Nov. | First organised moves against religion itself, campaign of 'dechristianisation' soon under way among extreme radicals. |
| | Dec. | 4: Law of 14 frimaire on revolutionary government tightens central control over government agents. |
| | Dec.–Feb. '94 | Protest at direction of Terror begins to emerge from former radicals, led by Danton; others are implicated in plots and corruption-scandals. Hébertist radicals demand even tougher measures, and talk of further popular insurrection. |
| 1794 | Feb.–Mar. | Measures taken for poor relief; proposal to confiscate suspects' land for redistribution to 'poor patriots' ('Ventôse Decrees'). |
| | Mar.–Apr. | Hébertist radicals and Dantonist moderates are successively arrested, tried and executed *en masse*, as terrorist measures tightened further. |
| | Apr.–May | Paris popular movement and local government neutralised as a political force by club closures and arrests. |
| | May | Cult of Supreme Being introduced to replace dechristianisers' Cult of Reason. |
| | Jun. | 8: Festival of Supreme Being, apotheosis of Robespierre. 10: Law of 22 prairial simplifies still further the mechanisms of trial by Revolutionary Tribunal; executions accelerate. Success in war, including victory at |

| | | |
|---|---|---|
| | | Fleurus (26), reduces clear reasons for continued violence of Terror. |
| | Jul. | Various political factions begin to fear Robespierre will purge them. He and his close colleagues increasingly politically isolated.<br>27: Coup of 9 thermidor outlaws Robespierre, Saint-Just, Couthon; Parisian forces fail to rally to them, they are executed (28). |
| | Aug.–Oct. | Gradual relaxation of terrorist measures, attempts by Jacobins and Paris sections to regain initiative are repressed. Suspects are released, and politics swing sharply rightwards. |
| | Nov. | Gilded Youth attack Paris Jacobin Club, it is ordered to close. Purge of radicals from Paris sections begins. |
| | Dec. | Trial of Carrier exposes 'horrors' of Terror.<br>24: Maximum on prices is suppressed. |
| | Dec.–Feb. '95 | Bitter winter of '*nonante-cinq*' leads to starvation, widespread deaths. |
| 1795 | Feb.–Jun. | 'White Terror' of reprisals against radicals, especially in cities of the south-east. |
| | Apr. | 1–2: Risings of germinal; Parisian crowds protest to Convention about hardship, calling for 1793 Constitution. Order restored and sympathisers in Convention arrested. |
| | May | 20–21: Risings of prairial, with similar demands, leading to further purges of radicals within the Convention, and throughout Paris. |
| | Jun. | 24: 'Verona Declaration' by Louis XVIII, confirms that restoration would take back church and *émigré* property, and be fatal to many revolutionary leaders. |
| | Aug. | 22: Constitution of Year III agreed, with separation of powers and executive 'Directory'. |
| | Oct. | 5: Vendémiaire rising in Paris, royalists attack measures to ensure continuity under new constitution. Bonaparte's troops suppress rising.<br>12: Elections to new legislative 'Councils'.<br>25: New law reimposes strict penalties on *émigrés* and priests. |
| | Nov. | Directory takes office. |

# GLOSSARY

Aristocrats: In a precise sense, the high nobility such as those who led the *émigrés*, but more generally used in the Revolution to designate anyone apparently in favour of a return to the Old Regime of privilege and inequality – thus over time an increasingly non-specific term of abuse and vilification. Counterposed to 'Patriots'.

Assignats: Paper currency of the Revolution, originally intended in 1790 as state bonds backed by National Property, but in use as money for everyday transactions, and subject to increasing inflation, by early 1791.

Brissotins: A name initially applied in 1791–1792 to members of what became more widely identified as the Girondins. Derived from the leading figure Jacques-Pierre Brissot, a journalist, activist and member of the Legislative Assembly.

*Cahiers de doléances*: 'Registers of grievances' recorded by communities and districts as they elected deputies to the Estates-General in 1789: a roll-call of discontent, widely seen as the harbinger of the structural upheaval to come.

*Chouans*: Anti-revolutionary guerrillas who attracted widespread sympathy from the rural populations of Brittany and Normandy. Some were committed royalists, others more concerned to evade the conscription of the Republic, but they rendered much of north-western France ungovernable in any normal sense through and beyond the Terror.

Committee of General Security: The 'police committee' of the Convention, taking responsibility for internal security of the country. Increasingly overlapped with the expanding remit of the Committee of Public Safety, causing tensions and resentments that would be part of the process that led to the fall of Robespierre and the end of the Terror.

Committee of Public Safety: The powerhouse of the Revolutionary Government, created by the Convention in the spring of 1793 to co-ordinate the war effort, becoming by the autumn the effective executive power of the Republic. Responsible for authorising all the major initiatives of the Terror. Twelve members of varying political persuasions, united by the war effort, but eventually splintering in the face of Robespierre's drive to purge ever more of the political apparatus.

Convention: The National Convention, elected in September 1792 after the fall of the monarchy to write a republican constitution. It had 745 deputies, divided between radical Montagnard and more cautious Girondin factions, with a large 'Plain' or 'Marsh' of uncommitted members in between. The rulers of France throughout the Terror, exercising power with no checks and balances, purged several times, and continuing to manipulate the handover to successor assemblies after finally producing a constitution in October 1795.

Cordeliers Club: Most prominent radical political club in Paris, founded in May 1790. Membership less elite than the Jacobins but largely confined to radical activists, journalists and municipal politicians. Associated strongly with the ultra-radicalism of Hébert by 1793, leading to its discrediting and closure in the spring of 1794.

Counter-revolution: An amorphous term, originally closely associated with the aristocratic *émigrés* and their close allies within the royal court, seeking the overthrow of the Revolution and a return to the Old Regime. By the time of the Terror, the label was applied to anyone who dissented in any way from the ruling orthodoxy – including, eventually, Robespierre and the 'terrorists' themselves.

Dechristianisation: A term coined by its enemies for the accelerating wave of attacks on the practices of the Catholic faith begun by radical activists in late 1793. The 'Cult of Reason' launched as part of this in November 1793 was replaced in May 1794 with the vaguely religious 'Cult of the Supreme Being'.

Departments: County-sized administrative units, created in 1790 and still in use today, the centrepiece of the administrative reformation of the early Revolution. Many of the department administrations sided with Federalism, if only passively, and they were bypassed under the Revolutionary Government's system of National Agents in favour of their subordinate smaller network of districts.

*Émigrés*: The 'emigrated', specifically nobles who left France after the popular uprisings of July 1789, with the explicit intention of fomenting opposition to the Revolution, and if possible overthrowing it by force. Led by the king's own brothers, and subject to intensifying penalties against their persons and property as the Terror developed.

Enragés: A loose grouping of Parisian ultra-radicals active in campaigning for stricter controls on prices and supplies in the first half of 1793. Initially received sympathetically by Marat and the Cordeliers, but marginalised by the late summer of 1793 by a concerted campaign by the Montagnard and *sans-culotte* leadership to play down the violence of Parisian opinions and attract support for the 1793 Constitution.

Estates-General: The historic representative assembly of France, last summoned in 1614, and originally a form of corporatist representation of the 'body politic'. The three Estates were the Catholic clergy, the nobility and the rest – a remainder that by 1789 had come to resent the privileges of the others, who were fewer than 500,000 in a population of 28 million. Met in May 1789, transformed into the National Assembly in June.

Federalists: Those who revolted against the 'anarchist' purge of the Girondins from the Convention in June 1793, especially in the centres of Caen, Lyon, Marseille and Bordeaux. Became a catch-all term for those who sought to resist centralised authority (and the effective domination of politics by Parisian radicals). Associated with overt counter-revolution, initially in radicals' minds, but eventually in the realities of civil war.

Feuillants: A group that broke away from the Jacobin Club in July 1789 to form a new club, representing the bulk of its membership in the National Assembly, and committed to the constitutional monarchy. Attempted to control the course of politics through the summer of 1791, both overtly in the Assembly and by covert negotiations with the royal family. Discredited by the autumn of 1791, and lost initiative rapidly to the resurgent Jacobins, especially as the mood in favour of war grew stronger. The 'Feuillant Club' itself, which like the Jacobins took its name from the monastic hall where it met, was driven into closure at the end of 1791, and the political agenda of the group faded thereafter.

Girondins: A political faction, originally on the left of politics and associated with the Jacobin Club in late 1791. Outflanked on the left by Parisian radicals and individual Jacobins such as Robespierre, the Girondins had effectively become the 'right wing' of the Convention by late 1792, and their leaders were purged on 2 June 1793 with the help of a massive *sans-culotte* mobilisation. This spurred Federalist revolt in several major centres. Named for the Gironde department, whence came three of its leaders.

Indulgents: Name given to those Convention deputies who seemed to want to relax the Terror in late 1793 and early 1794; also embracing those whose main objective was to attack ultra-terrorist excess. Associated with a series of corruption scandals, and with the former Cordeliers leader Georges Danton, the Indulgents were condemned and executed as a 'Dantonist faction' in April 1794.

Jacobins: Members of the network of 'Societies of the Friends of the Constitution', subsequently renamed under the Republic the 'Friends of Liberty and Equality'. The original 'Jacobin Club' was formed by members of the National Assembly and met in a monastic building that gave it its name. By the end of 1790 there were hundreds of provincial affiliates to this 'mother society'. The arbiter of radical politics on the national stage, although increasingly narrowly drawing the boundaries of orthodoxy as the Terror developed. Closed down in a right-wing backlash in November 1794.

Legislative Assembly: Elected under the Constitution of 1791, sat from October 1791 to September 1792. Saw the emergence of the Girondins as major political players, but otherwise eclipsed by the consequences of the declaration of war in April 1792. Rendered near-irrelevant by the Parisian assault on the monarchy on 10 August 1792, and shared power thereafter with the 'Insurrectionary Commune' until the meeting of the Convention.

Mass levy: Decreed in late August 1793, the mobilisation of the entire population for the war effort – placing essential industries under tighter discipline, compelling military service from all young men, and summoning a spirit of total national commitment. It created also widespread resistance, especially in rural areas, including the guerrilla *chouans* of Brittany and Normandy.

Montagnards: The radical side of the Convention, named for their habit of sitting high on its tiered benches. The 'Holy Mountain' became a figure of adulation in radical rhetoric in 1793–1794, although the Montagnards themselves were subject to increasingly bitter internecine disputes. Overlapped extensively with the Jacobin Club.

National Agents: Administrators placed in districts and municipalities by the Revolutionary Government at the end of 1793, supposed to maintain direct contact with the centre and oversee the imposition of terrorist measures. Although nominally under tight control from Paris, many were of necessity local appointees, and their influence was highly variable in practice.

National Assembly: Name taken on by the patriot elements in the Estates-General in June 1789, and subsequently made official in July as the 'National Constituent Assembly'. Produced the Constitution of 1791, but continually riven by disputes between extremists of left and right. It barred its members from election to the successor Legislative Assembly.

National property: '*Biens nationaux*', the property of the Catholic church effectively nationalised in November 1789, and also the confiscated property of *émigrés*, and of the royal domains. Used in the early Revolution to back the assignat paper currency, and later formed part of ambitious but unfulfilled plans for the redistribution of property to 'poor patriots'.

Non-jurors: Catholic priests who refused a loyalty oath imposed in January 1791 – around half of all priests. Initially allowed to continue ministering to the faithful, by early 1792 widely viewed as potential counter-revolutionary traitors, and subjected to increasingly punitive measures thereafter, amounting to complete proscription during the Terror.

Maximum: Controls on the price of 'goods of the first necessity' introduced as an emergency measure under *sans-culotte* pressure in September 1793. Allied to wage controls, an effort to keep supposedly artificial and nefarious price rises under political and popular control. Applied heavy-handedly, and with massive evasion, the measures nonetheless were seen by urban populations especially as vital to their survival. Hence unrest followed their withdrawal in early 1795.

Old Regime: All that had existed as the foundations of politics and society before the Revolution, a term invented to define the new start supposedly made in 1789, against privilege, nobility, corruption and self-interest in government.

Paris Commune: The municipal government of the city, which after the fall of the monarchy, and under the influence of leading *sans-culotte* and *ultra* radicals, became a significant force on the national stage. Led calls for the purging of the Girondins, and rallied physical force to ensure it was carried out, then did likewise for the installation of major measures of social and economic Terror. Increasingly seen as a destabilising influence by the Committee of Public Safety, the purge of the *ultras* destroyed its political power.

Patriots: Initially a fairly clear term designating those in favour of the general programme of the Revolution, but, like many such terms, exhausted by over-use by the time of the Terror, although exhortation to patriotic self-sacrifice remained commonplace.

Representatives-on-mission: Members of the Convention sent out in waves from March 1793, accruing effectively unlimited powers to combat counter-revolution and support the war effort, until taken in check by successive measures of late 1793 and early 1794. The abuses of their power became legendary, but they were prime engines of the massive mobilisation that won the internal and external conflicts of the Terror.

Revolutionary Armies: *Sans-culotte* militias raised after September 1793 to police the food supply and hunt down counter-revolutionary sympathisers. Initially effective, their enthusiasm and initiative – resulting in dechristianising violence and the alienation of the rural population – became a problem after a few months, and they were closed down in the spring of 1794.

Revolutionary Government: The array of institutions set up by successive decrees in late 1793 after the suspension of the constitution, centralising power in the Committee of Public Safety on behalf of the Convention, and authorising extra-legal 'revolutionary' solutions to ongoing problems.

Revolutionary Tribunal: Special court set up in Paris in March 1793 to judge enemies of the Revolution. Its only sentence was death, although it did not develop into a truly indiscriminate killing-machine until after the fall of the factions in spring 1794. Closed down in the thermidorian reaction, and its leading personnel executed as counter-revolutionaries.

*Sans-culottes*: 'Without breeches', originally a satirical term designating the disreputable nature of the supporters of radicalism, taken up from mid-1792 as a badge of honour by such radicals and their urban supporters, becoming by late 1793 a term designating any and all plebeian revolutionaries. Increasingly meaningless as an identifying label, and the pattern of dress associated with it – long trousers, short working-man's jacket, knitted red 'liberty cap' – itself became suspect by 1794 as a convenient mask for aristocratic agitators.

Sections: Administrative districts of major cities; neighbourhood councils and assemblies, in effect. Granted the right to meet daily in the run-up to the fall of the monarchy, though this was cut back to twice-weekly in September 1793. The forty-eight Sections of Paris were the home of the *sans-culotte* militants so influential in many of the measures of Terror. In the Federalist cities, the Sections produced many of the most ardent anti-Parisian activists.

September Massacres: Execution (or slaughter) of some 1500 suspected counter-revolutionaries in the prisons of Paris on 2–6 September 1792. Presented in many accounts as an outbreak of the most hideous barbarism, a surprising amount of concern for guilt and innocence was in fact on display – even if those qualities were attributed in arbitrary ways in many cases.

Supreme Being: A cult inaugurated in May–June 1794, vaguely religious, intended to replace what Robespierre saw as the 'aristocratic' atheism of dechristianisation with a more moral worship of the divinity, and the celebration of festivals to a series of virtues. It did not survive his fall.

Surveillance Committees: Formed in every community by order of the Convention in March 1793, these were to monitor the movements of outsiders, and acquired greater police powers as the Terror evolved. Known as 'revolutionary committees' in the Parisian Sections, they were prime sites of *sans-culotte* activism and the persecution of dissent.

Suspects: Individuals designated for house arrest or closer internment as a result of the 'Law of Suspects' on September 1793. Included any partisans of previous regimes, and a wide range of other categories. The threat of designation as suspect suppressed some dissent, although it was in no way a 'modern' watertight surveillance system.

Thermidorians: Those who overthrew Robespierre and his associates in the 'thermidorian reaction' of late July 1794. The leaders, figures like Tallien, Barras and Fouché, had been Montagnards who fell foul of Robespierre's obsession with personal virtue, a quality they tended to lack, and struck him down essentially in self-defence.

*Ultras*: A group of politicians associated with the Paris Commune and the Cordeliers Club, pursuing an extreme policy of *sans-culotte* revolution in 1793–1794. Due to their increasing opposition to the policies of the Revolutionary Government, they were branded as counter-revolutionaries, and executed as the 'Hébertist faction' after a ludicrous show trial in March 1794.

Vendée: One of the departments to the south of the lower Loire valley, became synonymous with the anti-republican, pro-Catholic revolt that erupted in the region in March 1793. Defeated in battle in December 1793, the Vendéans' guerrilla struggle was not finally crushed until several years later. Ruthless republican repression caused over 200,000 casualties.

Ventôse decrees: Measures for the confiscation of counter-revolutionaries' property and its redistribution to 'poor patriots' introduced in February–March 1794. Unclear even in outline, and never really put into practice, but totemic for those who wanted to see the Terror as having a genuine 'social' agenda.

# CAST OF CHARACTERS

Amar, Jean-Baptiste-André. 1755–1816. Prominent lawyer from Grenoble, elected to Convention, violently anti-royalist Montagnard. On Committee of General Security from June 1793, denounced various plots and corrupt conspiracies, while concealing his own machinations over the Indies Company scandal. Helped to bring down the 'factions' in spring of 1794, but turned on Robespierre. Imprisoned and then amnestied as a terrorist in 1795, then re-arrested after further radical plotting in 1796. Exiled to private life in Grenoble.

Artois, Charles-Philippe, comte d'. 1757–1836. Youngest brother of Louis XVI, suspected of involvement in 'aristocratic plot' of July 1789. Emigrated 16–17 July, settled in Turin, moved to Coblentz July 1791. Leading light in *émigré* activity and intrigue with the European powers. Fought in Allied armies once war broke out, including leading an unsuccessful expedition to Brittany in 1795. Lived in Britain thereafter, returned to France in 1814. Became King Charles X in 1824, forced to abdicate by July Revolution of 1830, retired to Britain.

Bailly, Jean-Sylvain. 1736–1793. Astronomer and historian, topped the poll for Parisian deputies to Estates-General, and was its president for the Tennis-Court Oath. Appointed Mayor of Paris after 14 July, emphasised social order in his rule, as against popular violence and demands of radical clubs: exemplified by the Champ de Mars Massacre of July 1791. Eventually worn out by the pressures put on him by radical activity. Left office in November 1791, but was guillotined on the site of the Massacre in November 1793.

Barbaroux, Charles-Joseph-Marie. 1767–1794. Marseille lawyer with a mercantile background, fiercely radical in local politics, led the *Marseillais* battalion to Paris to take part in the destruction of the monarchy. Soon became closer to Girondin leadership, and in the Convention fought against Montagnard and Parisian dominance. Fled after arrest in June 1793, joined ill-fated Federalist rising in Normandy, captured and executed after eight months on the run near Bordeaux.

Barère (or Barère de Vieuzac), Bertrand. 1755–1841. A brilliant lawyer from the Pyrenees, elected to the Estates-General, remaining centrist until radicalised by the king's flight in 1791. Progress leftwards continued in the Convention, spoke initially from the Plain, but joined Committee of Public Safety and became the defender of almost every act of the Terror. Role as a spokesman and committee organiser made him indispensable until thermidor, but then slowly fell from favour as a terrorist; spent directorial period in hiding from deportation.

Barnave, Antoine-Pierre-Joseph-Marie. 1761–1793. Barrister from Grenoble, leader in 'pre-Revolution' there. Prominent in Estates-General, leading figure by early 1791, one of the so-called 'Triumvirate'. Charmed by the queen as he escorted the royal family from Varennes, helped to negotiate king's reinstatement and tried to lead 'Feuillant' movement for stabilisation. Marginalised by Jacobin triumph, retired in early 1792, arrested after 10 August 1792.

Barras, Jean-Nicolas-Paul-François, vicomte de. 1755–1829. A dissolute aristocratic officer before 1789, entered the Convention as a radical, went on mission in 1793, led capture of Marseille and Toulon, and subsequent repression. In 1794 a leader of thermidorian coup, subsequently a Director. Corrupt and devious, organiser of coups, patron of Bonaparte. Forced into exile in 1810.

Batz, Jean-Pierre, baron de. 1754–1822. Financial speculator and noble deputy to the Estates-General, rapidly embroiled in royalist plots by his adventurous nature. Emigrated in 1792, returned to attempt to rescue the king, and thereafter took part in shadowy plotting throughout the Terror. Remained a royalist agent through the 1790s, but returned home openly under Napoleon.

Bentabole, Pierre-Louis. 1756–1798. Lawyer's son from Alsace and public prosecutor in the early Revolution. Elected to the Convention, displayed extreme hostility to the Girondins, and was sent on several missions. Conversion to thermidorian politics was assisted by falling in love with a wealthy heiress, and he became socially conservative as a directorial politician until his death.

Billaud-Varenne, Jacques-Nicolas. 1756–1819. Schoolmaster, lawyer and aspiring writer, Jacobin and Cordeliers member, served Insurrectionary Commune in 1792, elected to Convention, extreme Montagnard, elected to Committee of Public Safety in September 1793 as *sans-culotte* candidate. Threatened by Robespierre, took part in thermidor. Deported to Guiana for terrorism, later settled in Saint-Domingue as a farmer.

Bo, Jean-Baptiste-Jérôme. 1743–1814. A doctor, elected to Legislative Assembly and Convention from the Aveyron. Worked for poor relief and educational reforms, and also frequently sent on mission from 1793 to 1795. One of the 'humane terrorists'. Worked later as a bureaucrat, went into private practice in 1809.

Bonaparte, Napoléon. 1769–1821. Napoléon I, Emperor of the French, 1804–1814, 1815. Son of a Corsican lawyer with noble status, trained at Paris military school, artillery officer from 1785. Associated with Jacobinism from 1791, came to notice for commanding artillery at siege of Toulon. Commanded repression of Vendémiaire rising of 1795, sent to Army of Italy in 1796, led it on a series of brilliant victories and to peace with Austria in 1797. In 1798 commanded expedition to Egypt with dubious success, but evaded British blockade to reach France in October 1799, and brought to power in Brumaire coup the following month. His later career is well-known.

Bouchotte, Jean-Baptiste-Noël. 1754–1840. Career army officer, captain in 1789. Pro-revolution, and came to prominence in the north after Dumouriez's defection. Elected War Minister April 1793, introduced *sans-culotte* measures to administration. Returned to army April 1794, arrested in June, amnestied in 1795. Some Jacobin activities in later 1790s, but retired on military pension after Brumaire.

Breteuil, Louis-Auguste Le Tonnelier, baron de. 1730–1807. A career diplomat and, from 1783, relatively enlightened minister with responsibility for interior affairs. Slipped into reactionary views after clashing with Calonne, and involved in counter-revolutionary manoeuvres in July 1789. Emigrating, he became the king and queen's chief confidant and minister-plenipotentiary-in-exile, but all his plots came to nothing. Returned to France in 1802 and lived out his life in obscurity.

Brissot (or Brissot de Warville), Jacques-Pierre. 1754–1793. Pamphleteer and literary hack before 1789, allegedly reduced to police informing. Formed anti-slavery Société des Amis de Noirs (Society of Friends of the Blacks) in 1788, drawing in many future Girondin contacts. A prominent radical journalist in the early Revolution, entered Legislative Assembly, where he led calls for war, and subsequently Convention, grew increasingly opposed to the Jacobins and the violence of Parisian radicalism, arrested after 31 May–2 June insurrection.

Buzot, François-Nicolas-Léonard. 1760–1794. A lawyer from Evreux, noted Jacobin in the Estates-General, and overt republican after Varennes. Elected to the Convention, he shifted rightwards, perhaps under the influence of love for Madame Roland. Purged with other Girondins on 2 June 1793, failed to rally significant military support in Normandy. Killed himself to avoid capture after eight months on the run near Bordeaux.

Cabarrus, Thérèse de, Madame Tallien. 1773–1835. Daughter of Spanish minister, married to member of *parlement* of Paris, found by Tallien in prison in Bordeaux in 1793. They married, her influence swung him to the right, and her salon-keeping abilities made them an influential pair in thermidorian high society. Moved abroad after the marriage broke up, and married again into Spanish aristocracy.

Calonne, Charles-Alexandre de. 1734–1802. An *intendant* from the 1760s, Controller-General from 1783, lost out to noble and *parlementaire* opposition to his proposed reforms in 1787. After dismissal, went to England in disgrace, and from 1789 worked with *émigrés*, especially Artois. He was dropped as an adviser in 1792, and retired to London.

Carnot, Lazare-Nicolas-Marguerite. 1753–1823. A captain of engineers in 1789, entered politics through the Legislative Assembly and the Jacobins, and joined the Committee of Public Safety as its military expert after several missions to the provinces. The 'Organiser of Victory' thanks to his management of military supplies and administration. Later became a right-wing Director, and briefly War Minister under Napoleon before retiring.

Carrier, Jean-Baptiste. 1756–1794. Lawyer son of a prosperous farmer in the Cantal, elected to the Convention, became a hard-line Montagnard. On mission to Brittany and Nantes from August 1793 to February 1794, where he supervised thousands of executions. After thermidor, he was sent before the Revolutionary Tribunal, used as a show trial for the excesses of Terror.

Chabot, François. 1756–1794. Capucin priest, accepted clerical oath, elected to Legislative Assembly from Loir-et-Cher. Radical and conspiracy-theorist, denouncing 'Austrian Committee' at Court. Sent on mission by Convention, also served on Committee of General Security. His suspect private life associated him with 'foreign plotters' he had himself denounced, arrested November 1793, executed with the Dantonists.

Chalier, Marie-Joseph. 1747–1793. Trained as a monk in Lyon, but left, became travelling salesman around the Mediterranean. Took part in 14 July rising in Paris, returned to Lyon and took prominent role in radical politics. Leader of

Jacobin municipality in 1792–1793, noted for violent rhetoric, arrested and executed by Federalists after their rising.

Chaumette, Pierre-Gaspard. 1763–1794. A cobbler's son, medical student in Paris in 1789. Became a sectional activist, Cordeliers member and journalist. In August 1792 rose to prominence in the Commune, and became its procurator. A leading *sans-culotte* spokesman, and notably active in preaching dechristianisation. Arrested after the fall of Hébert and executed on the usual trumped-up charges.

Collot-d'Herbois, Jean-Marie. 1749–1796. Pre-revolutionary playwright and theatre director, moved to Paris in 1789, joined Jacobins, member of Insurrectionary Commune in 1792, elected to Convention. On mission for much of 1793, then elected to Committee of Public Safety in September 1793 as *sans-culotte* candidate. With Fouché, responsible for bloody repression in Lyon. Came under threat from Robespierre in summer 1794, and participated in thermidor. Left Committee of Public Safety, but prosecuted for terrorism and deported to Guiana.

Couthon, Georges-Auguste. 1755–1794. Lawyer from Clermont-Ferrand, wheelchair-bound by 1789. Elected to Legislative Assembly and Convention, a Jacobin friendly with Robespierre. Sent on mission, including to Lyon, and served on Committee of Public Safety from May 1793. Closely associated with Robespierrist Terror, drafted law of 22 prairial. Executed with Robespierre.

Danton, Georges-Jacques. 1759–1794. A barrister at Paris, took up radical stance from 1789 in Cordeliers District, and later Club, and Jacobins from 1791. Served as municipal prosecutor, involved in 10 August insurrection, Minister of Justice in Provisional Executive, turned blind eye to September Massacres, but rallied Paris to the war effort. Elected to Convention, Montagnard. Widely suspected of 'sticky fingers', especially when on mission to Belgium in late 1792/early 1793. Extravagant lifestyle aided suspicions. Supported terrorist institutions, retired due to ill-health in October 1793. Returned to politics later in the autumn, attacking dechristianisation and terrorist excess, became identified as an 'Indulgent', and thus suspect, arrested and executed as leader of a counter-revolutionary faction in April 1794.

David, Jacques-Louis. 1748–1825. Eminent neoclassical artist in 1780s, Parisian Jacobin from 1789, elected to Convention. Already organiser of Parisian festivals, took charge of national celebrations and plans for cultural regeneration as well as producing his 'martyr pictures' of Lepeletier and Marat. Served on Committee of General Security as a Robespierrist. Harassed after thermidor, but later patronised extensively by Napoléon.

Desmoulins, Lucie-Camille-Simplice. 1760–1794. Schoolfriend of Robespierre as scholarship-boys in Paris. Mediocre barrister at Paris, discovered talent for incendiary journalism in 1789. A Cordelier and, from 1791, Jacobin, closely linked to Danton, served as his secretary in Ministry of Justice. Elected to Convention, Montagnard. Like Danton, objected to Terror from December 1793, using a new journal, the *Vieux Cordelier* ('Old Cordelier') to denounce and satirise excesses. Like Danton, executed for this 'indulgent' attitude.

Dumouriez, Charles-François du Périer. 1739–1823. Professional soldier, entered revolutionary local politics in Cherbourg, soon moved to Paris, linked with Lafayette and Jacobin Club. Appointed foreign minister March 1792, dismissed with Girondins in June, returned to army command. Commander at victories of Valmy and Jemappes, responsible for invasion of Low Countries.

Girondin in politics; their problems in Paris, simultaneous with defeat in spring 1793, led him to try to lead his army on Paris. Failing, he fled to the enemy. *Emigré* organisations rejected him, settled in England.

Fabre d'Eglantine, Philippe-François-Nazaire. 1750–1794. A teacher and, from 1772, playwright. Moved to Paris in 1787, and became linked to Cordeliers from 1789, including Danton and Marat. Radical journalist, elected to Convention, Montagnard. Responsible for elaborating the final version of the Revolutionary Calendar in 1793. Denounced by Robespierre for financial corruption and profiteering, arrested in January 1794, executed with the Dantonists.

Fersen, count Axel von. 1750–1810. Aristocratic colonel of the Royal Swedish Regiment in French service, agent for *émigré* networks in France, and probable lover of Queen Marie-Antoinette. A key organiser of the Flight to Varennes, subsequently returning from exile on several occasions for secret discussion with the royal couple about counter-revolutionary diplomacy. Remained active in Swedish politics, beaten to death by a mob after accusations of poisoning a liberal prince.

Fouché, Joseph. 1763–1820. Schoolteacher at Nantes, elected to Convention, sent on mission to the west, the centre (where he was an early dechristianiser), and Lyon in November 1793, where he led mass executions. Recalled April 1794, a leader of thermidor. Protected by Barras from retribution for his terrorism, served as an ambassador in Italy in 1798, then made Minister of Police in 1799, repressing left- and right-wing elements equally. Served Napoléon in this position, and survived the Restoration.

Fréron, Louis-Stanislas. 1765–1802. Son of an Enlightenment literary critic, also a journalist before the Revolution. From 1790 produced the *People's Orator* in imitation of Marat. Cordelier, elected to Commune in 1792. Elected to Convention, on mission to Toulon conducted repression with extravagant violence, recalled January 1794. Thermidorian, then increasingly reactionary in politics, linked to Gilded Youth. Agent of government in the south during White Terror. Became a bureaucrat, died in the Caribbean as sub-prefect of Saint-Domingue.

Garat, Dominique-Joseph. 1749–1833. Lawyer and well-known writer elected to the Estates-General, avoided dangerous political entanglements through subsequent ministerial career at Justice and Interior in 1792–1793. Kept low profile through Terror, re-emerged as ambassador to Naples in 1797–1798, and as a bureaucrat under Napoléon.

Gensonné, Armand. 1758–1793. A surgeon's son and Bordeaux lawyer, one of the original three Girondins, like the others compromised by attempts to take power under the king in the summer of 1792, after their violent calls for war and denunciations of the *émigrés*. Also close to Dumouriez and tainted by his treason. Executed with his fellows in October 1793.

Gorsas, Antoine-Joseph. 1752–1793. A teacher and satirical journalist before 1789, son of a shoemaker. Significant Parisian newspaper editor from 1789, prominent in radical opinion-forming. Elected to Convention, became disillusioned with radical violence. A Girondin target of *sans-culotte* attacks, fled to Normandy in June 1793, went into hiding, but captured later in the summer visiting his mistress in Paris. Guillotined after the Girondins' show trial in October.

Guadet, Marguerite-Elie. 1758–1794. Like Gensonné and Vergniaud, a lawyer from Bordeaux who made his mark in the Legislative Assembly attacking court and *émigrés*. Subsequently prominent in stoking conflict with Parisian radicals, fled after 2 June 1793, eventually tracked down outside Bordeaux and executed.

Hanriot, François. 1761–1794. Clerk from peasant stock, active in the radical politics of Paris from 1789, rose in the ranks of the National Guard, particularly through the events of the summer of 1792. Commanded sectional forces at the fall of the Gironde, and subsequently became general of the Parisian National Guard. Tried and failed to rally its forces to protect Robespierre at thermidor, and perished with him.

Hébert, Jacques-René. 1757–1794. Son of a goldsmith, sought his fortune in Paris, but was scraping a living, for example selling theatre tickets, by 1789. Revolutionary journalism as 'Père Duchesne' brought him fame and influence. Cordelier, member of Insurrectionary Commune in August 1792, served as deputy municipal prosecutor. Although attacking Enragés, was himself a leader of Parisian extreme radical politics, involved in 31 May–2 June, 5 September 1793, dechristianisation, calls for extensions of Terror (and implicitly overthrow of Committee of Public Safety). By spring 1794 this call became explicit, and 'Hébertists' were condemned and executed.

Hérault de Séchelles, Marie-Jean. 1760–1794. Prosecutor in *parlement* of Paris, aristocratic background, linked to salons. Elected to Legislative Assembly as Feuillant, but became more radical. Elected to Convention, led committee drafting 1793 Constitution, joined Committee of Public Safety, but moderate by terrorist standards, linked to 'foreign plot', arrested and executed.

Herman, Armand-Martial-Joseph. 1759–1795. Senior judge before and during the Revolution in Robespierre's home region, brought to Paris by him to head Revolutionary Tribunal in 1793, moved sideways into the security apparatus as its chief bureaucrat in 1794. Betrayed his patron at thermidor, but was tried along with Fouquier-Tinville for the crimes of the Tribunal the following year.

Javogues, Claude. 1759–1796. Lawyer, made a name in local politics near Lyon before election to Convention. Brutally radical while on mission in Lyon region in 1793–1794, recalled in spring 1794. Critical of Robespierre, but also imprisoned as terrorist after thermidor. Amnestied in 1795, but involved in radical plotting, and joined an attempted insurrection. Executed by military commission.

Jullien, Marc-Antoine. 1775–1848. Son of a Convention deputy (who himself kept a very low profile through the Terror), still a teenager when sent by Robespierre on several provincial missions in 1793–1794, a radical patriot of the purest Robespierrist stripe. Imprisoned after thermidor, but pardoned. Fled France for Italy after involvement in radical plots under the Directory, protected there by Napoléon as a military administrator.

Lafayette, Marie-Joseph-Paul-Roch-Yves-Gilbert Motier, marquis de. 1757–1834. Aristocratic military hero of American War, liberal, called in 1787 for Estates-General after involvement in Assembly of Notables. Elected to Estates-General, and appointed to command Parisian National Guard after 14 July. Earned hatred of Marie-Antoinette after October Days, but also loathed by Parisian radicals for authoritarian stance, and alleged network of spies in the capital. Led Champ de Mars Massacre, defeated in elections for mayor of Paris in autumn 1791, rejoined army as general. Tried to lead Legislative Assembly in moves against Jacobins after 20 June 1792, and fled to the enemy after 10

August. Held in prison until 1797, returned to France under Napoléon, and would later be instrumental in creation of constitutional monarchy after Revolution of 1830.

Lebas, Philippe-François-Joseph. 1765–1794. Lawyer son of a wealthy notary from Robespierre's home region, elected to the Convention. Robespierrist member of the Committee of General Security, shared several important missions with Saint-Just, and was part of Robespierre's domestic circle. Volunteered for arrest at thermidor, and killed himself before recapture.

Legendre, Louis. 1752–1797. A butcher and early Cordeliers Club activist, prominent in patriotic mobilisations from 1789 onwards, and elected to the Convention. Close to Danton, became a thermidorian and launched increasingly bitter attacks on the terrorists. Had swung to the right by 1795, working against the *sans-culotte* risings of that year, and served as a directorial politician.

Lepeletier de Saint-Fargeau, Louis-Michel. 1760–1793. Parisian judge, elected to Estates-General for the nobility, joined Third Estate and became noted constitutional reformer. Elected to Convention as a Montagnard, assassinated before he could produce the scheme for national education he had devised.

Lindet, Jean-Baptiste-Robert. 1746–1825. A Norman lawyer, sat in the Legislative Assembly and Convention. A noted 'moderate' elected to the Committee of Public Safety, he served prominently in attempts to resolve the Federalist crisis peacefully before becoming involved with the administration of the Maximum for the rest of the Terror. Connected to radical plots after thermidor, but survived to serve as Finance Minister under the Directory before retirement.

Louis XVI. 1754–1793. King of France 1774–1789, King of the French, 1789–1792. An amiable, intelligent but indecisive man, lacking the drive to become great or the vices to become notorious. Widely mocked for his failure to consummate his marriage for seven years (1770–1777), and seen thereafter as a weak companion to Marie-Antoinette's allegedly libertine personality. Never accepted the agenda imposed on him by events in 1789, as revealed by manifesto during the Flight to Varennes in June 1791. As constitutional monarch from 1791, saw war as a means of liberation. Conducted himself with dignity during detention, trial and execution.

Louvet de Couvrai, Jean-Baptiste. 1760–1797. Novelist son of a printer, journalist and local activist in Paris from 1789, friend of Brissot and Roland. Elected to Convention from the Loiret with Roland's help, a vigorous defender of the Girondins and critic of Robespierre. Fled after proscription, hid successfully outside Bordeaux through the Terror, rejoined thermidorian Convention, and active as a conservative republican throughout the Directory.

Marat, Jean-Paul. 1744–1793. A trained doctor, one of the oldest of the revolutionaries. Scientific experimenter and anti-authoritarian writer, nonetheless he held the position of physician to the bodyguard of the comte d'Artois before 1789. Rapidly took up an extreme radical position in journalism. Often forced into hiding in the early Revolution, protected by Cordeliers District and Club, joined Insurrectionary Commune in 1792, allegedly largely responsible for September Massacres, for which Girondins loathed him. Elected to Convention, Girondin attempts to put him on trial were part of conflict leading to 31 May–2 June. After assassination in July 1793, many others tried to take up his journalistic mantle, and a short-lived 'cult' developed around him.

Marie-Antoinette, Joséphe-Jeanne. 1755–1793. Queen of France, 1774–1792.

Youngest daughter of Empress Maria-Theresa of Austria, married to future Louis XVI at fourteen. Widely mocked for her extravagance and reactionary opinions, even before 1789. After calling of Estates-General, blamed for Louis' apparent duplicity in July and September–October 1789, advocated flight, and viewed as centre of reactionary plotting at Court. Maintained contact with Austria after war declared. A blinkered and obstinate woman of little compassion, who would happily have seen the whole Revolution crushed, but was not the unnatural monster radical revolutionaries chose to paint her as.

Mirabeau, Honoré-Gabriel Riquetti, comte de. 1749–1791. Son of a physiocrat author, his dissolute youth included imprisonment via *lettre de cachet*, became outspoken liberal by late 1780s, elected by Third Estate of Provence to Estates-General, which he led through his oratory at crucial moments in spring and summer 1789. Through 1790, tried to set himself up as political broker between the Court and the Revolution, taking payment for his political advice to Louis, which was largely ignored. Died in April 1791 before this had emerged fully, but was rapidly discredited afterwards.

Necker, Jacques. 1732–1804. Banker from Geneva, Finance Minister of France, 1777–1781, reappointed after Brienne's dismissal in September 1788. Handled situation ineptly when Estates-General opened, dismissed as part of 'aristocratic plot' on 11 July. On his way to exile when recalled after 14 July, to popular acclaim, but never able to influence events thereafter. Emigrated to Switzerland in September 1790.

Orléans, Louis-Philippe-Joseph, duc d'. 1747–1793. Cousin of Louis XVI, a libertine of enormous wealth, became interested in liberal politics in late 1780s, and funded a network of pamphleteers (and allegedly agents). Influential in Assembly of Notables, elected to Estates-General and Convention. Suspicions that he wanted the throne for himself, and was using the Jacobin movement to that end, dogged him, and played a part, for example, in the politics of the post-Varennes period. Renamed himself 'Philippe Égalité' (equality) in late 1792 at the request of his local Section. Voted for king's death, but linked to Dumouriez, arrested and executed alongside the Girondins.

Pache, Jean-Nicolas. 1746–1823. Chief steward of the king's household from the early 1780s, a bureaucrat promoted by Roland into the Interior Ministry, later became War Minister, October 1792. Moved from Girondin to Montagnard sympathies, and dismissed February 1793. Elected mayor of Paris, helped plan 31 May–2 June events. Implicated with Hébertists in spring 1794, but survived, though dismissed as mayor. Harassed after thermidor, stayed in private life.

Payan, Claude-François de. 1766–1794. Artillery officer from the Dauphiné, entered local politics during the Revolution as a fervent, but intelligent, Jacobin activist, and joined the national bureaucracy of the Committee of Public Safety in 1793. Installed as National Agent of Paris in March 1794, controlling the city for the Robespierrists. A less reflective counterpart of Saint-Just, and like him perished with Robespierre.

Pétion, Jérôme. 1756–1794. Lawyer, elected to Estates-General, anti-slavery supporter, close associate of Robespierre, involved in agitation after Varennes. Elected mayor of Paris in November 1791, involved in plans for 10 August. Revulsion at September Massacres pushed his politics towards Girondins after election to Convention. On the run after 31 May–2 June, committed suicide.

Prieur de la Côte d'Or, Claude-Antoine. 1763–1832. An officer of military engineers, son of a tax official. Elected to Legislative Assembly and Convention, and joined Committee of Public Safety in August 1793 as a competent administrator. Played a significant role in military organisation, thus avoiding the taint of terrorism. Continued in politics until 1798, then rejoined army.

Prieur de la Marne, Pierre-Louis. 1756–1827. Lawyer, elected to Estates-General, noted radical. Elected to Convention from the Marne, and served on many missions to armies and provinces before and after joining the Committee of Public Safety. His radicalism led him to support the Parisian risings of the spring of 1795, and he had to go into hiding until the fall of the Directory, when he resumed his legal career.

Provence, comte de. 1755–1824. Louis XVIII, King of France, in theory from 1795, in practice 1814/15–1824. Elder of Louis XVI's brothers, involved in pre-revolutionary agitation, but soon swung to criticism of Revolution. Emigrated at time of Flight to Varennes. Joined Artois, declared himself Lieutenant-General of the Kingdom, and organised an *émigré* army. Declared himself regent in January 1793, and king in 1795. Moved around Europe, based in Russia from 1798, Britain from 1807.

Robespierre, Maximilien-François-Isidore. 1758–1794. Lawyer in Arras, elected to Estates-General, became notorious for extreme democratic views, and 'incorruptible' stance. Influential in Parisian politics during Legislative Assembly, and always prominent in Jacobins. Member of Insurrectionary Commune, elected to Convention, soon in open conflict with Girondins. Spoke out for king's death, and later for Girondins' proscription. Arguably the moral leader of Revolution after election to Committee of Public Safety in July 1793, largely responsible for discrediting Hébertist and Dantonist elements, while simultaneously taking a leading role in many policy areas. Seemed to be planning further purges when thermidorian coalition rounded on him. Attempted suicide after his outlawing on 9 thermidor, but survived to face the guillotine the next day. Inflexible, dogmatic, ill-equipped to deal with the ambiguities of politics, but an icon for radicals.

Roland de la Platière, Jean-Marie. 1734–1793. Royal factory inspector in Lyon in 1789, lobbyist in Paris for Lyon manufacturers in 1791, became linked to future Girondins socially at this point, brought in as Interior Minister in March 1792, dismissed June, reinstated after 10 August. Alienated from Montagnards over September Massacres and growing Girondin sympathies, resigned January 1793, fled Paris in June. Committed suicide on news of his wife's execution.

Roland, Marie-Jeanne or Manon Phlipon, Madame. 1754–1793. Parisian by birth, married Roland de la Platière in 1780. Intellectually inclined, aspired to emulate Old Regime salon hostesses' influence, and used her home to co-ordinate Girondin activities. Arrested after 31 May–2 June, executed in November 1793 during the repression of 'dangerous women'.

Romme, Gilbert. 1750–1796. A tutor before 1789, elected to Legislative Assembly and Convention from Puy-de-Dôme. Captured by Federalist rebels when on mission in Normandy, but released in summer 1793. Educational reformer, important in planning Revolutionary Calendar, and loyal Jacobin even after thermidor. Implicated in prairial rising, committed suicide on the way to execution.

Ronsin, Charles-Philippe. 1751–1794. Failed playwright of rural origins, became a club orator after 1789. National Guard officer in Paris, and from 1793 prominent in Bouchotte's War Ministry. Sent to Vendée, highly critical there of generals, recalled and imprisoned December 1793 as extremist, released in February, but began to call for *sans-culotte* insurrection, executed with Hébertists.

Roux, Jacques. 1752–1794. Priest, came to Paris in 1790, elected vicar of Saint-Nicolas-des-Champs, a poverty-stricken area of central Paris. Prominent orator in Cordeliers Club and Gravilliers Section, elected to Commune early 1793. Involved in protests of that year, calls for greater economic regulation and Terror. The leading 'Enragé', opposed by Montagnards, and imprisoned as counter-revolutionary on 5 September, when Terror was officially adopted. Committed suicide in prison five months later.

Roux-Fazillac, Pierre. 1746–1833. Army officer, elected to Legislative Assembly and Convention, highly critical of Girondins. Sent on mission, effective Jacobin reformer and regulator in areas less affected by conflict. Served Directory as local official in the Dordogne, then retired.

Saint-André, André Jeanbon. 1749–1813. After a mixed career as a merchant captain and protestant pastor, became a staunch Montagnard after election to Convention. Naval specialist on the Committee of Public Safety, spent most of the Terror on mission to naval ports, and much of the following year in the south on similar duties. Arrested and amnestied, sent to Turkey as a consul, but arrested and detained there for several years before returning to become a Napoléonic prefect.

Saint-Just, Louis-Antoine-Léon. 1767–1794. Officer's son, too young for political involvement in 1789. Emulated Robespierre's austere Rousseauism, elected to Convention, and came to attention with demands for the king's death and attacks on Girondins. Joined Committee of Public Safety in May 1793, frequently on mission to armies in east and north. Attacked Dantonists and Hébertists in 1794, and stood by Robespierre, thus sharing his fate at thermidor.

Santerre, Antoine-Joseph. 1752–1809. A wealthy brewer from the Faubourg Saint-Antoine, rose steadily in the Parisian National Guard, took a leading military role in toppling the monarchy, and escorted the king to his death. A general from July 1793, failed to win decisive glory after leading a volunteer force to the Vendée, and was arrested in April 1794. Released and returned to private life after thermidor.

Sieyès, Emmanuel-Joseph, abbé. 1748–1836. Church bureaucrat before 1789, wrote highly influential pamphlets condemning privilege in 1788–1789. Elected to Estates-General, instrumental in clashes May–July 1789, drafted Tennis-Court Oath and worked on Declaration of Rights. Worked on committees concerned with administrative reorganisation. Elected to Convention, but maintained low profile, more active after thermidor, and also served on Directorial Councils.

Tallien, Jean-Lambert. 1767–1820. A clerk who became a popular society leader and journalist in Paris after 1789, member of Insurrectionary Commune of 1792, involved in 10 August and September Massacres. Elected to Convention, Montagnard, made ferocious attacks on king and Girondins. On mission in autumn to Bordeaux his attitudes softened after he met Thérèse de Cabarrus, whom he later married. Returned to Paris, attacked by Robespierre, thermidorian who launched attacks on Revolutionary Tribunal and terrorist personnel. Madame Tallien's salon added to his influence, but they parted and his star waned. He later entered diplomatic service.

Thuriot, Jacques-Alexis. 1753–1829. Lawyer from the Marne, in Paris for the storming of the Bastille, and later elected to Legislative Assembly and Convention. Montagnard and friend of Danton, served on various missions, and on the Committee of Public Safety before and after the Terror. Presided over the Convention for part of Robespierre's overthrow. Remained Jacobin in politics. Arrested in 1795 after 'prairial' rising, but amnestied.

Turgot, Anne-Robert-Jacques, baron de l'Aulne. 1727–1781. Economist and administrator, from 1761 *intendant* of Limoges, where he experimented with rationalisation of local government. Key figure in 'advanced' economic thought in the mid-eighteenth century, and made Controller-General of Finances by Louis XVI in 1774. Proposed and implemented a series of radical liberalisations, resulting in outcry and the 'Flour War' of 1775. Removed from office in 1776.

Vadier, Marc-Guillaume-Alexis. 1736–1828. Magistrate and former officer, possibly the oldest terrorist. Served quietly in the Estates-General, attacked Girondins after election to Convention. Joined Committee of General Security in September 1793, attacked Dantonists. An ardent terrorist spymaster, but broke with Robespierre and helped his downfall at thermidor. Escaped deportation as a terrorist in 1795 by hiding until amnestied, but involved in further radical plotting, and kept under surveillance through 1790s.

Vincent, François-Nicolas. 1767–1794. A jailer's son and clerk, joined Cordeliers Club, involved in planning 10 August, moved into military bureaucracy under Bouchotte. A violent and impassioned speaker and plotter of *sans-culotte* supremacy. Denounced with Ronsin, like him seemed to preach insurrection in spring 1794, executed with the Hébertists.

# NOTES

## Introduction

1. For a conventional accounting of casualties, see Howard Peckham, *The Toll of Independence; Engagements and Battle Casualties of the American Revolution*, Chicago: University of Chicago Press, 1974. For a recent and 'anti-American' overview of the war, see Hugh Bicheno, *Rebels and Redcoats: The American Revolutionary War*, London: HarperCollins, 2003, and for a very different account, Ray Raphael, *A People's History of the American Revolution: How Common People Shaped the Fight for Independence*, New York: The New Bath Press, 2001. On the 'memory' of the war, see Sarah J. Purcell, *Sealed with Blood: War, Sacrifice, and Memory in Revolutionary America*, Philadelphia, Pa.: University of Pennsylvania Press, 2002. On its unorthodox nature, see Mark V. Kwasny, *Washington's Partisan War, 1775–1783*, Kent, Ohio: Kent State University Press, 1996, and for its general horrors, Harry M. Ward, *Between the Lines: Banditti of the American Revolution*, Westport, Ct.: Praeger Publishers, 2002.
2. Michael Broers, *Europe After Napoleon*, Manchester: MUP, 1996, usefully summarises the ideological fallout of the period.
3. François Furet, *Marx and the French Revolution*, Chicago: University of Chicago Press, 1988.
4. François Furet, *Interpreting the French Revolution*, Cambridge: CUP, 1981; J. Bosher, *The French Revolution: A New Interpretation*, London: Weidenfeld & Nicolson, 1989.
5. Gordon S. Wood, 'Conspiracy and the Paranoid Style: Causality and Deceit in the Eighteenth Century', *William and Mary Quarterly*, 39 (1982), pp. 399–441.
6. Taine's remark, and others, cited in George Rudé, *The Crowd in the French Revolution*, Oxford: OUP, 1959, pp. 2–3. Simon Schama, *Citizens: A Chronicle of the French Revolution*, New York: Viking Penguin, 1989, p. xv.

## Chapter 1: Night Flight

1. Marcel Reinhard, *La Chute de la royauté: 10 août 1792*, Paris: Gallimard, 1969, pp. 32–6.
2. Fersen and the queen were certainly deeply romantically attached: whether they ever consummated the relationship is unknowable, thanks in part to the

discretion of Fersen's nineteenth-century descendants in destroying his correspondence: see Munro Price, *The Fall of the French Monarchy: Louis XVI, Marie Antoinette and the Baron de Breteuil*, London: Macmillan, 2002, pp. 16–17.

3. Reinhard, *Chute*, pp. 91–3.
4. William Doyle, *The Oxford History of the French Revolution*, 2nd edn, Oxford: OUP, 2002, pp. 28–34.
5. For detailed accounts of these events, see for example Doyle, *Oxford History*, pp. 104–7; Colin Jones, *The Great Nation: France from Louis XV to Napoleon 1715–99*, London: Penguin, 2002, pp. 412–15.
6. See Durand Echeverria, *The Maupeou Revolution: A Study in the History of Libertarianism, France, 1770–1774*, Baton Rouge: Louisiana State University Press, 1985.
7. See Price, *Fall*, pp. 3–6.
8. John Hardman, *Louis XVI*, New Haven: Yale University Press, 1993, p. 35; Jones, *Great Nation*, p. 295.
9. See also John Hardman, *Louis XVI: The Silent King*, London: Arnold, 2000.
10. Arlette Farge, *Fragile Lives: Violence, Power and Solidarity in Eighteenth-Century Paris*, Cambridge: Polity Press, 1993, pp. 204–25. One hundred and thirty-two bodies were officially recovered, the actual death-toll may have been as much as several times higher.
11. Mary D. Sheriff, 'The Portrait of the Queen', in Dena Goodman (ed.), *Marie-Antoinette: Writings on the Body of a Queen*, London: Routledge, 2003, pp. 45–72. On the rumours of the queen's sexuality, and her posthumous status as a lesbian icon, see Terry Castle, 'Marie-Antoinette Obsession', in the same volume, pp. 199–238.
12. See Lynn Hunt, *The Family Romance of the French Revolution*, London: Routledge, 1992, chapter 1.
13. Simone Bertière, *Marie-Antoinette l'insoumise*, Paris: Fallois, 2002.
14. See John Hardman, *French Politics 1774–1789: From the Accession of Louis XVI to the Fall of the Bastille*, Harlow: Longman, 1995, p. 37; Jones, *Great Nation*, pp. 292–301.
15. Cynthia Bouton, *The Flour War: Gender, Class and Community in Late Ancien Régime French Society*, University Park, Pa: Penn State Press, 1993.
16. Steven L. Kaplan, 'Social Classification and Representation in the Corporate World of Eighteenth-Century France: Turgot's "Carnival"', in Steven L. Kaplan and Cynthia J. Koepp (eds), *Work in France: Representations, Meaning, Organization and Practice*, Ithaca, NY: Cornell UP, 1986, pp. 176–228.
17. Robert D. Harris, *Necker: Reform Statesman of the Ancien Régime*, Berkeley: University of California Press, 1979.
18. Bailey Stone, *Reinterpreting the French Revolution: A Global-Historical Perspective*, Cambridge: CUP, 2002, chapter 1.
19. For what follows, the classic account is Jean Egret, *The French Pre-revolution, 1787–1788*, Chicago: University of Chicago Press, 1977; William Doyle, *Origins of the French Revolution*, 3rd edn, Oxford: OUP, 1999, is a briefer overview.
20. William Doyle, *Venality: The Sale of Offices in Eighteenth-Century France*, Oxford: Clarendon Press, 1996.
21. Michael Kwass, *Privilege and the Politics of Taxation in Eighteenth-Century France: Liberté, Égalité, Fiscalité*, Cambridge: CUP, 2000.

22. Among the many writers on this topic, see notably Daniel Roche, *France in the Enlightenment*, Cambridge, Mass.: Harvard UP, 1998; Dena Goodman, *The Republic of Letters: A Cultural History of the French Enlightenment*, Ithaca, NY: Cornell UP, 1994; Roger Chartier, *The Cultural Origins of the French Revolution*, Durham, NC: Duke UP, 1991.
23. See the wide-ranging work of Robert Darnton, including *The Literary Underground of the Old Regime*, Cambridge, Mass.: Harvard UP, 1982, and *The Forbidden Best-sellers of Prerevolutionary France*, London: HarperCollins, 1996.
24. Gilbert Shapiro and John Markoff, *Revolutionary Demands: A Content Analysis of the 'Cahiers de Doléances' of 1789*, Stanford: Stanford UP, 1998.
25. David Andress, *The French Revolution and the People*, London: Hambledon & London, 2004, pp. 15, 24.
26. Andress, *French Revolution and the People*, pp. 6–10.
27. John Markoff, *The Abolition of Feudalism: Peasants, Lords, and Legislators in the French Revolution*, University Park, Pa.: Penn State UP, 1996.
28. Timothy Tackett, *Becoming a Revolutionary: The Deputies of the French National Assembly and the Emergence of a Revolutionary Culture (1789–1790)*, Princeton: Princeton UP, 1996.
29. Georges Lefebvre, *The Great Fear of 1789*, London: NLB, 1973, part 1.
30. Price, *Fall*, pp. 62–9.
31. The official record of the speech, and reaction to it, is translated in Keith Michael Baker (ed.), *The Old Regime and the French Revolution*, Chicago: University of Chicago Press, 1987, pp. 202–8.
32. Reproduced in full in Reinhard, *Chute*, pp. 437–51.
33. Reinhard, *Chute*, p. 438; Jacques Godechot, *The Taking of the Bastille, July 14th 1789*, London: Faber, 1970.
34. Barry M. Shapiro, *Revolutionary Justice in Paris, 1789–1790*, Cambridge: CUP, 1993.
35. Reinhard, *Chute*, pp. 438–9.
36. Reinhard, *Chute*, p. 450.
37. See Price, *Fall*, for a recent account of the Revolution that is definitely 'about' the king and queen.
38. See Doyle, *Oxford History*, pp. 108–15; D. M. G. Sutherland, *France 1789–1815: Revolution and Counterrevolution*, London: Fontana, 1985, pp. 49–88.
39. Lefebvre, *Great Fear*, parts 2 and 3.
40. William Doyle, 'Abolishing the Sale of Offices: Ambitions, Ambiguities, and Myths', *Canadian Journal of History*, 32 (1997), pp. 339–45.
41. Michael P. Fitzsimmon, *The Night the Old Regime Ended: August 4, 1789, and the French Revolution*, University Park, Pa.: Penn State UP, 2003.
42. Markoff, *Abolition of Feudalism*, chapter 9.
43. Anatoli Ado, *Paysans en révolution; terre, pouvoir et jacquerie 1789–1794*, Paris: Société des Études Robespierristes, 1996; Peter M. Jones, *The Peasantry in the French Revolution*, Cambridge: CUP, 1988.
44. Isser Woloch, *The New Regime: Transformations of the French Civic Order, 1789–1820s*, New York: W. W. Norton, 1994; Malcolm Crook, *Elections in the French Revolution: An Apprenticeship in Democracy, 1789–1799*, Cambridge: CUP, 1996; Patrice Gueniffey, *Le Nombre et la raison: la Révolution française et les élections*, Paris: Editions EHESS, 1993.
45. E. S. Brezis and F. Crouzet, 'The Role of Assignats during the French

Revolution: An Evil or a Rescuer?', *Journal of European Economic History*, 24 (1995), pp. 7–40.

46. Timothy Tackett, *Religion, Revolution and Regional Culture in Eighteenth-Century France: The Ecclesiastical Oath of 1791*, Princeton: Princeton UP, 1986.
47. Sutherland, *France 1789–1815*, pp. 109–10.
48. David Andress, *Massacre at the Champ de Mars: Popular Dissent and Political Culture in the French Revolution*, Woodbridge: Boydell Press, 2000, pp. 109–11.
49. Reinhard, *Chute*, p. 445.
50. Patrice Higonnet, *Goodness Beyond Virtue; Jacobins during the French Revolution*, Cambridge, Mass.: Harvard UP, 1998; Michael L. Kennedy, *The Jacobin Clubs in the French Revolution*, vol. 1, *The Early Years*, Princeton: Princeton UP, 1981.
51. Andress, *Massacre*, p. 136.
52. John Hardman (ed.), *The French Revolution Sourcebook*, London: Arnold, 1998, pp. 127–8.
53. For what follows, see Reinhard, *Chute*, chapter 4; Paul and Pierrette Girault de Coursac, *Sur la route de Varennes*, Paris: Table Ronde, 1984; Price, *Fall*, chapter 8.
54. Reinhard, *Chute*, p. 94.
55. Reinhard, *Chute*, p. 97.
56. A highly detailed account of the events at Varennes is contained in Timothy Tackett, *When the King Took Flight*, Cambridge, Mass.: Harvard UP, 2003, pp. 3–24.
57. Reinhard, *Chute*, p. 98.

### Chapter 2: Hankering After Destruction

1. David Garrioch, *The Making of Revolutionary Paris*, Berkeley: University of California Press, 2002.
2. Jeffrey Kaplow, *The Names of Kings: The Parisian Laboring Poor in the Eighteenth Century*, New York: Basic Books, 1972.
3. Farge, *Fragile Lives.*
4. Michael Sonenscher, *Work and Wages: Natural Law, Politics and the Eighteenth-Century French Trades*, Cambridge: CUP, 1989; Andress, *Massacre*, pp. 122–35.
5. Alan Williams, *The Police of Paris, 1718–1789*, Baton Rouge: Louisiana State UP, 1979.
6. Andress, *Massacre*, chapters 2–5.
7. Georges Lefebvre, 'Le Meurtre du comte de Dampierre', in *Études sur la Révolution française*, Paris: PUF, 1963, pp. 393–405.
8. Tackett, *When the King Took Flight*, pp. 78–80.
9. Tackett, *When the King Took Flight*, pp. 81–2.
10. Peter Burley, *Witness to the Revolution: British and American Despatches from France, 1788–1794*, London: Weidenfeld & Nicolson, 1989, pp. 139–40.
11. Charles-Elie, marquis de Ferrières, *Correspondance inédite, 1789, 1790, 1791*, ed. Henri Carré, Paris: Armand Collin, 1932, pp. 263–4, letter of 12 August 1790.
12. Andress, *Massacre*, p. 87.
13. Albert Mathiez, *Le Club des Cordeliers pendant la crise de Varennes et la massacre du Champ de Mars*, Paris, 1910, repr. Geneva: Slatkine-Megariotis Reprints, 1975.
14. Norman Hampson, *Danton*, London: Duckworth, 1978.

15. Isabelle Bourdin, *Les Sociétés populaires à Paris pendant la Révolution française jusqu'à la chute de la royauté*, Paris: Sirey, 1937.
16. R. B. Rose, *The Making of the Sans-Culottes: Democratic Ideas and Institutions in Paris, 1789–92*, Manchester: MUP, 1983.
17. Cited in Andress, *Massacre*, p. 114.
18. See Jeremy D. Popkin, *Revolutionary News: The Press in France 1789–1799*, Durham, NC: Duke UP, 1990; Jack Censer, *Prelude to Power: The Parisian Radical Press, 1789–1791*, London, 1976.
19. See two biographies of Marat: Ian Germani, *Jean-Paul Marat, Hero and Anti-hero of the French Revolution*, Lampeter: Edwin Mellen, 1992; Olivier Coquard, *Jean-Paul Marat*, Paris: Fayard, 1993.
20. David P. Jordan, 'The Robespierre Problem', in C. Haydon and W. Doyle (eds), *Robespierre*, Cambridge: CUP, 1999, pp. 17–34; p. 20.
21. Andress, *Massacre*, p. 145.
22. Andress, *Massacre*, pp. 148–51.
23. Andress, *Massacre*, p. 152.
24. Cited in Baker (ed.), *Old Regime*, p. 273.
25. Andress, *Massacre*, p. 153.
26. Andress, *Massacre*, pp. 160–7.
27. Tackett, *When the King Took Flight*, pp. 196–8.
28. Mathiez, *Club des Cordeliers*, pp. 146–7, and officers' testimony reproduced at pp. 249–50, 275–6, 280.
29. Andress, *Massacre*, p. 207.
30. Price, *Fall*, p. 208.
31. Burley, *Witness to the Revolution*, p. 147.
32. Price, *Fall*, pp. 49–54.
33. Munro Price, 'The "Ministry of the Hundred Hours": A Reappraisal', *French History*, 4 (1990), pp. 317–39.
34. Price, *Fall*, p. 115.
35. Price, *Fall*, p. 109.
36. Price, *Fall*, p. 210.
37. Price, *Fall*, p. 219.
38. Burley, *Witness to the Revolution*, p. 150.
39. Malcolm Crook, *Elections in the French Revolution: An Apprenticeship in Democracy, 1789–99*, Cambridge: CUP, 1996.
40. Barry M. Shapiro, 'Self-Sacrifice, Self-Interest or Self-Defense? The Constituent Assembly and the "Self-Denying Ordinance" of May 1791', *French Historical Studies*, 25 (2002), pp. 625–56.
41. Price, *Fall*, p. 227.
42. Higonnet, *Goodness Beyond Virtue*, pp. 30–2.
43. See John Hardman, *Robespierre*, London: Longman, 1999, a recent brief biography, and Haydon and Doyle (ed.), *Robespierre*, a collection of scholarly essays.
44. The speech is cited at length in Baker (ed.), *Old Regime*, pp. 282–6.
45. Burley, *Witness to the Revolution*, p. 153.
46. Reinhard, *Chute*, p. 216.
47. Reinhard, *Chute*, pp. 217–19.
48. Price, *Fall*, chapter 10.
49. Simon Burrows, 'The Innocence of Jacques-Pierre Brissot', *Historical Journal*, 46 (2003), pp. 843–71. See also Frederick A. de Luna, 'The Dean Street

Style of Revolution: J.-P. Brissot, *jeune philosophe*', *French Historical Studies*, 17 (1991), pp. 159–90, and Robert Darnton, 'The Brissot Dossier', *French Historical Studies*, 17 (1991), pp. 191–205.

50. The classic modern study of this grouping is M. J. Sydenham, *The Girondins*, London: Athlone Press, 1961. A useful recent supplement is Leigh Whaley, *Radicals: Politics and Republicanism in the French Revolution*, Stroud: Sutton Publishing, 2000.
51. Burley, *Witness to the Revolution*, p. 154.
52. Whaley, *Radicals*, p. 45.
53. Cited in David Andress, *French Society in Revolution, 1789–1799*, Manchester: MUP, 1999, pp. 177–8.
54. Claude Petitfrère, 'The Origins of the Civil War in the Vendée', *French History*, 2 (1988), pp. 187–207.
55. Jacques Godechot, *The Counter- Revolution: Doctrine and Action, 1789–1804*, Princeton: Princeton UP, 1971, p. 211.
56. Godechot, *Counter- Revolution*, pp. 207–10.
57. Godechot, *Counter- Revolution*, p. 209. See also Andress, *Massacre*, pp. 124–30.
58. On this topic, see David Barry Gaspar and David Geggus (eds), *A Turbulent Time: The French Revolution and the Greater Caribbean*, Bloomington: Indiana University Press, 1997.
59. Colin Jones and Rebecca Spang, 'Sans-culottes, *sans café, sans tabac*: Shifting Realms of Necessity and Luxury in Eighteenth-Century France', in Maxine Berg and Helen Clifford (eds), *Consumers and Luxury: Consumer Culture in Europe, 1650–1850*, Manchester: MUP, 1999, pp. 37–62; pp. 53–4.
60. D. M. G. Sutherland, *The French Revolution and Empire; The Quest for a Civic Order*, Oxford: Blackwell, 2002, pp. 129–30.
61. Michel Vovelle, *The Fall of the French Monarchy, 1787–1792*, Cambridge: CUP, 1972, pp. 196, 217.
62. Ado, *Paysans en révolution*, pp. 261–73.
63. Burley, *Witness to the Revolution*, p. 158.
64. Gwynne Lewis, *The Second Vendée: The Continuity of Counter-revolution in the Department of the Gard, 1789–1815*, Oxford: OUP, 1978, pp. 45–50.
65. Doyle, *Oxford History*, p. 176.
66. Burley, *Witness to the Revolution*, p. 157.
67. Cited in Schama, *Citizens*, pp. 594–5.
68. Doyle, *Oxford History*, pp. 177–80.
69. Georges Pernoud and Sabine Flaissier, *The French Revolution*, London: Secker & Warburg, 1962, pp. 117–20.
70. Price, *Fall*, pp. 248–53. On the night of his arrival, Fersen saw the queen alone, and stayed in her apartments until morning – the two words 'stayed there' in his journal, half-obliterated by a discreet descendant, being the only concrete evidence that the pair may finally have consummated their relationship. Whether they did or not, on subsequent nights Fersen stayed, and slept, with the mistress of another friend!
71. Price, *Fall*, p. 250.
72. Stone, *Reinterpreting the French Revolution*, pp. 166–8. See also T. C. W. Blanning, *The Origins of the French Revolutionary Wars*, London: Longman, 1986.
73. Burley, *Witness to the Revolution*, p. 158.
74. Whaley, *Radicals*, pp. 46–50.

## Chapter 3: The Fall

1. Rose, *Making of the Sans-Culottes*, pp. 150–1.
2. Schama, *Citizens*, p. 600.
3. Burley, *Witness to the Revolution*, p. 155.
4. Burley, *Witness to the Revolution*, p. 160.
5. Rose, *Making of the Sans-Culottes*, pp. 154–5.
6. Cited in Doyle, *Oxford History*, 2nd edn, p. 185.
7. Burley, *Witness to the Revolution*, p. 163.
8. *Archives parlementaires de 1787 à 1860*, première série, M. J. Mavidal *et al.* (eds), Paris, 1868–, vol. 45, p. 338.
9. Price, *Fall*, pp. 287–8.
10. Burley, *Witness to the Revolution*, p. 165.
11. Michael Sonenscher, 'Artisans, Sans-culottes and the French Revolution', in Alan Forrest and Peter Jones (eds), *Reshaping France: Town, Country and Region in the French Revolution*, Manchester: MUP, 1991, pp. 105–21, and 'The Sans-culottes of the Year II: Rethinking the Language of Labour in Revolutionary France', *Social History* 9 (1984), pp. 301–28.
12. Morris Slavin, *The Hébertistes to the Guillotine: Anatomy of a 'Conspiracy' in Revolutionary France*, Baton Rouge: Louisiana State UP, 1994, pp. 9–16.
13. See Ouzi Elyada, 'La Mère Duchesne: masques populaires et guerre pamphlétaire, 1789–1791', *Annales historiques de la Révolution française*, 271 (1988), pp. 1–16.
14. Cited in Jacques Guilhaumou, *L'Avènement des porte-parole de la République (1789–1792): essai de synthèse sur les langages de la Révolution française*, Lille: Presses Universitaires du Septentrion, 1998, p. 214.
15. Rose, *Making of the Sans-Culottes*, p. 155.
16. Schama, *Citizens*, p. 600.
17. Schama, *Citizens*, pp. 609–10; Price, *Fall*, pp. 288–9.
18. Rose, *Making of the Sans-Culottes*, p. 154.
19. Rose, *Making of the Sans-Culottes*, pp. 156–7.
20. Price, *Fall*, pp. 289–92.
21. Sutherland, *French Revolution and Empire*, p. 134.
22. Leigh Whaley, 'Political Factions and the Second Revolution: The Insurrection of 10 August 1792', *French History*, 7 (1993), pp. 205–24; pp. 206–7.
23. Reinhard, *Chute*, pp. 349–51.
24. Sydenham, *Girondins*, pp. 80–6.
25. Pierre Caron, *Les Massacres de septembre*, Paris: Maison du Livre Français, 1935, pp. 365–6.
26. Caron, *Massacres de septembre*, pp. 366–8.
27. *Gazette nationale, ou le Moniteur universel*, 3 August 1792, cited in Philip Dwyer and Peter McPhee (eds), *The French Revolution and Napoleon: A Sourcebook*, London: Routledge, 2002, pp. 68–9.
28. Godechot, *Counter-Revolution*, pp. 234–5.
29. The lyrics are given, in French and a variety of English translations, at <www.marseillaise.org>. I have made free with the metre of the original to convey the sense of some passages. A different analysis of the lyrics' meaning can be found in Schama, *Citizens*, pp. 598–9.
30. See David A. Bell, *The Cult of the Nation in France: Inventing Nationalism, 1680–1800*, Cambridge, Mass.: Harvard UP, 2001.

31. Pernoud and Flaissier, *The French Revolution*, p. 124.
32. Whaley, 'Political Factions', p. 210.
33. Whaley, 'Political Factions', pp. 215–16.
34. Whaley, 'Political Factions', pp. 218–19.
35. Some of these letters are cited in John Hardman, *The French Revolution: The Fall of the Ancien Régime to the Thermidorian Reaction, 1785–1795*, London: Arnold, 1981, pp. 141–2.
36. Whaley, 'Political Factions', pp. 213, 222–3.
37. Whaley, 'Political Factions', pp. 219–20.
38. Burley, *Witness to the Revolution*, p. 168.
39. Whaley, 'Political Factions', pp. 216–18.
40. Whaley, 'Political Factions', p. 222.
41. Price, *Fall*, pp. 297–8.
42. Pernoud and Flaissier, *The French Revolution*, p. 133.
43. Price, *Fall*, pp. 298–300. This draws on the detailed account of Rodney Allen, *Threshold of Terror: The Last Hours of the Monarchy in the French Revolution*, Stroud: Sutton, 1999.
44. Archives de la Préfecture de Police, Paris, AA88, fos 546–71, 10–15 August 1792. There were twenty-one deposits in total, four from corpses, nine from looters, and eight 'found'. Thirty-nine individuals all told made depositions.
45. Caron, *Massacres de septembre*, pp. 369–74.
46. Sutherland, *French Revolution and Empire*, p. 138.
47. Pernoud and Flaissier, *The French Revolution*, p. 110.
48. Price, *Fall*, pp. 304–6.
49. Pernoud and Flaissier, *The French Revolution*, p. 121.

## Chapter 4: The September Massacres

1. *Souvenirs d'un vieillard sur des faits restés ignorés: Journées des 10 août, 3, 4, 5, 9 et 12 septembre 1792*, 1843, cited in Antoine de Baecque, *Glory and Terror: Seven Deaths under the French Revolution*, London: Routledge, 2001, p. 62.
2. Jules Michelet, *La Révolution française*, vol. 3 (1849), cited in de Baecque, *Glory and Terror*, p. 61.
3. *La Famille royale préservée au Temple par la garde nationale de Paris*, undated manuscript, cited in de Baecque, *Glory and Terror*, p. 62.
4. Olivier Blanc, *L'Amour à Paris au temps de Louis XVI*, Paris: Perrin, 2002, pp. 32–3.
5. De Baecque, *Glory and Terror*, pp. 76–8.
6. Cited in de Baecque, *Glory and Terror*, p. 65.
7. Caron, *Massacres de septembre*, pp. 61–2, discusses briefly the legendary qualities of Lamballe's death. De Baecque's account, noted above, is comprehensive.
8. Caron, *Massacres de septembre*, pp. 4–5.
9. Caron, *Massacres de septembre*, pp. 29–30.
10. Caron, *Massacres de septembre*, pp. 30–2.
11. Caron, *Massacres de septembre*, pp. 33–4.
12. Caron, *Massacres de septembre*, pp. 56–9.
13. George Rudé, *The Crowd in the French Revolution*, Oxford: OUP, 1959, pp. 105–8.
14. Rudé, *Crowd*, p. 109.

15. Caron, *Massacres de septembre*, p. 418.
16. Caron, *Massacres de septembre*, p. 419.
17. Caron, *Massacres de septembre*, p. 422.
18. Hector Fleischmann (ed.), *Discours civiques de Danton*, Paris: Fasquelle, 1920, p. 14.
19. Hardman (ed.), *French Revolution Sourcebook*, pp. 156–7.
20. Burley, *Witness to the Revolution*, p. 173.
21. Caron, *Massacres de septembre*, pp. 325–6.
22. See Michel Foucault, *Discipline and Punish: The Birth of the Prison*, Harmondsworth: Penguin, 1977, pp. 3–5.
23. See Farge, *Fragile Lives*, pp. 173–204.
24. Caron, *Massacres de septembre*, pp. 103–20.
25. Pierre Caron's conclusions essentially seek to exculpate all revolutionary organisations from responsibility for the massacres, placing them at the door of popular spontaneity. This argument is a little forced, but so too is that of Frédéric Bluche, *Septembre 1792, logiques d'un massacre*, Paris: R. Laffont, 1986, which revisits some of the more conspiratorial explanations.
26. Caron, *Massacres de septembre*, pp. 324–39.
27. Caron, *Massacres de septembre*, pp. 76–102.
28. Caron, *Massacres de septembre*, pp. 27–54.
29. Caron, *Massacres de septembre*, pp. 33, 40.
30. Caron, *Massacres de septembre*, pp. 40–3.
31. Caron, *Massacres de septembre*, p. 44.
32. Caron, *Massacres de septembre*, pp. 44–6.
33. Arlette Farge, *Subversive Words: Public Opinion in Eighteenth-Century France*, Cambridge: Polity Press, 1994.
34. Rose, *Making of the Sans-Culottes*; Bourdin, *Les Sociétés populaires à Paris*.
35. Caron, *Massacres de septembre*, pp. 46–7.
36. Caron, *Massacres de septembre*, pp. 47–8.
37. Caron, *Massacres de septembre*, p. 46.
38. Caron, *Massacres de septembre*, pp. 49–51.
39. Caron, *Massacres de septembre*, p. 266.
40. See Andress, *Massacre*, pp. 124–8.
41. Andress, *Massacre*, chapter 2.
42. Farge, *Fragile Lives*, pp. 182–98.
43. Caron, *Massacres de septembre*, pp. 55–65.
44. Burley, *Witness to the Revolution*, p. 175.
45. Pernoud and Flaissier, *The French Revolution*, p. 151.
46. Caron, *Massacres de septembre*, pp. 66–70.
47. Hardman, *Robespierre*, pp. 48–9, 52.
48. Hardman, *Robespierre*, p. 53.
49. Hardman, *Robespierre*, p. 56.
50. Hardman (ed.), *French Revolution Sourcebook*, p. 157.
51. Price, *Fall*, p. 308.
52. T. C. W. Blanning, *The French Revolutionary Wars, 1787–1802*, London: Arnold, 1996, pp. 74–80.
53. Burley, *Witness to the Revolution*, p. 178.
54. Pernoud and Flaissier, *The French Revolution*, p. 296.
55. Schama, *Citizens*, p. 640.

## Chapter 5: Dawn of a New Age

1. Guy de la Batut, *Les Pavés de Paris: guide illustré de Paris révolutionnaire*, Paris: Editions sociales internationales, 1937, vol. 1, pp. 31–2.
2. Crook, *Elections in the French Revolution*; Gueniffey, *Le nombre et la raison*.
3. Burley, *Witness to the Revolution*, p. 177.
4. Whaley, *Radicals*, pp. 89–90.
5. Hampson, *Danton*, pp. 76–7.
6. Whaley, *Radicals*, p. 94.
7. Hampson, *Danton*, pp. 88–91.
8. Sydenham, *Girondins*, pp. 80–6.
9. Whaley, *Radicals*, pp. 96–7.
10. Whaley, *Radicals*, pp. 98–9.
11. J. M. Roberts and John Hardman (eds), *French Revolution Documents, Vol. 2: 1792–5*, Oxford: Blackwells, 1973, p. 32.
12. Whaley, *Radicals*, p. 100.
13. Hampson, *Danton*, pp. 90–1; Whaley, *Radicals*, p. 101.
14. See Popkin, *Revolutionary News*; Hugh Gough, *The Newspaper Press in the French Revolution*, London: Routledge, 1988.
15. On Jacobinism in general see Higonnet, *Goodness Beyond Virtue*.
16. Timothy Tackett, 'Conspiracy Obsession in a Time of Revolution: French Elites and the Origins of the Terror, 1789–1792', *American Historical Review*, 105 (2000), pp. 691–713.
17. Burley, *Witness to the Revolution*, p. 179.
18. See George A. Kelly, 'The Machine of the Duc d'Orléans and the New Politics', *Journal of Modern History*, 51 (1979), pp. 667–84.
19. David Andress, 'Liberty, Unanimity, and the Paradoxes of Subjectivity and Citizenship in the French Revolution', in I. Halfin (ed.), *Language and Revolution: Making Modern Political Identities*, London: Frank Cass, 2002, pp. 27–46.
20. On sensationism, see John C. O'Neal, *The Authority of Experience: Sensationist Theory in the French Enlightenment*, University Park, Pa: Penn State University Press, 1996.
21. A classic example of this is discussed by Robert Darnton, 'Readers Respond to Rousseau', in *The Great Cat Massacre and Other Episodes of French Cultural History*, Harmondsworth: Penguin, 1985, pp. 79–104. More generally, see David J. Denby, *Sentimental Narrative and the Social Order in France, 1760–1820*, Cambridge: CUP, 1994.
22. Kathryn Norberg, '"Love and Patriotism": Gender and Politics in the Life and Work of Louvet de Couvrai', in Sara E. Melzer and Leslie W. Rabine (eds), *Rebel Daughters: Women and the French Revolution*, Oxford: OUP, 1992, pp. 38–53, p. 38.
23. See William M. Reddy, 'Sentimentalism and Its Erasure: The Role of Emotions in the Era of the French *Revolution*', *Journal of Modern History*, 72 (2000), pp. 109–52. Reddy develops his themes at greater length in *The Navigation of Feeling: A Framework for the History of Emotions*, Cambridge: CUP, 2001.
24. The literature on Rousseau is voluminous. See a recent exploration, James Swenson, *On Jean-Jacques Rousseau, Considered as One of the First Authors of the Revolution*, Stanford: Stanford UP, 2000; Carol Blum, *Rousseau and the Republic of Virtue: The Language of Politics in the French Revolution*, Ithaca, NY: Cornell UP, 1986.

25. Paul Hanson, *The Jacobin Republic Under Fire: The Federalist Revolt in the French Revolution*, University Park, Pa: Penn State University Press, 2003, p. 233.
26. Antoine de Baecque, 'The Great Spectacle of Transparency: Public Denunciation and the Classification of Appearances', in *The Body Politic: Corporeal Metaphor in Revolutionary France, 1770–1800*, Stanford: Stanford UP, 1997, pp. 209–46.
27. Colin Lucas, 'The Theory and Practice of Denunciation in the French Revolution', *Journal of Modern History*, 68 (1996), pp. 768–85.
28. Hampson, *Danton*, pp. 86–7.
29. W. D. Edmonds, *Jacobinism and the Revolt of Lyon, 1789–1793*, Oxford: Clarendon Press, 1990, pp. 123–37.
30. Edmonds, *Jacobinism*, p. 133.
31. This and the following quotation cited in Ado, *Paysans en révolution*, pp. 325–6.
32. Pernoud and Flaissier, *The French Revolution*, p. 171.
33. Pernoud and Flaissier, *The French Revolution*, p. 172.
34. Pernoud and Flaissier, *The French Revolution*, pp. 234–5.
35. Pernoud and Flaissier, *The French Revolution*, pp. 291–3.
36. Michael Walzer (ed.), *Regicide and Revolution: Speeches at the Trial of Louis XVI*, Cambridge: CUP, 1974, p. 109.
37. Alison Patrick, *The Men of the First French Republic: Political Alignments in the National Convention of 1792*, Baltimore: Johns Hopkins UP, 1972, pp. 48–9.
38. Cited in Walzer (ed.), *Regicide*, p. 121.
39. Walzer (ed.), *Regicide*, p. 124.
40. Walzer (ed.), *Regicide*, p. 124.
41. Walzer (ed.), *Regicide*, p. 124.
42. Walzer (ed.), *Regicide*, pp. 126–7.
43. Andrew Freeman (ed.), *The Compromising of Louis XVI: The Armoire de Fer and the French Revolution*, Exeter: University of Exeter Press, 1989.
44. Freeman (ed.), *Compromising of Louis XVI*, pp. 12–16.
45. Freeman (ed.), *Compromising of Louis XVI*, pp. 42–4.
46. Cited in John Hall Stewart (ed.), *A Documentary Survey of the French Revolution*, New York: Macmillan, 1951, pp. 386–91.
47. Walzer (ed.), *Regicide*, pp. 166–7.
48. Price, *Fall*, pp. 318–19.
49. Patrick, *Men of the First French Republic*, pp. 40–1, note 7.
50. Patrick, *Men of the First French Republic*, pp. 42–3.
51. Cited in Schama, *Citizens*, p. 659. See pp. 657–60 on the trial in general.
52. Patrick, *Men of the First French Republic*, p. 59.
53. Patrick, *Men of the First French Republic*, pp. 60–1.
54. Patrick, *Men of the First French Republic*, p. 71.
55. Burley, *Witness to the Revolution*, p. 180.
56. Patrick, *Men of the First French Republic*, p. 84.
57. Schama, *Citizens*, p. 663.
58. See Schama, *Citizens*, pp. 662–3, for the high majority, and Price, *Fall*, p. 325, for mention of the tendentiously low one. The various totals are collated by Patrick, *Men of the First French Republic*, p. 104.
59. Pernoud and Flaissier, *The French Revolution*, pp. 195–6.
60. Schama, *Citizens*, pp. 668–9.
61. Price, *Fall*, pp. 308–9.

62. Price, *Fall*, p. 320.
63. Price, *Fall*, p. 324.
64. Price, *Fall*, p. 327; Schama, *Citizens*, p. 669.
65. See Daniel Arasse, *The Guillotine and the Terror*, Harmondsworth: Penguin, 1991, pp. 48–72, esp. pp. 68, 70.
66. For a post-Freudian view of the significance of king-killing at this point, see Hunt, *Family Romance.*

### Chapter 6: Things Fall Apart

1. Schama, *Citizens*, pp. 671–72.
2. Rebecca L. Spang, *The Invention of the Restaurant: Paris and Modern Gastronomic Culture*, Cambridge, Mass.: Harvard UP, 2000, pp. 133–7.
3. Schama, *Citizens*, pp. 672–3.
4. Freeman, *Compromising of Louis XVI*, pp. 43–5.
5. Colin Jones, *The Longman Companion to the French Revolution*, London: Longman, 1988, p. 349; Sydenham, *Girondins*, p. 149.
6. Robespierre's remark is cited in Blum, *Rousseau and the Republic of Virtue*, p. 198; Barère's in Rudé, *Crowd*, p. 118.
7. Burley, *Witness to the Revolution*, p. 182.
8. Stone, *Reinterpreting the French Revolution*, pp. 49–50.
9. Burley, *Witness to the Revolution*, p. 161.
10. Hampson, *Danton*, pp. 96–9.
11. Pernoud and Flaissier, *The French Revolution*, p. 282.
12. Doyle, *Oxford History*, pp. 201–2.
13. Burley, *Witness to the Revolution*, p. 186.
14. Schama, *Citizens*, pp. 688–9.
15. Burley, *Witness to the Revolution*, p. 187.
16. Doyle, *Oxford History*, p. 226.
17. R. B. Rose, *The Enragés: Socialists of the French Revolution?*, Sydney: Sydney UP, 1965, chapters 2 and 3 for biographies of Varlet and Roux.
18. Jean-Paul Marat, *Journal of the French Republic*, 25 February 1793: cited in Andress, *French Society in Revolution*, p. 186.
19. Sydenham, *Girondins*, pp. 149–51.
20. Pernoud and Flaissier, *The French Revolution*, pp. 283–4.
21. Dominique Godineau, *The Women of Paris and Their French Revolution*, Berkeley: University of California Press, 1998, pp. 244–7.
22. Pernoud and Flaissier, *The French Revolution*, p. 285.
23. Pernoud and Flaissier, *The French Revolution*, pp. 286–7.
24. Alan Forrest, *The Soldiers of the French Revolution*, Durham, NC: Duke UP, 1990, pp. 68–71.
25. Jones, *Peasantry*, pp. 223–5.
26. This and the following quotation cited in D. M. G. Sutherland, *The Chouans: The Social Origins of Popular Counter- Revolution in Upper Brittany, 1770–1796*, Oxford: Oxford University Press, 1982, pp. 260–1.
27. D. M. G. Sutherland, 'The Vendée: Unique or Emblematic?', in Colin Lucas (ed.), *The Terror*, vol. 4 of *The French Revolution and the Creation of Modern Political Culture*, Oxford: Elsevier Science, 1994, pp. 99–114; p. 100.
28. Jean-Clément Martin, 'Histoire et polémique: les massacres de Machecoul', *Annales historiques de la Révolution française*, 291 (1993), pp. 33–60.

29. Michel Biard, *Missionnaires de la République: les représentants du peuple en mission (1793–1795)*, Paris: Editions du CTHS, 2002.
30. See for example Jones, *Peasantry*, pp. 232–3.
31. Jones, *Longman Companion*, pp. 88–9.
32. Patrick, *Men of the First French Republic*, p. 109.
33. Sydenham, *Girondins*, pp. 162–3.
34. See Kelly, 'The Machine of the Duc d'Orléans'.
35. George Armstrong Kelly, *Victims, Authority and Terror; The Parallel Deaths of d'Orléans, Custine, Bailly and Malesherbes*, Chapel Hill, NC: U of North Carolina Press, 1982, esp. pp. 73–88.
36. Patrick, *Men of the First French Republic*, pp. 108–12.
37. Schama, *Citizens*, p. 718.
38. Morris Slavin, *The Making of an Insurrection; Parisian Sections and the Gironde*, Cambridge, Mass.: Harvard UP, 1986, pp. 14–15; Sydenham, *Girondins*, pp. 166–7.
39. Slavin, *Making*, p. 15.
40. Slavin, *Making*, chapter 2, esp. pp. 23–7.
41. Sydenham, *Girondins*, pp. 167–9; Schama, *Citizens*, pp. 719–20.
42. Slavin, *Making*, p. 16.
43. Patrick, *Men of the First French Republic*, pp. 116–17.
44. Slavin, *Making*, pp. 17–19.
45. Sutherland, 'The Vendée', p. 100.
46. Sydenham, *Girondins*, pp. 170–1.
47. Sydenham, *Girondins*, p. 172.
48. Hampson, *Danton*, pp. 111–12.
49. Slavin, *Making*, p. 17.
50. Slavin, *Making*, p. 70.
51. Sydenham, *Girondins*, pp. 174–5.
52. Batut, *Pavés de Paris*, vol. 1, p. 33.
53. Albert Soboul, *Les Soldats de l'An II*, Paris: Club Français du Livre, 1959, p. 123.
54. Patrick, *Men of the First French Republic*, p. 117.
55. Slavin, *Making*, pp. 12–13, summarises discussion on this; Sydenham, *Girondins*, and Patrick, *Men of the First French Republic*, consider the issues in depth.
56. Patrick, *Men of the First French Republic*, table on p. 30.
57. Slavin, *Making*, pp. 72–4.
58. Slavin, *Making*, pp. 74–5.
59. Slavin, *Making*, pp. 75–89, esp. pp. 78–9 on Loys.
60. Slavin, *Making*, pp. 93–101.
61. Slavin, *Making*, pp. 101–2; Paul Hanson, *The Jacobin Republic Under Fire; The Federalist Revolt in the French Revolution*, University Park, Pa.: Penn State University Press, 2003, pp. 57–8.
62. Slavin, *Making*, pp. 102–3.
63. Slavin, *Making*, pp. 112–14.
64. Slavin, *Making*, pp. 115–16.

## Chapter 7: Holding the Centre

1. Rudé, *Crowd*, p. 126.
2. R. R. Palmer, *Twelve Who Ruled: The Year of the Terror in the French Revolution*, Princeton: Princeton UP, 1941, p. 44.
3. *Archives parlementaires de 1787 à 1860*, vol. 73, p. 420.
4. Slavin, *Making*, p. 119.
5. Slavin, *Making*, p. 118.
6. Whaley, *Radicals*, p. 156.
7. Whaley, *Radicals*, p. 160.
8. Hanson, *Jacobin Republic Under Fire*, pp. 13–16.
9. Whaley, *Radicals*, p. 161.
10. Whaley, *Radicals*, p. 161.
11. Hanson, *Jacobin Republic Under Fire*, pp. 81–3.
12. Hanson, *Jacobin Republic Under Fire*, pp. 84–5; see William Scott, *Terror and Repression in Revolutionary Marseille*, London: Macmillan, 1973, pp. 88–9.
13. Cited in Andress, *French Society*, pp. 186–7.
14. Edmonds, *Jacobinism and the Revolt of Lyon*, pp. 186–201.
15. Hanson, *Jacobin Republic Under Fire*, p. 63. Several of the some eighty-four departments in existence were, of course, under foreign military occupation or royalist insurrection at the time.
16. Hanson, *Jacobin Republic Under Fire*, pp. 66–8.
17. Hanson, *Jacobin Republic Under Fire*, pp. 71–2.
18. Hanson, *Jacobin Republic Under Fire*, pp. 91–6.
19. Edmonds, *Jacobinism and the Revolt of Lyon*, p. 204.
20. Edmonds, *Jacobinism and the Revolt of Lyon*, p. 205.
21. Edmonds, *Jacobinism and the Revolt of Lyon*, pp. 206–8.
22. Edmonds, *Jacobinism and the Revolt of Lyon*, pp. 196–201.
23. Edmonds, *Jacobinism and the Revolt of Lyon*, p. 212.
24. Edmonds, *Jacobinism and the Revolt of Lyon*, pp. 226–7.
25. Edmonds, *Jacobinism and the Revolt of Lyon*, pp. 233–4.
26. Pernoud and Flaissier, *The French Revolution*, pp. 226–7.
27. Pernoud and Flaissier, *The French Revolution*, p. 228.
28. Schama, *Citizens*, p. 738.
29. Schama, *Citizens*, pp. 729–31, 735–41.
30. Pernoud and Flaissier, *The French Revolution*, p. 229.
31. David P. Jordan, 'The Robespierre Problem', in Haydon and Doyle (eds), *Robespierre*, pp. 17–34; p. 20.
32. Schama, *Citizens*, pp. 742–4.
33. The full text is displayed at <http://www.conseil-constitutionnel.fr/constitution/c1793.htm>.
34. Jacques-René Hébert, *Le Père Duchesne*, reprinted in 10 vols, Paris: EDHIS, 1969, no. 243, p. 7.
35. Hardman (ed.), *French Revolution Sourcebook*, p. 179.
36. Rose, *Enragés*, pp. 45–6.
37. Edmonds, *Jacobinism and the Revolt of Lyon*, pp. 236–43.
38. Doyle, *Oxford History*, p. 246.
39. Sutherland, *French Revolution and Empire*, p. 181.
40. Doyle, *Oxford History*, pp. 248–9.

41. Alan Forrest, *Society and Politics in Revolutionary Bordeaux*, Oxford: OUP, 1975, pp. 210–12.
42. Palmer, *Twelve Who Ruled*, pp. 87–8.
43. Pernoud and Flaissier, *The French Revolution*, pp. 303–4.
44. Sutherland, *French Revolution and Empire*, p. 222.
45. Ado, *Paysans en révolution*, p. 359.
46. Doyle, *Oxford History*, p. 247.
47. Soboul, *Soldats*, p. 218.
48. Slavin, *Hébertistes*, pp. 58–68.
49. Thomas E. Kaiser, 'From the Austrian Committee to the Foreign Plot: Marie-Antoinette, Austrophobia, and the Terror', *French Historical Studies*, 26 (2003), pp. 579–618; p. 598.
50. Kelly, *Victims, Authority and Terror*.
51. Schama, *Citizens*, pp. 752–3.
52. Palmer, *Twelve Who Ruled*, pp. 3–4.
53. Kaiser, 'From the Austrian Committee', pp. 598–9.
54. Alain Gérard, *'Par principe d'humanité': la Terreur et la Vendée*, Paris: Fayard, 1999, pp. 133–8.
55. Mona Ozouf, *Festivals and the French Revolution*, Cambridge, Mass.: Harvard UP, 1988, pp. 83–4.
56. Schama, *Citizens*, pp. 746–50.
57. Cited in Baker (ed.), *Old Regime*, pp. 340–1.
58. Sutherland, *The Chouans*, pp. 291ff.
59. Sutherland, *French Revolution and Empire*, p. 244.
60. Sutherland, *French Revolution and Empire*, p. 189.
61. Scott, *Terror and Repression in Revolutionary Marseilles*, pp. 123–6.
62. Doyle, *Oxford History*, p. 249.
63. Kaiser, 'From the Austrian Committee', pp. 600–1.
64. *Archives parlementaires de 1787 à 1860*, vol. 73, p. 411.
65. *Archives parlementaires de 1787 à 1860*, vol. 73, p. 412.
66. *Archives parlementaires de 1787 à 1860*, vol. 73, p. 415.
67. Hampson, *Danton*, p. 129.
68. Hampson, *Danton*, pp. 130–1.
69. *Archives parlementaires de 1787 à 1860*, vol. 73, p. 415.
70. Hampson, *Danton*, p. 132.
71. See Christian A. Muller, 'Du "peuple égaré" au "peuple enfant": le discours politique révolutionnaire à l'épreuve de la révolte populaire en 1793', *Revue d'histoire moderne et contemporaine*, 47 (2000), pp. 93–112; p. 98.
72. Rose, *Enragés*, pp. 46–8.

## Chapter 8: Saturnalia

1. Schama, *Citizens*, p. 780.
2. Edmonds, *Jacobinism and the Revolt of Lyon*, p. 280.
3. Palmer, *Twelve Who Ruled*, pp. 21, 40.
4. Jones, *Longman Companion*, pp. 123–4.
5. Cited in Baker (ed.), *Old Regime*, pp. 338–9.
6. Schama, *Citizens*, pp. 793–4.
7. See Sophie Wahnich, *La Liberté ou la mort: essai sur la Terreur et le terrorisme*, Paris: La Fabrique, 2003, esp. pp. 57–66, p. 62.

8. Rudé, *Crowd*, p. 252, table of workers' budgets, 1790 and 1793.
9. Palmer, *Twelve Who Ruled*, p. 70.
10. Rudé, *Crowd*, pp. 125–30.
11. Richard Cobb, *The People's Armies: The Armées Révolutionnaires, Instruments of the Terror in the Departments April 1793 to Floréal Year III*, New Haven: Yale UP, 1987, book 1, chapter 3.
12. Biard, *Missionnaires*, pp. 413–17.
13. J. M. Roberts and John Hardman (eds), *French Revolution Documents*, vol. 2, Oxford: Blackwell, 1973, pp. 151–2.
14. Paul Mansfield, 'The Repression of Lyon, 1793–4: Origins, Responsibility and Significance', *French History*, 2 (1988), pp. 74–101; p. 80.
15. Palmer, *Twelve Who Ruled*, pp. 92–4.
16. Palmer, *Twelve Who Ruled*, p. 71.
17. Palmer, *Twelve Who Ruled*, p. 96.
18. Doyle, *Oxford History*, p. 252.
19. Doyle, *Oxford History*, p. 253.
20. Baker (ed.), *Old Regime*, pp. 362–4; p. 363.
21. Baker (ed.), *Old Regime*, pp. 365–8.
22. Baker (ed.), *Old Regime*, p. 368.
23. Palmer, *Twelve Who Ruled*, pp. 72–3.
24. Baker (ed.), *Old Regime*, pp. 355–62; p. 356.
25. Baker (ed.), *Old Regime*, pp. 357–8.
26. Palmer, *Twelve Who Ruled*, pp. 78–9.
27. See Howard G. Brown, *War, Revolution and the Bureaucratic State: Politics and Army Administration in France, 1791–1799*, Oxford: OUP, 1995, esp. chapters 3 and 4; and Michel Bruguière, *Gestionnaires et profiteurs de la Révolution: l'administration des finances françaises de Louis XVI à Bonaparte*, Paris: Orban, 1986.
28. Baker (ed.), *Old Regime*, p. 355.
29. Baker (ed.), *Old Regime*, p. 361.
30. Hardman (ed.), *French Revolution Sourcebook*, p. 163.
31. See, classically, Joan McDonald, *Rousseau and the French Revolution, 1762–1791*, London: Athlone Press, 1965; and more recently, James Swenson, *On Jean-Jacques Rousseau*.
32. Blum, *Rousseau and the Republic of Virtue*.
33. Hunt, *Family Romance*, p. 92.
34. Chantal Thomas, 'The Heroine of the Crime: Marie-Antoinette in Pamphlets', in Goodman (ed.), *Marie-Antoinette*, pp. 99–116.
35. Hunt, *Family Romance*, pp. 93, 101.
36. Pernoud and Flaissier, *The French Revolution*, p. 210.
37. Pernoud and Flaissier, *The French Revolution*, pp. 211–18.
38. Schama, *Citizens*, pp. 798–9.
39. Hunt, *Family Romance*, p. 101.
40. David P. Jordan, 'The Robespierre Problem', in Haydon and Doyle (eds), *Robespierre*, p. 25.
41. Burley, *Witness to the Revolution*, p. 181.
42. Pernoud and Flaissier, *The French Revolution*, p. 218.
43. Pernoud and Flaissier, *The French Revolution*, p. 221.
44. Schama, *Citizens*, p. 800.
45. Schama, *Citizens*, p. 803.
46. Hardman, *French Revolution*, pp. 151–2.

47. Jordan, 'Robespierre Problem', pp. 25–6.
48. Schama, *Citizens*, p. 804.
49. Sutherland, *French Revolution and Empire*, p. 213.
50. Kelly, *Victims, Authority and Terror*, pp. 88–90; Schama, *Citizens*, p. 805.
51. Schama, *Citizens*, pp. 802–3.
52. Kelly, *Victims, Authority and Terror*, pp. 200–2.
53. Doyle, *Oxford History*, p. 253.
54. Alan Forrest, *The Revolution in Provincial France: Aquitaine, 1789–1799*, Oxford: OUP, 1996, pp. 237–8.
55. Rose, *Enragés*, pp. 68–70. See Richard Wrigley, *The Politics of Appearances: Representations of Dress in Revolutionary France*, Oxford: Berg, 2002, pp. 97–109, for a history of the cockade.
56. Darline Gay Levy, Harriet Branson Applewhite and Mary Durham Johnson, *Women in Revolutionary Paris, 1789–1795: Selected Documents*, Urbana: University of Illinois Press, 1979, pp. 215–16; p. 213.
57. Levy *et al.*, *Women in Revolutionary Paris*, p. 220.
58. Godineau, *The Women of Paris*, pp. 212–15.
59. Schama, *Citizens*, p. 800.
60. Forrest, *Revolutionary Bordeaux*, pp. 225–6.
61. Forrest, *Revolutionary Bordeaux*, p. 228.
62. Forrest, *Revolutionary Bordeaux*, p. 229.
63. Forrest, *Revolutionary Bordeaux*, pp. 237–9.
64. Edmonds, *Jacobinism and the Revolt of Lyon*, p. 284.
65. Edmonds, *Jacobinism and the Revolt of Lyon*, p. 283.
66. Edmonds, *Jacobinism and the Revolt of Lyon*, pp. 286, 252.
67. Edmonds, *Jacobinism and the Revolt of Lyon*, p. 287.
68. Edmonds, *Jacobinism and the Revolt of Lyon*, p. 288.
69. Malcolm Crook, *Toulon in War and Revolution: From the Ancien Régime to the Restoration, 1750–1820*, Manchester: MUP, 1991, pp. 139–41.
70. Crook, *Toulon*, pp. 142–3.
71. Crook, *Toulon*, pp. 147–9.
72. Crook, *Toulon*, p. 150.
73. Michel Vovelle, *The Revolution Against the Church: From Reason to the Supreme Being*, Cambridge: Polity Press, 1991, pp. 12, 179.
74. Baker (ed.), *Old Regime*, pp. 366–7.
75. Vovelle, *Revolution Against the Church*, p. 13.
76. Ozouf, *Festivals*, pp. 97–8.

## Chapter 9: Faction and Conspiracy

1. Pernoud and Flaissier, *The French Revolution*, p. 299.
2. Gérard, '*Par principe*', pp. 140–1, 532.
3. Pernoud and Flaissier, *The French Revolution*, p. 301.
4. Harvey Mitchell, *The Underground War Against Revolutionary France*, Oxford: Clarendon Press, 1965, pp. 36–7.
5. Jean-Clément Martin, *La Vendée et la France*, Paris: Seuil, 1987, pp. 167–83.
6. Pernoud and Flaissier, *The French Revolution*, pp. 312–13.
7. Gérard, '*Par principe*', p. 23.
8. Martin, *La Vendée et la France*, pp. 213–24; Jean-Clément Martin, *Blancs et bleus dans la Vendée déchirée*, Paris: Gallimard, pp. 102–4.

9. Cited in Muller, 'Du "peuple égaré" au "peuple enfant"', p. 100.
10. Pernoud and Flaissier, *The French Revolution*, pp. 302–3.
11. Bernard Lepetit and Maroula Sinarellis, *Atlas de la Révolution française*, vol. 8, *Population*, Paris: Editions EHESS, 1995, p. 33.
12. Martin, *La Vendée*, p. 232.
13. Martin, *La Vendée*, pp. 307–8.
14. Sutherland, 'The Vendée', pp. 107–8.
15. Gérard, *'Par principe'*, p. 26.
16. Sutherland, 'The Vendée', p. 104.
17. Cited in Sutherland, *French Revolution and Empire*, p. 217.
18. Martin, *La Vendée*, pp. 315–16.
19. Pernoud and Flaissier, *The French Revolution*, p. 298.
20. Hardman, *Robespierre*, p. 34.
21. Norman Hampson, 'François Chabot and His Plot', *Transactions of the Royal Historical Society*, 1975, pp. 1–14, p. 1.
22. Palmer, *Twelve Who Ruled*, p. 114.
23. Hampson, 'François Chabot', p. 6; Palmer, *Twelve Who Ruled*, pp. 114–15.
24. Hampson, *Danton*, p. 138.
25. Hampson, *Danton*, pp. 140–1.
26. Hampson, *Danton*, pp. 142–3.
27. Hampson, *Danton*, p. 143.
28. Sutherland, 'The Vendée', pp. 100, 103.
29. Slavin, *Hébertistes*, pp. 68–72.
30. Slavin, *Hébertistes*, pp. 73–7.
31. Slavin, *Hébertistes*, p. 75.
32. Hampson, *Danton*, pp. 145–6.
33. Hardman (ed.), *French Revolution Sourcebook*, p. 202.
34. Palmer, *Twelve Who Ruled*, p. 258.
35. Hampson, *Danton*, p. 147.
36. Slavin, *Hébertistes*, pp. 72, 76; Hampson, *Danton*, p. 148.
37. Andress, *French Society*, p. 192.
38. Palmer, *Twelve Who Ruled*, p. 261; Hampson, *Danton*, pp. 148–9.
39. Jones, *Longman Companion*, pp. 96–8.
40. Palmer, *Twelve Who Ruled*, p. 264.
41. Palmer, *Twelve Who Ruled*, pp. 265–6.
42. Elizabeth Sparrow, *Secret Service: British Agents in France, 1792–1815*, Woodbridge: Boydell Press, 1999, pp. 20–2.
43. Burley, *Witness to the Revolution*, p. 187.
44. Hampson, 'François Chabot', p. 8.
45. Sparrow, *Secret Service*, pp. 31–7.
46. Hampson, 'François Chabot', p. 7.
47. Hampson, 'François Chabot', pp. 7–8.
48. Hampson, 'François Chabot', pp. 9–10.
49. Slavin, *Hébertistes*, pp. 80–1.
50. Palmer, *Twelve Who Ruled*, pp. 266–8.
51. Hampson, *Danton*, p. 150.
52. Palmer, *Twelve Who Ruled*, pp. 268–9.
53. Hampson, *Danton*, p. 151.
54. Slavin, *Hébertistes*, p. 77.
55. Rudé, *Crowd*, pp. 132–3.

56. Laura Mason and Tracey Rizzo (eds), *The French Revolution: A Document Collection*, Boston: Houghton Mifflin, 1999, p. 238.
57. Rudé, *Crowd*, p. 132.
58. Slavin, *Hébertistes*, pp. 221–2.
59. Slavin, *Hébertistes*, p. 89.
60. Slavin, *Hébertistes*, pp. 82–4.
61. Slavin, *Hébertistes*, pp. 94–5.
62. Slavin, *Hébertistes*, p. 98.
63. Slavin, *Hébertistes*, p. 100.
64. Slavin, *Hébertistes*, pp. 100–1.
65. Slavin, *Hébertistes*, pp. 96–7.
66. Wrigley, *Politics of Appearances*, chapter 5.
67. Slavin, *Hébertistes*, p. 128.
68. Slavin, *Hébertistes*, pp.170–204, for potted biographies of all these figures.
69. Slavin, *Hébertistes*, pp. 208–32.
70. Slavin, *Hébertistes*, pp. 233–4; Schama, *Citizens*, p. 825.
71. Hampson, *Danton*, pp. 158–9; Palmer, *Twelve Who Ruled*, pp. 296–7.
72. Hampson, *Danton*, p. 156.
73. Baker (ed.), *Old Regime*, p. 369.
74. Baker (ed.), *Old Regime*, p. 370.
75. Baker (ed.), *Old Regime*, p. 374.
76. Baker (ed.), *Old Regime*, pp. 375, 378.
77. Hampson, *Danton*, p. 155.
78. Palmer, *Twelve Who Ruled*, pp. 297–8; Hampson, *Danton*, p. 162.
79. Hampson, *Danton*, p. 161.
80. Pernoud and Flaissier, *The French Revolution*, p. 269.
81. Hampson, *Danton*, pp. 162–3.
82. Palmer, *Twelve Who Ruled*, p. 298.
83. Palmer, *Twelve Who Ruled*, p. 299.
84. Burley, *Witness to the Revolution*, p. 190.
85. Hampson, *Danton*, pp. 168–9.
86. Hampson, *Danton*, p. 171.
87. Pernoud and Flaissier, *The French Revolution*, p. 270.
88. Palmer, *Twelve Who Ruled*, p. 303.
89. Hampson, *Danton*, p. 174.
90. Burley, *Witness to the Revolution*, p. 190.

### Chapter 10: Glaciation

1. Roberts and Hardman (eds), *Documents*, vol. 2, p. 177.
2. Alan Forrest, 'The Local Politics of Repression', in Keith Michael Baker (ed.), *The French Revolution and the Making of Modern Political Culture*, vol. 4, *The Terror*, Oxford: Elsevier Science, 1994, pp. 81–98; p. 86.
3. Forrest, 'Local Politics', pp. 87–9.
4. Gueniffey, *Le Nombre et la raison*, pp. 386–92.
5. Cited in Philippe Goujard, 'L'Homme de masse sans les masses ou le déchristianisateur malheureux', *Annales historiques de la Révolution française*, 58 (1986), pp. 160–80; see p. 163.
6. Roberts and Hardman (eds), *Documents*, p. 179.
7. Ozouf, *Festivals*, pp. 87–90.

8. Cited in Cobb, *The People's Armies*, p. 271.
9. Cobb, *The People's Armies*, p. 483.
10. Cited in Cobb, *The People's Armies*, p. 432.
11. Colin Lucas, *The Structure of the Terror: The Example of Javogues and the Loire*, Oxford: OUP, 1973, pp. 61–8.
12. Lucas, *Structure*, p. 77.
13. Lucas, *Structure*, p. 79.
14. Lucas, *Structure*, pp. 86–7.
15. Slavin, *Hébertistes*, p. 80.
16. Roberts and Hardman (eds), *Documents*, pp. 178–9; Lucas, *Structure*, p. 357.
17. Forrest, 'Local Politics', p. 86.
18. Lucas, *Structure*, pp. 294–5, 343–9.
19. Lucas, *Structure*, pp. xiv-xv.
20. Pierre-Henri Billy, 'Les Prénoms révolutionnaires en France', *Annales historiques de la Révolution française*, 322 (2000), pp. 39–60.
21. Cited in Goujard, 'L'Homme de masse', p. 171.
22. Scott, *Terror and Repression*, pp. 136–40.
23. Hardman (ed.), *French Revolution Sourcebook*, p. 219.
24. Hardman, *Robespierre*, pp. 104–5.
25. Hardman, *Robespierre*, pp. 106–7.
26. Hardman, *Robespierre*, p. 109.
27. Hardman, *Robespierre*, pp. 109–10.
28. Hardman, *Robespierre*, pp. 110–15.
29. Brown, *War, Revolution and the Bureaucratic State*, pp. 95–6.
30. Palmer, *Twelve Who Ruled*, p. 308.
31. Forrest, 'Local Politics', p. 93.
32. Hardman, *Robespierre*, pp. 116–17.
33. Hardman, *Robespierre*, pp. 128–30.
34. Hardman, *Robespierre*, p. 126.
35. Sutherland, *French Revolution and Empire*, pp. 221–2.
36. Hardman, *Robespierre*, pp. 143–4.
37. Jean-Pierre Gross, *Fair Shares for All: Jacobin Egalitarianism in Practice*, Cambridge: CUP, 1997, pp. 20–1.
38. Gross, *Fair Shares*, pp. 81–4.
39. Gross, *Fair Shares*, pp. 155–9.
40. Gross, *Fair Shares*, p. 87.
41. Gross, *Fair Shares*, pp. 56–60.
42. Hardman, *Robespierre*, p. 107.
43. Forrest, *Society and Politics*, p. 236; Sutherland, *French Revolution and Empire*, pp. 219–20.
44. Biard, *Missionnaires*, p. 586.
45. Forrest, *Society and Politics*, p. 237.
46. Forrest, *Society and Politics*, p. 237.
47. Forrest, *Society and Politics*, p. 238.
48. Schama, *Citizens*, pp. 822–7; Jones, *Longman Companion*, p. 345.
49. Jones, *Longman Companion*, pp. 363–4.
50. Palmer, *Twelve Who Ruled*, pp. 313–14.
51. Alan Forrest, *The French Revolution and the Poor*, Oxford: Blackwell, 1981, pp. 82–5.
52. Palmer, *Twelve Who Ruled*, p. 315.

53. Haim Burstin, 'Problems of Work During the Terror', in Baker (ed.), *The Terror*, pp. 271–93; p. 284.
54. Roberts and Hardman (eds), *Documents*, p. 244.
55. Roberts and Hardman (eds), *Documents*, pp. 244–5.
56. Palmer, *Twelve Who Ruled*, pp. 319–20.
57. David A. Bell, 'Lingua Populi, Lingua Dei: Language, Revolution and the Origins of French Revolutionary Nationalism', *American Historical Review*, 100 (1995), pp. 1403–37; p. 1417. See also David A. Bell, *The Cult of the Nation in France: Inventing Nationalism, 1680–1800*, Cambridge, Mass.: Harvard UP, 2001.
58. Forrest, *Revolution in Provincial France*, pp. 234–5.
59. Andress, *French Society*, pp. 189–90.
60. Palmer, *Twelve Who Ruled*, pp. 322–3.
61. Schama, *Citizens*, p. 836.
62. Ozouf, *Festivals*, pp. 111–16.
63. Ozouf, *Festivals*, p. 117.
64. Olwen Hufton, *Women and the Limits of Citizenship in the French Revolution*, Toronto: University of Toronto Press, 1992, pp. 116–17.
65. Jill Maciak, 'Of News and Networks: The Communication of Political Information in the Rural Southwest During the French Revolution', *French History*, 15 (2001), pp. 273–306; see pp. 297–8.
66. Patrice Gueniffey, *La politique de la terreur: essai sur la violence révolutionnaire, 1789–1794*, Paris: Fayard, 2000, p. 220.
67. Pernoud and Flaissier, *The French Revolution*, p. 320.
68. Schama, *Citizens*, pp. 831–6; Hardman, *Robespierre*, pp. 123–4.
69. Doyle, *Oxford History*, p. 277.
70. Hardman, *Robespierre*, p. 146.
71. Mason and Rizzo, *Documents*, pp. 241–3.
72. Hardman (ed.), *French Revolution Sourcebook*, pp. 231–2.
73. Richard T. Bienvenu, *The Ninth of Thermidor: The Fall of Robespierre*, Oxford: OUP, 1968, p. 104.
74. Hardman, *Robespierre*, p. 146.
75. Jones, *Longman Companion*, p. 121.

## Chapter 11: Triumph and Collapse

1. Jean-Paul Bertaud, *La Révolution armée: les soldats-citoyens et la Révolution française*, Paris: Robert Laffont, 1979, pp. 239–41.
2. Bertaud, *La Révolution armée*, p. 243.
3. Bertaud, *La Révolution armée*, p. 244.
4. Bertaud, *La Révolution armée*, pp. 240, 242–3.
5. Bertaud, *La Révolution armée*, pp. 235–6.
6. Forrest, *Soldiers*, p. 117.
7. Forrest, *Soldiers*, pp. 119–20.
8. Forrest, *Soldiers*, pp. 93–7.
9. Forrest, *Soldiers*, pp. 98–9.
10. Alan Forrest, *Napoleon's Men: The Soldiers of the Revolution and Empire*, London: Hambledon & London, 2002, pp. 89–90.
11. Palmer, *Twelve Who Ruled*, pp. 338–9.
12. Palmer, *Twelve Who Ruled*, pp. 340–2.

13. Palmer, *Twelve Who Ruled*, p. 343.
14. Sutherland, *French Revolution and Empire*, p. 218.
15. Palmer, *Twelve Who Ruled*, pp. 344–9.
16. Palmer, *Twelve Who Ruled*, pp. 350–3.
17. Pernoud and Flaissier, *The French Revolution*, p. 289.
18. Palmer, *Twelve Who Ruled*, pp. 353–4.
19. Palmer, *Twelve Who Ruled*, pp. 97–106, 350, 353.
20. Palmer, *Twelve Who Ruled*, pp. 351, 357.
21. Palmer, *Twelve Who Ruled*, p. 328.
22. Bienvenu, *Ninth of Thermidor*, pp. 117–18.
23. Hardman, *French Revolution Sourcebook*, p. 232.
24. Hardman, *Robespierre*, pp. 166–8.
25. Daniel Gordon, 'The Theater of Terror: The Jacobin Execution in Comparative and Theoretical Perspective', *Historical Reflections/Réflexions historiques*, 29 (2003), pp. 251–74, esp. pp. 264, 267–8.
26. Pernoud and Flaissier, *The French Revolution*, p. 252.
27. Pernoud and Flaissier, *The French Revolution*, p. 275.
28. Gordon, 'Theater of Terror', pp. 263–5.
29. Schama, *Citizens*, p. 840; Palmer, *Twelve Who Ruled*, p. 368.
30. Palmer, *Twelve Who Ruled*, p. 368.
31. Hardman, *Robespierre*, pp. 177–8.
32. Roberts and Hardman (eds), *Documents*, p. 251.
33. Bienvenu, *Ninth of Thermidor*, p. 119.
34. Hardman, *Robespierre*, p. 179.
35. Hardman, *Robespierre*, pp. 174–5.
36. Martin Lyons, 'The 9 Thermidor: Motives and Effects', *European Studies Review*, 5 (1975), pp. 123–46; p. 128.
37. Hardman, *Robespierre*, p. 174.
38. Roberts and Hardman (eds), *Documents*, pp. 251–2.
39. Hardman, *Robespierre*, p. 181.
40. Hardman, *Robespierre*, p. 182; Bienvenu, *Ninth of Thermidor*, pp. 124–5.
41. Bienvenu, *Ninth of Thermidor*, p. 135.
42. Bienvenu, *Ninth of Thermidor*, pp. 133–4.
43. Bienvenu, *Ninth of Thermidor*, p. 114.
44. Bienvenu, *Ninth of Thermidor*, p. 112.
45. Bienvenu, *Ninth of Thermidor*, p. 125.
46. Roberts and Hardman (eds), *Documents*, p. 250.
47. Hardman, *Robespierre*, pp. 179–80.
48. Hardman, *Robespierre*, p. 184.
49. Hardman, *Robespierre*, p. 195.
50. Bienvenu, *Ninth of Thermidor*, pp. 143–74.
51. Roberts and Hardman (eds), *Documents*, pp. 256–7.
52. Hardman, *Robespierre*, p. 187.
53. Bienvenu, *Ninth of Thermidor*, pp. 162–3.
54. Bienvenu, *Ninth of Thermidor*, p. 174. I have adjusted the translation here a little.
55. Bienvenu, *Ninth of Thermidor*, p. 174.
56. Roberts and Hardman (eds), *Documents*, p. 257.
57. Roberts and Hardman (eds), *Documents*, pp. 258–9.
58. Bienvenu, *Ninth of Thermidor*, p. 179.

59. Bienvenu, *Ninth of Thermidor*, p. 181.
60. Hardman, *Robespierre*, pp. 188–9.
61. Bienvenu, *Ninth of Thermidor*, p. 182.
62. Bienvenu, *Ninth of Thermidor*, p. 183.
63. Bienvenu, *Ninth of Thermidor*, p. 189.
64. Bienvenu, *Ninth of Thermidor*, pp. 190–3.
65. Bienvenu, *Ninth of Thermidor*, p. 198.
66. Hardman, *Robespierre*, p. 196.
67. Bienvenu, *Ninth of Thermidor*, pp. 199–200.
68. Hardman, *Robespierre*, pp. 190–2.
69. Hardman, *Robespierre*, pp. 197–8.
70. Bienvenu, *Ninth of Thermidor*, pp. 206–17; p. 217.
71. Hardman, *Robespierre*, p. 201.
72. Hardman, *Robespierre*, pp. 202–3.
73. Rudé, *Crowd*, pp. 139–41.
74. Pernoud and Flaissier, *The French Revolution*, p. 336.
75. Sutherland, *French Revolution and Empire*, pp. 232–3.
76. Pernoud and Flaissier, *The French Revolution*, p. 337.

## Chapter 12: Terror Against Terror

1. Hardman, *Robespierre*, p. 212.
2. Hardman, *Robespierre*, p. 206.
3. Bronislaw Baczko, *Ending the Terror: The French Revolution After Robespierre*, Cambridge: CUP, 1994, p. 1.
4. Baczko, *Ending*, pp. 16–17.
5. Baczko, *Ending*, pp. 8–9.
6. Baczko, *Ending*, p. 16.
7. Denis Woronoff, *The Thermidorean Regime and the Directory*, Cambridge: CUP, 1984, p. 1.
8. M. J. Sydenham, *The First French Republic*, London: Batsford, 1974, p. 28.
9. Woronoff, *Thermidorean Regime*, pp. 2–3; Sydenham, *Republic*, pp. 28–9.
10. Doyle, *Oxford History*, pp. 282–3.
11. Baczko, *Ending*, p. 46.
12. Baczko, *Ending*, p. 48.
13. Baczko, *Ending*, pp. 50–1.
14. Doyle, *Oxford History*, p. 283.
15. Sydenham, *Republic*, pp. 30–1; Woronoff, *Thermidorean Regime*, p. 4.
16. Baczko, *Ending*, pp. 36–8.
17. Doyle, *Oxford History*, p. 283.
18. Woronoff, *Thermidorean Regime*, pp. 3–4.
19. Sydenham, *Republic*, p. 32.
20. Baczko, *Ending*, pp. 142–3.
21. Baczko, *Ending*, p. 143.
22. Baczko, *Ending*, p. 144.
23. Baczko, *Ending*, p. 144.
24. Sydenham, *Republic*, p. 33.
25. Sydenham, *Republic*, p. 34.
26. Sydenham, *Republic*, p. 32.
27. Baczko, *Ending*, p. 147.

28. Sydenham, *Republic*, p. 37.
29. Doyle, *Oxford History*, p. 289.
30. Maurice Hutt, *Chouannerie and Counter-revolution: Puisaye, the Princes and the British Government in the 1790s*, Cambridge: CUP, 1983.
31. Sydenham, *Republic*, p. 38.
32. Richard Cobb, *Terreur et subsistances, 1793–1795*, Paris: Clavreuil, 1965, pp. 321–6.
33. Doyle, *Oxford History*, pp. 285–6.
34. Doyle, *Oxford History*, pp. 286–7.
35. Sydenham, *Republic*, p. 43.
36. Rudé, *Crowd*, chapter 10.
37. Sydenham, *Republic*, p. 43.
38. Sydenham, *Republic*, pp. 42–3.
39. Doyle, *Oxford History*, p. 287.
40. Sydenham, *Republic*, pp. 37–8.
41. Cited in Rudé, *Crowd*, p. 149.
42. Doyle, *Oxford History*, p. 290.
43. Sydenham, *Republic*, pp. 324, 326, 329.
44. Schama, *Citizens*, p. 851.
45. Sydenham, *Republic*, pp. 50–1.
46. Doyle, *Oxford History*, p. 294.
47. Sydenham, *Republic*, p. 54.
48. Hufton, *Women and the Limits of Citizenship in the French Revolution*, p. 48.
49. Sutherland, *French Revolution and Empire*, p. 250.
50. Sutherland, *French Revolution and Empire*, p. 251.
51. Sutherland, *French Revolution and Empire*, p. 249.
52. Sutherland, *French Revolution and Empire*, p. 250; Doyle, *Oxford History*, p.292.
53. Pernoud and Flaissier, *The French Revolution*, p. 186.
54. Doyle, *Oxford History*, p. 295.
55. Deborah Cadbury, *The Lost King: How DNA Solved the Mystery of the Murdered Son of Louis XVI and Marie Antoinette*, New York: Griffin, 2003. Note that even here 'murder' is introduced, and in the same year Jacques Rivière published *Le Mystère Louis XVII: histoire secrète de son évasion et de son exil aux Seychelles*, Corps: Les 3 Spirales, 2003.
56. W. R. Fryer, *Republic or Restoration in France? 1794–7: The Politics of French Royalism*, Manchester: MUP, 1965, pp. 13–17.
57. Sydenham, *Republic*, pp. 58–9.
58. Sutherland, *French Revolution and Empire*, pp. 274–7.
59. Harvey Mitchell, *The Underground War Against Revolutionary France: The Missions of William Wickham, 1794–1800*, Oxford: Clarendon Press, 1965, pp. 51–64.
60. Sydenham, *Republic*, pp. 60, 337.
61. Rudé, *Crowd*, pp. 162–5.
62. Rudé, *Crowd*, p. 163.
63. Rudé, *Crowd*, pp. 164–5.
64. Jones, *Longman Companion*, pp. 72–4.
65. Rudé, *Crowd*, p. 168.
66. Rudé, *Crowd*, p. 169.
67. Rudé, *Crowd*, pp. 172–3.
68. Rudé, *Crowd*, p. 174.

69. Sydenham, *Republic*, p. 324.
70. See Patrice Higonnet, *Class, Ideology and the Rights of Nobles During the French Revolution*, Oxford: Clarendon Press, 1981.
71. Jones, *Longman Companion*, pp. 234, 236.
72. Malcolm Crook, *Napoleon Comes to Power: Democracy and Dictatorship in Revolutionary France, 1795–1804*, Cardiff: University of Wales Press, p. 95. There are, of course, innumerable books devoted to the rise and fall of the First Empire.
73. On this concept, see Howard G. Brown, 'From Organic Society to Security State: The War on Brigandage in France, 1797–1802', *Journal of Modern History*, 69 (1997), pp. 661–95; and a forthcoming general study on the same area.
74. See Eugen Weber, 'The Nineteenth-Century Fallout', in Geoffrey Best (ed.), *The Permanent Revolution: The French Revolution and Its Legacy, 1789–1989*, London: Fontana, 1988, pp. 155–82.
75. Douglas Johnson, 'The Twentieth Century: Recollection and Rejection', in Best (ed.), *Permanent Revolution*, pp. 183–209; p. 192.

## Conclusion

1. Gueniffey, *Politique de la terreur*.
2. Théodore H. Barrau, *La Patrie: description et histoire de la France*, Paris: Hachette, 1877, p. 398.
3. Barrau, *La Patrie*, p. 399.
4. Barrau, *La Patrie*, p. 401.
5. For a summary of such issues, see Ronald Schechter (ed.), *The French Revolution: The Essential Readings*, Oxford: Blackwell, 2001, 'Introduction', pp. 1–30.
6. Hardman, *Robespierre*, pp. 143–4.
7. Gueniffey, *Politique de la terreur*, p. 225.
8. Marie-Hélène Huet, *Mourning Glory: The Will of the French Revolution*, Philadelphia: University of Pennsylvania Press, 1997, pp. 91–2.
9. Huet, *Mourning Glory*, p. 93.
10. Louis-Antoine Léon Saint-Just, *Oeuvres choisies*, Paris: Gallimard, 1968, p. 248.
11. Saint-Just, *Oeuvres*, p. 330.
12. Saint-Just, *Oeuvres*, pp. 341–3.
13. Saint-Just, *Oeuvres*, p. 344.
14. Louis-Antoine Léon Saint-Just, *Discours et rapports*, ed. Albert Soboul, Paris: Editions sociales, 1970, p. 217.
15. Saint-Just, *Oeuvres*, p. 310.
16. Saint-Just, *Oeuvres*, p. 312.
17. Saint-Just, *Oeuvres*, p. 325.
18. Saint-Just, *Oeuvres*, pp. 365–6.
19. Schama, *Citizens*, pp. 706–7.

# INDEX

Page numbers in *italics* denote glossary/cast of characters references.


Abbaye prison, 96–7, 104, 105, 106, 108
Aby, Ursule, 158
active citizens, 30, 45, 54, 55
address, form of, 221
Agde, 278–9
agriculture, 220
Amalgame law (1793), 159
Amar, Jean-Baptiste-André, 233, 252, 254, 271, 274, 323, 331, 348, 358, *391*
American Revolution, 1–2
American War of Independence, 15, 16
*Ami du Peuple, L'* ('People's Friend'), 47
Arc de Triomphe, 371
Armand, Antoine, 268
army, 312–15; conscription brought in and resistance to, 159–61, 163, 194–5; doses of Terror in, 314–15; education of soldiers, 315; improvements in, 312–14; legislation passed to reform, 159; newspapers distributed to, 315; organisation of, 157; problems in 1973 campaigns, 157, 158–9, 312; shrinkage of, 153–4, 157, 159; uniforms, 313; weapons, 312, 313; woman soldiers, 157–8
Army of the Eastern Pyrenees, 314
artistic competitions, 304–5
Artois, Charles-Philippe, comte d', 27, 32, 52–3, 63, 225, 363, *391*
Assembly of Notables, 17–18, 21
assignats, 31, 64, 109, 151, 214, 355, 359, 367, *385*
Auckland, Lord, 115
Austria, 52; alliance with Prussia, 69; and Peace of Campo Formio (1797), 368; war against France, 66–70, 72–3, 134–6, 154–5, 169, 195, 316–20, 354
'Austrian Committee', 73

Bailly, Jean-Sylvain, 48, 49, 61, 231, *391*
Baldwyn, agent, 260–1
Barbaroux, Charles-Joseph-Marie, 119, 129, 173, 174, 180, 188, 231, *391*
Barère, Bertrand, 125, 140, 305, 325, 332, 338–9, *391*; falls from favour, 348, 353, 357, 358; and insurrection against Girondins, 175–6, 180, 181; and Maximum, 264–5; and Robespierre's speech before arrest, 234, 235; spokesman for Committee of Public Safety, 164, 199, 248, 267, 302, 326, 330; stands for neutral ground in Convention, 151–2
Barnave, Antoine-Pierre-Joseph-Marie, 43, 52, 54, 57, 58, 66, *392*
Barras, Jean-Nicolas-Paul-François, 238, 288, 327, 329, 342, 346, 366, 367, *392*
Barry, Marie-Jeanne du, 234–5
Basire, Claude, 206

Basques, 305–6
Bastille, fall of (1789), 4–5, 25, 27, 107, 128
Batz, Jean-Pierre, baron de, 146–7, 261, 262, *392*
Beauge (citizen), 158
Bédoin, 295
Belgium, 153, 155, 318–20
Bentabole, Pierre-Louis, 277–8, 335, 342, 357, *392*
Bicêtre prison, 98, 104, 105, 321
Billaud-Varenne, Jacques-Nicolas, 120, 206, 207–8, 211, 218, 222, 256, 271, 332, 335, 337, 338, 348, 352, 353, 357, 358, *392*
Biron, duc de, 197, 198
Bo, Jean-Baptiste-Jérôme, 279–80, 297, *392*
Boisset, Joseph, 278–9
Bonaparte, Napoléon *see* Napoléon I (Bonaparte)
Bonchamps, Charles-Melchior, 245–6
Bonchamps, Madame, 247
Bordeaux, 184–6, 195, 235–6, 299–300
Bouchotte, Jean-Baptiste-Nöel, 197–8, 207, 255, 257, 315, *392*
Bouillé, Marquis de, 9, 37, 50
Bouillon, Rose, 158
Bourdon de l'Oise, François-Louis, 326–7, 334
Breteuil, Louis-Auguste Le Tonnelier, baron de, 53, 146, *392–3*
Breton Association, 63
Brienne, Loménie de (Archbishop of Toulouse), 18, 21
brigands, 27, 109–10, 119
Brissot, Jacques-Pierre, 67, 114, 120, 124–5, 129, 164, 168, *385*, *393*; arrest of, 180; attack on by Jacobin Club, 121, 122–3; background, 59–60; and *French Patriot*, 77, 122, 168, 169; as Girondin leader, 73, 77, 85, 119; trial of, 229
'Brissotins', 59, *385* *see also* Girondins
Britain *see* England
Brittany, 202
Brunswick, duke of, 82, 91, 99, 113–14, 114, 135, 194
Brunswick Manifesto, 82–3, 91, 99
Burke, Edmund, 5
Buzot, François-Nicolas-Léonard, 119, 169, 174, 180, 188, 231, *393*

Cabarrus, Thérèse de, Madame Tallien, 299–300, 329, 349, *393*, *400*
Caen, 184, 186, 188
*cahiers de doléances*, 22, *385*
Calendar, Revolutionary *see* Revolutionary Calendar
Calonne, Charles-Alexandre de, 16, 17, 18, 20, *393*
Cambon, Pierre-Joseph, 335
*capitation*, 17
Carmes prison, 105
Carmes, Society of the, 46
Carnation Plot, 226
Carnot, Lazare-Nicolas-Marguerite, 199, 216, 320, 332, *393*; and Robespierre, 326; as 'war minister', 318, 319, 325–6, 371
Carra, 85
Carrichon, Abbé, 322–3
Carrier, Jean-Baptiste, 248, 266–7, 299, 351, 352, 353, *393*
Carteaux, General, 204
Cassanyès, 309, 344
Castries, duc de, 43
Cathelineau, Jacques, 244
Catholic Church, 203; and Civil Constitution of the Clergy, 31, 32; reorganisation of under state control (1790), 30–1
Cazalès, Jacques-Antoine de, 43
Central Revolutionary Committee, 173–4, 176, 180
*certificat de civisme see* Civic Certificates
Chabot, François, 122, 131, 188, 239, 251, 251–2, 254, 261–2, 263, *393*
Chaillon, 143
Chaix, 'Marat', 282, 287
Chalier, Marie-Joseph, 183, 193, 290, *393–4*
Chambonas, 85
Champ de Mars Massacre (1791), 51–2, 61, 231, *391*, *396*
Charette, François, 355
Charleroi (Belgium), 319
Charles I, King of England, 143
Charles IV, King of Spain, 53
Châteaudun, 277

Châtelet, duc du, 104, 105, 261
Chaumette, Pierre-Gaspard, 132, 172, 174, 179, 205, 239, 254, *394*
Chénier, Marie-Joseph, 240
Choiseul, duc de, 9–10, 34, 36
*chouans*, 202–3, 246, 354, 355, *385*, *387*
*Chronicle of Paris*, 84
*citras see* Indulgents
Civic Certificates (*certificat de civisme*), 163, 211, 212, 365
Civil Constitution of the Clergy, 31, 32
Clavière, Etienne, 74, 146, 175, 177
Clémenceau, Georges, 370
clergy, 30–1; Civil Constitution of, 31, 32; and dechristianisation, 240, 242
Clootz, baron 'Anacharsis', 235, 242, 268
Coburg, General, 155, 319, 320
Collot-d'Herbois, Jean-Marie, 120, 256, 263, 271, 290, 321, 348, 353, *394;* arrest and deportation, 357, 358; criticism of Brissot, 122; elected to Committee of Public Safety, 211; repression of Lyon, 236, 237, 258; and Robespierre, 258
Commission of Twelve, 168, 170, 171–2, 174, 175
Committee of General Security, 233, 252, 292, *385*; dissension between Committee of Public Safety and, 323–5, 330–1, *385*; purging of after Robespierre's execution, 347; and Robespierre, 323–5, 330, 331, 333
Committee of Public Safety, 196, 206, 211, 221, 258, *388*; and Convention, 164, 217, 346–7; and dechristianisation, 239, 240, 241; dissension between Committee of General Security and, 323–5, 330–1, *385*; establishment of and remit, 164; and Girondins, 175, 181; members, 164, 194, 199; powers of, 198–9, 224; problems faced, 218; removal of obstacles to growing centralisation of power in, 292–4; renewal after Robespierre's execution, 346–7; and Robespierre, 194, 199, 326
Commune d'Armes (formerly Saint Etienne), 312
Commune of Paris *see* Paris Commune
'Concert of Europe', 3
Conciergerie, 104, 105
Condé, prince de, 364
Condorcet, marquis de, 50, 125, 129, 157
conscription, 159–61, 163, 194–5
Constitution, 116; (1791), 52, 54–5, 118; (1793), 191–2, 193, 194, 222, 358; (1795), 365
Convention, 113, 116–17, 131, *385–6*; abolition of feudal dues, 196–7; agreement on new Constitution, 116, 191–2; arrest and execution of *ultras* and Indulgents, 268–70, 272–6; attempt to purge Girondins from by Parisians, 166–7, 168, 169, 170–2, 174–7; attempt to reign in activity of Parisians, 191; and Committee of Public Safety, 164, 217, 346–7; conflict between Girondins and radicals within, 74, 77, 80–1, 102, 118, 119–25, 130, 131, 150, 155–6, 163–6; debate on fate of king, 136–9; and dechristianisation campaign, 240, 241; declaration of 'Terror', 179, 205–6, 207–9, 211; declares France a republic, 115, 116, 127; decree on Revolutionary Government, 222, 224; divisions and factionalism within, 116, 119–23, 131, 140, 253, 262–3, *388*; draconian legislation embarked on to put down rebellions (1793), 156–7, 162–3; electoral system, 117; and Enragés, 192, 193; expulsion of Girondins from, 177, 181, 218, *386*, *387*; gradual relaxation of terrorist measures, 347; introduction of the Cult of the Supreme Being (1794), 303–4; mass levy decree, 201–2; and Montagnards, 131; operation and power of, 118–19; passing of the Law of Suspects, 211–13; purging of radicals within, 357, 358–9; readmission of Federalists and Girondins, 357; readmission of 'Seventy-five' deputies, 353–4; reasons for divisions and conflict

Convention (*continued*)
within, 125–6; reassertion of control of the capital and the country, 198, 209; reversal of institutional centralisation within, 347; and rights of citizens, 372–3; rightwing swing in politics of, 349; risings against by Parisians over hardships, 178–9, 357–8, 359; and Surveillance Committees, 163; tensions with Parisian *sans-culottes*, 206–9, 211, 213; Terror agenda, 211–12; treatment of expelled Girondins, 180; trial of Louis XVI, 140–5; and *ultras*, 259, 266; uncertainty over future course after Robespierre's execution, 347–8; and war with Austria, 136; and women, 232, 233–4
Corday, Charlotte, 188–90, 322
Cordeliers Club, 44–5, 49, 86, 130, 132, 156, 190, 192, 196, 207, 241, 266, 293, *386*
Cottereau, Jean ('Jean Chouan'), 202
Coup of the 9 thermidor, 337–9, 340–1
Couthon, Georges-Auguste, 177, 194, 199, 210, 236, 257, 271, 290, 310, 311, 326, 330, 331, 334–5, 337, 339, 342, 343, 344, *394*
Cult of the Supreme Being *see* Supreme Being, Cult of the
cultural beliefs, 126–30
culture, 304–5; and artistic competitions, 304–5; decree to make French language universal, 306; and education, 306–7
Custine, comte de, 198

Damiens, Robert-François, 103
Dampierre, Maréchal-de-camp, 135–6
Danton, Georges-Jacques, 6, 51, 114, 125, 155, 164, 211, 258, 371, 376, *387*, *394*; arrest and trial of, 272–5; background, 45; and Cordelier Club, 45; criticism of *ultras*, 256; downfall, 269–70, 271–2; execution of, 275–6; feud with Rolands, 120–1, 131, 150; and Girondins, 169–70, 181; as an Indulgent, 253–4, *394*; involvement in financial wrongdoing suspicions, 131, 253, 256; Parisian hostility towards, 206–7; protest at direction of Terror, 253–4; removal from Committee of Public Safety, 198; and Robespierre, 270, 272–3; speech at speaker's tribune, 207–8, 211; speech prior to September Massacres, 101
David, Jacques-Louis, 150, 190, 200, 228, 251–2, 305, 340, 347, 348, 369, *394*
David, Nicolas, 51
de Kock, Jan, 268–9
de Séze, Raymond, 140, 142
dechristianisation, 203–4, 239–43, 253, 280–1, 287, *386*
Declaration of the Rights of Man (1789), 29
Delacroix, 272
departments, 30, *386*
Descombes, Antoine, 268
Desmoulins, Lucile-Camille-Simplice, 120, 168, 229, 256–7, 261, 263, 270, 272, 275, 291, *394*
Dillon, comte de, 198
Dillon, General, 73, 321
Directory, 365, 367, 368, 369, 372
Dobsen, Claude-Emmanuel, 173
Dordogne, 297, 298
Drouet (postmaster), 34, 35, 36, 362
Dubois-Crancé, Edmond-Louis-Alexis, 29, 186, 187, 236, 328, 331
Dufriche-Valazé, Charles, 230
Dumont, André, 239, 240
Dumont, Pierre, 99
Dumouriez, Charles-François du Périer, General, 135, 146, 153, 154–5, 164, 318, *394–5*
Duplay, Maurice, 251, 290
Duport, Adrien, 43
Duquet, Félicité, 157–8
Dutch *see* Holland
Duthy, Jean-Baptiste, 48–9

economy, 14–18, 367–8; impact of Revolution, 63–4; and Necker, 15–16; reforms by Calonne and failure of, 17–18, 20; Turgot's reforms, 14–15

education, 306–7
Egyptian campaign (1798), 368
Elbée, Maurice-Joseph d', 244, 246
electoral system, 30, 117–18
electors, 30, 54, 55
elite, social, 16–17
*émigrés*, 27, 48, 52, 68, 135, 163, 353, *386*; attacks on at end of 1790s, 367; attacks on by Girondins, 60, 61; and Brunswick Manifesto, 82–3, 91, 99; landing of in France (1795), 363–4; laws passed against (1791), 60; Louis' ultimatum to German princes to disperse, 67; selling of lands by Convention, 197
England: agents in France, 260–1; war against France, 152, 185, 195, 316, 317–18
'English letter', 199–200
Enragés, 156, 162, 167, 192, 193, 198, 205, 207, *386*
Eprémesnil, Jean-Jacques Duval d', 301
espionage, 260–2
Estates-General, 10, 11, 20, *386*; electoral process for and protests against, 21–2; meeting of at Versailles (1789), 23–4, 26, 27
executioners, 322–3
executions, 6, 110, 230–2, 300–1, 311, 321–3
executive, 365

Fabre d'Eglantine, Philippe-François-Nazaire, 120, 220, 240, 251–3, 254, 257, 263, *395*
Falaiseau, marquis de, 91
Favre (woman soldier), 157, 158
Federalists/Federalism, 280, 294, *386*; eradication of by republicans, 235–9; readmission back into Convention, 357; revolt of (1793), 183–9, 193, 195, 204; shrinking of influence and turning of tide in Republic's favour, 195–6; trial of and acquittal (1794), 350–1
*fédérés*, 74, 79, 83–4, 86, 133
*fermiers-généraux*, 301
Fersen, count Axel von, 9, 54, 68–9, 146, *395*
Festival of Federation (1790), 39, 79
Festival of the Law (1792), 74
Festival of the Supreme Being (1794), 307–10, 333, 374
Festival of the Unity and Indivisibility of the Republic (1793), 194, 200–1
feudal dues, abolition of, 196–7
feudalism, abolition of, 28, 29, 62
Feuillants, 51, 52, 53, 54–5, 56, 57, 64, 66–7, 75, 80, 139–40, 352, *386–7*
Firmont, Edgeworth de, 145
First Estate, 10
Fleuriot-Lescot, Jean-Baptiste, 293–4, 340, 341, 343
Fleurus, battle of (1794), 319–20, 325
'Flight to Varennes' (1791), 9–10, 24, 32, 34–7, 44, 46, 48, 49–50, 140, 362, *395*
Flour War (1775), 14–15, 65, *401*
food, 205, 298; and Maximum, 213–14, 218, 264–5, 298, 303, 356; prices, 23, 25, 134, 151, 192, 264, 356, 359, 364; and winter of 1994–95, 355
food riots, 66, 107, 264; (1793), 151–2, 156; (1795), 356
foreign agents, 260–1
Foreign Plot, 267, 321
forgery/forgers, 109
Fouché, Joseph, 203, 236, 237, 239, 282, 290, 291, 309, 327, 328, 329, 365, 368, *395*
Fouquier-Tinville, Antoine, 162, 166, 225, 229, 268, 274, 275, 324, 343, 345, 347, 358–9
Francis II, King, 70
Fraternal Society, 46, 49, 74, 130, 233
Frederick the Great, 12
French Indies Company Fraud *see* Indies Company affair
French language: decree to make it universal, 306
*French Patriot*, 77, 122, 168, 169
Fréron, Louis-Stanislas, 238, 288, 327, 339, 348, 350, 358, 366, *395*
*Friend of the People*, 266
Friends of Chalier, 290, 291, 327, 329
Friends of the Monarchical Constitution, 33

Garat, Dominique-Joseph, 150, 171, 256, *395*

Gard, 66
General Maximum *see* Maximum
Gensonné, Armand, 60, 62, 80, 125, 129, 164, 166, 180, *395*
Gerle, Dom, 324
Gilded Youth, 350, 352, 356, 360, 361, 366
Girondins, 59–60, 85, 112, 256, 354, *387*; abortive arrest of, 114; attacks against *émigrés*, 60, 61; calls for war against Austria, 66, 67–8; conflict between radicals and, 74, 77, 80–1, 102, 118, 119–25, 130, 131, 150, 155–6, 163–6; expulsion of from Convention, 177, 181, 218, *386*, *387*; house arrest after expulsion and fleeing to provinces, 177, 180, 181, 184; and Louis, 72, 74, 80–1, 142–3, 144; members, 60; Parisian hostility towards and attempt to purge from Convention, 166–7, 168, 169, 170–2, 174–7; political war between Montagnards and, 150, 155; reaction to expulsion and mounting resistance against Parisians, 183–5; readmission to Convention, 357; rehabilitation of outlawed survivors of leadership, 354; and Robespierre, 112–14, 123–4, 125, 139, 164–5, *399*; and transparency issue, 129–30; trial of and execution of detained, 228–30, 231
Glorious First of June battle, 317
Gorsas, Antoine-Joseph, 119, 123, 180, *395*
Gouges, Marie-Olympe de, 232, 234
Gower, Lord, 55, 66, 102
'Great Fear', 27–8
Great Register of National Welfare, 302
Gredelier, Madame, 109
Guadet, Marguerite-Elie, 67, 81, 129, 164, 165, 168, 169, 174, 180, 231, *395–6*
guilds, 14, 15, 39; abolition of (1791), 40
guillotine, 147–8
Gustavus III of Sweden, 68

Halles, Society of the, 46
hangman, 110
Hanriot, François, 174, 176, 181, 218, 341, 343, 344, *396*
Hébert, Jacques-René, 44–5, 132, 156, 170–1, 172, 179, 193, 205, 207, 251, 258, 263, *386*, *396*; arrest of and released, 170–1, 172; attack on Indulgents, 267; execution of, 269, 322; and Marie-Antoinette's trial, 225, 226; and *Père Duchesne*, 76–7; and radical journalism, 47, 241; trial of, 268–9
Hébertists: trial of and execution of, 268–9, 271, *389*
hell columns, 249–50
Hérault de Séchelles, Marie-Jean, 176, 200, 253, 260, 263, *396*
Herman, Armand-Martial-Joseph, 289–90, 293, 321, 324, 345, *396*
'hoarding commissioners', 292
Hoche, general Lazare, 354, 362, 363
Holland, 152–3; peace with France, 364; war with France, 153, 154, 354
Hondschoote, battle of (1793), 216, 223
Hood, Admiral, 204
Houchard, general, 216, 217–18, 223, 268, 315
Howe, Lord, 317

Indies Company Affair, 251–2, 261, 271, 274, *391*
Indigents, Society of, 46
Indulgents, 259, 271, *387*; conflict with *ultras*, 254–8, 259, 262–4, 263, 266–7; trial and executions of, 272–6
industry, 303
Inspecteurs de Police, 41
Insurrectionary Commune, 90, 120, 121, 123, *387*
Isnard, Maximim, 171, 357, 361
Issarts, Jean-Henri Bancal des, 114
Italian Campaign (1796), 368

Jacobin Club/Jacobins, 44, 45, 46, 55, 61, 74, 79, 118, 125–6, 130, 293, *387*; agenda of, 126; attack on Brissot, 121, 122–3; attempts to regain initiative, 348–9, 350;

closure (1794), *387*; and Convention, 178–9; and Feuillants, 51, 75; formation, 33; hostility towards, 352; Louis' view of, 33; national resurgence and reasons for, 56; persecution of, 367; public gallery of, 106; regrouping, 121–2; rise in popularity, 66; and Robespierre, 56, 327–8, 336, 342
James II, King, 143
Jarjayes, comte de, 52
Javogues, Claude, 283–4, 285–7, 336, *396*
Jemappes, battle of (1792), 372
Jourdan, Jean-Baptiste, 319–20
journals, 47
Jullien, Marc-Antoine, 299–300, *396*

Kéralio, Louise, 45

La Croix Castries, Charles-Eugène-Gabriel, 22
La Force prison, 98, 104, 105–6, 106, 109
La Lézardière, marquis de, 63
La Rochejacquelin, comte de, 244, 246
La Rouairie, marquis de, 63, 64
Ladmiral, 321
Lafayette, Marie-Joseph, marquis de, 25, 26, 43, 48, 49, 61, 67, 72, 73, 75, 78–9, 80, 87, 91, 225, *396–7*
Lamballe, princesse de, 93–5, 108, 109
Lameth, Alexandre de, 43
Lameth, Charles de, 43
Lamorlière, Rosalie, 227
land: demands for division and distribution of, 134; feudal dues abolished on, 133–4; proposal to confiscate suspects' land for redistribution *see* ventôse decrees
language, 305–6
Lanne, Marie Joseph, 290
Laplanche, 215, 216, 239
Latreille, Marie Anne, 268
Laumur, Michel, 268
Launay, Bertrand-René Jourdan de, 5
Lavoisier, Antoine-Laurent, 301
Law of 14 frimaire (1793), 258–9, 262, 278, 283, 285
Law of 22 prairial (1794), 310–11, 325, 330, 338, 347, 372–3
Law of General Police, 292
Law of Suspects, 211–13, 348, *389*
Le Bon, Joseph, 278
Le Roy, Louis, 99
Lebas, Philippe-François-Joseph, 290, 307, 338, 339, 342–3, *397*
Lebrun, 175, 177
Legendre, Louis, 44, 76, 273, *397*
Legislative Assembly, 57–8, 73, 84–5, 87, 133–4, *387*; arrangement with radicals, 90; detaining of royal family after storming of Tuileries, 88, 89; elections to new (1791), 55–6; Surveillance Committee of, 61; takes emergency powers, 80
Legros, 322
Lemain, Barthélemy, 315–16
Leopold II, Emperor, 67, 68
Lepeletier de Saint-Fargeau, Louis-Michel, 149–50, 190, *397*
Lequinio, Joseph-Marie, 250
Lescure, Madame de, 248
*lettres de cachet*, 53
Levy of Three Hundred Thousand, 159, 163, 171, 312
Lieutenant-General of Police, 41
Lindet, Jean-Baptiste-Robert, 180, 186–7, 199, 272, 326, 347–8, *397*
Lobjois, Antoine, 99
Lormes, 282
Louis XV, King, 11, 12, 20, 234
Louis XVI, King, 5–6, 75–6, *397*; accepts new constitution (1791), 6, 54–5, 140; and 'armed congress' objective, 59, 68–9; ascension to throne (1774), 11; attacks against by radicals and calls for dethronement, 77, 79, 83, 85–6; confrontation with Parisian radicals in palace (20 June 1792), 75–6; Convention's debate on fate of, 136–7; and death of children, 13; depression, 54, 59, 141; execution of (1793), 145–6, 147–8, 152; and failed 'Flight to Varennes', 9–10, 24, 32, 34–7, 49, 50; and Girondins, 72, 74, 80–1, 142–3, 144; 'iron cupboard' revelations, 138–40, 141–2, 146; and

Louis XVI, King (*continued*)
Jacobins, 33; manifesto, 24–5, 26, *397*; marriage to Marie-Antoinette, 12–13; move to Paris after march on Versailles by Parisians, 25–6, 29; nature, 11–12; plans to rescue, 145–7; politics of, 13–14; public opinion turning away from as republican sentiments increase, 79–80; refusal to sign National Assembly decrees, 29; reinstatement of after flight (1791), 50; restoration of *parlements*, 11, 12, 14, 18; return to Paris after failed escape, 41–2, 50; secret diplomacy efforts and foreign policy, 53–4, 58–9, 146; speech at Estates-General meeting, 24; speech to Legislative Assembly, 58; storming of Tuileries by Parisians and detaining of (10 Aug 1792), 72, 87–8, 88; trial of and sentenced to death (1792/3), 140–5; ultimatum given to German princes to disperse *émigrés*, 67; use of executive veto, 60, 74, 75, 118; view of war with Austria, 68–9
Louis XVII (Louis-Charles), 13, 362–3
Louis XVIII, King *see* Provence, comte de
Louis-Joseph, 13
Louvet de Couvrai, Jean-Baptiste, 85, 123–4, 128, 129, 130, 168, 174, 180, *397*
Loys, Jean-Baptiste, 173, 175
*lumières*, 18
Lyon, 186–8, 196, 287, 290–1; anti-Jacobin rising in, 177; breakdown of order (1792), 132–3; Federalist revolt in and fighting with Republicans, 187–8, 193, 195, 204; lobbying for return of autonomy by Friends of Chalier, 291; massacre of Jacobin prisoners (1795), 361; political tensions, 181, 183; repression of rebels in, 210–11, 236–7; and Robespierre, 291; scorning of by Parisian opinion after fall, 290
Machecoul, 162
Madame Royale, 362
Madelonnettes prison, 331
Maignet, Etienne, 294–5
Mailhe, Jean-Baptiste, 136–7, 144
Maillard, Stanislas, 105, 106, 108
Mainz, 193–4, 196
Malesherbes, Chrétien-Guillaume de Lamoignon de, 140–1, 145, 300–1
Mandat, marquis de, 87
Manège, 117
Marat, Jean-Paul, 52, 124, 139, 188, 348, *395*; funeral, 190–1; and Girondins, 120, 156, 164, 165; and Jacobins, 122, 164; journalism of, 47, 86, 131, 156; murder of, 188–9, 190; remains of, 356; and September Massacres, 113, 120; trial and acquittal of, 166, 167
Maria-Theresa, Empress, 12, 13
Marie-Antoinette, Queen, 9, 25, 33–4, 54, 59, 78, 85–6, 198, 205, *397–8*; appearance, 12; and Barnave, 52; and Carnation Plot, 226; and Feuillants, 54; friendship with princesse de Lamballe, 94; marriage to Louis XVI, 12–13; public perceptions of, 12, 42, 225–6; and storming of Tuileries, 88; trial and execution, 199, 218, 225–8; view of Legislative Assembly, 58
Marie-Thérèse-Charlotte, 13
*Marseillaise, La* (song), 83–4
Marseille, 181–2, 186, 195, 204, 288; anti-Jacobin coup by citizens in, 177; massacre of terrorists (1795), 361; political tensions in, 133, 181–3
Marx, Karl, 3
mass levy, 201–2, 279, 303, 312, *387*
Maximum, 213–14, 218, 264–5, 298, 303, 343, 356, *388*
Mazuel, Albert, 268
Mercy-Argenteau, comte de, 34, 78, 86
Meunier, Etienne, 315
Meynard, Léonard and Paule, 308–9
Mirabeau, Honoré-Gabriel Riquetti, comte de, 24, 140, *398*

Miranda, Francisco de, 154
Momoro, Antoine, 44, 132, 268, 269
Montagnards, 131, 150, 157, 166, 169, 175, *387*
Montbert, 249
Morris, Gouverneur, 43, 58, 73, 75, 86, 143, 155, 227, 274, 276
Munro, Colonel George, 111, 119, 127, 152, 260
Murat, 280

names, personal, 287–8
Nantes, 299, 350–2, 353
Napoléon I (Bonaparte), 238, 314, 367, 368–9, 372, *392*
Narbonne, 67
National Agents, 259, 280, 283, 285–6, *386*, *387*
National Assembly, 10, 27, 57, 106, 118, *387–8*; construction of system of democratic representation, 30; ending of, 57; produces Declaration of the Rights of Man (1789), 29; pronounces abolition of feudalism to calm the countryside (1789), 28, 29; reinstatement of Louis XIV after flight (1791), 50
National Convention *see* Convention
National Guard, 26, 41, 48, 54, 90, 119, 167–8, 360
Necker, Jacques, 15–16, 21, 25, 53, *398*
nobility, 22; exempt from the *taille*, 16
*nonante-cinq* ('ninety-five'), 355
non-juror priests, 61, 92, 160, *388*
Normandy, 202

*Old Cordelier*, 256–7, 261, 270
Orange Commission, 294–6, 310, 360, 372
Orléans, Louis-Philippe-Joseph, duc d', 21, 127, 165, 182, 230, *398*

Pache, Jean-Nicolas, 151, 166, 174, 181, 293, *398*
Paine, Thomas, 50, 354
Panis, Etienne, 335
Paré, Jules-François, 120, 207
Paris, 38–41, 49; clubs, 44, 74, 75; evolvement of internal politics, 167; mayorship elections (1793), 151
Pâris (bodyguard), 149
Paris Commune, 86, 92, 97, 125, 130, 166, 191, 196, 261, 341, *388*; and arrest of Robespierre, 341; and dechristianisation, 241, 242; and Girondins, 112, 168, 173, 176, *388*; influence of, 139; list of refusals for Civic Certificate, 212; and Louis' fate, 141; reduction of power, 294
Paris 'Police Legion', 365
Paris Revolutionary Army, 218, 237, 280–2, 290
Paris Sections, 44, 79, 86, 106, 151, 208, 209, 287, 294, 366, *389*; and arrest of Robespierre, 341; attempt to regain initiative, 349; limitation of meetings, 347; and rising against Girondins, 172, 173, 174–5, 176; role, 41; and September Massacres, 103–4; Surveillance Committees of, 163, 167, 181; uprising of and suppression of (1795), 366–7
Paris stock exchange, 196
Parisian National Guard, 338
Parisians, 166–8; and Convention, 191, 206–7; hostility towards Girondins and attempt to purge from Convention, 166–7, 168, 169, 170–2, 174–7; invasion of Tuileries (20 June), 75–6, 77, 122–3; protests against by southern and western France, 183–4; risings up of against Convention over hardships, 178–9, 357–8, 359; storming of Tuileries palace (10 Aug), 71–2, 87–9, 96, 98–9; *see also sans-culottes*
*parlements*, 15, 32, 301; abolition of (1771), 11, 20; abolition of (1788) and ensuing revolts, 20; opposition to reform, 17, 18; resistance to change, 20; restoration of (1774), 11, 12, 14, 18
*Patrie, La* (The Fatherland), 371–2
*Patriotic Annals*, 85
Payan, Claude-François de, 293, 295–6, 324, 325, 332, 334, 341, 343, 345, 372, *398*
Peace of Campo Formio (1797), 368

peasantry, 28, 62, 134, 160–1, 161–2, 197, 302–3
*People's Orator*, 100–1, 350, *395*
*Père Duchesne*, 76–7, 192, 228, 315
Pereira, 253, 268
Pétion, Jérôme, 60–1, 75, 79, 85, 87, 99, 105, 124, 129, 167, 169, 180, 188, 231, *398*
Philippeaux, Pierre, 255–6, 258, 263, 270, 272
physiocrates, 14
Pichegru, General Jean, 364
Pillnitz Declaration, 58–9
Pitt the Younger, William, 152, 200, 228, 267
Plain, the, 131
Poland, 154, 316
police bureau, 292, 323
Polignac, comtesse de, 94
political culture, 129; themes of French, 126–8
Pont-Charrault, 161, 162
Popular Commission for Public Safety (Bordeaux), 185, 195
Précy, comte de, 187–8
press, 47–8, 51–2
priests, non-juror *see* non-juror priests
Prieur de la Côte d'or, Claude-Antoine, 199, *398–9*
Prieur de la Marne, Pierre-Louis, 199, 318, 326, 260, *399*
Princes of the Blood, 13–14, 21, 127
prisons: and September Massacres *see* September Massacres
Proli, Pierre-Jean, 242, 253, 262, 268
Provence, comte de (later Louis XVIII), 52, 60, 91, 363, *399*
Prudhomme, Louis-Marie, 179
Prussia, 91, 115, 154; alliance with France, 69; peace with France, 354, 364; war with France, 73, 316
public opinion, 21; growth of, 19–20
Puisaye, comte de, 188, 354
punishments, 103

Quatresols, Anne, 158
Quiberon expedition, 364

radicals, 44–5; attacks on king and calls for dethronement, 77, 79, 83, 85–6; conflict with Girondins, 74, 77, 80–1, 102, 118, 119–25, 130, 131, 150, 155–6, 163–6; emphasis on performance of its virtues, 130; reprisals and purges against, 349, 356–7, 358–62, 367
Recollects, 123
religion, 31–2; and Cult of the Supreme Being, 303–4, 307–10, 333, 374, *386*, *389*; and dechristianisation, 203–4, 239–43, 253, 280–1, 287, *386*; *see also* Catholic Church
renaming, mania for, 287–8
Renault, Cécile, 321
representatives-on-mission, 162–3, 169, 182, 222, 278, 296–9, *388*; abolition of (1795), 358; in Bordeaux, 195, 235; combating and purging of counter-revolutionaries, 163, 215–16, 280, 311; limits put on powers of, 259, 347; power of, 215, 216; and war effort, 312, 318
Reubell, Jean-François, 352–3
Reunion Club, 81, 121–2
*Réveil du peuple, Le* (anthem), 356–7
Revolutionary Armies, 205, 208, 209, 214–15, 218, 259, 280–2, 283, *388*
Revolutionary Calendar, 219–21, 240, *395*, *399*
Revolutionary Government, *388*; Declaration of (1793), 222, 224; suspension of (1795), 358
Revolutionary Tribunal, 165, 213, 218, 300, 340, *388–9*; abolition (1795), 359–60; creation, 162; expansion, 209, 289–90; and Law of 22 prairial, 310–11; narrowing of remit, 347; show trials, 230
Rivarol, Antoine, 146
Robert, François, 45, 49, 120
Robespierre, Augustin (brother), 216, 339, 343, 344
Robespierre, Maximilien-François-Isidore, 5, 6, 56, 86, 151, 193, 224, 251–2, 257, 258, 262, 289–90, 349, *399*; address to Convention on revolutionary government, 258, 259–60; arrest of and failure of Parisian forces to rally to, 340–3;

attack on by Louvet, 123–4, 130; background, 56; backing away from public engagement, 326; and Carnot, 326; and Catherine Théot, 323–4; charges brought against and arrest of, 338–9; and Committee of General Security, 323–5, 330, 331, 333; and Committee of Public Safety, 194, 199, 326; and the Convention, 113, 217; criticism of by Hébert, 267; and Cult/Festival of Supreme Being, 307, 309–10, 323, 333, *389*; and Danton, 270, 272–3; and dechristianisation, 253; dependence on personal acquaintance for his work, 291–2; execution of, 343–4, 345; fear by political factions of being purged by, 323; Fouché as enemy of, 291, 309, 327, 329; and Friends of Chalier, 290, 291; and Girondins, 112–14, 123–4, 125, 139, 164–5, *399*; handling of Revolutionary Tribunal, 289–90; and idea of virtue, 292; and Louis, 140; and Lyonnais' struggle, 291; opposition to war against Austria, 70; patriot network, 289–90, 299, 311; political philosophy and approach, 56–7, 289, 291–2; religious views, 241; report 'On the Principles of Political Morality', 270–1; rise to power, 112–13; rising dissent against and enemies of, 310, 326–7, 335–6; rumours of plotting to make himself king, 345–6; running of police bureau, 292; speech to Convention in attempt to crush opposition and reaction to, 332–6; and trial of Marie-Antoinette, 227; and *ultra*/Indulgent conflict, 263, 271, 289; vision, 260
Robin, Jeanne, 248
Roederer, Pierre-Louis, 88
Rohan-Rochefort, prince de, 215
Roland de la Platière, Jean-Marie, 74, 120, 121, 138–9, 150–1, 176, 179–80, 230, *399*
Roland, Marie-Jeanne, Madam, 74, 85, 102, 114, 119, 120–1, 129, 150, 176, 179–80, 230, *399*
Roman-Fonrosa, 295
Romme, Gilbert, 219, 297, 298, 352, 360, *399*
Ronsin, Charles-Philippe, 132, 197, 198, 218, 237, 241, 254, 255, 257, 262, 264, 266, 268–9, 284, 285, *399–400*
Rossignol, Jean-Antoine, 197, 198
Rousseau, Jean-Jacques, 1, 128–9, 225, 233, 241, 304, 306, 374
Roux, Jacques, 156, 192, 193, 209, *400*
Roux-Fazillac, Pierre, 296–8, *400*
Rühl, Philippe-Jacques, 240, 360
Russia, 154

Saillans, comte de, 81–2, 83
St Bartholomew's Day slaughter (1572), 85
Saint-André, André Jeanbon, 317, 318, 326, *400*
Saint-Antoine, 39
Saint-Etienne, Jean-Paul Rabaut, 231
Saint-Firmin prison, 104
Saint-Just, Louis-Antone-Léon, 224, 271, 288–9, 292, 325, 337, 373, *400*; arrest of, 339, 343; background, 137; calls for king's execution without trial, 137–8, 140, 194; and Dantonists, 273–4; execution, 344; final speech to Convention, 374; *Republican Institutions*, 373–4; and trial of Indulgents, 275; and ventôse decrees (1794), 265, 269, 373; and war against Austria, 318, 319; writings, 373–5
Saint-Marcel, 39
Salpêtrière, La, 98, 104, 105, 108, 109
*sans-culottes*, 76, 79, 151, 167, 170, 171, 178, 280, *389*; campaign against, 356–7; crudity of, 284–5; and dechristianisation, 280–1; destruction of influence of in Paris, 360; dress of, 76, 267–8, *389*; and food riots, 264–5, 266; reduction in activism due to growth of government centralisation, 293–4; and Revolutionary Armies *see* Revolutionary Armies; rising

*sans-culottes* (*continued*)
against Convention over hardships (1795), 178–9, 357–8, 359; tensions with Convention, 206–9, 211, 213; view of peasantry, 280; *see also* Paris Sections
Santerre, Antoine-Joseph, 87, 145, 171, *400*
Sauce, 35–6
Savenay, battle of (1793), 244, 247
Schama, Simon, 5
Scheldt, River, 136
School of Mars, 306–7, 342
Second Estate, 10
Sections, *389 see also* Paris Sections
seigneurs, 22, 28, 29, 34, 65
sentimentalism, 128, 129
September Massacres, 6, 92, 93–115, 120, 122, 123, 130, 143, 372, *389*, *397*; brutality of killings, 111; conflict between Girondins and radicals over, 122, 124; consequences within new republican political class, 112; identity of instigators, 103–4; killing of prisoners, 97–8, 104; and murder of princesse de Lamballe, 94–5; number of prisoners spared and judicial procedures invoked, 104–6, 108–9; and Sections, 103–4; steps leading to, 99–102
Seven Years War (1756–1763), 12, 16
Sieyès, Emmanuel-Joseph, Abbé, 357, 368, *400*; *What Is the Third Estate?*, 21–2
Simmoneau, Louis, 65, 74
societies, 46–7, 51
Societies of the Friends of the Constitution, 32–3, *387*
Society of Friends of the Blacks, 59, *393*
Society of Revolutionary Republican Women, 232–3
Spain: treaty with France (1795), 364; war with France, 154, 354
spies *see* espionage
Subsistence Commission, 214
Supreme Being, Cult of the, 303–4, 307–10, 333, 374, *386*, *389*
Surveillance Committees, 163, 167, 181, 212, *389*
Swiss Guards, 88–9

*taille*, 16
Taine, Hippolyte, 5
Tallien, Jean-Lambert, 235, 267, 273, 299, 311, 327, 329–30, 337–8, 339, 347, 348, 349, *393*, *400*
Tallien, Madame *see* Cabarrus, Thérèse de
Tarente, Madame, 108
taxes, 16–17, 367–8
Tennis-Court Oath (1789), 13, 24, 140, *400*
Terror: declaration of by Convention, 179, 205–6, 207–9, 211; local impact of interventions of, 278–80; numbers detained under, 212–13; relaxation of, 347, 349, 353, 358, 365
Théot, Catherine, 323–4, 335, 339
thermidorians, 345, 348, 350, 353, 358, 360, *389*
Thionville, Merlin de, 351
Third Estate, 10–11, 21, 23, 24, 27
Thuriot, Jacques-Alexis, 327, 333, 347, 358, *401*
Tonnerre, 279
Toulon, 204, 206, 237–9
Tourzel, Madame de, 35, 42–3
towns, renaming of, 287
transparency, 128, 129–30, 130–1
Tronchet, 140
Tuileries palace, 25–6, 39; invasion of by Parisian radicals (20 June), 75–6, 77, 122–3; storming of (10 Aug) (1792), 71–2, 87–9, 96, 98–9
Turgot, Anne-Robert-Jacques, baron de L'Aulne, 14–15, *401*
Turreau, General, 245, 248–9, 250

ultra-revolutionaries, 282–4
*ultras*, 256, 262, 271, *389*; calls for insurrection of Convention, 266–7; conflict with Indulgents, 254–8, 259, 262–4, 263, 266–7; demand for tougher measures, 266; trial of Hébertists and execution of (1794), 268–9, 271, *389*

Vadier, Marc-Guillaume-Alexis, 271–2, 274, 323, 324, 332, 335, 339, 346, 348, 353, 357, *401*
Val de Dampierre, comte du, 41
Valmy, battle of (1792), 114–15, 119, 134, 372
Varenne, Maton de la, 111
Varlet, Jean-François, 156, 170, 173
Vendéan Revolt, 161–2, 171, 186, 193, 196, 198, 239, 244–50, 254, 256, 280, *389*; approach to warfare, 245; crushed at Savenay (1793), 244, 247–8; defeats, 246, 247; destruction of by 'hell columns', 249–50; indestructibility of on home territory, 244–5; origins, 161–2; republicans approach to, 247–8; treaty concluded with (1795), 354–5
Vendémiaire rising (1795), 366–7, *392*
ventôse decrees, 265–6, 267, 292, 302, 330, 373, *390*
Verdun, loss of in war, 96
Vergniaud, Pierre-Victurnien, 60, 67, 73, 80, 81, 89, 119, 125, 129, 143, 164, 169, 174–5, 177, 180, 229
Verona Declaration (1795), 363
Versailles, 22–3; march of Parisian woman on (1789), 25, 105
Vincent, François-Nicolas, 132, 207, 241, 255–6, 257, 262, 263–4, 266, 268–9, *401*
*vingtièmes*, 17
Violette, Jean-Denis, 105
Voltaire, 11

War Ministry, 197, 207, 255, 292
weights and measures, reform of, 219
Westermann, general, 247–8
White Terror, 360–2
Wimpffen, Félix, 184, 188
winter (1794–95) (*nonante-cinq*), 355–6
women, 232–4; in army, 157–8; crackdown on female political activity by Convention, 232, 233–4; presence in public galleries, 234; prohibitions against by thermidorian authorities, 360
workers' associations: banning of (1791), 40

Ysabeau, Claude-Alexandre, 235, 299, 300